THE ATLANTIC WORLD
AND VIRGINIA, 1550–1624

Published for the
Omohundro Institute of
Early American History
and Culture,
Williamsburg, Virginia,
by the
University of
North Carolina Press,
Chapel Hill

The

ATLANTIC WORLD

and

VIRGINIA,

1550–1624

EDITED BY PETER C. MANCALL

The Omohundro Institute of
Early American History and Culture
is sponsored jointly by the
College of William and Mary and the
Colonial Williamsburg Foundation.
On November 15, 1996, the Institute adopted
the present name in honor of a bequest
from Malvern H. Omohundro, Jr.

© 2007 The University of North Carolina Press
All rights reserved
Designed by Rich Hendel
Set in Monticello type by Tseng Information Systems, Inc.
Manufactured in the United States of America

Library of Congress Cataloging-in-Publication Data
The Atlantic world and Virginia, 1550-1624 / edited by Peter C. Mancall.
p. cm.
Essays from an international conference entitled The Atlantic world and
Virginia, 1550-1624, held in Williamsburg, Va., Mar. 4-7, 2004.
Includes bibliographical references and index.
ISBN-13: 978-0-8078-3159-5 (cloth : alk. paper)
ISBN-13: 978-0-8078-5848-6 (pbk. : alk. paper)
1. Virginia—History—Colonial period, ca. 1600-1775—Congresses.
2. America—History—To 1810—Congresses. 3. Great Britain—Colonies—
America—History—16th century—Congresses. 4. Great Britain—Colonies—
America—History—17th century—Congresses. 5. Europe—Colonies—America—
History—Congresses. 6. Acculturation—America—History—Congresses.
7. Virginia—Ethnic relations—History—16th century—Congresses. 8. Virginia—
Ethnic relations—History—17th century—Congresses. 9. America—Ethnic
relations—History—16th century—Congresses. 10 America—Ethnic relations—
History—17th century—Congresses. I. Mancall, Peter C. II. Omohundro
Institute of Early American History & Culture.
F229.A875 2007
975.5'02—dc22   2007000103

The paper in this book meets the guidelines for permanence and
durability of the Committee on Production Guidelines for Book Longevity
of the Council on Library Resources.

This volume received indirect support from an
unrestricted book publications grant awarded to the Institute by the
L. J. Skaggs and Mary C. Skaggs Foundation of Oakland, California.

cloth   11   10 09 08 07   5 4 3 2 1
paper   11   10 09 08 07   5 4 3 2 1

PREFACE

The contents of *The Atlantic World and Virginia, 1550–1624,* had their origin in an international conference of the same title, held in Williamsburg, Virginia, March 4–7, 2004. The intention of the conference and this resulting volume is to commemorate the four hundredth anniversary of the Jamestown settlement by approaching it from current historical perspectives on the encounters, collisions, and collaborations of peoples and political entities in North and South America, Africa, and Europe in the period surrounding contact between the inhabitants of Tsenacommacah and Englishmen.

The Omohundro Institute of Early American History and Culture organized the program. Recognizing the importance of adding an intellectual component to the mix of Jamestown commemorative events, Gillian Cell, then-provost of the College of William and Mary, endorsed the undertaking and authorized the College's financial backing. In addition, the Colonial Williamsburg Foundation, the Gilder Lehrman Institute of American History, the Reed Foundation, and the Virginia Foundation for the Humanities sponsored the conference, along with the Institute. The support of these organizations made possible the convening of Native American tribal representatives from the Chesapeake region and scholars from Africa, Australia, Europe, and the Americas. The sponsors' generous underwriting enabled the convocation of more than seventy participants and facilitated the attendance of about five hundred people at the public four-day event.

In conceptualizing the conference, I envisioned a mosaic of groups, regions, individuals, and influences in play around the Atlantic that formed the backdrop for the establishment of Jamestown in 1607 and the years following to 1624 (at which point the Virginia Company lost the political struggle to retain its outpost on the James, inaugurating royal control over the colony). Published here is a collection of essays developed from the original presentations. *The Atlantic World and Virginia's* premise is that reaching for a transnational vantage point can augment comprehension of the contacts between peoples from different continents and cultures and the resulting formations of new societies. Shifting forces and internal contests for political, economic, and cultural domination around the Atlantic littoral in the sixteenth and seventeenth centuries shaped the context in which the events at Jamestown occurred. The timing of the settlement came at a transition point between an early Atlantic era of regional exchanges and a transatlantic system of merchant capital centered in the Americas and based on slavery and the plantation economy. Displacements of populations and consolidations of power in many places contributed to this transformation. For the local inhabitants of Tsenacommacah, perhaps the most remarkable sight was not the arrival of three ships but the strangers' settling on an island the Paspaheghs deemed waste ground not fit for planting. The exchanges and conflicts between the Powhatans and the English constituted a local story most immediately meaningful for the participants; ultimately, though, their encounters and Africans' incorporation into their midst would have consequences for shaping the world in which we live. Most elusive to historical understanding is common people's experiences, sometimes remembered through oral traditions, often fragmented or lost to memory. Yet their quotidian existence is at the very core of the human story. Our grasp of others' lives is always incomplete; our task is always to do better.

At one time or another, nearly all the Institute staff played a role in the monumental undertaking of publicizing the conference, selecting the program, putting it into print, planning conference events, coordinating its logistics, and preparing this volume. Ronald Hoffman's directorial hand was there at every step of the way. He and Karen Ordahl Kupperman, Professor of History at New York University, were instrumental in shaping the conference program, and he gave helpful input on papers for the volume. Beverly Smith and Sally D. Mason were crucial to the success of the conference. Mendy C. Gladden efficiently organized the conference papers into a set for the publication process. Daniel H. Usner, Jr., and three other outside readers gave expert and constructive advice on the essays, and Peter C. Mancall provided important critical guidance to the authors in revising their essays for the volume. Manuscript editor M. Kathryn Burdette has demonstrated her editorial mastery in honing the contributors' prose, amassing the illustrations, and integrating the pieces into a volume fit for print. The final product is a testament to the collective endeavor that went into its making.

Fredrika J. Teute
Editor of Publications
Omohundro Institute of Early American History and Culture

CONTENTS

THE ATLANTIC WORLD
AND VIRGINIA, 1550-1624

NEWFOUNDLA[ND]

Stadacona
Hochelaga ✳ ACADIA
Port-
Royal ✳ ← Cape Breton
Plymouth ✳
Jamestown
TSENACOM-
MACAH
Ocute ✳
Altamaha ✳
Roanoke
Island
BERMUDA
St. Augustine ✳

Atlant[ic]

Ocea[n]

NEW
SPAIN
HISPANIOLA
CUBA
SANTO
DOMINGO
Veracruz ✳
Caribbean Sea
LESSER
ANTILLES
Portobello ✳ ✳ Maracaibo
Cartagena
PANAMA
Nombre
de Dios
VENEZUELA
GUIANA
São ✳
MARAN[HÃO]

Pacific

Ocean

PERU
BRAZIL
✳ Lima
Ba[hia]

The Atlantic World, ca. 1600. Drawn by Rebecca Wrenn

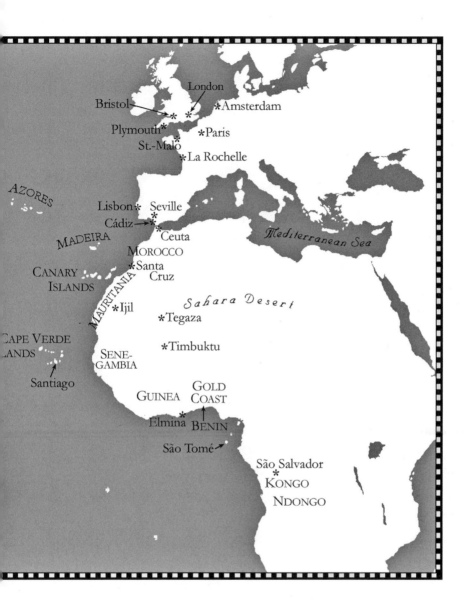

Peter C. Mancall

INTRODUCTION

The local inhabitants of Tsenacommacah, the Paspaheghs, knew their environment well. They used the best lands in the region for their home sites and fields, knew where to hunt and fish nearby, and eschewed swamp land since it attracted mosquitoes and could not be farmed. Hence, in the spring of 1607, they must have viewed askance the group of English colonizers who had sailed up the Chesapeake to establish a fortified camp on a marshy island that the Indians deemed unworthy of settling themselves. It was not much of a village, nor did the newcomers seem like much of a threat to the Powhatan Confederacy that dominated the peoples of Tsenacommacah. But unlike earlier English visitors who had arrived farther south in the mid-1580s at Roanoke in modern-day North Carolina, these immigrants proved to have more staying power. Despite difficult times at first, including periodic confrontations between the Powhatans and the English, the settlement named after King James survived. It became a permanent intrusion into In-

This volume grew from a remarkable and innovative conference sponsored by the Omohundro Institute of Early American History and Culture. Fredrika J. Teute designed the conference and subsequently played a crucial role in developing the individual essays here and the overall concept of the volume. Her energy led to a genuine circum-Atlantic effort and, in the process, made a lasting contribution to our understanding of the early modern world. Her vision for this book and wise counsel were invaluable for me from the moment I joined the project. I also want to thank Daniel H. Usner, Jr., and the other reviewers, who each provided detailed analyses of specific essays and helped the authors develop their arguments for this collection. Ron Hoffman, in addition to his role in the organization of the conference, also shaped particular essays here. Kathy Burdette performed remarkable copy-editing, and Mendy C. Gladden provided crucial support throughout the process of organizing the volume. All of the essays in this collection have benefited from the rigorous and thoughtful insights that are defining elements of the Omohundro Institute of Early American History and Culture's publication program.

In developing this introduction, I thank Lisa Bitel, Fredrika J. Teute, and Kathy Burdette for their extraordinary efforts, as well as the Huntington Library for permission to reproduce the images here.

dian Country and another uninvited outpost of Europeans along the margins of the Atlantic Ocean.[1]

Although the English managed to keep their outpost on the James River alive, it had no great significance at the time. Yet, when the English crossed the Atlantic bound for the shores of the Chesapeake, they joined a migratory stream that was altering the four continents bordering the ocean. By the mid-seventeenth century, that system had put in motion effects that would produce much of the modern world as we know it today—a Western Hemisphere in which most people speak European languages; an African diaspora that has spread people across the Americas and, to a lesser extent, Europe; a drastically reduced Native American population that has survived through cultural adjustment; and a global market that circulates goods around the world. Such transformations make the founding of Jamestown an almost trivial event. The essays in this volume aim to quite literally place the beginnings of Virginia in the history of the larger Atlantic Basin.

Over the last quarter-century, scores of historians have described how parts of the Atlantic world came into being in the early modern age. Some have focused explicitly on migration and argued that it was a common occurrence whose significance can only be understood by looking at the myriad movements of early modern peoples. Others have analyzed the environmental consequences of the transatlantic exchange, including the migration of animals, which (together with people) remade landscapes across the Atlantic Basin and facilitated the movement of devastating diseases.[2]

1. "George Percy's Account of the Voyage to Virginia and the Colony's First Days," in Warren M. Billings, ed., *The Old Dominion in the Seventeenth Century: A Documentary History of Virginia, 1606–1689* (Chapel Hill, N.C., 1975), 25; James Horn, *A Land as God Made It: Jamestown and the Birth of America* (New York, 2005), 56.

2. For works on the emergence of the Atlantic world, see, for instance, Bernard Bailyn, *Atlantic History: Concept and Contours* (Cambridge, Mass., 2005); Alison Games, "Atlantic History: Definitions, Challenges, and Opportunities," *American Historical Review,* CXI (2006), 741–757; J. H. Elliott, *The Old World and the New: 1492–1650,* The Wiles Lectures (Cambridge, 1970); J. H. Elliott, *Empires of the Atlantic World: Britain and Spain in America, 1492–1831* (New Haven, Conn., 2006); John Thornton, *Africa and Africans in the Making of the Atlantic World, 1400–1800,* 2d ed. (Cambridge, 1998); Alan Taylor, *American Colonies: The Settling of North America* (New York, 2001); David Armitage and Michael J. Braddick, eds., *The British Atlantic World, 1500–1800* (Basingstoke, 2002).

Migration: see esp. Bailyn, *The Peopling of British North America: An Introduction* (New York, 1986); Bailyn, *Voyagers to the West: A Passage in the Peopling of America on the Eve of the Revolution* (New York, 1986); Nicholas Canny, ed., *Europeans on the*

Many have examined the rise of the slave trade and Africans' participation in it, primarily as its victims, though other early modern peoples also became enslaved once Europeans decided to extract American natural resources and sought the labor to do so. But it is not only such grand topics that have attracted scholars. Historians and anthropologists have examined the movement of specific goods such as sugar, rice, and furs; one enterprising scholar compiled a five-volume work tracing the rise of tobacco and its spread across the Atlantic world. Even the potato, an American tuber that purportedly first traveled to England with Sir Walter Ralegh, has its own historians.[3] Yet while American plants improved the lives of Europeans, the westward movement across the Atlantic of infectious diseases took a horren-

---

Move: Studies on European Migration, 1500–1800 (Oxford, 1994); Alison Games, *Migration and the Origins of the English Atlantic World* (Cambridge, Mass., 1999); Ida Altman and James Horn, eds., *"To Make America": European Emigration in the Early Modern Period* (Berkeley, Calif., 1991); David Eltis, ed., *Coerced and Free Migration: Global Perspectives* (Stanford, Calif., 2002).

Environment: see William Cronon, *Changes in the Land: Indians, Colonists, and the Ecology of New England* (New York, 1983); Alfred Crosby, *Ecological Imperialism: The Biological Expansion of Europe* (Cambridge, 1986); Timothy Silver, *A New Face on the Countryside: Indians, Colonists, and Slaves in South Atlantic Forests, 1500–1800* (Cambridge, 1990); Jon T. Coleman, *Vicious: Wolves and Men in America* (New Haven, Conn., 2004), 1 143; Virginia DeJohn Anderson, *Creatures of Empire: How Domestic Animals Transformed Early America* (New York, 2004); Elinor G. K. Melville, *A Plague of Sheep: Environmental Consequences of the Conquest of Mexico* (Cambridge, 1997).

3. Few areas of early modern scholarship have received as much serious attention as slavery and the slave trade. See, for instance, Barbara L. Solow, ed., *Slavery and the Rise of the Atlantic System* (Cambridge, 1991); David Eltis, *The Rise of African Slavery in the Americas* (Cambridge, 2000); "New Perspectives on the Transatlantic Slave Trade," special issue of *William and Mary Quarterly,* 3d Ser., LVIII (January 2001); "Slaveries in the Atlantic World," special issue of *WMQ,* 3d Ser., LIX (July 2002); and Allan Gallay, *The Indian Slave Trade: The Rise of the English Empire in the American South, 1670–1717* (New Haven, Conn., 2002).

For sugar, see Sidney Wilfred Mintz, *Sweetness and Power: The Place of Sugar in Modern History* (New York, 1985), and Stuart B. Schwartz, ed., *Tropical Babylons: Sugar and the Making of the Atlantic World, 1450–1680* (Chapel Hill, N.C., 2004); for rice, see Peter A. Coclanis, *The Shadow of a Dream: Economic Life and Death in the South Carolina Low Country, 1670–1920* (New York, 1989); for the trade in fur (and deerskins), see, e.g., Eric R. Wolf, *Europe and the People without History* (Berkeley, 1982), 158–194; for tobacco, see Jerome E. Brooks, *Tobacco: Its History Illustrated by the Books, Manuscripts, and Engravings in the Library of George Arents, Jr.,* 5 vols.

dous toll on the indigenous peoples of the Americas. The most significant population decline probably took place before 1700, though viruses such as smallpox continued to devastate American populations well beyond 1800, when other lethal, infectious diseases, notably tuberculosis, also arrived in Indian Country.[4]

Ideas moved almost as efficiently as goods and diseases. Native American and African spiritual beliefs and nature knowledge spread among Europeans as well as between Indians and Africans. Catholic and Protestant missionaries carried their religious ideologies into Africa and across the Americas, and European concepts about politics, property, and power became rooted wherever newcomers established settlements. Cultures blended in the Atlantic world, evident in the spread of foods from one place to another, in peoples' dress, and in individuals' notions of history and cosmology. In French and Spanish America, the mixing of peoples led to intricate elaborations about different castes of individuals—ideas represented not only in legal codes and learned treatises about purity of blood but in several remarkable series of paintings categorizing racial groups.[5] Indigenous

<hr>

(New York, 1937-1952). The success of these plants was no coincidence; Europeans in particular continued to look for exotic (to them) plants that could improve their lives. See Londa Schiebinger, *Plants and Empire: Colonial Bioprospecting in the Atlantic World* (Cambridge, Mass., 2004).

Potato: Redcliffe N. Salaman, *The History and Social Influence of the Potato* (Cambridge, 1949); see also D. Humbert, *Histoire de la pomme de terre* (Nîmes, 1992); Larry Zuckerman, *The Potato: How the Humble Spud Rescued the Western World* (Boston, 1998); and Michael Pollan, *The Botany of Desire: A Plant's-Eye View of the World* (New York, 2001),181-238.

4. Scholars continue to debate the extent and effects of population loss in the Americas caused by the arrival of diseases from Eurasia, but all agree that increased exposure to Europeans and their animals meant repeated exposure to diseases for which Native Americans possessed no acquired immunities. See, among many sources, Russell Thornton, *American Indian Holocaust and Survival: A Population History since 1492* (Norman, Okla., 1987); Jared M. Diamond, *Guns, Germs, and Steel: The Fates of Human Societies* (New York, 1997); Noble David Cook, *Born to Die: Disease and New World Conquest, 1492-1650* (Cambridge, 1998); Suzanne Austin Alchon, *Native Society and Disease in Colonial Ecuador* (Cambridge, 1991); Elizabeth A. Fenn, *Pox Americana: The Great Smallpox Epidemic of 1775-82* (New York, 2001); Daniel K. Richter, *Facing East from Indian Country: A Native History of Early America* (Cambridge, Mass., 2001); David S. Jones, *Rationalizing Epidemics: Meanings and Uses of American Indian Mortality since 1600* (Cambridge, Mass., 2004).

5. For Native Americans' lifeways and ideas influencing Europeans' consciousness, see, e.g., Anthony Pagden, *European Encounters with the New World* (New Haven,

peoples resisted these new ways of ordering affairs in their temporal and spiritual worlds, but in the long run Europeans tended to prevail, even if that meant using violence to eradicate Native Americans' resistance. But the reshaping of Native America did not always involve armed struggle. By the late eighteenth century, and earlier in many places, Native American adaptations to European expansion across the Atlantic had effectively remade their communities. Some, including the Carolina Algonquians, painted by the English artist John White in Roanoke in the 1580s, disappeared as distinctive groups; others found ways to retain their cultural identity despite the continued presence of European colonists on lands they once controlled.[6]

1993); Anthony Grafton, *New Worlds, Ancient Texts: The Power of Tradition and the Shock of Discovery* (Cambridge, Mass., 1992); Stuart B. Schwartz, ed., *Implicit Understandings: Observing, Reporting, and Reflecting on the Encounters between Europeans and Other Peoples in the Early Modern Era* (Cambridge, 1994); Karen Ordahl Kupperman, ed., *America in European Consciousness, 1493–1750* (Chapel Hill, N.C., 1995); and Susan Scott Parrish, *American Curiosity: Cultures of Natural History in the Colonial British Atlantic World* (Chapel Hill, N.C., 2006). For the adoption of goods, see James Axtell, "The Indian Impact on English Colonial Culture," in Axtell, *The European and the Indian: Essays in the Ethnohistory of Colonial North America* (New York, 1981), 272–315; and Timothy J. Shannon, "Dressing for Success on the Mohawk Frontier: Hendrick, William Johnson, and the Indian Fashion," *WMQ*, 3d Ser., LIII (1996), 13–42.

For the images, see Ilona Katzew, *Casta Painting: Images of Race in Eighteenth-Century Mexico* (New Haven, Conn., 2004); for discussions of French and Spanish concerns with the purity of blood, see Guillaume Aubert, "'The Blood of France': Race and Purity of Blood in the French Atlantic World," and María Elena Martínez, "The Black Blood of New Spain: *Limpieza de Sangre,* Racial Violence, and Gendered Power in Early Colonial Mexico," *WMQ*, 3d Ser., LXI (2004), 439–478, 479–520.

6. The suppression of indigenous resistance and strategies of survival have been ably described by historians of Spanish America; see, among others, Steven W. Hackel, *Children of Coyote, Missionaries of Saint Francis: Indian-Spanish Relations in Colonial California, 1769–1850* (Chapel Hill, N.C., 2005); James F. Brooks, *Captives and Cousins: Slavery, Kinship, and Community in the Southwest Borderlands* (Chapel Hill, N.C., 2002); Ramón A. Gutiérrez, *When Jesus Came, the Corn Mothers Went Away: Marriage, Sexuality, and Power in New Mexico, 1500–1846* (Stanford, Calif., 1991); Nancy M. Farriss, *Maya Society under Colonial Rule: The Collective Enterprise of Survival* (Princeton, N.J., 1984).

There was no single strategy for success in Native American communities; some peoples managed to retain parts of their lands, while others moved. The best way to assess the situation is through case studies. Among the most revealing are James H. Merrell, *The Indians' New World: Catawbas and Their Neighbors from European Con-*

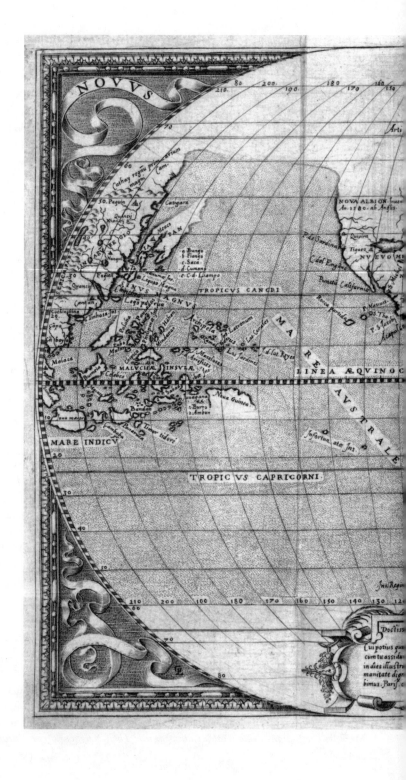

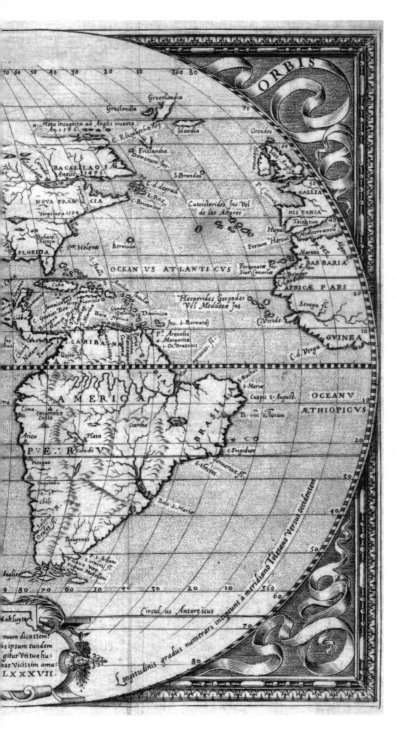

PLATE I.
Map from Pietro Martire d'Anghiera [Peter Martyr d'Anghera], De orbe novo, *ed. Richard Hakluyt (Paris, 1587). By permission of The Huntington Library, San Marino, California*

Many of the developments that had already begun and would eventually change the demography of the Atlantic Basin were not obvious before 1625, but the clues were there for canny observers. A map that appeared in a Latin edition of Peter Martyr's *De orbe novo,* published in Paris in 1587, provided a visual hint of the territorial expropriations and representational displacements occurring in the century after Christopher Columbus's historic first voyage to the West. The book was not just another edition of an important text describing parts of the Americas. Its publication was arranged by the younger Richard Hakluyt, the most avid promoter of the English colonization of eastern North America. As such, it is not surprising that the map included the term "Virginia," the first time any continental map had included the designation. (The map also included California and claimed it was English territory by right of Sir Francis Drake's circumnavigation several years earlier.) Despite these new place names, much of the Western Hemisphere remained in Native American hands. A generation later, however, European maps revealed more extensive claims, although most of the Americas and the African interior remained in indigenous hands. Who controlled the telling of the story is a factor that too many American historians have ignored, especially during major anniversaries of 1607.

The Anniversary Volume as Cultural Artifact

Just short of the centennial of Jamestown's founding, in 1705, Robert Beverley's *History and Present State of Virginia, in Four Parts* appeared in print in London. Unaware of, or indifferent to, the impending anniversary, he wrote not to commemorate it but because "no Body has ever presented the World, with a tolerable Account of our Plantations." There had been "some few General Descriptions" of the place earlier, but they had "been calculated more for the Benefit of the Bookseller, than for the Information of Mankind." Beverley celebrated the importance of his Virginia, but he made no great claims about the significance of its origins. Publications of French translations occurred in Paris and Amsterdam in 1707, not as anniversary volumes, but in response to a burgeoning European market for natural histories and travel accounts about the expanding world.[7] Beverley devoted one

tact through the Era of Removal (Chapel Hill, N.C., 1989); Daniel K. Richter, *The Ordeal of the Longhouse: The Peoples of the Iroquois League in the Era of European Colonization* (Chapel Hill, N.C., 1992); and Joshua Piker, *Okfuskee: A Creek Indian Town in Colonial America* (Cambridge, Mass., 2004).

7. Robert Beverley, *The History and Present State of Virginia, in Four Parts* (London, 1705), quotations at sig [A3v] ("Plantations") and sig. Ar ("Information of Man-

of the four parts of the *History* to an ethnographical account of the region's Indians, explicitly including them in his Virginia. Unlike later narrators of Virginia's beginnings for whom the ongoing role of Indians would be invisible, Beverley attended to Native Americans, their customs and values, as integral to the unfolding history of the colony, and he used Indians' habits as a means of critiquing the shortcomings of his fellow colonists' behavior.

Once the colonial era belonged to another time, the anniversary of Jamestown's settlement became noteworthy. During the bicentennial in 1807, Virginians gathered together in Jamestown to commemorate the colony's founding and to link their new state's storied past with the heroic efforts of its leaders during the American Revolution. A pamphlet from that bicentennial appropriated Jamestown's origins for political purposes. As such, it began a trend that would be repeated every fifty years. Like later celebrations, this one came with its festive trappings, including sailing ships, historical lectures, and ritual toasts. The 250th anniversary in 1857 inspired at least one poet to reflect on the glories of the past. With the nation then consumed by the passions that would soon ignite civil war, James Barron Hope wrote wistfully about the tragic passing of "the poor Indian" and celebrated the founding of the new settlement.

And here, at last, there rose the rambling town,
A smile contending with the forest's frown,
And busy sounds were borne upon the breeze,
The swarming hum of England's settling bees.[8]

---

kind"); Beverley, *Histoire de la Virginie . . .* (Amsterdam, 1707). Four new editions of John Smith's *Generall History* were published in Leyden or the Hague 1707 as part of Pieter van der Aa's *Naaukeurige versameling der gedenk-waardigste zee en land-reysen na Oost en West-Indiën . . .* , or his *De aanmerkenswaardigste en alomberoemde zee-en landreizen der Portugeezen, Spanjaarden, Engelsen, en allerhande natiën.* These works were only part of Aa's body of travel accounts published at the time, which also included a Dutch translation of Antonio de Herrera y Tordesillas's account of such authorities as Diego de Lopes and Amerigo Vespucci. See John Alden and Dennis C. Landis, eds., *European Americana: A Chronological Guide to Works Printed in Europe Relating to the Americas, 1493-1776* (New York, 1980-1997), V, 98-99; Antonius de Herrera et al., *Vyf verscheide voyagien der Kastiliaanen en Portugezen ter ontdekking gedaan naar de West-Indien, in de jaren 1500 en 1501 . . .* (Leyden, 1706). Aa also published some of the parts of his larger work as separate fascicules, including *Twee Scheeps-togten van Kapiteyn Johan Smith, beyde gedaan na Nieuw Engeland . . .* (Leyden, 1707).

8. *Report of the Proceedings of the Late Jubilee at James-town, in Commemoration of the 13th May, the Second Centesimal Anniversary of the Settlement of Virginia* (Petersburg, Va., 1807; HEH 78538), 3-6, 11, 16-17, 19, 46-48; James Barron Hope, *A Poem*

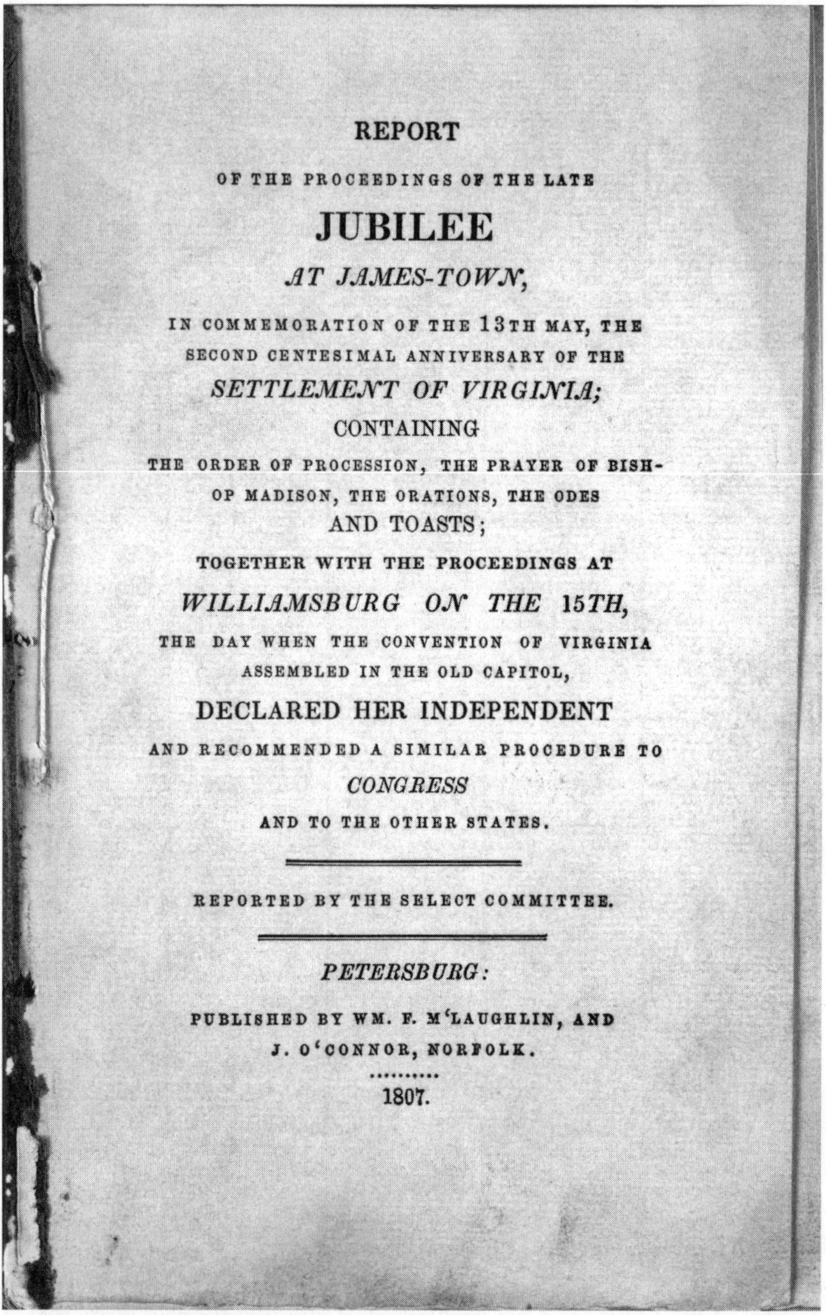

REPORT

OF THE PROCEEDINGS OF THE LATE

JUBILEE

AT JAMES-TOWN,

IN COMMEMORATION OF THE 13TH MAY, THE
SECOND CENTESIMAL ANNIVERSARY OF THE

SETTLEMENT OF VIRGINIA;

CONTAINING

THE ORDER OF PROCESSION, THE PRAYER OF BISH-
OP MADISON, THE ORATIONS, THE ODES
AND TOASTS;

TOGETHER WITH THE PROCEEDINGS AT

WILLIAMSBURG ON THE 15TH,

THE DAY WHEN THE CONVENTION OF VIRGINIA
ASSEMBLED IN THE OLD CAPITOL,

DECLARED HER INDEPENDENT

AND RECOMMENDED A SIMILAR PROCEDURE TO

CONGRESS

AND TO THE OTHER STATES.

REPORTED BY THE SELECT COMMITTEE.

PETERSBURG:

PUBLISHED BY WM. F. M'LAUGHLIN, AND
J. O'CONNOR, NORFOLK.
....
1807.

PLATE 2. *Title page from* Report of the Proceedings of the Late Jubilee at James-town . . . *(Petersburg, Va., 1807). By permission of The Huntington Library, San Marino, California*

Throughout the nineteenth century, serious historians showed no steady interest in Jamestown or its settling. Yet anniversary celebrations continued to inspire rhetorical flourishes. During the preparations for the tercentennial, observers once again traced direct links between the founding of Jamestown and the growth and development of the United States. None did so more effectively than Lyon G. Tyler, the president of the College of William and Mary. Tyler, who had recently completed a history of Jamestown and contributed to a multivolume history of the nation, summed up the meaning of Jamestown: "But for the plantation at Jamestown there would have been no Virginia, no New England, and no United States." To Tyler, what happened in Virginia was essentially a series of "firsts," or, as he put it, "the most important events affecting the destiny of the United States, viz.: The settlement itself at this place introducing the institutions of marriage, the right of trial by jury, the Protestant religion, and all the principles of English civilization; the birth of the first white child; the conversion of the first heathen; the arrival of the first cargo of negroes; the establishment of the first free school," and even the first stand against royal action. Tyler knew that Jamestown itself was "never anything more than a mere village with some considerable buildings of a metropolitan character; but as the first invention, it is, in the language of Bacon, 'of more dignity and merit' than the imperial cities of New York, New Orleans, Philadelphia, Washington, or Chicago." Jamestown's significance was that of a relic, valued because from its struggles came a nation. "Hither the pilgrim may come in years far distant," Tyler concluded, "to behold some last sign of those who laid the foundation-stone of the great republic." Others, too, promoted the importance of the anniversary, including the Daughters of the American Revolution, who wanted to see a statue of John Smith erected at Jamestown, and President Theodore Roosevelt, who encouraged other nations to send ships to Virginia to join in the celebration. At the same time, however, early-twentieth-century anthropologists were conducting field research to establish the cultural continuity and survival of specific Virginia tribal groups, and the American Anthropological Association dedicated most of its January 1907 issue to articles on Virginia Indians as a timely contribution to the Jamestown anniversary.[9]

---

on the Two Hundred and Fiftieth Anniversary of the English Settlement at Jamestown (Richmond, Va., 1857; HEH 77489), quotations at 6 and 14.

9. Lyon G. Tyler, *The Cradle of the Republic: Jamestown and the James River* (Richmond, Va., 1900); Tyler, *England in America, 1580–1652,* vol. IV of *The American Na-*

By the time scholars gathered in Williamsburg fifty years later, the scholarly academy had finally come to focus squarely on Jamestown. To be sure, filiopietism continued to mark the anniversaries, manifested in ephemera such as a special issue of the *Virginia Gazette*. But scholars who met in 1957 to recast the origins of the colony took a hard look at the colony's past. Some examined how Natives and newcomers dealt with each other, whereas others took a far more critical look at Virginia during its early decades. Still, despite the shift, some nationalist tendencies lingered in the scholarship. "At the beginning of the seventeenth century," wrote James Morton Smith, the editor of the Institute of Early American History and Culture's anniversary volume, "all America was a vast expanse of the unknown and the unexpected." By the end of the seventeenth century, as Smith put it, "it was becoming increasingly clear that the emerging civilization of the English colonies was something more than a transatlantic projection of England." If Smith's comments echoed the celebratory assertions of the past —he quoted John Locke's famous dictum that "in the beginning, all the world was America"—the scholarship in this volume nonetheless reflected the emergence of a more nuanced view of Jamestown and early Virginia.[10]

The 1957 volume, like all works of history, was a product of its specific moment. Reflecting postwar America's sense of distinctiveness, the overarching interpretation was an explanation of Virginia's history in situ as a growth of local attachments and separation from an English imperial outlook. The contributors emphasized the development of Virginia, including its historiography, its social structure and politics, and its relations with Native Americans. Two of the essays, though, were harbingers of historiographical turns that reached fruition in the latter part of the twentieth century. One provided a view from Indian Country; the other cast a glance toward the larger Atlantic world. Together, these essays point to the historical

tion: *A History* (New York, 1904); Tyler, *First Settlement at Jamestown* ([Williamsburg, Va.?], 1895; HEH 119972), 1, 5; Mrs. A. A. Blow, *An Address Delivered before the Daughters of the American Revolution at Their Congress Held in Washington, D.C., April, 1905* (n.p., [1905?]; HEH 118844), quotations at 3 and 4. Roosevelt's proclamation appeared in a brief pamphlet describing Jamestown's history for the benefit of those attending the commemoration; see *Address at the Opening of the Jamestown Exposition, April 26, 1907* ([Washington, D.C., 1907]; HEH 49942), 5; *American Anthropologist*, N.S., IX (1907), 31–152.

10. *Virginia Gazette: Jamestown Festival Edition, June 28, 1957* (Williamsburg, 1957; HEH 319634); "Introduction," in James Morton Smith, ed., *Seventeenth-Century America: Essays in Colonial History* (Chapel Hill, N.C., 1959), ix, xv.

perspective that shapes this current volume, the interplay of particular circumstances in the context of emerging global systems.[11]

The Essays

As this brief historical survey suggests, each generation creates the history of early Virginia that it needs, and the present is no exception.[12] The four hundredth anniversary of Jamestown's founding has arrived at a moment when scholars are crafting innovative ways to understand the occurrences in Virginia and putting forward new interpretations based on contemporary understanding of crucial events. One recent collection aimed to present early Virginia as the origin not of a great nation but of an empire. By contrast, scholars of the British Empire have paid little attention to what happened there. Jamestown scarcely appeared in the now-standard multiauthor history of the British Empire before 1700, nor does its founding matter in any significant way to a new generation of imperial historians who, together, have revived a once-stale field.[13]

11. "Introduction," in Smith, ed., *Seventeenth-Century America,* xv. Nancy Oestreich Lurie wrote an ethnohistorical account of the internal dynamics of the Powhatan confederacy that affected their reception of the English; Bernard Bailyn included material relating to migration to the colony from England. See Lurie, "Indian Cultural Adjustment to European Civilization," and Bailyn, "Politics and Social Structure in Virginia," in Smith, ed., *Seventeenth-Century America,* 33–60, 90–115.

12. For the historiography of Virginia specifically and the Chesapeake more generally, see Thad W. Tate, "Seventeenth-Century Chesapeake and Its Modern Historians," in Tate and David L. Ammerman, eds., *The Chesapeake in the Seventeenth Century: Essays on Anglo-American Society* (Chapel Hill, N.C., 1979), 3–50. Two preeminent modern historians have also examined Virginia as it appeared in the work of its historians in the seventeenth century, thereby revealing patterns in historical interpretation: see Richard S. Dunn, "Seventeenth-Century Historians of America," in Smith, ed., *Seventeenth-Century America;* and Alden T. Vaughan, "The Evolution of Virginia History: Early Historians of the First Colony," in Vaughan and George Athan Billias, eds., *Perspectives on Early American History: Essays in Honor of Richard B. Morris* (New York, 1973), 9–39.

13. Robert Appelbaum and John Wood Sweet, eds., *Envisioning an English Empire: Jamestown and the Making of the North Atlantic World* (Philadelphia, 2005) (it should be noted that, despite the title of the volume, the essays within it seem more concerned about establishing early Virginia's place in a larger Atlantic history than in its creation as a crucial stage in the development of the British Empire); Nicholas P. Canny, ed., *Oxford History of the British Empire,* I, *The Origins of Empire: British Overseas Enterprise to the Close of the Seventeenth Century* (Oxford, 1998). For the new generation of historians mentioned, see, for example, David Armitage, *The Ideological Origins of*

The authors whose work appears here reject the earlier teleological notions that emphasized the origins of democracy in America. Instead, these
scholars recognize the establishment of the settlement for what it was at the
time—namely, the creation of another outpost on the margins of expanding
European influence. Jamestown itself is in fact a minor player in the drama
described in these essays, and those who write about it see it as a community whose residents and neighbors included Africans and Native Americans along with Europeans. In this volume, non-Europeans are as important as the English.

The essays here all reveal the ways that large forces operating within the
Atlantic world shaped the lives of specific peoples from approximately 1550
to 1625. Some of the authors show Virginia as part of the larger story, but
others focus on different arenas in the Atlantic Basin. As a result, the volume's emphasis reflects this scholarly generation's understanding of the era
from the mid-sixteenth century to the early seventeenth century. This collection is an anniversary volume that deemphasizes the narrative of Jamestown's significance in favor of essays that examine the meeting of peoples
in different regions across the Atlantic world.

The first section in this volume focuses on eastern North America, the
homeland of the Powhatans and other Native American groups. Indigenous peoples had created complex societies and polities long before
Europeans arrived in the sixteenth century. Despite the rather facile gen-
eralizations about the likelihood of success offered by promoters, all of the
newcomers quickly recognized that they would need to master indigenous
protocols. As Daniel K. Richter demonstrates with extraordinary subtlety—
in an essay that uses anthropology and linguistics to explain this era—Europeans who dealt with Native Americans on either side of the Atlantic Ocean
often fell short of Natives' expectations. Few Europeans were able to master
the intricate play of trade, diplomacy, and spirituality that together guided
indigenous responses to the Spanish and English. Given the limitations
of the documentary record, it is often difficult to know exactly what Indians thought about these interlopers. Did they view Jesuits as open-minded
clerics who sought the improvement of indigenous souls or as murderous
sorcerers whose baptism of ailing children killed babies? Could leaders of
the English mission, most notably John Smith, ever understand how to deal

the British Empire (Cambridge, 2001); Niall Ferguson, Empire: The Rise and Demise
of the British World Order and the Lessons for Global Power (New York, 2002), 66–
67; Christine Daniels and Michael V. Kennedy, eds., Negotiated Empires: Centers and
Peripheries in the Americas, 1500–1820 (London, 2002).

properly with headmen? Smith and his colleagues could barely grasp Powhatan concepts such as *weroance.* The term, meaning "he is wealthy," referred to the authority that accrued to an individual who obtained and then redistributed goods. The newcomers had no obvious way to understand the individuals called *mamanatowick,* a word that included within it the idea of *manitou,* or power. No European who arrived in the Western Hemisphere had suitable preparation for dealing with such multilayered concepts.

By the time the English arrived, changes on the ground in Indian Country had already begun. As Joseph Hall argues, the story starts around 1540, when indigenous peoples in the southeast encountered Spanish explorers who had sailed to mainland North America. The Iberians never launched expeditions in this region as substantial as their invasion of Mexico, but their presence still had an effect on Native Americans, especially since the newcomers inadvertently brought Old World diseases that devastated Indian communities. From an indigenous perspective, the early Spanish forays constituted only the start of what later became a full-blown invasion.[14]

Though not obvious to many Europeans, indigenous polities were as complicated as those of the newcomers. Long-standing tensions existed between the Powhatans and their neighbors in Tsenacommacah. As James D. Rice reveals in an essay that breaks away from some historians' fixation on the Powhatans, other peoples of the Greater Chesapeake manipulated politics in the area, seeking to reduce the hold of the headman whose confederacy confronted the English. This region was not a land forgotten by time, as some of the newcomers might have believed since indigenous material culture and architecture differed so markedly from European standards. Instead, when the English arrived, they—like the Spanish conquistadores who traveled with Hernán Cortés to Mexico in 1519—entered into a fractious world suffering from conflicts produced by the expansionary visions of particular Native Americans. As a result, various indigenous groups responded to the English, who needed to make alliances if they were going to survive, with competing expectations and demands.

The second group of essays further complicates our understanding of the early modern Atlantic world. Here the focus is on Africa. The authors collectively explain the background to one of Virginia's most distinctive events:

14. As David S. Jones has recently argued, the transmission of pathogens alone did not lead to substantial mortality among Americans. Instead, as modern-day infectious disease experts have demonstrated, newly introduced viruses and bacteria proved so deadly because of other stresses placed on American bodies by colonizers, who sought land, goods, labor, and souls. See Jones, "Virgin Soils Revisited," *WMQ,* 3d Ser., LX (2003), 703–742.

the arrival in 1619 of "20. and odd Negroes" from Africa in Jamestown. The legal status of these emigrés is not clear from the surviving documents, though they likely were slaves. But why were they in Virginia before there was serious demand for their labor? Even if there was some demand for bound labor, why did these people come from Africa? The answers to these questions are not obvious. Unless these individuals were captured by Europeans on the African coast and bundled directly onto ships, their migration across the ocean necessarily involved other Africans. As the studies in this volume reveal, the emergence of the slave trade followed an indigenous logic and was not simply imposed by arriving Europeans.

The origins of the slave trade can be traced to commerce within Africa. As E. Ann McDougall reveals in her study of the Sahara, the salt trade in northern Africa was so advanced that its participants had developed the trade language *azayr* to facilitate long-distance exchange.[15] Profits from the Saharan salt trade allowed some participants to support towns with resident communities of scholars. The trade posed many challenges for African entrepreneurs, who had to deal with the powerful kin groups that controlled it as well as the regional rules for moving the product. The Saharan economy became part of a larger Atlantic commercial network through the efforts of the Sa'adien dynasty of Morocco, who used the port at Agadir (conquered by the Portuguese in 1541 and renamed Santa Cruz) to funnel the resources out of the desert and into the wider world.

Salt was only one good produced in parts of Africa. David Northrup's reconstruction of the economy of the Gulf of Guinea shows that Africans, especially the residents of Benin, had developed commercial networks long before Europeans established themselves in the region. Archaeological analysis reveals that African markets existed as early as the ninth century. By the turn of the first Christian millennium, the region boasted its own gold trade; gold fields were so rich that Africans were willing to trade their excess to Europeans during the fifteenth century. Before the first Europeans arrived, Africans had created sophisticated commercial systems that moved desirable goods from producers to consumers, created rules for the

15. A similar development had taken place in the interior of the southeast of the modern-day United States, where Americans had developed what scholars now refer to as "Mobilian," a lingua franca that facilitated trade from one group to the next before Europeans arrived. For its significance, see James M. Crawford, *The Mobilian Trade Language* (Knoxville, Tenn., 1978). The origins of the language remain obscure, but it became more important during the colonial period; see Daniel H. Usner, Jr., *Indians, Settlers, and Slaves in a Frontier Exchange Economy: The Lower Mississippi Valley before 1783* (Chapel Hill, N.C., 1992), 258–259.

exchange of goods, facilitated trade through the development of commercial languages and cowrie shell currency, and enabled economic development. When Europeans traveled to the capital city of the Benin region, they stood awestruck at its large palaces, highly trained artisans, broad thoroughfares, and great wealth. Even residents of smaller communities participated in the gold trade, a sign that the benefits of commerce stretched across the region.

Europeans who arrived in West Africa beginning in the fifteenth century recognized that they had to find ways to enter this network if they wanted to extract gold, pepper, and cloth from the region. The Dutch and the English, who began serious trade with West Africans by the latter decades of the sixteenth century, found discriminating consumers who appreciated some of Europe's finest wares, such as Dutch textiles. Africans traded for European cloth because it possessed an aesthetic appeal and an alluring novelty. By the early decades of the seventeenth century, Africans also developed a fondness for tobacco, a product from the Americas that Europeans transported across the Atlantic in order to enhance the prospects of acquiring African goods. Some Africans embraced trade to such an extent that, by the middle of the seventeenth century, they participated in the capture and sale of humans in exchange for commodities produced in Europe for use in the interior capital of Benin and along the coast.

The slave trade accelerated after 1650, but its origins lay in the long history of trade among African communities and between Africans and Europeans. Further, as Linda Heywood and John Thornton reveal in their highly detailed study of Central African elites, certain aspects of European culture had long held a powerful attraction, especially Christianity, literacy, and diplomatic protocols. A painting showing the Kongolese Dom Antonio Manuel receiving last rites from Pope Paul V in the Vatican reveals the extent of cultural borrowings and adaptations. Even Antonio Manuel's servants dressed like Europeans. By the time the English founded Jamestown, Europeans had long entertained embassies from Kongo, in large part because of the perception that at least the elite members of this Central African kingdom had converted to Christianity. By 1600, there were thirteen parishes in Kongo, and the church in São Salvador even had an organ and a bell tower. Not everyone in Kongo accepted the tenets of this European-based faith, of course; African churchmen battled those who still worshipped idols, fighting the same kinds of battles as European clerics trying to root out paganism at home. Religious conversion was only one sign of this process of appropriation; elites in Kongo and Ndongo also spoke and read Portuguese.

The cultural adaptations of African elites facilitated the developing slave trade. That noxious commerce had only begun to reach the shores of Virginia in 1619, but the buying and selling of Africans had already developed elsewhere in the Atlantic Basin; 58,000 African slaves had arrived in the Americas by 1580 and another 507,000 landed there, primarily in Iberian colonies, by 1640. The earliest African slave trade focused less on supplying slaves to staple plantations than to Spanish haciendas, which had less potential for profit and generated lower demand for bound laborers than later sugar plantations. The emergence into the Atlantic Basin of the English, Dutch, and French encouraged the rise of a more explicitly profit-oriented system with its far higher demands for laborers. The result was a massive expansion of the slave trade, especially after 1700. Yet even before the modern slave trade took hold, slavers nonetheless hauled bound laborers across the ocean. James H. Sweet's contribution to this volume shows the nature of slavery in the Portuguese world long before tobacco plantations began to crowd the shores of the Chesapeake Bay. From Lisbon to the island colony of São Tomé to the mainland of Brazil, Africans working for the Portuguese sought ways to escape their burden. Slavery had not yet spread as far as it would across the basin, but its brutality was already apparent.[16]

There are many lessons to be learned from these essays about Africans' participation in the Atlantic world, but despite the richness of modern scholarship, how many Europeans, or at least how many people in England, possessed a sophisticated view of Africa and its peoples' accomplishments remains unclear. On the other hand, the residents of Tudor and Stuart England were very familiar with developments on the European mainland and with European efforts to expand influence across the ocean.

The essays in the third group in this volume investigate elements of European activity that were of obvious relevance to the English, especially the efforts of the Spanish and the French. In the years following 1492, many Europeans became convinced that the Americas held potentially profitable resources. Though Europeans purchased some goods from Native Americans, they also employed violent means of extracting resources. Some Europeans found such conflicts unpleasant and even lamentable. The Dominican Bartolomé de Las Casas's excoriating critique of Spanish atrocities in the Indies, first published in 1552, still stands as a monument to imperial

16. Eltis, *Rise of African Slavery,* 9. On the distinction between the early and later systems of slavery in the Atlantic basin, see P. C. Emmer, "The Dutch and the Making of the Second Atlantic System," in Barbara L. Solow, ed., *Slavery and the Rise of the Atlantic System* (Cambridge, 1991), 76–81.

anxieties of the era. But the souls to be harvested for Christ and the goods that would flow to European markets made the pursuit worthwhile to explorers and colonizers.[17]

Europeans saw a variety of possibilities in the Americas. In places where the climate seemed appropriate, the newcomers hoped to cultivate well-known plants, such as grapes and (as the rise of plantations in São Tomé and Brazil reveal) sugar. But Europeans were also open to new commodities, such as chocolate. The most important of these was tobacco, which seemed able to heal a variety of human ailments and bring pleasure as well. Some Europeans, notably the English king James I, opposed the trade because they feared it would lead to the degradation of their societies. But as Marcy Norton and Daviken Studnicki-Gizbert reveal, such hesitance emerged long after the plant had become an international phenomenon. Merchants saw profits in tobacco well before English colonists considered planting it along the banks of the James River.[18]

Most historical interpretations of sixteenth-century European interest in the Americas emphasize the role of the Spanish and the Portuguese, but the French were also active participants in the Atlantic Basin. Scholars have earlier written at length about the inability of the French to establish populous colonies in the Western Hemisphere, and some have also addressed Americans' understanding of French efforts.[19] In this volume, Philip P. Boucher manages nothing less than what he calls a "tour d'horizon" of the French presence across the Atlantic world before 1635. During this formative era, major French interest was not in Canada but instead in Brazil and Florida. As Boucher reveals, matters of religion were central to their overseas efforts.

17. Bartolomé de Las Casas, *Brevissima relacion de la destruycion de las Indias* (Seville, [1552]).

18. See Marcy Norton, "Tasting Empire: Chocolate and the European Internalization of Mesomerican Aesthetics," *AHR,* CXI (2006), 660–691. For the history of Europeans' understanding of the plant during this era, see Peter C. Mancall, "Tales Tobacco Told in Sixteenth-Century Europe," *Environmental History,* IX (2004), 648–678.

19. For the French presence in North America see Peter Moogk, *La Nouvelle France: The Making of French Canada—A Cultural History* (East Lansing, Mich., 2000); for the long-term impact of the French in Canada, see J. M. Bumsted, "The Cultural Landscape of Early Canada," in Bernard Bailyn and Philip D. Morgan, eds., *Strangers within the Realm: Cultural Margins of the First British Empire* (Chapel Hill, N.C., 1991), 363–392; for indigenous views, see Cornelius J. Jaenen, "Amerindian Views of French Culture in the Seventeenth Century," *Canadian Historical Review,* LV (1974), 261–291.

But worldly concerns also mattered to the French, as Peter Cook demonstrates. When the French crossed the ocean, they paid attention to Native American organization of their communities. His close study of newcomers' words used in describing indigenous societies suggests that the French, to make sense of Native Americans, were breaking away from preexisting cultural and political categories. This shift in a European *mentalité* had ramifications in the three American locales where the French established overseas entrepôts during the sixteenth century. Even more, it suggests that the Atlantic experience—specifically European knowledge of indigenous American nations—altered intellectual constructs everywhere.

English policymakers knew about the overseas expeditions of the Spanish, Portuguese, and French, and they knew, too, the ways that continental Europeans profited from the Americas. When the time came to plant an English colony in Virginia in the early seventeenth century, the English also had a model of colonization that had worked for them in the Caribbean. This expansion into the West Indies is the subject of Philip D. Morgan's detailed re-creation of an English colonial effort that, though known to some historians, has not yet become central to our collective understanding of the early colonial era. No other area attracted so much English attention during the sixteenth century, and over time many of those whose initial overseas journeys took them to the islands found their way to the mainland. By the latter decades of the seventeenth century, this migration played a crucial role in the establishment of South Carolina as, in Peter Wood's memorable phrasing, a "colony of a colony."[20] That later colonial project was a long-term result of this earlier English venture and the documentation of its profits in published travel accounts and unpublished navigational maps. The islands also served as a laboratory for English experiments with the plant that would, in the long run, provide Virginia's economic salvation: tobacco.

The fourth section of this book follows English efforts to interpret the mass of information they had gathered about Native Americans, Africans, and other Europeans. Many of the English who prepared plans for what became Virginia drew on the history of their own nation. They located the settlement of eastern North America within the context of an ancient outward expansion of the Anglo-Norman population that began soon after the Norman invasion of 1066. Long before the Virginia Company tried to find investors and recruits, the English had already subdued much of Wales and Scotland. The Elizabethans had renewed the effort to bring Ireland into the

20. Peter Wood, *Black Majority: Negroes in Colonial South Carolina from 1670 through the Stono Rebellion* (New York, 1974), 13–34.

English realm. Sir Humphrey Gilbert was one of a number of individuals who had the opportunity to obtain lands in America because of his prior service in Ireland. Other Englishmen gained opportunities in the Western Hemisphere because of their individual experiences elsewhere. John Smith, Sir Walter Ralegh, and other men crisscrossed the Atlantic; their experiences link personal biography with the history of colonization.[21]

Further, the Elizabethans and early Stuarts knew that they were not the first Europeans to establish settlements in the Western Hemisphere. The most astute of these English observers might have read Richard Eden's mid-sixteenth-century translation of the history of early Spanish conquest written by the Italian linguist Peter Martyr (known to those on the Continent as Pietro Martire d'Anghiera). Others might have seen Richard Willes's collection of travel accounts, published in 1577, which included Peter Martyr's *Decades (De orbe novo)* as well as details about Europeans who made long-distance voyages. By the 1580s English readers could have found a translation of Las Casas's indictment of the conquistadores' treatment of Natives in the Western Hemisphere; this text later encouraged what became known as the Black Legend of the Spanish conquest. The Protestant English already believed in the superiority of their religion over that of Rome, as they demonstrated on the battlefield in Ireland and celebrated in their literature. Now they had proof that Catholics were despoiling the Americas and retarding the spread of Reformed Christianity. They knew that they could not repeat the errors of their European predecessors' ways. This anxiety forms the subject of Andrew Fitzmaurice's sensitive examination of the appropriation of indigenous property. The English approached the Americas with full understanding of the potential rights possessed by indigenous peoples, and they accused the Spanish of violating these rights. Drawing distinctions between the Spaniards' morality and their own, however, was not always easy, especially for members of the English elite who had great qualms about the entire overseas venture.[22]

21. R. R. Davies, *Domination and Conquest: The Experience of Ireland, Scotland, and Wales, 1100–1300* (Cambridge, 1990); Nicholas Canny, *The Elizabethan Conquest of Ireland: A Pattern Established, 1565–76* (Hassocks, 1976); Canny, *Making Ireland British, 1580–1650* (Oxford, 2001).

22. *The Decades of the Newe Worlde, or West India* (London, 1555); Willes, *The History of Travayle in the West and East Indies* (London, 1577); Bartolomé de Las Casas, *The Spanish Colonie, or Briefe Chronicle of the Acts and Gestes of the Spaniardes in the West Indies, Called the Newe World . . .* , trans. M. M. S. (London, 1583); a later edition, with ghastly engravings of purported Spanish atrocities, circulated again in the middle of the seventeenth century with a title that revealed its intent: Las Casas, *The*

As a result of the deep knowledge available in England during the sixteenth century, none of the founders of the Virginia Company could have imagined himself as an innovator. The entire purpose of their venture was to establish an English presence on the North American mainland before their European competitors used up its natural resources or converted the locals to Catholicism. This desire to colonize sprang from the efforts of individuals who believed that the future success of the realm lay in establishing developments abroad. No one promoted the venture more assiduously than the younger Richard Hakluyt. In the 1580s and 1590s, he collected and published historical travel narratives to goad the English into action. Englishmen, he argued, needed to pay attention to their own history as well as current-day adventures of other Europeans. David Harris Sacks investigates a long manuscript Hakluyt wrote in 1584 but never published, now known as the "Discourse of Western Planting." Hakluyt made an explicit argument for English colonization based on economic concerns, specifically the possibility of extracting material wealth from the Western Hemisphere and finding work for unemployed and underemployed Englishmen. He also urged the English to halt the spread of Catholic influence in North America. Sacks's essay explores compelling hints in Hakluyt's manuscript that suggest one way to overcome the kinds of qualms that Fitzmaurice describes: colonization, even if it meant appropriation of indigenous property, could be justified on the grounds that the English would bring reformed (Protestant) religion to the American mainland.[23]

Hakluyt was, in many ways, a man consumed with books and the les-

---

Tears of the Indians: Being an Historical and True Account of the Cruel Massacres and Slaughters of above Twenty Millions of Innocent People; Committed by the Spaniards in the Islands of Hispaniola, Cuba, Jamaica, Etc. . . . (London, 1656). Protestant English: see Thomas Churchyard, *A Generall Rehearsall of Warres* . . . (London, 1579); John Derricke, *The Image of Irelande* ([London?], 1581); Sir William Herbert, *Croftus sive de Hibernia Liber,* ed. Arthur Keaveny and John A. Madden (Dublin, 1992).

23. Richard Hakluyt, *Divers Voyages Touching the Discoverie of America, and the Ilands Adjacent* . . . (London, 1582); Hakluyt, *The Principall Navigations Voiages and Discoveries of the English Nation* . . . (London, 1589); and Hakluyt, *The Principal Navigations, Voyages, Traffiques, and Discoveries of the English Nation* . . . , 3 vols. (London, 1598–1600); and, now available in a superb modern edition, Hakluyt, *A Particuler Discourse concerninge the Greate Necessitie and Manifolde Commodyties That Are Like to Growe to This Realme of Englande by the Westerne Discoveries Lately Attempted* . . . , ed. David B. Quinn and Alison M. Quinn, Works Issued by the Hakluyt Society, Extra Ser., no. 45 (London, 1993).

sons they offered about the wider world.[24] Benjamin Schmidt's essay demonstrates the crucial influence that printed books had in this era—not only for the English but for continental Europeans as well. Schmidt focuses on Sir Walter Ralegh's reading and others' printing and reading of his texts. Ralegh's account of Guiana, specifically the details about the monsters he heard roamed the South American interior, have struck modern observers as extravagant. But the extravagance was crucial to this information's circulation. Schmidt depicts an explorer as reader and also as the object of readers' attention, made even more compelling by fantastic images later fabricated by continental publishers.

Books also figured centrally in the life and reputation of Captain John Smith, the most famous Englishman who actually saw Virginia during its formative years. In David Shields's interpretation, Smith was more than a heroic and battle-scarred warrior who proved himself in Turkey before setting sail for the Chesapeake. By the end of his life, he had also become a figure of great literary significance whose experience in the Americas testified to the next logical arena for English expansion. Schmidt's Ralegh and Shields's Smith share traits, but the differences are crucial: one spent years imprisoned in the Tower of London for advancing what he believed to be the goals of his nation, whereas the other, a blustering egomaniac, helped provide an ideological justification for overseas expansion. Why did Smith become so vital to the enterprise and its history? Because, as Shields cleverly reveals, Smith's biography evoked the ancient Britons, men of both action and contemplation. Smith's life story summed up British history and what the Stuarts hoped was the realm's boundless future.

The final essays in this volume bring the reader back to Tsenacommacah at the time of the English settlement of Jamestown. James Horn returns us to the shores of the Chesapeake and reconstructs a polyglot world from the perspective of the three peoples who hoped to control it. None of them possessed perfect information about where others could be found or their adversaries' true intentions. Though the Indians possessed the upper hand initially, the Spanish were at the time the most powerful European nation interested in North America, and the English ultimately prevailed in this region; Horn exposes "the half-baked impressions" that impeded

24. For an in-depth study of Hakluyt and how his understanding of printed books, among other sources, shaped his views on English overseas efforts, see Peter C. Mancall, *Hakluyt's Promise: An Elizabethan's Obsession for an English America* (New Haven, Conn., 2007).

each group's ability to devise appropriate strategies for coping with rapidly changing conditions. Horn's essay reminds us of the importance of contingency and error. It appears near the conclusion to make a very specific point: no matter how much the peoples of the territory the English labeled "Virginia" had learned about the aspirations, cultures, and mores of others in the region, travel across the Atlantic necessarily launched the putative colonists into a world of suspicion and rumor—a world still dominated by the Powhatans, at least until the 1620s.

Even as they tried to find their way in a world of imperfect knowledge, the English also knew all too well that some of those same Europeans they had been studying wished them ill. In the sixteenth century, as J. H. Elliott explains in his keynote address to the conference, Iberians controlled much of the North Atlantic. When other Europeans tried to challenge Spanish hegemony, as the French did in Florida in the mid-1560s, the Iberians believed they should be eradicated. The English could get away with establishing a colony in Jamestown in the early seventeenth century only because the Spanish saw no need to push them away: there was no gold or silver there, despite the occasional claims of some Englishmen, and so the Spanish were not interested. The English remained at Jamestown, then, because they were insignificant to European competitors and because they managed to survive, if at times only barely, the region's notorious ailments.[25]

The words of Stuart B. Schwartz, whose summary comment to the conference appears as the last substantive contribution to this volume, provide the ideal concluding message for a book that focuses on early Virginia—a place that he correctly notes "played simply a small part in a great global story." Although the repercussions of the founding of English colonies on the North American mainland would eventually be felt everywhere, the story told by the chapters in this book are more specifically Atlantic in focus because, by 1625, the later global story was not yet clear.

The Atlantic world of the late sixteenth and early seventeenth centuries was far more complex and interconnected than previous historians of Virginia acknowledged. The story of Jamestown cannot be understood by erecting a statue to Captain John Smith or beating a pilgrim's path to the shores of the James to worship at the shrine of democracy's birth in North

25. For the dangers facing the English, see Carville V. Earle, "Environment, Disease, and Mortality in Early Virginia," in Tate and Ammerman, eds., *The Chesapeake in the Seventeenth Century*, 96–125; Karen Ordahl Kupperman, "Apathy and Death in Early Jamestown," *Journal of American History*, LXVI (1979), 24–40.

America. Virginia's story only becomes intelligible when seen as a small, and not always significant, part of an Atlantic history.

Bishop Hall's Failure

Many early witnesses hoped that Virginia would fail. The Powhatans watched in dismay when colonists multiplied in Tsenacommacah by the early 1620s. Some English contemporaries, *pace* American lore, also thought that colonization was a bad idea. Among them was Joseph Hall, later the bishop of Norwich, who published a small book in an effort to halt what he believed was unnecessary travel. In a scathing pamphlet entitled *Quo Vadis? A Just Censure of Travell as It Is Commonly Undertaken by the Gentlemen of Our Nation,* published in London in 1617—soon after colonists along the James recognized that tobacco production might bring profit—Hall complained about the very fact of travel. He acknowledged the potential material reward of the "Earthly commodities" found abroad but concentrated on the soul-diminishing effects of the "unnecessary agitation" brought by travel. He sought to prevent travel among the elites who, for their part, saw visits to distant places as crucial stops on the path to civility.[26]

Hall had no qualms about travel for commercial benefit or diplomacy. God, after all, might have surrounded England with the sea, but the Almighty did not intend for the English or anyone else to remain always at home, for God "hath stored no parcell of earth with a purpose of private reservation." Hall sought to stop only what he termed "the Travell of curiosity." He feared that exposure to different people and alluring ideas would lead to moral bankruptcy. It was an act of desperation "to send forth our children into those places which are professedly infectious, whose very goodnesse is either impietie, or superstition[.] If wee desired to have sonnes poisoned with mis-beleefe, what could wee doe otherwise?" The most dreadful places were "those parts which are only thought worth our viewing, [as they] are most contagious; and will not part with either pleasure, or information, without some tang of wickednesse." Travel, so Hall argued, had become too popular. The English seemed to believe that "he should not bee worthy to tread upon the earth, that would not emulate *Drake,* and *Candish* [Cavendish], in compassing it." Hall admonished the

---

26. Frederic W. Gleach, *Powhatan's World and Colonial Virginia: A Conflict of Cultures* (Lincoln, Neb., 1997); [Joseph Hall], *Quo Vadis? A Just Censure of Travell as It Is Commonly Undertaken by the Gentlemen of Our Nation* (London, 1617), sig. A4r, [A5r].

gentry to stay put. "God hath given us a world of our owne, wherein there is nothing wanting to earthly contentment." The Almighty had already provided whatever a rational individual could want, and so Hall told his English readers to "enrich your selves with your owne mines, improve those blessed opportunities which God hath given you, to your mutuall advantage; and care not to be like any but your selves." He enjoined Englishmen to preserve their identities by remaining at home and eschewing the stimulation of eye-opening wonders.[27]

Had Hall's plea succeeded, Virginia would not have become a permanent New World settlement. Jamestown and Virginia survived because individuals converged there who used their imagination and curiosity to engage with their new circumstances. Their motivations are mostly lost to history, but two things remain clear. Despite Joseph Hall's caveat, people traveled to strange and different lands, some voluntarily and many not, expanding the Atlantic world's compass. Second, the indigenous residents of Tsenacommacah, seeing certain advantages in the English presence, allowed them to remain near the shores of the Chesapeake, thus ensuring their survival even though the newcomers proved unreliable and annoying neighbors.

In the end, neither the Powhatans, other European nations, nor English skeptics could halt the development of Virginia in the seventeenth century. By 1624, the struggling outpost had become a colony under royal auspices, survived an uprising by Powhatans who had decided that the English had overstayed their welcome, incorporated Africans into the labor force, and begun to make a profit from shipping tobacco across the ocean. In the process, Native Americans, Europeans, and Africans together made Virginia a critical arena of the emerging Atlantic world.

27. Hall, *Quo Vadis?* 2 (distribution of commodities by God), 5 (curiosity), 11–13 (children), 24 (Drake and Cavendish); 87 (happy at home), 97 (misnumbered as 91) ("enrich your selves").

part one

NATIVE AMERICAN SETTINGS

Daniel K. Richter

TSENACOMMACAH AND THE ATLANTIC WORLD

In what may be the only surviving early-seventeenth-century example of the genre, William Strachey, secretary of the Virginia Company of London, did his best to reduce to Roman letters a "scornefull song" that victorious Powhatan warriors chanted after they killed three or four Englishmen "and tooke one Symon Score a saylor and one Cob a boy prisoners" in 1611:

> 1. Mattanerew shashashewaw crawango pechecoma
> Whe Tassantassa inoshashaw yehockan pocosak
> Whe, whe, yah, ha, ha, ne, he wittowa, wittowa.
>
> 2. Mattanerew shashashewaw, erawango pechecoma
> Captain Newport inoshashaw neir in hoc nantion matassan
> Whe weh, yah, ha, ha, etc.
>
> 3. Mattanerew shashashewaw erowango pechecoma
> Thomas Newport inoshashaw neir in hoc nantion monocock
> Whe whe etc.
>
> 4. Mattanerew shushashewaw erowango pechecoma
> Pockin Simon moshasha mingon nantian Tamahuck
> Whe whe, etc.

Strachey explained that the refrain—which almost needs no translation— mocked the "lamentation our people made" for the deaths and captive-

Earlier versions of this chapter were presented at the Atlantic World Workshop at New York University, Feb. 24, 2004; "The Atlantic World and Virginia, 1550–1624," conference, Williamsburg, Va., Mar. 4, 2004; and Centre interuniversitaire d'études sur les lettres, les arts et les traditions, Université Laval, Québec, Feb. 11, 2005. I thank the participants in those events and, especially, Lauren Benton, Kathleen J. Bragdon, Anna C. Brickhouse, William H. Carter, Nicole Eustace (whose "very big Rolodex" analogy did not make it into the text but clarified many things), J. Frederick Fausz, April Lee Hatfield, Juan José Ponce, Sharon Richter, Larry E. Tise, Laurier Turgeon, and Alden T. Vaughan for their comments and assistance.

taking. But far more interesting is the gloss he provided for the verses. The Powhatans sang of

> how they killed us for all our Poccasacks, that is our Guns, and for all Captain [Christopher] Newport brought them Copper and could hurt Thomas Newport (a boy whose name indeed is Thomas Savadge, whome Captain Newport leaving with Powhatan to learne the Language, at what tyme he presented the said Powhatan with a copper Crowne and other guifts from his Majestie, sayd he was his sonne) for all his Monnacock that is his bright Sword, and how they could take Symon . . . Prysoner for all his Tamahauke, that is his Hatchett.[1]

In spite of all their material goods—their guns, their copper, their swords, their hatchets—and in spite of the fact that many of these same vaunted items had been given to the Powhatans by Virginia's leader, Newport, in the name of the mighty King James, the Englishmen had, at least on this occasion, been made subject to Native people's power.[2]

Like the song, this essay tells a story about goods and power. Or, rather, it tells three related stories about Chesapeake Algonquian men and what appear to have been their quests for goods and power from the emerging Atlantic world of the late sixteenth and early seventeenth centuries: Paquiquineo (Don Luis), who left the Chesapeake around 1561 and returned with a party of Spanish Jesuit missionaries in 1570; Namontack, who traveled to England with Christopher Newport in 1608 and again in 1609 (while the Thomas "Newport" Savage of the song took up residence in Powhatan country); and Uttamatomakkin (also known as Tomocomo or Tomakin), who made the oceanic voyage with Pocahontas in 1616–1617. We know

1. William Strachey, *The Historie of Travell into Virginia Britania (1612),* ed. Louis B. Wright and Virginia Freund, Works Issued by the Hakluyt Society, 2d Ser., no. 103 (London, 1953), 85–86. On Strachey's linguistic skills, see Frank T. Siebert, Jr., "Resurrecting Virginia Algonquian from the Dead: The Reconstituted and Historical Phonology of Powhatan," in James M. Crawford, ed., *Studies in Southeastern Languages* (Athens, Ga., 1975), 291–294. Except in direct quotations, wherever possible I have standardized the spelling of Algonquian words according to the usage in Helen C. Rountree, *Pocahontas's People: The Powhatan Indians of Virginia through Four Centuries* (Norman, Okla., 1990).

2. Strachey's gloss, of course, also needs a gloss, thanks to the irregularities of seventeenth-century punctuation and the ambiguity of the word *for.* While it is possible that Strachey meant that the English had been killed *for* their weapons—to take possession of them—the references to Newport and Savage and, especially, the combination of the word *all* with the singular sword and hatchet makes "in spite of" a more likely reading, for all April Hatfield's much-appreciated efforts to convince me otherwise.

very little about any of these men, their status, or their motives, and what we do know comes down to us in highly colored tales written by Europeans who were not exactly their friends. Nonetheless, for all the dangers of skimpy sources, of European chroniclers' distortions, and, possibly, a historian's overactive imagination, the stories deserve serious attention. Traveling at crucial moments in their people's early engagement with Europeans, the three voyagers allow us to glimpse what the emerging Atlantic world meant to the elite of the Powhatan paramount chiefdom—if not to the common people who gave their "densely inhabited land" its name, *Tsenacommacah*. In their travels, Paquiquineo and Namontack apparently attempted to exert control over the access to the goods the 1611 song would mock in order to build power for their people, their political superiors, and themselves. Uttamatomakkin's travels, by contrast, confirmed what the singers by then already knew: that power would have to be asserted in spite of, not by way of, "guifts from his Majestie."[3]

Chiefdoms and the World of Goods

Just as the arrival of Spaniards and English in the Chesapeake cannot be understood apart from the political and economic characteristics of competitive early modern nation-states, the exploits of these three voyagers from Tsenacommacah—and the significance of material goods in the Powhatan song—cannot be understood apart from the political and economic characteristics of the social forms known as chiefdoms. In the classic definition by anthropologist Elman R. Service, "Chiefdoms are *redistributional societies* with a permanent central agency of coordination" and a "profoundly inegalitarian" political order in which redistributive functions center on exalted hereditary leaders. For Service and his contemporary Morton Fried, the

3. Strachey, *Historie of Travell*, ed. Wright and Freund, 86. Most scholars translate *Tsenacommacah* (or *Tsenacomoco*) as "densely inhabited land" (Frederic W. Gleach, *Powhatan's World and Colonial Virginia: A Conflict of Cultures* [Lincoln, Neb., 1997], 25). According to David Beers Quinn, drawing on the work of James A. Geary, the word combines a root meaning "'land dwelt upon,' 'dwelling-house,' 'house-site,'" with a prefix meaning "close together" ("The Map of Raleigh's Virginia," in Quinn, ed., *The Roanoke Voyages, 1584–1590: Documents to Illustrate the English Voyages to North America under the Patent Granted to Walter Raleigh in 1584*, 2 vols., Works Issued by the Hakluyt Society, 2d Ser., nos. 104–105 [London, 1955], II, 854). On another occasion, Geary proposed "it is a nearby dwelling-place" ("Strachey's Vocabulary of Indian Words Used in Virginia, 1612," in Strachey, *Historie of Travell*, 211). Helen C. Rountree suggests "our place" (*Pocahontas, Powhatan, Opechancanough: Three Indian Lives Changed by Jamestown* [Charlottesville, Va., 2005], 8).

material underpinnings of stratified chiefdoms lay in "differential rights of access to basic resources . . . either directly (air, water, and food) or indirectly" through the control of such basic productive resources as "land, raw materials for tools, water for irrigation, and materials to build a shelter." Subsequent comparative archaeological work, however, moves beyond such straightforward materialist definitions to embrace a much more complex variety of cultural forms.[4]

Much of this work roots chiefdoms in what is known as a "prestige-goods economy." As archaeologists Susan Frankenstein and Michael Rowlands explain, in such an economy, "political advantage [is] gained through exercising control over access to resources that can only be obtained through external trade." These resources are not the kind of basic utilitarian items described by Service and Fried but instead "wealth objects needed in social transactions." They may be, in the words of anthropologist Mary Helms, "crafted items acquired ready-made from geographically distant places" or things "valued in their natural, unworked form as inherently endowed with qualitative worth—animal pelts, shells, feathers, and the like." In either case, they "constitute a type of inalienable wealth, meaning they are goods that cannot be conceptually separated from their place or condition of origin but always relate whoever possesses them to that place or condition." The social power of such goods thus comes from their association with their source, often described as "ancestral beings—creator deities, culture-heroes, primordial powers—that are credited with having first created or

4. Elman R. Service, *Primitive Social Organization: An Evolutionary Perspective* (New York, 1962), 143-177, quotations on 144, 150; Morton H. Fried, *The Evolution of Political Society: An Essay in Political Anthropology* (New York, 1967), 52 (quotation), 185-226. Fried's four-stage evolutionary scheme of "egalitarian," "ranked," and "stratified" "societies" and "the state" does not entirely coincide with Service's "band," "tribe," "chiefdom," and "state" levels of "sociocultural integration," but clearly the two scholars had similar views on the political-economic principles at work. The literature critiquing and elaborating evolutionary typologies is vast. For useful overviews, see Thomas E. Emerson, *Cahokia and the Archaeology of Power* (Tuscaloosa, Ala., 1997), 12-18; and Timothy Earle, "Archaeology, Property, and Prehistory," *Annual Review of Anthropology,* XXIX (2000), 39-60. For comments on the continued heuristic value of such an approach, see Robert D. Drennan, "Regional Demography in Chiefdoms," in Drennan and Carlos A. Uribe, eds., *Chiefdoms in the Americas* (Lanham, Md., 1987), 313-315; Patricia Galloway, *Choctaw Genesis, 1500-1700* (Lincoln, Neb., 1995), 38-40; and Earle, *How Chiefs Come to Power: The Political Economy in Prehistory* (Stanford, Calif., 1997), 1-16. For an introduction to chiefdom forms in the southeast during the period of European contact, see Charles Hudson, *The Southeastern Indians* (Knoxville, Tenn., 1976), 202-211.

crafted the world, its creatures, its peoples, and their cultural skills." Indeed, inalienable goods never fully belong to those to whom they have been given; they always remain in some sense the property of the giver. Those who control such prestige goods wield power because of their connection to—and control over—power at the goods' source.[5]

In eastern North America, the prestige goods that shaped the power of chiefdoms were the crystals, minerals, copper, shells, and mysteriously crafted ritual items that moved through the ancient trade routes of the continent. Their potency came from their rarity and their association with distant sources of spiritual power. But those same characteristics made eastern North America's prestige-goods chiefdoms inherently unstable. Lacking a monopoly of force to defend their privileges, chiefs depended for their status on a fragile ideological consensus at home and on equally fragile external sources of supply and trade routes they could not directly control. Chiefdoms thus perched on a fine line between slipping "back" into less hierarchical forms or moving "forward" toward the coercive apparatus of a state while "cycling" between periods of centralization and decentralization. As a result, as social forms, they were forever in flux.[6]

The basic political units of late-sixteenth- and early-seventeenth-century Tsenacommacah were just such unstable prestige-goods chiefdoms, headed by men and women called, respectively, *weroances* and *weroansquas,* whose

5. Susan M. Frankenstein and Michael J. Rowlands, "The Internal Structure and Regional Context of Early Iron Age Society in South-western Germany," *Institute of Archaeology Bulletin,* XV (1978), 73-112, quotation on 76; Mary W. Helms, "Political Lords and Political Ideology in Southeastern Chiefdoms: Comments and Observations," in Alex W. Barker and Timothy R. Pauketat, eds., *Lords of the Southeast: Social Inequality and the Native Elites of Southeastern North America,* Archaeological Papers of the American Anthropological Association, no. 3 (Washington, D.C., 1992), esp. 187–188 (quotations); Pauketat, "The Reign and Ruin of the Lords of Cahokia: A Dialectic of Dominance," ibid., 31–51. Important theoretical statements on the political economy of gift giving include Marcel Mauss, *The Gift: The Form and Reason for Exchange in Archaic Societies,* trans. W. D. Halls (1924; London, 2002); Marshall Sahlins, *Stone Age Economics* (Chicago, 1972); Mary Douglas and Baron Isherwood, *The World of Goods* (New York, 1979); Annette B. Weiner, *Inalienable Possessions: The Paradox of Keeping-While-Giving* (Berkeley, Calif., 1992); and Maurice Godelier, *The Enigma of the Gift,* trans. Nora Scott (Chicago, 1999).

6. Timothy K. Earle, "Chiefdoms in Archaeological and Ethnohistorical Perspective," *Annual Review of Anthropology,* XVI (1987), 281, 297; Galloway, *Choctaw Genesis,* 67–74; Emerson, *Cahokia and the Archaeology of Power,* 17–18; Frankenstein and Rowlands, "Internal Structure and Regional Context of Early Iron Age Society," *Institute of Archaeology Bulletin,* XV (1978), 78–79.

titles descended, as John Smith explained, to "the first heyres of the Sisters, and so successively the weomens heires."[7] Most of these local chiefdoms were subordinate to a larger paramount chiefdom that Powhatan, or Wahunsonacock, presided over as *mamanatowick* in the early seventeenth century. The weroances and particularly the mamanatowick owed their status in part to kinship, through their own matrilineages and through marriage alliances with the multiple spouses to which apparently only the elite were entitled. (Wahunsonacock reputedly had a hundred wives strategically placed in subordinate towns.) In a way Service and Fried would recognize, weroances also to some extent controlled food surpluses through tribute from subordinates and through corn, bean, and squash fields their people planted and harvested to be stored in their granaries. (These food stores might have taken on additional significance during the repeated droughts and crop failures of the late sixteenth and early seventeenth centuries.) But most important, weroances' power evidently rested on their control of such goods as copper from the continental interior and pearls from the Atlantic coast. As archaeologist Stephen R. Potter puts it, "Chiefs handled worldy risks confronting their societies by serving as both a banker to their people and a culture broker to outsiders."[8]

To a significant degree, the power that derived from these functions came from a weroance's ability to distribute prestige goods to followers and thus create bonds of asymmetrical obligation. "He [who] perfourmes any remarkeable or valerous exployt in open act of Armes, or by Stratagem," ob-

7. Helen C. Rountree, *The Powhatan Indians of Virginia: Their Traditional Culture* (Norman, Okla., 1989), 103–125; John Smith, *A True Relation . . .* (1608), in Philip L. Barbour, ed., *The Complete Works of Captain John Smith (1580–1631),* 3 vols. (Chapel Hill, N.C., 1986), I, 61 (quotation).

8. Kathleen M. Brown, *Good Wives, Nasty Wenches, and Anxious Patriarchs: Gender, Race, and Power in Colonial Virginia* (Chapel Hill, N.C., 1996), 45–53; Alex W. Barker, "Powhatan's Pursestrings: On the Meaning of Surplus in a Seventeenth Century Algonkian Chiefdom," in Barker and Pauketat, eds., *Lords of the Southeast,* 61–80; E. Randolph Turner III, "Native American Protohistoric Interactions in the Powhatan Core Area," in Helen C. Rountree, ed., *Powhatan Foreign Relations, 1500–1722* (Charlottesville, Va., 1993), 78–83; Stephen R. Potter, *Commoners, Tribute, and Chiefs: The Development of Algonquian Culture in the Potomac Valley* (Charlottesville, Va., 1993), 149–173, quotation on 169; Martin D. Gallivan, *James River Chiefdoms: The Rise of Social Inequality in the Chesapeake* (Lincoln, Neb., 2003), esp. 1–8, 21–31; Margaret Holmes Williamson, *Powhatan Lords of Life and Death: Command and Consent in Seventeenth-Century Virginia* (Lincoln, Neb., 2003), esp. 129–172. On the droughts and crop failures of this period, see David W. Stahle et al., "The Lost Colony and Jamestown Droughts," *Science,* CCLXXX (1998), 564–567.

served Strachey, "the king taking notice of the same, doth . . . solemnely reward him with some Present of Copper, or Chayne of Perle and Beades." Lavish feasts from chiefly stores and perhaps the bestowal of sexual favors from young women in the weroance's household served similar redistributive functions for diplomatic visitors. Such actions merged into a broader pattern that might best be described as the conspicuous display of chiefly power. Wahunsonacock "hath a house in which he keepeth his kind of Treasure, as skinnes, copper, pearle, and beades, which he storeth up against the time of his death and buriall," wrote Smith. The structure was "50 or 60 yards in length, frequented only by Priestes," and at each corner stood "Images as Sentinels, one of a Dragon, another a Beare, the 3[d] like a Leopard and the fourth a giantlike man, all made evillfavordly, according to their best workmanship." Smith—who, it should be recalled, appeared to be an emissary from a strangely female-less society—also went out of his way to note that the mamanatowick "hath as many women as he will, whereof when hee lieth on his bed, one sitteth at his head, and another at his feet, but when he sitteth, one sitteth on his right hand and another on his left."[9]

Such conspicuous display embodied the strength and wealth of the people and their connection to the sources of the power that prestige goods and marriage connections represented; indeed, the term *weroance* roughly translates as "he is wealthy." Such goods visibly accumulated at the apex of the social and political order, in the person regarded "not only as a king but as halfe a God": the mamanatowick, a word incorporating the term *manitou,* or "spiritual power." The material, the spiritual, and the political were inseparable in the person of the mamanatowick and the people for whom he acted. "The wealth of the chief and his distribution of it are alike means by which he confers life and prosperity on his people," anthropologist Margaret Holmes Williamson explains. "Indeed, he really has nothing of 'his own' as a private person. Rather, he is the steward of the group's wealth, deploying it on their behalf for their benefit." The mamanatowick, "by being rich and generous and by living richly . . . makes bountiful the macrocosm that he represents."[10]

The material, the spiritual, and the political also came together in the fact that most of the powerful goods that chiefs accumulated were interred with

9. Strachey, *Historie of Travell,* ed. Wright and Freund, 114; Brown, *Good Wives,* 66–67; John Smith, *A Map of Virginia* . . . (1612), in Barbour, ed., *Works of Smith,* I, 173–174.

10. Gallivan, *James River Chiefdoms,* 169; Gleach, *Powhatan's World,* 28–34; Williamson, *Powhatan Lords of Life and Death,* 152. See also Sahlins, *Stone Age Economics,* 185–191.

them when they died. Weroances' "bodies are first bowelled, then dryed upon hurdles till they bee verie dry, and so about the most of their jointes and necke they hang bracelets or chaines of copper, pearle, and such like, as they use to weare," Smith observed and archaeologists confirm. "Their inwards they stuffe[d] with copper beads and covered with a skin, hatchets and such" before wrapping the corpses "very carefully in white skins" and laying them on mats in a temple house with "what remaineth of this kinde of wealth . . . set at their feet in baskets." In effect, then, because prestige goods died with the chief, weroances and would-be weroances always had to create for themselves anew the tribute networks, the trade connections, the diplomatic and marriage alliances, the masses of prestige goods that undergirded their power. This fact, more than some abstract historical force called "cycling," undergirded the inherent instability of these chiefdoms. And it brings us at last to our three travelers, who apparently sought just such connections, alliances, and goods, either as rising chiefs themselves or on behalf of the weroances who sent them.[11]

Paquiquineo

We cannot be absolutely certain that the man usually known by the Spanish name Don Luis or Don Luis de Velasco was originally from Tsenacommacah, or even that Tsenacommacah was the same place that he and the Spanish called *Ajacán*. Yet through careful detective work, Clifford M. Lewis and Albert J. Loomie reasonably concluded in the mid-twentieth century that "there are enough indications available to link Don Luis with the ruling Powhatan clique" and that Ajacán included territories between the James and York rivers that were later known to be part of the Powhatan paramount chiefdom.[12] Spanish sources variously describe Paquiquineo as "a young *ca-*

11. Smith, *Map of Virginia,* in Barbour, ed., *Works of Smith,* I, 169 (quotation); Strachey, *Historie of Travell,* ed. Wright and Freund, 94–95; Potter, *Commoners, Tribute, and Chiefs,* 210–220. As Helen C. Rountree observes, "'things' is the operative word" in describing the Powhatans' agenda in dealing with Europeans ("The Powhatans and the English: A Case of Multiple Conflicting Agendas," in Rountree, ed., *Powhatan Foreign Relations,* 110, 177–183, quotation on 178). Seth William Mallios, "In the Hands of 'Indian Givers': Exchange and Violence at Ajacan, Roanoke, and Jamestown" (Ph.D. diss., University of Virginia, 1998), begins from similar premises about the importance of material exchange in relations between Powhatans and Europeans.

12. Clifford M. Lewis and Albert J. Loomie, *The Spanish Jesuit Mission in Virginia, 1570–1572* (Chapel Hill, N.C., 1953), 28–40, 58–62, quotation on 58; Rountree, *Pocahontas's People,* 15–20. None of the documents in Lewis and Loomie give Paquiquineo's

cique," as "a person of note" who "said he was a chief," as "the Indian son of a petty chief of Florida" who "gave out that he was the son of a great chief," as a chief's son "who for an Indian was of fine presence and bearing," or as "the brother of a principal chief of that region." Unhelpfully, the same sources say that, in 1570, he was either "more than twenty years of age" or "a man of fifty years." It is quite possible that, as Lewis and Loomie suggest, Paquiquineo was either the brother or father of Wahunsonacock and his successors Opitchapam and Opechancanough. Given the matrilineal descent of chiefs' titles and European chroniclers' unfamiliarity with the intricacies of Algonquian kinship terms, Paquiquineo might also have been the uncle of these later paramount chiefs. There is less reason to believe that, as Carl Bridenbaugh proposed, Paquiquineo actually *was* Opechancanough, although nearly anything is possible. Whatever the case, he was almost certainly a member of a chiefly lineage, if not that of the paramount mamanatowick, then of a subsidiary weroance. The one surviving Spanish document that uses his Algonquian name suggests his high status by referring to his traveling companions as his Indian servants *("su criado indios").*[13]

And, whatever the case, Paquiquineo seems to have gone into the Atlantic world because of his chiefly lineage, either on his own initiative, or at the behest of his weroance, or because the Spanish perceived him as a high-value captive. We do not know exactly how he found his way onto what was probably Antonio Velázquez's ship *Santa Catalina* in 1561. Ac-

------

Algonquian name, which, as far as I know, first appeared in English-language scholarship in Paul E. Hoffman, *A New Andalucia and a Way to the Orient: The American Southeast during the Sixteenth Century* (Baton Rouge, La., 1990), 184.

13. "Relation of Luis Gerónimo de Oré," ca. 1617, in Lewis and Loomie, *Spanish Jesuit Mission,* 179; "Relation of Juan de la Carrera . . . March 1, 1600," ibid., 131; "Relation of Juan Rogel between 1607 and 1611," ibid., 118; "Relation of Bartolomé Martínez," Oct. 24, 1610, ibid., 156; Francisco Sacchini, *Borgia, the Third Part of the History of the Society of Jesus* (1649), ibid., 221; Lewis and Loomie, *Spanish Jesuit Mission,* 58-62; Carl Bridenbaugh, *Jamestown, 1544-1699* (New York, 1980), 10-17; Rountree, *Pocahontas's People,* 18-19; entry 85, contaduría 286, no. 1, datas, fol. 171v, Archivo General de Indias, Seville. Ralph Hamor reported that the Chickahominies, who were not part of Powhatan's paramount chiefdom, considered the Spanish "odious" because *"Powhatans* father was driven by them from the *west-Indies* into those parts" (Raphe Hamor, *A True Discourse of the Present Estate of Virginia, and the Success of the Affaires There till the 18 of June, 1614* [London, 1615], 13). Helen Rountree argues that Paquiquineo was from a different kin group than Powhatan and that his chiefdom was not yet part of the paramount chiefdom in 1570 (*Pocahontas, Powhatan, Opechancanough,* 27-29).

counts written more than a generation later give three different versions of the story. Francisco Sacchini wrote that "the brother of a principal chief of that region gave himself up to some Spaniards sailing near Ajacán," although "none of his family knew of this." In much more detail, Luis Gerónimo de Oré explained that "while the *Adelantado* Pedro Menéndez, was governing the *presidios* of Florida, a ship from the port of Santa Elena lost its course toward the north, at a latitude of $37\frac{1}{2}°$ and put into a large bay which the sailors called the Bahía de Madre de Dios" and that "from among some Indians who came aboard they retained a young *cacique*." Bartolomé Martínez improbably had Menéndez himself sailing into the Chesapeake. Native people "came alongside in canoes and boarded the flagship," where "His Excellency, as was his custom, like another Alexander, regaled them with food and clothing." The boarding party included "a chief who brought his son." The *adelantado* "asked the chief for permission to take [Paquiquineo] . . . along that the King of Spain, his lord, might see him" and "gave his pledged word to return him with much wealth and many garments." According to Martínez, "The chief granted this and His Excellency took him to Castile, to the Court of King Philip II," who was "very pleased with him" and bestowed on him "many courtly favors and rich garments."[14]

The emphasis on clothing and material goods in these stories may capture something about how Paquiquineo understood his mission in an Atlantic world he would come to know too well. It is reasonable to assume that he planned to establish a relationship with Europeans who could provide him, his lineage, and his chiefdom with a source of the goods that brought power. Compared to other locations on the Atlantic coast, the Chesapeake had experienced few European visitors, shipwrecks, and their associated influxes of material goods before Paquiquineo's departure. Verrazano missed the bay in 1524. An English ship apparently blew in on a storm in 1546 and found "over thirty canoes" full of Native people who already knew enough about Europeans to bring along "as many as a thousand marten skins in exchange for knives, fishhooks and shirts." But such episodes were rare on a coast much off course for Europeans plying routes to and from either the West Indies and the Spanish Main or Newfoundland. With enough knowledge of Europeans to understand their potential as a source of copper, beads, and other prestige goods, Paquiquineo would have set off to establish a personal alliance, and a personal exchange relationship, that would substantially re-

14. Sacchini, *Borgia,* in Lewis and Loomie, *Spanish Jesuit Mission,* 221; "Relation of Martínez," "Relation of Gerónimo de Oré," in Lewis and Loomie, *Spanish Jesuit Mission,* 156, 179; Hoffman, *New Andalucia,* 181–187.

inforce the power of his lineage and chiefdom by bringing Europeans and their goods into the Chesapeake on a regular basis.[15]

Of course, in 1561, he could not know that it would be nearly a decade before he could return home or just how much of the Atlantic world he would see in the interim. Paquiquineo seems to have spent most of his time in Mexico City, living with Dominican priests, learning Spanish, undergoing catechization, and acquiring his new name in honor of his baptismal sponsor, the viceroy of New Spain. If he left home with any illusions that Spaniards were beneficent beings who would readily bestow their riches on Ajacán, those illusions must have been quickly dashed in the flesh-and-blood reality of the colonial capital that was rising on the ruins of Tenochtitlán — and on the backs of oppressed Native people. Yet he must also have seen the ways in which caciques from outlying districts could extract favors from the imperial regime and in general how indigenous people with claims to elite heritage could carve out positions of relative power. Whatever he (and his Dominican teachers) did to attract the attention and favors of the viceroy must have encouraged Paquiquineo to believe he could turn his situation to his advantage — if only he could get back home under the right conditions. "A clever talker," he touted "the grandeurs of his land," the willingness of his people to hear the Gospel, and his eagerness to provide "the help which Timothy gave to Saint Paul."[16]

Such talk helped get him from Mexico to Havana where, in 1566, he set sail with a party of thirty soldiers and two Dominican friars to establish a mission in Ajacán. The expedition never reached its goal, however. Paquiquineo claimed to be unable to recognize the entrance to Chesapeake Bay (which could have been a ruse because he distrusted the soldiers or just the honest ignorance of a landlubber), and a storm finally blew the party so far out to sea that they gave up.[17]

But Paquiquineo did not. Menéndez had "chanced upon" him in Havana at some point during the 1565–1566 expedition that slaughtered the French

15. Lewis and Loomie, *Spanish Jesuit Mission,* 13 (quoting deposition of "John, an Englishman born in Bristol"), 16; William C. Sturtevant, "Spanish-Indian Relations in Southeastern North America," *Ethnohistory,* IX (1962), 54–56; Potter, *Commoners, Tribute, and Chiefs,* 161–166; Turner, "Native American Protohistoric Interactions," in Rowntree, ed., *Powhatan Foreign Relations,* 92.

16. Charlotte M. Gradie, "The Powhatans in the Context of the Spanish Empire," in Rountree, ed., *Powhatan Foreign Relations,* 154–172; "Relation of Rogel," "Relation of Carrera," in Lewis and Loomie, *Spanish Jesuit Mission,* 118, 131, 133.

17. Gradie, "Powhatans in the Context of the Spanish Empire," in Rountree, ed., *Powhatan Foreign Relations,* 168–169.

Huguenot colony at Fort Caroline and planted Spanish garrisons at Saint Augustine, Santa Elena (modern-day Parris Island, South Carolina), and elsewhere in La Florida. Perhaps Menéndez brought Paquiquineo with him to Spain in 1567. Certainly, at least according to Father Juan Rogel, who was stationed in Santa Elena at the time, the adelantado brought him back to Havana when he returned from Spain in 1569 or 1570. According to Father Gerónimo de Oré, who visited Florida in 1614 and 1616 and drew upon interviews and manuscripts of those who remembered the events, when Paquiquineo learned in Spain that Jesuits were already at work in other parts of La Florida, he announced "that he would venture to take some priests to his country and that with the help of God and his own industry, the Indians of that land would be converted to the Faith." The Jesuits then "offered themselves to the King, and asked for his permission as well as for the necessary provisions to go to those parts, and to take with them the *cacique* Don Luis." Whatever might have happened in Spain, some such exchange took place in Havana, among Paquiquineo, Menéndez, and the vice-provincial of the Jesuit mission to La Florida, Father Juan Baptista de Segura. The provincial had become increasingly disillusioned with the slow pace of conversions at Santa Elena and points adjacent and imagined in Ajacán a fresh mission field where, with Paquiquineo's help and without the corrupting influence of Spanish soldiers and laymen, the Jesuits could win souls, or martyrdom, or both.[18]

Thus Paquiquineo, Segura, a freshly arrived priest named Luis de Quirós, three Jesuit brothers, three novices, and Alonso de Olmos, a boy whose father lived at Santa Elena, sailed for the Chesapeake late in the summer of 1570. When their ship stopped at Santa Elena, Father Juan de la Carrera, who was stationed there, tried to talk Segura out of his plan to establish a mission without an armed guard—a scheme he chalked up partly to the naïveté of Segura's "holy, sincere Christian heart" but mostly to the verbal wizardry of Paquiquineo, who had somehow sold Segura and Menéndez on the idea. "I pointed out the difficulty in the execution of the plan, saying that the Indian did not satisfy me, and judging from what he had told me, I saw that he was a liar," Carrera wrote, thirty years after the fact, when he had long since been proved correct. Segura not only

18. "Relation of Rogel," "Relation of Gerónimo de Oré," in Lewis and Loomie, *Spanish Jesuit Mission,* 118, 180; Noble David Cook, "Beyond the *Martyrs of Florida:* The Versatile Career of Luis Gerónimo de Oré," *Florida Historical Quarterly,* LXXI (1992), 169, 182.

stood his ground but, said Carrera, sent Quirós to demand that the expedition be given "the best and the larger portion of everything I had in my charge, especially the church goods." Laden with "the best and richest articles . . . in the way of chalices, monstrances, and vestments and other articles besides church furnishings," the ship sailed for Ajacán. If Paquiquineo had set out a decade earlier in search of prestige goods, he had them now.[19]

Everyone arrived safely in the Chesapeake on September 10, 1570. A few days later, the ship that brought them departed with much of the meager food with which the expedition had been "ill-provisioned for the journey." Also on board was the only letter Quirós and Segura ever sent from the mission, which made clear that things were already going horribly wrong. The paradise Paquiquineo had described had, unbeknown to him, endured "six years of famine and death." Many of those who had not perished had "moved to other regions to ease their hunger," and those who stayed behind said "that they wish[ed] to die where their fathers have died, although they have no maize, and have not found wild fruit, which they are accustomed to eat." No one on either side, Spanish or Indian, had enough food.[20]

Nonetheless, Paquiquineo had brought the Spanish and their goods. The people of Tsenacommacah "seemed to think that Don Luis had risen from the dead and come down from heaven, and since all who remained are his relatives, they are greatly consoled in him"—at least according to Quirós and Segura, who believed that those relatives had "recovered their courage and hope that God may seek to favor them, saying that they want to be like Don Luis, begging us to remain in this land with them." This might well have been true if the Jesuits were to provide the powerful gifts for which Paquiquineo hoped. But two other things happened almost immediately, one spiritual and one material, that might have determined the course of everything else that followed. "The chief has kept a brother of Don Luis, a boy of three years, who lies seriously ill, 6 or 8 leagues from here and now seems certain to die," Quirós and Segura reported. As the priests understood it, the chief "requested that someone go and baptize him, for which reason it seemed good to Father Vice-Provincial [Segura] to send . . . one of Ours to baptize the boy so close to death." There is no hint in the records of what happened on that sacramental journey. But there are many indications

19. "Relation of Carrera," in Lewis and Loomie, *Spanish Jesuit Mission,* 131–133.
20. Luis de Quirós and Juan Baptista de Segura to Juan de Hinistrosa, Sept. 12, 1570, ibid., 89, 90.

from elsewhere in North America of the conclusions that Native people drew when Jesuits wielded their water and spells and a child died anyway.[21]

The Jesuits might or might not have thus sealed a reputation as murderous sorcerers, but there is no question that they quickly dashed any hopes that they might be conduits for powerful prestige goods. "By a bit of blundering (I don't know who on the ship did it) someone made some sort of a poor trade in food," Quirós complained. Previously, "the Indians whom we met on the way would give to us from their poverty, [but] now they are reluctant when they see they receive no trinkets for their ears of corn." To nip such expectations of reciprocity—almost certainly the Native people did not see their provision of food to people who brought exotic goods in terms of barter—Segura "had forbidden that they be given something, so that they would not be accustomed to receiving it and then afterwards not want to bargain with us." Not surprisingly, "the Indians took the food away with them." For the moment, at least, Segura held firm in his conviction that the fathers "must live in this land mainly with what the Indians give" them. "Take care," Quirós warned his correspondent, "that whoever comes here in no wise barters with the Indians, if need be under threat of severe punishments, and if they should bring something to barter, orders will be given that Don Luis force them to give in return something equal to whatever was bartered, and that they may not deal with the Indians except in the way judged fitting here."[22]

Over the starving months of winter, the fathers apparently did break down and exchange some goods for food, but with local villagers, rather than with Paquiquineo, his chief, or his somewhat more distant town. Paquiquineo himself had almost immediately fled to that town, where he supposedly refused all communication with the fathers and settled down to what Jesuit chroniclers delighted in describing as the life of a "second Judas" who "allowed himself free rein in his sins, marrying many women in a pagan way." The story as usually told then reached a gruesome end. Paquiquineo supposedly responded to a final desperate Jesuit plea for aid with a brutal attack, first on the messengers and then on the mission station, where Segura and the others died from blows with their own axes. As evidence of the murders—and, we might add, of the power of exotic goods—

21. Ibid., 89–90; James Axtell, *The Invasion Within: The Contest of Cultures in Colonial North America* (New York, 1985), 122–123.

22. Quirós and Segura to Hinistrosa, Sept. 12, 1570, in Lewis and Loomie, *Spanish Jesuit Mission*, 92 (quotations); Mallios, "In the Hands of 'Indian Givers,'" 105–153.

Spanish sailors dispatched the next summer to supply the mission claimed that Native men were wearing the slain priests' cassocks as they tried to lure them ashore.[23]

But everything the chroniclers and subsequent historians have thought they knew about what happened after September came from the lips of the only one of the Spaniards who survived the experience, the young boy Alonso—as embroidered by the rhetorical conventions of Catholic hagiography and by what might have been poorly translated boasts from Native people. Who knows what combination of survivor guilt and intimidation shaped the tales of a boy who, nearly two years after the crisis, found himself delivered up to a vengeful Menéndez? The governor had sailed up the river in "an armed *fragatilla* with 30 soldiers," had lured aboard Paquiquineo's uncle "with five of his leaders and eight other Indians," and had then forced Alonso to act as interpreter while Rogel hastily "catechized and baptized" eight or nine of the Tsenacommacans, "after which they were hanged from the rigging of the Governor's ship." To Rogel, it was "a marvelous thing in how short a time the Governor learned what was happening there from the mouth of the boy." Marvelous, indeed, given that Menéndez was in too much of a hurry to follow up on the boy's story about where the priests were buried and that Alonso admitted he had not actually witnessed the murders. All we can know for certain is that the Jesuits died, that they utterly failed to live up to behavioral expectations of a prestige-goods economy, and that their deaths—whether by assassination or starvation—provoked a brutal retaliation by the Europeans. The lessons Paquiquineo took away from his effort to master the Spaniards and their goods can only be imagined.[24]

Namontack

If we know little with certainty about Paquiquineo, we know even less about Namontack, the man who joined the English in the transaction that sent Thomas Savage to live with the Powhatans in 1608, as recalled in the song of 1611. But at least in his case, thanks to the work of scholars such as J. Fred-

23. "Relation of Carrera," in Lewis and Loomie, *Spanish Jesuit Mission,* 134. An excellent summary of the standard narrative of Paquiquineo, on which an alternate perspective appears here, is James Horn, *A Land as God Made It: Jamestown and the Birth of America* (New York, 2005), 1–10.

24. Lewis and Loomie, *Spanish Jesuit Mission,* 46–47; Juan Rogel to Francis Borgia, Aug. 28, 1572, and "Relation of Juan Rogel," ibid., 108–109, 120–121 (quotations); Hoffman, *New Andalucia,* 261–266; Gleach, *Powhatan's World,* 89–97.

erick Fausz, Martin Quitt, and Frederic Gleach, we have a clearer sense of the broader historical narrative in which he fits, a narrative that begins shortly after the first arrival of the Jamestown colonists in 1607.[25]

As Wahunsonacock and his subordinates apparently understood it, the weroance figure among the English was Christopher Newport, not John Smith, who consistently portrayed himself as Newport's subordinate. Newport's initial voyage of exploration up the James River in May 1607 thus assumed crucial significance for chiefs of Tsenacommacah seeking connections to goods and power. According to Gabriel Archer, Newport and his entourage "were entertayned with much Courtesye in every place." Two weroances subordinate to Wahunsonacock fairly tripped over themselves to arrange ceremonial welcomes that displayed their wealth and generosity. Escorted to the presence of the weroance of Arrohateck, Newport's entourage found the chief "satt upon a matt of Reedes, with his people about him" and another mat ready "layd for Captain Newport." After the visitors had feasted on roast deer, mulberries, corn and bean soup, and cornbread, the weroance presented Newport with "his Crowne which was of Deares hayre dyed redl [redd]." While everyone "satt merye banquetting with them, seeing their Daunces, and taking Tobacco, Newes came that the greate kyng Powatah was come: at whose presence they all rose of their mattes (save the kyng Arahatec); separated themselves aparte in fashion of a Guard, and with a long shout they saluted him." Believing the newcomer was *the* Powhatan, rather than, as turned out to be the case, a subordinate weroance named Parahunt from the *town* called Powhatan, the English did their best to act like proper chiefs. "Him wee saluted with silence sitting still on our mattes, our Captaine in the myddest," reported Archer. Newport then "presented (as before . . . [he] dyd to kyng Arahatec) gyftes of dyvers sortes, as penny knyves, sheeres, belles, beades, glasse toyes etc. more amply then before."[26]

25. J. Frederick Fausz, "An 'Abundance of Blood Shed on Both Sides': England's First Indian War, 1609-1614," *Virginia Magazine of History and Biography,* XCVIII (1990), 3-56; Rountree, *Pocahontas's People,* 29-55; Martin H. Quitt, "Trade and Acculturation at Jamestown, 1607-1609: The Limits of Understanding," *William and Mary Quarterly,* 3d Ser., LII (1995); Gleach, *Powhatan's World;* James Axtell, *After Columbus: Essays in the Ethnohistory of Colonial North America* (New York, 1988), 182-221.

26. [Gabriel Archer?], "A Relatyon . . . Written . . . by a Gent of the Colony . . . ," May 21-June 21, 1607, in Philip L. Barbour, ed., *The Jamestown Voyages under the First Charter, 1606-1609,* 2 vols., Works Issued by the Hakluyt Society, 2d Ser., nos. 136-137 (Cambridge, 1969), I, 83-84. It took the better part of a month for the colo-

On the evening of the same day, ten miles farther upriver at a hilltop town that Archer called "Pawatahs Towre," the two weroances jointly presided over another feast, at which the mats prepared for the guests were "layde right over against the kynges." As night came on, Newport "certifyed" to Parahunt that the English "were frendes with all his people and kyngdomes." In response, the weroance, according to Archer, "very well understanding by the wordes and signes we made; the significatyon of our meaning," proposed "of his owne accord a leauge of fryndship with us; which our Captain kyndly imbraced." Newport, "for concluding therof gave him his gowne, put it on his back himselfe, and laying his hand on his breast saying Wingapoh Chemuze (the most kynde wordes of salutatyon that may be) he satt downe." The chiefly exchanges of gifts and food continued somewhat more awkwardly the next day when Newport invited Parahunt to a Sunday dinner of "two peeces of porke . . . sodd . . . with pease." Not surprisingly, the weroance and his party brought along some more appetizing food of their own—which might have been as much a political as a gastronomic statement—but everyone "fedd familiarly, without sitting in . . . state as before." Parahunt ate "very freshly of" the salt pork stew and washed it down with enough "beere, Aquavite, and Sack" to feel "very sick, and not able to sitt up long."[27]

As the competitive feasting continued, more than just a hangover troubled the ceremonial displays of chiefly harmony and asymmetrical redistribution.[28] A particularly tense moment occurred just before that informal Sunday meal, when "two bullet-bagges which had shot and Dyvers trucking toyes in them" turned up missing. On Newport's protest, the two weroances "instantly caused them all to be restored, not wanting any thing." That the recovery was so easy suggests that the chiefs themselves had been the ones who redistributed "the shott and toyes to (at least) a dozen sever-

---

nists to figure out that the Parahunt was merely "a wyroaunce, and under this great Powaton" (Edward Maria Wingfield, "A Discourse of Virginia," 1608, ibid., 215).

27. Archer, "Relatyon," in Barbour, ed., *Jamestown Voyages*, I, 84–87, 89.

28. In Archer's firsthand account, the next day Parahunt simply concluded that his guests' "hott Drynckes he thought caused his greefe, but that he was well agayne, and . . . [the English] were very wellcome" (ibid., 89). But if the comments of Sir Walter Cope a couple of months later are accurate, Newport might have used the occasion to further increase his reputation among the Powhatans: "One of ther kinges syck with drinkinge our aquavite, thought him selfe poysoned[.] newport tolde him by signes that the nextday he showld be well and he was so: and tellinge hys cuntry men thereof they came apace olde men and old women upon Every belliach to him, to know when they showld be well" (Cope to Lord Salisbury, Aug. 12, 1607, ibid., 110).

all persons." This provided an opportunity for Newport, whether he fully understood his actions or not, to assert his superiority to the two weroances by reenacting the redistribution of prestige goods and claiming the sole right to provide them. As Archer put it, he "rewarded the theeves with the same toyes they had stollen, but kept the bulletes, yet he made knowne unto them the Custome of England to be Death for such offences."[29]

More troublesome for the future of Anglo-Powhatan relations were Newport's stubborn insistence that the weroances provide guides for an overland expedition beyond the falls of the James; Parahunt's more stubborn explanations of why that would be impossible; and Newport's defiant erection, before he turned back, of "a Crosse with this inscriptyon Jacobus Rex. 1607. and his owne name belowe." Parahunt did not see the cross go up at the base of the falls or the Englishmen as they prayed for their monarch and their "owne prosperous succes in this his Actyon, and proclaymed him kyng, with a greate showte." If Parahunt's family maintained any tradition of the travels of Paquiquineo in the world of Europeans, however, they must have scoffed when the Tsenacommacans who witnessed the spectacle repeated Newport's disingenuous explanation "that the two Armes of the Crosse signifyed kyng Powatah and himselfe, the fastening of it in the myddest was their united Leaug, and the shoute the reverence he dyd to Pawatah."[30]

Against this uneasy backdrop, as the English returned downriver to Jamestown, they participated in feasts offered with progressively less enthusiasm, until, ominously, their guide (who was the brother-in-law of the weroance of Arrohateck) "tooke some Conceyt, and though he shewed no discontent, yet would he by no meanes goe any further." The reason soon became clear; the previous day, some two hundred Tsenacommacans had attacked the English fort. As one colonist succinctly put it, "The people used our men well untill they found they begann to plant and fortefye, Then they fell to skyrmishing." The fighting continued for several weeks until the mamanatowick unilaterally declared a truce, while colonist after colonist succumbed to dysentery, salt poisoning, and malnutrition. "Throughout the summer and autumn," Fausz concludes, "Wahunsonacock kept the depleted, disease-ridden colonists alive with gifts of food until he had restored their trust and earned a formal recognition of their grateful dependence"—a recognition driven home by the capture and ritual adoption of Smith at the end of the year.[31]

29. Archer, "Relatyon," ibid., 87.
30. Ibid., 87–89.
31. Ibid., 89–95, quotations on 94; Cope to Salisbury, Aug. 12, 1607, ibid., 110 (quo-

It is significant that, from a few days after the initial attack on Jamestown through the difficult period of skirmishing and truce, famine and disease, Newport was, as George Percy put it, "gone for England, leaving us (one hundred and foure persons) verie bare and scantie of victualls, furthermore in warres and in danger of the Savages." Among the Powhatans, the reputation of the great man Newport, who knew something of how to behave at a feast and to distribute prestige goods, can only have risen in his absence, particularly in contrast to his underling Smith. In his official capacity as "Cape Marchant," Smith ran about the countryside dickering with and bullying weroances for the foodstuffs that, as Quitt has pointed out, could be given or received, but never appropriately bartered for, in a prestige-goods economy.[32]

If we trust the Pocahontas-free version of Smith's captivity contained in his 1608 *True Relation,* the cape merchant reinforced Newport's reputation during his audience with Wahunsonacock. When the mamanatowick "asked mee the cause of our comming," Smith reported, "I tolde him, being in fight with the Spaniards our enemie, beeing over powred, neare put to retreat, and by extreame weather put to this shore, where . . . our Pinnasse being leake[y] wee were inforced to stay to mend her, till Captaine Newport my father came to conduct us away." And what a father Newport was:

> In describing to . . . [Wahunsonacock] the territories of Europe, which was subject to our great King whose subject I was, and the innumerable multitude of his ships, I gave him to understand the noyse of Trumpets, and terrible manner of fighting were under captain Newport my father, whom I intituled the Meworames which they call King of all the waters. At his greatnesse hee admired, and not a little feared: hee desired mee to forsake Paspahegh, and to live with him upon his River, a Countrie called Capahowasicke: hee promised to give me Corne, Venison, or what I wanted to feede us, Hatchets and Copper wee should make him, and none should disturbe us. This request I promised to performe: and thus

tation); Rountree, *Pocahontas's People,* 29–34; Horn, *A Land as God Made It,* 54–59; Fausz, "An 'Abundance of Blood Shed,'" *VMHB,* XCVIII (1990), 17; Gleach, *Powhatan's World,* 106–122.

32. George Percy, "Observations Gathered out of a Discourse of the Plantation of the Southerne Colonie in Virginia by the English, 1606," in Barbour, ed., *Jamestown Voyages,* I, 143; Smith, *True Relation,* in Barbour, ed., *Works of Smith,* I, 35–39, quotation on 35; Smith, *The Generall Historie of Virginia, New-England, and the Summer Iles* . . . (1624), ibid., II, 142–146; Quitt, "Trade and Acculturation," *WMQ,* 3d Ser., LII (1995), 247.

having with all the kindnes hee could devise, sought to content me: hee sent me home with 4 men, one that usually carried my Gowne and Knapsacke after me, two other loded with bread, and one to accompanie me.[33]

In January 1608, shortly after Smith's return to Jamestown with no intention of demonstrating his subordination by relocating to the place Powhatan had assigned him, Newport — "father," "King of all the waters," font of "Hatchets and Copper," better known among his own people as what James Axtell has called "a one-armed, one-time pirate" — returned at last to Tsenacommacah with the "First Supply." Copper flowed out of Jamestown, traded by Newport's seamen so liberally that Indian corn and furs "could not be had for a pound of copper, which before was sold for an ounce." Meantime, Wahunsonacock and his people "confirmed their opinion of Newport's greatnes . . . by the great presents Newport often sent him." In return, said Smith, "the Emperour Powhatan each weeke once or twice sent me many presents of Deare, bread, [and] *Raugroughcuns* [raccoons], halfe always for my father, whom he much desired to see, and halfe for me: and so continually importuned by messengers and presents, that I would come to fetch the corne, and take the Countrie their King had given me, as at last Captaine Newport resolved to go see him." At about this point, Smith began to regret the whoppers he had told the Powhatans during his captivity: "The President, and the rest of the Councell, they knewe not, but Captaine Newports greatnesse I had so described, as they conceyved him the chiefe, the rest his children, Officers, and servants."[34]

The chiefly progress of Newport and Smith to visit Wahunsonacock in February 1608 had many rough moments, including some comical English efforts to cross fragile bridges or wade out to a barge marooned at low tide, several far less comical English refusals to lay down their arms during diplomatic ceremonies, and (on the way back to Jamestown) a tragic English episode of shooting first and asking questions later that left at least one Native man dead. But as on his former embassies, Newport provided just enough evidence to confirm his reputation as a chief who might fulfill the Natives' economic and political expectations and take his subordinate place in Powhatan's domain. For his part, Wahunsonacock spared no

33. Smith, *True Relation,* in Barbour, ed., *Works of Smith,* I, 53–57.

34. James Axtell, *Beyond 1492: Encounters in Colonial North America* (New York, 1992), 187; John Smith, *The Proceedings of the English Colonie in Virginia since Their First Beginning from England in the Yeare of Our Lord 1606, till This Present 1612 . . .* (1612), in Barbour, ed., *Works of Smith,* I, 215 (quotations); Smith, *True Relation,* ibid., 61–63 (quotations).

PLATE I. *Pendants cut from sheet copper at Jamestown.*
Courtesy of APVA Preservation Virginia

effort to display his own power, wealth, and generosity. "Before his house stood fortie or fiftie great Platters of fine bread," said Smith, who entered to the sound of "loude tunes" and "signes of great joy" during a preparatory embassy while Newport waited for a future grand entry. Wahunsonacock, "having his finest women, and the principall of his chiefe men assembled, sate in rankes," presided "as upon a Throne at the upper ende of the house, with such a Majestie as I cannot expresse, nor yet have often seene, either in Pagan or Christian; with a kinde countenance hee bad mee welcome, and caused a place to bee made by himselfe to sit." When Smith presented the mamanatowick "a sute of red cloath, a white Greyhound, and a Hatte; as jewels he esteemed them, and with a great Oration made by three of his Nobles . . . , kindly accepted them, with a publike confirmation of a perpetuall league and friendship."[35]

But, lest Smith get too comfortable over the turkey dinner that "the Queene of Appomattoc, a comely yong Salvage," then served him, Wahunsonacock reminded him of whom the welcome had really been prepared for: "Your kinde visitation doth much content mee, but where is your father whom I much desire to see, is he not with you?" After Smith assured him that "the next day my Father would give him a child of his, in full assurance of our loves, and not only that, but when he should thinke it convenient, wee would deliver under his subjection the Country of Manacam and Pocoughtaonack his enemies," the mamanatowick put his visitor in his place in a different way. "With a lowd oration," Smith reported, "he proclaimed me a werowanes of Powhatan, and that all his subjects should so esteeme us, and no man account us strangers nor Paspaheghans, but Powhatans, and that the Corne, weomen and Country, should be to us as to his owne people." Smith, "for many reasons," made no objections to this declaration of dependence and, "with the best languages and signes of thankes" he could improvise, beat a hasty exit. But not before Wahunsonacock further displayed his power. "The King, rising from his seat," said Smith, "conducted me foorth, and caused each of my men to have as much more bread as hee could beare, giving me some in a basket, and as much he sent a board for a present to my Father."[36]

In Smith's account (and probably because it *is* Smith's account), Newport's subsequent audiences with Wahunsonacock seem almost anticlimactic. But in at least three ways beyond keeping the great man waiting, New-

35. Rountree, *Pocahontas's People,* 40–43; Smith, *True Relation,* in Barbour, ed., *Works of Smith,* I, 63–65.

36. Smith, *True Relation,* in Barbour, ed., *Works of Smith,* I, 65–67.

port acted his peaceful and generous chiefly part. When he arrived, he presented the mamanatowick with the thirteen-year-old Thomas Savage, "whom he gave him as his Sonne." When the issue of weapons at the council fire again came up, he commanded his "men to retire to the water side, which was some thirtie score [paces] from thence." And when, in response to Smith's efforts to start haggling over the price of provisions, Wahunsonacock announced to Newport that "it is not agreeable with my greatnes in this pedling manner to trade for trifles, and I esteeme you a great werowans," Newport bestowed on him "not . . . lesse then twelve great Coppers [to] try his kindnes." Although Smith carped that this gift of large kettles pried from the Powhatans no more grain than a single smaller one could have purchased elsewhere, Newport's display of asymmetrical generosity apparently had a great effect. "Thanks to God, we are at peace with all the inhabitants of the surrounding country, trading for corn and supplies," colonist Francis Perkins wrote from Jamestown in March. Not only did Native people "value very highly indeed [our] reddish copper," but "their great Emperor, or Werowance, which is the name of their kings, has sent some of his people to show us how to plant the Native wheat [maize], and to make some gear such as they use to go fishing."[37]

In April, Newport again sailed for England, taking with him Namontack, described as Wahunsonacock's "trusty servant, and one of a shrewd subtill capacity," whom the mamanatowick "well affected to goe with him for England in steed of his Sonne." The thaw in Anglo-Powhatan relations after Wahunsonacock declared the English his subordinates and received a massive gift of prestige goods from the newcomers' weroance suggests that Namontack went off into the Atlantic world with expectations similar to those of Paquiquineo. He would broker the connections to bring his people a secure supply of the Europeans' exotic goods and thus master their power. But Namontack's people must also have realized something that those who initially welcomed Paquiquineo home did not. The alliance symbolized by prestige goods also opened the way to an array of more mundane, but economically vital, items: copper for tools and weapons as well as for display,

37. Ibid., 69–71 (quotations); Smith, *Proceedings of the English Colonie,* ibid., 215–217 (quotation); Francis Perkins "to a Friend in England," Mar. 28, 1608, in Barbour, ed., *Jamestown Voyages,* I, 160 (editor's bracketed words omitted). The four great kettles of the *True Relation* are not mentioned in Smith's later versions of this story, which instead say only that "Newport [was] thinking to out brave this Salvage in ostentation of greatnes, and so to bewitch him with his bounty" and that the transaction "bred some unkindnes betweene our two captaines" (*Proceedings of the English Colonie,* in Barbour, ed., *Works of Smith,* I, 217 [quotations]; *Generall Historie,* ibid., II, 156).

iron axes and knives, cloth, perhaps even firearms. Solidifying the incorporation of the people who made these things into a polity of Tsenacommacah was important work indeed.[38]

It was work that was not going well during Namontack's absence. Smith repeatedly reinforced the contrast between his own parsimony and Newport's chiefly generosity as well as his unwillingness to play the subordinate weroance role the mamanatowick had assigned him. Wahunsonacock had, "to express his love to Newport, when he departed, presented him with 20 Turkies, conditionally to returne him 20 Swords, which immediatly were sent him." Smith, however, refused to make a similar exchange, and the mamanatowick, "not finding his humor obaied in sending him weapons, . . . caused his people with 20. devises to obtain them, at last by ambuscadoes." The skirmishing only ended when Wahunsonacock "sent his messengers and his dearest Daughter Pocahuntas" to try to patch things up—and Smith had convinced himself that the Tsenacommacans were "in such feare and obedience, as his very name wold sufficiently affright them." With Smith hardly able to conceal his contempt for the mamanatowick's authority, for the London Company policies, and for what he considered Newport's coddling of Indians who should be ruled by force, the Powhatans might well have pinned much of their hopes on Namontack's successful return.[39]

No doubt, as Smith suspected, Namontack had carried instructions "to know our strength and countries condition." In England, Newport tried to show him some impressive sights, or at least to show him off to all the right people who could contribute to the expedition back to Jamestown that would be known as the "Second Supply." According to Spanish ambassador Don Pedro de Zúñiga, "This Newport brought a lad who they say is the son of an emperor of those lands and they have coached him that when he sees the King he is not to take off his hat, and other things of this sort." Although Zúñiga was "amused by the way they honour[ed] him, for . . . he must be a very ordinary person," the royal treatment probably gave Namontack a simpler impression of the possibilities for mobilizing European material and political power than Paquiquineo had taken home from his longer and more difficult travels. Whatever the case, the consensus among English on

38. Smith, *Proceedings of the English Colonie,* in Barbour, ed., *Works of Smith,* I, 216 (quotation); Smith, *True Relation,* ibid., 79 (quotation). On the dangers of over-emphasizing the symbolic aspects of the underlying economic relationships prestige goods represent, see Camilla Townsend, *Pocahontas and the Powhatan Dilemma* (New York, 2004), 62–63.

39. Smith, *Proceedings of the English Colonie,* in Barbour, ed., *Works of Smith,* I, 220–221.

both sides of the Atlantic seemed to be that "they treated him well" and that "the Emperor, his father, and his people were very happy over what he told them about the good reception and entertainment he found in England."[40]

Whatever Namontack might have said when the English were not listening, his return to Tsenacommacah with Newport in the fall of 1608 brought the Powhatans' efforts to integrate English chiefs into a prestige-goods economy to their climax, in the remarkable episode of Wahunsonacock's coronation. Historians have almost universally agreed with Smith that the whole scheme was as cockamamie as the company's orders that Newport was not to return to England "without a lumpe of gold, a certainty of the south sea or one of the lost company of Sir Walter Rawley" or that he deliver to the Chesapeake a shipload of "Poles and Dutch to make pitch and tarre, glasse milles, and sope-ashes" with no plans for how they would be fed. "As for the coronation of Powhatan and his presents of Bason, Ewer, Bed, Clothes, and such costly novelties, they had bin much better well spared, then so ill spent," Smith concluded. "We had his favour much better, onlie for a poore peece of Copper, till this stately kinde of soliciting made him so much overvalue himselfe, that he respected us as much as nothing at all." Of course, from Wahunsonacock's perspective, a "stately kinde of soliciting" and the prestige goods that Namontack's embassy had apparently acquired from the English king were exactly the point. Indeed, it is even possible that the only one of the English for whom the mamanatowick had any real respect was Newport, whose status as his subordinate weroance was about to be confirmed.[41]

As at the previous ceremonial meeting between Newport and Wahunsonacock, Smith was in charge of the preliminaries and set off to deliver Namontack and an invitation that Wahunsonacock "come to his Father Newport to accept those presents, and conclude their revenge against the Monacans." A ceremonial welcoming dance that Smith utterly failed to understand—involving "30 young women [who] came naked out of the woods" carrying arrows, swords, clubs, "a pot-stick," and other items as they "cast themselves in a ring about the fire, singing, and dauncing with excellent ill varietie"—certainly gave no hint of subordination to the English. A message from Wahunsonacock about his power might also have

40. Smith, *True Relation,* in Barbour, ed., *Works of Smith,* I, 79; Pedro de Zúñiga to Philip III, June 26, 1608, in Barbour, ed., *Jamestown Voyages,* I, 163; "Relation of What Francis Magnel, an Irishman, Learned in the Land of Virginia during the Eight Months He Was There," July 1, 1610, ibid., 154.

41. Smith, *Proceedings of the English Colonie,* in Barbour, ed., *Works of Smith,* I, 234.

been conveyed when, having "solemnely invited Smith to their lodging . . . all these Nimphes more tormented him then ever, with crowding, and pressing, and hanging upon him, most tediously crying, love you not mee?"[42]

In any event, there was no question who was in charge the next day when Wahunsonacock gave Smith an audience:

> If your king have sent me presents, I also am a king, and this my land; 8 daies I will stay to receave them. Your father is to come to me, not I to him, nor yet to your fort, neither will I bite at such a baite: as for the Monacans, I can revenge my owne injuries. . . . But for any salt water beyond the mountaines, the relations you have had from my people are false.

So much for the South Sea; so much for English military might; so much for Smith, who then watched politely as Wahunsonacock literally drew him a map to show him the facts.[43]

Perhaps Paquiquineo had hoped for a scene like the one that played out next: Newport and fifty of his men processing overland to the capital while three barges brought prestige goods up the river. Like Smith, most historians play the scene for a laugh:

> All things being fit for the day of his coronation, the presents were brought, his bason, ewer, bed and furniture set up, his scarlet cloake and apparel (with much adoe) put on him (being perswaded by Namontacke they would doe him no hurt.) But a fowle trouble there was to make him kneele to receave his crowne, he neither knowing the majestie, nor meaning of a Crowne, nor bending of the knee, indured so many perswasions, examples, and instructions, as tired them all. At last by leaning hard on his shoulders, he a little stooped, and Newport put the Crowne on his head. When by the warning of a pistoll, the boates were prepared with such a volly of shot, that the king start up in a horrible feare, till he see all was well, then remembring himselfe, to congratulate their kindnesse, he gave his old shoes and his mantle to Captain Newport.

Wahunsonacock and the Native people who witnessed the ceremony almost certainly were not laughing. Tribute had been brought, prestige goods displayed, unbalanced reciprocity practiced, and the mamanatowick's power demonstrated.[44]

42. Ibid., 235–236.
43. Ibid., 236–237.
44. Ibid., 237. See also Francis Jennings, *The Invasion of America: Indians, Colo-*

PLATE 2. *"Powhatan's Mantle," perhaps the ceremonial garment given to Christopher Newport at Powhatan's coronation in 1608. Denver Public Library, Western History Collection, X-31119. Original at the Ashmolean Museum, Oxford, England*

And "Captain Newport [who] brought them Copper," as the Tsenacom-macan song called him, once again went off into the Atlantic world, taking Namontack with him and leaving Smith in charge. Namontack would never return. It is likely that, sailing on the *Sea Venture,* flagship of the "Third Supply," he was shipwrecked in Bermuda and then killed in a brawl with a fellow Tsenacommacan named Matchumps. Meanwhile, in the Chesapeake, everything that could have gone wrong in the Anglo-Powhatan relationship did. Private trade among colonists, mariners, and Indians at Jamestown undercut the authority of both Smith and Wahunsonacock to manage the flow of prestige goods. "Of 2. or 300. hatchets, chissels, mattocks, and pick-axes" brought on the Second Supply, Smith complained, "scarce 20 could be found" six weeks later. All had been illicitly traded to Native people for furs, skins, baskets, and other commodities. Food remained skimpy at Jamestown, and Smith, using ever more aggressive tactics to extract it from Indian neighbors, finally "resolved . . . to surprise Powhatan, and al his pro-vision." Almost simultaneously, Wahunsonacock—much as he had the last time Newport sailed away—tested Smith's willingness to maintain the con-trolled, ritualized flow of prestige goods and allow the mamanatowick to reassert the authority that private trade threatened to undermine. If Smith "would send him but men to build him a house, bring him a grin[d]stone, 50. swords, some peeces, a cock and a hen, with copper and beads," Wahun-sonacock's messengers said, "he would loade his shippe with corne." Smith, "knowing there needed no better castel, then that house to surprize Pow-hatan," quickly shipped off five craftsmen he could not feed anyway to start construction on the mamanatowick's house while he mobilized some thirty-eight troops for an expedition to the Powhatan capital in January 1609.[45]

---

nialism, and the Cant of Conquest (Chapel Hill, N.C., 1975), 116-117; Alden T. Vaughan, *American Genesis: Captain John Smith and the Founding of Virginia* (Boston, 1975), 41-46; Axtell, *Beyond 1492,* 187-188; Rountree, *Pocahontas's People,* 47-48; Gleach, *Powhatan's World,* 126-127; Williamson, *Powhatan Lords of Life and Death,* 35; Rountree, *Pocahontas, Powhatan, Opechancanough,* 112-114. Two exceptions to the general dismissal of the coronation ceremony are Gallivan, who concludes that, "upon receiving exotic symbols of authority, purportedly from King James, Powhatan had in many ways reached the pinnacle of his status as Mamanatowick" (*James River Chief-doms,* 169); and April Lee Hatfield, who takes seriously Newport's "intention to overlay Powhatan territory with an English unit of governance" ("Spanish Colonization Litera-ture, Powhatan Geographies, and English Perceptions of Tsenacommacah / Virginia," *Journal of Southern History,* LXIX [2003], 245-282, quotation on 265).

45. Strachey, *Historie of Travell,* ed. Wright and Freund, 85-86; Alden T. Vaughan, "Powhatans Abroad: Virginia Indians in England," in Robert Appelbaum and John

Smith, told along way at the town of Weraskoyack that Wahunsona-cock "hath sent for you only to cut your throats," needed no convincing. The mamanatowick similarly needed little convincing from the house build-ers who (perhaps encouraged by their first decent meals since arriving in the Chesapeake) "revealed to him as much as they knew of . . . [English] projects, and how to prevent them." Not surprisingly, the meeting between Smith and Wahunsonacock was strained. The English had to ask for the re-ception feast that earlier embassies had received as a matter of course, and Wahunsonacock almost immediately inquired when the visitors "would bee gon, faining hee sent not for" them. Multiplying the insult, the mamana-towick both drove a hard bargain and mocked Smith for his insistence that the expedition was about trading for food rather than about alliance and prestige goods. "Neither had hee any corne, and his people much lesse, yet for 40 swords he would procure . . . 40 bushels," Wahunsonacock declared. Indeed he would not trade at all "without gunnes and swords, valuing a basket of corne more pretious then a basket of copper, saying he could eate his corne, but not his copper." When Smith protested that, "as for swords, and gunnes, I told you long agoe, I had none to spare," Wahunsonacock re-sponded bluntly. "Many do informe me, your comming is not for trade, but to invade my people and possesse my Country, who dare not come to bring you corne, seeing you thus armed with your men," he announced. "To cleere us of this feare, leave abord your weapons, for here they are needlesse we being all friends and for ever Powhatans."[46]

The next day, having got nowhere with Smith on the incompatibility of arms and petty trade with the status of "being all Powhatans," the mamana-towick starkly outlined the contrast between Smith and Newport:

Captaine Smith, I never used anie of [my] Werowances, so kindlie as your selfe; yet from you I receave the least kindnesse of anie. Captaine Newport gave me swords, copper, cloths, a bed, tooles, or what I desired, ever taking what I offered him, and would send awaie his gunnes when I intreated him: none doth denie to laie at my feet (or do) what I desire, but onelie you, of whom I can have nothing, but what you regard not, and yet you wil have whatsoever you demand. Captain Newport you call

Wood Sweet, eds., *Envisioning an English Empire: Jamestown and the Making of the North Atlantic World* (Philadelphia, 2005), 51–55; Smith, *Proceedings of the English Colonie,* in Barbour, ed., *Works of Smith,* I, 239–244 (quotations); Smith, *Generall His-torie,* ibid., II, 185–193.

46. Smith, *Proceedings of the English Colonie,* in Barbour, ed., *Works of Smith,* I, 244–246.

father, and so you call me, but I see for all us both, you will doe what you list, and wee must both seeke to content you.

Smith utterly rejected the status of a subordinate weroance: "Powhatan, you must knowe as I have but one God, I honour but one king; and I live not here as your subject, but as your friend." Many specific affronts and skirmishes led up to the bloodbath that J. Frederick Fausz has rightly termed "the First Anglo-Powhatan War" of 1609 to 1614. But Smith's rejection of the basic assumptions of subordination and asymmetrical exchange in a prestige-goods chiefdom might well have served as that war's declaration.[47]

Yet even through the years of fighting, the goods that Namontack and Newport brought from across the Atlantic retained their power for both sides. At least one English raiding party "ransaked" the temple of the subordinate Nansemond chiefdom and "Tooke downe the Corpes of their deade kings from of their Toambes, and caryed away their pearles Copp[er] and braceletts wherew[i]th they doe decore their kings funeralles." Tsenacommacans, meanwhile, "stopped full of Breade" the mouths of Englishmen they slew. Most suggestive of the continued power of goods, however, was a ceremony described by Henry Spelman, who lived among the Powhatans from late 1609 to late 1610. Spelman explained that Wahunsonacock kept most of the more ordinary "goods and presents *that* are sent him, as the Cornne," in a house built for that purpose at the town of Oropikes. "But the beades or Crowne or Bedd which the Kinge of England sent him are in the gods' house at Oropikes, and in their houses are all the Kinge ancesters and kindred commonly buried." At least once a year, on the day after the

47. Ibid., 246–250; Fausz, "An 'Abundance of Blood Shed,'" *VMHB*, XCVIII (1990), 19–47; Quitt, "Trade and Acculturation," *WMQ*, 3d Ser., LII (1995), 251–258. The omission of what must be the word "my" from Powhatan's description of Smith as a weroance seems more than a slip. As Smith's modern editor notes, "Both the *Generall Historie* and Purchas's *Pilgrimes* omit 'of'" from the same sentence (Barbour, ed., *Works of Smith,* I, 248n). My suspicion is that this declaration of English subordination was hastily (and thus incompletely) edited out of *Proceedings of the English Colonie* and then further cleaned up in later versions. On any subordination implied by kinship, Smith was a little more ambiguous but also seemed to declare his independence: "I call you father indeed, and as a father you shall see I will love you," he claimed to have told Wahunsonacock, "but the smal care you had of such a child, caused my men [to] perswade me to shift for my selfe." Significantly, the paragraph containing this exchange bears the marginal note "Captaine Smith's discourse to delay time, that hee might surprise Powhatan" (*Proceedings of the English Colonie,* in Barbour, ed., *Works of Smith,* I, 249).

PLATE 3. *Glass trade beads, most in shades of blue, from Jamestown.*
Courtesy of APVA Preservation Virginia

people planted the corn fields that belonged to the mamanatowick, Wahunsonacock

> takes the croune which the Kinge of England sent him beinge brought
> him by tow men, and setts it on his heade which dunn the people goeth
> about the corne in maner backwardes for they going before, and the king
> followinge ther faces are always toward the Kinge exspectinge when he
> should flinge sum beades amonge them which his custum is at that time
> to doe makinge those which had wrought to scramble for them But to
> sume he favors he bids thos that carry his Beades to call such and such
> unto him unto whome he giveth beads into ther hande and this is the
> greatest curtesey he doth his people.

This was a prestige-goods chiefdom in action. That ceremony, that crown,
those beads were exactly what Paquiquineo and Namontack hoped to bring
home from the Atlantic world, confirming Powhatan's power over Europeans and their goods even—perhaps especially—in the midst of war with
the English.[48]

48. Mark Nicholls, ed., "George Percy's 'Trewe Relacyon': A Primary Source for the
Jamestown Settlement," *VMHB,* CXIII (2005), 244–245, 247; Henry Spelman, "Re-

PLATE 4. *Ralph Hamor's embassy to Powhatan. 1619.*
Engraving by Theodore de Bry. Virginia Historical Society, Richmond, Virginia

Uttamatomakkin

As is well known, the First Anglo-Powhatan War came to an end with the kidnapping of Pocahontas in 1613, her diplomatic marriage to John Rolfe in 1614, and their voyage to England in 1616. Joining the traveling couple were several others, including Uttamatomakkin. A high-ranking priest—the prefix *uttama-* connotes "spiritual" or "priestly"—and "an experienced Man and Counseller to *Opochancanough* their King and Governour in *Pow-*

---

lation of Virginea," in Edward Arber, ed., *Travels and Works of Captain John Smith, President of Virginia, and Admiral of New England, 1580-1631,* 2 vols. (Edinburgh, 1910), I, cv, cxii. Rountree and Williamson are among the few scholars who seem to have recognized the significance of this account. Rountree minimizes the significance of "the paste-jewel crown" (*Powhatan Indians of Virginia,* 110). Williamson, pointing out that "in the deep Southeast beads were structurally analogous to white body emissions," elaborates upon the fertility symbolism of Powhatan's acts: "Powhatan circled his newly planted field symbolically shooting semen all over his subjects, his workers, who faced him just as a woman might face a man during intercourse" (*Powhatan Lords of Life and Death,* 157). On beads as fertility symbols, see Townsend, *Pocahontas,* 86–87.

hatans absence," Uttamatomakkin was, said Samuel Purchas, "sent hither to observe and bring newes of our King and Country to his Nation." To Wahunsonacock and Opechancanough—the rising chief whose emissary Uttamatomakkin was—the trip to England might have been a final attempt to establish the kind of relationship envisioned since 1608 or 1561.[49]

Shortly after Pocahontas's marriage, colonist Ralph Hamor visited Wahunsonacock in hopes he could persuade him to marry off another daughter to the English. He quickly learned that the mamanatowick had a quite different agenda, focused on prestige goods and his image of the long-absent Christopher Newport. Wahunsonacock's first words were to Hamor's interpreter, Thomas Savage: "You . . . are my child, by the donative of Captaine *Newport,* in lieu of one of my subjects *Namontacke,* who I purposely sent to King James his land, to see him and his country, and to returne me the true report thereof." Unaware, as was Hamor, of Namontack's death in Bermuda, the mamanatowick complained that he had "yet . . . not returned, though many ships have arrived here from thence, since that time, how ye have delt with him I know not." If Namontack's quest to harness the power of the Atlantic world for Tsenacommacah's paramount chiefdom remained unfinished, it was the fault of the English.[50]

And at Jamestown, the English also continued to ignore the demands of prestige-goods relationships. Before Wahunsonacock spoke to Hamor, he felt the Englishman's neck and demanded to know "where the chaine of pearle was" that he had sent to his "Brother Sir *Thomas Dale* for a present, at his first arrivall" and that was to be worn by any future official English emissary. Having talked his way out of this breach of protocol, Hamor grandiloquently announced that "Sir *Thomas Dale* your Brother, the principal commander of the English men, sends you greeting of love and peace, on his part inviolable," and presented "in testimonie thereof . . . a worthie present, *vid,* two large peeces of copper, five strings of white and blew beades, five wodden combes, ten fish-hookes, and a paire of knives." Wa-

49. Fausz, "An 'Abundance of Blood Shed,'" *VMHB,* XCVIII (1990), 43–49; Samuel Purchas, *Purchas His Pilgrimage; or, Relations of the World and the Religions Observed in Al Ages and Places Discovered, from the Creation unto This Present* (London, 1617), 954. On *uttama-*, see Townsend, *Pocahontas,* 149–150.

50. Hamor, *True Discourse,* 38. After Wahunsonacock's coronation, Namontack had left with Newport as his guide on the ill-conceived expedition against the Monacans (Smith, *Proceedings of the English Colonie,* in Barbour, ed., *Works of Smith,* I, 237) and exploration of "the head of the Falls which takes the name of Namantack the Fynder of yt" (Strachey, *Historie of Travell,* ed. Wright and Freund, 131). It is possible the mamanatowick never saw him again.

hunsonacock expressed polite "thankes" but made it clear that such gifts given in the king's name were "not so ample; howbeit himselfe a greater *Weroance,* as formerly Captaine *Newport,* whom I very well love, was accustomed to gratefie me with." To drive home the point about impudent English stinginess, he announced that the daughter whose hand the English sought was already pledged to "a great *Weroance* for two bushels of *Roanoke* [wampum]." Moreover, he considered "it not a brotherly part of your King, to desire to bereave me of two of my children at once."[51]

After a meager meal of nothing but sodden cornbread, presented with the excuse that Wahunsonacock had not expected guests, the mamanatowick "caused to be fetched a great glasse of sacke, some three quarts or better, which Captain *Newport* had given him sixe or seaven yeeres since, carefully preserved by him, not much above a pint in all this time spent." To each of the English he dispensed "in a great oister shell some three spoonefuls." After redistributing this powerful substance associated with Newport, Wahunsonacock sent the emissaries on their way the next day with explicit instructions for Dale. Hamor was

> to remember his brother to send him these particulars, Ten peeces of Copper, a shaving knife, an iron frow to cleave bordes, a grinding stone, not so bigge but four or five men may carry it, which would be bigge enough for his use, two bone combes, such as Captaine Newport had given him; the wodden ones his own men can make: an hundred fishhookes or if he could spare it, rather a fishing saine, and a cat, and a dogge, with which things if his brother would furnish him, he would requite his love with the returne of skinnes.

Wahunsonacock insisted that Hamor repeat each item and, the Englishman said, "yet still doubtful that I might forget any of them, he bade me write them downe in such a Table book as he shewed me, which was a very fair one." Like the bottle of sack and the crown from England, the notebook (which might or might not have come from Newport and which Hamor was not allowed to mark) was a prestige item that ratified the mamanatowick's power. "He tolde me," said Hamor, "it did him much good to shew it to strangers which came unto him."[52]

There is no record that Dale sent the goods Wahunsonacock demanded; this would have been an unlikely course for a man who a few years earlier had directed that some colonists who "did Runne Away unto the Indyans . . .

---

51. Hamor, *True Discourse,* 38–43.
52. Ibid., 43–45.

be hanged some burned some to be broken upon wheles others to be Staked and some to be shott to deathe . . . To terrefy the reste for attempteinge the Lyke." That Uttamatomakkin returned from England filled with "rails against England English people and particularly his best friend Thomas Dale" suggests Dale did nothing to meet the Powhatans' expectations. So too does Pocahontas's embittered complaint when she met Smith in England that "they did tell us alwaies you were dead, and I knew no other till I came to Plimoth; yet Powhatan did command Uttamatomakkin to seeke you, and know the truth, because your Countriemen will lie much."[53]

Clearly Uttamatomakkin was not impressed with the truths he found in England, where he became the brunt of a running English joke. Wahunsonacock "sent him, as they say, to number the people here, and informe him well what wee were and our state," Smith reported. "Arriving at Plimoth, according to his directions, he got a long sticke, whereon by notches hee did thinke to have kept the number of all the men hee could see, but he was quickly wearie of that taske." Purchas said he also tried to count trees, "till his Arithmetike failed. For their numbring beyond an hundred is imperfect, and somewhat confused." Still, Uttamatomakkin held his own in a theological debate with Purchas (who found him "very zealous in his superstition") and presumably sat gamely through the theatrical productions and other events where the Powhatans were paraded. Although the Tsenacommacans had been "graciously used" at the court of James I, Uttamatomakkin vociferously "denied ever to have seene the King," because the monarch acted nothing like a proper chief. When Smith finally persuaded him otherwise, "He replyed very sadly, You gave Powhatan a white Dog, which Powhatan fed as himselfe, but your King gave me nothing, and I am better than your white Dog."[54]

Christopher Newport was probably in England during part of Uttamatomakkin's unsuccessful quest for prestige goods; in November 1616, he sailed for the East Indies, where he died in August of the next year. There is no record that the two men met, although it is hard to imagine that Uttamato-

53. Nicholls, ed., "Percy's 'Trewe Relacyon,'" *VMHB*, CXIII (2005), 261–262; Samuel Argall to Council for Virginia[?], June 9, 1617, in Susan Myra Kingsbury, ed., *The Records of the Virginia Company of London*, 4 vols. (Washington, D.C., 1906–1935), III, 73; Smith, *Generall Historie*, in Barbour, ed., *Works of Smith*, II, 261.

54. Smith, *Generall Historie*, in Barbour, ed., *Works of Smith*, II, 261 (quotations); Purchas, *Purchas His Pilgrimage*, 954–955 (quotations); Norman Egbert McClure, ed., *The Letters of John Chamberlain* (Philadelphia, 1939), II, 12, 50 (quotation), 56–57, 66; Vaughan, "Powhatans Abroad," in Appelbaum and Sweet, eds., *Envisioning an English Empire*, 58–65.

makkin failed to ask after him, to hear talk of him, or to take additional um-brage if there was no response. Whatever the case, he returned home with nothing good to say about the English or Dale. Samuel Argall was con-vinced that "all his reports are disproved before opachankano and his Great men whereupon (to the great satisfaccion of the Great men) Tomakin is dis-graced." Uttamatomakkin's disgrace might have been real, but less because of the rhetorical brilliance of English counterarguments than the plain proof that Powhatan's vision of incorporating the Atlantic world into Tsenacom-macah had been so utterly wrong and that Opechancanough would have to build chiefly authority through other means. Those who sang the taunting song of 1611 already realized as much.[55]

Tsenacommacah and the Atlantic World

I have speculated here at great length but also endeavored to operate within an accepted model of how chiefdoms work and to stay very close to the texts of the few documents that describe the exploits of Paquiquineo, Namon-tack, and Uttamatomakkin in the Atlantic world. Those texts glimpse the attempts of envoys from Tsenacommacah to incorporate European things into their prestige-goods economy, to subordinate representatives of Euro-pean kingdoms to their paramount chiefdom, and to use the new world of the Atlantic to multiply their people's power. Control of supplies of cop-per, sacred chalices, exotic crowns, blue glass beads, bottles of sack, and volumes of blank paper reinforced the power of the mamanatowick and his subordinate weroances—and, in turn, displayed to Tsenacommacans their power over Captain Newport and King James. As copper and beads became ever more accessible to ever more ordinary people, the need to display ever more esoteric items—and to send someone like Uttamatomakkin to find out exactly how things worked at the source—became ever more pressing.

This particular Native world of goods perhaps had already died with Pocahontas, Powhatan, and Newport in 1617 and 1618. Perhaps it died with Namontack in 1609. But it certainly died in the devastating Powhatan as-sault on the English in 1622—an assault that, few have noticed, came within months of the arrival of word about a new Virginia Company scheme. To forestall Dutch exploitation "of a trade of Furrs to be had in Hudsdons and

<hr />

55. K. R. Andrews, "Christopher Newport of Limehouse, Mariner," *WMQ*, 3d Ser., XI (1954), 39–40; David R. Ransome, "Newport, Christopher," *American National Biography* Online, http://www.anb.org/articles/20/20-00718.html (accessed Feb. 2, 2004); Argall to Council for Virginia, June 9, 1617, in Kingsbury, ed., *Records of the Virginia Company*, III, 73–74.

De La Ware River," a ship was to be dispatched from Virginia, loaded with trade goods and "two or three [men] skilfull in the languages and maners of the Indians, and expert in those places, wherein the trade is to be, that may serve for guides and Interpreters." Virginia colonists who spoke Algonquian were hardly known for their tight lips. Opechancanough surely overheard their talk and understood what this expedition to competing distant shores meant for the economic basis of his, and his people's, power over the English and their goods.[56]

56. "Treasurer and Company. Letter to Governor and Council in Virginia," July 25, 1621, in Kingsbury, ed., *Records of the Virginia Company*, III, 488 (quotation); "Council of the Virginia Company. A Letter to the Governor and Council in Virginia," Nov. 26, Dec. 5, 1621, ibid., 526–527 (quotation), 530.

Joseph Hall

BETWEEN OLD WORLD AND NEW

OCONEE VALLEY RESIDENTS AND THE SPANISH

SOUTHEAST, 1540–1621

In 1621, Lieutenant Marmaduke Parkinson and his English companions made an intriguing discovery on their way up the Potomac River. While the English were visiting their Patawomeck allies, their chief showed them "a China Boxe." According to Governor George Yeardley and his council's summary of Parkinson's report,

> This Boxe or Casket was made of braided Palmito, painted without, and lined in the inside with blue Taffata after the China or East India fashion. They enquiring whence it came, the King of Patomeck said, it was presented him by a certaine people of the Mountaines toward the Southwest, who got it from another Nation beyond them some thirtie dayes journie from Patomacke, called Acana Echinac, beeing of small stature, who had Houses, Apparell, and Houshold stuffe like us, and living within foure dayes journey of the Sea, had ships come into their River.

Believing this intelligence confirmed that the "South Sea," or Pacific Ocean, was a manageable journey beyond the Appalachian Mountains, the governor reported enthusiastically that the Virginia Colony would soon benefit from "a most rich Trade to Cathay, China, Japan, and those other of the East Indies."[1]

Unfortunately for Yeardley, no amount of enthusiasm could compensate for the vast expanses that separated Virginians from Chinese. So what was one of their taffeta-lined palmetto boxes doing just upriver from Chesapeake

Thanks to the anonymous reader, Peter Mancall, Marvin Smith, Melissa Sundell, Mark Williams, and the Jamestown and the Atlantic World conference attendees for their comments and to Sylvia Hawks for retyping various drafts.

1. Samuel Purchas, *Hakluytus Posthumus; or, Purchas His Pilgrims,* 20 vols. ([1625]; Glasgow, 1905–1907), XIX, 151–152.

Bay? Answering that question and addressing its larger significance runs the risk of taking a flight of fancy similar to the Virginians', to imagine a world that might enthrall but did not exist. If there are not clear answers to such a question, though, there are striking clues, which demonstrate that, in 1621, the English of Virginia inhabited the northern fringes of a region already adjusting to the demands and opportunities of colonization.

To understand this region and the exchange networks through which the small box passed, we must look not to the Pacific Ocean, as Yeardley believed, but to the lands of La Florida and the town its colonists called San Augustín. To equate the sounds of Acana Echinac with the name of the Spanish colonial outpost is a stretch, and it appears even more tenuous when we note that a separate summary of Parkinson's expedition referred to it as "Acanackchina," but sketchy linguistic evidence is not the only liability of such an orientation.[2] To all appearances, the Spaniards of La Florida were far too weak to be conducting a regional trade. It was with more reach than grasp that Spaniards had already claimed the Atlantic lands stretching from the Gulf of Mexico to the Grand Banks as La Florida, and their efforts to enforce some claim to the Chesapeake, whose lands they called Ajacán, only confirmed this fact. Although they did establish a short-lived mission on the bay in 1570–1571 and sailed north again with two timid reconnaissance missions in 1609 and 1611, none of these efforts had lasting results, and Spaniards exercised little control beyond the limits of today's central and northern Florida.[3]

Such failures, though, should not mask the impact of the colony on the wider Southeast. Many scholars have mistaken La Florida's marginal position in North America and in Spain's empire more generally for a lack of influence on the southeastern lands that lay beyond Spanish control. In fact, it was precisely thanks to colonial debility that Spaniards reshaped the region. More accurately, Native Americans, using Spanish resources, were re-

2. Ibid., 147. Helen C. Rountree, noting the chief's comments about a bay four days' journey from the sea, has speculated that the Indians had originally acquired their unusual gift from Spaniards visiting Mobile Bay. Although fishermen and traders from Cuba might have been journeying along the Gulf Coast, there is little evidence for such activity. Even if she is right, it does not diminish the larger point of this essay (Rountree, "The Powhatans and Other Woodland Indians as Travelers," in Rountree, ed., *Powhatan Foreign Relations, 1500-1722* [Charlottesville, Va., 1993], 23).

3. Charlotte M. Gradie, "The Powhatans in the Context of the Spanish Empire," in Rountree, ed., *Powhatan Foreign Relations*, 154-172; David B. Quinn, ed., *New American World: A Documentary History of North America to 1612*, V, *The Extension of Settlement in Florida, Virginia, and the Spanish Southwest* (New York, 1979), 141-158.

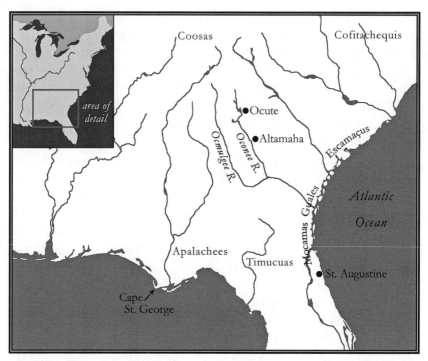

The Oconee Valley and Its Neighbors, ca. 1600. Drawn by Rebecca L. Wrenn

fashioning their societies from within. The profound consequences of these adjustments require a more careful look at two poorly understood inhabitants of the seventeenth-century Southeast: Indians whose histories suffer from an obvious lack of documentation and Spaniards whose histories suffer from an alleged lack of regional relevance.[4]

4. As David J. Weber has noted, "[Spanish] missionaries failed to advance permanently, defend effectively, or Hispanicize deeply North American frontiers in the seventeenth century." Unfortunately, this cogent observation says little about Spaniards' unintended influences on the lands around and beyond their missions. Equally regrettably, scholars of the Southeast continue to believe that Spain's regional influence was small primarily because they have not examined it. Paul E. Hoffman's history of the colony's frontiers, for example, confines itself primarily to the state boundaries of Florida, and John E. Worth's admittedly "very preliminary exploration" of Spanish and English relations with southeastern Indians before 1700 has little to say about the Natives of the deep interior, who, he notes, "remained in virtually complete isolation from direct European contact." Consequently, it is no surprise that Charles Hudson believes that the Spanish mission system was unable "to shape Indian societies at a distance" and that Alan Gallay asserts, "After the initial forays of Spanish explorers, Spain's influence did not reach much farther into the South than Florida." What fol-

Spaniards founded Saint Augustine in 1565, and in the following century, the Spanish population of La Florida grew feebly to fewer than two thousand.[5] Within that same period, though, tens of thousands of Native Americans inhabiting a broad territory east of the lower Mississippi valley reoriented economic and political structures in response to the new and prestigious goods available from the Spanish outpost.[6] The extent to which Natives effected such changes is difficult to tell from a single china box, but the larger patterns become clearer, if still only faintly so, in the history of the Oconee Valley in north central Georgia. Close to the colony but still beyond its effective control, Oconee peoples by 1600 were using Spanish goods to reorganize their societies. Taking advantage of Spanish goods, leaders of the polity known as Altamaha managed to sever their tributary relation-

lows in this essay should suggest the limitations of these assessments. See Weber, *The Spanish Frontier in North America* (New Haven, Conn., 1992), 121; Hoffman, *Florida's Frontiers* (Bloomington, Ind., 2002); Worth, "Spanish Missions and the Persistence of Chiefly Power," in Robbie Ethridge and Charles Hudson, eds., *The Transformation of the Southeastern Indians, 1540-1760* (Jackson, Miss., 2002), 45, 47; Charles Hudson, "Introduction," ibid., xxv; Alan Gallay, *The Indian Slave Trade: The Rise of the English Empire in the American South, 1670-1717* (New Haven, Conn., 2002), 33. For examples of works that discuss Spanish missions in their regional contexts, see Cynthia Radding, *Wandering Peoples: Colonialism, Ethnic Spaces, and Ecological Frontiers in Northwestern Mexico, 1700-1850* (Durham, N.C., 1997); James F. Brooks, *Captives and Cousins: Slavery, Kinship, and Community in the Southwest Borderlands* (Chapel Hill, N.C., 2002); Susan M. Deeds, *Defiance and Deference in Mexico's Colonial North: Indians under Spanish Rule in Nueva Vizcaya* (Austin, Tex., 2003).

5. In 1598, the population of the colonial city was seven hundred. That estimate might have included one hundred African slaves mentioned in a separate letter ten years later. By 1689, on the eve of the collapse of the missions and Spain's larger colonial project in Florida, the population in Saint Augustine was about fifteen hundred. A small number of ranching families also lived to the west in Apalachee, but these did not begin arriving there until the middle 1670s. See Gonzalo Méndez de Canzo to king, Feb. 23, 1598, Archivo General de Indias, Seville, Audiencia of Santo Domingo 224, doc. 31 (hereafter cited as AGI, SD); Pedro de Ibarra to king, Jan. 4, 1608, ibid., doc. 62; Ebelino de Compostela to king, September 1689, ibid., SD 151; John H. Hann and Bonnie G. McEwan, *The Apalachee Indians and the Mission San Luis* (Gainesville, Fla., 1998), 148-149. All correspondence is written from Saint Augustine unless otherwise noted.

6. Gregory A. Waselkov, "Seventeenth-Century Trade in the Colonial Southeast," *Southeastern Archaeology,* VIII (1989), 117-133; Peter H. Wood, "The Changing Population of the Colonial South: An Overview by Race and Region, 1685-1790," in Wood, Waselkov, and M. Thomas Hatley, eds., *Powhatan's Mantle: Indians in the Colonial Southeast* (Lincoln, Neb., 1989), 90.

ship with their Ocute neighbors to the north.[7] More subtly and strikingly, even as Spaniards recorded struggles for preeminence among rival elites, archaeological evidence suggests that their followers were also challenging the wider political and ceremonial life of the Oconee Valley.

Spaniards offered gifts because southeastern Indians successfully thwarted any efforts to impose Spanish imperial will. Although sixteenth-century Spaniards generally favored pacifying and colonizing frontier areas of their American empire with sword, pike, and arquebus, Spanish colonial ambitions in La Florida shattered repeatedly against persistent and widespread Native hostility. The region's most famous invader, Hernando de Soto, frequently resorted to torture and kept his Indian porters (and sometimes their leaders) as prisoners during his expedition of 1539-1543, but Soto, who had gained renown as one of Pizarro's most ruthless lieutenants in Peru, died on the banks of the Mississippi River without ever sighting a chiefdom worthy of his avarice. By the 1590s, Florida officials knew that Natives' military and demographic strength required quieter means of conquest.[8] The gifts Spaniards offered in turn provided the leaders who received them with new materials to buttress sagging prestige. Although the evidence for these political modifications appear earliest in the lands, like the Oconee Valley, that lay relatively close to Spanish missions and fortifications, the consequences extended not only as far as the Chesapeake but also west to the Mississippi River. In these shifts lie clues into what a china

7. Regarding the location of the Ocute and Altamaha chiefdoms, see John E. Worth, "Late Spanish Military Expeditions in the Interior Southeast, 1597-1628," in Charles Hudson and Carmen Chaves Tesser, eds., *The Forgotten Centuries: Indians and Europeans in the American South, 1521-1704* (Athens, Ga., 1994), 118 n. 20.

8. "The Account by a Gentleman from Elvas," ed. and trans. James Alexander Robertson and John H. Hann, in Lawrence A. Clayton, Vernon James Knight, Jr., and Edward C. Moore, ed. and trans., *The De Soto Chronicles: The Expedition of Hernando De Soto to North America in 1539-1543,* 2 vols. (Tuscaloosa, Ala., 1993), I, 95, 146; Rodrigo Rangel, "Account of the Northern Conquest and Discovery of Hernando de Soto," ed. and trans. John E. Worth, ibid., 276, 285-288; Paul E. Hoffman, "Hernando de Soto: A Brief Biography," ibid., 439-441, 457-459. For a discussion of broader imperial policy, see Richard W. Slatta, "Spanish Colonial Military Strategy and Ideology," in Donna J. Guy and Thomas E. Sheridan, eds., *Contested Ground: Comparative Frontiers on the Northern and Southern Edges of the Spanish Empire* (Tucson, Ariz., 1998). For two roughly contemporary examples of Spaniards' abandoning military conquest in favor of gifts, diplomacy, and what one scholar has called peace "by purchase" and another has characterized as a temporary truce, or "counterfeit peace," see Philip Wayne Powell, *Soldiers, Indians, and Silver: The Northward Advance of New Spain, 1550-1600* (Berkeley, Calif., 1952), 181-203; Deeds, *Defiance and Deference,* 56-85.

box from Florida was doing on the banks of the Potomac and how it formed part of some Indians' efforts to use Spanish goods to adjust to—and construct—a colonial world long before the arrival of colonial settlers.

The roots of Spanish influence lay partly in their willingness to offer gifts to compensate for their military weakness, but it also depended on the political nature of the chiefdoms—like those of the Oconee—that accepted those offerings. The concept of the chiefdom is one that scholars have employed for societies ranging from pre-Roman Gaul to contemporary New Guinea. Across this range of human experience, chiefdoms are generally understood to be societies ruled by hereditary elites who define and maintain their power by receiving tribute from subordinates and mediating with the supernatural and the exotic in order to maintain and even improve their societies. Rather than depend on bureaucracies, standing armies, or other institutions frequently associated with states, chiefs depend on a degree of control over surplus food and the rare objects that indicate religious and political power.[9]

Southeastern chiefdoms readily impressed the explorers who witnessed them during the sixteenth and seventeenth centuries, and Spaniards intent on controlling the region paid close attention to the political hierarchies atop which they hoped to situate themselves. Some of the best eyewitness descriptions come from the accounts of those who accompanied Soto on his fruitless search for a southeastern empire. He and his followers were the first to document the societies of Altamaha, Ocute, and other neighboring polities in the Oconee Valley. Ocute's "cacique" impressed the Spaniards with his ability to command "two thousand Indians" to bring gifts of food to the invaders. He also wielded enough influence over neighboring chiefdoms to compel some, like Altamaha, to offer tribute as signs of submission. So powerful was he (or so great were his pretensions to power) that he personified his town. "Ocute" referred both to the town and its leader.[10]

9. My understanding of the chiefdom draws in part upon the following works: Robert L. Carneiro, "The Chiefdom: Precursor of the State," in Grant D. Jones and Robert R. Kautz, eds., *Transition to Statehood in the New World* (Cambridge, 1981); Christopher S. Peebles and Susan M. Kus, "Some Archaeological Correlates of Ranked Societies," *American Antiquity,* XLII (1977), 421–448; Paul D. Welch, *Moundville's Economy* (Tuscaloosa, Ala., 1991); Timothy Earle, *How Chiefs Come to Power: The Political Economy in Prehistory* (Stanford, Calif., 1997); Robin A. Beck, Jr., "Consolidation and Hierarchy: Chiefdom Variability in the Mississippian Southeast," *American Antiquity,* LXVIII (2003), 641–661.

10. "Account by a Gentleman from Elvas," ed. and trans. Robertson and Hann, in

In calling him a *cacique,* Spaniards were importing from the Caribbean an Arawak term for "chief." Ocute's followers understood him and other leaders in terms common to other Muskogean speakers in the Southeast. In the powerful Cofitachequi and Coosa chiefdoms of the South Carolina and Georgia interiors, the complex hierarchy required a variety of titles. An *orata,* which the chronicler Juan de la Bandera translated as *señor menor,* led small villages or groups of villages. These recognized the influence of a *mico,* or *gran señor,* who, in addition to enjoying the respect of oratas, also headed a town of his own. In both Coosa and Cofitachequi, these micos in turn owed respect to one above them. In the case of Coosa's paramount, Bandera referred to him only as "un cacique grande" called Cosa. Apparently, the most powerful mico did not need a new title; he simply embodied the town and province over which he ruled.[11]

As prospective supreme rulers coming from a society that was itself extremely conscious of rank, Spaniards had a tendency to exaggerate the social hierarchies of most of the American societies they described. Micos or their superiors nonetheless had significant personal power, which appeared most obviously in the shape of massive earthen platform mounds. As the sites of chiefly residences and temples, these earthworks powerfully symbolized the authority of their elevated inhabitants. From these heights, chiefs celebrated important rituals or called their followers to war. Because southeasterners usually built their mounds in stages, the structures served two other significant purposes. The additions of new layers were themselves ceremonial acts, allowing the community to simultaneously elevate their chief and connect themselves with the earth that the mounds represented. Furthermore, these ceremonial additions usually followed the death of one leader and the succession of another, with the new layer covering the remains and the goods of the deceased. Thus, although new leaders lost access to powerful symbolic items associated with the previous chief, such burials and new layers enabled a successor to stand quite literally on the power of his predecessor.[12]

___
Clayton, Knight, and Moore, ed. and trans., *De Soto Chronicles,* I, 77; Rangel, "Account of the Northern Conquest," ed. and trans. Worth, ibid., 272.

11. Charles Hudson, *The Juan Pardo Expeditions: Exploration of the Carolinas and Tennessee, 1566–1568* (Washington, D.C., 1990), 62–63.

12. Pietro Martire d'Anghiera [Peter Martyr d'Anghera], *De Orbe Novo: The Eight Decades of Peter Martyr D'Anghera,* ed. and trans. Francis Augustus MacNutt, 2 vols. (New York, 1912), II, 262–265; Vernon J. Knight, Jr., "The Institutional Organization of Mississippian Religion," *American Antiquity,* LI (1986), 678–679; Richard A. Krause, "The Death of the Sacred: Lessons from a Mississippian Mound in the Tennessee River Valley," *Journal of Alabama Archaeology,* XXXVI (1990), 92–95; Chester B.

The ritually and symbolically powerful goods that leaders held close in both life and death provided crucial elements of political control. A former resident of South Carolina's coast, Francisco Chicorana, explained one such example to the Spanish imperial historian Peter Martyr d'Anghera in the early 1500s. According to this native of Chicora now living in Spain, the people of Chicora's neighboring province of Duhare venerated two idols "as large as a three-year old child, one male and one female," which "had their residence in the palace." Twice a year, during sowing season and harvest season, the chief Duhare displayed these idols for the necessary ceremonies of supplication and thanksgiving. Appearing atop his mound with the idols on the appropriate days, "he and they are saluted with respect and fear by the people." During the two days of rituals, Duhare remained closely associated with these idols that assured "rich crops, bodily health, peace, or if they are about to fight, victory." Throughout the Southeast, finely crafted objects, frequently of rare materials, occupied the focal point of ceremonies of cosmological order, communal cohesion, and military strength.[13]

In many instances, these goods owed their power to their exotic origins and the perilous journeys that leaders undertook to acquire them. Travel beyond the immediate protection of one's kin and community entailed significant risk, and the ceremonies of return acknowledged both the risk that a traveler took and the prestige that accompanied success. In 1595, the leader of the recently converted village of San Pedro, just north of Saint Augustine, returned from a journey. The man, named Juan, and his wife entered the town with the entire populace "wailing in a high voice as if they had dropped dead before their eyes," and the townspeople repeated these lamentations in Juan's presence for "many days." The Franciscan who recorded this event did not allude to death incidentally. After his arrival in Saint Augustine, he learned that nearby mission Indians cried in a similar manner to memorialize a recently dead leader.[14]

DePratter, *Late Prehistoric and Early Historic Chiefdoms in the Southeastern United States* (New York, 1991), 139–147.

13. Martyr, *De Orbe Novo,* ed. and trans. MacNutt, II, 262–263; Knight, "Institutional Organization," *American Antiquity,* LI (1986), 675–687.

14. Andrés de San Miguel, *An Early Florida Adventure Story,* trans. John H. Hann (Gainesville, Fla., 2000), 70–71. Other accounts of mourning that accompany the return of travelers in the upper Mississippi valley and coastal Brazil were, according to Native sources, ceremonies that recalled those who had died since the traveler's last visit. This association between long-distance travel and death is an interesting and potentially helpful one, especially because it seems incomplete: the Europeans arriving at these towns and recording these ceremonies were visiting for the first time and

In the perilous and poorly known world beyond the town, leaders conducted the negotiations and exchanges that gave them access to rare and powerful objects. Outsiders provided chiefs with information and goods unavailable to the less privileged. These, in turn, entered into the ceremonies and exchanges that maintained inequality. Thus, thanks to a series of short-distance exchanges among a chain of neighbors, a chief in piedmont Georgia might be able to display ceremonial objects manufactured from Gulf Coast conch shells, Appalachian chert, or Great Lakes copper.[15] It also meant that a Patawomeck leader who died some time after 1607 could leave this world in the company of a shell gorget probably manufactured by someone in the province of Guale on the Georgia coast. In addition to conferring significant prestige on a fortunate few, these objects and the exchanges that moved them around the region knitted the Southeast in a loose but expansive network.[16]

These exchanges, and the power they bestowed, required constant maintenance, and the regularity of these interactions knitted leaders and their polities into a wider web of relationships. Perhaps the most striking evidence of chiefs' ability to cross linguistic, political, and geographic barriers

---

thus must have been the objects of such rituals for the mere fact of their arrival and not their departure and return. Apparently, just as Mary Helms has shown in other regions, travel over great distances had powerful links to travel outside of this world. See Robert L. Hall, *An Archaeology of the Soul: North American Indian Belief and Ritual* (Urbana, Ill., 1997), 3; Mary W. Helms, *Ulysses' Sail: An Ethnographic Odyssey of Power, Knowledge, and Geographical Distance* (Princeton, N.J., 1988).

15. Peebles and Kus, "Some Archaeological Correlates of Ranked Societies," *American Antiquity,* XLII (1977), 421–448. For a discussion of this phenomenon in the Americas more generally, see Helms, *Ulysses' Sail.*

16. Jeffrey P. Brain and Philip Phillips, *Shell Gorgets: Styles of the Late Prehistoric and Protohistoric Southeast* (Cambridge, Mass., 1996), 39–40. For a number of examples of broad distribution of very similar manufactured goods, see 360–394. Brain and Phillips do not provide a date for the shell gorget from Virginia, but John Scarry and Mintcy Maxham mention that it was part of a burial from the early historic period. See Scarry and Maxham, "Elite Actors in the Protohistoric: Elite Identities and Interaction with Europeans in the Apalachee and Powhatan Chiefdoms," in Cameron B. Wesson and Mark A. Rees, eds., *Between Contacts and Colonies: Archaeological Perspectives on the Protohistoric Southeast* (Tuscaloosa, Ala., 2002), 159. For a more complete discussion of the Virginia burial site where the gorget was found, see Stephen R. Potter, "Early English Effects on Virginia Algonquian Exchange and Tribute in the Tidewater Potomac," in Wood, Waselkov, and Hatley, eds., *Powhatan's Mantle,* 162–166.

is the remarkable consistency to the rituals that gave order to these power-ful and potentially dangerous exchanges. During the two years that Soto's force menaced and met the peoples of Georgia, South Carolina, Tennessee, and Alabama, his chroniclers recounted an amazingly uniform array of ritu-als to welcome and propitiate the powerful newcomers with gifts. Whether visiting the towns of the Oconee Valley or arriving at the provinces of Cofi-tachequi or Coosa, Soto regularly received offerings of food, valuables, and burdeners—provided he and his men did not violate the norms of such en-counters by taking things not set aside for them.[17]

Although many of Soto's hosts addressed him as "Brother," these ex-changes frequently reinforced unequal relations among chiefs.[18] Various leaders accepted these unequal regional relations because they secured them a modicum of influence at home. Amid the relatively fractious politics of the Oconee Valley, some apparently sought out powerful benefactors. When Oconee residents established a town on the western edge of the valley around 1500, they probably did so to take advantage of exchanges with the powerful chiefdom of Coosa, some 150 miles to the northwest.[19]

Followers in the thousands, monuments of earth, and knowledge of a wider world all protected and demonstrated significant authority, but chiefs'

17. Marvin T. Smith and David J. Hally, "Chiefly Behavior: Evidence from Six-teenth Century Spanish Accounts," in Alex W. Barker and Timothy R. Pauketat, eds., *Lords of the Southeast: Social Inequality and the Native Elites of Southeastern North America,* Archaeological Papers of the American Anthropological Association, no. 3 (1992), 99–110. As further evidence of the extent to which elite ideas crossed language barriers, Apalachees of the Florida panhandle, Timucuas of central Florida, and Apa-lachicolas of the Georgia-Alabama border all shared common leadership terms such as *inija,* meaning "second-in-command," and *holahta,* meaning "chief," even though all three groups spoke distinct languages (John H. Hann, "Political Leadership among the Natives of Spanish Florida," *Florida Historical Quarterly,* LXXI [1992], 207).

18. One of the most extreme examples of this political phenomenon appears in Moundville in west central Alabama. By controlling the production and distribution of an array of items, including utilitarian ceramics and copper ornaments, Moundville's leaders ensured that all neighboring ceremonial and political centers depended in some form on Moundville and also that Moundville's leaders possessed the most prestigious items. As a result, the chiefdom remained stable for a relatively long period between 1100 and 1400. See Paul D. Welch, "Control over Goods and the Political Stability of the Moundville Chiefdom," in John F. Scarry, ed., *Political Structure and Change in the Prehistoric Southeastern United States* (Gainesville, Fla., 1996).

19. Mark Williams, "Growth and Decline of the Oconee Province," in Hudson and Tesser, eds., *Forgotten Centuries,* 191.

personal power had limits. Regardless of their regional connections, leaders had to accommodate the interests of the commoners. Early French explorers of coastal Florida noted that, though council houses included an elevated seat for the chief, he still consulted with the members of his town before making decisions of any importance. Tribute, another marker of subordination, also required careful management because overburdened tributaries might simply leave if tributary demands interfered excessively with their own subsistence. Ocute the chief might personify Ocute the town, but without a standing army or other bureaucratic institutions, he also possessed very personal limits on his power.[20]

Amid intense internal and external competition for preeminence, southeastern chiefdoms experienced volatile and sometimes short lives. Chiefdoms dominated the central region of Georgia from the eleventh through the sixteenth centuries, for instance, but few lasted more than one hundred years. Internal rivalries most likely caused the demise of most of those chiefdoms, but environmental stresses such as droughts could provide the necessary impulse for unrest. Regardless of the reasons, as chiefs lost access to reliable food stores, important esoteric knowledge, or rare goods, they became less valuable to their followers. Lacking leaders to coordinate the storage and distribution of surpluses or dissatisfied with those who remained in charge, townspeople abandoned their homes in favor of the protection of still-extant chiefdoms or the resources available in less-populated regions.[21]

Soto's chroniclers described signs of instability among the polities of the Oconee Valley in 1540. With mounds significantly smaller than those of their distant neighbors of Cofitachequi and Coosa, the Oconee chiefdoms evidently experienced intense political rivalries that periodically disrupted the valley. Precisely because mounds contained the remains of and the associations with earlier chiefs, successful claimants who challenged older lineages evidently sought to disassociate themselves from these constructions by moving their principal community to a new site or an abandoned site free from reminders of the discredited order. Ecological considerations might

20. René Goulaine de Laudonnière, *Three Voyages,* ed. and trans. Charles E. Bennett (Gainesville, Fla., 1975), 14; Alex W. Barker, "Powhatan's Pursestrings: On the Meaning of Surplus in a Seventeenth Century Algonkian Chiefdom," in Barker and Pauketat, eds., *Lords of the Southeast,* 61–80; Beck, "Consolidation and Hierarchy," *American Antiquity,* LXVIII (2003), 645–655.

21. DePratter, *Chiefdoms,* 162; David J. Hally, "Platform-Mound Construction and the Instability of Mississippian Chiefdoms," in Scarry, ed., *Political Structure and Change,* 92–127; David G. Anderson, *The Savannah River Chiefdoms: Political Change in the Late Prehistoric Southeast* (Tuscaloosa, Ala., 1994).

also have influenced these decisions, as leaders and followers sought more fertile soil for their crops.[22]

Whether or not he recognized the meaning of Oconee political geography, Soto could not have helped but note how the opportunism of subordinates regularly strained the unequal bonds between leaders and followers. Before entering the valley, Soto learned from a neighboring and perhaps tributary leader that "a great lord lived on ahead; that his domain was called Ocute." When he arrived at the Oconee town of Altamaha, though, Soto discovered that some thought less reverentially of Ocute's influence. Upon meeting the imposing Spanish force, the cacique of Altamaha asked "to whom he had to give the tribute in the future, if he should give it to the Governor [Soto] or to Ocute."[23] Refusing to confront Ocute or concede his own pretended supremacy, Soto shrewdly enjoined Altamaha to continue offering tribute to Ocute until Soto declared otherwise. Despite Altamaha's implicit challenge to Ocute's preeminence, Soto still considered Ocute the leader with the greatest influence, and he offered his gifts accordingly. Where the cacique of Altamaha received a silver-colored feather from the Spaniard, Soto offered Ocute a yellow satin hat and a shirt in addition to a similar feather.[24]

Soto paid close attention to such hierarchies and instabilities in the misguided hope that they would help his search for a new Incan or Mexican empire. His failure and the repeated failures of his successors to extract riches from the interior condemned La Florida to a marginal place in Spain's American empire. Nonetheless, Natives' deep respect for the power of rare

22. Hally, "Platform-Mound Construction," in Scarry, ed., *Political Structure and Change,* 112–113; Mark Williams and Gary Shapiro, "Mississippian Political Dynamics in the Oconee Valley, Georgia," ibid., 147–148.

23. "Account by a Gentleman from Elvas," ed. and trans. Robertson and Hann, in Clayton, Knight, and Moore, ed. and trans., *De Soto Chronicles,* I, 77; Rangel, "Account of the Northern Conquest," ed. and trans. Worth, ibid., 272. The tenuous nature of hierarchy even suffuses outsiders' descriptions of the Oconee Valley polities: where most of Soto's chroniclers emphasized Ocute's preeminence in the valley, the admittedly taciturn Luís Hernández de Biedma made no distinction between the power of "Altapaha" and "other caciques, who were named Ocute and Cofaqui." Of more recent vintage, one of the archaeologists most familiar with the Oconee Valley believes that the town of Cofaqui was the principal center during Soto's visit in 1540. See Luys Hernández de Biedma, "Relation of the Island of Florida," ed. and trans. John E. Worth, in *De Soto Chronicles,* I, 229; Williams, "Growth and Decline," in Hudson and Tesser, eds., *Forgotten Centuries,* 179.

24. Rangel, "Account of the Northern Conquest," ed. and trans. Worth, in Clayton, Knight, and Moore, ed. and trans., *De Soto Chronicles,* I, 272.

goods would tie many southeastern societies, even if indirectly, to Spanish colonial efforts. As Native peoples, especially those of the Florida and Georgia coasts, thwarted Spanish missionary and military impositions, they forced Spaniards to abandon the pretensions of the rigid rule of empire for the more carefully negotiated and personal forms of chiefly influence. By courting the allegiance of peoples near and far with gifts, Spaniards were offering something that Native leaders could use, and Spaniards were then able to evangelize tens of thousands of people from Saint Augustine north to the coastal province of Guale in Georgia and west to the powerful Apalachees of the Florida panhandle. More broadly and more significantly for the history of the Southeast, they also provided a new array of materials for reorganizing many uncolonized Indians' politics and polities. Ironically, the very weakness that has convinced later historians of Spain's regional irrelevance is precisely what convinced leaders in Saint Augustine to pursue policies that promoted regionwide consequences.[25]

These later Spanish successes first required a series of painful lessons in southeastern politics. When Pedro Menéndez de Avilés founded Saint Augustine in 1565, he and his royal sponsor, Philip II, focused their efforts on securing a strategic point along Spanish sea lanes. Menéndez was already a successful military leader and administrator, and he enjoyed support from Europe's most powerful monarch, but the colony would flourish or flounder less on the dreams of two men and more on the very real and varied interests of the new colony's neighbors. Even the very act of seeking Native leaders as allies posed serious challenges. In lands stretching from the Atlantic to the Gulf coasts lived perhaps twenty-four thousand Timucuas whose chiefs exercised significant influence over the people of their town and who in turn acknowledged the power of one of several leaders. These paramount chiefs struggled with one another for preeminence.[26] Among these politi-

25. My history of the colony's early years draws on the following works: Eugene Lyon, *The Enterprise of Florida: Pedro Menéndez de Avilés and the Spanish Conquest of 1565–1568* (Gainesville, Fla., 1976); Paul E. Hoffman, *A New Andalucia and a Way to the Orient: The American Southeast during the Sixteenth Century* (Baton Rouge, 1990), esp. 169–290; Hoffman, *Florida's Frontiers,* 51–82; Amy Turner Bushnell, *Situado and Sabana: Spain's Support System for the Presidio and Mission Provinces of Florida,* Anthropological Papers of the American Museum of Natural History, no. 74 (Athens, Ga., 1994), 36–48.

26. John E. Worth, *The Timucuan Chiefdoms of Spanish Florida,* I, *Assimilation,* and II, *Resistance and Destruction* (Gainesville, Fla., 1998), I, 13–18, II, 2–6; John H. Hann, *A History of the Timucua Indians and Missions* (Gainesville, Fla., 1996), 73–84, 257–261; Jerald T. Milanich, "Native Chiefdoms and the Exercise of Complexity

cally diverse and linguistically related peoples were the Mocamas of the coast just north of Saint Augustine. Just to the north of the Mocamas lived the Guales. Unlike the more politically cohesive Timucuas, the Guale towns of the Georgia coast accorded a wavering allegiance to the paramount leaders of two or three towns and spoke a Muskogean language distinct from the Timucuan but related to those of inland peoples like the Altamaha. The peoples of the Deep South—even those immediately adjacent to the fledgling colony—resisted a simple template.[27]

Spaniards nonetheless sought to impose one. In the five years following the establishment of Saint Augustine, Spanish soldiers, missionaries, and colonists experienced breathtakingly rapid success and failure. After wiping out the nascent French colony of Fort Caroline near today's Jacksonville, Florida, fortifying seven other harbors from Santa Elena near today's Beaufort, South Carolina, south to the Florida Keys and then north along the Gulf Coast to Tampa Bay, and establishing a chain of forts from Santa Elena inland to the western slopes of the Appalachians, the colony suffered a series of local uprisings that destroyed nearly everything. By 1570, Spaniards in Saint Augustine and Santa Helena inhabited European islands in a sea of Indians who were at best mildly friendly and at worst openly hostile. Another revolt against the newly established Jesuit mission on the Chesapeake in 1571 convinced the missionaries to abandon the colony, and many colonists followed suit after Santa Elena's Guale and Escamaçu neighbors overran Santa Elena in 1576.[28] The template had been simple and the consequences, for Menéndez, simply devastating. When he died in Spain in 1574, the colony showed few prospects for success. La Florida lacked the ex-

in Sixteenth-Century Florida," in Elsa M. Redmond, ed., *Chiefdoms and Chieftaincy in the Americas* (Gainesville, Fla., 1998). The number twenty-four thousand comes from Worth, *Timucuan Chiefdoms,* II, 6, but he acknowledges it as speculation "virtually incapable of proof."

27. Grant D. Jones, "The Ethnohistory of the Guale Coast through 1684," in D. H. Thomas, G. D. Jones, R. S. Durham, and C. S. Larsen, eds., *The Anthropology of St. Catherines Island,* I, *Natural and Cultural History,* Anthropological Papers of the American Museum of Natural History, no. 55 (1978), 155–210; John E. Worth, *The Struggle for the Georgia Coast: An Eighteenth-Century Spanish Retrospective on Guale and Mocama,* Anthropological Papers of the American Museum of Natural History, no. 75 (Athens, Ga., 1995), 12.

28. Hudson, *Juan Pardo Expeditions,* 23–46, 175–176; Bushnell, *Situado and Sabana,* 38–41, 61–62; Hoffman, *New Andalucia,* 266; Hann, *History of Timucua Indians,* 50–72; Luís Gerónimo de Oré, *The Martyrs of Florida (1513–1616),* ed. and trans. Maynard Geiger (New York, 1936), 33–38.

ploitable resources that would finance colonization on Spanish terms, and Natives throughout the region had no interest in promoting their own sub-jugation.

As if to reinforce what was already painfully evident to La Florida's offi-cials, in 1573 Philip II issued new policies that pressured his representa-tives to incorporate "unpacified" peoples into the empire through kindness rather than conquest. Such an unfunded mandate offered little help to the struggling colony, but a more significant shift came in 1593, when the king authorized La Florida's governor to receive funds specifically to pay for gifts to visiting friendly caciques. By offering the "clothes and tools and flour" that Philip II stipulated, the governor would demonstrate not only his kind-ness but also his power. By 1597, that list had come to include hatchets and hoes; cloth of wool, linen, and a little silk; shirts, stockings, hats, glass beads, and even a pair of shoes. The Native dignitaries who received these small quantities of goods recognized them as unusual new equivalents for the copper ornaments, finely dressed skins, and shell beads that confirmed their high status and spiritual power. New goods soon began joining more familiar ones in the internments of their dead possessors.[29]

Leaders not only recognized the power of these objects; they needed it. The first European diseases arrived in the Southeast no later than 1526, when Lucas Vázquez de Ayllón brought six hundred colonists to establish a short-lived and disease-ridden colony on the coast of South Carolina. As coastal and interior peoples acquired a taste for the pigs that escaped from the supply trains of this and other Spanish expeditions, they also encoun-tered new diseases that swine could transmit to humans. Archaeologists have not found mass graves that would suggest high and sudden mortality, but they have noticed that settlements diminished in number and size after contact.[30] In addition, by the end of the 1500s, inhabitants of one town near

29. Joseph del Prado to king, Dec. 30, 1654, AGI, SD 229; Francisco Mugado to king, July 27, 1597, ibid., SD 231; Weber, *Spanish Frontier,* 107; Vernon James Knight, Jr., *Tukabatchee: Archaeological Investigations at an Historic Creek Town, El-more County, Alabama, 1984,* Office of Archaeological Research, Alabama State Mu-seum of Natural History, University of Alabama Report of Investigations, no. 45 (Moundville, Ala., 1985), 169–185; Cameron B. Wesson, "Prestige Goods, Symbolic Capital, and Social Power in the Protohistoric Southeast," in Wesson and Rees, eds., *Between Contact and Colonies,* 110–125; Hudson, *Juan Pardo Expeditions,* 138–140.

30. Ann F. Ramenofsky, *Vectors of Death: The Archaeology of European Contact* (Albuquerque, N.M., 1987), 55–63; Marvin T. Smith, *Archaeology of Aboriginal Cul-ture Change in the Interior Southeast: Depopulation during the Early Historic Period* (Gainesville, Fla., 1987), 60–85; Ramenofsky and Patricia Galloway, "Disease and the

the Georgia coast began to decorate their pottery with an increasing number of ceremonial motifs in a much "sloppier" manner than their predecessors. Less experienced potters, deprived of the benefits of their stricken elders, apparently sought to confront these invisible scourges and sustain their societies as best as their craftswomanship would allow.[31]

Chiefs pursued remedies of a different sort. As new and powerful (if also tactless and sometimes ineffective) players in the Southeast, the Spanish deserved careful attention. Not only did they seem more resistant to these dangerous diseases, but they possessed new sources of power that perhaps could thwart future epidemics or at least mitigate the political and religious instability that usually accompanied them. Acquiring these Spanish gifts might provide leaders with access to a new ceremonial power. Many also requested the powerful and unusual Franciscans who had replaced the frustrated Jesuits. In accepting missionaries, remarkable men who walked unarmed among unfamiliar peoples and enjoyed the respect of imposing governors and military men, Indian leaders were wisely allying with spiritual leaders who possessed access to important new sources of cosmological power.[32] In addition, by placing themselves strategically between their people and the powerful people of Saint Augustine, Indian leaders ensured that they would not lose influence to opportunistic rivals who might seek out the Spanish ahead of them.[33]

This access came at a price. Native leaders visiting Saint Augustine to acquire gifts also participated in larger ceremonies that Spaniards understood as the Indians' "rendering of obedience" to the Spanish king. Spanish officials also expected these new subjects to submit to a new spiritual

Soto Entrada," in Galloway, ed., *The Hernando de Soto Expedition: History, Historiography, and "Discovery" in the Southeast* (Lincoln, Neb., 1997).

31. Rebecca Saunders, *Stability and Change in Guale Indian Pottery, A.D. 1300–1702* (Tuscaloosa, Ala., 2000), 177. For a different example of stress on craft production possibly caused by disease, Marvin T. Smith notes the decline of craft specialization during the early seventeenth century. It could be that, as he surmises, diseases were disrupting chiefly hierarchies and the craftspeople they supported. It could also be that the arrival of Spanish goods supplanted these indigenous crafts. In either case, Spanish goods perhaps caused and certainly filled a crucial gap in the iconography of power (Smith, *Aboriginal Culture Change,* 108–112).

32. Franciscans took pride in their ability to impress Native leaders, and later historians consider it important to the Franciscans' success in New Mexico as well as Florida. See Francisco de Marrón to king, Jan. 23, 1597, AGI, SD 235; Luís Gerónimo de Oré to king, [1617?], Santo Domingo, ibid.; Weber, *Spanish Frontier,* 115–116.

33. Worth, *Timucuan Chiefdoms,* I, 37–38.

monarch along with their temporal one. Spaniards could not compel Indian leaders to render obedience or seek conversion, but both such acts placed Native leaders in a Spanish hierarchy that included Spaniards at the top.[34] They acted on this assumption, too, with the governor approving the succession of head caciques. Although no governor wanted to risk the hostility or instability that would accompany excessive interference, the governor's supervisory role ideally reminded Natives of their new place in the developing colonial system and helped ensure that loyal leaders supervised its development at the town and village level. Some Indians accepted this new relationship with alacrity: at Mission San Pedro in the Timucuan coastal province of Mocama, the leader known as Cacique Juan went so far as to expel those who refused to convert. Twenty-five years old, he had come of age familiar with Christian practice and might have owed some of his youthful prominence to Spanish support.[35]

Others were less enthusiastic about any Spanish attempts at subordination. A series of Indian revolts and reprisals over the course of the seventeenth century made very clear that Indians and Spaniards occasionally operated under divergent norms.[36] The Guale revolt of 1597, which I discuss in more detail below, provided Spaniards with the first lesson in this political reality. In many instances, these revolts might have been the product of Spaniards' abusing an authority that Natives had conceded, but in other instances, Native Americans approached Spaniards and their goods with a sense not of submission but of entitlement. During the middle 1620s, when Governor Luís Rojas y Borja was trying to invigorate the colony's regional influence through liberal gift giving, budget-conscious royal officials complained that he offered gifts of clothing and other items to all comers, regardless of their evangelical intentions or their rank. According to the officials, such largesse actually weakened the colony because "today the Indians come for this clothing as if for tribute, and they say so."[37]

This sense of entitlement to Spanish goods, and the belief that they constituted tribute rendered by a subordinate rather than gifts offered by a superior, suggests the complicated misunderstandings that surrounded these

34. Ibid., 36–43.

35. Consejo de Indias to king, June 20, 1596, Madrid, AGI, SD 6. Juan was twenty-six in 1597. See Hann, *History of Timucua Indians,* 150.

36. For some of the works that review parts or all of this history, see Worth, *Timucuan Chiefdoms,* II; Weber, *Spanish Frontier,* 141–145; Hoffman, *Florida's Frontiers,* 122–147.

37. Francisco Ramírez, Juan de Cueva, and Francisco Menéndez Márquez to king, Jan. 30, 1627, AGI, SD 229.

objects and the ways that Indians were incorporating them into their political and ceremonial worlds on their own terms.[38] It also suggests the ways that Indians understood Saint Augustine to be the center of a new chiefdom in the region, one to which they owed respect, but also one from which they could expect a political support commensurate with their allegiance to the Spaniards. After years of bitter lessons on the impotence of imposition, the governor who spearheaded this campaign of generosity in the 1590s, Gonzalo Méndez de Canzo, acknowledged Indian leaders' needs, protesting to the king that "I spend much of my own resources on the Natives, which is necessary because they are poor people . . . in order to attract them to conversion and your royal service."[39] Whether he realized it or not, Méndez was describing himself as a new chief in the region. That he described his generosity in a letter pleading for a larger royal salary for his services suggests just how much he believed that the hierarchy of gifts continued eastward across the Atlantic.

The carefully reciprocal and intensely competitive relationships of chiefdoms that Méndez intimated and many Indians experienced was easy for Spaniards to forget in the midst of a new string of successes following 1587. Thanks to the respect that royal officials showed to the Franciscans and that Indians showed to all Spaniards, it was easy to see why the custodian of the Franciscan mission, Francisco de Marrón, could claim in 1597 that the Indians thought of the missionaries as "gods on earth." By that year, Franciscans could claim a decade of evangelizing in Mocama and two years in Guale. Months after Marrón had declared Franciscans' apotheosis, Governor Méndez sent additional expeditions north, west, and south of the limits of colonial and evangelical control. The northerly embassy attempted to establish ties with Altamaha and Ocute, where Spaniards once again learned the importance of negotiation rather than imposition. Two Franciscans, Fray Pedro de Chozas and Francisco de Veráscola, led the evangelical

---

38. Such misunderstandings over the meanings of European-Native relationships occurred everywhere, but they appear most compellingly in Richard White, *The Middle Ground: Indians, Empires, and Republics in the Great Lakes Region, 1650–1815* (Cambridge, 1991). One passage is particularly helpful by way of comparison. "Often, in the examples that follow, when the French sought the imposition of hard-and-fast rules, the Algonquians sought the 'power' that comes from knocking the order off balance, from asserting the personal, the human exception" (52). Although White is describing Native polities significantly different from chiefdoms, the power of the person and the personal resonates in the history of southeastern Indians' relations with the Spanish during the decades that closed the sixteenth and opened the seventeenth centuries.

39. Méndez to king, Feb. 23, 1598, AGI, SD 224.

expedition north to the Oconee Valley early in the summer of 1597. Accompanying them were Gaspar de Salas, a soldier and interpreter who spoke Guale, and thirty Indians, who could provide protection for the expedition. Chozas loaded them, as the Franciscan Alonso Gregorio de Escobedo put it in his epic poem, *La Florida,* "with Castillian blankets, with knives, fish hooks, and scissors, and with very fine glass beads, with sickles and cutting axes." The party set out from the Guale mission of Tolomato, expecting that the people of Altamaha and Ocute "would know the power of our people and the little which they enjoyed in their western lands." Chozas supplemented these material demonstrations with suitably dramatic preaching, and the formidable Veráscola further exhibited the power of the Spaniards and their god by successfully wrestling "chest to chest" many challengers in the towns they visited. Escobedo was writing an epic of Franciscan achievement, and we should expect some exaggeration, but clearly he and his heroes knew that they needed to demonstrate to chiefs and their followers the material, physical, and cosmological power that resided in Saint Augustine and across the ocean in Spain.[40]

Having ventured north to impress the supposedly benighted peoples of the Oconee Valley, the Spaniards for their part marvelled at what they saw. In 1597, Saint Augustine still struggled to feed itself; but even the poor food of that sandy outpost must have sounded good as the party of thirty-three spent seven days heading northwestward from Tolomato through uninhabited wilderness. The sight of the Oconee Valley with its populous villages and towns and fields filled with a "quantity of food" that included corn, beans, grapes, and watermelons must have indeed been a feast for the eyes.[41]

One day after their arrival in the valley, they were in the town of Altamaha, where Chozas met the members of the leading family in the council house and presented to each a blanket.[42] Impressed with the offer, the leaders granted his request to preach to the town. The following day, Cho-

40. Marrón to king, Jan. 23, 1597, AGI, SD 235; Alonso Gregorio de Escobedo, *La Florida,* excerpted in Atanasio López, ed., *Relación histórica de la Florida, escrita en el siglo XVII,* 2 vols. (Madrid, 1931), I, 27–28. For a summary of this *entrada,* see Worth, "Late Spanish Military Expeditions," in Hudson and Tesser, eds., *Forgotten Centuries,* 105–108. For Salas's linguistic abilities, see Maynard Geiger, *The Franciscan Conquest of Florida (1573–1618)* (Washington, D.C., 1937), 82–83.

41. Testimony of Gaspar de Salas, Feb. 2, 1600, AGI, SD 224, doc. 35.

42. Escobedo, *La Florida,* in López, ed., *Relación histórica de la Florida,* I, 28. Two lines ("y luego se pusieron en presencia / de toda la familia endemoniada") suggest that Chozas first sought the approval of the members of Altamaha's closely related elite before meeting with the entire town.

zas had "the king" place a cross in the center of the plaza, and then he and Veráscola called the community to meet inside the council house, where, after first beginning with a grave and prolonged silence, Chozas proceeded to instruct the people about the Christian faith. A sudden rain shower convinced his listeners of his spiritual power, and the town accepted baptism en masse and reciprocated with gifts to the Spaniards. In both acts, Altamahas expressed their own desire to build a deeper relationship.[43]

Continuing inland one more day to Ocute, the visitors were again "well received." They noted with surprise and hope that the women of Ocute wore shawls similar to those of New Spain. All seemed well, but as soon as they indicated a desire to continue farther on their journey, perhaps to determine the proximity of the other colony, the chief Ocute "obstructed them with much pleading and crying," explaining that many of those farther inland still recalled Soto's visit and hoped to kill some of those related to the ruthless invader. The warm reception was cooling, and the missionaries failed to convert anyone in Ocute.[44] The situation became even more grim when, on their return through Altamaha, the formerly friendly chief suddenly seemed more interested in removing Chozas's scalp. Chozas evidently possessed great power, and the chief had decided that the hair on his head—rather than the ideas in it—might improve Altamaha's chances of winning an imminent competition against another chief. Only a timely shot from Salas's arquebus saved the missionary. Before hastily departing, though, Chozas still insisted on asking for burdeners to carry his goods because those who had accompanied him inland "had hid themselves in the wilds." In addition to refusing the request, the mico Altamaha bellowed threats forcefully enough to hasten Chozas and his companions on their way. They returned home by a different route, following settled areas and spending only two days crossing uninhabited lands, before arriving at the coast, not in Tolomato, but farther south at San Pedro in Mocama.[45]

For Chozas, Veráscola, and Salas, the expedition had failed. They returned from the province they called La Tama with glorious accounts of conversions and tantalizing rumors of silver mines, but the obstructions of

43. Ibid., 28–30.

44. The reason for Ocute's reticence is difficult to determine, but the best evidence comes from Escobedo. Although he mistranscribes Ocute as "Quaque," he elliptically refers to Chozas's failure there by listing "Quaque" along with "Tama" (alias Altamaha) and two towns of Fatufas and Usatipass, then saying that Chozas "converted three kingdoms, but not the first" (ibid., 28–29). For the quotes about Ocute's obstructionism, see testimony of Salas, Feb. 2, 1600, AGI, SD 224, doc. 35.

45. Escobedo, *La Florida*, in López, ed., *Relación histórica de la Florida*, I, 31, 32.

Oconee elites and brewing problems in Guale made this modest expedition the last of its size for decades to come. Far from Saint Augustine and its ambitions and preoccupations, Altamahas and Ocutes, and especially their leaders, had much more to look forward to. They had acquired items from the powerful new people of the coast, and perhaps the Spaniards' ally and tributary, Juan of Tolomato, might return by way of the newly blazed trail with more such items.[46] For his part, Ocute could proudly reflect that he had maintained effective control over his subordinates and his guests. Altamaha's sudden interest in Chozas's scalp probably had something to do with Ocute's refusal to accept conversion, and the shift probably reassured the paramount leader in Ocute that the chief of Altamaha remained loyal to him. The Spaniards had visited without trying venture farther inland, and they had left respectful of but not angered by Ocute's and Altamaha's displays of independence. From Ocute's town square, this new relationship looked promising indeed.

Despite these positive developments, Oconee peoples' hopes of deriving new benefits from Saint Augustine, whether via the hands of Franciscans, Guales, or others, took an unexpected turn not long after Chozas's hasty departure. Late in September 1597, Guales revolted, destroying the missions, killing five Franciscans, and capturing a sixth. Despite Spaniards' remarkable successes with promoting Native loyalties and conversions through gifts, old coercive habits died hard. Having stacked ample tinder by attacking important Guale traditions and restricting converts' movements among the province's towns, Franciscans then provided an incendiary spark by passing over Juan of Tolomato as principal mico of the province in order to appoint his more tractable uncle, Francisco. The outraged Juan "went into the interior among the pagans, without saying anything or without obtaining permission as they were wont to do on other occasions." After "a few days," Juan returned to Tolomato with some of these inland supporters (probably Guales who had fled the missions) and rallied Francisco and other followers against the missionaries.[47]

46. Juan probably shared these ambitions. Unlike the many Indian escorts who deserted Chozas, Juan probably remained with the expedition—and he collected on this loyalty when he returned to Saint Augustine to request gifts from the governor for his service. He probably imagined that such loyalty would secure him similar Spanish generosity in the future, a generosity he might share with trips inland along the new path from Tolomato to the Oconee Valley. See Alvárez de Castrillón to king, Sept. 14, 1597, AGI, SD 231.

47. Oré, *Martyrs of Florida,* ed. and trans. Geiger, 73. For summaries of the revolt, see Geiger, *Franciscan Conquest,* 86–115; Hoffman, *Florida's Frontiers,* 82–86; Bush-

Although not directly involved in the revolt, Oconee Valley peoples were never far from the minds of those who were. Juan's initial foray inland suggested that the coastal Guales recognized the value of the interior, and Spaniards confirmed these perceptions when they responded to the revolt in October by sailing along the coast to burn the insurgents' cornfields and towns. The following spring, Governor Méndez met with Guale leaders to ransom the captive Franciscan, offering axes, hoes, and blankets for his return. When the Guale leaders demurred, insisting on the return of some of their own sons who had been living in Saint Augustine for several years, the governor shifted tactics, becoming enraged and threatening to send for three hundred soldiers "and put them to the sword, and cut down all their maize and food, and follow them as far as La Tama."[48] Guales promptly returned the missionary. Spaniards possessed unmistakable military power, but both they and Guales also recognized that the Oconee Valley's peoples, however distant, played a pivotal role; they could either be the refuge to which Guales might flee or the anvil against which Spaniards could crush them.

Unfortunately for Méndez, his hammer was small and his anvil a figment of his rhetoric. The reality was more complex because the governor's army was strong enough only to conduct coastal raids and because Altamahas had little incentive to undertake a military campaign for him. As a result, in addition to his strong words and a scorched-earth campaign against the coastal towns, he also used gifts of "tools, axes, and hoes" to entice some of the Guales' old enemies, the Escamaçus from Santa Elena, just north along the coast from Guale, to resume their traditional hostilities. Spanish reprisals and Escamaçu raids convinced many Guale leaders to visit Saint Augustine to renew their allegiance to the Spanish in early 1600, and the governor used these contacts to make new offers of gifts to those who visited. Some royal officials in the colony considered such gifts wasted on peoples whose "friendship is feigned," and others worried that Méndez's generosity would upset those who had remained loyal. The governor contented himself with this imperfect strategy because he had little choice. Despite his threats of fire and blood to the Guales, he acknowledged to the king that, because the rebels had retreated to lands so far from the coast, "there was no way that one could punish them there unless it were by the hand and order of the same Indians," especially the newly loyal leader of the Guale town of Asao. Even the new friendship had its shortcomings, as the nominally paci-

nell, *Situado and Sabana,* 60–66. For a documentary overview, see Quinn, ed., *New American World,* V, 69–92. For quote, see ibid., 69.

48. Quinn, ed., *New American World,* V, 87.

fied towns continued to defy Spanish authority by welcoming French traders, and they would continue to do so for another three years. No Spaniard was foolish enough to think that Guales were ready to welcome new missionaries.[49]

Saint Augustine's officials courted Altamaha alliance with gifts, but Oconee leaders did not pursue these objects or their purveyors blindly. If they were going to associate themselves with Spanish beads, cloth, or hoes, they also needed to be sure Spaniards showed themselves to be a formidable chiefdom in their own right. The Spaniards had proved to be powerful benefactors during their visit inland during the summer of 1597. One year later, a royal official noted that the "inland Indians" probably approved that the governor was demanding greater tribute payments from those Indians who remained loyal. And yet, two months after that, as the governor sent sixteen soldiers to help defend the Mocama mission of San Pedro, the same official noted that the governor needed to send rations with these soldiers instead of expecting the Mocamas to feed them because "the inland Indians are watching to see how we aid our friends." By exacting appropriate tribute for subordinate polities and providing necessary support for these same dependents, Spaniards could demonstrate their power—and the power of their goods—to observant Altamahas.[50]

49. Bartolomé de Argüelles to king, Aug. 3, 1598, Feb. 20, 1600, AGI, SD 229; Alonso de Alas to king, Jan. 12, 1600, ibid.; Alonso de Cano to king, Feb. 23, 1600, ibid.; testimony of Gonzalo Méndez de Canzo to king, Nov. 27, 1601, ibid., SD 224, doc. 41; Joseph M. Hall, Jr., "Making an Indian People: Creek Formation in the Colonial Southeast, 1590–1735" (Ph.D. diss., University of Wisconsin, 2001), 87–93; Bushnell, *Situado and Sabana*, 66. Hoffman describes the Spanish response as "swift, brutal, prolonged, and effective in restoring Spanish control in Guale," and Bushnell shares a similar assessment of the Spanish military response. Although scorched-earth tactics played an important role in ending the revolt, Spaniards could not have pacified the province without the assistance of Indians who exacted their own concessions, such as a reduction in tribute or, as I describe below, Spanish gifts. See Hoffman, *Florida's Frontiers*, 83; Bushnell, *Situado and Sabana*, 66.

50. Argüelles to king, Aug. 3, 1598, AGI, SD 229. Argüelles's statement is difficult to parse, but it offers intriguing insight into the politics of power, gifts, and tribute. It reads, "Les alço El dho gobernador el tributo y aunque no era de mucha ynportancia parece que era una manera de Reconocimiento con lo qual se ganaba opinion con los de la tierra adentro q no estiman en mas de quanto ben que a cada uno se le tributa." I translate the passage literally as "The said governor raised their tribute and although it was not of much importance, it seems that it was a form of acknowledgment [of authority] with which we gained [a good] opinion from those from the inland who do not esteem those except according to how much they exact as tribute."

Although Méndez probably did not decide to provision the San Pedro garrison, he was doing his best to convince inland peoples like the Altamahas that his friendship could be of great service to them. Not surprisingly, he also had need of their friendship. As he had already acknowledged to the king, Indians would be crucial to suppressing the last of the insurgents, and Altamaha assistance would prevent Francisco, Juan, and their followers from fleeing further inland. As the Spaniards well knew, gifts would make this alliance possible, but to distribute these gifts, Governor Méndez enlisted the help of two Christian chiefs from Mocama, the coastal province just south of Guale. The two Mocamas, Cacique María of the mission town of Nombre de Dios and Cacique Juan of San Pedro, received gifts valued at 350 ducats—roughly the equivalent of three years' pay for a common soldier—to take "into the interior land to the caciques with whom they have contact." Offering such gifts to their friends, the Christian leaders could also explain that all who joined the Spaniards could expect similar generosity from His Majesty. Such generosity might encourage recalcitrant Guales to reciprocate with allegiance rather than continued hostility. If not, then perhaps by attracting other interior peoples like the Altamahas, the governor could expand the mission system and simultaneously pressure Guales from the south and interior.[51]

Spaniards could not have guessed the result. Nor could they control it. By placing colonial policy in Native hands, La Florida's royal and religious officials initiated a series of changes that enabled Indian peoples to adjust to colonial neighbors on indigenous terms. No longer orchestrating the ceremonies of "rendering obedience" in the course of presenting their gifts, Spaniards were supplying Native leaders with valuable items that they then introduced to the southeastern political economy on their terms. Although we know little about Cacique María's ambitions, Cacique Juan clearly molded Spanish interests to fit his own. In 1598, two years before his generous gift to Juan, Governor Méndez had noted approvingly that "he spends himself into poverty giving gifts to other caciques to bring them to our obedience."[52] Although Spaniards doubtless approved of such generosity in the service of their temporal and divine monarchs, Juan also had more personal interests in mind. Some time before receiving the governor's

51. Méndez to king, Feb. 23, 28, 1600, AGI, SD 224, 229, doc. 35. Between 1583 and 1723, soldiers were paid 115 ducats a year (Bushnell, *Situado and Sabana,* 45).

52. Méndez to king, Feb. 23, 1598, AGI, SD 224, doc. 31. Among the beneficiaries of his largesse were the Spaniards themselves, who by 1595 had apparently received some nine thousand reales' worth of supplies from the cacique and his people. See San Miguel, *Early Florida Adventure Story,* trans. Hann, 7.

gifts in 1600, he requested Méndez to appoint him head cacique of Guale. Perhaps the Mocama leader hoped that his growing influence among Spaniards and Indians would enable him to capitalize on the apostasy of Guale's most recent head cacique. The governor balked at the request, but what is significant is that Spaniards were placing gifts in the hands of Native intermediaries who had their own interests at heart.[53]

Altamahas—especially their mico Altamaha—used this influx of gifts to restructure their polity. Gifts probably arrived from Juan of San Pedro, with Juan directly or indirectly sending them up the same path that Chozas and others had followed back from the Oconee three years earlier. Although there is no documentation of these gift exchanges, evidence of their consequences appears in the shifting political fortunes of Altamaha in the Oconee Valley. In 1540, Altamahas owed some allegiance to Ocute's chief, and as Fray Chozas knew, Ocute still influenced the actions of its downriver tributary as late as 1597. Despite this long-standing relationship, Altamahas had evidently severed ties with Ocute by 1601, when they joined Guales and a number of other peoples in a final, decisive attack on the remaining Guale recalcitrants. The next year, another Spanish visitor noted Altamahas' independence and perhaps rising prominence when he referred to it as "the capital of the province." Such success, though, came at the price of hostility with Ocute: when the visitor expressed interest in continuing northward toward Ocute, his hosts urged him to reconsider "so that they might not kill him."[54] With a warning that mirrored the one Ocute issued to Chozas and his companions, Altamahas proclaimed a new line of independence and even hostility in the Oconee Valley. The Spaniards' influence on this new political situation probably owed something to the gifts that came from Juan and traveled the well-populated route from San Pedro. Whether or not Juan could claim credit for this success, Ocutes themselves recognized and resented this new Spanish influence in their valley.

The struggles among elites masked more fundamental shifts among the

53. Governor Méndez feared that Guale resistance to a Mocama leader would "undercut what I have done with so much work to attract and reduce the province [to Spanish allegiance]." Juan apparently did not respond to the rejection before he died later that year, perhaps from disease. See Méndez to king, Feb. 28, June 26, 1600, AGI, SD 224, docs. 35, 36.

54. Testimony of Juan de Lara in "Información de orden de Su Majestad sobre el estado general de las provincias de la Florida y si conviene o no desmantelar el fuerte de San Agustín," Sept. 3–9, 1602, AGI, SD 2533, excerpted and translated in Worth, "Late Spanish Military Expeditions," in Hudson and Tesser, eds., *Forgotten Centuries*, 109.

general population of the Oconee Valley. Spanish gifts might have promoted a new Altamaha independence, but they apparently did not halt the decline of elite power. That Spaniards placed these goods in the hands of leaders probably encouraged southeastern elites to draw upon these new resources in a time of political flux, but the results did not always favor chiefs' authority. One suggestive clue appears in 1604, when Governor Pedro de Ibarra met Altamahas in Guale and gave only passing mention to the "cacique of La Tama." Rather than the head of the famed inland province, he appeared in a list as one of many other dignitaries welcoming Ibarra. Perhaps Spanish contact with Altamaha had become routine, or perhaps the visiting cacique was not the mico of Altamaha but one of his subordinate oratas. Regardless, the lack of emphasis suggests that this leader was not as powerful as his Spanish title suggested.[55] Archaeology confirms a power shift that the documents can only suggest. For more than a century before Cacique Juan or any other emissaries ventured with gifts from Saint Augustine, the Altamahas, Ocutes, and their neighbors were abandoning their towns, dispersing their homes throughout the valley. By 1580, valley residents no longer used their mounds, and the fact that Fray Chozas met with Altamaha leaders in a council house suggests that the decisions of individual chiefs were becoming increasingly communal. In other words, Altamaha leaders probably sought Spanish goods not just to escape Ocute's influence but also to maintain their own influence over an increasingly segmented population.[56]

In some respects, the new strategies worked. Following the turn of the century, at a time when many interior populations were consolidating dwindling communities at the fall line frontiers between piedmonts and coastal plains, Oconee peoples were also relocating. Although many peoples moved in order to build new communities at locations that afforded the greatest op-

55. "Relación del viage que hizo el señor Pedro de Ibarra, gobernador y capitán general de la Florida, á visitar los pueblos indios de las provincias de San Pedro y Guale," in Manuel Serrano y Sanz, ed., *Documentos históricos de la Florida y la Luisiana, siglos XVI al XVIII* (Madrid, 1913), 183–184.

56. People began moving into scattered farmsteads in the second half of the fifteenth century, probably as a result of relative peace and the growing population that accompanied it. Although such population dispersal likely did not induce people to abandon the mounds, it certainly exacerbated the mounds' declining role toward the end of the century. See Mark Williams, "Chiefly Compounds," in J. Daniel Rogers and Bruce D. Smith, eds., *Mississippian Communities and Households* (Tuscaloosa, Ala., 1995); James W. Hatch, "Lamar Period Upland Farmsteads of the Oconee River Valley, Georgia," ibid., 135–155.

portunities for subsistence, some residents of the Oconee Valley were actually moving downstream of the fall line to the coastal plain. They now inhabited lands less ecologically diverse and less agriculturally fertile than their former homes, but they had much easier access to the respected clothing, beads, and tools from Saint Augustine. Like other inland peoples, they once again began settling in more nucleated towns rather than dispersed farmsteads, and this shift might have been a product of their mico's rising authority. The mico might have sought additional Spanish support for his precarious position as an independent leader by requesting Franciscans at the short-lived mission of Santa Isabel, which was founded by 1616 along the Altamaha River and lasted at least another two decades. Depopulation from epidemics could have just as easily caused a dwindling population to seek the mutual protection of towns and the spiritual protection of Franciscans. Whether dealing with the problems of leadership or depopulation, some Indians were looking to Saint Augustine for solutions.[57]

Altamahas did not pursue this strategy alone. In 1612, Governor Fernández de Olivera claimed that unnamed southeastern Natives' widespread interest in trade and missionaries signified both "God's miraculous work" and the influence of the gifts and aid the governor offered to those who came. The most significant sign of this attractive power was that "[Some] have arrived here from the very Cape of Apalachee and from much further away. They assured me that they have been walking for two and a half months and that all along the way they have had safe passage and warm reception knowing that they come here." Seven decades after the Apalachees of the Florida panhandle had hounded Soto's forces out of their province, their descendants were joining others to seek Spanish friendship and trade goods. More strikingly, other peoples were journeying eastward perhaps five hundred miles to do so.[58] Gifts and the power that they conferred and

57. Smith, *Aboriginal Culture Change,* 77-80; Smith, "Aboriginal Population Movements in the Postcontact Southeast," in Ethridge and Hudson, eds., *Transformation,* 10-12; Williams, "Growth and Decline," in Hudson and Tesser, eds., *Forgotten Centuries,* 191-193; Mark Williams, personal communication, May 13, 2004. So little is known about the Pine Barrens site and the Santa Isabel mission that any conclusions must be tentative. See Frankie Snow, "Pine Barrens Lamar," in Mark Williams and Gary Shapiro, eds., *Lamar Archaeology: Mississippian Chiefdoms in the Deep South* (Tuscaloosa, Ala., 1990), 82-89; Oré, *Martyrs of Florida,* ed. and trans. Geiger, 129, 135 n. 22; Worth, *Timucuan Chiefdoms,* I, 73; Worth, "The Timucuan Missions of Spanish Florida and the Rebellion of 1656" (Ph.D. diss., University of Florida, 1992), 68-69, 76 n. 14.

58. Fernández de Olivera to king, Oct. 13, 1612, AGI, SD 225, doc. 4. According to

confirmed gradually insinuated themselves into the power structures of a variety of peoples beyond the echoes of Spaniards' cannon or the peal of their mission bells.

Unfortunately for the Altamahas, or at least for our history of them, Olivera's news also represented a shift in Spanish interest. Beginning in 1607, Spaniards directed their evangelical and diplomatic efforts to the lands west of Saint Augustine. The very fact that the Santa Isabel mission remains poorly understood and lacks almost any documentation attests to their declining interest in the lands north and west of Guale. Altamahas and missionaries continued to express intermittent hopes for a mission on the Oconee, but this, too, ceased after 1636.[59]

Increasingly silent documents should not distract us from what was already under way in the Georgia interior. Altamaha leaders and followers were drawing on Spanish goods to shape their own struggles for survival, prominence, and cosmological order. In these efforts lie clues to the ways that Indians were laying the political and ceremonial groundwork for the more trying challenges that would appear later in the century. A number of scholars have pointed out that, in the interval between contact and colonization, southeastern societies adjusted to the idea of Europeans before they had to confront the reality of the newcomers. As one china box suggests and as the larger history of the Oconee Valley confirms, this interval provided more than just time.

Spanish gifts to indigenous leaders replaced or augmented the rare and prestigious objects that held together many southeastern political and cosmological orders. The diseases and violence that accompanied the arrival of colonists had posed serious challenges to these orders. In the wake of these disruptions, chiefs struggled to maintain the populations and cosmic harmony that would build the inspiring mounds and maintain the crucial food surpluses. So, too, did skilled craftspeople lose the time and the expertise to endow their pottery, shells, deerskins, or copper with the powerful designs that leaders and followers both needed for social stability. In the midst of these crises—some grave, some merely troubling—chiefs also rec-

---

Amy Turner Bushnell, traveling the 150 miles between Saint Augustine and the center of the province of Apalachee took roughly fifteen days. The cape, today's Cape Saint George, is located where the Apalachicola River empties into the Gulf of Mexico and would probably have been about another week's travel distant. Two and a half months' travel could mean that the visitors had arrived from a location as much as four times farther away than Apalachee (Bushnell, *Situado and Sabana,* 114).

59. Luís Gerónimo de Oré to king, [1617?], Santo Domingo, AGI, SD 235; Lorenzo Martínez to king, Oct. 22, 1636, ibid.; Hoffman, *Florida's Frontiers,* chap. 5.

ognized some of the opportunities that accompanied the Europeans. Spaniards, lacking the authority to impose a colonial order, provided gifts that enabled leaders to salvage some of their own influence. As leaders and followers must have recognized, axes and hoes did not carry indigenous designs; glass beads did not come from the traditionally sacred sites of the coast. These new objects coming from Saint Augustine did, however, enjoy a prominence of their own that could compensate for and perhaps replace older items and older symbols. Furthermore, by focusing their gift giving and diplomacy on chiefs, Spaniards inadvertently ensured that the people who most needed these objects actually got them. These same leaders then incorporated the new items relatively smoothly into older ceremonies and distribution networks. Thus, by 1630, Spanish beads were arriving in towns as far west as Alabama and as far north as Tennessee. So too, in 1621, china boxes were joining shell gorgets on long journeys from Guale to the Potomac.[60]

And English gifts were heading south. In 1633, an Escamaçu ventured south along the coast to a Guale mission to report that the English had established a colony in his province, that "the English were giving away gifts of tools and other things," and, more troubling, "that they gave away more [than the Spaniards]."[61] The lack of any further documentation on the matter suggests that the Escamaçu was grossly mistaken about English settlement activities, but he probably made no mistake about the English objects. Indians throughout much of the Southeast had been exchanging indigenous objects for centuries and Spanish goods for decades. That Jamestown, Virginia, was a new source of rare objects should hardly surprise.

Like the Spanish, the English also sought to maintain a fragile colonial foothold with gifts to powerful neighbors, first with the Powhatans and then, as relations with the Powhatans soured, with their principal rivals.[62] As the Escamaçu made clear in 1633, these localized efforts also had far-reaching consequences. The Escamaçu's additional claim that the English offered their goods on better terms also foreshadowed a radical transformation of the exchanges that brought these goods from European ships into Native hands. The consequences became clearest a half-century later.

60. Smith, *Aboriginal Culture Change,* 46–51; Knight, *Tukabatchee,* 107.

61. Order of Sergeant Major Eugenio de Espinosa to Sergeant Major Antonio Herrera López y Mesa, Sept. 9, 1633, enclosed in "Relation of Merits of Antonio Herrera López y Mesa," Apr. 22, 1649, AGI, Indiferente General 114, doc. 23.

62. Potter, "Early English Effects," in Wood, Waselkov, and Hatley, eds., *Powhatan's Mantle,* 154–160.

As the later colony of South Carolina expanded its trade inland during the 1670s and 1680s, English emissaries regularly offered rare goods (including firearms) to broad segments of the male population. The exchange of gifts among elites had become the exchange of goods between traders.

Had elites not already adjusted to the growing presence of European items during the previous century, the sudden availability of these prestigious objects could have promoted a form of inflation catastrophic to Native notions of authority. Natives' ability to maintain many precontact structures of influence, however attenuated, likely owed much to the gradual transition that Spaniards initiated.[63] Spaniards hardly orchestrated their colonial efforts with this transition in mind, but they clearly provided Natives near to and far from the missions not just time but resources to reorganize their societies. Chozas's evangelical campaign and Méndez's need for help against the Guales introduced Oconee peoples to new items for their political struggles. The close of these evangelical and diplomatic overtures, however, marked not an end but a beginning. The inter-Indian exchanges that had explicitly begun with Juan of San Pedro and María of Nombre de Dios only continued.

The consequences were broad, but not all experienced them the same way. The same gifts that promoted Altamaha's authority did so in part at the expense of the formerly paramount Ocute. After 1659, as Altamahas, Ocutes, and other peoples suffered increasing violence and upheaval with the beginning of English-sponsored slave raids, the Altamahas became the heart of a new, confederated people known as the Yamasees. Altamahas could not have attributed their town's prominence among the late-seventeenth-century Yamasees entirely or even primarily to Spanish goods and the political changes that they facilitated. The prominence that Altamaha elites did retain in the early part of the century, though, at least helped the efforts of their descendants to take a leading role in addressing the crises that accompanied the slave raiders. Similar patterns would also enable the descendants of other chiefdoms to contemporaneously assemble the larger confederacies known as the Catawbas, Creeks, Cherokees, Choctaws,

63. Worth, "Spanish Missions," in Ethridge and Hudson, eds., *Transformation*, points out the importance of Spanish colonial policies for the maintenance of precontact hierarchies in the missions. This study of Altamaha's fortunes suggests that some of the same materials that supported the power of Christian chiefs might have also stabilized the uncertain footing of their unconverted neighbors. On the growing presence of European goods in southeastern graves, see Wesson, "Prestige Goods," in Wesson and Rees, eds., *Between Contact and Colonies*.

and Chickasaws. Still-powerful leaders, wielding new icons of prestige, re-assembled a new political order from the remains of the old.[64]

Europeans' arrival in North America, which the Spanish initiated, frequently appears in the scholarship as the beginning of a cataclysm. It was. Ruthlessly torturing Natives in their quests for indigenous empires, inadvertently more destructive and disruptive thanks to the pathogens they left behind, early Spanish conquistadors introduced Native Americans to new forms of power and brutality. Although chiefdoms certainly suffered for the arrivals of Soto and other, less-belligerent visitors, to imagine chiefdoms' collapse as an immediate consequence is to exaggerate Europeans' ability to project their influence (and their microbes) throughout the region. It also exaggerates Natives' inability to ask the questions that would enable them to address these new challenges. What is most important to note, though, is that Altamahas, Ocutes, and—as Governor Olivera's letter suggests—countless other peoples were answering some of these questions with Spanish goods in the first decades of the seventeenth century. Peoples to the north of the missions did not flock to Saint Augustine in similarly noteworthy numbers, but they, too, appreciated the power of things from Acana Echinac. Indeed, they incorporated these goods into age-old and frequent contests for influence within and among their polities. These goods and this political competitiveness endowed Native societies with a flexibility that would serve them well amid the crises that accompanied colonial competition after 1607.

64. Hall, "Making an Indian People," 200–206. Vernon James Knight, Jr., "The Formation of the Creeks," in Hudson and Tesser, eds., *Forgotten Centuries,* 385–386, points out that "the resilience of the local chiefdoms" in some parts of what would later be the Creek Confederacy played crucial roles in the consolidation of the larger network of alliances.

James D. Rice

ESCAPE FROM TSENACOMMACAH

CHESAPEAKE ALGONQUIANS AND

THE POWHATAN MENACE

One of the best-known images of life in early Virginia, frequently reprinted in textbooks, popular histories, and scholarly monographs, depicts
a malevolent-looking Indian named Iopassus as he attempts to lure Pocahontas into the hands of the English captain Samuel Argall. Iopassus, the
brother of the powerful *weroance* (chief) of the Patawomeck nation (and a
tribute-paying subordinate of Pocahontas's father, Powhatan), holds behind
him a copper pot given him by Argall, while his wife cradles a cask and
some trade beads under her right arm. Pocahontas is clearly uneasy about
boarding Argall's ship, and with good reason: as most American schoolchil-
dren know, Iopassus succeeded in luring Pocahontas into English captivity.
This 1617 engraving by the Frankfurt-born artist Georg Keller, originally
an illustration for a German translation of Ralph Hamor's *True Discourse
of the Present State of Virginia,* adorns countless modern retellings of Pocahontas's capture, typically over a caption such as "Pocahontas being persuaded to board the English ship before her capture" or "Iapassus and his
wife persuade Pocahontas to visit Captain Argall's ship."[1]

Thanks to Kathleen Bragdon, J. Frederick Fausz, Joshua Piker, Stephen Potter, and
participants in the Toronto Area Early Canada/Colonial North America Seminar for
their comments on earlier drafts of this essay. Thanks also to Dennis Blanton, Keith
Egloff, Stuart Fiedel, and Alice Kehoe for their guidance in matters archaeological, to
Christian Feest, Laura Rice, and Jeffrey Ruggles for their help in tracing the history of
Georg Keller's print, and to Joseph Miller, Helen Rountree, Timothy Shannon, Margaret Holmes Williamson, and Cynthia Van Zandt for their generous and helpful advice.

1. Christian F. Feest, "The Virginia Indian in Pictures, 1612–1624," *The Smithsonian Journal of History,* II (1967), 13–17. The most commonly reprinted version of
the engraving is a copy made by Johann Theodore de Bry in 1618. The examples of
modern captions are from Karen Ordahl Kupperman, *Indians and English: Facing Off*

PLATE I. *Anglo-Powhatan relations, 1613–1614, according to Georg Keller.*
By Johann Theodore de Bry after Georg Keller. Virginia Historical Society,
Richmond, Virginia

Only rarely, however, does the modern-day caption make any reference
to the rest of the engraving. Although it is often cropped to exclude everything except the exchange between Pocahontas, Iopassus, and Iopassus's
wife, in the original engraving that scene occupies only the lower left corner
of the image. From there, the story continues, unfolding in a zigzag course
from the foreground on the lower left to the far background at the upper
edge of the print. In the following scene, which Keller placed to the right of
and behind Iopassus's wife, Pocahontas boards Argall's boat together with
Iopassus and his spouse. They then sit down to dinner at Argall's table, at
which point Pocahontas is seized and taken prisoner. Next, English ships
come to a Powhatan village to negotiate Pocahontas's return. The discus-

in Early America (Ithaca, N.Y., 2000), viii, 209; and Philip L. Barbour, *Pocahontas
and Her World: A Chronicle of America's First Settlement in Which is Related the Story
of the Indians and the Englishmen . . .* (Boston, 1970), xvi.

sions are not going well: smoke and flames billow from the village because the Indians have attacked the English negotiators and the English have responded by sacking and plundering the Powhatans' town and fields. The engraving then chronicles a series of negotiations in 1614 that led to the end of a five-year war between Powhatan's people and the Jamestown colonists.

Seventeenth-century viewers, guided by the text of Ralph Hamor's firsthand narrative, would have read the entire image from beginning to end, and they would have recognized the story of Pocahontas's captivity as but a single element in a broader narrative encompassing the history of Anglo-Powhatan relations up to 1614. And on a deeper level, they would have taken in the artist's potent, highly compressed representation of all colonial relations, in which the Natives are innately treacherous, yet simpleminded (why else would Iopassus ask so for little in return for so great a prize as Pocahontas?), and Indians' and Europeans' interests are utterly irreconcilable.

The image's potency derives in large part from its simplicity, and that simplicity is, in turn, the result of Keller's decision to gloss over some potentially messy distinctions between different times, places, and Indian nations. One does not learn from this image, for example, that Argall captured Pocahontas on the Potomac River in 1613, whereas the conflict in the background took place a year later and eighty miles away, on the Pamunkey River. Nor does one learn that the 1614 battle did not involve the Patawomecks (who had delivered Pocahontas to Argall in the first place) or that Iopassus's people had ample reason to dislike Powhatan. Had Keller drawn such distinctions, it would have been harder to portray Iopassus as treacherous and simpleminded. But at the same time, a more complex portrayal would have obscured some essential truths contained in the engraving: for example, that a great many Europeans were truly convinced that Indians were inherently duplicitous, and that Europeans' and Native Americans' interests were indeed ultimately irreconcilable. In short, the image is so compelling precisely because it oversimplifies what was, in fact, a complex set of colonial encounters in the Chesapeake region.

Modern writers such as J. Frederick Fausz, Frederic Gleach, Karen Ordahl Kupperman, Martin Quitt, Helen Rountree, E. Randolph Turner III, and Margaret Holmes Williamson have created a genuine renaissance of scholarship on seventeenth-century Virginia. Collectively, these authors have made it nearly impossible to tell a story about early Jamestown that does not take Powhatan culture into account. Like Georg Keller, they have arrived at their best insights, not by trying to tell the whole story, but rather by going directly to the heart of the matter, to the deepest insights about how Europeans and Native Americans—so startlingly different in their very conceptions of the universe—struggled to assimilate their new awareness of each other into their existing worldviews. For these writers, the heart of the matter is to be found in Anglo-Powhatan relations; thus "the Powhatans'" experiences are treated as normative, as central to the story or analysis, whereas other Native groups are considered part of the "Powhatan fringe." It follows logically from this that the geographical center of the action was in the Powhatan (and Virginia) heartland, along the James and York rivers. Because a focus on Anglo-Powhatan relations requires the presence of the English, most writers take as their starting point the arrival of Europeans (though an opening chapter may address the state of Native America on the eve of contact). And since the central problem is to understand how such radically different people responded to encounters with each other, "culture" and "colonialism" are the key concepts; significantly, these concepts lead those who wield them to privilege analysis over narrative and structure over events. In short, modern scholars have, like Keller, collapsed time and space in order to produce accounts of early Virginia that speak powerfully to their contemporaries.[2]

2. This is not to say that modern writers invariably stay within these boundaries, but these are the norms. E. Randolph Turner III's writings, for example, focus on developments long before 1571, but he emphasizes cultural analysis and is Powhacentric. Helen Rountree sometimes subordinates analysis to narrative, but most of her publications are Powhacentric and begin with the arrival of Europeans. J. Frederick Fausz's focus on politics, tendency toward narrative, and sensitivity to geography make him a model for the kind of approach I take in this essay—though he, too, picks up the story with the arrival of Europeans. Stephen Potter's impressive work on the Potomac River is a rare departure from the Powhacentric norm, though he does not employ narrative. See Edwin Randolph Turner III, "An Archaeological and Ethnohistorical Study on the Evolution of Rank Societies in the Virginia Coastal Plain" (Ph.D. diss., Pennsylvania State University, 1976); Helen C. Rountree, *The Powhatan Indians of Virginia: Their Traditional Culture* (Norman, Okla., 1989); Rountree, *Pocahontas's People: The Powhatan Indians of Virginia through Four Centuries* (Norman, Okla., 1990); Rountree and Thomas E. Davidson, *Eastern Shore Indians of Virginia and Maryland* (Charlottesville, Va., 1997); Rountree and Turner, *Before and after Jamestown: Virginia's Powhatans and Their Predecessors* (Gainesville, Fla., 2002); J. Frederick Fausz, "Merging and Emerging Worlds: Anglo-Indian Interest Groups and the Development of the Seventeenth-Century Chesapeake," in Lois Green Carr, Philip D. Morgan, and Jean B. Russo, eds., *Colonial Chesapeake Society* (Chapel Hill, N.C., 1989), 47–98; Stephen R. Potter, *Commoners, Tribute, and Chiefs: The Development of Algonquian Culture in the Potomac Valley* (Charlottesville, Va., 1993). See also Frederic W. Gleach, *Powhatan's World and Colonial Virginia: A Conflict of Cultures* (Lincoln, Neb., 1997); Margaret Holmes Williamson, *Powhatan Lords of Life and Death: Command and Consent in Seventeenth-Century Virginia* (Lincoln, Neb., 2003); Karen Ordahl Kupperman, *Set-*

Yet this impressive body of recent scholarship misses much of the story —or, more properly, stories—of which Jamestown, and Powhatan, were only a part. Just as the attention lavished on colonial societies has left, until lately, little room for the Native peoples of the Chesapeake, so, too, do studies focusing on the Powhatans far outnumber those focusing on the non-Powhatans who made up the majority of the Chesapeake's Native population. We need to explore more fully the Native American Chesapeake beyond the Powhatan core; to expand our view to encompass the fifteenth century, the fourteenth century, and even earlier eras; to apply the ethnographic insights we've gained since the 1980s to the study of Algonquian political and diplomatic history; and to integrate those ethnographic insights into narratives. Then we might gain new insights into some particularly compelling questions: who had the power to make things happen in early-seventeenth-century Virginia? How did the specific features of Algonquian political culture structure relations between different polities in the region? What calculations guided Native leaders' interactions with other Indian and English people? And why were so many Indian leaders willing to help the Jamestown colonists?

The short answer to this bundle of questions is that Indian political histories, and particularly the histories of Powhatan's enemies and his more reluctant subjects, are the key to understanding colonial encounters in early Virginia. The rise of chiefdoms in the centuries preceding 1607 produced a political order and a regional diplomatic configuration to which the small, troubled Jamestown colony was forced to adapt. This was no static structure. Paramount chiefdoms, in particular, had a dramatic and surprisingly brief history—so brief, in fact, that many people could recall a time when things had been very different. They keenly remembered when Tsenacommacah, the territory encompassed by Powhatan's paramount chiefdom, was limited to parts of the upper James and Pamunkey rivers. This historical memory, together with certain deep-seated habits of mind rooted in Algonquian cosmology and political culture, created widespread resentment of the expansionist chief Powhatan. Thus many people in the early seventeenth century regarded Powhatan, and not the English, as the primary menace

tling with the Indians: The Meeting of English and Indian Cultures in America, 1580–1640 (New York, 1980); Michael Leroy Oberg, *Dominion and Civility: English Imperialism and Native America, 1585–1685* (Ithaca, N.Y., 1999); Martin D. Gallivan, *James River Chiefdoms: The Rise of Social Inequality in the Chesapeake* (Lincoln, Neb., 2003); and James Axtell, "The Rise and Fall of the Powhatan Empire," in Axtell, *Natives and Newcomers: The Cultural Origins of North America,* 233–258 (Oxford, 2001).

to their independence. They viewed the troubled relations between Powhatan and the Jamestown colonists as an opportunity to cast off the Powhatan yoke and to escape from Tsenacommacah.

Histories

More than thirty thousand Native people lived in the Chesapeake region when the Jamestown colonists arrived. Most were broadly Algonquian in culture, though the Susquehannocks were Iroquoian, and the piedmont Monacans and Manahoacs were likely Siouan. The majority lived within chiefdoms, a type of political hierarchy in which hereditary rulers commanded tribute, coordinated foreign policy, and served as vital intermediaries between humans and the spiritual world. Moreover, by the late sixteenth century, an increasing number of people found themselves living within paramount chiefdoms, which were comprised of multiple chiefdoms owing tribute (and varying degrees of obedience) to a chief of chiefs such as Powhatan. The circumstances that gave rise to these Algonquian chiefdoms, and historical memories of the tumultuous sixteenth century, profoundly shaped each nation's relations with outsiders in the seventeenth century.[3]

Before about 1300 C.E., the peoples of the Chesapeake were accustomed to a relatively egalitarian social, religious, and political order.[4] In the three centuries after 1300, however, most local societies created ever more hierarchical systems, with the majority of the population submitting themselves to village and even paramount chiefs. At least five fundamental and thoroughly interrelated forces led the inhabitants of Chesapeake in this direction: accelerating population growth, an increasing dependence on agriculture, the onset of the Little Ice Age, intensifying competition for prime village locations, and a marked increase in both warfare and long-distance trade.

Chesapeake societies began to experiment with maize by at least 900 C.E. Although they were slow to integrate it into their annual subsistence cycle, maize was a seductive plant, calorie rich and not overly labor intensive. It grew especially well during the consistently warm centuries between about 900 and 1300 C.E., which are often labeled "the Medieval Optimum." The more the peoples of the Chesapeake experimented with agriculture, the more their grain-fed populations grew, so much so that by 1300 it was

3. The Patuxent River nations and possibly the Monacans and Mannahoacs formed confederacies, but not paramount chiefdoms.

4. The key word here is "relatively." As Gallivan notes, "Ethnographies of supposedly egalitarian hunter-gatherer and peasant communities demonstrate that true equality may be a social impossibility" (Gallivan, *James River Chiefdoms,* 45).

becoming increasingly difficult for the region's enlarged populations to sustain themselves by fishing, gathering, and hunting alone. By the fourteenth century, beans and squash supplemented the maize crop, providing more dietary diversity, greater security against crop failures, and more calories, while also reducing the need for hoeing weeds (spreading vines suppressed their growth) and extending the life of fields (beans helped to fix nitrogen in the soil). Thus communities modified their ways to more fully incorporate cultivated plants into their annual subsistence cycles: they altered their ceramic technologies and settlement patterns and became noticeably more insular and territorial.[5]

5. For general treatments, see Bruce D. Smith, "Origins of Agriculture in Eastern North America," *Science,* CCXLVI (1989), 1566–1571; and Linda S. Cordell and Bruce D. Smith, "Indigenous Farmers," in Bruce G. Trigger and Wilcomb E. Washburn, eds., *The Cambridge History of the Native Peoples of the Americas,* I, *North America* (New York, 1996), part 1, 234–250. On experimentation with cultigens in the Chesapeake region, see Paul Randolph Green, "Forager-Farmer Transitions in Coastal Prehistory" (Ph.D. diss., University of North Carolina, 1987), 1–9, 26–31; Dennis C. Curry and Maureen Kavanagh, "The Middle to Late Woodland Transition in Maryland," *North American Archaeologist,* XII (1991), 6–7, 21–26; Laurie Cameron Steponaitis, "Prehistoric Settlement Patterns in the Lower Patuxent Drainage" (Ph.D. diss., SUNY-Binghamton, 1986), 2, 269–276, 287–288; Joan Walker and Glenda Miller, "Life on the Levee: The Late Woodland Period in the Northern Great Valley of Virginia," in Theodore Reinhart and Mary Ellen Hodges, eds., *Middle and Late Woodland Research in Virginia: A Synthesis* (Courtland, Va., 1992), 166–170; William Gardner, *Lost Arrowheads and Broken Pottery: Traces of Indians in the Shenandoah Valley* (Manassas, Va., 1986), 77–79; Potter, *Commoners, Tribute, and Chiefs,* 91–100, 138–145, 170–173, esp. 144–145; Michael John Klein, "An Absolute Seriation Approach to Ceramic Chronology in the Roanoke, Potomac, and James River Valleys, Virginia and Maryland" (Ph.D. diss., University of Virginia, 1994), 70; John P. Hart, David L. Asch, C. Margaret Scarry, and Gary W. Crawford, "The Age of the Common Bean *(Phaseolus Vulgaris L.)* in the Northern Eastern Woodlands of North America," *Antiquity,* LXXVI (2002), 377–383. On settlement patterns and ceramic technologies, see Walker and Miller, "Life on the Levee," in Reinhart and Hodges, eds., *Middle and Late Woodland Research in Virginia,* 168–170; Curry and Kavanagh, "Middle to Late Woodland Transition," *North American Archaeologist,* XII (1991), 3–28; Potter, *Commoners, Tribute, and Chiefs,* 138–145, 170–173 (esp. 144–145); J. Sanderson Stevens, "Examination of Shepard and Potomac Creek Wares at a Montgomery Complex Site (44LD521)," *Journal of Middle Atlantic Archaeology,* XIV (1998), 95–126; Klein, "An Absolute Seriation Approach," 22–28, 70; R. Michael Stewart, "Prehistoric Settlement and Subsistence Patterns and the Testing of Predictive Site Location Models in the Great Valley of Maryland" (Ph.D. diss., Catholic University of America, 1980), 384; Stewart, *Prehistoric Farmers of the Susquehanna Valley: Clemson Island Culture and*

But in a singularly unhappy coincidence, accelerating population growth and a deepening commitment to agriculture after 1300 C.E. coincided with the onset of the Little Ice Age, a centuries-long phase in which temperatures averaged several degrees cooler than in the thirteenth century.[6] Cooler

the St. Anthony Site (Bethlehem, Conn., 1994), 11–13, 186. On cultural insularity and declining long-distance trade, see Melburn D. Thurman, "A Cultural Synthesis of the Middle Atlantic Coastal Plain, Part I: 'Culture Area' and Regional Sequence," *Journal of Middle Atlantic Archaeology,* I (1985), 7–32; Stewart, "Catharsis: Comments on Thurman's Coastal Plain Synthesis," *Journal of Middle Atlantic Archaeology,* III (1987), 111–124; Potter, *Commoners, Tribute, and Chiefs,* 77–81, 100, 114–122, 141–145; Gardner, *Lost Arrowheads,* 83–85; Curry and Kavanaugh, "Middle to Late Woodland Transition," *North American Archaeologist,* XII (1991), 10–16, 22–25; Klein, "An Absolute Seriation Approach," 26, 85–86; Green, "Forager-Farmer Transitions in Coastal Prehistory," 106, 143; Frederic W. Gleach, "A Rose by Any Other Name: Questions on Mockley Chronology," *Journal of Middle Atlantic Archaeology,* IV (1988), 85–98; Lewis Binford, "Archaeological and Ethnohistorical Investigations of Cultural Diversity and Progressive Development among Aboriginal Cultures of Coastal Virginia and North Carolina" (Ph.D. diss., University of Michigan, 1964), 485; Steponaitis, "Prehistoric Settlement Patterns," 2.

6. Concerns about global warming have inspired an explosion of research on climate history, which has largely confirmed the existence of both the Medieval Optimum and the Little Ice Age while also complicating earlier portrayals of the Little Ice Age as a relatively uniform cold snap. Current research on climate change points to switching mechanisms connected to oceanic currents (and to the associated atmospheric circulation patterns). The best known of these are the ENSO phenomenon, which encompasses the El Niño and La Niña events that can alternately drown and parch such far-flung places as California and Peru; and the jet stream, relative to which the Chesapeake occupies a transitional position. The Little Ice Age, then, was characterized, not by numbing cold, year after year, but rather by a greater tendency toward switching mechanisms that, when activated, caused lower average temperatures and short growing seasons. Thus even in the midst of the Little Ice Age, some years were hot and dry; others were warm and wet; and still others were cold and wet. The problem was that people couldn't be content with having good harvests in some years or even in most years; they needed to be able to feed themselves every year.

Historians have just begun to take advantage of the new climate research. Though scholars often cite David W. Stahle et al., "The Lost Colony and Jamestown Droughts," *Science,* CCLXXX (1998), 564–567, there is much more still to absorb. Good entry points into this literature include H. H. Lamb, *Climate, History, and the Modern World,* 2d ed. (New York, 1995); Brian Fagan's adroit popularization, *The Little Ice Age: How Climate Made History, 1300–1850* (New York, 2000); and Thomas Cronin, *Principles of Paleoclimatology* (New York, 1999). For studies specific to the Chesapeake region, see Debra A. Willard, Thomas M. Cronin, and Stacey Verardo, "Late-Holocene Climate and Ecosystem History from Chesapeake Bay Sediment Cores, USA," *The Holo-*

temperatures translated into significantly shorter growing seasons: in the uplands of the interior and to the north and the west of the Chesapeake region, the growing season frequently dropped below the minimum 120 days required for maize, making such places particularly susceptible to crop failures and lowered yields.[7] Groups in central New York and on the upper Susquehanna River, who had also committed themselves to agriculture, were particularly hard-hit by the changing climate. In response, many groups gravitated to lower latitudes and elevations—and often into the Chesapeake region.[8] Once they arrived in the Chesapeake, migrants from the north and west gravitated toward a few vital enclaves of rich, well-

cene, XIII (2003), 201-214; Grace Brush, "Natural and Anthropogenic Changes in Chesapeake Bay during the Last 1000 Years," _Human and Ecological Risk Assessment,_ VII (2001), 1283-1296; John Kutzbach and Thompson Webb III, "Climate and Climate History in the Chesapeake Bay Region," in Philip D. Curtin, Grace S. Brush, and George W. Fisher, eds., _Discovering the Chesapeake: The History of an Ecosystem_ (Baltimore, 2001); United States Geographical Service, "Effects of Climate Variability and Human Activities on Chesapeake Bay and the Implications for Ecosystem Restoration," U.S.G.S. Fact Sheet FS-00-116 (Reston, Va., 2000); and Dennis B. Blanton, "Drought as a Factor in the Jamestown Colony, 1607-1612," _The Journal of the Society for Historical Archaeology,_ XXXIV (2000), 74-81.

7. Victor A. Carbone, "Environment and Prehistory in the Shenandoah Valley" (Ph.D. diss., Catholic University of America, 1976); Dean R. Snow, _The Iroquois_ (Cambridge, Mass., 1994), 22, 33; Green, "Forager-Farmer Transitions in Coastal Prehistory," 139-143; Steponaitis, "Prehistoric Settlement Patterns," 287-288; Potter, _Commoners, Tribute, and Chiefs,_ 100-102; Curry and Kavanagh, "Middle to Late Woodland Transition," _North American Archaeologist,_ XII (1991), 24.

8. It is hard to say exactly who migrated where, for archaeological evidence is notoriously unhelpful on this score. It is easier to spot an intrusive culture than to identify its source and easier to note a group's disappearance than to pinpoint its destination. See Irving Rouse, _Migrations in Prehistory: Inferring Population Movement from Cultural Remains_ (New Haven, Conn., 1986). The general trend of migrations, though, was clearly down the latitudes and downward in altitude, sloping along toward warmer weather and fertile soils. See Green, "Forager-Farmer Transitions in Coastal Prehistory," 53, 104-106, 139-143; Potter, _Commoners, Tribute, and Chiefs,_ 119-161; Stewart, _Prehistoric Farmers,_ 26-27, 188, 194-197, 200-202; Barry Kent, _Susquehanna's Indians_ (Harrisburg, Pa., 1984), 14-21; Gardner, _Lost Arrowheads,_ 79-89; Stevens, "Examination," _Journal of Middle Atlantic Archaeology,_ XIV (1998), 110, 122-123; Dennis B. Blanton, Stevan C. Pullins, and Veronica L. Deitrick, _The Potomac Creek Site (44ST2) Revisited,_ Virginia Department of Historic Resources Research Report, no. 10 (Richmond, Va., 1999); Snow, _Iroquois,_ 19-20, 26-46; John P. Hart, "Maize, Matrilocality, Migration, and Northern Iroquoian Evolution," _Journal of Archaeological Method and Theory,_ VIII (2001), 151-182.

drained soils along major waterways, setting off an intensifying competition for these prime village locations. Whole new villages sprang up, particularly near the fall line and in the piedmont and interior valleys.[9] Paradoxically, population growth turned out to be part of the solution to the problems created by population growth. A community that controlled good farmland, fishing places, and gathering places could feed growing populations and thus produce more warriors to defend its privileged location. Not coincidentally, a number of villages in the western and northern reaches of the Chesapeake region sprouted palisades, a substantial commitment of labor and resources that would only make sense when the inhabitants were under constant threat of attack.[10]

Yet palisades were not enough to save the communities that lay in the path of raiders from the north. The Little Ice Age had forced the proto-Iroquoian peoples who remained in modern-day New York into increasingly compact and populous agricultural settlements situated on relatively warm bottomlands, where they gradually consolidated into a smaller number of ever larger and better-defended villages. The transition did not go smoothly: the Iroquois Great League of Peace and Power (the Five Nations) was intended to bring an end to a maelstrom of fifteenth and early-sixteenth-century warfare between these northern villages, in which (according to oral tradition) "feuds with brother nations, feuds of sister towns and feuds of families and of clans made every warrior a stealthy man who liked to kill." The Great League resolved many of these feuds, establishing peace

9. E. Randolph Turner III, "The Virginia Coastal Plain during the Late Woodland Period," in Reinhart and Hodges, eds., *Middle and Late Woodland Research,* 106–108; Walker and Miller, "Life on the Levee," ibid.; Curry and Kavanagh, "Middle to Late Woodland Transition," *North American Archaeologist,* XII (1991), 18–24; Blanton, Pullins, and Deitrick, *Potomac Creek Site Revisited;* Green, "Forager-Farmer Transitions in Coastal Prehistory," 139–143; Kavanagh, *Archaeological Resources of the Monocacy River Region, Frederick and Carroll Counties, Maryland,* Maryland Geological Survey, Division of Archaeology File Report no. 164 (Crownsville, Md., 1982), 79–81.

10. Blanton, Pullins, and Deitrick, *Potomac Creek Site Revisited;* Richard Dent, *Chesapeake Prehistory: Old Traditions, New Directions* (New York, 1995), 250–251; Walker and Miller, "Life on the Levee," in Reinhart and Hodges, eds., *Middle and Late Woodland Research,* 167, 172–182; Gardner, *Lost Arrowheads,* 88–90; Stevens, "Examination," *Journal of Middle Atlantic Archaeology,* XIV (1998), 123; Kavanagh, *Resources,* 77–82; Potter, *Commoners, Tribute, and Chiefs,* 130–131, 147–148, 153–155; Klein, "An Absolute Seriation Approach," 114–115; Stewart, *Prehistoric Farmers,* 201–205; and Stewart, "Clemson's Island Studies in Pennsylvania: A Perspective," *Pennsylvania Archaeologist,* LX (1990), 97.

between the Five Nations and fusing them into a loose polity by the middle of the sixteenth century, but the cultural imperatives that inspired Iroquois men to go to war each summer continued unabated. Five Nations warriors therefore redirected their efforts outward, placing neighboring peoples not included in the league under tremendous pressure.[11]

The Susquehannocks were especially hard-hit, so much so that, after about 1525, they moved from their homeland on the upper Susquehanna River to the lower Susquehanna River, with some continuing southward in the late sixteenth century to establish palisaded villages on the upper Potomac. Their presence made the Chesapeake interior a very dangerous place indeed. Susquehannock warriors harassed their neighbors; and what was worse, those who were unfortunate enough to live in the Shenandoah Valley or western Maryland were caught in a deadly crossfire between the Five Nations and the Susquehannocks. Most abandoned their villages during the course of the sixteenth century, transforming their former homelands into a vast hunting ground and war zone. Those who remained in the Shenandoah Valley built palisades and otherwise mobilized for war. Even after the Potomac River Susquehannocks relocated to the lower Susquehanna River in the early seventeenth century, Iroquoian raiders—Five Nations, Susquehannocks, and a people known to Chesapeake Algonquians as the Massawomecks—continued to harass the northern and western Chesapeake. By 1608, the rivers on the Western Shore north of the Patuxent River had been abandoned, as had virtually all of the roughly ten thousand square miles of the Potomac basin above the fall line.[12]

11. Arthur C. Parker, *The Constitution of the Five Nations; or, The Iroquois Book of the Great Law,* New York State Museum Bulletin, no. 184 (Albany, N.Y., 1916), 16–17 (quotation); William N. Fenton, *The Great Law and the Longhouse: A Political History of the Iroquois Confederacy* (Norman, Okla., 1998); Daniel K. Richter, *The Ordeal of the Longhouse: The Peoples of the Iroquois League in the Era of European Colonization* (Chapel Hill, N.C., 1992), chap. 2.

12. On the Susquehannocks' ordeals, see Daniel K. Richter, "War and Culture: The Iroquois Experience," *William and Mary Quarterly,* 3d Ser., XL (1983), 528–559; Kent, *Susquehanna's Indians,* 15–18. On their sojourn in the Potomac basin, see Janet G. Brashler, "A Middle 16th Century Susquehannock Village in Hampshire County, West Virginia," *The West Virginia Archaeologist,* XXXIX (1987), 1–30; Robert D. Wall, "Late Woodland Ceramics and Native Populations of the Upper Potomac Valley," *Journal of Middle Atlantic Archaeology,* XVII (2001), 15–37; Wall and Heather Lapham, "Material Culture of the Contact Period in the Upper Potomac Valley: Chronological and Cultural Implications," *Archaeology of Eastern North America,* XXXI (2003), 151–177. Wall's work suggests that the Susquehannocks came from the

The thirty-plus Algonquian nations below the fall line withstood the migrations and warfare of the fourteenth, fifteenth, and sixteenth centuries by consolidating authority in the hands of hereditary chiefs who could exact tribute, send men to war, discipline their subjects, and coordinate the resistance against northern raiders and rival claimants to their homelands. Over the course of the sixteenth century, a hierarchy of places and rulers emerged around the rim of the bay. On the lowest level were hamlets without hereditary rulers. Such hamlets paid tribute to a nearby village whose weroance appointed a "lesser king" to each dependent settlement. Increasingly during the sixteenth century, the weroance was, in turn, subject to a paramount chief who ruled a number of village / hamlet clusters.[13]

------

lower Susquehanna in the late sixteenth century and remained on the upper Potomac into the early seventeenth century. Not coincidentally, radiocarbon dates at sites in western Maryland and the lower Shenandoah Valley reveal a distinct gap in the sixteenth century: villages occupied in earlier centuries yield a sharply declining number of dates after 1500. See Hettie L. Boyce and Lori A. Frye, *Radiocarbon Dating of Archeological Samples from Maryland* (Baltimore, 1986), 8, 10-11, 19-29, 44; Donna C. Boyd and C. Clifford Boyd, "Late Woodland Mortuary Variability in Virginia," in Reinhart and Hodges, eds., *Middle and Late Woodland Research,* 252-253; Dent, *Chesapeake Prehistory,* 256-257, 262; Walker and Miller, "Life on the Levee," in Reinhart and Hodges, eds., *Middle and Late Woodland Research,* 175-182; Kavanagh, *Resources,* 52, 75-82; Potter, *Commoners, Tribute, and Chiefs,* 175-176; R. Michael Stewart, "Early Archeological Research in the Great Valley of Maryland," *Maryland Archeology,* XXXIII (1997), 1-44; Joan W. Chase, "A Comparison of Signs of Nutritional Stress in Prehistoric Populations of the Potomac Piedmont and Coastal Plain" (Ph.D. diss., American University, 1988), 60. For accounts of Susquehannock and Massawomeck raiders, see Kent, *Susquehanna's Indians,* 17-19, 311-319; Andrew White, "A Briefe Relation of the Voyage unto Maryland" (1634), in Clayton Colman Hall, ed., *Narratives of Early Maryland, 1633-1684* (New York, 1910), 74, 89; John Smith, *The Proceedings of the English Colonie in Virginia since Their First Beginning from England in the Yeare of Our Lord 1606, till This Present 1612* . . . (1612), in Philip L. Barbour, ed., *The Complete Works of Captain John Smith (1580-1631),* 3 vols. (Chapel Hill, N.C., 1986), I, 230-232; Smith, *The Generall Historie of Virginia, New-England, and the Summer Iles* . . . (1624), ibid., II, 105-106, 119, 165, 170-172, 176; Smith, *A Map of Virginia* . . . (1612), ibid., I, 149-150, 166; "Instructions to Sir Thomas Gates," in Barbour, ed., *The Jamestown Voyages under the First Charter, 1606-1609,* 2 vols. (Cambridge, 1969), I, 237; Henry Spelman, "Relation of Virginea," in Edward Arber, ed., *Travels and Works of Captain John Smith, President of Virginia, and Admiral of New England, 1580-1631* (Edinburgh, 1910), cv-cvi.

13. Smith, *Map of Virginia,* in Barbour, ed., *Works of Smith,* I, 147-148; George Percy, "Observations Gathered out of a Discourse of the Plantation of the Southerne

According to Piscataway oral tradition, the first paramount chief in the region likely emerged on the Potomac River some thirteen generations before 1634 (probably somewhere between 1440 and 1530) when "there came a King from the Easterne Shoare." Called the *tayac*, he and his successors expanded Piscataway influence all along the Potomac.[14] By the mid-sixteenth century, however, an even more powerful chief was consolidating his hold over a half-dozen subordinate weroances near the falls of the James and Pamunkey rivers. The man commonly known today as Powhatan inherited these chiefdoms sometime in the 1560s or 1570s; over the next few decades, according to Indian accounts, another two dozen Algonquian nations had "bene either by force subdued unto him, or through feare yielded" to this charismatic leader. By 1607, Powhatan was collecting tribute from nearly all of the Algonquian nations in Virginia below the fall line, from the Nansemond River to the south bank of the Potomac, and he was still adding to Tsenacommacah when the Jamestown colonists arrived. The Kecoughtans, a prosperous nation of about one thousand, fell to Powhatan in the late 1590s, while the Chesapeakes were destroyed and their territory colonized by Powhatan loyalists within a year or two of 1607. And in the fall of 1608, Powhatan showed Jamestown colonists a string of two dozen fresh Piankatank scalps, bragging that he had scattered the survivors and

------

Colonie in Virginia by the English, 1606," in Alexander Brown, *The Genesis of the United States: A Narrative of the Movement in England, 1605–1616, Which Resulted in the Plantation of North America by Englishmen* . . . (New York, 1890), I, 158–161; William Hand Browne et al., eds., *Archives of Maryland,* 72 vols. (Baltimore, 1883–1972), XV, 251 (hereafter cited as *Arch. Md.*); Rountree, *Powhatan Indians,* 117.

14. Not all chiefs were men, but the means of succession—from the oldest brother to the youngest, then to the oldest sister, then to her sons—meant that few chiefs were women. The dates suggested here for the origins of the tayac's paramount chiefdom coincide with both the formation of the Iroquois League and with the archaeological evidence of increasingly hierarchical societies on the inner coastal plain. James H. Merrell calculated an average of nine years in office for each tayac, based on the average tenure between 1634 and 1700, which yielded a founding date of 1534. But Merrell assumed that exotic, European-introduced epidemics struck the Piscataways in the sixteenth century, an assumption for which there is as yet no solid evidence. Merrell was also deliberately conservative in his assessment so as not to exaggerate the paramount chiefdom's antiquity, so 1534 should be taken as the latest likely date for the beginning of the tayac's' paramount chiefdom. It is possible that other paramount chiefdoms preceded this one; this is simply the earliest for which we have evidence. See Browne et al., eds., *Arch. Md.,* III, 403 (quotation); Merrell, "Cultural Continuity among the Piscataway Indians of Colonial Maryland," *WMQ,* 3d Ser., XXXVI (1979), 551.

replaced them with the "remayne" of the recently conquered Kecoughtans. Powhatan had even begun to extend his influence to the lower Eastern Shore, though he had not yet incorporated the nations there into Tsenacommacah.[15]

Powhatan's paramount chiefdom, then, was still a work in progress when the Jamestown colonists arrived on the scene. Most people were well aware that Powhatan's chiefdom was not the only game in town; they knew of the independent Chickahominies, living in the heart of Tsenacommacah without being part of it, the Piscataway tayac's paramount chiefdom on the north bank of the Potomac, or the piedmont confederation of Monacans and Mannahoacs. In nearly every village, there were people who could remember when they had become a part of Powhatan's chiefdom. Thus those who had voluntarily joined with Powhatan to avoid some greater threat knew that they could always recalculate their chances of surviving outside of Tsenacommacah. Those who had been conquered by Powhatan or "through feare yeilded" could remember a time when they had neither paid tribute to Powhatan nor done his bidding; they, too, had every reason to seek opportunities to regain their independence. And of course those who lived uncomfortably close to the edges of Tsenacommacah were anxious to retain their independence. In short, many Algonquian weroances had an interest in diminishing Powhatan's power and influence.

Structures

One might reasonably ask what it means to call these polities "chiefdoms" and why it matters. What difference did it make that Chesapeake Algonquians had organized themselves into chiefdoms rather than fashioning themselves into bands, tribes, or states? And what did the specific features of Algonquian chiefdoms have to do with diplomatic relations in the contact era? In fact, the particulars of Algonquian political culture did much to determine the up-and-down fortunes of the Jamestown colony. If we are to appreciate the logic that guided the Chesapeake nations' varied responses to the English presence, it is critical that we first understand the spiritual sources of all power in the Algonquians' world, as well as the cosmological vision that explained and sustained chiefly authority—and, above all, that

15. William Strachey, *The Historie of Travell into Virginia Britania (1612)*, ed. Louis B. Wright and Virginia Freund, Works Issued by the Hakluyt Society, 2d Ser., no. 103 (London, 1953), 43–45 (quotation), 57 (quotation), 63–69, 104–105, 108; Smith, *Map of Virginia*, in Barbour, ed., *Works of Smith*, I, 147, 173, 178. On Powhatan's multiple names, see Williamson, *Powhatan Lords*, 56–57, and Gleach, *Powhatan's World*, 32–33.

we grasp the utter inseparability of spiritual power, trade, diplomacy, and chiefly authority.[16]

We might begin by contrasting chiefdoms with other forms of political organization. Tribal societies, for example, are generally egalitarian. Age and sex place some limits on a person's power, but otherwise anyone with sufficient personal charisma and achievements can exercise leadership. Whoever can lead may lead, for there is no fixed limit on the number of people who can serve a given function. Shamans, for instance, thrive if they seem to do good work, not because they've been initiated into an exclusive priestly caste. In contrast, chiefdoms limit the number of people who may exercise authority, and they vest some key leadership positions with an authority independent of the charisma and achievements of the officeholder. A priest, for example, possesses authority because he's been consecrated, and not simply because he attracts a following. Although a little charisma never hurts, a chief has authority by virtue of his birth. Chiefly authority is based on commoners' acceptance of his legitimate sovereignty, not just on the chief's ability to persuade and inspire his people.[17] Chiefs in the Chesapeake region used their authority to exact tribute, compel men to go to war, and order executions—all of which marked a real departure from tribal politics, in which tribute was virtually unknown, waging policy-driven wars required an almost impossible degree of consensus, and no one person could order an execution. Yet chiefdoms were also fundamentally unlike a modern nation state; they lacked bureaucracies, centralized record keeping, police, courts, standing armies, and other trappings of modern nation-states.[18]

16. Strachey, *Historie of Travell,* ed. Wright and Freund, 57. The theoretical literature on chiefdoms is impressive and ever growing. See, for example, Morton H. Fried, *The Evolution of Political Society: An Essay in Political Anthropology* (New York, 1967); Elsa M. Redmond, ed., *Chiefdoms and Chieftaincy in the Americas* (Gainesville, Fla., 1998); Timothy Earle, ed., *Chiefdoms: Power, Economy, and Ideology* (Cambridge, 1991); and esp. Earle, *How Chiefs Come to Power: The Political Economy in Prehistory* (Stanford, Calif., 1997). Each of these works is broadly comparative; all but one is global in scale.

17. Elsa M. Redmond, "The Dynamics of Chieftaincy and the Development of Chiefdoms," in Redmond, ed., *Chiefdoms and Chieftaincy,* 1–13; Earle, "Chiefdoms in Archaeological and Ethnohistorical Perspective," *Annual Review of Anthropology,* XVI (1987), 279–308.

18. Tribute: Spelman, "Relation," in Arber, ed., *Travels and Works of Captain John Smith,* cxii–cxiii; John Smith, *A True Relation . . .* (1608), in Barbour, ed., *Works of Smith,* I, 69; Smith, *Map of Virginia,* ibid., 158–159, 169, 174; Strachey, *Historie of Travell,* ed. Wright and Freund, 87. Initiated wars: ibid., 44, 54, 104. Ordered exe-

All power, authority, and legitimacy had its origins in the world of the spirits. The creator Ahone was "the good and peceable" god, the ultimate source of *manit* (spiritual power) and "the giver of al the good things." Ahone was too awesome for humans to really know. He took a hands-off approach, leaving humans "to make the most of their free will and to secure as many as they can of the good things that flow from him." Therefore, "it was to no purpose either to fear or worship him." Instead, Ahone had another spirit, Okeus, to deal directly with humans; Okeus was "always busying himself with our affairs and frequently visiting us, being present in the air, in the thunder, and in the storms." A morally neutral spirit with whom Algonquians needed to maintain a right relationship, Okeus "expected adoration and sacrifice." On the whole, though, he served as a guardian who spoke directly to priests and taught humans how to live: how to dress, how to wear their hair, how to cultivate plants, and to otherwise "fashion themselves" according to his will.[19]

On a day-to-day basis, however, Algonquians had less to do with Okeus than they did with *quiyoughcosughs,* a broad term encompassing a veritable host of lesser gods—including their weroances and priests. As embodiments of quiyoughcosughs, chiefs and priests straddled the already indistinct, porous frontier connecting humans and spirits. Only they could enter the sacred precincts of the *quioccasan,* or temple. Only they went on to the lair of the Great Hare after they died, lived a full life there, then returned to this world. While on this earth, quiyoughcosughs maintained contact with their fellow spirits; and while away from earth, they served as intercessors on behalf of their living relatives.[20] But priests and chiefs were

---

cutions: Spelman, "Relation," cxi; Strachey, *Historie of Travell,* 77. See also White, "Briefe Relation of Maryland," in Hall, ed., *Narratives of Early Maryland,* 26.

19. Strachey, *Historie of Travell,* ed. Wright and Freund, 88-103 (quotations); Smith, *Map of Virginia,* in Barbour, ed., *Works of Smith,* I, 169 (quotation); White, "Briefe Relation of Maryland," in Hall, ed., *Narratives of Early Maryland,* 44-45; "A Relation of Maryland," ibid., 88 (quotation); "Occurants in Virginia" (1619), in Samuel Purchas, *Hakluytus Posthumus; or, Purchas His Pilgrimes . . .* , 20 vols. (1625; rpt. Glasgow, 1905-1907), XIX, 118; Spelman, "Relation," in Arber, ed., *Travels and Works of Captain John Smith,* cv.

20. William White, "Fragments Published before 1614," in Barbour, ed., *Jamestown Voyages,* I, 149-150; Smith, *Map of Virginia,* in Barbour, ed., *Works of Smith,* I, 169-170; Smith, *Proceedings of the English Colonie,* ibid., 170; Strachey, *Historie of Travell,* ed. Wright and Freund, 77, 88, 94-95, 100-103; Purchas, *Hakluytus Posthumus,* XIX, 954; Spelman, "Relation," in Arber, ed., *Travels and Works of Captain John Smith,* xv. Piscataway oral tradition describes the dead as intercessors for the living. See Gabri-

only part of this pantheon of quiyoughcosughs; according to one Algonquian, "there are many of them of the same nature," and "there are tutelar deities in every town." Manit was incarnate in many things, as John Smith observed: "All things that were able to do them hurt beyond their prevention, they adore with their kinde of divine worship; as the fire, water, lightning, thunder, our ordinance, peeces, horses, etc."[21]

Relations between flesh-and-blood quiyoughcosughs mirrored those between the greater gods. Ahone created order and stability, whereas Okeus, assigned to deal with humans, held out the threat of war and famine. Like Ahone, weroances and paramount chiefs served as sources of order and stability within their communities. Primarily concerned with mediating between more powerful spiritual beings and their own people, each hereditary chief delegated Okeuslike external relations such as war and diplomacy to an external chief, normally a relative who was a lesser chief in his own right. The Patawomeck weroance, for example, deputized his brother Iopassus (chief of a Patawomeck hamlet) to deal with outsiders, while Opechancanough, not his elder brother Powhatan, normally came forward to negotiate with the Virginia colonists.[22]

Chiefly lineages emphasized their foreign origins in order to demonstrate that they were part of a universal spiritual order rather than local parvenus. The brother of the Piscataway tayac recalled that their line of chiefs began with "a King from the Easterne Shoare." Similarly, Powhatan was born an outsider to all but a half-dozen of the thirty-plus chiefdoms he acquired during his lifetime, and oral tradition consistently maintained that his predecessor came from the West Indies or the Southwest.[23] Yet with-

----

elle Astra Tayac, "'To Speak with One Voice': Supra-Tribal American Indian Collective Identity Incorporation among the Piscataway, 1500–1998" (Ph.D. diss., Harvard University, 1999), 54, 75.

21. Smith, *Map of Virginia,* in Barbour, ed., *Works of Smith,* I, 169.

22. Smith, *True Relation,* in Barbour, ed., *Works of Smith,* I, 65; Smith, *Generall Historie,* ibid., II, 156, 243–244, 268; Spelman, "Relation," in Arber, ed., *Travels and Works of Captain John Smith,* cii–civ; [Ralph] Hamor, *A True Discourse of the Present Estate of Virginia, and the Successe of the Affaires There till the 18 of June, 1614* (London, 1615), rpt. in *Virginia: Four Personal Narratives* (New York, 1972), 4–6; Strachey, *Historie of Travell,* ed. Wright and Freund, 46, 101; "Letter of Sir Samuel Argoll," in Purchas, *Hakluytus Posthumus,* XIX, 91–93; Williamson, *Powhatan Lords,* 95–123, 132–133; Gleach, *Powhatan's World,* 28–36.

23. Browne et al., eds., *Arch. Md.,* III, 402–403 (quotation); Robert Beverley, *The History and Present State of Virginia,* ed. Louis B. Wright (Chapel Hill, N.C., 1947), 61; Hamor, *True Discourse,* rpt. in *Virginia,* 13; Earle, "Chiefdoms in Perspective,"

out a continuing stream of evidence that they possessed unusual spiritual power, exogamous chiefly lineages would have been little more than pushy outsiders. Priests, bound in a deeply symbiotic relationship with chiefs, provided that evidence. Through rituals, images, architecture, clothing, and bodily markings, priests constantly reminded people of the hereditary and personal spiritual power of chiefs. Priests also tended temples containing sacred images, the bodies of deceased chiefs, and the stored wealth of the current chief.[24]

Although ordinary people could not match the spiritual potency of chiefs and priests, almost anyone could forge some connection with the spirits through rituals, sacrifices, smoking, and dreaming. Indeed, such connections were critical to success in life. Ordinary people constantly tended to their relations with the spirits who inhabited their world. They routinely sacrificed the "first fruits of their Corne, and of that which they get by hunting and fishing." Tobacco and other sacred objects opened paths of communication at such moments. Ordinary people also offered tobacco and other goods "when they returne from the warrs, from hunting, and upon many other occasions," and after their customary morning bath. Dreams also connected humans and spirits.[25] For young men, however, there was no substitute for a successful *huskanaw,* a rigorous coming-of-age ritual reserved for the "choicest and briskest . . . and such only as have acquired some treasure by their travels and hunting." A young man who successfully completed the huskanaw established a personal relationship with a spirit who would henceforth serve as a source of power and wisdom, not to mention help him to fight, hunt, and fish better. Having emerged from the ceremony fortified with the power of their tutelatory spirit, they had much to offer their

Annual Review of Anthropology, XVI (1987), 299; Redmond, "Introduction," in Redmond, ed., *Chiefdoms and Chieftaincy,* 10–12.

24. Smith, *Map of Virginia,* in Barbour, ed., *Works of Smith,* I, 169–170, 173; Spelman, "Relation," in Arber, ed., *Travels and Works of Captain John Smith,* civ–cv; Strachey, *Historie of Travell,* ed. Wright and Freund, 88–89.

25. White, "Briefe Relation of Maryland," in Hall, ed., *Narratives of Early Maryland,* 45, 88 (quotation); Smith, *Map of Virginia,* in Barbour, ed., *Works of Smith,* I, 170–171 (quotation); Smith, *True Relation,* ibid., 59; Smith, *Generall Historie,* ibid., II, 124–125; Tayac, "'To Speak with One Voice,'" 75; Spelman, "Relation," in Arber, ed., *Travels and Works of Captain John Smith,* cv; Strachey, *Historie of Travell,* ed. Wright and Freund, 97–98, 123; White, "Fragments," in Barbour, ed., *Jamestown Voyages,* I, 150; Stanley Pargellis, ed., "An Account of the Indians in Virginia," *WMQ,* 3d Ser., XVI (1959), 232–233, 235–236; "Annual Letters of the Jesuits" (1639), in Hall, ed., *Narratives of Early Maryland,* 124–126.

weroance and their community. A few became priests or conjurors. Others, having ritually "died" to their families in the course of the huskanaw, were "qualified . . . equally and impartially to administer justice, without having respect either to friend or relation." The weroance selected his "best trusted Councellors and Freindes" from this class of men, consulting them before making important decisions.[26]

People could improve their access to spiritual power if they possessed copper, shell beads, or other potent objects. Such items permitted spiritually gifted users to more readily invoke and more fully employ the power of spiritual beings. These things were literally otherworldly: in Native traditions throughout the eastern woodlands, they were represented as gifts from guiding spirits. As such, they formed connecting links through which spiritual power and guidance could flow, allowing their users to boost their own power and well-being. The specific uses to which they were put depended upon their color—the reddest copper was especially prized, as were particularly white or dark beads—and upon the ceremonies in which they were used. In very concrete ways, copper and beads were the keys to power.[27]

In fact, one can trace the flow and exercise of power by following the transit of beads and copper through networks of trade, tribute, and gifting. Each of these networks tended to funnel spiritually potent items through the region's weroances and paramount chiefs. Like chiefly lineages, the most spiritually potent trade goods came from the outside: copper came from the Great Lakes region, whereas the best shell beads came from the Eastern Shore. They tended to accumulate in the hands of chiefs, who were already presumed to possess spiritual power and thus had the authority to regulate

26. Susan Myra Kingsbury, ed., *The Records of the Virginia Company of London,* 4 vols. (Washington, D.C., 1906–1935) (hereafter cited as *RVC*), III, 438; Samuel Purchas, *Purchas His Pilgrimes . . .* , 3d ed. (London, 1617), 955; Spelman, "Relation," in Arber, ed., *Travels and Works of Captain John Smith,* cv–cvi; White, "Briefe Relation of Maryland," in Hall, ed., *Narratives of Early Maryland,* 85; Pargellis, "Account of the Indians," *WMQ,* 3d Ser., XVI (1959), 234–235; White, "Fragments," in Barbour, ed., *Jamestown Voyages,* I, 147–149; Strachey, *Historie of Travell,* ed. Wright and Freund, 58, 85–86, 98–100, 104 (quotation); Smith, *Map of Virginia,* in Barbour, ed., *Works of Smith,* I, 171–172; White, "Briefe Relation," 43, 45; Hamor, *True Discourse,* rpt. in *Virginia,* 6; Purchas, *Hakluytus Posthumus,* XIX, 93; Beverley, *History,* ed. Wright, 84, 108–109 (quotation), 115; and Gleach, *Powhatan's World,* 38–43.

27. Gleach, *Powhatan's World,* 56–59; Christopher L. Miller and George R. Hamell, "A New Perspective on Indian-White Contact: Cultural Symbols and Colonial Trade," *Journal of American History,* LXXIII (1986), 311–328; George E. Lankford, "Red and White: Some Reflections on Southeastern Symbolism," *Southern Folklore,* L (1992), 53–80; Williamson, *Powhatan Lords,* 247–254.

long-distance trade. Chiefs traded directly with outsiders for these goods and attempted (with partial success) to monopolize the trade.[28] But even trade goods acquired by ordinary people were subject to regular demands for tribute, which also channeled them into chiefs' hands. Consequently, weroances and paramount chiefs accumulated tremendous stores of valued goods, some of which was conspicuously displayed as a reminder of chiefly legitimacy.[29]

Smart chiefs, however, also gave away much of their wealth. Gifts conjured up a general sense of indebtedness on the part of recipients, and such obligations could be called in at important moments to gain support for the chiefs' decisions. Yet gift giving was not necessarily a coercive or even calculated act; it could just as easily be conceived of as a way of maintaining a sense of reciprocity and balance within a relationship. Indeed, a weroance who gratefully accepted a gift of copper from Powhatan might soon afterward turn around and offer copper as tribute to Powhatan—an act more consistent with the cultivation of reciprocity than with the cold calculation of debts owed. Moreover, when a chief distributed copper to his clients, the reddish metal identified its recipients with the spiritual sources of authority, power, and influence. Thus copper was not used to "wage" hireling weroances and war leaders, as the English thought, but rather to enhance the spiritual power they needed if they were to command respect at home and to succeed in war abroad.[30]

28. William Wallace Tooker, "On the Meaning of the Name Anacostia," *American Anthropologist,* VII (1894), 389–393; Philip L. Barbour, "The Earliest Reconnaissance of Chesapeake Bay Area: Captain John Smith's Map and Indian Vocabulary," *Virginia Magazine of History and Biography,* LXXIX (1971), 296; Strachey, *Historie of Travell,* ed. Wright and Freund, 46, 56–57, 107, 132; Smith, *True Relation,* in Barbour, ed., *Works of Smith,* I, 59, 69, 81; Smith, *Map of Virginia,* ibid., 160, 166, 173–174; Smith, *Proceedings of the English Colonie,* ibid., 242, 247; Hamor, *True Discourse,* rpt. in *Virginia,* 4–6; "Letter of Sir Samuel Argoll," in Purchas, *Hakluytus Posthumus,* XIX, 91–93; Boyd and Boyd, "Mortuary," in Reinhart and Hodges, eds., *Middle and Late Woodland Research,* 256–257.

29. Strachey, *Historie of Travell,* ed. Wright and Freund, 56–57, 61, 63, 87, 107; White, "Briefe Relation," and "Letters of the Jesuits," in Hall, ed., *Narratives of Early Maryland,* 43, 125, 127; Spelman, "Relation," in Arber, ed., *Travels and Works of Captain John Smith,* cv, cxii–cxiii; Smith, *True Relation,* in Barbour, ed., *Works of Smith,* I, 69, 81, 93; Smith, *Generall Historie,* ibid., II, 201; Smith, *Map of Virginia,* ibid., I, 173–174; Percy, "Observations," in Brown, *Genesis of the United States,* I, 12–15; Tayac, "'To Speak with One Voice,'" 63; Potter, *Commoners, Tribute, and Chiefs,* 170–173.

30. Strachey, *Historie of Travell,* ed. Wright and Freund, 68–69 (quotation), 104,

Long-distance trade, tribute, and the ethic of gifting merged almost seamlessly into diplomacy. The Native peoples of the Chesapeake expected the exchange of goods between chiefs to take the form of mutual generosity rather than competitive bargaining, especially when the diplomatic stakes were high. More than mere goods were exchanged in such encounters. When John Smith's men reconnoitered the Chesapeake Bay in 1608, each nation they came upon wanted to exchange presents "to expresse their loves." The English party, for example, gave the Massawomecks two bells in order to establish peaceable relations, while the Tockwoghs and Susquehannocks gave gifts to Smith to pave the way for an attempt at enlisting the English as allies against the Massawomecks. Gifting in a diplomatic setting created a sense of reciprocity that made peaceable relations possible. That the goods exchanged normally included copper and beads should serve as a reminder that diplomacy constituted an encounter not just between humans but also between the spiritual beings from which the participants derived their power.[31]

In sum, chiefs were generalists: unlike more specialized priests, warriors, or political advisors, chiefs took the lead in religious, military, political, economic, and diplomatic affairs. Because they combined spiritual, military, and economic power, chiefs could hold their own against fellow elites whose sources of power were more narrowly defined. By 1607, virtually every Algonquian nation in the Chesapeake region had institutionalized the position of weroance. A hereditary chief's authority and power were now as much ascribed as achieved, rooted as much in his right to command as in his personal characteristics. Chiefly power and authority were now of a piece with the very structure of the universe: the weroance, Ahone, the outer chief, Okeus, the priest, the shaman, the quiyoughcosugh, the warrior, and the commoner all had their place within the cosmos and in society. Yet each source of chiefly power—spiritual, military, and economic—could cut both ways, either working to consolidate the chief's rule or to undermine it. An individual weroance had access to spiritual power independent of his para-

<hr/>

107, 114; Spelman, "Relation," in Arber, ed., *Travels and Works of Captain John Smith*, cvi–cxiii.

31. Smith, *Proceedings of the English Colonie,* in Barbour, ed., *Works of Smith,* I, 228, 231–232 (quotation). On trade, gifting, power, and diplomacy, see James Axtell, *The Invasion Within: The Contest of Cultures in Colonial North America* (New York, 1985), 88–89; Peter Burke, *History and Social Theory* (Ithaca, N.Y., 1992), 70–73; and Richard White, *The Middle Ground: Indians, Empires, and Republics in the Great Lakes Region, 1650–1815* (New York, 1991), 103, 180–182.

mount chief's connections to the spirit world; the warriors who deferred to a chief could also turn on him; and the inherently decentralized nature of exchange networks made them impossible to fully control. Since no weroance or paramount chief could monopolize power, there remained a real tension between the way things were supposed to work (from a chief's perspective) and the way things actually did work. This tension helps to explain why early-seventeenth-century Algonquian political life and diplomacy was so complicated, fluid, and diverse.[32]

The cosmology that structured and sustained chiefdoms did much to determine the course of Anglo-Indian relations after 1607. To begin with, chiefdoms had a longer history in the region than did paramount chiefdoms. The difference between (on the one hand) the century or two of chieftaincy in an Algonquian town and (on the other hand) ten or twenty years of paying tribute to Powhatan created a gap into which the English could easily slide; people who were ideologically committed to their own weroance's sacred lineage but who merely acquiesced in Powhatan's rule were perfectly willing to consider working with the English to rid themselves of Powhatan. For, notwithstanding the accumulation of power in Powhatan's hands, the Chesapeake was actually composed of a number of local power cores; each weroance, including Powhatan's thirty-plus tributary chiefs, remained the head of a distinct nation.

The existence of multiple power cores, each with its own semidivine chiefly lineage, created a complex diplomatic configuration in the Chesapeake region. This presented the English with a plethora of diplomatic possibilities: English observers noted with keen interest the "many severall nations of sondry Languages, which envyron Powhatans Territories." To the south, on Albemarle Sound, lay Algonquian nations that were independent of Powhatan, whereas the Monacans and Mannahoacs, who lived in the Virginia piedmont, were "deadly enemyes ever unto Powhatan." With the exception of the two southernmost chiefdoms, the Eastern Shore nations showed no interest in developing closer relations with the paramount chief. Just across the Potomac River from Powhatan's northernmost tributary nations lay the Piscataway tayac's paramount chiefdom, and above them were the resolutely independent chiefs of the Patuxent River. Beyond them, of course, lay the Massawomecks and Susquehannocks, people of modest concern to those living in the Powhatan core area but of intense interest to the northern Chesapeake nations.[33]

32. Earle, *How Chiefs Come to Power,* 4–14.
33. Strachey, *Historie of Travell,* ed. Wright and Freund, 49 (quotation); Kings-

The concentration of authority in the hands of chiefs, together with the practice of delegating external relations to an outer chief such as Iopassus or Opechancanough, simplified diplomatic relations and rendered their protocol at least superficially comprehensible to Europeans. Englishmen found this much easier than dealing with more egalitarian societies. Later generations of English colonists, for example, were confused when the diffusion of power among the Iroquois made it difficult to come to an agreement that was binding upon even a single community, let alone the League as a whole.[34] In contrast, when a weroance or outer chief in the Chesapeake region committed to an exchange or an alliance, the odds were good that his community would comply with the terms of the pact.

Finally, the utter inseparability of spiritual power, tribute, copper and beads, chiefly legitimacy, long-distance trade, and diplomacy inadvertently played into English hands. The tribute system put surplus corn—of which the English were often desperately in need—into the hands of chiefs, whereas the English could lay their hands on vast quantities of copper and glass beads. The resulting trade instantly made the English major players in the region's diplomacy, despite their small numbers and military weakness. An influx of spiritually potent goods from this new source could be used to strengthen a weroance's position, both within his nation and in diplomatic affairs. In Algonquian eyes, the English trade created a sense of reciprocity that would ensure the newcomers' friendship. English copper and beads, as well as more mundane items such as metal tools, also made the newcomers sufficiently useful that they need not be killed or left to starve. It gave at least some Native people a good reason to keep the English around.

Calculations

But how did all of this work out in practice? How did the rise of chiefdoms, Algonquians' historical memories, and Algonquian cosmology and political structure enter into the calculations of specific weroances who wondered how they might best exploit the English presence at Jamestown? The Chesapeake's diplomatic configuration was so complex, and the histories of the region's dozens of nations so diverse, that the arrival of the English at Jamestown meant something different to each weroance and his people. No two nations' interests, geographies, or histories were alike, and

---

bury, ed., *RVC,* III, 17–20; Smith, *True Relation,* in Barbour, ed., *Works of Smith,* I, 55, 67; Smith, *Proceedings of the English Colonie,* ibid., 236; Smith, *Map of Virginia,* ibid., 148–150, 165–166, 173, 230–232.

34. A major theme in Richter, *Ordeal of the Longhouse.*

each weroance's calculations were thus based on a unique formula. The weroances' initial responses to the English presence were strikingly varied and fluid; there were no two-sided Anglo-Indian relations but rather an intricate web of relations encompassing dozens of nations with hundreds of "sides." Thus to understand why the establishment of Jamestown had such a dramatic effect on the Native peoples of the Chesapeake, we must view the English from the perspective of the region's lesser weroances.

Weroances and leading elders among the Quiyoughcohannocks, Chickahominies, Accomacks, and Patawomecks (to cite but four examples) had to begin by discerning the ways in which Powhatan and the English dealt with each other—but only in order to calculate how they might assimilate the Powhatans and English into their own diplomatic strategies. Keeping track of Anglo-Powhatan relations was not an easy task, for each party pursued multiple diplomatic strategies. Powhatan, for example, alternated between trying to absorb, kill, and coexist with the English. At first, the small, disease-ridden colony at Jamestown seemed to pose little danger to Powhatan's people, and the colonists' willingness to trade their fine, reddish copper and smooth glass beads seemed to recommend them. Thus Powhatan initially tried to integrate the colonists into his chiefdom, with their leaders serving as subordinate weroances. As John Smith understood it, his four-week captivity among the Powhatans in December 1607 culminated in a ceremony designed to make the Jamestown colony a new tributary nation within Tsenacommacah. Powhatan gave Smith a new territory (called "Capahowasicke"), a new name, and a fictive kinship to the great weroance to mark his new status, and he expected that his new English subjects would henceforth offer him regular tribute such as "hatchets . . . bells, beads, and copper."[35] At the ceremony's conclusion, wrote Smith, Powhatan "proclaimed me a werowanes of Powhatan" and directed that "all his subjects should so esteeme" the Jamestown colonists as "Powhatans."[36]

35. *The Complete Works of Captain John Smith* suggests this interpretation (Smith, *Generall Historie,* in Barbour, ed., *Works of Smith,* II, 148 n. 4, 151 [quotation]), and J. Frederick Fausz commits himself to this interpretation in his doctoral dissertation (Fausz, "The Powhatan Uprising of 1622: A Historical Study of Ethnocentrism and Cultural Conflict" [Ph.D. diss., College of William and Mary, 1977], 237–238). See also Gleach, *Powhatan's World,* 109–122.

36. Smith, *True Relation,* in Barbour, ed., *Works of Smith,* I, 67 (quotation), and see 57, 73–75; Smith, *Proceedings of the English Colonie,* ibid., 248; Smith, *Generall Historie,* ibid., II, 152. Christopher Newport was to be the "great Werowance" who tended primarily to internal affairs, whereas Smith was to serve as his external chief.

But Smith proved a wayward weroance. He failed to move the colony from Jamestown to Capahowasick, he spent the summer of 1608 reconnoitering the Chesapeake Bay in a transparent attempt to formulate an independent English foreign policy, and he forcibly extracted corn from his fellow Powhatan weroances.[37] By 1609, Powhatan had apparently given up hope of incorporating the English into Tsenacommacah. He henceforth treated the English as interlopers—as potentially useful people, but as outsiders nonetheless. He and his successor Itoyatin alternated between enmity and amity toward the English: from 1609 to 1614, and again in 1622, they chastised the English by withholding corn, killing livestock, and attacking colonial settlements; whereas, between wars, the paramount chief sanctioned extensive trade with the colonists.[38]

The English, too, pursued more than one diplomatic strategy. As April Hatfield has noted, some thought it best to follow the Spanish example by "appropriating Powhatan's paramount chiefdom" and making it their own. Thus the English consistently described the boundaries of Virginia as corresponding to those of Tsenacommacah. Thus Christopher Newport countered Powhatan's ritual incorporation of the English into Tsenacommacah with a coronation ceremony designed to reduce Powhatan to a vassal of James I. Thus the English repeatedly asserted their willingness to join Powhatan's people in attacking their mutual enemies. And thus Thomas Dale asserted in 1611 that a victory over Powhatan would force the paramount chief "to accept of a well liked condition of life with us," bringing all of Tsenacommacah into the English fold and paving the way for the conquest of "the neighbor Salvadges."[39]

More often, however, the colonists sought to ally themselves with Powhatan's enemies. Smith discussed an alliance with virtually everyone he encountered during his 1608 reconnaissance of the bay, and Deputy Gover-

Smith deliberately led Powhatan to believe that the English had accepted their tributary status by delivering the tribute (*True Relation,* 73–75).

37. Smith, *Generall Historie,* in Barbour, ed., *Works of Smith,* II, 191; Smith, *Proceedings of the English Colonie,* ibid., I, 220.

38. J. Frederick Fausz, "Patterns of Anglo-Indian Aggression and Accommodation along the Mid-Atlantic Coast, 1584–1634," in William W. Fitzhugh, ed., *Cultures in Contact: The Impact of European Contacts on Native American Cultural Institutions, A.D. 1000–1800* (Washington, D.C., 1985), 235–252.

39. April Lee Hatfield, "Spanish Colonization Literature, Powhatan Geographies, and English Perceptions of Tsenacommacah/Virginia," *Journal of Southern History,* LXIX (2003), 245–282; Brown, *Genesis of the United States,* I, 503 (quotation).

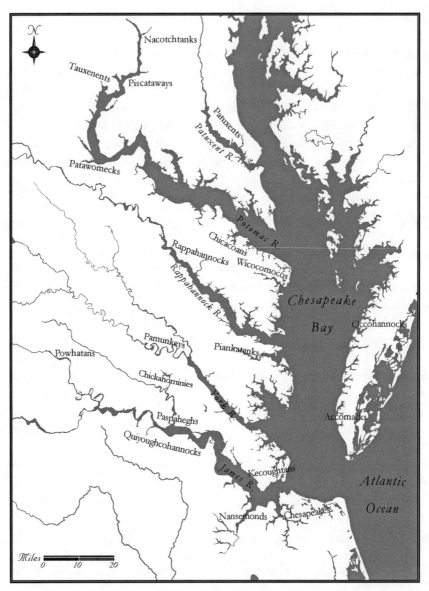

PLATE 2. *Selected Algonquian Nations in the Chesapeake Bay Region, ca. 1608.*
Drawn by Rebecca L. Wrenn

nor Thomas Gates's 1609 instructions from the Virginia Company made this strategy explicit. Gates was advised to consider reseating the colony on the Choanoke River, "under the proteçion of a wiroane called Gepano-con enemy to Powhaton." If he stayed at Jamestown, Gates was to "make freindeship" with the nations "that are farthest from you and enemies unto those amonge whom you dwell." Such people, not having had much contact with the English, would be particularly impressed with the newcomers' copper and beads; "with those you may hold trade and freindship good Cheape." With Powhatan under attack from the enemies who "environed" him, the English could then liberate "all other his weroances . . . from the Tirrany of Powhaton." Gates's successor, the Lord de la Warr, was given the same instructions, which the secretary of the colony, William Strachey, wholeheartedly endorsed: "There was never any Invasion, Conquest, or Far off-plantacion that had successe without some partie in the place itself or neere it." People who had but recently been absorbed into Powhatan's chiefdom, Strachey thought, "maie peradventure be drawne from him for some rownd Rewardes and a plentifull promise of Copper."[40]

While English and Powhatan leaders tried out their various diplomatic strategies, other chiefs considered the advantages to be gained from the ever-changing Anglo-Powhatan relationship. Even the Quiyoughcohannocks, living on the James River in the very heart of Tsenacommacah, toyed with the idea of an English alliance. Though the Quiyoughcohannocks had joined a combined Powhatan force that attacked Jamestown within days of the colonists' arrival in 1607, they also had reason to resent Powhatan.[41] They were not among the six nations originally inherited by Powhatan and thus retained memories of their incorporation into Tsenacommacah. Moreover, their weroance, Pepiscunimah, had recently run afoul of Powhatan. Pepiscunimah had lured away "a Chief woman" from Powhatan's brother Opechancanough, upon which Powhatan installed one of his own sons (still

40. Kingsbury, ed., *RVC,* III, 17–20 (quotation), 29; Strachey, *Historie of Travell,* ed. Wright and Freund, 106–108 (quotation); Smith, *Proceedings of the English Colonie,* in Barbour, ed., *Works of Smith,* I, 224–233.

41. [Gabriel Archer?], "A Relatyon . . . Written . . . by a Gent of the Colony . . . ," May 21–June 21, 1607, in Barbour, ed., *Jamestown Voyages,* I, 97–98; Percy, "Observations," in Brown, *Genesis of the United States,* I, 136–137, 143; Edward Maria Wingfield, "A Discourse of Virginia," 1608, in Barbour, ed., *Jamestown Voyages,* I, 216. The Quiyoughcohannocks were also known to the English as the Topahannocks and Rappahannocks; sorting out these references from the other Topahannocks and Rappahannocks (on the Rappahannock River) requires careful attention to context.

a child) in Pepiscunimah's place and banished the former weroance to a small, dependent hamlet. (Pepiscunimah retained some of his influence, however, not least because his brother Choapock served as a chief advisor to the new weroance.)[42]

Given this recent history, it should come as no surprise that the Quiyoughcohannocks grew closer to the English after 1609 even though their putative ruler Powhatan was by then at war with the colonists. The Quiyoughcohannocks sent a guide to accompany an English expedition in search of the lost colonists of Roanoke, hinted that they might be receptive to Christianity, and regularly sent gifts to the president of the Jamestown colony. And although Powhatan directed his weroances to try to starve out the colonists between 1609 and 1614, Smith noted that the "weeroance [of?] the Quiocqua[ha]nocks did a[ll]wayes at o[ur] greatest nee[de] supply us w[ith] victualls." Choapock and Pepiscunimah urged the Quiyoughcohannocks to forever "keepe good qu[iet] with the English," which they apparently did even when the colonists established a settlement in the Quiyoughcohannock homeland.[43] Although the Quiyoughcohannocks never quite crossed the line to place themselves in outright opposition to Powhatan, neither did they show much eagerness to join Powhatan in direct opposition to the English.[44]

Yet there was no simple correspondence between resisting Powhatan and aiding the English. Take, for example, the independent Chickahominies, whose homeland lay in the very center of the Powhatan core area. Though they paid some sort of tribute to Powhatan and occasionally agreed to "helpe him in his Warrs" on an ad hoc basis, they had already held off Powhatan for more than thirty years by the time the English arrived and were still governed by a council of their own elders. It helped that the Chickahominies, "a warlick and free people," could field three hundred warriors, far more than all but a handful of nations in the region and as many as Powhatan's three brothers combined could muster from their home villages.[45]

Since trade and diplomacy were so thoroughly intertwined, we can use

42. Strachey, *Historie of Travell,* ed. Wright and Freund, 64–65.

43. Smith, *Proceedings of the English Colonie,* in Barbour, ed., *Works of Smith,* I, 265–266; Smith, *True Relation,* ibid., 34n–35n (quotation); Strachey, *Historie of Travell,* ed. Wright and Freund, 64–65, 101.

44. Not, at least, until 1622, when the remnants of the Quiyoughcohannocks apparently joined in the Powhatans' surprise attacks against the English. See Fausz, "Powhatan Uprising," 362, 375.

45. Strachey, *Historie of Travell,* ed. Wright and Freund, 68–69.

the Chickahominies' willingness to trade with the English as a rough index of their willingness to act independently of Powhatan. In the fall of 1607, the English, mere days from starvation, canvassed their neighborhood for people willing to trade corn. Most of the weroances they approached dragged their feet, offering but little to the worried colonists. The Kecough-tans contributed just sixteen bushels of corn, and the Paspaheghs a mere ten or twelve. The Chickahominies, however, traded hundreds of bushels to Smith's trading party, which had to make three trips to carry it all to Jamestown.[46] Yet each of Smith's trips up the Chickahominy River yielded a smaller quantity of corn, suggesting that he had imposed too much on his potential allies. When Smith returned in December 1607, he was captured by large party that included both Chickahominies and Powhatan's outer chief, Opechancanough.[47]

Throughout 1608, the Chickahominies edged closer to Powhatan, hold-ing secret talks with the paramount chief in the spring and refusing to trade corn to the English in the fall. (The English forced them to trade any-way.)[48] The Chickahominies had only to look to their closest neighbors, the Paspaheghs, to see where an expanded English presence along the James River might lead. The Jamestown colonists' treatment of their Paspahegh hosts was truly vile: they destroyed Paspahegh crops and dwellings, killed dozens of people and chased the survivors into the woods, and cut off a Paspahegh emissary's hand. They captured a wife of the weroance, threw her children into the river and shot "owtt their Braynes in the water," and finally ended her agony by taking her into the woods and putting her to the sword.[49] Nothing in this series of events suggested that the English would make good neighbors. Thus when war between the English and Powhatans broke out in 1609, the Chickahominies could be found squarely on Powha-tan's side (though still not in his chiefdom).

Resolutely self-governed even as they cleaved to Powhatan's foreign pol-icy, the Chickahominies hastened to make a separate peace with the En-glish as soon as they learned of the end of the war in 1614; according to this

46. Smith, *True Relation,* in Barbour, ed., *Works of Smith,* I, 39–41; Smith, *Pro-ceedings of the English Colonie,* ibid., 212.

47. Smith, *True Relation,* ibid., 45–47, 91; Smith, *Proceedings of the English Colonie,* ibid., 212–213.

48. Smith, *Proceedings of the English Colonie,* ibid., 239, 259–260; Smith, *True Re-lation,* ibid., 91.

49. George Percy, "'A Trewe Relacyon': Virginia from 1609 to 1612," *Tyler's Quar-terly,* III (1921–1922), 271–272 (quotation); Smith, *Generall Historie,* in Barbour, ed., *Works of Smith,* II, 236.

agreement, the Chickahominies were to provide the English with corn each year.[50] In 1616, however, the thin facade of peaceable Anglo-Chickahominy relations began to crumble. The English killed a dozen Chickahominies in a dispute over that year's tribute, a tragedy that Opechancanough skillfully exploited to draw the Chickahominies even closer to the Powhatans.[51] The episode forced the Chickahominies to take stock of their relations with neighboring peoples, and their deliberations yielded a clear decision to reaffirm their alliance with Powhatan. One band of Chickahominy warriors became "Runnagados" who attacked English outposts in 1617, whereas the majority of the nation remained outwardly at peace with the English until the moment the Chickahominies joined in the Powhatans' massive surprise attacks of March 22, 1622. The Chickahominies cooperated with the Powhatan war chief Opechancanough and fought alongside the Pamunkeys (the core nation of Tsenacommacah) until the bitter end, enduring English attacks against their crops, food stores, and homes as late as 1627. The Chickahominies once again followed Opechancanough into the Third Anglo-Powhatan War in 1644. Although retaining some degree of political autonomy throughout (in 1632 they signed another peace treaty independently of the Pamunkeys), after the 1616 disaster they never deviated from the Powhatans' foreign policy.[52]

Thus even in the heart of Tsenacommacah, some Algonquian leaders gave serious consideration to how their interests might be served by the English newcomers. Ultimately, however, the Jamestown colonists were of little help to reluctant Powhatans who lived in the core of Tsenacommacah. Not even the Chesapeakes and Piankatanks, who had been so brutally subjugated by Powhatan, were able to exploit the English to gain a degree of independence from the paramount chief. But what about the many people who lived at a safer remove from Powhatan and the English? Might they find the English more useful than the Chickahominies and Quiyoughcohan-

50. Smith, *True Relation,* in Barbour, ed., *Works of Smith,* I, 91–93; Smith, *Proceedings of the English Colonie,* ibid., 239; Smith, *Generall Historie,* ibid., II, 246; Hamor, *True Discourse,* rpt. in *Virginia,* 14.

51. Smith, *Generall Historie,* in Barbour, ed., *Works of Smith,* II, 256–257; Kingsbury, ed., *RVC,* IV, 117–118.

52. Smith, *Generall Historie,* in Barbour, ed., *Works of Smith,* II, 264–265, 291 (quotation), 318; Kingsbury, ed., *RVC,* III, 245, IV, 9, 250; H. R. McIlwaine, ed., *Minutes of the Council and General Court of Colonial Virginia [1622-1632, 1670-1676]* (Richmond, Va., 1924), 480; William Waller Hening, *The Statutes at Large, Being a Collection of All the Laws of Virginia from the First Session of the Legislature, in the Year 1619* (Richmond, Va., 1809–1823), I, 287, 293.

nocks had? For weroances in the eastern and northern reaches of Tsenacom-macah, this was a question well worth exploring.

The Accomack and Occohannock nations together formed a mini-paramount chiefdom in their own right, with a combined population of per-haps a thousand. Their location on the lower Eastern Shore put them out of reach of the Massawomecks and Susquehannocks, and their immediate neighbors on the Eastern Shore apparently posed no expansionist threat (their neighbors' attention tended to be directed toward the north and the west rather than to the southern tip of the Eastern Shore). But rather than live in total isolation, the Accomacks and Occohannocks developed close ties with Powhatan. They might have had little choice, for Powhatan was rapidly expanding his chiefdom to the east between 1590 and 1610, reach-ing Kecoughtan (almost directly across the fifteen-mile-wide bay from Ac-comack) in 1597. Soon Powhatan claimed the Accomacks and Occohan-nocks as his subjects. This was probably an exaggeration on Powhatan's part, since he made this claim while attempting to impress upon the En-glish the wisdom of accepting him as their paramount chief, but the East-ern Shore weroances nevertheless had good reason to desire close relations with Powhatan. The Eastern Shore, Powhatan said, provided him a regular tribute in shell beads—probably the relatively rare and sought-after wam-pumpeake, which was made from shells that were far more common on the Eastern Shore than to the west. In exchange, Powhatan could provide the Eastern Shore weroances with copper and poccune (a plant used to make a red dye), neither of which was readily available on the Eastern Shore. The resulting trade was likely beneficial to the lower Eastern Shore chiefs and Powhatan alike, for each gained access to spiritually potent goods that con-ferred power on those who possessed them.[53]

In short, in 1608, the Accomacks and Occohannocks were merely pro-spective (or, at most, recent and incomplete) additions to Tsenacommacah.

53. Smith, *True Relation,* in Barbour, ed., *Works of Smith,* I, 69; Smith, *Map of Vir-ginia,* ibid., 150; Smith, *Generall Historie,* ibid., II, 168; Strachey, *Historie of Travell,* ed. Wright and Freund, 57, 68, 104-105; Rountree and Davidson, *Eastern Shore Indi-ans,* 30-31, 45, 48-49. Eastern Shore shell beads were still being traded to the Western Shore in the 1680s, according to naturalist John Banister in "Of the Natives," in Joseph Ewan and Nesta Ewan, eds., *John Banister and His Natural History of Virginia, 1678-1692* (Urbana, Ill., 1970), 373. The trade in copper is a reasonable inference based on what Powhatan had to offer in return. So, too, is the trade in poccune, which Eastern Shore Indians still got from the Western Shore as late as 1681 (Browne et al., eds., *Arch. Md.,* XV, 369).

There is no evidence that they were particularly oppressed by Powhatan and no indication that the Eastern Shore weroances bore a personal grudge against the paramount chief, as the Quiyoughcohannocks did. But they also had more and better opportunities than most Chesapeake nations to form an English alliance. They had likely been among the first to encounter European sailors during the sixteenth century, and the Roanoke colonists had mapped the lower Eastern Shore in 1585.[54] Moreover, English seagoing vessels could navigate the open waters of the Chesapeake Bay more easily than could Powhatans in dugout canoes. The trip was well worth an English captain's trouble, for the Accomacks often had large surpluses of corn to trade and were willing to exchange it for English trade goods that surpassed Powhatan's offerings.

Perhaps this explains why the Accomacks and Occohannocks gave John Smith a friendly reception during his June 1608 reconnaissance of the bay, despite the fact that Anglo-Powhatan relations were very tense at that moment. The English "were kindly intreated" at Accomack; the weroance there, Smith judged, "was the comliest proper civill Salvage wee incountred."[55] Similarly, when Captain Samuel Argall set out to explore the Eastern Shore in 1613 (in the middle of an Anglo-Powhatan war), he found a "great store of Inhabitants, who seemed very desirous of our love . . . whom I found trading with me fore corne, whereof they had great store."[56] Nor did the Accomacks turn against the English after 1616, when seventeen men assigned to a saltworks at Smith Island set up a fishing camp on the mainland, very close to the main Accomack village.[57]

A rare conflict on the Eastern Shore in 1619 provides a glimpse into the

54. David Beers Quinn, ed., *The Roanoke Voyages, 1584–1590: Documents to Illustrate the English Voyages to North America under the Patent Granted to Walter Raleigh in 1584,* I, Works Issued by the Hakluyt Society, 2d Ser., nos. 104-105 (London, 1955), 245-246.

55. Smith, *Proceedings of the English Colonie,* in Barbour, ed., *Works of Smith,* I, 220, 224-225 (quotation).

56. Purchas, *Hakluytus Posthumus,* XIX, 92.

57. Kingsbury, ed., *RVC,* III, 116, 253, 279-280; John Rolfe, "Virginia in 1616," *Virginia Historical Register,* I (1848), 100, 106; Joe Jones, *Additional Archaeological Survey and Artifact Survey, the Arlington Site (44NH92)* (Williamsburg, Va., 2001), 4, 39; Darrin Lowery, *Archaeological Survey of the Chesapeake Bay Shorelines Associated with Accomack County and Northampton County, Virginia,* March 2001, MSS, Virginia Department of Historic Resources, Richmond, Va., 96. The fishing camp might have been seasonal, as according to Rolfe, they fished in the spring and fall.

complex calculations of interest on the part of the Accomacks, Powhatan, and the English. Agents of Captain John Martin went to trade that summer with the Accomacks, "with whom," according to the governor, "wee were in league and peace." The men had trouble finding anyone willing to trade for corn, possibly because it was still early in the summer (a time when food was at its scarcest). Fortunately (or so they thought), Martin's men came upon "a Canoa coming out of a creeke," loaded with corn. When the Indians refused to trade, the Englishmen took the canoe by force, "measuring out the corne with a baskett they had" and "giving them satisfaction in copper beades and other trucking stuffe." The outraged Accomacks could have complained directly to the English governor, which would have implied the Accomacks' independence from the Powhatans. Instead, they appealed to Opechancanough, signaling to the colonists that they could not count on the Accomacks to choose them over Powhatan's successor Itoyatin. The English, who were simultaneously embroiled in a dispute with the Chickahominies over a similar incident, were well aware of the stakes: after Opechancanough took the Accomacks' complaint to Jamestown, the governor asked the newly established Virginia Assembly to sanction Martin for fear that "such outrages as this might breede danger and loss of life to others of the Colony."[58]

After this incident, however, the Accomacks and Occohannocks turned their backs on the Powhatans for good. Thomas Savage, the colonists' best translator and a former protégé of Powhatan, had established a regular trade on the Eastern Shore by 1620. He proved so successful that he soon cut Opechancanough out of the Eastern Shore trade. Savage further embarrassed Opechancanough by outmaneuvering thirteen Pamunkey warriors in a skirmish with just four Englishmen while a hundred "Easterlings" looked on. The "Easterlings," according to the Accomack weroance, "derided" the Pamunkeys for their inept performance. Enraged, Opechancanough tried to have Savage killed, but the "laughing king" of the Accomacks exposed the plot. Later in 1620, the Accomack weroance solidified the English alliance by permitting Virginia Secretary John Pory to settle twenty men near his main town and allowing another new plantation nearby.[59] Given these

58. Kingsbury, ed., *RVC*, III, 157 (quotation), IV, 515 (quotation); H. R. McIlwaine, ed., *Journals of the House of Burgesses of Virginia, 1619-1658/59* (Richmond, Va., 1915), 5 (quotation).

59. Smith, *Generall Historie*, in Barbour, ed., *Works of Smith*, II, 288-290 (quotation); Kingsbury, ed., *RVC*, I, 340, 343-344, 349, III, 585, 641, 705, IV, 585.

overtures, it is not surprising that Opechancanough met with a brisk refusal in 1621 when he dispatched gift-bearing messengers to enlist the Accomack weroance in a plan to poison the English. Instead, the Accomacks leaked news of the Powhatans' impending surprise attack against the English, forcing Opechancanough to delay his plans until the following year. The rupture was now complete: Pory reported that "they on the West [the Powhatans]" would have liked to "invade" the lower Eastern Shore, except that they lacked "Boats to crosse the Bay."[60]

The Accomacks declined to join in the Powhatan uprising of 1622, choosing instead to trade corn to the English throughout the ten-year Anglo-Powhatan War. So firm was the alliance that Governor George Yeardley took refuge on the lower Eastern Shore for six weeks during the summer of 1622, and there was some talk of moving the entire colony there. But Virginia's leading men were anxious not to impose too much on the Accomacks and Occohannocks: they continued to chastise Captain Martin for allowing his men to steal corn on the Eastern Shore, they closely regulated trade with the Eastern Shore nations, and as late as 1625 they discouraged settlers from taking up additional territory on the Eastern Shore. Consequently, the handful of English settlers on the Eastern Shore placed little pressure on the Accomacks. Only nine men lived on Pory's plantation in January 1622, and only fifty-three English settlers lived on the Eastern Shore in 1625. The English alliance had allowed the "Easterlings" to assert their independence, at least for the time being—though ultimately, of course, they were overwhelmed by the slow but inexorable spread of the English population on the lower Eastern Shore.[61]

No one, however, enjoyed more success at using the English as a pawn in their own diplomacy than did the Patawomecks. The Patawomecks were among the most numerous and powerful people in the Chesapeake region, but their location near the frontier of settlement on the Potomac River left them exposed to attacks from all directions. The expansionist Piscataway tayac controlled the north bank of the river, directly across from the Patawomecks; the dreaded Massawomecks regularly swept down the Potomac

60. Kingsbury, ed., *RVC,* III, 556, IV, 10; Smith, *Generall Historie,* in Barbour, ed., *Works of Smith, II,* 290–291 (quotation), 298.

61. Kingsbury, ed., *RVC,* III, 116, 656–657, 696–697, 705–707, IV, 10–11, 61, 73, 275–276, 515, 559; McIlwaine, ed., *Minutes of the Council,* 48–50, 156; Smith, *Generall Historie,* in Barbour, ed., *Works of Smith,* II, 311; "Muster of the Inhabitants of Virginia, 1624/25," in Annie Lash Jester, *Adventures of Purse and Person: Virginia, 1607–1625* (Princeton, N.J., 1956), 68–71.

River to attack villagers there; and the Susquehannocks attacked upward from the mouth of the river. Clearly, it was in the best interests of the Potomac River nations to coordinate their wars and diplomacy against these multiple threats. One possibility was to join the tayac's paramount chiefdom, but the Piscataways and Patawomecks, roughly equal in resources and power, had long been competitors; could one truly accept subjugation at the hands of the other?[62]

Powhatan offered another option. Shortly before the arrival of the English, all but one of the nations on the south bank of the Potomac began paying tribute to Powhatan. Powhatan paid regular visits to collect tribute and reinforce his authority; he directed the overall diplomatic policy of the Patawomecks and their south-bank neighbors and served as a counterweight against the Piscataway tayac. At the same time, the eighty miles between the Patawomecks and Powhatan's home village prevented Powhatan from meddling much in the Patawomecks' everyday affairs. Thus Powhatan offered protection, but at a price that the Patawomecks were willing, for the moment, to pay. Indeed, the price was lower than it was for people living closer to the Powhatan heartland: Powhatan's inability to maintain close surveillance over the Patawomecks, the Patawomecks' military power, and Powhatan's need to cultivate Patawomeck goodwill so as to maintain them as a buffer on his northern frontier all combined to make Powhatan's hold over the Patawomecks very tenuous indeed. To reassert their independence, the Patawomecks needed just one good ally, one solid trading partner who would enable them to defend themselves without seeking shelter under Powhatan or the Piscataway tayac.

From the moment of John Smith's 1608 *entrada* up the Potomac, it appeared that the Patawomecks had found their ally in the English. Although Smith frankly admired the Spanish way of subjugating Indians and thought the Patawomecks "generally perfidious," he nevertheless recognized that the Patawomecks' and Virginians' mutual antipathy to Powhatan constrained both parties to "a kinde of constancy." Thus the Patawomecks, warned of Smith's approach by emissaries of Powhatan, followed the letter of Powhatan's instructions by ambushing Smith's party—and then immediately violated the spirit of those instructions by setting aside their weapons and welcoming the English. At Patawomeck, Smith met the weroance's brother and outer chief, Iopassus, who permitted the visitors to travel throughout the Patawomeck homeland. Thus began a mutually beneficial

62. Browne et al., eds., *Arch. Md.,* III, 402–403.

(though often rocky) relationship that allowed the Patawomecks and English alike to operate ever more independently of Powhatan.[63]

The Patawomeck weroance fairly leaped to cultivate the English as allies when the First Anglo-Powhatan War broke out in the fall of 1609. Part of Powhatan's strategy was to cut off Jamestown's food supplies, and he soon had the colonists teetering on the brink of starvation. The Patawomecks, however, defied Powhatan's trade embargo by selling the captain of an English ship as much corn as he could carry—and this despite an ugly incident in which the English cut off "towe of the Salvages heads." (The ship sailed directly to England without delivering the food, consigning many of the colonists to death in the famous "starving time," but that was hardly the Patawomecks' fault.) A few months later, the Patawomeck weroance again defied Powhatan, this time by helping a young man named Henry Spelman to escape from Powhatan's household. Later in 1610, Iopassus handed Spelman over to Captain Samuel Argall and again traded a boatload of corn to the English. Iopassus filled Argall's ships with another 1,100 bushels of corn in 1612, then delivered Pocahontas into Argall's hands in 1613—an act that eventually brought the war to an end.[64]

The Patawomecks and English had relatively little contact during the peace that followed Pocahontas's 1614 marriage to John Rolfe, but Iopassus was poised to renew the alliance when Anglo-Powhatan relations worsened at the end of the decade in the wake of Pocahontas's death in 1617 and Powhatan's in 1618. (Powhatan's younger brother Itoyatin became the new permanent chief, and Opechancanough remained the outer chief.) In September 1619, Iopassus surprised the English by appearing unannounced in Jamestown, ostensibly to ask that "2 shipps might be speedyly to Patawamack where they should trade for greate stoore of corne." Iopassus also surprised the governor by insisting that he dispatch an Englishman to accompany him back to Patawomeck by an overland route—a troublesome and inefficient way of traveling in the Tidewater region. Still another surprise awaited the two English ships that arrived at Patawomeck in October: there was no corn to be had! Angered, the two English captains acquired their corn mainly "by force from Jupasons [Iopassus's] Country who deceyved them." Then, despite the fact that Iopassus had clearly duped the English

63. Smith, *Generall Historie,* in Barbour, ed., *Works of Smith,* II, 316 (quotation); Smith, *Proceedings of the English Colonie,* ibid., I, 226–227, 232.

64. Percy, "Trewe Relacyon," *Tyler's Quarterly,* III (1921–1922), 265–269 (quotation); Spelman, "Relation," in Arber, ed., *Travels and Works of Captain John Smith,* ciii–civ; Purchas, *Hakluytus Posthumus,* XIX, 89, 91–92; Smith, *Generall Historie,* in Barbour, ed., *Works of Smith,* II, 236, 243–244.

in some way, and although the English had just taken the Patawomecks' corn, Iopassus "made a firme peace againe" just before the English ships departed in late November.[65]

Iopassus's strange behavior makes better sense when understood in the context of 1619—a year, according to English leaders, of increasingly "doubtful times between us and the [Powhatan] Indians." The Governor's Council noted in October that Opechancanough had "stood aloofe upon termes of dout and Jealousy" of late and that he "would not be drawne to any treaty at all."[66] Amid this uncertainty, Iopassus's 1619 mission to James-town stands out as a dashing and rather daring declaration of independence. By traveling overland through the heart of Itoyatin's paramount chiefdom, with English emissaries in tow, Iopassus clearly signaled that the Patawo-mecks could make their own deals with the English. Yet Iopassus's initiative amounted to more than a change of masters; he also made fools of the En-glish, thus indicating the Patawomecks' independence of both of the pow-ers to their south.[67]

The Patawomecks' greatest opportunity, however, came on March 22, 1622, when Powhatan warriors struck almost simultaneously against settle-ments all along the James River. Seizing the colonists' own weapons and tools, the Powhatans cut, bludgeoned, and speared the woefully unprepared settlers to death. They killed more than a quarter of the English popula-tion in the space of a few hours, without "sparing eyther age or sexe, man, woman or childe." At least 347 colonists died, and survivors reported that the attackers mutilated English corpses.[68]

Henry Spelman learned of the attacks while trading at Chicacoan, on the south bank of the Potomac near the river's mouth. One of Spelman's acquaintances there told him that Opechancanough had tried and failed to enlist the Chicacoans in the March 22 attack, but that the Wicocomocos,

65. Smith, *Generall Historie,* in Barbour, ed., *Works of Smith,* II, 268; Kingsbury, ed., *RVC,* III, 244-247 (quotations).

66. Sickness had swept through the English settlements that summer, weakening the colonists' ability to withstand an attack despite considerable migration from En-gland in the previous eighteen months. At the same time, a terrible epidemic among the Powhatans reminded them of the costs of hosting the English. The colony's first-ever representative assembly met that summer and passed several acts betraying their nervousness about Indian relations. See Kingsbury, ed., *RVC,* III, 152, 161-175, 220, 228, 246; McIlwaine, ed., *Journals of the House of Burgesses,* 15 (quotation).

67. Kingsbury, ed., *RVC,* III, 244-245; Rountree, *Pocahontas's People,* 70.

68. Edward Waterhouse, *A Declaration of the State of the Colony and Affairs in Vir-ginia* (London, 1622), 13-20.

who lived at the end of the peninsula formed by the Potomac and Rappahannock rivers, had agreed to support Opechancanough's plans. Spelman, accompanied by another ship captained by Raleigh Croshaw, sailed directly to Wicocomoco. The Wicocomocos denied any complicity with Opechancanough, and they agreed to provide enough corn to fill Spelman's pinnace. Spelman returned to Jamestown, while Croshaw went on to Patawomeck.[69]

Croshaw arrived in Patawomeck at a delicate moment. The Patawomeck weroance had not yet committed himself to either side in the new Anglo-Powhatan war. Now he "earnestly entreated" Croshaw "to be his friend, his countenancer, his Captaine and director against the Pazaticans [on the Rappahannock River], the Nacotchtanks, and Moyaons [Piscataways] his mortall enemies." In exchange, he implied, the Patawomecks might serve the English cause "as an opposite to Opechancanough." Croshaw sent his ship back to Jamestown after finishing his trading, but he stayed behind at Patawomeck to keep an eye on the situation.[70] Shortly after Croshaw's ship left, messengers from Opechancanough appeared at Patawomeck. They bore two baskets of beads—an impressive gift—and bragged of the Powhatans' successful exploits of March 22. The Patawomeck weroance, they suggested, should kill his English guests. The weroance considered his position for two days, then decided to remain on the fence. The English, he announced, "were his friends, and the Salvage Emperour Opitchapam now called Toyatan [Powhatan's successor], was his brother." He refused to accept the beads.[71]

When Captain Ralph Hamor sailed to the Potomac in May 1622, he joined Croshaw in trying to persuade the Patawomecks to commit to an English alliance. The weroance, however, held out for direct military assistance from the English in the Patawomecks' own conflicts along the Potomac River. He told Croshaw and Hamor that he had no corn to spare, but that "the Nacotchtanks and their confederats had, which were enemies both to him and them." If the English wished to "fetch" the corn at Nacotchtank (at modern-day Washington, D.C.), he would provide "40. or 50 choise Bowmen to conduct and assist them." Hamor agreed to the scheme. The Patawomecks and English sailed upriver and laid waste to the Nacotchtanks, killing numerous villagers and driving the rest into the woods. Taking as much corn and loot as they could carry, and "spoiling the rest," they returned in triumph to Patawomeck. Hamor went on to Jamestown, but Croshaw de-

69. Smith, *Generall Historie,* in Barbour, ed., *Works of Smith,* II, 304–313.
70. Ibid., 305.
71. Ibid., 308–309.

cided to stay at least through the coming harvest, when he would procure much-needed corn for Jamestown.[72]

The arrival of another English ship in late July or early August 1622 set in motion a chain of events that threatened to destroy the renewed Patawomeck-Virginia alliance. Captain Isaac Madison had been commissioned to assist the Patawomeck weroance against "our enemies, and to defend them *and theire Corne* to his uttmost power." Just as Madison's ship arrived at Patawomeck, Croshaw received an urgent letter from his wife, a prisoner of Opechancanough on the Pamunkey River. Croshaw hastily departed for Jamestown to help arrange her release. This left the inept Captain Madison in charge of trade and diplomacy on the Potomac.[73] Madison relied heavily upon Robert Poole, an often troublesome interpreter who quickly made himself unpopular with the Patawomecks. The inexperienced and ill-advised Madison almost immediately committed the blunder of trading with the Piscataways, enemies to the Patawomecks; given the close association between Algonquian trade and Algonquian diplomacy, this must have made the Patawomeck weroance very apprehensive.[74]

Amid all of this uncertainty, a fugitive weroance who had recently been "beat out of his Country" by the Nacotchtanks took refuge at Patawomeck. The chief, most likely from a Tauxenent town near the falls of the Potomac, "professed much love to the Patawomeks" but, in fact, bore a grudge against the Patawomeck weroance for not coming to his aid against their mutual Nacotchtank enemy. Shortly after arriving at Patawomeck, the "expulsed King" told Poole that the Patawomeck weroance and his "great Conjurer" were plotting with Opechancanough to kill the Englishmen at Patawomeck.[75] The day after the rumor of a Patawomeck plot reached Madison's ears, a shallop from Jamestown brought a message requesting that some Patawomeck "great men" come to Jamestown. The Patawomecks refused, and Madison suddenly went berserk. He locked the weroance, his son, and four other Patawomeck men inside the English stronghouse where they had been meeting, and "setting upon the towne with the rest of his men, slew thirty or forty men, women and children." The survivors took refuge in the woods. After the killings, Poole and Madison accused the weroance of plotting with Opechancanough, which the weroance immediately recognized as

72. Ibid., 309.

73. Ibid., 309-310 (quotation, with emphasis added); Kingsbury, ed., *RVC*, III, 654.

74. Smith, *Generall Historie*, in Barbour, ed., *Works of Smith*, II, 310-312.

75. Ibid.

a rumor designed to break up the Patawomeck-English alliance. But Madison, dissatisfied with the weroance's explanation, abandoned Patawomeck and carried his hostages back to Jamestown.[76] Experienced Potomac River hands such as Spelman, Hamor, and Croshaw were all in Jamestown when Madison arrived with his prisoners, and they quickly convinced Governor Wyatt that Madison had blundered. Wyatt hastily commissioned Hamor to return the prisoners to their home on the Potomac, but the damage was already done.[77]

Although the future of the Patawomeck alliance seemed doubtful in the fall of 1622, the summer's trade and diplomacy on the Potomac (and the Eastern Shore) had at least bought the English time to develop a strategy for repaying the Powhatans. The strategy that emerged was cold, calculating, and devastatingly effective. At first, the colonists held back: "to lull them the better in securitie," the Virginians deliberately "sought no revenge till thier Corne was ripe." Then, throughout the fall and early winter of 1622–1623, Englishmen attacked villages from the Rappahannock to the Nansemond rivers, timing their raids to "surprize their Corne." Governor Wyatt's instructions to his officers and his reports to the Virginia Company emphasized corn over conquest, and when he reckoned up his military assets, he counted men who were "serviceable for Caryinge of Corne" as well as fighters.[78] Even diplomacy pointed toward ecological warfare: the English agreed to a truce in the spring of 1623, all the while planning to resume their attacks after the corn ripened.[79]

The announcement of the spring 1623 Anglo-Powhatan truce coincided with an attempt at making amends with the Patawomecks. Spelman arrived on the Potomac in March and immediately set to trading. On March 27, he went ashore at Nacotchtank—the same town that the Patawomecks and English had sacked in 1622. Suddenly, a flotilla of canoes appeared, so swiftly overtaking and overwhelming Spelman's party that the English managed to fire only a single shot. Some of the canoes raced for the larger English ship, whose skeleton crew frantically raised the sails just in time to outpace their pursuers. As they sped away, the survivors "heard a great brute amongst the Salvages a shore, and saw a man's (Spilman's) head throwne downe the banke," then retrieved and displayed on a pole. All told, the Nacotchtanks

76. Ibid., 312–313.

77. Ibid., 314; Kingsbury, ed., *RVC,* III, 697.

78. Kingsbury, ed., *RVC,* III, 678–679, IV, 6–7, 9, 10, 12 (quotation); Smith, *Generall Historie,* in Barbour, ed., *Works of Smith,* II, 314–315 (quotation), 318.

79. Kingsbury, ed., *RVC,* II, 482, IV, 37, 71, 89, 98–99, 102.

killed twenty men, took prisoner a boy named Henry Fleet, and captured guns, armor, and swords.[80]

A Patawomeck-English rapprochement followed quickly on the heels of Spelman's death at Nacotchtank. Opechancanough agreed to meet Captain William Tucker at Patawomeck in May 1623, apparently confident that Madison's rampage there in the summer of 1622 had rendered the Patawomecks neutral or hostile to the English. The Patawomecks, however, had lured Opechancanough into a trap: after the negotiations, Captain Tucker provided poisoned drinks to toast the accord, then fired on the deathly ill Powhatan delegates. Some of the English took scalps, and Tucker bragged (mistakenly) of killing Opechancanough.[81]

Although the Patawomecks' willingness to conspire against Opechancanough was encouraging to the English, the Virginians had yet to make full reparations for Madison's murders and kidnappings of the previous summer. Indeed, the plot to poison Opechancanough had simply put the English further in debt to the Patawomecks. Making amends would require a grand gesture, which Governor Wyatt performed in the fall of 1623. As soon as the English harvest had been secured, Wyatt personally led a ninety-man force to the Potomac River. Wyatt, anxious to "settle the trade with our freends," still did not know who had killed Spelman, but for diplomacy's sake, he accepted the Patawomecks' manifestly false assertion that the Piscataways had done the deed. Together, bragged Wyatt, the English and Patawomecks attacked the Piscataways, "putt many to the swoorde," and took "a marvelous quantetie of corne."[82]

Now reconciled with the English, the Patawomecks finally agreed to support an attack against the Pamunkeys, the core nation in Itoyatan's paramount chiefdom—"not only to asiste us in that revenge, but to accompeny

---

80. Ibid., IV, 61, 89; Smith, *Generall Historie,* in Barbour, ed., *Works of Smith,* II, 319–321 (quotation).

81. Kingsbury, ed., *RVC,* II, 478, 483, IV, 102, 221–223 (quotation), 234, 250, 261; *Calendar of State Papers,* Colonial Series, *America and West Indies* (London, 1860), II, 48, III, 69; "Lord Sackville's Papers Respecting Virginia, 1613–1631," *American Historical Review,* XXVII (1922), 507.

82. Kingsbury, ed., *RVC,* II, 478, IV, 221, 250–251, 292, 399–400, 450–451 (quotation). Henry Fleet, the boy taken captive in the incident, later revealed that it had taken place at Nacotchtank (which the Patawomecks and English had sacked in the summer of 1622), but he remained a captive until 1627 and thus could not explain things to Governor Wyatt. See Fleet, "A Brief Journal of a Voyage in the Barque 'Warwick' to Virginia," in Edward D. Neill, ed., *The Founders of Maryland as Portrayed in Manuscripts, Provincial Records, and Early Documents* (Albany, N.Y., 1876), 25.

us and bee our guides in a warr against the Pomunkeys." Defeating the Pamunkeys would guarantee the Patawomecks' recently won independence from Itoyatan and make it harder for Opechancanough to retaliate against them for their role in his poisoning in the spring of 1623. It is not clear what role the Patawomecks actually played, but in a decisive battle in the summer of 1624, an English force confronted the Pamunkey warriors while an equal number of Virginians took advantage of the diversion by laying waste to the Pamunkeys' fields. When the Pamunkey warriors finally realized how much damage the English had done, they "gave over fightinge and dismayedly, stood most ruthfully lookinge one while theire Corne was Cutt downe." For the first time, the English clearly had the upper hand in Tsenacommacah.[83] Yet Virginia's leaders deliberately prolonged the war for another eight years after the climactic victory of 1624. Year after year, the Virginians inflicted light casualties and took large quantities of grain. Periodic truces and aborted peace treaties encouraged the Powhatans to plant more food, which the English took as booty when the peace invariably failed.[84]

The Patawomecks, however, took no part in these raids, for as far as they were concerned, the English alliance had already served its purpose. Under the cover of the war, the Patawomecks had fully detached themselves from Tsenacommacah and struck major blows against the Piscataway tayac and his Nacotchtank clients. The fundamental rhythms of their lives remained unchanged: Patawomeck villagers followed the same annual round of seasonal work and social life as they had before the war, and they followed the same steps through the life cycle. The old rules still governed the workings of political systems, intercultural trade, and warfare. Above all, the Patawomecks still controlled their own territory: the nearest tobacco plantation was as yet nearly a hundred miles to the south. This post-independence disengagement between the Patawomecks and Jamestown was a mutual affair. After 1624, the English returned to their habitual focus on Powhatan's

83. Kingsbury, ed., *RVC,* IV, 450–451 (quotation), 507–508 (quotation).

84. Ibid., 568–569; McIlwaine, ed., *Minutes of the Council,* 151, 172, 184, 483–484. As early as December 1622, John Martin circulated a manuscript on "the manner howe to bringe in the Indians into subjection without makinge an upper exterpation of them." This system of "harshe visitts" and "feede fights" especially served the interests of Virginia's elites, who used the spoils of battle to consolidate even more power and wealth in their hands. See Kingsbury, ed., *RVC,* III, 704, IV, 507; J. Frederick Fausz and John Kukla, "A Letter of Advice to the Governor of Virginia, 1624," *WMQ,* 3d Ser., XXXIV (1977), 127; Fausz, "Patterns of Anglo-Indian Aggression," in Fitzhugh, ed., *Cultures in Contact,* 225–268; and Fausz, "Merging and Emerging Worlds," in Carr, Morgan, and Russo, eds., *Colonial Chesapeake Society,* 47–98.

chiefdom; not until 1629, when George Calvert began scouting the northern Chesapeake for a potential new colony, did the Patawomecks again attract much attention from the English.

This disengagement between the English and most of the Native peoples of the Chesapeake Bay region was reflected in the dearth of engravings and other images of Virginia Indians after 1624. Europeans were treated to quite an array of visual representations of Indians in the critical years of 1585–1624, including John White's drawings based on his experiences at the aborted colony at Roanoke, Theodore de Bry's engravings based on those drawings, a broadside advertising a lottery to raise money for the Virginia Company, an engraving of Pocahontas in English clothing, and various illustrations in the writings of Captain John Smith. In contrast, only a handful of new images were produced after 1625. Reflecting the declining need to understand the complex diplomatic configuration of the Chesapeake Bay region, these post–1624 images were noticeably more generic and stereotyped than their predecessors: ethnographic details specific to Virginia grew scarce, and none contained anything like the narrative and historical specificity of Georg Keller's 1617 engravings.[85]

The English habit of worrying primarily about the Powhatans and only secondarily about other Indian nations has persisted down to the present day. Early English observers were deeply impressed by the extent of Powhatan's power, which extended into Jamestown itself. Consequently, their reports had to focus on Powhatan in order to provide the information needed if the English were to survive in the heart of Tsenacommacah. Historical accounts of Virginia's Native peoples have generally followed suit, going along with the main flow of information from English writers such as William Strachey and John Smith. Modern scholars, however, need not perpetuate this Powhacentric worldview. If read against the grain and combined with archaeological evidence (and a few precious snippets of oral tradition), the classic eyewitness accounts from Jamestown can help us to understand how the rise of chiefdoms and paramount chiefdoms in the centuries preceding 1607 produced historical memories, a common Algonquian political culture, and a regional diplomatic configuration that profoundly shaped subsequent Anglo-Indian relations. If read with an appreciation of the polycentric nature of Native American politics on the eve of colonization, then these familiar sources yield more complex stories than can be found in tales featuring only the Powhatans and the English as protago-

85. Feest, "Virginia Indian in Pictures," *Smithsonian Journal of History*, II (1967), 1–30.

nists. In a polycentric account of the contact era, it is impossible to sustain the fiction that places beyond the Powhatan core area were merely smaller stages on which the larger story of Anglo-Powhatan relations was played out; instead, they emerge as distinctive places with stories of their own and as vital centers of action that played unique and formative roles in the history of seventeenth-century Virginia. If we moderns read the sources in full awareness that the inhabitants of Quiyoughcohannock, Accomack, and Patawomeck each regarded their homeland as the center of the universe rather than as part of a borderland, or fringe area, then we, too, might escape from Tsenacommacah and begin to see early Virginia with a newly independent vision.

part two

AFRICA AND THE ATLANTIC

E. Ann McDougall

THE CARAVEL AND THE CARAVAN

RECONSIDERING RECEIVED WISDOM

IN THE SIXTEENTH-CENTURY SAHARA

The image of a plucky, seaworthy caravel that epitomizes the fifteenth- and early-sixteenth-century beginnings of the Atlantic world seems far removed from that of the Sahara's centuries-old camel caravan, rhythmically meandering its way across desert sands. But in the course of the next century or so, both image and reality became intertwined along a dynamic West African frontier stretching from modern-day Morocco to Senegambia. The economic, political, and cultural dynamics generated by this frontier intersection varied in nature and impact, affecting the development of both the Atlantic and Sahara in different ways, at different times, through to at least the late nineteenth century. However, it was during the sixteenth and early seventeenth centuries that both worlds took on characteristics that set the context for these later relationships. This essay explores the role of the caravel and the caravan in this process—as it shaped both the writing of its history and the unfolding of history itself.[1]

The chronological parameters historians place upon "moments" in history quite literally define the content of that history. In this case, the years 1550–1624 derive from the history of a people and a place far removed from the Sahara, its Atlantic littoral, and its neighbors—namely, Jamestown, Virginia, and its inhabitants. What using this era as a lens through which to

The author would like to thank the conference organizers for the invitation and support to participate in what was a very stimulating intellectual endeavor. In addition, thanks to the University of Alberta, Support for the Advancement of Scholarship Endowment Fund, for its generous and ongoing support of my research and conference activity.

1. It is my intent to show readers how important the *history of the writing of history* actually is in shaping what we conceive of as knowledge. Just as this volume challenges conceptions of the Atlantic world, I am taking this opportunity to challenge one that has dominated almost all discussion of Saharan-Atlantic relations in this region.

view this part of West Africa will produce is uncertain at best, problematic at worst, for it is not consistent with extant African historiography and marginalizes by exclusion critical contextual developments of the earlier fifteenth century and the later seventeenth. That said, sometimes precisely this kind of reformatting reveals aspects of development hitherto obscured or distorted and brings into one discussion elements previously addressed only in discrete discourses.[2] The effort in this volume can only explore those aspects and elements deriving from the Saharan side of things; however, it is fair to say that the conversations generated by the conference's probing of the Atlantic world have influenced revisions to this exploration.[3] I genuinely hope that, in turn, drawing the Sahara into the discussion of the Atlantic world will provoke further reflection of interacting influences (historiographic and historical) among Africanist and non-Africanist scholars alike.[4]

Even among Africanists, the Sahara is largely invisible. It tends to be relegated into North Africa, where it disappears, and it is excluded from the dominant "sub-Saharan Africa" paradigm that shapes the field. In Middle Eastern Studies, it is (at best) the periphery of the Maghreb and the Mediterranean.[5] The situation was not so different in the fifteenth century, when interest in the desert interior was, for the most part, mediated by northern concerns. Not unlike the Atlantic itself, the Sahara appeared on pictorial maps as a kind of "ocean" around which (or at least to the north and south of

2. One example of such a discourse is the metaphor reflected in the title of this paper. As we will see below, the "caravel versus caravan" imagery has been used extensively both in early modern and modern West African historiography; as such, it is readily recognizable to Africanists. It seems, however, to be a concept new to those who study the Atlantic world. Other examples are the discourses generated (respectively) within the worlds of Middle Eastern and African studies — the tendency of scholars to speak of "sub-Saharan" Africa further exacerbates the discrete nature of discussions that often overlap in terms of subject and geography.

3. In particular, extensive discussions of cultural meetings on the margins of the Atlantic world raised new questions about comparable approaches to the Saharan frontier. They may well provide a needed counterbalance to the "dichotomous" and "conflictual" conceptual models currently prevailing in the historiography (for example, James Webb, Jr., and Omar Kane, discussed below).

4. By "the Sahara," I mean as distinct from Morocco. Although Morocco (in particular the Sa'adien dynasty that had roots in the south, in the so-called pre-Saharan region) might have seen the Sahara as an extension of its territories, the Sahara was an entity distinct unto itself, engaging (or not) with the Atlantic world on its own terms.

5. Under the Middle East Studies Association's geographical regions of expertise, for example, only one country (Sudan) that can truly claim to be Saharan (other than those that border the Mediterranean) is included.

which) various peoples and cultures existed, and across which commodities of value were transported, in this case, by turbaned Bedouin on camelback.[6] On the southern shores, those commodities included manufactured goods (cloth, paper, metal goods) and salt; on the northern, ostrich feathers, wax, slaves, and gold. Morocco was one of those regions whose southern realms bordered the Sahara and whose northern shores opened onto the Mediterranean.

As a receptor of trans-Saharan goods—especially gold—Morocco was an irresistible target for its close neighbor Portugal. The initial conquest in 1415 was of Morocco's northern port of Ceuta: occupation of the city, the Portuguese assumed, would bring control of Saharan wealth. But, as Vincent Cornell puts it so evocatively, soon "that dream of easy riches became an expensive nightmare." Portuguese policy thereafter aimed more at seeking West African gold through interception and diversion: interception of the Saharan trade on the Atlantic coast (first the northern coast through the towns of Safi and Azemmour, then the western Atlantic at the trading post of Arguin), and diversion "at source" (with São Jorge da Mina on the Gold Coast intended to divert gold to the coastal rather than the desert trade). This shift in policy shaped relations with Morocco significantly: much subsequent attention was given to producing and assuring regular access to grain and cloth specifically intended for the African gold trade, as well as assuring that other goods in demand south of the desert were supplied through Moroccan commercial connections:

> Just as they reactivated the medieval exchange loop based on the trade in grain between Morocco and the Iberian peninsula, the Portuguese also attempted to take over the trans-Saharan trade routes that went through Morocco by diverting caravan traffic from Fez to the Atlantic coast. . . . By thus making Morocco the linchpin of two highly profitable commercial circuits (grain, leather, wax, fish and medicinal herbs flowing north to the Iberian Peninsula; woven goods, copper, horses, and salt flowing south to sub-Saharan Africa) the Portuguese were able to reap high short-term profits.[7]

This Portuguese influence in northern towns and surrounding plains had effected major economic and social change. So when, in the 1490s, Portu-

6. See the famous Catalan Atlas of 1375 (http://www.the153club.org/africa1.html).

7. Vincent J. Cornell, "Socioeconomic Dimensions of Reconquista and Jihad in Morocco: Portuguese Dukkala and the Sadid Sus, 1450–1557," *International Journal of Middle East Studies,* XXII (1990), 379–418, esp. 380–392 (quotations on 381, 389).

gal established a trading factory at the southern location of Santa Cruz in an attempt to cut off Spanish competition (and exploit the fertile agricultural region of the Sus), the move drew strong opposition from those local clans that did not wish to lose their own power. The south was home to Sufi Muslim clerical groups who resented the invasive presence of the infidels. They quickly exploited traditional alliances to generate a centralized, powerful resistance. This process (spanning the first few decades of the sixteenth century), which involved declaring loyalty to a strong, secular military leader, was the origin of the Sa'adien state. It was also a catalyst for war with the north (still to some extent under the control of the royal Merinid family established in Fez). In economic terms, it generated investment in the region's sugar industry in order to provide payment for arms.[8] In 1541, the Portuguese enclave of Santa Cruz was conquered and renamed Agadir. This meant that, on the eve of the period we are looking at here, southern Morocco, under the leadership of the new Sa'adien dynasty, was pursuing its own, independent "Atlantic policy" through the port of Agadir.[9] For its ruler, Muhammed al-Shaykh, the nearby Sahara was critical to sustaining the economy that would support that policy. Consequently, it is not surprising that Morocco and Moroccans are, from the outset, part of this Saharan story. But as the Saharan version of that story begins, the Sahara becomes more than Portugal's competitor and Morocco's periphery—it emerges as a world unto itself.

Historiography: Caravel vs. Caravan

The extent to which historians understand the early history of the Sahara bordering the Atlantic is literally dependent upon the caravel and the caravan, although not in that order. It was the camel caravans from the ninth and tenth centuries onward, or rather the merchants who captained those "ships of the desert," who delivered to the Mediterranean and the Near East information about the flora, fauna, geography, and ethnology of the Afri-

8. Cornell, "Reconquista and Jihad," *International Journal of Middle East Studies,* XXII (1990), 380–407. Cornell traces the growth of the sugar industry on 403–404. Contrary to assumptions that slave labor was involved and that this industry was tied into the Saharan trade through the importation of labor, Cornell argues convincingly for wage labor and a "latifundia" organization.

9. Atlantic contacts were now England, France, and the Netherlands rather than Portugal or Spain; in Cornell's words, the economic policy was an adaptation of traditional political alliances in that it leapfrogged hostile states (in this case, the Iberian Peninsula). See ibid., 401.

PLATE I. *Tuareg salt caravan, Timbuktu-Gao region, Mali, 1978–1979.*
Photo by author

can Sahara and its "sub"-regions.[10] That knowledge, rendered intelligible at the time to a wide, Islamic, Arabic-speaking world by a range of authors (some of whom wrote from firsthand experiences, others of whom compiled secondhand evidence), found its way in part into Europe through the cosmopolitan scholarship of Muslim Spain.[11] The "medieval Arabic" view of the Sahara was predicated on the understanding that a river (or other large body of flowing water) linked the Atlantic to the Nile and that rich sources of gold lay beyond it.[12] From the ninth century onward, some Africans (both

10. "Ships of the desert": A. G. Hopkins, *An Economic History of West Africa* (London, 1973).

11. Among the better-known examples of the former are Ibn Batutta (fourteenth century) and Leo Africanus (sixteenth century); of the latter, Ibn Hawqal (wrote 988), Al-Bakri (wrote 1068), and Al-Idrisi (wrote 1154). According to N. Levtzion and J. F. P. Hopkins: "Al-Idrisi is perhaps the best known in Europe of all Arab geographers, no doubt because an abridgement of his work was printed in Rome as early as 1592, thus being one of the first Arabic books ever printed" (Levtzion and Hopkins, eds., *Corpus of Early Arabic Sources for West African History* [Cambridge, 1981], 104).

12. John Thornton, *Africa and Africans in the Making of the Atlantic World, 1400–1800,* 2d ed. (Cambridge, 1998), 19. The Senegal, Gambia, Niger, and Benue rivers

in and to the south of the Sahara) were understood to be converting to Islam. Of interest to most writers in this Arabic-speaking, Muslim world was what these realities meant for commerce, as represented by the caravans that facilitated the exchange of goods and information in all directions along Saharan trade routes.[13]

When Henry the Navigator launched the Portuguese caravel upon the Atlantic Ocean, leaving the familiar waters off northern Morocco and the Canary Islands, he challenged the Muslim, Arab (and Arabic) monopoly on knowledge of the Sahara as surely as he challenged the commerce of its caravan "ships." In effect, the first arena of interaction between what would become the Atlantic and Saharan worlds was intellectual. What early Africanists and leading European historians long regarded as the first written records of African history, the accounts of Portuguese voyages along the West African Atlantic coast, brought a radically different perspective to understanding the Sahara.[14] Ironically, the underlying interests of the Portuguese were similar to those of their predecessors: assessing the potential for the spread of religion (in this case, Christianity) and the trade in gold. The information about the Sahara and its peoples that now filtered through the Portuguese lens was acquired initially from coastal raids (random kidnappings of Saharans along the coast) and subsequently from ex-

---

were conflated into one "Nile of the Blacks." The origin of this appears to have been the above-mentioned Al-Idrisi in his twelfth-century text. Much influenced by the Ptolemaic geographical tradition, he tried to fit new information emanating from travelers in the Sahara and Sudan into the existing conceptual framework. Consequently, he postulated a divided Nile, one flowing north into Egypt, the other across the Sudan. And as in Egypt, he imagined that all major towns must lie along the river.

13. See annotations of texts like Al-Bakri's and Al-Idrisi's (as above) in Levtzion and Hopkins, *Corpus*.

14. African historians (like most others, until recently) sought out the written record before the oral. There has long been a kind of divide, however, between those who study Africa through the written records in European languages and those who do so using Arabic accounts (and usually have a primary interest in Islam, not Africa per se). Only recently has this begun to change as new generations of Africanists acquire Arabic as an African language.

The shorthand "Portuguese" refers to most fifteenth- and sixteenth-century voyages, even though several were captained by Venetian and Genoan personnel. The parallels with transatlantic voyages are reflected in a discourse that refers to this as "the Portuguese discovery of Africa" (J. Suret-Canale, "The Western Atlantic Coast, 1600–1800," in J. F. A. Ajayi and Michael Crowder, eds., *A History of West Africa,* I [London, 1971], 387–440, esp. 387).

changes at the trading factory of Arguin and along the extensive Senegambian coast.[15]

In 1487, Portugal decided to extend its efforts at interception by penetrating the Saharan world itself: a second trading factory was established in the oasis of Wadan (in the central Mauritanian region of Adrar). We know little about the venture, other than that it survived for only a few years.[16] Presumably, Portugal undertook this enterprise based on information that, in this major salt entrepôt, the gold and slaves crossing the desert were divided into cargoes destined either for Arguin or (north) for the Barbary Coast.[17] The intent was most probably to influence more slave trade to flow toward the former. It was this knowledge, highlighting the operations of the gold, salt, and slave trades, as well as information about tribal participation in commerce and conflict between indigenous clerics *(zawaya)* and immigrant Arab warriors *(hassan),* that formed the base of European understanding from the sixteenth century onward.[18] And it was this knowledge that shaped the perceptions of the new Atlantic competitors, the Dutch, the French, and the British, in the centuries of Atlantic competition to follow.[19]

The failure of the Wadan venture had both real and symbolic import. Realistically, it meant that Portuguese (and later other European) efforts to

15. This became the equivalent of firsthand knowledge, especially as compared to information filtering through Moroccan multilayered sources.

16. Duarte Pacheco Pereira, *Esmeraldo de situ orbis,* ed. and trans. George H. T. Kimble, Works Issued by the Hakluyt Society, 2d Ser., no. 79 (London, 1937), 75. Local tradition claims they were driven out; Pereira speaks of the "hostile reception" by the local people, eventually forcing them to leave. No year is given for the closure of the fort. See also Abdel Wedoud Ould Cheikh, "Nomadisme, Islam et pouvoir politique dans la société maure pre-colonial (XIe siècle–XIXème siècle)" (Ph.D. diss., L'Université René Descartes—Paris V, 1995), 70, 89.

17. G. R. Crone, ed. and trans., *The Voyages of Cadamosto and Other Documents on Western Africa in the Second Half of the Fifteenth Century,* Works Issued by the Hakluyt Society, 2d Ser., no. 80 (London, 1937), 17–22.

18. Information was supplied by Cadamosto (fifteenth century) and Valentin Fernandes and Duarte Pacheco Pereira (early sixteenth century). See discussion in E. A. McDougall, "The Question of Tegaza and the Conquest of Songhay: Some Saharan Considerations," in *Le Maroc et l'Afrique subsaharienne aux débuts des temps modernes,* Institute des Etudes Africaines, Colloque International, Marrakech, 1992 (Rabat, 1995), 251–282, esp. 256–257.

19. Succinct accounts of the emergence of this competition are Boubacar Barry, *Senegambia and the Atlantic Slave Trade* (Cambridge, 1998), 36–54; and Thornton, *Africa and Africans,* 13–71.

physically integrate Atlantic and West African networks (commercial and cultural) subsequently focused on the more southerly, sahelian regions of the Senegal and Gambia rivers.[20] Indeed, historians discussing the making of the Atlantic world and the role of Greater Senegambia overlook entirely this early effort to include the Sahara.[21] Symbolically, however, the Wadan failure marks a moment now lost to history, when interests generated by the growth of Atlantic trade sought deliberately to incorporate those of the western Sahara, to make the western Sahara a part of the Atlantic world, not merely a periphery through the mediation of Morocco. Failure meant that the caravel and the caravan each continued to carve out, thereafter, its own distinctive reality.

Historians, however, like to think linearly, chronologically. They seek to construct "the narrative," the story that brings parallel worlds into a single universe. It is not surprising, therefore, that they have knitted medieval

20. This does not mean that they ceased to appreciate the importance of the coastal island factory of Arguin. It continued to be the focus of rivalry for control between the Portuguese, Dutch, and French over the next couple of centuries (Barry, *Senegambia,* 46–48). Nor was Morocco overlooked, but its role in European affairs was changing.

21. For example, see Philip D. Curtin, in his influential *Economic Change in Precolonial Africa: Senegambia in the Era of the Slave Trade* (Madison, Wis., 1975), 61:

> The Portuguese, as the leading alien power on the African coast, were not interested in controlling local competition so much as they were in keeping other Europeans out of their private commercial preserve. They therefore seized and fortified offshore islands, not coastal enclaves. Their three strongpoints of the late fifteenth century were Arguin Island, some 500 kms north of the Senegal [River], the Cape Verde Islands, 800 kms due west, and Elmina far away on the Gold Coast. Portuguese went ashore to trade, but they did so under the peaceful conditions of a nonmilitarized trade diaspora. With the exception of the brief attempt to seize a post at the mouth of the Senegal about 1490, the Europeans remained a set of enclaved merchant communities on the African Mainland. The first attempts to switch to trading post empire came only with the mid-seventeenth century.

Barry outlines the activities of the Portuguese during this era similarly, noting failed attempts to build forts in the Senegal River estuary and on the Gambia River; he makes no mention of the failure to penetrate inland over the desert route from Arguin in spite of discussing the activities and ultimate decline of Arguin itself (*Senegambia,* 40–41). John Thornton's masterful *Africa and Africans* also omits any reference to this venture in his discussion of Portuguese early trade organization (see esp. 58, 59). Although both Curtin and Barry include consideration of the Sahara and Arguin in their conceptualization of Senegambia—for Barry, the region's northern frontier is explicitly marked by Arguin (46)—Thornton makes no mention of either; his Africa is clearly sub-Saharan, his Africans exclusive of Saharans.

"views from the caravan" and observations from the voyages of discovery together sequentially. The image of the caravan and the caravel symbolizes economic competition, social friction, and ultimately (in the late seventeenth century) military conflict. Gradually, a new paradigm emerged that began, in turn, to shape how we would look at this region of West Africa.[22]

Ironically, this symbolism, and the subsequent intellectual discourse it generated, had its roots not in the writing of African history but in Vitorino Magalhães-Godinho's seminal work on Portuguese economic history, *L'Economie de l'empire portugais,* that appeared in 1969. It was in his analysis of the impact of early Portuguese trade along the western Atlantic coast of Africa that the metaphor of an Atlantic "caravel commerce brutally eliminating the caravan trade of the desert" first came into play. French scholar Jean Devisse took issue with this argument in his own influential work on trans-Saharan trade routes in 1972. But in suggesting that the model fell down on grounds that the Atlantic competition developed trade in different commodities than the Saharan—Godinho's focus on gold as "the" measure of the success, he argued, obscured important changes occurring in the nature of Saharan traffic—he inadvertently reinforced the model defined by the imagery's "competition."[23]

The imagery itself was put front and center first by Senegalese historian Boubacar Barry. He used it to shape both his regional study of Senegal's Waalo (1972) and his later magnum opus on Greater Senegambia (1988). In the former, he characterized the late-seventeenth-century war that straddled southwestern Mauritania and riverine Senegal (known from the Senegalese side as the War of the Marabouts and in Mauritania as the Shurr Bubba war) as an ideological (religious) and military extension of the antagonism that had emerged between coastal European commerce and trans-Saharan trade. Saharan groups of zawaya and hassan were the protagonists in this lengthy conflict; Barry argues that the former fought in defense of the traditional Saharan-based commerce, whereas the latter sought to benefit from the new Atlantic opportunities. Mauritanian scholar Abdel Wedoud Ould Cheikh notes that Barry took this war, considered formative

22. Constructing the medieval "view from the caravan" was greatly facilitated by the appearance of two collections of annotated translations: Joseph Cuoq's *Recueil des sources arabes concernant l'Afrique occidentale du VIIIe au XVIe siècle: (Bilād al-Sūdān)* (Paris, 1975); and Levtzion and Hopkins's *Corpus.*

23. Vitorino Magalhães-Godinho, *L'Economie de l'empire portugais aux XVe et XVIe siècles* (Paris, 1969), 181–188; Jean Devisse, "Routes de commerce et échanges en Afrique occidentale en relation avec la Méditerranée," *Revue d'histoire economique et sociale,* L (1972), 357–397, esp. 387.

in the making of Senegambia, "to be the political and military outcome of the antagonism between two types of trade, between the *champions of caravans and of caravels.*"[24]

In his later work, Barry continued to draw upon this imagery to articulate the significance of the challenge posed by the bourgeoning Atlantic trade (first in gold, then in slaves) to Saharan desert commerce in general. Arguing that it was only by "opening out onto the Atlantic seaboard" that Senegambia came to play a significant regional role, he went on to underscore the import of this development: "Strictly speaking, the Sahara did not really become a desert until Atlantic fleets supplanted its camel caravans. This vast turnabout totally ruined the trans-Saharan trading system as from [sic] the fifteenth century." More specifically among the Europeans, it was

> [the Portuguese whose] impact was the most spectacular. The seacoast became, from then on, the leading front for acculturation. The settlement of the Portuguese at Arguin around 1445 was the *first victory of the caravel over the caravan.* Its consequence was the rerouting of trade circuits towards the Atlantic. . . . Because of the steady decline of the trans-Saharan trade, the entire southern region of the country now known as Mauritania, beginning from Arguin, came within the orbit of Senegambia, attracted by the Atlantic trading system.[25]

Henceforth, that region would be driven by Senegambia's political economy. The Atlantic world's overshadowing of the Sahara, Barry argues, climaxed in the late-seventeenth-century Shurr Bubba war that was critical to the shaping of both Mauritania and Senegal.[26]

In the wake of Barry's argument, there have been some challenging variations on this caravel-versus-caravan theme. Ould Cheikh's as-yet-unpublished thesis poses directly the question of the impact of the caravel on the caravan, engaging in an extensive discussion with Godinho and Barry that draws heavily on Saharan sources. In effect, he fleshes out Devisse's early work to look more closely at the commodities that supported Sa-

---

24. Boubacar Barry, *Le royaume du Waalo, 1659–1859: Le Sénégal avant la conquête* (Paris, 1972); Barry, *La Senegambie du XVe au XIXe siècle: Traite negrière, Islam et conquête coloniale* (Paris, 1988); Abdel Wedoud Ould Cheikh, "Herders, Traders, and Clerics: The Impact of Trade, Religion, and Warfare on the Evolution of Moorish Society," in John G. Galaty and Pierre Bonte, *Herders, Warriors, and Traders: Pastoralism in Africa* (Boulder, Colo., 1991), 199–218, esp. 205–206 (emphasis added).

25. Barry, *Senegambia*, 5, 15, 36–37 (emphasis added); "as from" is a translation awkwardness repeated throughout the book.

26. Ibid., 50–54.

haran trade—drawing heavily on my own work to magnify the special role of salt in that commerce. He also expands Devisse's analysis to consider which Saharan groups were involved in managing that trade over time. The longevity of the regionally based commerce and organization argues strongly against the hypothesis that "the Atlantic commerce marked the ruin of the trans-Saharan commerce." Provocatively, he suggests that the opposite may well hold, that the fifteenth-century development of several Saharan market centers like Wadan, Shinqit, and Tishit (all were well-watered oases, sources of dates and grain, termini of trans-Saharan trade routes in what is today Mauritania) indicates that the installation of the Portuguese coincided with a growing importance of the caravan that continued until the late seventeenth century.[27]

Omar Kane, a senior Senegalese historian, draws a very different picture of the competitive interests involved that nevertheless relates to the evolution of the caravel-caravan model. He shifts attention away from gold and salt, Atlantic and Saharan interests, and focuses instead on the slave trade. Where others see the slave trade gradually becoming a factor in the so-called caravel-caravan competition, Kane argues that, in these early days, it was Moroccan interests in trading and raiding for slaves, not Atlantic influence, that dominated trans-Saharan trade and shaped Senegambia. For Kane, the Moroccan state was the principal "manager" of sub-Saharan slave raiding, and the desert populations were but manipulated extensions of Moroccan policy. Leaving aside for the moment the extent to which one can legitimately speak of unified Moroccan state interests during this era and the degree to which they were themselves also tied to the Atlantic world, one can infer from Kane that the caravan remained the dominant commercial factor in the region. But because it served interests both external and detrimental to the integrity of the Sahara, he argues, it weakened the region's ability to resist later incorporation into the Atlantic world.[28]

Kane's analysis becomes even more relevant to our discussion when con-

27. Ould Cheikh, "Nomadisme, Islam et pouvoir politique," I, esp. chap. 1, 70–107; he labels this medieval phase in the trans-Saharan trade "The Age of Salt" (62). See also Elizabeth Ann McDougall, "The Ijil Salt Industry: Its Role in the Pre-colonial Economy of the Western Sudan" (Ph.D. diss., University of Birmingham, 1980), 70–87, esp. 85. Cornell gives further support to this argument, as will be discussed below.

28. Omar Kane, "Les relations entre le Maroc et les états riverains du fleuve Sénégal de la fin du XVe au milieu du XVIIIe siècle," in Le Maroc et l'Afrique subsaharienne, 25–46, esp. 26–28. On the unified Moroccan state interests and their ties to the Atlantic world, see Cornell's article "Reconquista and Jihad," International Journal of Middle East Studies, XXII (1990).

sidered along with James Webb, Jr.'s *Desert Frontier.* Webb picks up on the central dynamic of slaving in the Senegal region, affirming Morocco's role, while also acknowledging Saharan commerce in gold, gum, and salt. But he situates his argument firmly in opposition to Barry's conclusions about the growing Atlantic trade. He argues instead that the measure of competition should be slaves and that the Saharan trade in this commodity was more important than the Atlantic one, even into the eighteenth century. Consequently, when Webb offers a critique of Barry's version of the Shurr Bubba war, he argues that "the number of slaves sold into the Atlantic slave trade was a very small percentage of those sold into the desert and across the desert to North Africa"; therefore, there is no justification for an analysis rooted in one group's defense of the caravan against the threat of the caravel. During the period under consideration here, the caravan continued to dominate the economy of the Senegambian region; the Atlantic world had not yet found inroads into it, even though both the Atlantic and Senegambia were defined increasingly by slaving and the slave trade.[29]

In Search of a Saharan World: The Fifteenth and Sixteenth Centuries

This historiographical introduction to an era Ould Cheikh once referred to as "these 'dark ages' of western Saharan history" allows us to focus the remainder of this essay on questions central to that history and to its relation with the emerging Atlantic world. Where exactly did the frontier lie between the Atlantic and Saharan worlds? What were the contours of the latter? The caravel-caravan paradigm follows the Senegambian coast geographically, sometimes extending as far north as Arguin but often stretching only as far as the Senegal River; as mentioned above, it peaks chronologically with the war of Shurr Bubba in the 1670s, ultimately focusing attention on southwestern Mauritania and the lower Senegal River region. But the continued interest of European powers in controlling Arguin and the significance of the growing salt trade to the trans-Saharan commerce draws us into the Sahara of the Mauritanian Adrar, source of its own desert salt (Ijil) and location of the earliest Portuguese attempt at an in-

29. James L. A. Webb, *Desert Frontier: Ecological and Economic Change along the Western Sahel, 1600–1850* (Madison, Wis., 1995), 34, and see esp. the chapters "The Southwestern Frontier" (32–35) and "The Horse and Slave Trade" (82–90). Kane's "Les relations entre le Maroc et les états riverains," in *Le Maroc et l'Afrique subsaharienne,* although appearing simultaneously with *Desert Frontier,* was originally presented at a conference in Marrakech in 1992.

land presence (Wadan). Following the development of that commerce, then, takes us, not southwest toward the war of the marabouts and the establishment of Europeans on the Senegal (as the historiography would have it), but southeast, into the market region of the upper Senegal and its relatively unknown hinterland, the Tagant-Hodh.[30]

What role should be assigned to the Moroccans and Saharans with whom these Europeans interacted? Is the emphasis on slave raiding and trading illuminating (or even legitimate)? Again, this perception of Moroccan activity and impact has been shaped by the view from the caravel, so to speak —literally by sources generated from and pertaining to Senegambia and the question of Atlantic-Saharan competition. But if we are drawing on the conceptual innovation suggested by this conference in exploring as many realities as possible being created around the margins of the Atlantic world, we should be doing the same with its Saharan counterpart. From this perspective, as suggested in the introduction, Morocco and Moroccans constitute facets of the Saharan world as much as the Mediterranean. Clearly they were contributing to the dynamics of the desert, deliberately, in an attempt to shape its reality. But what reality, exactly? Morocco itself remained another frontier linking the Saharan and Atlantic worlds throughout the period we are examining here. This context is significant in understanding the nature of Morocco's Saharan activities in the sixteenth and early seventeenth centuries. Similarly, it shapes how Moroccans saw themselves vis-à-vis "Saharans." In the Saharan world of the late sixteenth and early seventeenth centuries, did Moroccans and Saharans generate the same kind of cultural and social hybrids we saw emerging in the Atlantic world? Can we see comparable economic partnerships and networks, drawing on increasingly large human, cultural, and geographical hinterlands? It is too ambitious to think we can satisfactorily answer these questions in the pages that remain. However, we can glimpse the potential for pushing them fur-

30. Ould Cheikh, "Herders, Traders, and Clerics," in Galaty and Bonte, *Herders, Warriors, and Traders,* 202. See Barry's explicit identification of Arguin as marking the northern frontier of greater Senegambia (*Senegambia,* 37); Curtin's implicit inclusion of desert regions as developed in his chapter "Religion and Political Change" (*Economic Change in Precolonial Africa,* 46–58); Suret-Canale's statement that the Senegal River marked the "natural boundary" of the region ("Western Atlantic Coast," in Ajayi and Crowder, eds., *History of West Africa,* I, 387); and Thornton's exclusion of anything "Saharan" in the African part of the Atlantic world (*Africa and Africans,* 13–71).

Saint Louis was established by the French on the small island strategically located at the mouth of the Senegal River in 1659; the Dutch had occupied the island of Gorée just off the coast of today's Dakar in 1621.

ther and thereby decrease our obsession with the carvel-caravan competition that has dominated the discourse to date.

It has long been my contention that the development of the Sahara's salt industries underpinned growth in desert social, economic, religious, and political life. What we know of the history of the Ijil industry supports that contention. The medieval "salt network" our Portuguese sources drew attention to had already given rise to its own commercial language, *azayr* (a mixture of Saharan Berber and Sahelian Soninke), and provided a skeletal frame for cultural and religious interaction spanning the desert edge. A class of specialized traders converted Ijil and other desert salts into the wealth needed to support a growing stratum of indigenous, Islamic scholars by the twelfth and thirteenth centuries. By the fourteenth and fifteenth centuries, they and their hundreds of students *(telamidh)* followed the proliferation of salt markets springing up along the desert edge. Tinigi was home to the Tajakant, a clan said to be descended from the famed Almoravids; the town seems to have given way in importance in the fifteenth century to nearby Shinqit, where other clerical clans established themselves. Wadan, so inhospitable to the Portuguese, welcomed more of the same, including the famous Aqit family, who, in the course of the sixteenth and seventeeth centuries, became prominent scholars in both Timbuktu and Morocco. Other salt-trading centers like Tishit and Walata attracted learned emigrants from declining centers of the former sahelian Ghana empire. All of them nurtured scholars—teachers, *qadis* (judges), grammarians, calligraphers—who, in turn and in time, drifted back south. Some, like migrants from Tishit during precisely the era that interests us here, moved into the Togba region of the western Tagant-Hodh; others moved toward the Senegal River. Many of these scholars and their families were, like their places of origin, directly associated with the trade and marketing of salt. This is epitomized in the probably apocryphal but oft-cited oral tradition from Shinqit: "'One Day' it is said, 'a caravan of 32000 loaded camels left Shinqit with salt: 20000 belonging to its inhabitants, 12000 to the inhabitants of Tishit. The entire caravan was sold in Zara [in the Tagant] and the people with one accord wondered which of the two towns was the more prosperous."[31]

31. McDougall, "Ijil Salt Industry," 88–93; McDougall, "The View from Awdaghust: War, Trade, and Social Change in the Southwestern Sahara, from the Eighth to the Fifteenth Century," *Journal of African History,* XXVI (1985), 1–31, esp. 27–28 for azayr; McDougall, "Salts of the Western Sahara: Myths, Mysteries, and Historical Significance," *International Journal of African Historical Studies,* XXIII (1990), 231–257, esp. 241–251 (there were many forms of salt available); McDougall, "The Economics of Islam in the Southern Sahara: The Rise of the Kunta Clan," *Asian and African Studies,*

Two of these many clans are of particular interest to us. The Tajakant, mentioned above, were widely influential through the networks established by their clerics and *telamidh*. They were also known for their fifteenth-century prosperity (contemporary with that of Wadan), based on the marketing of salt and slaves. In the sixteenth century, they dispersed from the Adrar. Some moved to the southeast into the Tagant-Hodh and established Togba as their capital. It is said that, on their arrival, the resident warrior clan in the region demanded a fee for the right to settle: "one young female slave and 4 ozs of gold for every house built." This tradition, possibly apocryphal, suggests a continuing Tajakant involvement in the trade for slaves and gold, replicating their earlier commercial interests in Tinigi and suggesting continued access to the Adrar's salt.[32]

The second clan of interest is the Kunta. Contrary to its own latterly constructed tradition of origin that claims a fifteenth-century influence in the western Sahara, it likely emerged as a recognized zawaya clan from the Adrar's Tajakant dispersal during the sixteenth century. Its so-called "founder" originated from Tinigi and is said to have had long-standing commercial relations with eastern Mauritania, where he owned date palm groves in the salt market of Tishit. Around the beginning of the sixteenth century, he is said to have moved to Walata, where he knew fame as both trader and cleric. Upon his death in 1515, he became the "patron saint" of travelers to Walata; mentioned among those seeking his spiritual approval were merchants from Ijil as well as southern Morocco, Tuat (an area of extensive oases in what is today southern Algeria), and the eastern mine of Tegaza (to the north of Timbuktu). Toward the end of the century, the Kunta are said to have replicated the Tajakant dispersal. Although the parallels are a bit too similar for historical comfort, it seems that the Kunta split their clients and tributaries between themselves. Over the seventeenth century, one of these groups moved permanently into the Tagant, leaving one family in the Adrar (Wadan) and another in southwest Brakna. This distribution of the Kunta positioned them well, as the earlier dispersal had done for the Tajakant, to build on the salt trade from Ijil along the east-west interregional exchange bordering the sahel and to tap into north-south trans-Saharan networks with which they intersected.[33]

XX (1986), 45–60; McDougall, "The Quest for 'Tarra': Toponymy and Geography in Exploring History," *History in Africa*, XVIII (1991), 271–289, esp. 276 n. 38; see also Ould Cheikh, "Nomadisme, Islam et pouvoir politique," 71–72.

32. McDougall, "Quest for 'Tarra,'" *History in Africa*, XVIII (1991), 278.

33. McDougall, "Ijil Salt Industry," 81–98, draws heavily on Aziz A. Batran, "Sidi

The stories of the Tajakant and the Kunta draw us into a larger sixteenth-century Sahara where we encounter both Moroccan interests and a competing salt industry. When they dispersed from the Adrar, the Tajakant also moved north to Tinduf. The town was well placed to channel the trans-Saharan commerce into Moroccan territories: northwest to the rich agricultural Sus (discussed earlier as a terrain of conflict between the Portuguese and the incipient Sa'adien state), north to the Dra'a valley (heartland of the Sa'adi interests), and northeast to the luxurious oases of the Tafilelt (also a frequently contested resource between Moroccan competitors for power). Similarly, it served as a staging post for caravans traveling south into the Sahara, both toward the Adrar and the middle Niger. The Tajakant became recognized masters of the trade between southern Morocco and the Adrar, thereby also becoming valuable to Sa'adien rulers. Togba remained patched into the interregional salt network as well, as is evidenced by vestiges of *azayr* (probably via the migrations from Tishit) in the region. This network operated east-west along the desert edge, with its eastern terminus at Timbuktu, and intersected with the trans-Saharan trade whose northern termini were under Moroccan control. The Kunta also had a second distinct group that settled to the north, nomadizing between the Atlantic coastal hinterland and Tuat. This group established a number of scholarly communities *(zawiya)* and from there launched trading activities between Tuat and southern Morocco. This group began to drift south toward the middle Niger in the seventeenth century, at which point they also were reportedly involved with the Timbuktu commerce in Tegaza salt.[34]

As these Saharan clerical and merchant diasporas were reaching north and northeast into Moroccan spheres of influence, the southern Sa'adien state was also reaching well into the Sahara. Beginning around 1540, rulers began launching various efforts to acquire revenue from the desert salt mines of Tegaza and Ijil.[35] What is important to note is that those efforts

al-Mukhtar al-Kunti and the Recrudescence of Islam in the Western Sahara and the Middle Niger, c. 1750–1811" (Ph.D. diss., University of Birmingham, 1971), for the analysis of early Kunta genealogy.

34. McDougall, "Quest for 'Tarra,'" *History in Africa,* XVIII (1991), 278; McDougall, "Ijil Salt Industry," 81–98, esp. 88–93; McDougall, "Economics of Islam," *Asian and African Studies,* XX (1986), 50–52. Tinduf lies just south of the southern Moroccan Dra'a region, the Dra'a being the extensive *wadi* extending from the inland Sahara in an east-southwest direction all the way to the Atlantic that supported hundreds of date-palm oases.

35. McDougall, "The Question of Tegaza," in *Le Maroc et l'Afrique subsaharienne,*

involved simple requests to the Sudanese Muslim ruler of the large, sub-Saharan empire of Songhay for the right to tax production and trade, the offer of gifts in exchange for that right, shows of force expressed by military expeditions (two of which passed by way of the Adrar—one of which was likely targeting Ijil itself), and outright annexation of Tegaza in the 1550s and again in the 1580s.[36] In each of the latter two cases, occupation was short-lived but did involve the presence of Moroccans as "agents" of the emperor and tax collectors.[37] Other mines in the Tegaza-Tawdeni plains were brought into production as a response to the Moroccan presence, and these, in turn, affected the local economy, but we know little more about exactly how Saharan traders like the Tajakant and Kunta responded to these efforts in this early phase. Finally, at some point during the century, the Moroccans established a garrison in Shinqit as a consequence of an alliance with a local clerical clan—presumably this venture was in some fashion related to interest in (if not control over) the nearby mine of Ijil; it was later used as a base from which to launch the slave raids Kane spoke of in the seventeenth century. What other functions it served, what other Moroccan personnel were posted there, and when it was abandoned is all information we lack—information nonetheless critical to really understanding the nature of the cultural frontier that might have been developing, however fleetingly.[38]

In 1591, Morocco surpassed the goal of controlling Tegaza's wealth by staking claim to the Songhay Empire itself; as part of the conquest, Morocco occupied Timbuktu. Tradition recounts an "oath swearing" carried

---

but see esp. "Appendix 1: A Chronology of Pre-conquest Relations," 273–277 (page 278 was not printed; page 277 ends in mid-sentence).

36. I have argued for an association between the expedition and an interest in exercising some form of control over Ijil on largely circumstantial evidence (ibid., 253–255). Cornell states categorically that the Moroccan sultan Muhammed al-Shaykh sought to reestablish the trans-Saharan trade network that had been disrupted by Portuguese and Bedouin raids since 1517 and as part of this goal took control of the Ijil mine. He sees the subsequent taking over of the Tegaza mines in 1556–1557 as a similarly motivated action ("Reconquista and Jihad," *International Journal of Middle East Studies,* XXII [1990], 401–402, 415 nn. 78–79).

37. This occurred first in 1556–1557, later in 1583–1584; neither appears to have been long-lived.

38. McDougall, "Quest for 'Tarra,'" *History in Africa,* XVIII (1991), 277. The alliance and garrison are rarely discussed; it is interesting that Cornell makes no reference to them in his discussion of Ijil (see n. 36, above). See "Epilogue: The Eighteenth Century" (below) for reference to a Kunta response to the situation in the Tegaza-Tawdeni plains.

out according to the organization of established merchant quarters: the first day concerned "foreigners" from the Fezzan (southern, modern-day Libya) and Tuat; the second, merchants from Walata, Wadan, and "the West."[39] Interesting as they are, these urban-based affiliations obscure the clan connections—the "dispersals," scholarly networks, and commercial diasporas that linked, rather than separated, the markets, oases, and zawiya of the desert. These "itinerants" included clerics and merchants from southern Morocco, especially from the Dra'a region. And that demographic profile gave definition to a late-sixteenth-century Sahara that was clearly contested territory between those who lived and worked within its environs, as well as with and between those on its northern and southern "shores." This Sahara was seen as a great source of wealth to all who could negotiate its terms.

In Search of the Saharan World: The Seventeenth Century

Unfortunately, the first half of the seventeenth century remains largely silent in terms of internally generated voices. However, there are a few that emerge later in the 1600s from a variety of sources—Moroccan, Saharan, and European, written and oral—that both individually and collectively articulate the nature of the Saharan world that had emerged by this time. They give us every reason to believe our sense of a dynamic society and economy continuing to flourish on the margins of the Atlantic in the early part of the century.

Speaking most directly to this is the 1690 account of one Cornelius Hodges. An employee of the English Royal African Company, he had a goal "to reach the gold-mines and slave-markets [of the interior], and thus to enable his company to frustrate the French in their attempt to tap the sources of labour-supply," the inland slave trade. Although he personally never reached the sought-after markets, an expedition of his men did. According to his report, they were directed to a large town named "Tarra," "verry neare as bigg as the Citty of London with the walls . . . [in] the Moores Countrey," said to be "the only mart for slaves in all those western parts of Affrica." Although there is still uncertainty about Tarra's exact location, its commercial structure was well described: any merchants carrying European goods, wishing to purchase slaves here, had first to "turn" their goods into cloth and with the cloth purchase the "Salt of the Moores who bring it above 1100 miles on Camells and will Truck it for no othr soart of commodities than Cloathes, Gold and Slaves." After acquiring the salt, merchants could "truck it for slaves," Hodges went on to explain, "wch is the

---

39. Elizabeth Hodgkin, "Social and Political Relations on the Niger Bend in the Seventeenth Century" (Ph.D. diss., Birmingham University, 1987), 479.

Reason that many times before they can dispatch the goods of 4 or 5 slaves that it costs them 1/2 as much for Lodging and Provisions. But it goes with 500 ozs of gold, pays no customes and may turne it into what commodity he pleaseth, In less than two Dayes If he pleaseth." Tarra was a desertside market, where the demands of Saharans for cloth, gold, and slaves intersected with those of sub-Saharans for salt, structuring commercial transactions in such a way as to make penetration by Europeans and European goods difficult.[40]

At least, this was how it appeared from the point of view of Atlantic interests. We actually have several additional Saharan perspectives on Tarra, one provided by oral tradition that is inadvertently enriched by Hodges, one by a locally generated source in which the town is called "Zarra," and a third derived from archaeological information on the region. According to tradition, the Tajakants' dispersal that effectively allowed their traders and transporters to exploit trade in salt, slaves, and gold between Morocco and the Tagant-Hodh culminated toward the late seventeenth century in an important wedding. The emperor of Morocco (since 1649 under the new Alawite dynasty) gave his daughter in marriage to the Tajakant chief of Togba, thereby staking (or confirming) a familial claim to influence, if not direct political power, in the area. It is said that initial Tajakant acceptance of local warrior overlordship had given way to a refusal to make the annual slave gold payments, and that the emperor had subsequently placed a military force at his son-in-law's disposal to battle these overlords and their allies.[41]

In 1690, Hodges's men recounted that, three days after their arrival in Tarra, some "40,000 horsemen and camels [arrived] to Lay siege to It. The Emperour Drew his forces up and incamped without the towne to receive them there." This "siege" has been characterized as typical of Morocco's slave raids into Senegambia. But given the history of relations between Morocco, the Tajakant, and the commerce of the region, another interpretation

40. Thora G. Stone, "The Journey of Cornelius Hodges in Senegambia, 1689–90," *English Historical Review,* XXXIX (1924), 89–95, esp. 89, 92–93. See also McDougall, "Quest for 'Tarra,'" *History in Africa,* XVIII (1991), 273. The English Royal African Company was founded in 1672 following on the heels of the unsuccessful Company of Royal Adventurers Trading to Africa that had established itself in the River Gambia in 1661 for pursuing the trade in slaves.

41. Mohammed el-Chennafi, "Sur les traces d'Awdagust: Les Tagdāwəst et leur ancienne cité," in D. Robert, S. Robert, and J. Devisse, eds., *Tegdaoust I, tome I: Recherches sur Aoudaghost* (Paris, 1970), 101. With no exact date known, we can only surmise that the emperor in question was either Mulay Mohammed al-Rashid (1664–1672) or Mulay Ismail (1672–1727).

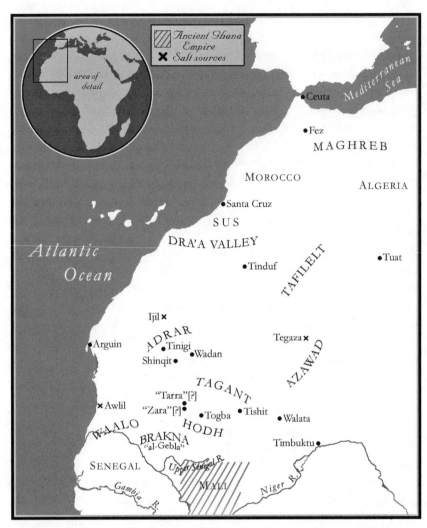

PLATE 2. *The Saharan World, 15th–17th Centuries. Drawn by Rebecca L. Wrenn*

suggests itself. Tradition also tells us that the battle against the Tajakants' enemies involved a joint Tajakant-Moroccan force, personally led by the Tajakant chief. We are also told he died and was buried in Togba ca. 1690–1691. I have suggested elsewhere the possibility that Hodges's men actually witnessed the battle in which the Tajakant chief resisted his overlords, assisted by the sultan's army, and lost his life. This must remain conjecture at present, but from the perspective of the regional political economy, the likelihood that this siege was a slave raid of any kind appears unlikely. Indeed, Hodges's men were drawn into assisting "the Moores": "It pleased

162 | E. ANN MCDOUGALL

God to give them such good success, they being all very good firemen, *that the Emperor attributed the victory and safeguard of his countrey wholely to Mahamit.*" Clearly, Moroccans saw this region, its commerce, and the Taja-kant as constituting their world, and the Saharan Tajakant acknowledged this perspective while simultaneously seeking to increase their own power vis-à-vis neighboring clans. And although all this seems to have constituted a historical moment that was not repeated, for that moment, the Atlantic world was truly drawn into that of the Sahara, not merely as observer but as participant in the victory.[42]

I have, in the past, postulated that Tarra might, in fact, have been Togba, but a mid-to-late-seventeenth-century Saharan document called a *nawazil* eliminates that possibility. Although compiled and recorded later in Walata, this document consists of about 240 questions put to a learned Adrar scholar over a period of many years before 1696 (the date of his death). The questions are posed by Saharans from the Adrar, as well as from far away—the Tagant-Hodh, Timbuktu, southern Morocco, the Sudan in general. Although it covers many subjects, one of the two largest groups of questions concerns commerce, and half of these are either directly related to salt transactions or use salt to illustrate the issue at hand. In discussing how these merchants should conduct their commerce in order to be consistent with the laws of Islam, the texts reveal that the major salt markets between the Adrar and Tagant-Hodh were Shinqit, Togba, and a place called "Zara." The last was unquestionably the principal entrepôt for the salt commerce from the Adrar, the source of the "salt of the Moores" referred to by Hodges; it was also almost certainly Tarra. This salt passed through Togba on occasion, confirming that Zara / Tarra and Togba were indeed independent markets. The nawazil also confirms that there were several different salts traveling in these desert edge networks, one of which came from Awlil, a medieval coastal mine of uncertain location. There are several possible places to the north of the Senegal River where salt formed by evaporating seawater in large depressions could have been removed in blocks (as was Awlil salt); and, of course, we have no way of knowing for sure that it was the same Awlil last mentioned in twelfth-century Arabic accounts. But the reference, suggesting that "bars" of salt from Ijil and Awlil were being traded in the

---

42. Stone, "Journey of Hodges," *English Historical Review,* XXXIX (1924), 93; Curtin, *Economic Change in Precolonial Africa,* 51; el-Chennafi, "Sur les traces d'Awda-gust," in Robert, Robert, and Devisse, eds., *Tegdaoust I,* 106 n. 2; McDougall, "Quest for 'Tarra,'" *History in Africa,* XVIII (1991), 279, in the context of a larger discussion of Tarra's identity.

same markets at a time when this part of the Senegambian coast was fully incorporated into the Atlantic economy, confirms the continuing existence of a commercial frontier bordering both Atlantic and Sahara. And, at least in this case, the frontier was characterized by market dynamics firmly rooted in Saharan networks and Islamic exchange practices.[43]

It also appears to have been centered firmly in the Mauritanian Tagant-Hodh, a region about which we know far too little, other than that it had once housed a famous medieval trans-Saharan market called Awdaghust. Awdaghust appears to have declined considerably with the growing prosperity of the salt markets of the Adrar-Tagant (Shinqit, Wadan, Tishit, Walata) and the contemporaneous development of the middle Niger salt industry. However, archaeological work in this area published in the 1980s records a seventeenth-century revival of Awdaghust, presumably tied to the emergent economy we have been describing. In addition, more sites have been located near the Wadi Togba that seem to have been agricultural centers (two of them boasted grain silos that could have stored twenty to thirty tons of grain); other evidence argues that the region also became a center of cotton cloth manufacture about the same time. We also know of several additional migrations of Saharan clans from Wadan (including another Kunta family) into the Tagant during this same century. The date palm oases and scholarly centers they built reflected, as well as contributed to, the healthy prosperity of the larger regional economy. The difficulties encountered by European traders in penetrating the Tarra market were in fact the consequence of a whole economic system supported by a very widespread religious, cultural, and commercial Saharan diaspora.[44]

Three letters provide a final glimpse into this world; they were written

43. McDougall, "Quest for 'Tarra,'" *History in Africa,* XVIII (1991). Muhammed bin al-Muktar Bel-La'mash al-Shanqiti (d. 1696), "Nawazil," MS no. 5742, al-Khizana al-Hassaniyya, microfilm, Archives Royales, Rabat, Morocco. Thanks to Mohamed Lahbib Nouhi for his generous assistance. Zara / Tarra: see McDougall, "A Qadi from Shingit and the Question of Salt: The *Nawazil* of Mohammed bin al Mukhtar bin La'amech (Late 17th C.)," paper presented at the African Studies Association meeting, Philadelphia, November 11-14, 1999. For a discussion of Awlil as a medieval source, see ibid.; and McDougall, "Salts of the Western Sahara," *International Journal of African Historical Studies,* XXIII (1990), 241-242.

44. McDougall, "View from Awdaghust," *Journal of African History,* XXVI (1985); Denise Robert-Chaleix, "Fusaioles décorées du site de Tegdaoust," in *Tegdaoust III, recherches sur Aoudaghost: Campagnes 1960-65, enquêtes générales* (Paris, 1983), 510-512; see also McDougall, "The Ijil Salt Industry"; and with reference to an even broader set of migrations, see Webb, *Desert Frontier,* 50-53.

by the Moroccan emperor to his son, then governor of the Saharan regions Wadi Dra'a and Tafilelt, between 1692 and 1699.[45] Although they may seem to be as unrelated to the Atlantic world as our medieval camel caravans appeared to be, when understood in the context of the Sahara we have been revealing, they become important insights into its dynamics and contours. The emperor refers to the lands now governed by his son—the Saharan hinterland—as the traditional "heartland" of the empire, one whose resources, especially the caravans arriving regularly from the Sudan, should allow for the building-up of a significant power base.[46] The letter continues:

An effective governor would have written to the Arabs of al-Gebla [the Trarza, Brakna of southern Mauritania] and of Teghaza and the Kings of Sudan and would have addressed all of these countries and planted spies in all of these directions such that you know every tribe and its intentions and every leader and his situation. And if you saw anyone of the Arabs of these areas go astray, you would bide your time, and then you would chose the right opportunity and take him to task wherever he might be. Had you done this all the Arabs would have come to respect and fear you and had you established yourself in that manner they would have sent presents to you and they would have come to visit you and you would have had the right or the ability to do to any of them near or far, what you wanted. And as a result everyone would know your name, and they would send delegations to where ever you are and your country would become prosperous, you would be able to make the caravan routes safe and [collect appropriate taxes].

At this moment, about a century after Morocco's conquest of the region, the emperor's specific Saharan concern was Tegaza and the failure of his representative there to collect the required salt taxes. He gave explicit instructions as to what his son should say in the letter that he, in turn, was supposed to send with the emperor's emissary to the mine. He was to threaten the Tegaza agent with replacement unless the overdue taxes were delivered immediately, and he was to outfit his father's emissary with twenty of his own best camels. This order was not to be questioned.[47]

45. Letters from Moulay Ismail (sultan of Morocco) to his son, al-Mamoun, governor of Tafilelt and Dra'a, 1692, 1699, and n.d., in "Notes from Mohamed al-Gharbi, Rio Oro" *(As-supiya al-hamra wa wadi dhahab dar al Kibab)* (Casablanca, n.d.), 217–243.
46. One that could be supported by an army, as his ancestors had done (ibid., 228–229.)
47. Ibid, 241–243.

Apart from providing insight into the stormy relationship between the emperor and his son, this correspondence reveals the continuing centrality of the Sahara to the Moroccan political economy, specifically the importance of trans-Saharan trade and the salt mines of Tegaza.[48] It also reveals how Saharans—the "Arabs" of the letters—were regarded by the Moroccan state as subjects to be kept in line and from whom gifts were to be received. It is perhaps notable that none were referred to from the Adrar or Tagant-Hodh as needing such "close observation," a reflection (one might postulate) of the close ties and important commercial connections the state had already established with the prominent zawiya families of these regions. Geographically, this perception pushes the Saharan world, viewed from Morocco as a kind of natural extension of its territories in familial, political, and economic terms, from the Adrar, Brakna ("al-Gebla"), and Tagant-Hodh into the Azawad north of Timbuktu (Tegaza) and as far north as the extensive oases of Tafilelt and Tuat. Delineating the contours of this world were the western and eastern salt networks rooted in Ijil and Tegaza, respectively— networks that might have intersected in some of the same markets in the southern desert edge and certainly drew on some of the same Saharan clan diasporas as transporters and traders.

This Sahara was very much the preoccupation of a Moroccan state seeking legitimacy in Islam among clerical desert zawaya and establishing its heartland among the Arabs, who could assure access to, and protection of, desert resources. As allies were cultivated, family connections cemented through marriage, and representatives of the state settled in various Saharan markets to collect taxes (and assure supplies of slaves), distinctions between being Moroccan and being Saharan surely blurred.[49] Not, as Kane would argue, because the Saharans were simple extensions of Morocco's slave-raiding interests but because identities—cultural and political—were refashioned continuously as the Saharan economy drew people from its margins and simultaneously extended its commercial tentacles into an increasingly larger domain. It was along these dynamic margins that European

48. Mentioned specifically is the son's inability to deliver information about rebellious Arabs, to keep track of what the people of Tafilelt owed in taxes, and to deal with loyal Jewish families who had served well the Crown (ibid., 232–233).

49. In 1679, Emperor Mulay Ismail married the daughter of the emir of Brakna while touring in Mauritania. It is said that all the warrior emirs renewed their allegiance to him at this time (Kane, "Les relations entre le Maroc," in *Le Maroc et l'Afrique sub-saharienne,* 27).

interests (first Portuguese, later French and English) articulated themselves and the Atlantic world began to make itself felt in the Sahara.[50]

Epilogue: The Eighteenth Century

A letter from the governor of the French Fort Saint Joseph (on the Senegal River) to the director of the Compagnie des Indes (ca. 1732) reported that the merchants were complaining that the "Moors" were taking all the gold and cloth of the upper Senegal region in exchange for their (Saharan) salt. The frontier with which the Atlantic world continued to interact was itself evolving. But whereas the caraval was by this time unquestionably shaping the history of Senegambia, the caravan apparently still frustrated European interests therein.[51] Moreover, its continued commercial strength reflected the development of a Saharan world in which desert politics, economics, and religion continued to generate a powerful attraction for Saharans, including Moroccans, who wrestled each other for control.[52] Negotiations over whose

50. It is ironic that Kane and Webb, who portray this complexity of relations as sets of dichotomies, also provide the best evidence for an argument to the contrary (see ibid., 26–28; Webb, *Desert Frontier,* "The Southwestern Frontier"). One example is the oft-cited story of the emir of Trarza who traveled to Morocco to seek assistance in his war with the Brakna in the early eighteenth century. In addition to the military support, he received gifts from the Moroccan emperor—a copper drum, white turban, and white trousers—that have since become symbols of emiral authority in Trarza. This is as clear a melding of the cultural and political, reflecting a particular historical moment as one could imagine (Webb, *Desert Frontier,* 40 n. 56).

The gum trade also began in the early 1600s at Arguin but only became significant during the latter part of the century. Although it does not feature prominently as part of an analysis focusing on the period 1550–1624, it added an important element to that frontier between the Atlantic and Saharan worlds by the eighteenth century (see Barry, *Senegambia,* 68, and Webb, *Desert Frontier,* "The Trade in Gum Arabic," 97–131, for further discussion of the nature of that role).

51. Governor of Fort Saint Joseph cited in McDougall, "The Question of Tegaza," in *Le Maroc et l'Afrique subsaharienne,* 270 n. 75. I take issue here with Barry's conclusion (reiterated in the introduction to his section on the eighteenth century) that "from this time on, Senegambia became the natural outlet from most of western Sudan toward the Atlantic. This redirection of trade routes toward the sea signaled the final victory of the caravel over the caravan. It also marked the definitive decline of the trans-Saharan trade" (*Senegambia,* 57).

52. Michel Abitbol eloquently explained one of the region's driving dynamics when he concluded that "Islam and commerce became in the eyes of the eighteenth-century sultans, the best 'tools' for penetrating [the Mauritanian Sahara and Sahel], as effective as they were peaceful in nature" ("Le maroc et le commerce transsaharien du XVIIe

Sahara this was to be were not yet over. In a letter believed to have been written between 1760 and 1790 from a Kunta shaykh (Sidi al-Mukhtar al-Kabir) to the Moroccan sultan, the shaykh alludes to earlier letters sent by the Sultan to his Moroccan representative at the salt mine of Tegaza.[53] They had apparently instructed the representative to collect taxes from everyone extracting Tegaza's salt. "Everyone" included the Kunta. The shaykh objected, first, because his respected zawiya family should not be required to submit to the authority of a mere *qaid* (that is, a layperson, uneducated and "without value")—in this case, a direct challenge to the religious legitimacy of the Moroccan ruler; and second, because the sultan had no right to charge fellow Muslims for accessing salt. According to ancient traditions, the shaykh claimed, "water, fire, pasture *and salt* should be free to all." Both aspects of the complaint drew on religious authority and juxtaposed it to secular power, the inference being, of course, that the former should hold sway in this instance. At stake were wealth and status: whose was to characterize the Saharan world? A final glimpse of these dynamics, generated by a local tradition often relegated to myth, offers yet another insight into how they were operating in the mid-eighteenth century. It is said that, in 1766–1767, a Kunta shepherd from Wadan was led by a giant lizard to the Ijil saline; it then disappeared into the middle of the *sebkha,* and salt was discovered. Some versions of this tale continue by saying that the Kunta kept this a secret for a long time because the mine lay close to wells dug by another tribe from southern Morocco, and therefore, by Islamic law, belonged to them. Eventually, the Kunta chief bought the wells, thereby gaining the right to exploit the surrounding lands and the resources lying beneath them (another reference to religious law). When the previous owners discovered this deceit, they appealed to the local emir to annul the purchase. The Kunta took the case to the sultan of Morocco, who in turn issued a certificate that the deal had been made in good faith and that the Kunta were indeed the new proprietors of Ijil. Apart from casting some doubt on interpretations that might have had the Moroccan sultan controlling the mine from the sixteenth century, this account affirms the complexity of power as it was exercised and understood in the eighteenth-century Sahara. The intersection of politics, economics, and religion in this world was still one of

siècle au debut du XIXème siècle," *Revue de l'occident musulman et de la méditerranée,* XXX (1980), 5–19, esp. 9.

53. A partial copy of this letter was obtained in Nouakchott, Mauritania, and made available to me by Mohamed Lahbib Nouhi.

uncertainty—but it was clearly not a world subsumed into the Atlantic hinterland. Not unlike the dynamics unfolding in the rapidly evolving Atlantic world, even a century after the mid-sixteenth– early-seventeenth-century era, the long-term consequences of early Atlantic-Saharan interactions were far from clear, far from inevitable.[54]

54. D. Brosset, "La saline d'Idjil," *Bulletin du comité de l'Afrique français, renseignements coloniaux,* XLIII (1933), 259–265 (for the legend, see 259–260); Lt. Berges, "Salines: Etude sur la Sebkha d'Idjil," unpublished paper, Département de Géologie et des Minières, Nouakchott, Mauritania, n.d. For a discussion of the legend and its various versions, see E. Ann McDougall, "Snapshots from the Sahara: 'Salt,' the Essence of Being," in David Mattingly et al., eds., *The Libyan Desert: Natural Resources and Cultural Heritage,* Society for Libyan Studies, monograph no. 6 (London, 2006), 295–303. See also footnote 36, above.

David Northrup

THE GULF OF GUINEA AND
THE ATLANTIC WORLD

In August 1553, Captain Thomas Windham set sail from Portsmouth for the Gulf of Guinea, the middle section of the Atlantic coast of sub-Saharan Africa, below the western bulge the Portuguese called Upper Guinea and above the coast of what they called Angola (West Central Africa). This pioneering English trading expedition had been carefully organized to gain a share of the trade established by Portuguese mariners during the previous century, and its two "goodly ships" were laden with bolts of woolen and linen cloth, iron bars, brassware, and other small items. Windham called first at the Gold Coast on the western shores of the Gulf of Guinea, where he was successful in exchanging some of his cargo for 2,400 ounces of gold, despite having to stay clear of the main trading sites that the Portuguese had established and fortified. Unsatisfied with this cargo of gold, however, the captain had forced his Portuguese guide to conduct them five hundred miles eastward in search of other goods from the kingdom of Benin in the western Niger Delta.

When palace officials in Benin learned of the arrival of Windham's ships, they dispatched messengers to the port town, who escorted the English merchants and their Portuguese guide to the capital, also known as Benin. In an audience chamber off one of the many courtyards of his sprawling palace, the *oba* (ruler) welcomed the visitors. Addressing them in Portuguese, a language he had learned from missionaries as a child, the oba asked their purpose in coming to his kingdom. When the English explained their interest in purchasing a large quantity of Benin's pungent pepper, which the Portuguese had been sending to Europe for several decades, the oba arranged for the visitors to inspect some sacks of peppercorns stored in a nearby warehouse. In short order, eighty casks of pepper were loaded aboard the English ships anchored offshore.

The oba's eagerness to open trade with a new European country was evident not just in these actions but as well in his offer to sell some pepper on credit, repayable on the next voyage, should the English lack sufficient trade goods. Yet in his hospitality toward the English, the oba was not neglectful of what he would receive in return, for the English account says he instructed his commercial agents to assess the quality of the goods the English had brought. Negotiations were successfully completed for the English to purchase a large quantity of pepper, but the commercial success of the expedition came at a high cost. Windham and 100 of the 140 men on the ships perished of tropical diseases while at Benin or after the precipitous departure in a single ship. The health risks of the Niger Delta led the English to center their early West African trade on the healthier Gold Coast and even more in Senegambia.[1]

The details of Windham's voyage should make it clear that Africans were able to deal with Europeans from positions of strength and understanding in the mid-sixteenth century and needed no persuasion to enlarge their Atlantic trade. The reasons for African interest and for their trading skills are not hard to find. Whereas, for the English, 1553 marked the beginning of a risky new trading venture in tropical Africa, for the Africans of the Gulf of Guinea, it marked the opening of a third period in their commercial exchanges with distant lands. African encounters with the English between the mid-sixteenth and mid-seventeenth centuries—and with the Dutch and French, who soon joined them—were built upon several decades of Atlantic exchanges with the Portuguese. Before that, there had been several centuries of commercial and cultural interactions among the peoples in the hinterland of the Gulf of Guinea and between them and the other regions of Africa extending all the way to the Mediterranean. A review of the two prior phases will enable one to see the period after 1550 in its African historical context.

Trade before the Opening of the Atlantic

Long-distance trade in West Africa has a long history. Even if some of the history cannot be fully documented, exchanges of local surpluses between different ecological zones and of unevenly distributed minerals must have existed for a considerable time. A startling archaeological discovery provides a convenient point from which to begin the analysis of the centuries before the opening of the Atlantic. From two sites excavated in 1959 in the

---

1. Richard Eden's memoir of Thomas Windham's voyage to Guinea and Benin, in John William Blake, ed. and trans., *Europeans in West Africa, 1450–1560* (London, 1942), 314–320. For a broader treatment of the English at Benin, see A. F. C. Ryder, *Benin and the Europeans, 1485–1897* (London, 1969), 76–84.

village of Igbo-Ukwu, due east of Benin City on the other side of the Niger River, came dramatic evidence of concentrated wealth and long-distance trade that dated to the ninth century. More than seven hundred metal objects survived a millennium of concealment in the earth. Iron objects had been degraded by their long burial, but a number of well-preserved, large objects in bronze provide evidence of great artistic skill and technical casting ability as well as a wide network of trade. Analysis of the mixture of metals in the castings conclusively linked them to sites in the Benue River valley 200 miles to the northeast. The subsequent development of the artistic and technological skills evident at Igbo-Ukwu can be traced through other copper-based castings from Benin and from Ife and other Yoruba sites northwest of Benin that are now displayed in museums throughout the world. These objects also confirm an even broader range of trade, since the copper alloys used in them have a distinctively different composition from those at Igbo-Ukwu. The most likely sources for these ores are in the Sahara. It has also been argued that some of the 165,000 beads in various materials recovered from Igbo-Ukwu were made in India and the Mediterranean.[2]

Other details of trading activities before the opening of the Atlantic can be inferred from descriptions by early Portuguese visitors. The ready market that the Portuguese found on the Gold Coast for cloth, beads, slaves, and other items from Benin and adjacent areas strongly suggests that such a trade had been conducted before the arrival of the first Europeans, through the intercoastal lagoons and creeks that connect these two distant locations. In addition, early Portuguese accounts appear to confirm that trade goods were already moving up and down the lower Niger River in giant canoes through networks of regularly spaced markets. Some form of this trading system must have existed as far back as the time of Igbo-Ukwu.[3]

No speculative guesses are necessary when it comes to explaining the antiquity of gold trade from West Africa. Both Muslim and European sources attest to the prominence of gold in the trade across the Sahara and to its importance in the rise of the giant and wealthy medieval African states of the western Sudan. At least from 1415, the Portuguese were well aware that the

2. Thurstan Shaw, *Igbo-Ukwu: An Account of Archaeological Discoveries in Eastern Nigeria* (London, 1970); Peter Garlake, *Early Art and Architecture of Africa,* Oxford History of Art (London, 2002), 117–139.

3. David Northrup, *Trade without Rulers: Pre-colonial Economic Development in South-eastern Nigeria* (Oxford, 1978), 22–29.

sources of the gold lay below the Sahara, and getting access to it was a major reason their ships sailed south along the Atlantic coast of Africa. The gold fields in the hinterland of the Gold Coast became part of this trading system from about 1000. The rapid growth of the gold exports from the Gold Coast via the Atlantic after 1480 (examined below) shows the existence of surplus production that could be diverted to new markets.[4] Another piece of evidence for the importance of trade to the north comes from the transformation of the name of the Portuguese main outpost on the Gold Coast. The Portuguese named the coastal fort they erected in 1482 São Jorge da Mina, which was commonly shortened to Mina in early documents. However, by the seventeenth century, European accounts were identifying it as Elmina, not, it would seem, as the result of some corruption of a Romance language, but because to local Africans, *mina* (the mine) sounded like the Arabic *el mina* (the port). The influence of Arabic this far south confirms the strength of the trading connections to the north.

Finally, the existence of regional currencies demonstrates that the trade of coastal West Africa before the opening of the Atlantic was not confined to limited luxury goods but permeated general activities. A trading currency based on the shell of the cowrie, a tropical marine gastropod found in the Indian Ocean, became established in the western Sudan through the trans-Saharan trade at least by the eleventh century and gradually spread southward. The evidence is too slender to confirm that the shell currency at Benin was based on Indian Ocean cowries instead of an Atlantic shell, as was the case at the Kingdom of Kongo farther south along the coast, but the former possibility is consistent with the fact that the demand for cowrie shells at Benin was so great that, by about 1540, the kingdom was importing vast quantities of them from the Portuguese, whose ships carried them from the Indian Ocean as ballast. In parts of West Africa, cowries and gold functioned as dual currencies with fixed rates of exchange. Gold Coast Africans calculated values using standardized weights of gold, the earliest of which were based on weights used in the distant trading cities of Jenne and Timbuktu in the western Sudan.[5]

4. This evidence is summarized by E.W. Bovill, *The Golden Trade of the Moors*, 2d ed. (London, 1968), 79-119.

5. Marion Johnson, "The Cowrie Currencies of West Africa," *Journal of African History*, XI (1970), 17-49; Ray A. Kea, *Settlements, Trade, and Politics in the Seventeenth-Century Gold Coast* (Baltimore, 1982), 186-193; Ryder, *Benin*, 60-61.

The arrival of the Portuguese opened a new link in this commercial chain. It seems instructive that the three West African coasts that attracted the greatest amount of European trade before 1650—Senegambia, the Gold Coast, and the Niger Delta—were locales that already had strong long-distance trading connections to the interior. Africans in these coastal areas were most prepared to respond to new trading connections, and such African responses shaped the patterns of trade at least as much as did the activities of the Europeans. It may also be instructive (though beyond the scope of this essay) that West Central Africa, where trade grew fastest and became the most disruptive, had no such long-distance connections.[6]

For Africans along the Gulf of Guinea, the Atlantic brought a number of advantages they were eager to exploit—and a minimum of risks. Although the goods that came via the Atlantic were not essentially different from what they already possessed, these new sources were potentially cheaper, since they avoided the heavy carriage costs and many middlemen of the overland trade. Ships were also capable of providing more abundant quantities of sought-after items, whether rare and precious or commonplace. The Portuguese records make it plain that, once Africans recovered from the alien appearance of their unexpected visitors from the sea, they quickly moved to encourage European contacts and to keep the visitors under control.

The Portuguese request to establish their first official trading post on the Gold Coast in 1482 provides a clear example of this dual strategy. As the Portuguese account relates, the local ruler showed a strong appreciation of the advantages of making his territory the site of a fixed trading post and a realistically low assessment of the dangers that might result from this new connection. The local delegation processed to the place of negotiations dressed in their best attire and accompanied by music. In response to the Portuguese spokesman's request for permission to erect a trading structure near the coast, the chief (whose name, the Portuguese recorded, was Caramansa) welcomed them, noting how superior these well-dressed official delegates appeared compared to the few scruffy Portuguese freebooters who had preceded them. Caramansa archly suggested that any attempts at high-handed dealings would be incompatible with the aristocratic status of such men as these, but he went on to warn that, should they or future Portuguese be tempted to try any improper tactics, he had only to withdraw a

6. For some discussion, see David Northrup, *Africa's Discovery of Europe, 1450–1850* (New York, 2002), 53–54.

short distance to deprive them of access to the gold they sought. Trouble emerged almost immediately when Portuguese workmen began clearing the site before Caramansa had received the rich present he required for allowing a foreign presence on his soil. The leaders of the expedition moved quickly to provide him with Moroccan cloths, brass basins and bracelets *(manillas)*, and other cloths, and they were careful to compensate local Africans for any damage they did to existing dwellings.[7]

In short order, São Jorge da Mina became the Portuguese headquarters on the Gold Coast, but Europeans continued to receive sharp reminders when they neglected to respect their hosts. In 1570, in retaliation for a Portuguese attack, an alliance of two African communities captured and killed over three hundred Portuguese at Mina, decorating the grave of an African king with the skulls of fifty of them. Eight years later, another Gold Coast community avenged Portuguese violence by seizing the Portuguese outpost at Accra, razing it to the ground, and killing its inhabitants.

Africans had reason to be as mindful of restoring good relations as they were in defending against European aggression. A Dutch account by Pieter de Marees relates that, after a group of Dutchmen on another part of the Gold Coast in 1598 had disregarded African warnings not to cut branches in a sacred grove, a group of villagers chased the Dutch away by force and killed and beheaded one of them. The next day, inhabitants of the village brought the man who had done the beheading to the Dutch and decapitated him in recompense. "From this one can see," de Marees observes, "how eager they were to maintain their friendship with the Dutch."[8]

The kingdom of Benin had responded to the first official Portuguese contacts in 1486 in a welcoming way and with a degree of sophistication befitting so powerful a kingdom. After listening to the request for trade, the oba dispatched the head of his port town to Lisbon, where, Portuguese accounts say, the ambassador made a very favorable impression:

> This ambassador was a man of good speech and natural wisdom. Great feasts were held in his honour, and he was shown many of the good things of these kingdoms. He returned to his land in a ship of the king's, who at his departure made him a gift of rich clothes for himself and his wife;

7. Ruy de Pina's chronicle of King João II, in Blake, ed. and trans., *Europeans in West Africa,* 70–78.

8. Pieter de Marees, *Description and Historical Account of the Gold Kingdom of Guinea (1602),* ed. and trans. Albert van Dantzig and Adam Jones (Oxford, 1987), 44–97, quotation on 83.

and through him he also sent a rich present to the king of such things as he understood he would greatly prize.[9]

There is no record of exactly what the ambassador reported upon his return to Benin, but his impressions of Portugal were clearly positive enough for Benin officials to engage in significant trade with Portugal, while taking great care to turn this new relationship to their advantage. In a custom that became widespread along the Gulf of Guinea, visiting ships had to make rich gifts to the ruler and other officials to "open" the markets. In 1522, for example, officers of the Portuguese vessel *São Miguel* presented the oba with 20 ounces of coral, 4 Indian caps, and 10.5 yards of red satin. By that date, three other Benin officials had been assigned to handle the Atlantic trade, and each of them also received a customary gift consisting of 20 yards of cloth. The kingdom additionally collected tribute from neighboring African states that wished to remain on good terms with their powerful neighbor. In the total context of Benin's commercial activities, the Portuguese trade was modest in importance, but it provided useful and attractive items.[10]

By 1550, the Gulf of Guinea's connection to the Portuguese was past its peak, as the Portuguese focused their attention on the expanding trades of Angola and the Indian Ocean. The fading of the once-flourishing Portuguese trades made West Africans eager to open new relations with the other European nations that were beginning to penetrate the Portuguese monopoly. As illustrated earlier by the account of the oba of Benin's reception of English merchants in 1553, the experience Africans had gained in dealing with the Portuguese made them well prepared to do so from positions of understanding and strength.

For their part, the new northern European visitors had much to learn about their African trading partners. Although ethnocentrism inevitably colored their understanding, their accounts of what they saw do not display the racial bias that would distort accounts from centuries later. Unlike the piratical approach John Hawkins would adopt in Upper Guinea, these practical men were concerned to establish trading relations that were profitable and long-term.

A revealing example of this strategy and the reasons for it comes from a member of a prominent London merchant family, John Lok, who led a trading expedition to the Gold Coast in 1554. In his account of the expe-

9. Ruy de Pina's chronicle of King João II, in Blake, ed. and trans., *Europeans in West Africa*, 78–79.

10. Ryder, *Benin*, 32–75, 164–168, 295–306.

dition, written for the benefit of others in England, he stressed the wealth of Gold Coast Africans, who adorned themselves with ivory and gold. He also noted that they were very skilled traders, a point that the Dutch commented on in detail a half-century later. De Marees emphasized that African traders were adept in detecting any attempt to defraud them and noted how particular they were in their preferences for goods brought from Europe: "When we have brought them things they did not like, they have mocked us in a scandalous way." Lok returned to England from a second voyage to the Gold Coast with five African men whom he set to learning English so that they might serve future English merchants as interpreters. At least three of these men later became brokers and intermediaries in the trade on the Gold Coast, roles that Africans would dominate for the next three centuries.[11]

However, the English lacked the resources to establish an important trading settlement on the Gold Coast until the 1630s, by which time they had been surpassed by the Dutch. Having initially failed to capture the Portuguese castle at Mina, the Dutch set up their first permanent Gold Coast settlement, Fort Nassau, in 1612. Whether through better connections or as a result of other circumstances, the annual exports of gold expanded in 1618 to three times what they had been in the later sixteenth century. In 1637, they seized Elmina for good.[12]

Relations at Benin followed a similar pattern, though Europeans there were even more subordinate since the powerful kingdom did not permit them to erect any outposts on its territory. For their part, Europeans were impressed with Benin not just because of the commercial possibilities of the kingdom's pepper *(Piper guineense)*, its cotton textiles, and its ivory, but also because of its striking capital city, its large palace complex, and its artisans' great skill. Many sixteenth- and seventeenth-century visitors commented extensively on Benin's capital city, which was surrounded by a massive earthen wall five or six miles in circumference and pierced at intervals by large gates fashioned from the trunk of a single tree. From the gates, broad streets ran in straight lines across the city, intersecting at right angles. Dutch accounts deemed the thirty main streets to be as wide as the great avenues of Amsterdam. Within the city, the houses of ordinary citizens had

11. Richard Eden's account of John Lok's voyage to Mina, 1554-1555, in Blake, ed. and trans., *Europeans in West Africa*, 326-346; Peter Fryer, *Staying Power: The History of Black People in Britain* (London, 1984), 5-7; de Marees, *Description*, 54; P. E. H. Hair and Robin Law, "The English in Western Africa to 1700," in Nicholas P. Canny, ed., *Oxford History of the British Empire*, I, *The Origins of Empire: British Overseas Enterprise to the Close of the Seventeenth Century* (Oxford, 1998), 250-255.

12. Kea, *Settlements*, 192-194.

earthen walls and thatched roofs, which European observers considered airy and very pleasant. Their walls and floors were polished "as smooth and even as any plastered wall in Holland and as shining as a looking-glass."[13]

The city's notables lived within the palace complex, which was a veritable city in itself, said by the Dutch to be easily as big as the town of Haarlem. A German account of 1603 estimated the palace precincts were as large as the entire city of Tübingen and compared the size and ceremony of the oba's annual public procession on horseback through the city to a papal appearance in Rome in a jubilee year. The palace complex was enclosed by a second set of earthen walls. Between the many structures inside ran "beautiful long galleries about as big as the Exchange at Amsterdam." The pillars of the galleries were covered with bronze castings of scenes from the kingdom's history. A Spanish account judged the representations of men, animals, and birds on the brass plaques to be as finely worked as if they had been made with an engraving tool by a Spanish silversmith. Today, examples of these plaques, removed during the British expedition of 1897, are prized collections of the Metropolitan Museum, the British Museum, and other collections.[14]

In addition to their praise of Benin's city planning, architecture, and bronze casting, European visitors commented favorably on the quality of Benin's cotton textiles (blue or blue with white stripes), stone beads, woven baskets and mats, as well as pottery. A late-sixteenth-century English account lauded the skill of Benin's ivory carvers, who made spoons adorned with depictions of fowl and wild animals. In addition, the kingdom's armorers made swords, spears, arrowheads, shields, and bows. Some Europeans brought examples of these objects back home as curiosities, along with souvenirs of Benin's musical instruments (horns, drums, and flutes). Nor were the skills of Benin's farmers confined to the cotton they grew for the local textile industry and the peppercorns they grew for export. Benin's farmers also raised yams, oranges, plantains and bananas (which, an English account explained, resembled cucumbers), along with hot peppers, palm oil, and palm wine.[15]

13. Newly translated from the Dutch account of Olfert Dapper (1668) in Thomas Hodgkin, ed., *Nigerian Perspectives: An Historical Anthology,* 2d ed. (Oxford, 1975), 159–161.

14. Andreas Josua Ultzheimer, translated in Basil Davidson, *African Civilization Revisited: From Antiquity to Modern Times* (Trenton, N.J., 1991), 235–236; Alonso de Sandoval, *De instauranda Aethiopum salute: El mundo de la esclavitud negra en América* (Bogotá, 1956), 78–79, a reissue of Sandoval's 1627 work.

15. James Welch, "A Voyage to Benin beyond the Countrey of Guinea . . . in the

The tone of these European accounts is reminiscent of the awestruck accounts early European visitors wrote of the empires and cities of Asia. To be sure, the earthen walls of the palace complex in Benin were worlds apart from the precincts of the Forbidden City of Beijing. However, in many ways, Benin was perceived as closer to that world than to the Native American nations of the Chesapeake and New England.

Nevertheless, the size of Benin's capital, its palace complex, and its elaborate bureaucratic governance were unique in coastal West Africa. Elsewhere along the Gulf of Guinea, centralized political institutions were hard to find until well after 1650. So it is all the more remarkable that the small communities on the Gold Coast and east of Benin, which were often little more than clusters of a few neighboring villages, were also so successful in dealing with Atlantic traders. As has been seen, minor rulers on the Gold Coast proved adept at supplying gold for export, driving hard bargains, and defending their rights against Europeans. Two factors worked to the advantage of these small polities. First, although there is little direct evidence of the particulars of their political and social structures, it is clear that even small-scale societies possessed sufficient internal organization to put forward a united front and maintain reasonable order in commercial relations. Second, their political fragmentation was balanced by the widespread trading networks and the professional traders who plied them. It is notable that, despite their intense interest in gaining direct access to the gold exported from the Gold Coast, the Portuguese and northern Europeans were absolutely unable to penetrate inland or even to learn with any degree of accuracy how far the gold deposits were from the coast.

The small-scale societies, rather than centralized monarchies, were also characteristic of other parts of the Gulf. The coast between the Gold Coast and Benin attracted only a few European visitors before 1600, but thereafter, the local ports began to rise in importance and eventually became known as the Slave Coast. To the east of Benin, along the Bight of Biafra, political and social organization were similarly fragmented, but it, too, proved capable of considerable involvement in the Atlantic trade after 1650. Any penetration inland by Europeans was effectively blocked until after 1800.

Although contemporary European accounts are quite clear on the bal-

Yeere 1588," in Richard Hakluyt, ed., *The Principal Navigations, Voyages, Traffiques, and Discoveries of the English Nation* . . . , 8 vols. (London, 1927), IV, 295–297; D. R., "A Description and Historical Declaration of the Golden Kingdom of Guinea . . . ," in Samuel Purchas, comp., *Purchas His Pilgrimage* . . . , 4th ed. (London, 1626), 716.

ance of mutual interests that existed, it is necessary to emphasize this point because older historiographies continue to influence popular understanding of these relations. After the rise of European imperial power in the nineteenth century, it became common to rewrite the histories of earlier interactions in Africa in terms of heroic and all-powerful Europeans and weak and inept Africans. This tradition survives in a curious way. Much as Marx wrote that he had found Hegel standing on his head and turned him right side up, neo-Marxist champions of Africa turned the pro-imperial argument upside down: Africans became more central to the story but primarily as victims subordinate to all-powerful Europeans, who were now villains rather than heroes. No work did more to spread this revisionist message than *How Europe Underdeveloped Africa,* published in 1972 by the Afro-Guyanese scholar Walter Rodney and still widely read. This angry and tendentious work projected the unhappy situation of colonial and postcolonial Africa backward through the centuries. The earlier the era being discussed, the more distortion his simple message of inequality seemed to introduce.

Fortunately, modern historians of Africa and the Atlantic have moved back to reading the influence of Africa in a more balanced matter. Much of this work has focused on the era after 1650, when slaves dominated Africa's exports, a factor that creates its own problems. A few brave souls have tackled the earlier period, notably Basil Davidson in his pioneering first edition of *The African Slave Trade* (1961) and, more recently, John Thornton in *Africa and Africans in the Making of the Atlantic World, 1400–1680* (1992). These works effectively challenged readers to contemplate an Atlantic world in which Africans and Europeans had different strengths but worked out mutually satisfactory relationships that endured for centuries until interrupted by the New Imperialism of the late nineteenth century.[16]

Africa's Imports and Exports

Although older accounts of Africa's involvement in Atlantic trade tended to concentrate on what Africans exported, modern historians of Africa have found that goods they chose to import provide even more insight into their engagement with the Atlantic. For the most part, as Thornton has argued, the imports were nothing new, consisting of the kinds of goods that Africans

16. Davidson's book first appeared in Britain under the title *Black Mother;* a revised edition appeared from Atlantic Monthly Press in 1980. Thornton subsequently published a second edition (1998) with Cambridge University Press that included a new chapter taking parts of the story as far as 1800.

were already producing themselves—textiles, metals, and items of personal adornment. However, two things made the imports particularly desirable: they included novel designs and materials and they were attractively priced.

One his first voyage to West Africa in 1555, William Townsend noted that the more important men at the western end of the Gold Coast wore locally made cloth wrapped around their middles and locally made cloth caps, whereas some of their servants wore smaller waist cloths and simpler caps. He indicated that their ropes and fishing lines were made from the backs of trees and that they possessed very finely made iron hooks, fish-hooks, "darts," and much larger double-sided "daggers" with finely curved edges. A half-century later, de Marees also noted that Gold Coast Africans were "very clever at making weapons" as well as skilled using them, a point he illustrated by recounting their military success against the Portuguese.[17]

After some hard bargaining, Townsend's African partners agreed to ex-change some of their gold for English cloth, brass basins, and other small items. Two-thirds of the items Gold Coast Africans bought from the Dutch between 1593 and 1607 were also textiles. That Gold Coast Africans im-ported textiles in such quantities from the Atlantic (both European-made and made elsewhere in Africa) clearly did not reflect their inability to pro-duce such goods themselves. Two other factors point to the logic of this de-mand. First, the demand for cloth was highly elastic, especially when the price was attractive. Second, European cloths were novelties; their wool, linen, and silk fibers were not those used by West African weavers, and most of the forty different designs, colors, and textures that the Dutch fur-nished were particularly novel. Sometimes novelty commanded a premium price, as in the case of luxurious textiles and clothing intended for the elite, but most of the cloths were intended for a broader market where they had to compete with African-made textiles for attention and price.

After textiles, metals and metalware had the next largest share of the trade goods brought by the Dutch. Although this category included basins, buckets, pots, and pans made of copper or tin that were high-priced counter-parts to African vessels made of pottery, wood, or gourds, most of the metal goods were also aimed at a broader market. Some were fabricated tools and weapons (axes, hatchets, spades, knives) of familiar and unfamiliar designs, but it is notable that iron bars constituted the greatest share of metal im-ports.[18] Iron smelting was widespread in sub-Saharan Africa and had been around since remote antiquity, so the high demand for iron bars (and cop-

17. De Marees, *Description,* 92.
18. Kea, *Settlements,* 207–209.

per rods in some places) strongly suggests that these imports were desired to supplement an inadequate supply and that the cost of European-made metals was part of the attraction. Skilled African blacksmiths found new employment in turning the iron into familiar goods.

The Atlantic traders also brought a number of goods that were innovations in the West African market. American tobacco, introduced by the Portuguese, found a ready market on the Gold Coast by the mid-1600s. A German observer reported both men and women were great smokers and carried tobacco in little bags around their necks "as if it were a precious jewel." The Portuguese also supplied small quantities of firearms, and African pressures on Dutch traders led them to sell muskets to some Gold Coast communities in sufficient quantities in the early seventeenth century that, with some training by Dutch and Portuguese instructors, some Africans became adept in their use. However, the Dutch suspended these firearm sales until 1660, so such weapons had little impact until the 1700s.[19] By the mid-seventeenth century, some Africans on the Gold Coast, both men and women, had acquired a taste for another novelty, distilled spirits in the form of French brandy, although neither Dutch gin nor English gin was yet found desirable. All of these products would greatly expand in volume in the centuries after 1650, but none was yet a significant import.

There is little reason to think that the growth of Atlantic imports diminished existing African production of cloth or metals. As later European accounts attest, West Africans continued to produce their own textiles and metalware for several centuries while supplementing them with additional supplies and novel designs from abroad. In the seventeenth century, for example, Benin continued to weave its own cotton textiles and to export this highly prized cloth via the Dutch, who resold them on the Gold Coast, where the Portuguese had found a ready market for Benin cloth in the previous century. Between 1644 and 1646, the Dutch purchased at least sixteen thousand Benin cloths, and a single English vessel is known to have loaded some four thousand pieces of the prized cloth. It is not clear whether the extensive transshipments of locally made beads from Benin to the Gold Coast also continued past the early Portuguese period.[20]

19. Otto Friedrich von der Groeben, translated in Adam Jones, *Brandenburg Sources for West African History, 1680–1700* (Stuttgart, 1985), 25; R. A. Kea, "Firearms and Warfare on the Gold and Slave Coasts from the Sixteenth to the Nineteenth Centuries," *Journal of African History*, XII (1971), 185–213; Kea, *Settlements,* 154–163.

20. Duarte Pacheco Pereira, *Esmeraldo de situ orbis: Côte occidentale d'Afrique du sud marocain au Gabon,* ed. and trans. Raymond Mauny (Bissau, 1956), 134, 138, 146; Ryder, *Benin,* 93–95; Kea, *Settlements,* 216, 234.

It also seems that the Atlantic trade of this period produced only incremental alterations in established African trading relations. The significant quantities of gold exported the first two centuries of the Atlantic trade obviously represented a new outlet for local miners and merchants, one that brought in attractive new trade goods. Because shipping costs via the ocean would have been much lower than those occasioned by the sending of gold northward and the receiving of similar trade goods overland from the Mediterranean, the terms of the new Atlantic trade were probably very attractive to Gold Coast Africans. However, if the opening of Atlantic trade provided new outlets for gold, there is no evidence that it seriously diminished older overland trading networks in this period. Rather, the Atlantic became an additional link in the already existing chain of relationships.

As the actions of the oba of Benin in 1553 vividly illustrate, Africans on the Gulf of Guinea were eager sellers in that trade and had numerous commodities to offer. The next English expedition to Benin, in 1588, brought home pepper, ivory, palm oil, cotton cloth, and bark cloth. Pepper remained Benin's principal export to the English (and to the Dutch, who displaced them in the 1590s), along with some ivory and, as already seen, considerable quantities of cottons and akori beads intended for resale on the Gold Coast. As Asian supplies of pepper became more abundant by the 1630s, the Dutch purchased less from Benin, but strong demand for the kingdom's cotton cloth and beads on the Gold Coast made up the difference.[21]

Benin's exports were very largely produced locally and were under close direction of the state, but the gold exported from the Gold Coast, the most valuable export of this period from the entire Gulf of Guinea, was imported from some distance inland and thus passed through a number of hands on its way to the many outlets on the Atlantic. Between 1601 and 1636, the Gold Coast exported an average of 32,000 ounces of gold a year into the Atlantic. At century's end, it was considerably higher. Another valuable export was ivory (about 160,000 pounds a year in 1601–1636). Although records for this period are fragmentary, inanimate goods constituted about 95 percent of the value of exports from the Gulf of Guinea and Upper Guinea in 1623–1632, the rest being made up of slaves.[22]

21. Ryder, *Benin,* 76–98.

22. Calculated from Ernst van den Boogaart, "The Trade between Western Africa and the Atlantic World, 1600–1690: Estimates of Trends in Composition and Value," *Journal of African History,* XXXIII (1992), 372–377. See also David Eltis, "The Relative Importance of Slaves and Commodities in the Atlantic Trade of Seventeenth-Century Africa," *Journal of African History,* XXXV (1994), 237–249. Boogaart estimated that slaves represented 27 percent of the value of Atlantic Africa's exports in

TABLE I. *Estimated Volume of the Atlantic Slave Trade, 1500–1700 (in thousands)*

	Upper Guinea	Gulf of Guinea	West Central Africa	Total
1500–1600	45.0	53.3	284.4	382.7
1601–1650	6.4	33.1	461.9	501.4
1651–1675	18.5	115.9	104.3	238.7
1676–1700	40.7	325.3	132.6	498.6

Note: Allocation by coast of origin of the slave trade to Europe and Atlantic islands in 1522–1600 follows Eltis's allocation of the transatlantic slave trade for 1519–1600. The table combines Senegambia and Sierra Leone (as Upper Guinea) and excludes the slave trade from Mauritania and from Southeast Africa.

Source: David Eltis, "The Volume and Structure of the Transatlantic Slave Trade: A Reassessment," *William and Mary Quarterly,* 3d Ser., LIII (2001), 44, table 2; Ivana Elbl, "The Volume of the Early Atlantic Slave Trade, 1450–1521," *Journal of African History,* XXXVIII (1997), 73, table 7; Paul E. Lovejoy, *Transformations in Slavery: A History of Slavery in Africa,* 2d ed. (Cambridge, 2000), table 2.3.

Despite the modest value of the export slave trade to West Africa in this period, there is an understandable temptation to focus one's attention on that trade, especially when looking at Africa's involvement in the Atlantic world from an American perspective. For this reason, it is useful to look more closely at slave exports. Although the proportions and sources of the transatlantic slave trade from Africa before 1650 cannot be tallied with the precision possible after that date, numerous modern studies enable one to demonstrate how unimportant slaves were in the trade of the Gulf of Guinea before the mid-seventeenth century. Table 1 shows the current estimates of the numbers of slaves who passed through the Atlantic to destinations in Europe, to European-controlled islands off the coast of Africa, and to the Americas. Because the roughness of the early data has led researchers to divide their estimates by time periods of unequal length, the scope of the trade is easier to comprehend when the total numbers are converted to annual averages in Table 2. The tables show that the involvement of West Africa in the Atlantic slave trade was modest in the century before 1650,

1623–1632 (measured against the value of the goods imported). But when one excludes the large slave trade from West Central Africa (92 percent of the Atlantic slave trade in 1601–1650, as expressed in Table 1), the share for the coasts north of the equator falls to 5 percent.

TABLE 2. *Estimated Volume of the Atlantic Slave Trade, 1500–1700 (average per annum)*

	Upper Guinea	Gulf of Guinea	West Central Africa	Total
1500–1600	450	533	2,844	3,827
1601–1650	128	662	9,238	10,028
1651–1675	740	4,636	4,172	9,548
1676–1700	1,628	13,012	5,304	19,944

Source: Table 1.

especially compared to West Central Africa, which supplied 86 percent of slave exports. Indeed, the average annual flow of slaves from Upper Guinea, the Gold Coast, and the kingdom of Benin and its neighbors in the western Niger Delta actually fell in the first half of the seventeenth century.

The slave trade from these coasts shrank for three reasons. First, the demand for slaves in Europe dried up. Second, the new English merchants were disinclined to buy slaves, at least until English colonies in the Americas created a new market at midcentury. As late as 1620, an English trader named Richard Jobson rejected a Gambian's offer of slaves with the assertion that English people "did not deale in any such commodities, neither did wee buy or sell one another, or any that had our owne shapes."[23] Third, for reasons that are unknown, the kingdom of Benin also cut back on its participation in the slave trade into the Atlantic for a time, establishing separate markets for female and for male slaves by 1516, raising prices, and then refusing to sell male slaves at all.

As Table 2 indicates, however, the average annual volume of the slave trade from the Gulf of Guinea in the third quarter of the seventeenth century would grow to seven times what it had been during the first half of the century. The average annual volume would nearly triple again during the last quarter. However, the greater importance of the Atlantic slave trade after 1650 is no reason to ignore the fact that the number of slaves leaving the Gulf of Guinea averaged only a few hundred per year from 1550 to 1624. Nor was this later expansion some sort of natural outcome of the modest slave trade of the previous century. Rather, the sharp increase of the Atlan-

23. Richard Jobson, *The Golden Trade; or, A Discovery of the River Gambra* . . . (1623; rpt. London, 1932), 120; Hair and Law, "English in Western Africa," in Canny, ed., *Oxford History of the British Empire,* I, 250–255.

tic slave trade in the mid-seventeenth century resulted from the marriage of new demands for labor in the Americas with rising African interest in the trade goods available from the Atlantic.

As David Eltis has argued, it was not foreordained that American colonial labor had to be African, nor was it initially. Indeed, if African labor was to be used, it would have been much more efficient to site the plantations in Africa, as the Portuguese had done when turning the island of São Tomé in the Bight of Biafra into the world's greatest sugar producer during the mid-sixteenth century. That logical outcome did not occur because Europeans were not strong enough to gain and maintain control over more lands in Africa. The depopulated West Indies were an easier target. As Eltis puts it, the plantation system created "in the Americas was what Europeans wanted to happen in Africa, but could not bring about" because Europeans did not have the power to move into West Africa. Two African elements were essential to this new phase of Atlantic trade: Africans were willing to trade in slaves, and the high price Europeans were willing to pay for African laborers translated into sufficient quantities of consumer goods that ended up not just in the coffers of West African rulers and merchants but also on the bodies and in the households of an expanding number of more ordinary people. As John Thornton concludes, the existence of a well-established African system for "the capture, purchase, transport, and sale of slaves was . . . as much responsible as any external force for the development of the Atlantic slave trade."[24]

Africans in the Americas

Even though the size of the Atlantic slave trade from the Gulf of Guinea coast would be far greater after 1650, by the early seventeenth century, slaves from the region had become important enough demographically, economically, and culturally in some parts of the Americas to merit examination. An unusually rich set of observations from this era sheds light both on the lives of those unfortunate victims of the Atlantic trade and on the internal trade, culture, and political organization of the area east of the Niger they came from.

The merger of the thrones of Portugal and Spain from 1580 to 1640 had enabled the growing demand for slaves in Spanish Peru to be met from the

24. David Eltis, *The Rise of African Slavery in the Americas* (Cambridge, 2000), 1–28, 137–192, quotation on 139; Northrup, *Africa's Discovery*, 77–106; John Thornton, *Africa and Africans in the Making of the Atlantic World, 1400–1800*, 2d ed. (Cambridge, 1998), 97.

slaving networks the Portuguese had pioneered in West and West Central Africa. A Jesuit missionary estimated that a dozen or more ships arrived each year in the port of Cartagena, each carrying several hundred slaves from Upper Guinea (Senegambia to Sierra Leone), Angola, or São Tomé. Some of the slaves from São Tomé came from adjacent parts of the Bight of Biafra. From Cartagena, most of the slaves were moved to the silver-mining enterprises in the western part of the viceroyalty of Peru. In the city of Lima alone, the African population grew from 4,000 in 1586 to some 20,000 in 1640.[25]

It goes without saying that these African immigrants strove to incorporate as much as they could of their social and cultural experiences in Africa and during the Middle Passage into the new cultural contexts of their lives in the Americas. What had they experienced in Africa? Here we should recall Thornton's point that political institutions in Atlantic Africa were generally small, diverse, and kinship based. But I am suspicious of his second thesis that these diverse peoples can be grouped "at most" into three culture zones—Upper Guinea, Lower Guinea (the Gulf of Guinea), and Angola—and that these three culture zones (and "only seven distinct subcultures" within them) were a primary underpinning of the cultural identities that came into existence in the Americas.[26]

The first problem is that the precise nature of cultural affinities in West Africa is not explicitly specified and is probably not specifiable, since there is no way to measure whether degrees of nonlinguistic cultural commonality were greater within these zones than across zonal lines during this period. Thornton seems aware of this problem and bases his argument very largely on linguistic affinities that are more measurable, but the facts do not appear to support his thesis. As elsewhere in the world, affinities that may be evident to modern linguists were not necessarily so apparent to individual speakers of these languages, especially when most people lived in relative isolation from communities at any distance from their homes.[27] Moreover,

25. Sandoval, *De instauranda,* 107; Herbert S. Klein, *African Slavery in Latin America and the Caribbean* (New York, 1986), 28–29, 32. See also James Lockhart, *Spanish Peru, 1532–1560: A Colonial Society* (Madison, Wis., 1968), 171–198.

26. Thornton, *Africa and Africans,* 183–192. The subcultures he identifies are linguistically based: Mande, the northern West Atlantic languages of Wolof and Fula, and the southern West Atlantic languages of Upper Guinea; the western (Akan) and eastern (Aja) clusters of the Kwa languages of Lower Guinea; and the Bantu languages of Angola. He asserts these subgroups were "often quite homogeneous" (192).

27. In a personal communication, linguist Victor Manfredi points out that specialists are still debating a number of West African language classifications.

Thornton's central assertion that linguistically related West African languages are today mutually intelligible is demonstrably untrue and appears based on a false analogy with more closely related languages in West Central Africa.[28]

Because there is little direct evidence from these decades that could be used to test hypotheses about cultural affinities, it is worth considering the cultural parameters of Gulf of Guinea societies in a broader comparative context. As a rule, even in stable societies, cultures change over time, and similar cultures may change in divergent ways unless constrained by countervailing forces. For this reason, it is dangerous to assume that geographical proximity and linguistic affinity can be used to define large culturally homogeneous zones. In parts of the world where such cultural zones do exist, they are usually the product of active promotion by imperial systems, centralized religious traditions, and/or by formal indoctrination usually associated with a canon of written texts. The classical Sinitic, Indic, or Greco-Roman "high cultures," or "great traditions," were associated with elite literacy, commerce, urbanization, and political centralization.

In the year 1000, for example, Europe was likely as diverse as West Africa in its spoken languages and folkways, but thereafter, a more powerful overlay of cultural unity came about as a result of the revival of intra-European trade and urban life, the spread of formal education and literacy (primarily in Latin), the revival of Roman legal and administrative traditions, the expansion of Latin Christianity, and the revival of Greco-Roman artistic and literary norms. Folk cultures persisted and political disunity was the norm, but the spread of this "great tradition" among the elite provided a significant degree of cultural commonality before the invention of nationalist identities in the nineteenth and twentieth centuries.[29]

The societies in the hinterland of the Gulf of Guinea interacted commercially but lacked the centralized political, religious, and educational institutions necessary to reinforce widespread cultural commonality. Other than Benin, there were no large states in the seventeenth century. Most Africans in the region shared a belief in a Supreme Being, but their creation myths focused on the origins of their ancestors (not humanity in general), and religious practice was similarly communal and focused on placating and ma-

28. This issue is discussed in detail in David Northrup, "Igbo and Myth Igbo: Culture and Ethnicity in the Atlantic World, 1600–1850," *Slavery and Abolition,* XXI (2000), 1–20.

29. See Patrick J. Geary, *The Myth of Nations: The Medieval Origins of Europe* (Princeton, N.J., 2002).

nipulating the spirits of departed ancestors and other capricious spirits that inhabited the community. Among the Yoruba, there existed some kingship traditions that had reached as far as Benin, but, inferring from later ethnographic evidence, religious practice in general seems to have been highly diverse. In the absence of widespread centralized political and religious traditions and without literacy and a classical tradition, it is extremely difficult to imagine what the cultural unity Thornton proposes could have been based on. Diversity was, of course, no weakness at this point in time, and people of the Gulf of Guinea showed far more openness to other cultures than seems to have been the case in parts of the world with established great traditions.

To the north, some elites in the western and central Sudan of West Africa had joined the Islamic "great tradition," adopting in varying degrees religious beliefs and practices, Islamic law and science, and the Arabic language and script. By 1550, the rulers of Bornu, Songhai, and some Hausa states had become Muslims, as had some commercial classes. However, such growth came slowly. In the sixteenth and seventeenth centuries, Islam was very largely an urban religion in the Sudan, much as Christianity had been in early medieval Europe.[30] With some exceptions (especially among pastoralists), the rural masses were untouched. Their religious practices were oral and thus malleable and intensely local. Although some Muslims might have reached the coast of the Gulf of Guinea, Islamic culture did not have any substantial influence there in this period.[31]

It is likely that some of the Africans from the eastern Niger Delta might have been exposed to elements of Christianity through the agency of Portuguese missionaries or the influence of enslaved Kongolese Christians they might have met on São Tomé and traveled with across the Atlantic. However, the fundamental point is that neither Islam nor Christianity was sufficiently influential in the Gulf of Guinea area to act as a unifying cultural force. Nor were other aspects of contact with Europeans, limited in any case to coastal peoples, of sufficient magnitude to create a pan-African culture.

These speculations about diversity and the weakness of any unifying great tradition in West Africa are useful to keep in mind when examining an unusually rich description of the linguistic, cultural, and commercial developments in this period. Southeast of the kingdom of Benin in the

30. "The Christian Church began as a city Church; it was only slowly and gradually that it moved out into the country" (Stephen Neill, *A History of Christian Missions,* Pelican History of the Church, VI, rev. ed. [Harmondsworth, 1986], 27).

31. Nehemia Levtzion, "Islam in the Bilad al-Sudan to 1800," in Levtzion and Randall L. Pouwels, eds., *History of Islam in Africa* (Athens, Ohio, 2000), 63–73.

eastern Niger Delta, the fishing community of Elem Kalabari by 1550 was becoming an important trading port that would be known in Europe and the Americas under variations of the name (New) Calabar. While working among slaves newly arrived in Cartagena for eighteen years, the Jesuit missionary Alonzo de Sandoval had collected remarkably precise information about the people he knew as Caravalies. Father Sandoval carefully distinguished two categories of Caravalies: the "native or pure" Caravalies from the port town and its immediate vicinity and *"caravalies particulares,"* who came from forty or fifty places farther inland. He recorded the name of eighteen of these inland locations, most of which can be identified with actual places and peoples within fifty or sixty miles of Elem Kalabari. Sandoval stated that the each of these inland communities had its own language, although most of the places one can identify would have spoken versions of the Ijo language of Elem Kalabari. Two names appear to refer Efik-speaking communities and one to Igbo speakers. To overcome their diversity of dialect and language, Sandoval noted, all the Caravalies used a Portuguese pidgin to communicate among themselves. He used a version of that same pidgin in his work among slaves arriving in Cartagena.[32]

Sandoval's remarkable evidence reveals much about the process of ethnogenesis under way among transported Africans in Peru at the beginning of the seventeenth century. The Calabar nation there was made up of diverse people, not a single community. The name that united them was not their own but that of the port from which they had been shipped. Little is known of what the enslaved Africans from Elem Kalabari's hinterland thought of their new grouping or what particular cultural traits they incorporated into it from their home communities. Because the "national" names and cultures that emerged in the New World were amalgams of the identities and communities that existed in Africa, it is important to appreciate how much they owed to the experiences of enslavement and transport overseas and to the circumstances of the Americas. In contrast to contemporary Europeans, who were content to sort Africans into a few rough and static regional boxes, modern historians should pay heed not just to the elements

32. Sandoval, *De instauranda,* 17, 94. P. E. H. Hair, "Ethnolinguistic Continuity on the Guinea Coast," *Journal of African History,* VIII (1967), 263, initially identified the communities Sandoval named. I have developed some of these arguments at greater length in "Igbo and Myth Igbo," *Slavery and Abolition,* XXI (2000). Mayra E. Beers, "Alonso de Sandoval: Seventeenth-Century Merchant of the Gospel," http://www .jayikaslakfoundation.org/prize/199702.html (accessed Dec. 22, 2003), provides a good account of the missionary's life and work.

of African cultures that survived the passage to the Americas but also to Africans' rich diversity and their capacity for change.

Cultural Imports and Exchanges

In the early seventeenth century, the volume of West Africa's Atlantic trade was much too small in comparison to the population to have much impact, nor were there any changes attributable to African production of goods for export. However, there were some notable cultural changes in coastal West African communities under way before 1624. The most obvious and widespread of these was the adoption of numerous Portuguese words and the use of the Portuguese language, not just in communicating with Europeans of various nationalities but also for communication among West Africans of different languages.

Some Africans had also responded positively to Portuguese missionary efforts to bring them into the fellowship of Christians. With the reigning oba of Benin's endorsement in 1516, missionaries had begun instruction of some royal youths, and churches might have been built. Benin had abandoned this experiment before 1550, but Christianity persisted longer in other parts of West Africa. In 1600, for example, the Catholic ruler of the kingdom of Warri in the western Niger Delta sent his eldest son to Lisbon with written instructions that he was to be educated in European ways. After spending eight years in various schools and making a pilgrimage to the famous shrine of Saint James at Compostela, the son (by then known as Domingos) returned to Warri, accompanied by his well-born Portuguese wife, a chaplain, and ten servants. After succeeding his father as ruler, Domingos built a church and actively encouraged those around him to practice Christianity.[33] Farther west, there was also a small number of African Christians, as de Marees observed about the Gold Coast:

> I have found some who could tell a lot about the birth of Christ, the Last Supper, his bitter passion, death and resurrection, and other points related to our Christian religion. One in particular, whom I knew very well and who was also my good friend, could read and write Portuguese very well and was well versed in the Scriptures.[34]

33. A. F. C. Ryder, "Missionary Activity in the Kingdom of Warri to the Early Nineteenth Century," *Journal of the Historical Society of Nigeria,* II (1960), 1–26.

34. De Marees, *Description,* 74. See also Robin Law, "Religion, Trade, and Politics on the 'Slave Coast': Roman Catholic Missions in Allada and Whydah in the Seventeenth Century," *Journal of Religion in Africa,* XXI (1991), 42–77.

Cultural contacts on the Gold Coast (and in Upper Guinea and Angola) had a sexual dimension as well. De Marees relates that the Portuguese resident in the trading forts regularly purchased women as steady sexual partners. Over time, a preference developed for women who were half white, who would have been lighter skinned as well as more apt to be able to speak Portuguese. He says that the Portuguese treated these mistresses as their wives and maintained them "in grand style and . . . in splendid clothes." At least in the early seventeenth century, the Dutch do not seem to have taken up this practice. The English would not have permanent residents on the coast until the 1630s, and over time, Anglo-African offspring were also known, although little specific information is known until the eighteenth century.[35]

Both commercial contacts and these more intimate relations shaped the growth of African cultural brokers, who were essential to the functioning of the commercial exchanges. Around the European trading forts on the Gold Coast, sizeable African villages grew up, whose residents were employed as laborers and in far more important roles. No position was more important than that of the "linguist," who not only possessed the skills to translate from one or more European language to one or more African languages but who was also a skilled interpreter of culture. Europeans almost never learned an African language, so all such individuals were wholly or partly of African descent. As was seen earlier, some Africans Lok had taken from the Gold Coast in 1554 returned to play these essential roles. The absence of any European residents and the smaller volume of trade in the Niger Delta meant such cultural brokers were fewer in number. At Benin, as already mentioned, the oba appointed special chiefs to handle these roles. Little is known about specific individuals in the period 1550–1624, but in later times, such individuals were often rich and powerful.[36]

A more widespread influence from the Atlantic was on diet. De Marees praised the Portuguese for introducing a number of new livestock species, including pigs, sheep, chickens, and pigeons, as well as sugarcane, pineapples, and a form of bananas. He said local Africans were initially willing

35. De Marees, *Description,* 216–217. For Upper Guinea, see George E. Brooks, *Eurafricans in Western Africa: Commerce, Social Status, Gender, and Religious Observance from the Sixteenth to the Eighteenth Century* (Athens, Ohio, 2003); for the eighteenth-century Anglo-Africans, see Margaret Priestley, *West African Trade and Coast Society: A Family Study* (London, 1969).

36. For a general treatment of cultural brokers in West Africa, see Philip D. Curtin, *Cross-Cultural Trade in World History* (Cambridge, 1984), esp. 38–41; see also Priestley, *West African Trade,* and Northrup, *Africa's Discovery,* 59–69.

to pay high prices for the new fruits because of their novelty. The most important of the new cultigens was maize, which the Portuguese had brought from the West Indies to the Cape Verde Islands before 1540 and which spread from there to the island of São Tomé. Its cultivation was introduced around their forts on the Gold Coast by the beginning of the seventeenth century. That it was possible to harvest two crops a year made the unfamiliar crop attractive to Africans, who gradually expanded maize cultivation for their own consumption. They ate it roasted on the cob, brewed beer from it, and baked bread of cornmeal mixed with local grains, some of which they sold to the Portuguese. By the eighteenth century, maize had surpassed rice as the principal grain cultivated on the Gold Coast.[37]

This survey of the Gulf of Guinea in the decades around 1600 demonstrates that African societies there were diverse, adept, and adaptable. Whether living in large political units or small ones, Africans used the accumulated wisdom from centuries of experience in regional and long-distance trading systems to secure the goods they wanted from the Atlantic on terms they found acceptable. Their exports demonstrated their skills in gold mining, elephant hunting, agriculture, and textile production. Europeans brought great skills and capital to the Atlantic trade with Africa, but it is instructive that their cultural impact was slight. Not just during the decades around 1600 but also for three centuries thereafter, it was African trading techniques, currencies, weights, and preferences that dominated the trade at the coast as well as inland.

Although these dealings showed much continuity with established African ways of acting, West Africans also demonstrated their capacity for change and innovation. Many acquired new goods and ate new food. Some experimented with new beliefs; quite a number learned, at the least, the rudiments of Portuguese. Africans from this region who passed into slavery in Spanish America exhibited similar qualities, but in those circumstances, the capacity for change looms larger than continuity with their particular cultural roots.

37. De Marees, *Description*, 113-114, 216; James McCann, "Maize and Grace: History, Corn, and Africa's New Landscapes, 1500-1999," *Comparative Studies in Society and History*, XLIII (2001), 250-251.

Linda Heywood & John Thornton

CENTRAL AFRICAN LEADERSHIP AND THE

APPROPRIATION OF EUROPEAN CULTURE

On January 3, 1608, Dom Antonio Manuel, the marquis of Funta (in the Kingdom of Kongo) and Kongolese ambassador to Rome, arrived in the Holy City. He came at the head of a small entourage of six, "black in appearance, but of noble and serious customs," and "above all he was pious and devout" as a Catholic, possessor of "value and prudence in negotiations." He had come from and represented "a Christian Ethiopian king to this Holy See." He had finished a turbulent four-year journey to Rome from Kongo, thrice robbed by Dutch pirates, held up by hostile Spanish authorities, and now, mortally ill, had to be carried in a litter. The pope, Paul V, had a wing of the Vatican palace, recently occupied by Cardinal Roberto Bellarmino, nobly prepared for him, and he was accorded all the honors that were customary for royal ambassadors. The patriarch of Jerusalem, master of the house, received him with honor in the wing called Paradise. Upon his arrival at the apartments, Antonio Manuel, though barely strong enough to walk, said a short prayer "as a sign of his piety." Although the pope provided him with the best doctors, they could offer no remedy, and his sickness worsened. Finally, three days after his arrival, on the eve of the Epiphany, Pope Paul visited him, blessed him, and pronounced the last rites. Shortly after midnight, "he rendered his soul to the lord."[1]

The pope, perhaps remembering the black Magus King Baltasar and seeing that Antonio Manuel had died the day before the Epiphany, dedicated the procession, the day of the Magi Kings, to this ambassador "come from a distant country in Ethiopia" to pay homage to the Holy See. Antonio Manuel received all the honors due a royal ambassador of a Christian king.

---

1. Account of the Embassy of Antonio Negrita, 1608, in António Brásio, ed., *Monumenta Missionaria Africana,* 1st Ser. (Lisbon, 1952–1988), V, 406–408 (hereafter cited as *MMA*).

PLATE I. *"Paulo V visita o Embaixador do Congo no leito da morte,"*
Fresco in Vatican Library. In António Brásio, ed., Monumenta Missionaria Africana,
1st Ser. (Lisbon, 1952–1988), V, 417

The top echelon of Roman society came to the cavalcade and participated
in an elaborate procession with musicians, the Swiss Guards, brothers of
various orders, and a great concourse of people. Antonio Manuel was eventually buried in the church of Santa Maria Maggiore, accompanied by religious friars of the city with one hundred white torches and the brothers of
the company of the Holy Sacrament of Saint Peter. A Jesuit priest delivered the funeral oration, promising to fulfill the one diplomatic issue that
Antonio Manuel had been able to raise, that of sending priests from Rome to
Kongo. The famed sculptor Francesco Caporelli created a bust in his honor.
The Vatican issued a commemorative medallion to celebrate the occasion,
with an image of Pope Paul on one side and of Antonio Manuel on the
other. Finally, a fresco was commissioned, which still stands in the Vatican
Library and depicts Antonio Manuel receiving the pope's blessing from his

deathbed. In a fitting modern commemoration of his mission, the Italian and Angolan governments cooperated to issue two Angolan stamps in his honor in 2002 to recognize Angola's nomination to the Security Council of the United Nations.[2]

Antonio Manuel in his person and his mission embodied the fruits of the appropriation of European diplomacy and some elements of European culture by the elite of the Kingdom of Kongo. He bore a Christian name of Iberian origin, and its unusual form of two given names was a Central African naming practice, common among African Christians, of placing a father's name as a second name. His title of marquis of Funta, like titles of other Kongolese nobles such as the duke of Mbamba or the count of Soyo, paralleled European and Christian titles. According to all accounts, he was a deeply devout and pious Christian. He was literate, and, indeed, the bundle of letters that he left testifies to his literacy in Portuguese (and perhaps Spanish) and the level of literacy among the elite in his country. In fact, he was educated entirely in Kongo and before leaving on the mission had served as a teacher in the Kongolese county of Soyo, in the marquisate of Mpemba, and at São Salvador, Kongo's capital.[3] Antonio Manuel car-

2. Ibid. For a good synthesis of materials on the whole mission and its context, see Teobaldo Filesi, *Roma e Congo all'inizio del 1600: Nuove testimonianze* (Como, 1968); another summary, with details, is found in Graziano Saccardo, *Congo e Angola con la storia dell'antica missione dei capuccini* (Venice, 1982-1983), I, 122-125. An English account with many details and background is in Richard Gray, "A Kongo Princess, the Kongo Ambassadors, and the Papacy," *Journal of Religion in Africa,* XXIX (1999), 140-154.

3. John Thornton, "Central African Names and African Naming Patterns," *William and Mary Quarterly,* 3d Ser., L (1993), 727-729. It is unclear when titles were first adopted. They were not in use in the earlier sixteenth century; for example, Duarte Lopes, who left Kongo as its ambassador to Rome in 1583, does not use them in his report on Kongo in 1591, in Filippo Pigafetta, *Relatione del Reame di Congo e delle circonvicine contrade tratta dalli scritti et ragiomente di Odardo Lopez portoghese* (Rome, 1591). The first attestation of such a title is in 1593, Archivo Segreto Vaticano, Miscellania, Armadio I (hereafter cited as ASV, Misc., Arm.), vol. XCI, Collettione di Scritture di Spagna, II, fols. 125-126, Papers of Antonio Manuel, Provisão de Miguel, conde de Sonho, Feb. 13, 1593. The Kongolese ambassador to Spain noted the full use of these titles in his report to the Vatican in 1594 (*MMA,* III, 502). For Antonio Manuel's personal papers, see ASV, Misc., Arm. I, vol. XCI, fols. 125-256. The bundle contains sixty-nine letters, notes, and documents in Portuguese and Spanish. Several documents (fols. 125-125v, 129) are in his hand.

On his education and life as a teacher, see fols. 137-137v, Carta de mestre de pemba de D. Antonio Manuel, 1600. He paid 3 *lefuku* (a local measure of *nzimbu,* the shell money of Kongo), for the right. It identifies him as a teacher at the capital at the time;

PLATE 2. *Bust of Antonio Manuel. By Francesco Caporelli. In Brásio, ed.,*
Monumenta Missionaria Africana, *V, 401*

ried with him a variety of administrative documents that had been issued in
Kongo. Some concerned his appointment to official positions, others were
grants of privileges or orders to carry out taxation policies, and still others
provided for a diplomatic mission between Kongo and Soyo. One was a
statement of an oath made by the count of Soyo. Even though his trip to
Rome was his first foreign travel, he seemed remarkably comfortable in the
milieu of noble Europeans and in the courts of Spain and Portugal. His let-

---

see fol. 230, provision of Gonçalo da Silva Mendonça, Procurador of Congo, Oct. 19,
1593, for his ecclesiastical position in Soyo.

ters reveal that he was in contact with a wide range of religious leaders in Portugal, Spain, France, and Italy.[4]

Caporelli's bust and the papal medallion show him dressed in an interesting combination of African and European clothing; while he has a fine European cape, beneath it he wears the familiar netted shirt *(nkutu)* characteristic of Kongolese nobility.[5] At the same time, he is depicted carrying a quiver full of arrows, another African touch. In the fresco at the Vatican Library, five of his six servants are shown dressed entirely in European clothing.

European-style diplomacy, Christianity, and literacy were major appropriations of European culture of the leaders of Central Africa and will be the main focus of this essay: they distinguished Central Africans from the inhabitants of the rest of Africa that participated in the Atlantic world.

In the sixteenth and seventeenth centuries, the portion of Central Africa that dealt regularly with Europeans included the two kingdoms of Kongo (on the north around the Congo River) and Ndongo (along the Kwanza River in modern-day Angola and Democratic Republic of Congo). In addition, less important kingdoms like Loango on the north coast of modern Congo-Brazzaville, Matamba in Angola, and still smaller ones between these larger states were also drawn into the Atlantic world. Other countries in West Africa engaged in trade and occasionally sent missions to Europe; as a result of this trade, many indulged in items of European culture, including clothing items, military technology, and European and American food crops. The Central African case, and in particular in Kongo, differs be-

4. ASV, Misc., Arm. I, vol. XCI, fols. 125–125v, Provisão de conde D. Miguel de Sonho, Feb. 4, 1593; fol. 137, appointment as mestre of Mpemba by church with salary, Dec. 16, 1600; fol. 202, appointment as master of Mpemba by Álvaro II, June 19, 1599; fol. 230, provision of Visitor of Congo, Oct. 19, 1593; fol. 243, Alvará of Álvaro II, Aug. 23, 1600; fol. 244, order of Álvaro II to Simão Manipemba, Feb. 22, 1600; fol. 245, testimony of oath of Miguel, count of Soyo, Dec. 20, 1591. These are original documents that once had seals (though all are now lost, their remains can be seen on the texts).

On his European travel, see Gray, "Kongo Princess," *Journal of Religion in Africa,* XXIX (1999), 140–154.

5. A near-contemporary description of this is found in Garcia Simões to Provincial, Oct. 20, 1575, *MMA,* III, 132. The term for this shirt is found in the now lost Jesuit chronicle, probably written by João de Pavia around 1640 of events in the kingdom that formed the source for Antonio Franco, *Synopsis annalium societatis Jesu in Lusitania ab anno 1540 usque ad annum 1725* (Augsburg, 1726), anno 1627, no. 11, 249, as "encute" (with relevant Latin grammatical alterations).

cause of the degree to which European culture was accepted and was used to benefit Central African elites.[6]

From the time of the arrival of the first Portuguese explorers in 1483, Central Africans, as did those in West Africa who had been dealing with the Portuguese since the 1440s, quickly adopted food crops from Europe and America as the New World opened up, though even here the borrowing was wider than elsewhere. Maize, called "masa ma Mputu," for example, was being grown in Kongo by the 1580s, though at that time it was considered only fit for pigs. Tobacco was also incorporated into the inventory, and a report of 1612 notes that the people smoked it to keep hunger in check. No doubt it was also smoked for pleasure, as we see in illustrations of Queen Njinga of Ndongo and Matamba (ruled 1624-1663) smoking on her pipe. Such borrowings were so common, a Dominican report suggested with some exaggeration, that the Kongolese grew "all" Portuguese crops. When Carmelite missionaries arrived in Kongo in 1583, King Álvaro I sent them "some gifts from here [Kongo] and Portugal, baskets of sweet bread, heads of garlic, a little vinegar, because all this is very much esteemed here."[7]

In common with other Africans, Central Africans also took advantage of European weapons. In 1583, soldiers in the Kongolese province of Mbamba bore long swords, like those of the Slavonians, imported from Portugal, which Duarte Lopes believed "could cut a slave in two." Firearms were perhaps more important. European soldiers served in Kongo armies at the very

6. By "kingdom," we mean a polity with bounded territory in which a clearly defined, self-reproducing leadership group created rules and laws, enforced them, adjudicated disputes, and could command resources to carry out its tasks through taxation in money, labor, or kind. That there were gaps in the kingdom's ability to perform these duties should not deter us from applying the term in Africa, for it is routinely used in historical sources to describe France, where the king was regularly challenged by rivals, where his jurisdiction was limited by local charters, privileges, and exemptions, where there existed domains where his officers could neither tax nor enter, and where significant portions of his army were privately owned.

7. Pigafetta, *Relatione,* 40; Samuel Brun, *Schiffarten* (Basel, 1624), 26, English trans. in Adam Jones, ed. and trans., *German Sources for West African History, 1599-1669* (Wiesbaden, 1983), 61; Luis de Cácegas and Luis de Sousa, *Historia de S. Domingos* (Lisbon, 1662), part 2, book 4, chap. 12, in *MMA,* V, 610; "Relação de Frei Diogo do Frei Santissimo Sacramento," ibid., IV, 367.

For smoking, see the illustrations found in MSS Araldi (papers of the Araldi family), Giovanni Antonio Cavazzi da Montecuccolo, "Missione evangelica . . . al Regno di Congo" (1665-1668), vol. A, as extracted and published in Ezio Bassani, "Un Cappuccino nell'Africa nera nel Seicento: I disegni dei *Manoscritti Araldi* del Padre Giovanni Antonio Cavazzi da Montecuccolo," *Quaderni Poro,* IV (1987), plate 10.

PLATE 3. *Queen Njinga smoking her pipe. MSS Araldi,*
Giovanni Antonio Cavazzi da Montecuccolo, "Missione evangelica . . .
al regno di Congo" (1665–1668), vol. A

beginning of their relationship, in 1491, when Portuguese artillery helped to suppress rebels. Portuguese soldiers were still being employed in the Kongo army in the early seventeenth century, for Dutch witnesses in 1608 recorded that Portuguese troops helped the count of Soyo in his wars, being paid in slaves taken from the survivors. However, as early as 1583, Kongo also equipped its soldiers with muskets, though only the king and the Mwene (lord of) Mbata, located on the eastern border where there were dangerous enemies, had them. The king still preferred Portuguese soldiers with guns, and so he forbade others of his subjects to have guns, as they might "rebel and face him with one or two thousand arquebusiers," whom he could not resist. In fact, musketeers did participate in a civil war in 1587, and in the early 1600s, the count of Soyo had sons who were "very experienced in using all guns."[8]

Ndongo, like Kongo, soon came to adopt guns as well, faced as it was, after 1579, with a long war against the Portuguese. In 1586, one of the Sobas, who had been baptized and served for a time with the Portuguese, raised a company of arquebusiers, which he put at the disposal of his king, and used them to fight the Portuguese army in the province of Ilamba. Portuguese merchants also sold weapons to the Africans of Ndongo; when the Portuguese army attempted to storm Queen Njinga's fortified island of Kindonga in 1625, the chronicler Antonio de Oliveira Cadornega noted that they met considerable fire from *espingardas* (muskets), "which they did not lack," thanks to the short-sighted greed of the Portuguese, and now these weapons were "being used against us."[9]

Diplomacy: Kongo

It was their mastery of European-style diplomacy, however, that set West Central Africans apart from other elites in West Africa. One of the consistent aims of the diplomatic missions was to ensure that Kongo be regarded as a Christian power with the same status as European powers. Antonio Manuel's mission to Rome was a telling illustration of this, but it was not the

8. Pigafetta, *Relatione*, 26, 37; Brun, *Schiffarten*, 28, English in Jones, ed. and trans., *German Sources*, 62; a Jesuit to Provincial of Portugal, Dec. 15, 1587, *MMA*, III, 352.

9. "História da residência dos Padres da Companhia de Jesus em Angola, e cousas tocantes ao reino, e conquista," May 1, 1594, *MMA*, IV, 568–569 (this portion of the text was actually written by Baltasar Afonso); Antonio de Oliveira Cadornega, *História geral das guerras angolanas (1680–81),* ed. Matias Delgado and M. Alves da Cunha (Lisbon, 1940–1942; reed. 1972), I, 132.

first embassy to Europe or even to Rome from this part of Africa. Kongo's first diplomatic mission to Europe took place in 1488, led by a member of the Kongolese nobility whose Kikongo name was Chrachafusus (perhaps Nkanga Mfusu) but who had been baptized João da Silva in Portugal. The goal of this mission was to obtain technical support such as carpenters, masons, farmers, and priests, so that from that point onward "men of each of the two kingdoms would be equal." Kongo's Christian king Afonso I Mvemba Nzinga (1509-1542) sent a second mission to Portugal in 1512 led by his cousin Pedro de Sousa to make obedience to the pope "as was the custom of Christian kings." Sousa's mission was accompanied by the king's young son Henrique, who had been studying in Portugal and already knew Latin and therefore became the spokesperson of the mission while in Rome. Pope Leo X received them "in solemn audience" in 1513 and "gave thanks to God for seeing people so barbarous and with customs so different and remote from Europe converted to the faith of Jesus Christ." They delivered a letter of obedience from Afonso to the pope.[10]

Afonso sent a more elaborate embassy in 1535 whose aim was to make obedience to Pope Paul III and request the "graces and spiritual gifts that other Christian kings and princes receive." Although the mission never reached Rome, the members did spend time in Lisbon, returning to Kongo only in 1543. By the time Afonso died, Kongo was deeply involved in the diplomacy of the Catholic world. His son Pedro, overthrown by his grandson Diogo, tried to plot with friends in Rome to get a papal bull dismissing Diogo's claims and legitimizing his own position. Pedro believed that such a bull would have a decisive effect in Kongo. At the same time, Jacome de Fonseca, who handled Kongo's affairs for Diogo, attempted to negotiate a Kongolese embassy to Rome to give obedience to the pope. By that time, there was a resident Kongolese ambassador in Lisbon, Antonio Vieira, "a black man" who had gone to Portugal in the 1520s and served as ambassador of Pedro I (1542-1545). Vieira married Margaryda da Syllva, a lady in waiting of Queen Catharina of Portugal, and handled affairs for several successive Kongolese kings. By 1566 Vieira had taken up residence in São

10. Rui de Pina, "Relazione del Regno di Congo" (1492), 86va, 88ra, in Carmen M. Radulet, *O cronista Rui de Pina e a "Relação do Reino do Congo"* (Lisbon, 1992) (later versions and editions give his name as Caçuta, which seems less likely phonologically than the version in the Italian manuscript). On the second mission, see Damião de Góis, *Chronica del Rei Emmanuel* (Lisbon, 1556), part 3, chap. 39; see also Teobaldo Filesi, *Le Relazioni tra il Regno del Congo e la sede apostolica nel XVI secolo* (Como, 1968), 35-40. Strangely enough, the events are not recorded in any Roman documentation, though the Portuguese chronicle is quite explicit.

Tomé but saw fit to advise Queen Catharina (then ruling and reigning) on Kongo's affairs and to offer counsel concerning the strengthening of relations between the two countries, especially concerning mineral exploration and trade. His letter reveals close knowledge of affairs in both Central Africa (including Ndongo) and Portugal.[11]

Kongolese diplomatic efforts in Europe intensified after 1575, when the Portuguese began building their colony in Angola, presenting a real threat to Kongo sovereignty. Hence, Álvaro I saw an aggressive diplomatic effort as one means to ensure the independence of his kingdom. He sent many missions to Portugal, including two headed by his relatives, Sebastião Álvares, the royal secretary, and Pedro Antonio, "the second person in his government." Adopting the posture of European Christian kings, he called on his European counterparts to assist his missions to Rome, but Spain and Portugal were hostile to Kongo's initiative and starved the missions of funds. Álvaro I's son and successor, Álvaro II, continued the tradition, especially as Portuguese aggression against Kongo vassals deepened. In spite of hindrances, his ambassador to Spain, a "close relative" named Antonio Vieira (not the same person as Pedro I's ambassador), presented Álvaro's request that Kongo be established as a diocese separate from São Tomé under its own bishop, because it had all the trappings of a well-established Christian kingdom. Álvaro was encouraged in his efforts to obtain an epsicopal see by the papal hierarchy, which was hostile to Portuguese intentions. As a result, Clement VIII erected the Kongo capital of São Salvador as an episcopal see on July 18, 1596. On September 20, 1596, both Clement VIII and the papal collector urged Álvaro II to send an ambassador to Rome "to show that he is a obedient son," as "all the Christian kings do," which would cause "the glorious name of your majesty to be known in this part of Europe and principally in Rome, which is the seat and head of all Christianity." However, the potential advantage that Kongo could claim by having its own bishop, whose authority was extended to the Portuguese colony of Angola, was weakened when the king of Portugal succeeded in winning the right to

11. For the Rome mission, see Afonso I to Pope Paul III, Feb. 21, 1535, *MMA*, II, 39; details can be found in Saccardo, *Congo e Angola,* I, 39–41. On the bull, see Pedro I to Rodrigo de Santa Maria, undated, but added to the inquest into Pedro's treason by Diogo's officials in 1550, *MMA*, II, 261–262. On Fonseca's negotiations, see Comendador Mor to João III, Nov. 18, 1553, ibid., II, 310. On Vieira, see "Informação das Cousas do Congo," 1553, ibid., II, 330 (a Jesuit document that denounced Vieira as being of little service to Portugal). He also handled financial affairs: Alvará of Diogo I to Diogo Gomes, Aug. 15, 1546, ibid., II, 149–150; see his own account of affairs in Kongo, Aug. 18, 1566, giving his biography, ibid., II, 543–544.

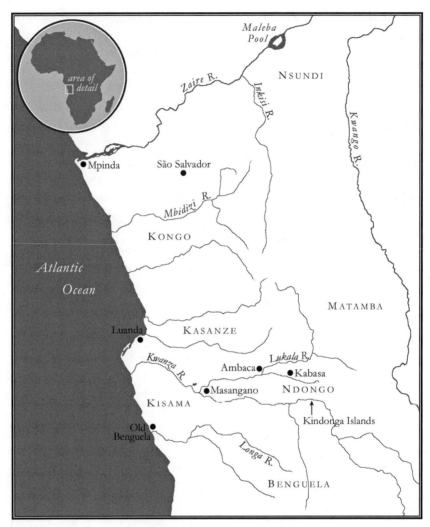

PLATE 4. *Angola in West Africa, ca. 1620. Drawn by Rebecca L. Wrenn*

nominate the bishops and quickly used this power to its advantage. When Antonio Vieira, who had returned to Kongo to obtain instructions to take up this post, died, eventually the task fell to Antonio Manuel.[12]

Indeed, Álvaro II took the opportunity to use Antonio Manuel's mis-

12. Pigafetta, *Relatione,* 62–63; see also "Relação dos Carmelitas Dẽsalços," *MMA,* IV, 404; Saccardo, *Congo e Angola,* I, 112–125. On Vieira's role, see account of embassy, *MMA,* V, 406. The see was erected by the bull *Dilatatum est,* July 18, 1596, ibid., III, 541; the papal collector (in a letter to Álvaro II, Sept. 20, 1596) added that Vieira would be a good choice (ibid., III, 543).

sion to continue to promote the theme of Kongo as a full-fledged member of the Christian community, demanding that he be held as a feudatory of the pope, a sign in European Christendom of full membership and independence. He requested a supply of the full range of Christian paraphernalia, an Agnus Dei, relics, indulgences, and other marks of the ancient roots of the religion. He expected church officials, especially those from Europe, to treat him with respect, at least as much as any European ruler would expect. Detailing the abuses of power that the Portuguese bishops and senior dignitaries had committed in order to belittle him and promote Portugal's agenda, Álvaro requested that his royal chapel of Saint James be exempt from their jurisdiction, as was customary in other Christian kingdoms, and that it become a center of his own religious life immune from threats by hostile church authorities. He also asked that his private confessor be exempt as well, to have full rights to carry out religious duties on his behalf, and to have judicial authority outside the cathedral. Anxious to control the finances of the church, Álvaro insisted that the collection of the tithe follow "ancient custom" so that his own officials could gather it and pay church expenses. Perhaps with an eye to obtaining papal support for the imposition of primogeniture, he asked that one of his illegitimate sons be recognized as his heir if his legal wife bore no son. His correspondence reveals an intimate knowledge of European customs regarding the relationship between Christian monarchs, the local church authorities, and the papacy. He demanded that the Portuguese be censured for their illegal seizure of Kongo's mines (presumably in the Dembos area), denounced the governor of Angola, and insisted that all Portuguese in his country staying more than six or seven years be considered citizens and thus subject to Kongo law. Finally, he asked for permission to expel the New Christians (Christians of Jewish ancestry) from his domains. This request was aimed at the many Portuguese priests and settlers in Angola and Kongo who were New Christians.[13]

This diplomacy accelerated as relations between Kongo and Angola deteriorated with the arrival of aggressive and ruthless governors like Luis Mendes de Vasconcelos (1617–1621), who commenced a period of devastating military aggressions against Kongo, thanks to his alliance with the cannibal mercenary Imbangala (called "Jagas" in the documents of the era). Mendes de Vasconcelos's campaigns had reached into the Dembos region, subordinate to Kongo, as well as Kongo's vassal Kasanze in the hinterland of Luanda. Álvaro III, Kongo king since 1615, complained continually that the governors of Angola intercepted his letters and hindered his diplomacy.

13. Petitions of Antonio Manuel to king of Spain, June 29, 1604, *MMA*, V, 110–111.

One of Álvaro II's letters complained, "They fear that this king of Congo would register a complaint with the pope and with his Catholic majesty [of Spain] concerning the thievery, cruelty, and insults that they have committed in the company of the Jagas, enemies of these our kingdoms." He felt that he might have to send an ambassador again but expressed concerns that a Kongolese ambassador would be discovered, so that he might have to send one secretly, perhaps "some priest."[14]

The struggle with Portugal pushed King Pedro II (1622–1624) to carry his diplomatic strategy in new directions. Facing a Portuguese army that invaded Kongo with Imbangala soldiers in 1622, Pedro looked to Kongo's traditional Christian allies elsewhere in Europe for help. In his letters to Spain and Rome, he complained that a Portuguese army sent by the governor of Angola, João Correia de Sousa, had invaded Kongo in 1622 with Portuguese and Imbangala troops. They had killed the duke of Mbamba and the marquis of Mpemba during a battle at Mbumbi, giving their bodies to the Imbangala to be eaten. To counter Portuguese aggression, Pedro had moved an army down to drive the Portuguese off and launched a major diplomatic offensive. He dispatched letters to King Philip III of Spain and to the pope through his permanent ambassador Juan Baptista Vives, complaining of "an army of more than 200,000 Jagas, barbarous heathens, who sustain themselves on human flesh, outside the army of the Portuguese . . . and desolated many provinces . . . where they are infinite Christians, who were killed and eaten. Others were made slaves . . . [in the] Duchy of [M]Bamba, where there was also the marquis of [M]Pemba and other nobles; all were killed and eaten." Philip III promised a full investigation and eventually had his officials in Brazil return some of those Kongolese who had been enslaved there.[15]

Pedro also took the important additional step of courting the Dutch West India Company as a counterweight to the Portuguese. In 1623, he wrote to the Dutch States General shortly after the Battle of Mbumbi. After relating that the Portuguese had killed two of his nobles, he proposed a joint Kongo-Dutch naval-military attack on Portuguese Angola. He offered to pay the company in gold, silver, and ivory if its ships would assault Luanda by sea while he sent an army down the coast to attack it from the land. The Dutch obliged by sending a fleet under the famous admiral Piet Heyn, which ar-

14. Álvaro III to Giovanni Battista Vives, Feb. 26, 1622, *MMA,* VII, 4.
15. Pedro II to Giovanni Battista Vives, Nov. 28, 1623, *MMA,* VII, 161; Felipe III to Pedro II, June 17, 1623, *MMA,* VII, 116–117. On the complex negotiation of the return of slaves, see Saccardo, *Congo e Angola,* I, 187–188.

rived on Kongo's shores in 1625 only to learn that Pedro had died and his son and successor Garcia I (1624-1626) was not willing to press the attack, offering as an explanation that, as Catholics, the Kongolese were not ready to attack their fellow religionists by joining the Calvinists. But the plan was never shelved, and it continued to be discussed until it was carried out when the Dutch invaded Angola in 1641.[16]

Diplomacy: Ndongo

Like the rulers of Kongo, Ndongo's king Ngola Kiluanje (ca. 1515-1556) wanted to establish diplomatic relations with Europe to promote its independence and prestige in the Atlantic world. But his efforts were continually frustrated and undermined by Kongo's interference. Ndongo's first effort to establish diplomatic relations with Portugal in 1518 was accompanied by a request for missionaries, probably because its rulers realized that, as with Kongo, conversion might be the first step to direct relations with Christian Europe. Although Ndongo's mission passed first through Kongo, Portugal responded in 1520 by sending a mission directly to Ndongo, which Kongo's King Afonso frustrated by spreading rumors in Ndongo. As a result Ngola Kiluanje gave an order to arrest the members of the Portuguese mission. Ndongo remitted the captives to Afonso and in turn accepted a Kongo mission headed by a priest named Afonso Anes.[17]

If Ndongo failed to establish direct relations with Portugal in 1518-1520, it was no more successful in avoiding Kongo's interference in its diplomatic initiatives when it sent a new mission to Portugal in 1548. After many delays, Portugal sent a mission with four Jesuits to Ndongo, headed by Paulo Dias de Novais, in 1560. Members of this mission found a chapel and reli-

16. Nationaal Archief (Netherlands) Staten Generaal 5751, session of Oct. 27, 1623; Piet Heyn, "Journael van de Brasiliese Reyse, gehouden opt Schip De Neptunus . . . 15 January 1624 tot den 16 July 1625," fols. 24v-25, published with original pagination marked in L. M. Akveld, "Journaal van de Reis van Piet Heyn naar Brazilië en West-Afrika, 1624-25," *Bijdragen en medelingen van het historisch genootschap,* LXXVI (1962), 85-174, esp. 144-145. The best work on the planned attack is Klaas Ratelband, *Nederlanders in West Afrika, 1600-1650: Angola, Kongo en São Tomé* (Zutphen, 2000); for an English account, David Birmingham, *Trade and Conflict in Angola: The Mbundu and Their Neighbours under the Influence of the Portuguese, 1483-1790* (Oxford, 1966).

17. Regimento to Manuel Pacheco and Baltasar de Castro, Feb. 16, 1520, *MMA,* I, 431-432; Baltasar de Castro to João III, Oct. 15, 1526, ibid., I, 485-487; João III to Afonso, ca. 1529, ibid., I, 532; Saccardo, *Congo e Angola,* I, 76-77, see also Ilídio do Amaral, *O Reino do Congo . . .* (Lisbon, 1996), 75-82.

gious items left over from Father Anes's mission still there, which had been reverently guarded. However, there was no other sign of the kind of religious conversion that early Portuguese missions to Kongo had inspired. As happened in 1520, the 1560 mission found out that the king of Ndongo, Ndambi a Ngola, had been informed by the king of Kongo that the purpose of the Portuguese mission was "to see whether we had silver or gold in order for the king of Portugal to take the land." As the Jesuits commented, the king of Kongo "would not suffer that we were in Angola and that he alone would send presents of things which he got from Portugal before they came there." These suspicions caused Dias de Novais to leave Ndongo, though the king retained the Jesuit missionary, Francisco de Gouveia, who accompanied him.[18]

Dias de Novais's renewed mission to Ndongo in 1575 ran into exactly the same problems that all the earlier ones did. When Dias de Novais came to Kabasa, Ndongo's capital, he encountered two Kongo diplomats who had been dispatched to warn Ndongo that Portugal intended to conquer it. This time, however, the king of Ndongo, Ngola Kiluanje kia Ndambi, arrested the Kongolese diplomats and turned them over to the Portuguese, who subsequently sent them to São Tomé for trial. During this time of friendly relations, Ngola Kiluanje kia Ndambi sent Dom Pedro da Silva Manuel, a Kongolese "raised in Portugal" who had come with Dias de Novais, as his ambassador to Lisbon, carrying gifts of silver and copper, slaves, and pieces of Kikongo wood. Silva Manuel was received well, inducted into the order of Santiago, and given grants for his support.[19]

But Kongo interfered again, and in 1578 the Portuguese priest Francisco Barbuda, who had lived in Kongo since 1556 as vicar general and who was now a confidant of Álvaro I, arrived in Ndongo's capital of Kabasa, once again with warnings about Portuguese motives.[20] This time, Ngola Kiluanje kia Ndambi accepted his advice and had those Portuguese resident

18. "Apontamentos sobre Paulo Dias de Novais" (copies of old documents, summarizing document of July 17, 1560), *MMA*, II, 466–467; "História," ibid., IV, 553; Pedro Mendes to Jesuit General, May 9, 1563, ibid., II, 502.

19. "História," ibid., IV, 555–557; minute of Apr. 5, 1600, ibid., V, 7.

20. Pigafetta, *Relatione*, 61; see Michel Chandeigne, ed., *Le royaume de Congo et les contrées environnantes (1591): La description de Filippo Pigafetta et Duarte Lopes,* trans. Willy Bal (Paris, 2002), 320 n. 3. Barbuda arrived in Angola in 1578: Paulo Dias de Novais, Oct. 22, 1578, *MMA,* IV, 304. He argued loudly, claiming to be loyal only to the king of Angola before the Portuguese representative in Kabasa; see Act of Pero da Fonseca, Cabaça, Apr. 18, 1579, ibid., IV, 308–309.

in his capital massacred. However, he also killed nearly a thousand Kongolese who were there, provoking a war that would permanently damage relations between the two. Kongo subsequently aided Portugal in the war against Ndongo that followed. Duarte Lopes, who was residing in Kongo from 1578 to 1583, noted that, by the time he left to serve as Kongo's ambassador to Rome, the two kings were dealing with each other and were "friends," but Ndongo's ruler had "reason to regret the reprisals and massacre that were committed against the people of Kongo and the Portuguese" at Kabasa.[21]

The outbreak of this war stranded Ndongo's ambassador in Portugal, where he was implicated in the ill-fated revolt of Dom Antonio, prior of Crato, in 1580. Despite his protestations that he was "a man of Guiné, ignorant of the things of the world," he was found guilty of treason and exiled to North Africa for twelve years. Still alive at the age of eighty-five in 1600, he petitioned for pardon and asked to be sent to Lisbon so he could return to Angola.[22]

Following this debacle, for the next eighty years Ndongo abandoned attempts to have direct diplomatic missions to Europe. Instead, Ndongo's diplomacy was directed to the Portuguese in Angola. In 1603, King Mbandi a Ngola sent an embassy to the Portuguese governor Manuel Cerveira Pereira proposing an alliance and eventually a possible acceptance of vassalage to the Portuguese. Nothing is known of the outcome of this endeavor, and in 1617 the new Portuguese governor, Luis Mendes de Vasconcelos, launched a massive attack on Ndongo, which destroyed its capital and forced Ngola Mbandi to take refuge in one of his alternative capitals on the island of Kindonga in the Kwanza River.[23]

From there, Ngola Mbandi sent "petitions" to Mendes de Vasconcelos asking that his wife and two of his sisters who had been captured in the war be returned to him. Following this, he sent a formal embassy headed by his eldest sister, Njinga Mbandi, to the new Portuguese governor, João Correia de Sousa, in 1622. The goals of this mission were to end the war, to achieve the return of captured dependent populations, to secure the withdrawal of the Portuguese fort recently built at Ambaca near Ndongo's tradi-

21. "História," *MMA*, IV, 572; Pigafetta, *Relatione*, 14.

22. Minute of Apr. 5, 1600, *MMA*, V, 7.

23. "Relaçion del Governador d'Angola sobre el Estado en que tem Aquella Conquista . . . ," Sept. 28, 1603, *MMA*, V, 61; see also Guerreiro, "Missão dos Jesuitas em Angola," ibid., V, 55.

tional capital, and to obtain Portuguese assistance in removing marauding Imbangala bands from Ndongo's land.[24]

Like Antonio Manuel arriving in Rome, Njinga arrived in Luanda with great pomp, accompanied by an escort of "pages and waiting women," and she was received with a great public show of muskets and music with the "sound of various instruments both abbondi [Mbundu] and European." But Njinga's mission also had distinct differences from the missions of Kongo to Portugal and Rome. Whereas Kongo's ambassadors were anxious that their country be treated as an equal on the same terms as other Christian countries, Njinga came as an African ruler who was not Christian but still wanted to be treated as the representative of a sovereign state in West Central Africa.

Njinga was well received by the governor, who offered her a "cushion on the ground according to the custom of black people" while he was seated on a chair, making it appear she was a vassal and subordinate. Nearly forty years later, Njinga recalled that, "when she saw she was not given a magnificent and showy chair, she called one of her waiting-women, and sat on her as if she had been a chair, rising and sitting down as necessary, and explained her embassy with much acuteness and intelligence of mind."[25]

24. For a full explication of the mission and its antecedent and immediate consequences, see Beatrix Heintze, "Das Ende des unabhängigen Staates Ndongo (1617–1630)," in Heintze, *Studien zur Geschichte Angolas im 16. und 17. Jahrhundert: Ein Lesebuch* (Cologne, 1996), 120–126.

25. MSS in the possession of Carlo Araldi, Modena (hereafter cited as MSS Araldi), Giovanni Antonio Cavazzi da Montecuccolo, "Missione evangelica al Regno de Congo" (1668), A, book 2, 24–25. Cavazzi collected this information at Njinga's court around 1662, from Njinga herself and others in her court, including her sister Barbara Kambu, as he wrote in the margin at this point, "The following case has been told me by several people, and having known and frequented Queen Ginga I have no difficulty in believing it, or even making others believe it . . . [Ginga] does not lack great powers of observation and curiosity and what follows from them." Heintze, who favors a different reconstruction of events, has pointed out that the reports of Fernão de Sousa written in 1624–1625, closer in time to the events, have a different chain of events, with the Portuguese initiating negotiations through the mission of Dionisio de Faria Baretto and Manuel Dias, and with Njinga and her two sisters coming to Luanda as "hostages" at the same time (Heintze, "Ende," in Heintze, *Studien zur Geschichte Angolas*, 210–217). She discounts Cavazzi's version as reflecting legendary elements of Njinga's life through the passage of time. We have favored Cavazzi's account, however, which, even though written later, was certainly that of eyewitnesses (including Njinga), on the strength of its logic: the "hostages" would not negotiate a treaty and be allowed to return without some immediate exchange, and Sousa was not an eyewitness (un-

Njinga's mission was successful in a diplomatic sense, as she won important concessions from the Portuguese concerning the ending of the war and restitution of Ndongo subjects. Njinga accepted baptism in Luanda, and on her return Ngola Mbandi proposed the establishment of more formal diplomatic relations and agreed to be baptized. By doing this Njinga began down her own road in dealing with European powers on their own terms.[26]

When the Portuguese reneged on their negotiated agreements, Ngola Mbandi sent Njinga a second time to Luanda, again winning acceptance of the initial terms. In the end the Portuguese did not keep to the terms of the agreement, and as a result Ngola Mbandi committed suicide, for "seeing these delays, [he] supposed that they were deceits and died from depression, and they said that it was poison that he himself took in desperation."[27]

Following her brother's death, Njinga took over rule of Ndongo herself and immediately began a new diplomatic front with the newly arrived Portuguese governor Fernão de Sousa. But too much was at stake in Angola for the Portuguese to agree to Njinga's insistence that, in order to resolve their political differences, they first remove the fort that they had constructed in Mbaca. As a result, the Portuguese resumed their war against Ndongo, despite the several embassies that Njinga continued to send to the Portuguese governors during this period. The war came to an end only when Njinga and the Portuguese signed a new treaty in 1657 after Njinga had failed to oust the Portuguese within the Ndongo-Dutch-Kongo alliance. Following the treaty, Njinga renewed her international diplomacy by sending an embassy to Pope Alexander II in 1662 to join Christendom as a sovereign state.[28]

---

like Njinga and Cavazzi's other informants) but received his information from the confused and charged atmosphere of Luanda after the expulsion of Correia de Sousa (in 1622). Sousa, moreover, frequently put the Portuguese in the best light and as having the upper hand in their dealings with Africans, as witnessed by his accounts of Kongo and elsewhere where independent witnesses are available.

26. "Relação de Dongo," in Beatrix Heintze, ed., *Fontes para a história de Angola no século XVII*, 2 vols. (Stuttgart, 1985-1988), I, *Memórias, relações e outros manuscritos da colectânea documental de Fernão de Sousa, 1622-1635*, 198 (hereafter cited as *FHA*); other details in Fernão de Sousa to Governo, Aug. 15, 1624, ibid., II, *Cartas e documentos oficiais da colectânea documental de Fernão de Sousa (1624-1635)*, 86; Sousa, "Lembrança," ibid., I, 196. Also see Heintze, "Ende," in Heintze, *Studien zur Geschichte Angolas*, 210-217.

27. Sousa, "Lembrança," *FHA*, I, 196. Further details worked out in Heintze, "Ende," in Heintze, *Studien zur Geschichte Angolas*, 218-219.

28. *MMA*, VII, 249; Njinga to Pope Alexander VII, Aug. 25, 1662, ibid., XII, 402-403. There are frequent mentions of these embassies in Fernão de Sousa's long letter

Kongo's diplomatic success in Europe was greatly aided by the fact that it was perceived as a Christian country that often followed European ways, at least among the elite. As the descriptions of Antonio Manuel's Christian comportment in Rome attest, Christianity was well established in Kongo by the time of his mission in 1608. The acceptance of the Christian religion and the education of the Kongolese elite in the Christian faith had first begun with the baptism of Kongo's King Nzinga Nkuwu in 1491 and were fully established by his son Afonso Mvemba Nzinga (1509–1542). Afonso sent many of his children and other Kongolese nobles to Portugal to study and to become priests. His son Henrique became a bishop and returned to Kongo in 1526, the first sub-Saharan bishop in the Catholic tradition. Afonso's successor, Diogo I (1545–1561), pushed the Christianization model beyond Kongo's borders and, with the help of Jesuit teachers, deepened and systematized Christianity at home. By the end of his reign, Diogo had sent missionaries to most nearby countries. Already in 1550, Kongolese nobles had appropriated Christian practices, such as swearing oaths on the cross and the Gospels and taking ecclesiastical sanctuary, according to a locally conducted treason inquiry. Late-sixteenth-century elite Kongolese had great fear of being excommunicated. They had an attachment to foreign and special religious symbols; in 1583, priests found a crucifix brought from Spain in a hermitage outside São Salvador. Kongo's self-identification as a missionary center continued, for in 1604 Álvaro II announced the conversion of four neighboring heathen kings, "Cundi, Cala, Ocanga, and Zareacacongo."[29]

By the time of Antonio Manuel, the appropriation of Christianity could be easily seen in the organization of Kongo's church. A report of 1600 noted some thirteen parishes in Kongo, each with a vicar and the parish church in provincial capitals. Much of the church's income and power was spent

---

to his sons, written 1631 and incorporating summaries and copies of much of his correspondence, in *FHA,* I, 227, 230, 240–244 and passim.

29. "Apontamentos que fez o Padre Sebastião de Souto . . ." (ca. 1561), *MMA,* II, 478–480; "Devassa de d. Diogo Rei do Congo," Apr. 10, 1550, ibid., II, 248–262; "Relação dos Carmelitas Dĕsalços," ibid., IV, 408; Santissimo Sacramento, "Relação," ibid., IV, 366; "Sommario dell'instruttione che portò à Roma Don Antonio Manoele Ambasciatore del Re di Congo . . . ," June 29, 1604, ibid., V, 118.

On the politics of the Jesuits and their mission, see John Thornton, "Early Kongo-Portuguese Relations, 1483–1575: A New Interpretation," *History in Africa,* VIII (1981), 183–204.

in the capital city of São Salvador (formerly Mbanza Kongo, renamed by Álvaro I in 1570). In 1604 São Salvador had an organ, choir, bell tower with bell, cemetery (maybe of rough stone), and a Santa Casa de Misericordia (almshouse). Control over this establishment was hotly contested, however, between the kings of Kongo and Portugal. The crown of Portugal insisted on paying the prebends of the church dignitaries and making their appointments, but Álvaro paid and supported the curates in the parishes. The success of Álvaro's diplomatic initiatives carved out separate areas in the church, such as the Chapel of Saint James, where he would control finance and personnel, through the tithe, instituted since 1516 and bringing the equivalent of more than five hundred cruzados annually by 1613. Álvaro took every opportunity to create and fund new lay confraternities. When the Dominicans proposed establishing a brotherhood of the rosary in 1610, Álvaro II sent an offering of twenty-five thousand reis in *nzimbus* (the Kongolese shell currency), and the duke of Mbamba added the same amount, as did other nobles who followed the king. A royal cousin became the judge, and the duke of Mbamba was the procurator of the fraternity.[30]

Although Álvaro III (1614–1622) pushed the same religious programs as his predecessors, his personal life was widely regarded as irregular and dissolute. When he died suddenly, his successor, Pedro II, was immediately hailed by Jesuits, who believed that he "would return the kingdom to the purity of faith that they had in the time of Dom Affonso." Pedro was indeed a model of Christian piety, driving out the concubines of his predecessors as soon as he arrived in São Salvador, so that he could be devoted to his one legal wife. He promptly set about ensuring that the recipients of *rendas* (revenue-bearing lands) set up schools "where they would teach the nobles to know God and to read and write." Bras Correa, his confessor, described him as "a truly Catholic baron, mostly truly and extremely devoted to the Divine Cult . . . [he] spent the major part of the day reciting the canonical hours and almost all the Psalms." Jesuit supporters said that he went to church every day, "even on stormy nights," was chaste, fasted regularly, confessed, scourged himself, and on Holy Thursday washed the feet of the poor. During this time "he meditated on the meaning of the Passion of the

30. Royal order, Jan. 18, 1600, *MMA*, V, 4; "Probationes qualitatum R. P. Fratis Antonij de S.to Stephano . . . prasenatti ad ecclesiam Congensem et Angolensem . . . ," Dec. 19, 1603–Jan. 31, 1604, testimony of Licenciate Simão Rangel, deacon of Congo, Jan. 16, 1604, ibid., V, 72; "Relação da Costa de Guiné, 1607," ibid., V, 387; Cácegas and Sousa, *Historia,* part 2, book 4, chap. 12, ibid., V, 610–622; Álvaro II to Pope Paulo V, Feb. 27, 1613, ibid., VI, 131.

Lord." He was generous to the poor, consoled the sick, and often gave sermons on advancing the faith to neighboring kingdoms.[31]

More than churches in Europe, however, the Kongo church suffered from lack of an ordained clergy. For the most part, one secular priest served for an extensive parish with thousands of parishioners, according to Dominican visitors in 1610. At best the vicar visited his parish once a year, during Lent. However, the lack of clergy did not mean a lack of Christian teaching or even religious worship among the commoners, because of Kongo's active laity. When Carmelite missionaries crossed rural Mbamba in southwest Kongo in 1583-1584 they reported that lay preachers, whom the people called teachers *(mestres)*, were found in many villages. These lay ministers were like Dom João, a member of the royal family who had a license to perform baptisms, the only Catholic rite that was universally observed in Kongo. João—and no doubt others like him—had lived in Portugal during his youth and was thus bilingual. Antonio Manuel had also exercised these functions, as is attested by a certificate appointing him as teacher in Mpemba in 1600 that noted that he had performed the same functions in São Salvador before that, which was left among his papers when he died in Rome.[32]

By the end of the sixteenth century, people in Kongo followed regular Christian ways in areas near the parish churches and in the capital of São Salvador with its cathedral, five other churches, and many private oratories where both priests and lay ministers were concentrated. However, Kongo's settlement pattern also concentrated the population in those very areas. Baptismal records suggest that nearly 100,000 Kongolese lived within about ten kilometers of São Salvador in the early seventeenth century, representing about 20 percent of the country's population. When Carmelite priests arrived at São Salvador in 1583, they were met by a large, solemn procession that they believed had thirty thousand people when they brought images into the city. People from all walks of life residing in this area attended Mass regularly and usually knew the principal elements of the faith, and many of the wealthier classes received regular education. Frequently, services were so massive they were held on the public square to

31. [Mateus Cardoso], "Morte de D. Álvaro III Rei do Congo e eleição de D. Pedro II Affonso," 1622, *MMA,* XV, 493; Bras Correa to Juan Bautista Vives, July 23, 1623, ibid., VII, 46; Franco, *Synopsis annalium,* 1624, nos. 14-18, 241-242, based probably on the chronicle (now lost) of João de Paiva, Jesuit resident in Kongo at the time.

32. Cácegas and Sousa, *Historia,* part 2, book 4, chap. 12, *MMA,* V, 611, which recounts a visit in 1610; ASV, Misc., Arm. XCI, 137-137v, Carta de mestre de pemba de D. Antonio Manuel, 1600.

accommodate the thousands. This level of religious life was not confined to São Salvador but could also be found in other towns.[33]

Kongolese villagers shared in this religious culture, although they received less in the way of regular church services than did the townspeople, and were instructed only by the noble teachers and had sacraments at best only during annual visits in Lent. By the end of the sixteenth century, however, they did recognize and accept the principal rituals and symbols of Christianity. They identified the cross, religious paintings, priestly garb and paraphernalia, and other blessed objects (perhaps religious medals) as a part of their own religious lives. They became Catholics formally through baptism and sought to have their own children baptized when the opportunity arose. In all likelihood the custom of taking a saint's name in Portuguese form was also widespread among the common people, as it was among the elite.

For their part, the country people flocked to the priests to hear Mass, confess, marry, and baptize their children. Some simply came to get a blessing or to have something blessed for them to carry away. Mbanza Mbamba, a modest country town and parish seat, had a spotless church with a well-painted retable behind it, and some three thousand came to hear Mass. People were particularly devoted to the cult of the Virgin Mary, for the priests carried her image, and droves of people came to them, expecting miracles in her name. Later, in rural parts of another province, Nsundi, the priests met a woman who had walked from her home for four days just to ensure that they could hear her confession, as she had learned to do from a priest. Carmelites in 1583 noted that in Nsundi, the home town of João the interpreter who had been to Portugal, the priests sang Mass on the road, and the people knew how to sing songs to an organ. Dominicans observed that in a procession in 1610 the people had "shawms in the Portuguese usage" to which they sang. Dutch visitors to Soyo in 1608 thought Kongolese there were "mostly Christians and go to mass every day, twice a day when it rains. They maintain five or six churches." Moreover, in 1622,

33. Arquivo de Instituto Historico e Geografico Brasiliero, Rio de Janeiro, Lata 848, doc. 16, "Descrição das necessidades do reino do Congo sobre assuntos religiosos" (ca. 1650), fol. 2, indicating 4,500 annual baptisms in the parish of São Salvador, which at a birth rate of 47 per thousand equals approximately 94,000 people, from a population of roughly 500,000; Santissimo Sacramento, "Relação," *MMA,* IV, 366; "Relação dos Carmelitas Dèsalços," ibid., IV, 395; testimony of Kongolese ambassador, Antonio Vieira, 1595, "Interrogatoria de statu Regni Congensis . . . ," ibid., III, 502; testimony of Martinho de Ulhoa, bishop of São Tomé, "De Statu Regni Congi," 1595, ibid., III, 511–512; testimony of Rangel, Jan. 16, 1604, ibid., V, 71.

when Father Mateus Cardoso, a Jesuit resident, wrote a detailed description of the funeral of King Álvaro III, the pageantry and rituals that took place were strongly reminiscent of the funerals that might have been held for a European king.[34]

Kongolese, however, did not adopt outright these Christian elements, for many people retained many of their older beliefs within the forms of Catholic rites, worship, and devotion. For example, local custom created marriage rules that recognized a wife married in church but allowed for keeping of concubines, and many Kongolese did not partake in the Christian sacrament of marriage, especially in rural areas or across class and educational lines. Many Kongolese also continued to revere local deities in their traditional locations by identifying them as Catholic saints or as angels; no doubt many a rural crucifix was planted on an ancient shrine. Kongolese religious terminology crept into Christian prayers, converting the Bible into a charm, for example. And it is likely that placing the emphasis on the receiving of salt in baptism (as evidenced by the Kikongo term for it, *kudia mungwa*) related to the protective power of salt in many West Central African religious traditions. These practices, however, merely mirrored the folk Christianity of Europe, where various pre-Christian practices and customs entered the church's customs.[35]

Carmelites observed that in Kongo the people were very devoted to idols and their priests, whom they called *ganga (nganga,* a term used for both Catholic clergy and local religious practitioners) and that, advanced as they were in Christianity, they "follow them in all things." Although this was widespread, it seemed to them most prominent in Mbata, the easternmost of Kongo's provinces. Clergy, and sometimes the Kongolese educated elite, usually denounced this as "fetishism" (witchcraft) and sought to end it.[36]

34. Santissimo Sacramento, Dec. 2, 1584, *MMA,* III, 296, and "Relação," fols. 117–118v, ibid., IV, 361–365 (these testimonies are possibly the only ones that give direct evidence of rural life at the time); Cácegas and Sousa, *Historia,* ibid., V, 612–613; Pieter van den Broecke, "Journal of My Voyage . . . to Angola . . . ," September [1608], in J. D. La Fleur, ed. and trans., *Pieter van den Broecke's Journal of Voyages to Cape Verde, Guinea, and Angola (1605–1612),* Works Issued by the Hakluyt Society, 3d Ser., no. 5 (London, 2000), 59 (hereafter cited as Van den Broecke, "Journal"); [Cardoso], "Morte de D. Álvaro III," *MMA,* XV, 487–493.

35. Santissimo Sacramento, "Relação," *MMA,* IV, 386; Cácegas and Sousa, *Historia,* ibid., V, 611–612.

36. "Relação dos Carmelitas Dēsalços," ibid., IV, 406–407, 409 (Mbata reference), and 412–413; Santissimo Sacramento, "Relação," ibid., 369–371. See also John Thorn-

Typically, foreign priests thought that a lack of education rather than of will was to blame for any problems in Kongo's Christianity. Jesuits who came in 1575 found Kongo's Christianity to be "very weak," because the people had been baptized by "idiot priests" and their customs were "heathen." But they believed that the level of Christianization in Kongo was such that they could easily eliminate the defective elements by teaching. Carmelites voiced the same sentiments. In challenging claims that the Kongolese returned to "idolatry" and that many had not seen a priest for years, Diego de Santissimo Sacramento observed: "On the contrary, I did not find anyone who was apostate from the faith or returned totally to idolatry, because it was a point of honor to be Christian and they know well the error in which they sin. I only found that they go for reasons of sickness to their fetishers and priests of idols, and these are very cautious and do it secretly." Public disdain for those who abandoned the faith made them fearful that they would be reprehended and punished should they do so.[37]

Later missionaries generally made the same observations, though by the second decade of the seventeenth century the detailed reports of Jesuit missionaries rarely speak of any survivals of traditional religion. In fact, Jesuit Mateus Cardoso went so far as to write in 1624 that the Kongolese "never had idols or temples where they adored them, [as] they only knew God, whom they adored as the author of all good, whom they called Zambia-pungu, that is supreme lord of the sky, they also had knowledge of the devil; but they did not praise him, but they had reverence for him because he was the author of all evil, because they would not do it, they call him Cariam-pemba." Visiting Jesuits only occasionally mentioned the presence of "fetishes," and then only in the context of the inhabitants of the far eastern provinces. Otherwise, they seemed to believe that Kongo's shortcomings were those not of a newly converted people but of the normal sins of disrespect of the clergy.[38]

ton, "The Development of an African Catholic Church in the Kingdom of Kongo, 1491–1750," *Journal of African History,* XXV (1984), 147–167.

37. Diogo da Costa to Jesuit General, Mar. 20, 1592, *MMA,* XV, 317; "Relação dos Carmelitas Dēsalços," ibid., IV, 413.

38. [Mateus Cardoso], *História do Reino de Congo . . .* , ed. António Brásio (Lisbon, 1969), chap. 3, fol. 3, 20. For examples of the fetishes, see chronicle of Paiva, as used in Franco, *Synopsis annalium.*

Christianity arrived in Ndongo as a result of the first Portuguese (and then Kongolese) mission in 1520–1526 (mentioned above), but the people of Ndongo never took to it with the same enthusiasm as the Kongolese did. Dias de Novais's first mission, with its Jesuit priests, made some more converts, but still the general population was not involved. In 1564, Ngola Kiluanje kia Ndambi took an interest in Jesuit preaching, telling Father Francisco de Gouveia that "the time would come in which he would call me to teach him." When Gouveia died in 1575, the king noted that Gouveia "had raised and trained him since he was small," and he respected Gouveia enough that he called his "holy men and fetishers" to treat Gouveia's final illness, for whom he "had a lot of affection," calling him "his ganga." He sent his royal musicians to play as Gouveia was dying, gave him a lavish funeral, and had the priest buried in the Jesuit church. But neither he nor his sons took up Christianity.[39]

Jesuits also made some conversions among Ndongo subjects who lived near Kongo's territory at Luanda, where there were "ancient Christians of the land" governed by delegates sent from Kongo, especially in the land located just south of the Kwanza River. Soba Songa, whose lands lay in the same area, was baptized in 1581. An "in-law of the King of Angola [Ndongo]," whose lands lay south of the Kwanza's mouth across from Kongo territory, he was baptized on the Epiphany (January 6) 1581. Songa's ceremony reveals the pattern of appropriation that took place in Ndongo's territory. His baptism was a combination of feast (usually held on a feast day) and public celebration. Songa took the Christian name of Constantino to honor the Emperor Constantine, and then, wearing his Portuguese clothing, traveled through his lands with the priest, Baltasar Afonso, planting crosses in key locations and identifying and burning "houses of idols." Yet the priest noted that idols were still found in some of the houses. Elsewhere, even where they were not converted, Ndongo's people sometimes put European religious objects in their own shires as objects of worship.[40]

39. Francisco de Gouveia to Jesuit General Mirão, Nov. 1, 1564, *MMA,* XV, 232, and ibid., II, 527; Garcia Simões to Provincial, Oct. 20, 1575, ibid., III, 141; "História," ibid., IV, 555–556.

40. "Residençia de Angola," 1588, ibid., III, 378; Baltasar Barreira to Jesuit General, Jan. 31, 1582, ibid., XV, 269–278, and to Sebastião de Morais, Jan. 31, 1582, ibid., III, 209–210 (for a similar ceremony to Songa's a few weeks later, see Barreira to Jesuit General, Jan. 31, 1582, ibid., XV, 276); anonymous Jesuit letter to Provincial, Nov. 20, 1583, ibid., XV, 283–284.

The pattern of appropriation would continue even as the Portuguese advanced their conquest. The Portuguese began missionary activity in conquered areas as soon as they subdued sections of Ndongo's people in the wars that began in 1580. For example, Dias de Novais asked for ten priests in 1582 to minister to the new converts in lands conquered from Ndongo, as he had already had mass baptisms of five or six thousand people. Jesuits who accompanied the conquest sent out "chapel boys," some of whom had been trained to play European musical instruments, to teach and preach, and still others were to prepare the people for baptism. But even these conversions were hardly spontaneous or voluntary, as they were closely connected to Portuguese expansion and domination. Many people came to Dias de Novais "because of the cruelty of the king [Njinga Ngola Kilombo kia Kasenda]," as the Jesuit Diogo da Costa wrote. "Many of his vassals come to the governor; this year I baptized a few more than one hundred." Such membership in the Christian community could easily be put aside, and in 1594 the Jesuits realizing this complained, "Too many heathens have been baptized without instruction."[41]

It was in this context that Njinga's brother authorized her to accept baptism when she went as his ambassador to Luanda in 1622. But no sooner had she left the city than she put aside the rosary and other Christian objects she had received at her baptism and put her trust in local religious rituals, though she did keep them in her *misete* (ritual repository). Eventually, Njinga did return to Christianity with much more enthusiasm following the treaty of 1657.[42]

Although Ndongo formally adopted Christianity, the people never embraced the religion to the same degree that those of Kongo did. Christianity was associated with Portuguese domination and colonialism, so resistance to the Portuguese sometimes took on an anti-Christian air, and churches were attacked during rebellions. Imbangala raiders took up religious beliefs that were rooted in African concepts of witchcraft and formed a positively anti-Christian component that they spread to their captives. Njinga herself and many of her followers followed Imbangala rites from time to time.

41. Paulo Dias de Novais to king, Jan. 12, July 3, 1582, ibid., IV, 337, 342; Barreira to Jesuit General, Jan. 31, 1582, and May 15, 1593, ibid., XV, 278, 332; Diogo da Costa, May 31, 1586, ibid., III, 339; Pero Rodrigues, "Visita da Residencia de Angola . . . , 1594," ibid., III, 477.
42. MSS Araldi, Cavazzi, "Missione evangelica," A, book 2, 27.

The appropriation of Christianity in Central Africa by the elite also brought with it literacy in Portuguese. As early as 1491, for example, a Kongolese who had visited Portugal wrote letters for the newly baptized king and established a school. Afonso also had many schools established, one of which had at least one thousand students. A treason inquest of 1550 written in Portuguese reveals the plotters' writing to each other and shows the king's sending letters and other written orders to officials. Some elite Kongolese went to Portugal to study and be ordained, like Dom Juan (João), a relative of kings of Kongo whom Carmelite missionaries met in Mbamba in 1583. One of his companions, Álvaro, spoke Portuguese and was studying Castilian but had not yet mastered it when he met the Spanish priests. Although Kongolese usually did not write in Kikongo, a Kikongo catechism was produced in 1557; another in 1624 was a translation of a Marcos Jorge's Portuguese catechism done by the "best teachers of São Salvador." Outside of that, all written works were in Portuguese (and in a few other European languages, such as Latin and Spanish).[43]

Most of the nobility of Kongo also learned to speak Portuguese, another example of their appropriation of European culture. When visited by the Spanish Carmelites, however, King Álvaro I chose to speak to them in Kikongo, though they noted he could speak Portuguese. In 1607, Count Miguel of Soyo had no difficulty in reading aloud in Portuguese, in "perfect form," the letter of credentials presented to him by Dutch ambassadors. Education in Soyo was in the hands of a Portuguese priest named Don Gonsalves, "who teaches them everything." But literacy extended beyond this priest, for the same report noted the existence of "eight to ten schools here like those in Portugal, where all the children are instructed and taught in Portuguese," where "everyone goes the whole day with a book in hand and with a rosary." Another German visitor, Samuel Brun, a physician in Dutch employment, thought that the people of Soyo spoke Portuguese better than

43. "Devassa de d. Diogo Rei do Congo," *MMA*, II, 260–261, both a letter as an attachment and mention of other letters used as certificates; Santissimo Sacramento, "Relação," ibid., IV, 362–363; Pigafetta, *Relatione*, 68. Lopes claimed that they kept no records of litigations, but there exist inquiries and other court records in written form conducted in Kongo. Apparently his reference is to property litigations, which he said were nonexistent, as all land belonged to the king. The preface of the catechism of 1624 notes its production by Kongolese teachers under the supervision of the Jesuit Mateus Cardoso; see *Doutrina Christãa* (Lisbon, 1624).

most non-Iberians who adopted it. "They make their prayers in Latin and Portuguese and are with the Portuguese every day, they learn the language better. They also have schoolmasters as in Spain, but only in Spanish and Portuguese; in their own language they have none, for the latter is very hard to write and learn." Not surprisingly, Kongolese kept archives and had done so since at least the mid-sixteenth century, as their references to earlier letters in their correspondence amply attest. Extant Kongolese letters are signed and sometimes bear wax seals, and others once had them. The Carmelites received such a letter bearing the five armed swords of Kongo's official seal. Antonio Manuel's private papers, which contain sixty-nine documents dating between 1591 and 1608, attest to the proclivity for keeping documents even among private persons. There were, of course, public archives in the care of the state, for, in 1613, Álvaro II complained that his archives had been destroyed earlier during the "Jaga" invasions (1568–1571), precluding him from retrieving earlier papal bulls and pronouncements that had been stored there.[44]

Some nobles of Ndongo also became literate, though many fewer than in Kongo. Queen Njinga, for example, wrote letters and kept archives. In 1626, she sent a letter to the Portuguese commander at Ambaca, the first known written correspondence by a Ndongo ruler. Njinga was not herself literate, for she made a mark on the treaty of 1657, and her some dozen known letters were written by trusted secretaries. These letters dealt with trade, politics, and even personal matters. Her sister, Graça Kifunji, however, was literate. When she was captured by the Portuguese in 1629 and kept in captivity until 1646, she sent regular letters to Njinga, and she received letters from Kongo as well. (These letters were kept in an archive that fell into Portuguese hands when they defeated Njinga in 1646.) Njinga's rivals at Pungo Andongo, whom the Portuguese supported in their wars against her, also wrote occasional correspondence, as did Henrique in 1643. (In recent years, local archives of correspondence going back as far as the late seventeenth century have been found in towns and villages in Angola, though the antiquity of this correspondence cannot be fully established.)[45]

44. "Relação dos Carmelitas Dēsalços," *MMA,* IV, 396, and Santissimo Sacramento, "Relação," ibid., 363; Van den Broecke, "Journal," 59; Brun, *Schiffarten,* 28, English in Jones, ed. and trans., *German Sources,* 62; Álvaro II to Paulo V, Feb. 27, 1613, *MMA,* VI, 130.

45. Njinga's 1626 letter transcribed in Sousa to sons, 1630, *FHA,* I, 245; Cadornega, *História,* I, 418; Henrique, king of Dongo, to João IV, Mar. 10, 1643, *MMA,* IX, 39–40. Cadornega saw some of Graça Kifunji's letters himself; she kept them under an altar

Aside from adopting European and American crops, technology, diplomacy, Christianity, and literacy, Central African elites also sampled a wide range of European cultural offerings, including clothing, etiquette, and style. These especially complemented the diplomatic and religious initiatives. The Kongo elite went a bit further than elsewhere in Africa in incorporating European clothing into their own apparel. As early as the 1580s Duarte Lopes noted with regard to Kongo that the people, especially the nobility, took up European clothing styles after their conversion to Christianity. They wore "capes, mantles, scarlet cloaks, cloth of silk, berets" after the "Portuguese manner," including velvet and leather slippers and Portuguese half boots "according to their possibilities." Soldiers especially wore these boots frequently in operations. Women of the court, for their part, especially among the elite, veiled their heads and wore black velvet berets decorated with jewels, with gold chains around their necks.

Court etiquette also became more European. Álvaro I had decided to reform court etiquette in the 1570s, "in some degree in imitation of the king of Portugal," notably in table manners. When he ate in public, his table, covered with velvet tablecloth decorated with gold appliqué, was set on a three-step raised dais covered with an Indian tapestry. He had a sideboard with gold and silver vessels from which he ate and drank. The king maintained a courtly demeanor as well, for, when he went about to attend Mass or give his twice weekly audiences, all the nobles followed him, including trusted Portuguese who resided at court. Other elements of European culture were on display as well, for the king sat on a throne of European style with red velvet covering adorned with gold nails, placed on carpet. Although African music was still in use, missionaries reporting on life at court noted that there was already a "small chamber choir called Saint Joseph" performing European religious music. The king's "very richly ornamented chalice" had been "sent from the kings of Portugal when that land was dis-

---

in a shrine she had built. As a result of finding the letters from her sister Graça, the Portuguese ordered her to be drowned in the Kwanza by throwing her in a whirlpool.

For the beginnings of a larger effort to publish these documents, see Ana Paula Tavares and Catarina Madeira Santos, eds., *Africae Monumenta: A apropriação da escrita pelos africanos* I, *Arquivo Caculo Cacahenda* (Lisbon, 2002). This is a state archive of the "Dembo" Caculo Cacahenda containing 210 documents dating from 1677 to the early twentieth century. Other documents were recovered by Eva Sebastyén, mostly dating from the eighteenth century, during her stay in Angola in the early 1980s.

covered." The same throne was displayed when Álvaro III died forty years later in 1622, along with the carpet and a cushion on which the king put his knees in church at his funeral.[46]

Imitation of European nobility was not limited to the royal court. When the count of Soyo received the Dutch trader Pieter van der Broeke, he, like the king, was seated on a "Spanish chair with a red velvet covering and covered with gold tacks, and this chair stood on an expensive carpet." His clothing was a red damask robe with three wide gold trimmings, a black embroidered hat with gold and pearls that his subjects had made themselves." In 1612, Samuel Brun noted that in Soyo the count used local money to buy "silk and velvet" with which they decorated the churches. Rich cloth could be displayed at other provincial towns as well, for Dona Christina, wife of Dom Sebastião, the duke of Mbamba, gave the Spanish Carmelite Diego de Santissimo Sacramento a good piece of red damask in 1583. Even in the distant northeastern province of Nsundi, merchants bought and sold costly Portuguese and Indian cloth, paying for it in their own high-quality palm cloth.[47]

Some members of Ndongo's elite were also prepared to borrow the rich clothing style of the Portuguese elite. In 1582, when Portuguese Jesuits baptized the lord of Songa, a subject of Ndongo living near the mouth of the Kwanza River, he appeared wearing an outfit of Portuguese clothing. His son wore some red pearls, with yellowish boots and a cassock and clothing, with a white damask guoro that was newly made for him, and with an illustrious short-sleeved gown with a hood. Often when Ndongo elites allied with the Portuguese as they expanded their colony, they added some items of Portuguese clothing to their attire. Some of them, like Francisco Mwenge a Kiluanje, one of Portugal's important allies and a powerful noble, adopted full Portuguese attire. Most people, however, only added some items from Europe. Both men and women in Ndongo, for example, used imported pearls (locally called *anzolas*) made in Venice as money and ornamentation. When these beads were strung together in the manner of a rosary, they were called *missanga*. This taste for European items was found even among enemies of Portugal, for, following a large battle in the 1580s against the lord of Mosenque a Nzenza, Portuguese soldiers captured porcelain, cloth,

46. Pigafetta, *Relatione,* 67–68 (on the military half boots, see 21, with illustration); Santissimo Sacramento, "Relação," *MMA,* IV, 367; [Cardoso], "Morte de D. Álvaro III," ibid., XV, 285–286.

47. Van den Broecke, "Journal," 59; Brun, *Schiffarten,* 28, English in Jones, ed. and trans., *German Sources,* 62; Santissimo Sacramento, "Relação," *MMA,* IV, 365.

silk clothes, and Portuguese weapons as well as European chests. Certainly these were items of Portuguese provenance that the soba valued.[48]

Central African appropriation of European forms of diplomacy, religion, and a range of European material culture represented an early African reaction to globalization. Their willingness to be part of the community formed by European expansion differed sharply from the reactions of their counterparts in West Africa, in spite of the notable attempts by the Portuguese to spread their culture there as well. Kongo's receptivity to Europe contrasts strongly with that of Benin, for example, especially with regard to literacy and religion. Although much of this appropriation took place among the elite, who led the process, even common people participated, particularly in the adoption of Iberian names, most notably among the Kongolese. Those who might not have owned European clothing were likely to have seen it at festivals or other public gatherings where nobles met commoners and to have associated it with their own, rather than a foreign, culture.

Kongolese and Angolans who came to the Americas were therefore likely to be familiar with aspects of European culture in Virginia. This familiarity might engender both accommodation and resistance: they willingly participated in Christianity, had their children baptized and used their Christian background as a means to gain freedom; alternatively, they resisted as their counterparts in northern Brazil did when they created the runaway republic of Palmares, or as later arrivals in South Carolina did during the Stono Rebellion. In contrast, West Africans who followed them to the Chesapeake, who came from areas whose leaders were less accepting of European culture, were more likely to develop autonomous communities in the newly developing slave quarters. As slavery took root, the two strategies merged in the world of eighteenth-century slave society.[49]

48. Barreira to Jesuit General, Jan. 31, 1582, *MMA,* XV, 272; Cadornega, *História,* I, 115-116; Pigafetta, *Relatione,* 23-24; "História," *MMA,* IV, 570.

49. Ira Berlin, *Many Thousands Gone: The First Two Centuries of Slavery in North America* (Cambridge, Mass., 1998). On Palmares, see R. K. Kent, "Palmares: An African State in Brazil," *Journal of African History,* VI (1965), 161-175, for an account that focuses on its Angolan background; on the Stono Rebellion, see John Thornton, "African Dimensions of the Stono Rebellion," *American Historical Review,* XCVI (1991), 1101-1013.

James H. Sweet

AFRICAN IDENTITY AND SLAVE RESISTANCE
IN THE PORTUGUESE ATLANTIC

Every good historian of early English North America is familiar with the story of the "20. and odd Negroes" that arrived in Jamestown in 1619, purchased from a Dutch "man of Warr" by English settlers who themselves arrived in the Chesapeake only some twelve years earlier. We now know that this Dutch ship arrived at Point Comfort from the Caribbean, where it teamed up with the English corsair *Treasurer* to commandeer the Portuguese slave ship *São João Bautista*. The *São João Bautista* was on its way to Veracruz, Mexico, directly from the Angolan port of Luanda, where it collected a cargo of enslaved Africans, most likely from the Kingdom of Ndongo, about two hundred miles into Central Africa.[1]

Despite the almost certain Central African provenance of the pirated "20. and odd Negroes," some scholars have embraced the idea that these Africans, along with the hundreds who followed them over the next generation, were "Atlantic Creoles." Atlantic Creoles originated in coastal Africa and were intimate with European sociocultural norms. They were multilingual, culturally flexible, and socially agile. According to at least one proponent of this argument, these enslaved Africans "found the settlements around

I would like to thank John Coombes, Neil Kodesh, and Jessica Krug for commenting on early drafts of this essay. I would also like to thank the anonymous reviewers for their insightful suggestions.

1. Engel Sluiter, "New Light on the '20. and Odd Negroes' Arriving in Virginia, August 1619," *William and Mary Quarterly,* 3d Ser., LIV (1997), 395–399; John Thornton, "The African Experience of the '20. and Odd Negroes' Arriving in Virginia in 1619," ibid., LV (1998), 421–434. These were not the first Africans in the Virginia colony. William Thorndale has demonstrated that, in the March 1619 census, thirty-two Afro-Virginians were already in the colony. See Thorndale, "The Virginia Census of 1619," *Magazine of Virginia Genealogy,* XXXIII (1995), 155–170.

Chesapeake Bay little different from those they had left along the Atlantic rim . . . [and were] very much at home in the new environment."[2]

Several distinguished American historians have criticized the exaggeration of the Atlantic Creoles argument; yet the idea remains salient, not only in university classrooms but also in the realm of public history, through PBS documentaries like *Slavery and the Making of America*.[3] Debates over the character of North America's "charter generation" of African slaves likely will not cease anytime soon. Nevertheless, everyone seems to agree that the identities of the enslaved were forged through various cultural dialogues that encompass the breadth of the Atlantic world. Nowhere is this more suggestive than in the case of those enslaved Central Africans who passed from Imbangala, to Portuguese, to Dutch, and, finally, to English settlers' hands in Jamestown in 1619.[4]

This essay attempts to contextualize the "Creole" identities of Virginia's charter generation of African slaves, especially those "20. and odd" who arrived in the Americas on board a Portuguese vessel. Comparing and contrasting three different Portuguese Atlantic settings between 1550 and 1624 will demonstrate the historical contingencies of identity formation and suggest some of the variables that shaped the identities of runaway Africans in the early Portuguese Atlantic world. In Portugal, "Jolof" slaves used their Islamic identity to forge connections with "Turks" and "Moors," with whom they plotted to run away to North Africa. Kinship ties between ethnic Jolofs remained important, but the conditions of enslavement necessitated newer, broader alliances. In São Tomé and Brazil, enslaved Africans did not have the option of escaping back to their homelands; thus, they formed runaway communities in their new environments. Throughout history, these

2. Ira Berlin, *Many Thousands Gone: The First Two Centuries of Slavery in North America* (Cambridge, Mass., 1998), 40.

3. For critiques of the Atlantic Creoles argument, see "Tapestry of Shame," Peter Kolchin's review of Ira Berlin's *Many Thousands Gone* in *Los Angeles Times Book Review,* Nov. 22, 1998, 12. Also see James Oakes's review ("Slaves without Contexts") in *Journal of the Early Republic,* XIX (1999), 103-109. Finally, see Peter Coclanis's trenchant review of Berlin's more recent work, *Generations of Captivity: A History of African-American Slaves,* in *WMQ,* 3d Ser., LXI (2004), 544-556. As evidence of the traction of the Atlantic Creole idea, see Edward Countryman, ed., *How Did American Slavery Begin?* (Boston, 1999). The PBS documentary, *Slavery and the Making of America,* premiered on Feb. 9, 2005.

4. Imbangalas were Central African mercenary warriors who were responsible for the enslavement of thousands of Ndongo people between 1618 and 1620. See Thornton, "The African Experience," *WMQ,* 3d Ser., LV (1998), 421-434.

runaway communities have been characterized as essentially "Angolan." Closer examination reveals the complex and mixed ethnic heritage of runaway communities in both São Tomé and Brazil, particularly in their early years.

In the end, this examination may also shed light on the continuing debates over the complexities of identity formation in early British North America. Like the Jolofs in Portugal, the Central Africans who arrived in the Chesapeake in 1619 carried with them ideas and understandings that were deeply etched in their African pasts. Some of these ideas cohered with those that existed in the lands of their enslavement, and Africans capitalized on this confluence as a means to improve their condition. Still, as the São Tomé and Brazil cases will demonstrate, we must be careful not to generalize the early processes of identity formation in the Chesapeake. Enslaved Africans in early-seventeenth-century Virginia did not forge themselves as Atlantic Creoles, but neither were they able to create Ndongo, Angolan, or even Central African communities. Indeed, unlike the situation in other parts of the Atlantic world, the atomization of Africans in early Virginia precluded the creation of slave communities until at least the middle of the seventeenth century.

Portuguese Beginnings

The Atlantic slave trade began, not with the trade to the Americas, but rather with a substantial trade to Portugal and the Atlantic islands. As early as the second decade of the sixteenth century, Portuguese ships carried one thousand African slaves per year to various destinations in Africa, the Atlantic islands, and Portugal itself, making the enslaved the most commonly offered commodity on the African side of the Portuguese-African trade.[5] Such a start to the Atlantic slave trade was a clear expression of the potential for African supply and European demand. By the 1520s, more than 156,000 African slaves had been transported to Portugal and its Atlantic island colonies, roughly a third of the number that would be delivered during the entire 250-year history of the slave trade to the territories that would eventu-

5. Ivana Elbl, "The Volume of the Early Atlantic Slave Trade, 1450–1521," *Journal of African History*, XXXVIII (1997), 31–76. Elbl shows that slaves were 60–95 percent of all African exports to Europe during this period. For a further articulation of this argument, see Elbl, "'Slaves Are a Very Risky Business . . .': Supply and Demand in the Early Atlantic Slave Trade," in José C. Curto and Paul E. Lovejoy, eds., *Enslaving Connections: Changing Cultures of Africa and Brazil during the Era of Slavery* (Amherst, N.Y., 2004), 29–55.

ally become the United States. Though the trade to Portugal abated by the 1530s as the export market to the Americas blossomed, by the 1550s African slaves were once again arriving in Portugal in numbers that rivaled those from the earlier period.[6]

The largest concentration of Portugal's slaves resided in and around Lisbon, although significant numbers also lived in the major cities of the north and in the southern region of the country. Sub-Saharan Africans represented the largest contingent of slaves by the middle of the sixteenth century, but North African "Moors," Ottoman "Turks," and East Indians still accounted for a small portion of the country's enslaved population. By 1550, Lisbon had nearly ten thousand slaves, or roughly 10 percent of the city's population. In the southern region, slaves were widely scattered but overall represented around 6 percent of the population. Most urban slaves engaged in tasks that placed them in close contact with their masters—as body servants, apprentices, fishermen, and so forth. In rural areas, slaves worked as herdsmen, grape pickers, and in the production of olive oil.[7]

The level of discomfort in the daily lives of Portugal's African captives varied according to the nature of their work and the attitudes of their masters; some were treated cruelly. Chaining, whipping, and burning with hot wax were not unusual punishments for those accused of being derelict in their duties. Some slaves lacked adequate clothing and food. Africans were also susceptible to European diseases. By law, slaves were prohibited from gathering in groups, and nighttime curfews were also enforced. In short, slaves' lives in sixteenth-century Lisbon were not altogether unlike those of slaves in the urban areas that would later emerge in the Americas.[8]

6. A. C. de C. M. Saunders, *A Social History of Black Slaves and Freedmen in Portugal, 1441-1555* (Cambridge, 1982), 23.

7. Saunders, *Social History*, 50-58, 63-72. On southern Portugal, see Jorge Fonseca, *Escravos no sul de Portugal, séculos XVI-XVII,* Rota do escravo, no. 2 (Lisbon, 2002). Fonseca found that Africans and their descendants represented 83.7 percent of the south's slave population in the sixteenth century, followed by Mouriscos (9.3 percent), East Indians (6.5 percent), and a negligible number of Chinese (29-34). His data reveal that slaves made up only 5.5 percent of the population in southern Portugal in the sixteenth century, with only the Algarve reaching as high as 8.4 percent (28). These figures significantly reduce the estimated 10 percent claimed by Saunders for southern Portugal (54-55). Earlier histories of slavery in Iberia minimized the importance of slave labor in agriculture, but Fonseca notes that they were by no means inconsequential. In the southern region of Portugal, slaves were more likely to be engaged in agricultural pursuits than in any other tasks (36, 77-92).

8. Saunders, *Social History*, 107-108.

The African response to slave life in Portugal was rather predictable. Petty thievery was probably the most common form of resistance. Slaves stole fish, grapes, clothes, and such—all items to improve their daily living conditions. Others defied Portuguese law and the Catholic Church, gathering to socialize and gamble on Sundays and holy days. Still others took out their frustrations on their fellow slaves, violently lashing out with fists, clubs, and knives.[9] For those who found their lives particularly intolerable, flight was an option. Unlike most places in the Americas, no runaway slave communities existed in Portugal; there simply were not enough slaves to sustain such communities, and isolated runaways were easily identified. Those who made it across the Castilian border were frequently extradited to their Portuguese masters. The only sure way to effect successful flight was to land in North Africa, or *terra dos mouros* (land of the Moors), as it was more commonly known, some three hundred miles from the southern coast of Portugal. Such a trip required a boat and navigational skills or the financial means to pay a boat captain. Although the majority of slaves had none of these resources, some still tried to escape.

African slaves in Portugal attempted to steal boats and return to Africa from as early as the fifteenth century, but not until the 1550s do we see a rash of these attempts, almost always by Senegambian slaves. Indeed, among the slaves imported into Lisbon (and parts of the Americas) in the mid-sixteenth century were large numbers of Islamic Jolofs. The majority of these slaves were captured through warfare in Senegambia, as the coastal provinces of Kajoor, Waalo, and Baol broke away from the centralized rule of the Jolof interior.[10] As the Jolof confederation disintegrated in the middle of the sixteenth century, Portuguese traders took advantage of deep political divisions, purchasing slaves from all sides. Whether the political divisions of Senegambia continued to manifest themselves in the slave communities of Europe and the Americas is unclear. The Portuguese identified all en-

9. Ibid., 122–125. See, for instance, the case of the slave Manoel, who was arrested for playing dice games "only on Sundays" (Arquivo Nacional da Torre do Tombo [hereafter cited as ANTT], Chancelería D. Filipe III, Perdões e Legits, livro 14, fols. 308–308v [Oct. 18, 1623]). On slaves' stabbing other slaves, see ibid., fols. 310v–311 (Nov. 6, 1623), and livro 12, fol. 5v (July 23, 1633).

10. Boubacar Barry, *Senegambia and the Atlantic Slave Trade* (Cambridge, 1998), 8, 43–44. On the earliest attempts to steal boats and return to Africa, see Saunders, *Social History*, 137–138. James Lockhart found 45 "Jelofs" in a sample of 207 Africans in Peru between 1548 and 1560. These Jelofs constituted the largest group of Africans in his sample. See Lockhart, *Spanish Peru, 1532–1560: A Social History* (Madison, Wis., 1968), 173.

slaved peoples from the region as Jolofs, regardless of their former political affiliations. For slave traders and slaveowners, Jolofs came from the same broad region, spoke the same language, and had at least a marginal belief in Islam. The Portuguese were thus responsible for creating a homogenizing Jolof identity that ignored obvious divisions in northern Senegambia. At the same time, former enemies in Senegambia now had common cause in opposing their enslavement and Portuguese sociocultural hegemony. Many, if not most, of the enslaved quickly recast their identities to adhere to their new condition and context. Ironically, some had to embrace the very Jolof identity they had fought to shed in Senegambia.

Perhaps nowhere is the transformation and expansion of identity in the diaspora clearer than in the realm of religion. As slaves funneled out of Senegambia, they carried their Islamic beliefs with them. This Islamic identity allowed them to forge alliances with fellow slaves in Portugal, not only among fellow Jolofs but also among their Moorish and Turkish religious brethren. Indeed, one of the most striking features of Portuguese slavery for Jolof, Fula, and other Islamic Africans must have been the realization that many slaves shared Islamic faith, regardless of their race or place of birth. Thus, Islam became a central node of identity for many enslaved West Africans in Portugal.

The emergence of an enslaved Muslim community that included significant numbers of Jolofs facilitated the organization of plots to return to Islamic Africa. The majority of these escape attempts failed, but an examination of the individuals involved reveals a great deal about slave identity. Between 1553 and 1566, at least eight Jolof slaves were accused of attempting to return to North Africa. In some of these cases, religious affiliations among diverse Muslims were the inspiration for collective action. In 1561, for instance, an Islamic African named Antônio joined six white Mouriscos in a flight attempt. The seven men had already approached an East Indian boatman to carry them to North Africa, but the plot fell apart when one of the ringleaders was arrested and confessed to the Inquisition. Similarly, in 1564, a Jolof slave, also named Antônio, allied himself with two Turks in his attempt to flee to North Africa. Antônio claimed that, despite his baptism in the Catholic Church, he remained a Muslim and never truly became a Christian. The three men procured a boat and were prepared to depart when their plot was uncovered.[11]

In spite of zealous attempts by some Jolofs to escape, others determined that the risks of flight were too great. In 1554, two Turkish slaves asked a

11. ANTT, Inquisição de Lisboa, Processos, nos. 10845, 12869.

Jolof slave named Francisco to help them get to the "land of the Moors." Francisco, who operated a fishing boat for his master in the town of Setú-bal, agreed to carry the two Turks to North Africa. The three men decided to leave during the celebration of Nossa Senhora do Rosário, or, as it was also known, the "festa dos negros." On this day, however, the docks were closely guarded, perhaps in response to the flight threat posed by slaves on holy days. Francisco then told the men that any Saturday would probably be a better time to depart.[12]

Similar delays persisted for nearly a year, during which time Francisco prayed the *shahada* as well as other Muslim orations with his religious brethren. When the plot finally unraveled and Francisco was questioned by inquisitors, he claimed that it was not his will to go to North Africa; the Turks had coerced him. Furthermore, he stated, as a forty-year-old man, he was too old to earn money to feed himself in a new land. Francisco told the inquisitors that, when he arrived in Portugal, his master never taught him Catholic prayers and orations, and so he continued his Islamic ways. Francisco's efforts to throw himself at the mercy of the church worked. His only punishment was a short stay in jail and instruction in the faith. When he was reconciled to the church nine months after his arrest, the Inquisition demanded that he continue his religious instruction and attend Mass on Sundays and holy days. The inquisitors also ordered that his master not sell him under penalty of confiscation or payment of the equivalent of his value.[13]

Although religious brotherhood formed the basis for some runaway plots, other escape attempts were almost certainly the result of African kinship affinities. In 1566, a Jolof slave named Antônio tried to persuade another Jolof named Zambo to escape to the "land of the Moors." At the time, the masters of both slaves were imprisoned in the Castle of Lisbon. Antônio complained to Zambo that they were ill clothed and poorly fed. After many hours of conversation, Zambo finally relented and told Antônio, "Brother, let's go."[14]

The two men consulted a boatman named Antônio Fernandes, who agreed to deliver them to "any land of the Moors" in exchange for cash. They

12. Ibid., 7565. This association of the celebration of Nossa Senhora do Rosário with "the party of the negros" is significant in that Africans and their descendants were the most prominent devotees of Our Lady of Rosary. Saunders posits that the majority of black religious brotherhoods were dedicated to Our Lady of Rosary because of the "semi-magical, almost talismanic nature of the rosary itself." See Saunders, *Social History*, 152.

13. ANTT, Inquisição de Lisboa, Processos, no. 7565.

14. Ibid., 10870.

arranged a day and time for their departure and agreed to meet at the boat-man's house. In the interim, Zambo met an older Jolof man named Pedro, who asked if he could come along with them. Zambo agreed and also per-suaded a thirteen-year-old Jolof girl, Antônia, to make the journey. Zambo, Antônia, and Pedro arrived at the boatman's house at the appointed time. After waiting several hours for Antônio, the three Jolofs departed without their comrade. Just as they were launching their boat, they were captured by the police.[15]

In his defense before the Inquisition, Zambo claimed that Antônio had tricked him, forcing him to make the trip against his will. He noted that Antônio was an old man and had been in Portugal for many years. Explain-ing his own naïveté and that of the other Jolofs, Zambo told inquisitors that he had been in Portugal for only five years; Antônia had arrived the same year he had; and Pedro was "very boçal," having arrived only within the year. Zambo attempted to further protect the young girl, Antônia, by tell-ing inquisitors that he had forced her to join them. Ultimately, Zambo was sentenced to march in the Auto da Fé of 1567 and to undergo instruction in the faith.[16]

In the course of his interrogation, Zambo confessed that, even after being baptized in the Catholic Church, he remained committed to Mohammed and continued to recite Islamic orations. Nevertheless, his involvement in the plot to escape seemed to have far more to do with kinship than reli-gion. The kinlike relationship that was forged between him and the older man, Antônio, was cemented at the moment Zambo told him, "Brother, let's go." Moreover, Zambo took responsibility for a young Jolof girl who was particularly vulnerable. Finally, the recently arrived Pedro also was taken under Zambo's wing. Given Pedro's neophyte status in Portugal, he prob-ably could communicate only in the Wolof language. Indeed, the first lan-guage of all the conspirators was likely the language of their common home-land.

Several lessons can be learned from the escape attempts of Jolof slaves in sixteenth century Portugal. Even though Jolofs formed only a small group in Portugal, they found a much larger community of enslaved Muslims who could serve as potential allies. From as early as 1455, European travelers in Africa noted that the Jolof were "not . . . very resolute" in their practice of Islam, "especially the common people."[17] Islam in Senegambia remained

15. Ibid.
16. Ibid.
17. Alvise da Cadamosto, *The Voyages of Cadamosto and Other Documents on West-*

intertwined with beliefs in ancestral spirits and spirits from the natural world. Nevertheless, in Portugal, religious solidarity between enslaved Jolofs, Turks, and Moors served as a basis for resistance to slavery. For some Jolofs, religious identity probably took on far greater importance in Portugal than it had in their homeland, strengthening the Islamic presence that Portuguese Catholics sought to eradicate.

Moreover, even as Islamic religious identity took on new importance, kinship and kinlike networks remained paramount. Where they could, Jolofs sought out one another, engaged one another in conversation, and sought solutions to their collective condition. As Zambo's case illustrates, runaway attempts were not conspiracies by random slaves. They were built on affiliations that began in Africa through a shared language, a shared understanding of age and kinship obligations, and so on. In the end, Jolof identity in Portugal was simultaneously shaped by the Portuguese present and the African past, as the various cultural strands fused to create a new culture of resistance to slavery in Portugal.

Developing Communities of Runaways: São Tomé and Brazil

During roughly the same period that Jolof slaves were banding together to run away from their masters in Portugal, similar groups of slaves formed the Portuguese Atlantic's first runaway communities in São Tomé and Brazil. The history of runaway slave communities is intimately tied to some of the most important foundational myths of each of these countries. In São Tomé, the communities of *Angolares* have been held up as a bastion of Angolan-derived resistance to Portuguese colonialism. Similarly, in Brazil, the communities of Palmares have served to demonstrate the rejection of the colonial slave regime and the creation of an independent, Angolan-inspired "republic" in Pernambuco (present-day Alagoas). Although there is some degree of truth in each of these myths, the history of these societies is often collapsed into a timeless composite. In fact, it often seems that these runaway communities have no history at all. As rendered in much of the scholarly literature, these communities attained their essential characters almost from their inceptions and carried them forward into subsequent centuries. Following is an attempt to unravel the earliest histories of these famous runaway communities and to add some historical specificity to the foundational myths.

In the sixteenth century, São Tomé became the Atlantic's first true "sugar

---

ern Africa in the Second Half of the Fifteenth Century, trans. and ed. G. R. Crone, Works Issued by the Hakluyt Society, 2d Ser., no. 86 (London, 1937), 31.

society," its very creation and economic sustenance resting solely on the backs of African slaves. By the 1550s, the island had between sixty and eighty sugar mills that produced a total of 150,000 arrobas (2,150 tons) of sugar per year. The average sugar plantation had between one hundred and three hundred slaves, creating a slave labor force of around ten thousand for the entire island. Living conditions for the island's slaves were abysmal. Their huts were infested with fleas and lice. Disease and malnourishment were common. And it was not unheard of for masters to murder disobedient slaves. As would be the case some years later in Brazil, the ill treatment of São Tomé's slaves prompted one priest to comment that they were treated "worse than cattle."[18]

São Tomé's slaves responded to their daily hardships in much the same way as other slaves across the diaspora—they fled. From the very beginnings of sugar production on the island, slaves began running away from the cane fields, and the pace of slave flight increased rapidly by the second decade of the sixteenth century. Between 1514 and 1527, nearly 5 percent of the slaves that arrived in São Tomé escaped, accounting for almost 700 runaways. By the 1530s, long periods of famine prompted even more slaves to abandon the sugar plantations, swelling the ranks of the runaway communities. In 1530, the royal factor counted 230 slaves that fled to the interior. These slaves, from a variety of African backgrounds, usually ran to the densely wooded areas of the island. There, they formed communities that survived, in part, by raiding Portuguese villages. Planters and government officials became so concerned with the threat that they dispatched armed troops to destroy the runaway settlements. Only a year later, in 1531, the runaways defeated the troops that were sent to subdue them, prompting planters who lived nearest to the forest to abandon their properties and move closer to the city. Fearing imminent attack by the runaways, in 1535 residents of the island asked the Crown to send troops to aid in the *guerra do mato* (bush war). Entries into the bush were frequent but largely ineffective, as the runaway communities continued to grow. In 1545, one resident complained of an army of 600 to 800 armed slaves who attacked his

18. Robert Garfield, *A History of São Tomé Island, 1470–1655: The Key to Guinea* (San Francisco, Calif., 1992), 72–73; J. Cuvalier and L. Jadin, *L'Ancien Congo d'apres les archives romains (1518–1640),* Memoires de l'academie royale des sciences coloniales, XXXVI (1954), 154–155 (report of Bishop Ulhoa, ca. 1590). For the treatment of slaves in Bahia in the 1630s, see Father Antônio Rodrigues's comment that an overseer knew "how to treat the bulls better than the Negroes" (ANTT, Cartório dos Jesuítas, maço 69, no. 75).

homestead. By this time, the communities were self-replicating. During one entry in 1547, a planter and his armed slaves captured 40 fugitives, including women and children.[19] The cycle of runaways, assaults on the island's city, and the responses of armed militias continued throughout the second half of the sixteenth century, culminating in the 1590s in a series of bold attacks by the runaways on the island's major city, led by a man named Amador. The city of São Tomé was nearly overthrown in 1595. Though Amador was arrested and executed in 1597, runaways continued to plague the island well into the seventeenth century.

Despite the clear narrative of events leading to the buildup of São Tomé's runaway slave communities, described above, the dominant historiography of the island reveals a very different account. Indeed, the early history of runaway communities is practically erased in favor of a more dramatic story emanating from eighteenth-century oral history.[20] A group of enslaved Africans, known as Angolares, were shipwrecked off the coast of São Tomé in 1554. Supposedly, they were on their way from Angola to Brazil. The survivors of the wreck swam ashore and settled in the southern hinterlands of the island, building several small *quilombos* (runaway communities) on Mount Cambumbé. There, they continued to speak the Kimbundu language and to live according to Angolan customs. The first contacts between the Angolares and the island's other inhabitants allegedly came when runaways from the island's sugar plantations were welcomed into the Angolan community. Not until 1574 did the Portuguese learn of the Angolares, when the residents of the quilombos made their first raids on the city of São Tomé. Throughout the latter part of the sixteenth century, the Portuguese attempted to eradicate the Angolares, conducting military expeditions against the villages, but the Angolares were never vanquished.[21] Supposedly, the Angolar communities maintained their ethnic integrity well into the nineteenth century, as the inhabitants remained "fetishists and su-

19. Catarina Madeira Santos, "A formação das estruturas fundiárias e a territorialização das tensões sociais: São Tomé, primeira metade do século XVI," *Studia,* LIV–LV (1996), 77, 78; Rui Ramos, "Rebelião e sociedade colonial: 'Alvoroços' e 'levantamentos' em São Tomé (1545–1555)," *Revista internacional de estudos africanos,* IV–V (1986), 31, 34, 35.

20. Father Manuel Rosário Pinto recorded the oral history in 1734. For a transcription of this "Relação," see António Ambrósio, "Manuel Rosário Pinto," *Studia,* XXX–XXXI (1970), 205–329.

21. This version of events can be found in Francisco Tenreiro, *A ilha de São Tomé* (Lisbon, 1961), 63–73; and Garfield, *History of São Tomé Island,* 76–79.

perstitious like the Negro from Angola." They also purportedly held property in common, elected kings and chiefs, and spoke a language that was a mix of São Tomé dialect and Kimbundu.[22]

Several historians have questioned the veracity of the Angolar legend, noting that the mention of shipwrecks and the term "Angolar" do not appear in the documents until the eighteenth century. Moreover, until the middle of the sixteenth century, the majority of São Tomé's slaves were imported from Kongo, not Angola. Others came from the Bight of Benin and the Bight of Biafra.[23] The early runaway communities of São Tomé were thus a peculiarly Sãotomense phenomenon, reflecting the mixture of various African and Portuguese cultural influences. The later emphasis on Angola may be explained by the increased presence of Angolans in São Tomé beginning in the last decades of the sixteenth century, or it may be an error of the eighteenth-century oral sources, since the ethnic signifier "Angola" had come to mean any area along the West Central African coast, including Kongo. Certainly, São Tomé's "bush wars" of the late sixteenth century were not the direct legacy of a single shipwreck of Angolans; rather, they were the result of a mixed group of Africans who came together in the slave communities and forests of the island to assert their freedom.

Even as the city of São Tomé withered under Amador's siege in the mid-1590s, African slaves were creating the first significant runaway communities in Brazil. The connection between the two situations was not lost on the Portuguese. In 1597, the Jesuit priest, Pedro Rodrigues, noted that among the enemies of the Portuguese in Brazil were "the runaway negros from Guiné who are in some of the mountains of Brazil from whence they come to make raids, and there could come a time when they will dare to destroy

22. Almada Negreiros, *Historia ethnographica da ilha de S. Thomé* (Lisbon, 1895), 296–300. Gerardo A. Lorenzino's work on the Angolar language complicates the formulation of Almada Negreiros, noting the significant contribution of Kwa to the Bantu-Sãotomense mix. See Lorenzino, *The Angolar Creole Portuguese of São Tomé: Its Grammar and Sociolinguistic History* (Munich, 1998).

23. See Jan Vansina, "Quilombos on São Tomé; or, In Search of Original Sources," *History in Africa,* XXIII (1996), 453–459; and Gerhard Seibert, "A Questão da origem dos Angolares de São Tomé," Brief Papers, no. 5/98, Centro dos Estudos Africanos, Lisbon, 1998. John Thornton shows that imports from Mpinda to São Tomé rose from 2,000–3,000 in the 1520s to 4,000–5,000 in the 1530s, to as many as 6,000–7,000 in 1548 (Thornton, "Early Kongo-Portuguese Relations: A New Interpretation," *History in Africa,* VIII [1981], 183–204. Philip D. Curtin, *The Atlantic Slave Trade: A Census* (Madison, Wis., 1969), 99–100, estimates that roughly 20 percent of São Tomé's slaves came from the Bight of Benin and the Bight of Biafra.

the *fazendas* [cane farms], as their relatives do on the island of São Tomé." Of course, Father Rodrigues's prediction soon came to pass. By the beginning of the seventeenth century, runaways plagued Portuguese settlements from Bahia to Pernambuco. In a report describing the Jesuit mission to the Bahian Recôncavo in 1617, an anonymous priest wrote:

> The people from Angola who come to these parts . . . have the custom of fleeing to the woods, joining together in small groups and living from the assaults that they make on the residents, stealing livestock and destroying their crops and cane fields, which results in much damage and many losses, beyond those losses that come from the lack of their daily services. And many of them live for many years in the woods, and some never return because they go to the Mocambos, which are some . . . small villages . . . where they live many leagues inside the forest. And from there, they make their assaults, robbing and attacking and often times killing many. And in these assaults they try to carry away their male and female kinsmen to live with them as pagans.[24]

Little detail is known about these first African runaways, but Brazil's most famous runaway slave community, Palmares, also allegedly emerged during this early period in the southern part of Pernambuco. Like the history of the Angolares in São Tomé, the long history of Palmares has been distorted to reflect a dominant Angolan presence, albeit with influences from Brazilian-born blacks, Indians, and even whites. Based largely on documentation from the late seventeenth century, scholars have focused on the characterization of Palmares as an Angolan-derived quilombo. They also have emphasized important symbolic connections to Angola: members of the community called it "Angola janga" (little Angola), its leader was known as Ganga Zumba, and so on.[25] Robert Anderson has raised questions about the extent to which Palmares was Angolan in the late

24. Archivum Romanum Societatis Iesu (hereafter cited as ARSI), Brasilia 26, fol. 218, Brasilia 8, I, fols. 46–47. The report is also quoted in Stuart B. Schwartz, *Slaves, Peasants, and Rebels: Reconsidering Brazilian Slavery* (Urbana, Ill., 1992), 105.

25. The seminal study of Palmares is Edison Carneiro, *O Quilombo dos Palmares,* 4th ed. (São Paulo, 1988), orig. publ. as *Guerras de los Palmares* (Mexico City, 1946). Also see Décio Freitas, *Palmares: A Guerra dos Escravos,* 2d ed. (Rio de Janeiro, 1978). For African influences on Palmares, see Nina Rodrigues, *Os Africanos no Brasil* (São Paulo, 1933). The best-known English work on Palmares is still R. K. Kent, "Palmares: An African State in Brazil," *Journal of African History,* VI (1965), 161–175. Also see Stuart B. Schwartz, "Rethinking Palmares: Slave Resistance in Colonial Brazil," in Schwartz, *Slaves, Peasants, and Rebels,* 103-136.

seventeenth century. He notes that the population of Palmares was, by that time, largely Brazilian-born. Moreover, recent archaeological evidence suggests that there was a strong indigenous presence at Palmares in its later years.[26] These findings clearly demonstrate that Palmares underwent important transformations over the course of its history, but they reveal very little about the earliest years of the famous runaway community. When did Palmares take on its Angolan qualities? Were the Angolan influences a result of the first generations of slaves in Pernambuco, or did they come later?

Though we may never be able to answer these questions completely, one thing is clear: there is little evidence to suggest a preponderance of Angolan influences in the earliest manifestations of Palmares. Some scholars claim that the first runaway communities of Palmares emerged in the late sixteenth century.[27] If so, we can be almost certain that Palmares began as a mixed community of Indians and Africans of various backgrounds. Until the last decades of the sixteenth century, Brazil's slave population was made up largely of indigenous peoples. Africans began arriving in significant numbers around the middle of the sixteenth century from a variety of destinations, although Central Africa became the dominant source for the colony's slaves by the 1590s. Evidence suggests that the first groups of runaways were a reflection of this mixed slave population. In particular, runaway Africans joined so-called santidades, renegade communities that have long been associated with indigenous millenarianism. The santidade cult of Jaguaripe, Bahia, is perhaps the best known. There, Indian, African, and mixed-race runaways formed a religious community that sought to overthrow Portuguese slaveowners and to make themselves "lords of the white

26. Robert Nelson Anderson, "The *Quilombo* of Palmares: A New Overview of a Maroon State in Seventeenth-Century Brazil," *Journal of Latin American Studies,* XXVIII (1996), 545–566. Anderson uncovers a number of problems with Kent's research, including errors in Portuguese translation and faulty historical interpretations. Pedro Paulo de Abreu Funari, "A arqueologia de Palmares—Sua contribuição para o conhecimento da história da cultura afro-americana," in João José Reis and Flávio dos Santos Gomes, eds., *Liberdade por um fio: História dos quilombos no Brasil* (São Paulo, 1996), 26–51. More recently, see Funari, "Conflict and the Interpretation of Palmares, a Brazilian Runaway Polity," *Historical Archaeology,* XXXVII (2003), 81–93.

27. Freitas, *Palmares,* 15. See also Ronaldo Vainfas, "Deus contra Palmares: Representações senhoriais e idéias jesuíticas," in Reis and Gomes, eds., *Liberdade por um fio,* 62–63; and Flávio dos Santos Gomes, "Palmares," in Colin A. Palmer, ed., *Encyclopedia of African American Culture and History: The Black Experience in the Americas,* 2d ed., IV (New York, 2005), 1713–1716.

people." Adherents engaged in prayers, baptisms, speaking in tongues, and trances induced by alcohol and tobacco. Believers claimed that, once God freed them from the yoke of white supremacy, crops would grow abundantly without any attention, hunters' arrows would travel through the woods in search of prey while the hunters rested, and so on.[28]

Whether Africans understood the full implications of the Christian message elicited by santidades is impossible to know; the message of freedom was one that would have appealed to all slaves, however, regardless of background. The prospect of freedom in the santidades thus might have facilitated a redemptionist form of Christianity in some Africans. This message would have been particularly resonant with those handfuls of Central Africans who already had some contact with Christianity in Africa, a Christianity that was itself endowed with a healthy dose of redemptionist magic.[29]

Regardless of whether religion was part of what drew Africans to santidades, across Brazil during the sixteenth century the formula held that Africans joined Indians in *their* communities. For example, in 1588, Philip I wrote to the governor of Brazil, Francisco Giraldes: "I am informed that . . . between the captaincy of Bahia and Pernambuco, along the coast, there are more than three thousand Indians that have made fortifications, and they make . . . great damage on the farms of my vassals in those parts, drawing to their sides all the Guiné negros that have run away, and they impede the ability to travel from one captaincy to another."[30] Given the preponderance of Indian slaves in the sixteenth century, runaway and renegade communities were usually characterized as Indian. The earliest Africans found themselves more isolated from their African brethren than would later cohorts.

28. See Stuart B. Schwartz, *Sugar Plantations in the Formation of Brazilian Society: Bahia, 1550-1835* (Cambridge, 1985), 47-50; and, more recently, Alida C. Metcalf, "Millenarian Slaves? The Santidade of Jaguaripe and Slave Resistance in the Americas," *American Historical Review,* CIV (1999), 1531-1559.

29. For Christianity in Central Africa, see the various works of John K. Thornton, especially "The Development of an African Catholic Church in the Kingdom of Kongo, 1483-1750," *Journal of African History,* XXV (1984), 147-167; "Perspectives on African Christianity," in Vera Lawrence Hyatt and Rex Nettleford, eds., *Race, Discourse, and the Making of the Americas: A New World View* (Washington, D.C., 1995), 169-198; and "Religion and Cultural Life in the Kongo and Mbundu Areas, 1500-1800," in Linda Heywood, ed., *Central Africans and Cultural Transformations in the American Diaspora* (Cambridge, 2002), 71-90.

30. Instituto do Açúcar e do Álcool, *Documentos para a história do açúcar* (Rio de Janeiro, 1963), I, 359-360.

As such, they allied themselves with Indians in a variety of settings, usually known as santidades, as a way of escaping their servitude.

Over time, as more and more Africans began to arrive in Brazil, the Portuguese conflated the meanings of "santidade" and "mocambo" (the Kimbundu word for "hideout").[31] On the one hand, this was a logical shift in the perception of the residents, as prototypical runaway communities shifted from Indian to African. On the other hand, this conflation was an expression of continued alliances between Indians and Central Africans. In 1612, for example, Diogo de Campos Moreno claimed, "Indians run away to the forest . . . where they create . . . abominable rituals and behaviors, joining the negros from Guiné, who have also run away, which results in deaths, thefts, scandals, and violence, so that nobody is able to cross the backlands safely from one part to the other, nor are they able to expand the settlements further into the interior." Moreno noted that these were "mocambos among the negros, or gatherings of runaways that are called Santidades."[32] Not only did Moreno use the terms "mocambos" and "santidades" synonymously, but also his statements demonstrate that, by the second decade of the seventeenth century, Indians were beginning to join well-established African communities, rather than the other way around. Slowly but surely, santidades were giving way to mocambos, as Central Africans supplanted other Africans and Indians in Brazil's slave population.

The use of the Kimbundu term "mocambo" as early as 1612 is a watershed in the history of Brazilian runaway communities. Distinctly Central African ideas were already becoming salient enough to penetrate into the Portuguese vernacular, as the Kimbundu "hideout" became the preferred way of describing runaway slave communities. Yet there is no evidence that these communities were quilombos, the lineageless warrior groups of Angola that were allegedly the inspiration for the social organization of Palmares. The first known use of the term "quilombo" in Brazilian documents does not occur until 1691. Indeed, the first use of the term in the entire Portuguese-speaking world appears as late as 1622 in Angola.[33] That Palmares, or any of the early runaway communities in Brazil, were called quilombos by their inhabitants, or by the Portuguese, is thus highly unlikely.

31. Other scholars have noted this same trend. See, for instance, Ivan Alves Filho, *Memorial dos Palmares* (Rio de Janeiro, 1988), 10–11; and Metcalf, "The Santidade of Jaguaripe," *AHR*, CIV (1999), 1531–1559.

32. Diogo de Campos Moreno, *Livro que dá razão do estado do Brasil—1612* (Recife, 1955), 110, 113.

33. Schwartz, *Slaves, Peasants, and Rebels,* 125; Vansina, "Quilombos on São Tomé," *History in Africa*, XXIII (1996), 453.

So how and when did Palmares shift from "mocambo" to "quilombo"? Events on both sides of the Atlantic probably contributed to this shift. Marauding bands of warriors, who called themselves Imbangala, emerged in Central Africa from as early as the 1580s, organizing themselves into *kilombo,* merit-based, male warrior societies that cut across lineage boundaries, erasing ties based on natal descent. These lineageless warrior societies were a pragmatic solution to the fracturing of natal kinship units caused by drought, famine, war, and forced migration that plagued Central Africa from the 1570s to the 1590s. By the 1620s, Portuguese governors in Angola employed kilombo warriors as mercenaries to capture hundreds of slaves in the regions around Luanda. These slaves, large numbers of whom were funneled into Brazil, came from diverse backgrounds, but generally they were from the Kikongo-speaking regions to the north of Luanda and the Kimbundu-speaking regions south of the Kwanza River. In the ensuing chaos created by Imbangala assaults, many people were forced to abandon their ancestral homes and regroup in the rugged highlands, often with unrelated strangers. The military-corporate organization of these refugee communities was not at all unlike the maroon communities that would later emerge in the Americas.[34] Nor was the social hierarchy of these refugee communities far removed from the organization of the Imbangala. For those who would arrive in Brazil from diffuse Central African refugee communities, the kilombo provided a unifying template for lineageless social organization, despite the associations with their own enslavement.[35]

On the Brazilian side, the Dutch invasion of Pernambuco in the early 1630s provided slaves with ripe opportunities to abandon the plantations and flee for the forests. The Dutch probably imported small numbers of slaves through the 1640s, but the conflict and disruption caused by the power struggles in Pernambuco and Luanda almost certainly inhibited the flow of slaves to the region.[36] Meanwhile, the Dutch engaged in a series of

34. Joseph C. Miller, *Way of Death: Merchant Capitalism and the Angolan Slave Trade, 1730–1830* (Madison, Wis., 1988), 142; Beatrix Heintze, *Asilo ameaçado: Oportunidades e consequências da fuga de escravos em Angola no século XVII* (Luanda, 1995); Miller, "Central Africa during the Era of the Slave Trade, c. 1490s–1850s," in Heywood, ed., *Central Africans,* 46-47. For the development of the kilombo in Central Africa, see Miller, *Kings and Kinsmen: Early Mbundu States in Angola* (Oxford, 1976), 112–175.

35. The inhabitants of Palmares allegedly enslaved some of the people that they captured in their raids. From this perspective, enslavement is simply a potential outcome of warfare.

36. The Dutch invaded Pernambuco in 1629 and were not expelled until 1654. They

campaigns against the runaway communities of southern Pernambuco, indicating the growing strength and unity of these communities. During this period, the social organization of the quilombos likely began to take shape.

Thus, there were no quilombos in Brazil before 1624. Historians continue to cast the earliest runaway communities as quilombos, however, particularly owing to the nature of the source materials on Palmares. Since almost all of our knowledge about the Palmares comes from documents written in the 1680s and 1690s, historians tend to collapse the first ninety years of its history into the final ten years, distilling the community's long history into a snapshot of the quilombos. Moreover, the term "quilombo" has come to mean any runaway slave community in Brazil, significantly broadening the narrower, seventeenth-century definition of the term, thus casting a more unified, militant, African light on slave resistance and black power in Brazil.[37] To the extent that the term "quilombo" homogenizes a much more complicated early history of Palmares, it is not unlike the foundational myth of São Tomé's Angolar communities.

The three cases of slave resistance presented here—Portugal, São Tomé, and northeast Brazil—demonstrate the complex interplay between history, politics, and identity. In particular, they reveal how early histories are subject to contestation, transformation, and even erasure. In sixteenth-century Portugal, African slavery was not uncommon; yet there is a fairly widely held belief among educated Portuguese that there were never slaves in Portugal. Others believe slaves arrived in Portugal only as appendages of their Brazilian masters. In other words, African slavery in Portugal was incidental to the colonial and, especially, the Brazilian experience. The early history of Africans in Portugal is often forgotten as a result, because slavery is tied to colonial exploits in the Atlantic world outside Portugal. This erasure of slavery in Portugal is particularly unfortunate, since so many facets of it tie directly to the burgeoning Atlantic world.[38]

---

also seized Luanda in 1641, only to be removed in 1648. On the slave trade, see David Eltis, "The Volume and Structure of the Transatlantic Slave Trade: A Reassessment," *WMQ,* 3d Ser., LVIII (2001), 17–46.

37. For a fuller elaboration of the meaning of *quilombo,* see Schwartz, "Rethinking Palmares," in Schwartz, *Slaves, Peasants, and Rebels,* 125. On the political symbolism of Palmares, see Abdias do Nascimento, "Quilombismo: An Afro-Brazilian Political Alternative," *Journal of Black Studies,* XI (1980), 141–178.

38. An example of the Portuguese apology for slavery can be found in no less a figure than the duke of Bragança, who in August 2000 wrote that works by foreign scholars, emphasizing Portugal's slave past, are examples of the "falsification of his-

São Tomé and northeast Brazil demonstrate different, but no less problematic, trends. The combination of sloppy methodology and the influences of presentist politics can significantly alter the ways we interpret the past. The early histories of the most famous runaway slave communities in São Tomé and Brazil, as shown above, are more complicated than the foundational myths allow. Though the romanticism and political power of revisionist histories might be transformed when we dig deeply into these myths, we more clearly reveal the complex historical processes of an Afro-Atlantic world in formation.

In Portugal, African identity was a determining factor in who attempted to escape from slavery in the middle of the sixteenth century, but this identity was far more nuanced than simple ethnicity. Jolofs shared cultural traits with other Jolofs, but they were also marginally Islamic. As such, Jolofs forged alliances with other non-Jolof Turks and Moors to mitigate the effects of their shared slavery. For some Jolofs, their Muslim identity likely became dominant in Portugal. For others, however, the ethnic past took precedence, as atomized Jolofs sought out one another in urban settings like Lisbon. The bottom line was much the same: the recasting or reassertion of identities in Portugal was aimed, in part, at liberation from enslavement.

For Central Africans in São Tomé and Brazil, the possibility of escape to an ethnic or religious homeland was not possible in the same way that it was for Jolofs in Portugal. The alternative was the formation of runaway communities in the countries of their enslavement. All evidence suggests that the earliest runaways went in small groups of two or three, only constituting larger communities as these small groups came together over time. In São Tomé, these runaways included slaves from the Bight of Benin and the Bight of Biafra as well as those from Central Africa. In Brazil, the first small groups of runaways ran to settlements that had already been established by Indians. Thus, identity was shaped largely by conditions of the particular slave society. Only under the influence of increasing numbers of Central Africans did these diffused groups come together to form what would later be characterized as African-derived quilombos.

Ultimately, the identities of runaway slaves in the Atlantic world shifted in accordance with transformations in Africa and the diaspora. Joseph Miller's conclusion that "the transatlantic connection lies less in the transfer of

tory," prompted by a "war which some countries launched against Portugal" (Letters to the Editor, *Anglo-Portuguese News* [Lisbon], Aug. 17, 2000). See Howard B. Johnson, "Storm over Sagres; or, How a Book Review Caused a Duke to Lose His Cool," http://www.people.virginia.edu/~hbj8n/storm.pdf.

an integral set of practices than in ad hoc strategies of assembling new communities out of refugees of the most disparate backgrounds" is, to a large extent, correct.[39] Beliefs and practices evolved and were cast anew in the environments of the diaspora, but no more so than they were under similar shifts in the social, political, or economic conditions of Africa itself. Indeed, it is very difficult even to talk about "integral" (that is, ethnic) practices in early-seventeenth-century Angola, where thousands of people were already dislocated refugees and runaways before their entry into the Atlantic slave trade. Nevertheless, many of these Central Africans shared the refugee experience and equipped themselves with commonly understood ways of reformulating their identities. Assembling new communities often went hand in hand with the creation of new sets of social and cultural practices that could be understood by all. The development of shared languages, religious beliefs, and social structures resulted in integrally Central African forms that were transferred to places like Brazil through a Kimbundu lingua franca, a broadly shared belief in the power of ancestral spirits *(kilundu)*, and lineage hierarchies like the kilombo. The peculiarities of various American slave settings no doubt led to alterations in the function of Central African practices, but the forms often remained the same. Thus, the cultural flexibility and adaptability that have so often been associated with slave communities in the Americas were already institutionalized in various Central African social and cultural forms, forms that were also essential to cultural survival and transformation in the diaspora. These integrally Central African forms were especially evident in places like seventeenth-century Brazil, where Central Africans made up more than 90 percent of the enslaved population.

The dynamic interplay between the history of Africa and the history of the diaspora transcends the three cases discussed here, bearing strongly on the history of the entire Atlantic world. Research on the slave trade increasingly enables us to trace the origins of groups of enslaved Africans, if not by particular ethnicity, then certainly by "provenance."[40] By reading the history of enslaved African peoples, moving forward in time we are able to gain a much better insight into historical change among Africans in various diasporic destinations. Moreover, we can begin to compare the experiences

39. Joseph C. Miller, "Retention, Reinvention, and Remembering: Restoring Identities through Enslavement in Africa and under Slavery in Brazil," in Curto and Lovejoy, eds., *Enslaving Connections,* 92.

40. For the useful conceptualization of "provenance groups," see Mariza de Carvalho Soares, *Devotos da cor: Identidade, étnica, religiosidade e escravidão no Rio de Janeiro, século XVIII* (Rio de Janeiro, 2000), 95-127.

of common sets of Africans, noting how their identities diverged from one another in the diaspora.

During roughly the same period that Jolofs tried to flee from Portugal to North Africa, for example, runaway Jolof slaves in Santo Domingo stole horses from their Spanish masters, attacking colonial settlements on the island. In this way, they capitalized on cavalry skills learned in their homelands.[41] The toolbox from which these Jolofs drew their weapons of resistance was the same one that was used by Jolofs in Lisbon; however, their tool of choice was dictated by the context of their enslavement. Whereas Jolofs in Lisbon drew on their Islamic identity and their knowledge of nearby North Africa, Jolofs in Santo Domingo capitalized on their knowledge of Spanish horses. Ironically, the tools of resistance that were used by these widely scattered, enslaved Jolofs were the result of knowledge gained in earlier cultural exchanges with Arab Muslims and Portuguese in Africa. To that end, what was integrally Jolof was already integrally Atlantic, even in the sixteenth century.

These same lessons regarding continuity, change, and disjuncture in the diaspora can be seen in the experiences of the first African slaves in English-speaking North America. If the "20. and odd" Africans arriving in Virginia in 1619 were Central Africans from the Kingdom of Ndongo, how might they have been the same or different from those from Ndongo in northeastern Brazil who would contribute to the early manifestations of Palmares? How might they have compared to others from Ndongo who were arriving in Cartagena, New Granada (Colombia)?

Among other things, many of these Central Africans likely shared a rudimentary understanding of Catholicism. In the 1620s, Jesuit Father Alonso de Sandoval commented at length on the instruction needed to prepare African slaves for baptism in Cartagena. In discussing Central Africans, he noted, "If they are from Loanda, Angolas, Angicos, Congos, and Malemba, etc., they ordinarily *bring* enough knowledge to be validly baptized."[42] This prior knowledge of Catholicism was only one of the possible tools that could be used by Central Africans to help ameliorate their condition as slaves. In Brazil, as already noted, a certain form of redemptionist Christianity

41. Carlos Esteban Deive, *La esclavitud del Negro en Santo Domingo (1492–1844)*, 2 vols. (Santo Domingo, 1980), II, 445–454. On the increasing importance of horses in Senegambian warfare, see Ivana Elbl, "The Horse in Fifteenth-Century Senegambia," *International Journal of African Historical Studies*, XXIV (1991), 85–110.

42. Alonso P. de Sandoval, *De instauranda aethiopum salute: El mundo de la esclavitud negra en America* (Bogotá, 1956), 380 (emphasis added).

might have animated the first Africans who fled to the santidades. During this period, the idiom of resistance was a shared Indian-African millenarianism that included elements of Christianity. But, over the course of the seventeenth century, as Central Africans came to dominate the slave population, they were able to re-create core cultural expressions from their African pasts, calling upon their ancestors in a variety of healing and divination rituals aimed at curing physical ailments and contesting their enslavement. In places where Central Africans constituted the majority of the population, as in much of northeastern Brazil, these beliefs and rituals had far greater resonance than the elemental, Africanized Catholicism that some might have learned in their homelands. Moreover, Catholicism in Brazilian slave society often came with Bible in one hand and whip in the other. Ultimately, Central African healing and divination were viewed as more powerful weapons against the institution of slavery than the Catholicism that was most closely associated with the raw power of masters.[43]

In places like early Virginia, the possibilities of re-creating distinctly Central African beliefs were far more remote than in seventeenth-century Brazil. Isolated and atomized from their countrymen, the "20. and odd" Central Africans were more likely to find an outlet for their Christian beliefs than for any other forms of Ndongo or even broadly conceived Central African beliefs. Their proximity to their masters and, particularly, to white indentured servants meant that these earliest Central Africans, and those that followed them in the seventeenth century, were more fully integrated into the day-to-day affairs of English colonial life, including the practice of Christianity. Here, Central Africans quickly came to understand that Christian practices (however Catholicized or Africanized) were a potential passageway to an improved condition, perhaps even freedom. Indeed, this nascent African-Christian identity, combined with integration into communities of British indentured laborers, some of whom were Irish Catholics, probably goes further to explain the development of cultural expressions in early Virginia than the presence of so-called Atlantic Creoles among the first

43. The Catholic Church was among the largest slaveholders in Brazil, especially during the early colonial period. In particular, the Benedictines and the Jesuits owned large sugar estates. See Dauril Alden, *The Making of an Enterprise: The Society of Jesus in Portugal, Its Empire, and Beyond, 1540–1750* (Stanford, Calif., 1996); and Stuart B. Schwartz, "The Plantations of St. Benedict: The Benedictine Sugar Mills of Colonial Brazil," *Americas*, XXXIX (1982), 1–22. On Central African religious practices in Brazil, see James H. Sweet, *Recreating Africa: Kinship, Culture, and Religion in the African-Portuguese World, 1441–1770* (Chapel Hill, N.C., 2003).

slaves.[44] Like the first runaway Africans in Brazil who adapted themselves to the redemptionist Christianity of Indian communities, Central Africans in Virginia used their prior knowledge of Christianity as a tool to integrate the community of servants in Virginia. These Central Africans would have found it in their best interest to elide the differences between themselves and British servants, who were ultimately freed after their period of indenture. By becoming like servants instead of like slaves, Central Africans challenged notions that they were chattel, opening the way for manumission and roles as freedmen.[45]

Ultimately, the first Central Africans that arrived in the Chesapeake were not unlike those that arrived in other parts of the diaspora; the conditions of their enslavement were, however, markedly different. As with Central Africans in Brazil, the culture and the society of the Chesapeake determined their possibilities and shaped the choices they made. By comparing and contrasting the experiences of enslaved Africans with similar pasts and charting the processes by which their identities were transformed across diverse spaces, we can begin to realize wider possibilities in the study of the so-called Black Atlantic.

44. During the seventeenth century, several Irish women were known to have had relationships with black slaves in the Chesapeake. The most famous of these, "Irish Nell" Butler, married the "saltwater" slave, Charles, in a Catholic wedding in 1681. Similarly, in 1713, an "Irish woman named Grace [was] married to a Negro man" (Martha Hodes, *White Women, Black Men: Illicit Sex in the Nineteenth-Century South* [New Haven, Conn., 1997], 19–38). The extent of Irish-African alliances and Catholic resistance in early Virginia can only remain speculation. By 1700, however, the rising numbers of Irish servants alarmed some English colonists, who feared the growth of Catholicism. See Margaret M. R. Kellow, "Indentured Servitude in Eighteenth-Century Maryland," *Histoire Sociale / Social History,* XVII (1984), 236–237. For Irish-African alliances in the British Caribbean, see Hilary McD. Beckles, "A 'Riotous and Unruly Lot': Irish Indentured Servants and Freemen in the English West Indies, 1644–1713," *WMQ,* 3d Ser., XLVII (1990), 505–522. For a fine reexamination of the cultural exchanges between white servants and blacks slaves, see John C. Coombs, "Building 'the Machine': The Development of Slavery and Slave Society in Early Colonial Virginia" (Ph.D. diss., College of William and Mary, 2003).

45. Perhaps the most obvious case of Christian expression is that of Anthony Johnson, who almost immediately after arriving in the colony in 1621 married a woman named Mary. Their four children were also baptized in the Anglican Church.

part three

EUROPEAN MODELS

Marcy Norton & Daviken Studnicki-Gizbert

THE MULTINATIONAL COMMODIFICATION

OF TOBACCO, 1492–1650

AN IBERIAN PERSPECTIVE

Some twenty years after the settling of Jamestown, Charles I remained openly ambivalent about the prospects of Virginia. The problem was tobacco, a plant that never found much favor with his predecessor, James I, who in 1604 penned the famous tract *A Counterblaste to Tobacco.* "This plantation," Charles wrote in 1627, "is wholly built upon smoke, tobacco being the only means it has produced."[1] Given the dangerously precarious nature of the fledgling colony, he advised the Governor and Council of Virgnia to diversify, to explore more substantial possibilities such as mining, pitch making, or lumbering. Time would show that Charles had little reason to be concerned. Virginia's dedication to the commercial planting of tobacco charted a remarkably successful path of colonial development. In that same year, Virginia planters exported some 300,000 pounds of tobacco to England. Ten years later, this volume would have quadrupled. Smoky and ephemeral as they might have seemed at first, Virginia's tobacco foundations ultimately proved robust and long lasting.[2]

In addition to the input offered by many conference participants, we would like to acknowledge the following colleagues and assistants for their timely and generous help with the research and writing of this paper: Peter Cook, Alejandro de La Fuente, Kate Desbarats, Chouki El-Hamel, Jessica Julius, and Christian Krelling.

1. Charles I to the Governor and Council of Virginia, November 1627, in Karen Ordahl Kupperman, John C. Appelby, and Mandy Banton, eds., *Calendar of State Papers,* Colonial Series (hereafter cited as *CSP,* Col.), *North America and the West Indies, 1574–1739,* I, *1574–1660,* CD-ROM (London, 2000), 86. The smoke motif was also taken up in William Bullock's *Virginia Impartially Examined . . .* (London, 1648).

2. "Brief Answer to the Propositions Touching Tobacco Lately Delivered . . . ," July 1624, *CSP,* Col., I, 69; and petition of the Governor, Council, and Burgesses of Virginia to the king, Mar. 26, 1628, ibid., 89. Long-term data are given in Russell R. Menard,

This essay provides background and context for the development of the trade and production of English tobacco in the Americas. Although it is possible to enclose the history of the Virginia plantation with the history of seventeenth-century English empire building or American nation making, there is a case to be made for placing this history within the broader frame of the commodification of tobacco in the Atlantic. Transformed into a plantation crop at the turn of the seventeenth century across the Caribbean basin, tobacco quickly became one of the principal staples circulating in the transatlantic trades. Tobacco progressed as it did in large part because of multinational exchanges and alliances between a wide set of actors—Amerindians, Africans, and Europeans of different nations and communities; that is, the early history of tobacco ranged across national boundaries and spheres of colonial empire.

The alternate view is that tobacco cultivation was a product of imperial, or at least colonial, designs. In the case of Virginia, tobacco was the staple struck upon to assure the economic sustenance of the first English colonies, colonies that were key pieces in a policy aimed at challenging, and then breaking, the Spanish Empire's hegemony over the Atlantic. Success in Virginia, wrote an English contemporary, would put "a bit in our ancient enemies' mouth."[3] This view fits into a narrative keyed to the story of David and Goliath: a narrative of imperial rivalry in which England, a small but plucky European power, resists invasion in 1588 by the most powerful armada of the century, goes on to repeatedly "singe the beard of the king of Spain" through a well-directed campaign of naval raids, and then gets down to the more serious matters of settling plantations, establishing colonial trading circuits, and creating an Atlantic empire that would, in time, eclipse that of Spain. Its central cast includes some of the most signal figures of Elizabethan England—Raleigh, Drake, Grenville, Hawkins—men who made their name in this Atlantic theater of war, privateering, and raiding. Within this context, the development of Anglo-American tobacco production and trade, the vital underpinning of a successful colonization strategy, was simply the continuation of war by economic means.[4]

"The Tobacco Industry in the Chesapeake Colonies, 1617-1730: An Interpretation," *Research in Economic History,* V (1980), 109-177.

3. Sir Thomas Dale to Sir Ralph Winwood, June 3, 1616, *CSP,* Col., I, 17.

4. Carole Shammas, "English Commercial Development and American Colonization, 1560-1620," in K. R. Andrews, N. P. Canny, and P. E. H. Hair, eds., *The Westward Enterprise: English Activities in Ireland, the Atlantic, and America, 1480-1650* (Liverpool, 1978), 153-154, 160.

The adoption of tobacco was Virginia's primary staple in a broader pattern of colonial economic development that unfolded, quasi-simultaneously, across the western Atlantic seaboard. Consider the dates. Tobacco was planted by English settlers in Virginia for the first time in 1607. Six years later, the first major shipment of Virginia tobacco was unloaded on the London docks. These dates fall in the middle of a rather narrow chronological slice, a moment, really, of other first times for the planting and marketing of the crop. The first tobacco plantation was established in 1589 in Trinidad by a Luso-Spanish consortium of merchants, planters, and officials who settled the island with laborers—both European servants and African slaves. Almost immediately thereafter, tobacco appeared as a colonial staple across the Spanish Caribbean, in Cuba, Santo Domingo, Puerto Rico, and Venezuela. Tobacco was then taken up by other nations, both Amerindian and European, so that, by the 1610s, it was possible to find tobacco being grown for Atlantic markets from the Chesapeake to the Bahian Recôncavo, the heartland of the Brazilian plantation economy.[5]

The first matter this essay addresses is the origins of this sudden flourishing of tobacco plantations. Tobacco, as a plantation crop, was different from sugar, which was transposed from the eastern Atlantic as early as 1514.[6] The commodification of tobacco was slower and more complex. Its consumption was noted in the very first European accounts of discovery and was clearly a key piece of pre-Conquest Amerindian life across the continents. But it would take close to a century before it was raised for market on plantations. Tobacco had to move from indigenous consumers and traders to Afro-Caribbean market women, to the popular classes of Europe, until it finally became a crop that was raised by servile labor and sold on transatlantic markets.

The remarkable takeoff of tobacco as a staple was made possible by numerous commercial connections lacing across the Atlantic—this is the second theme of the essay. These connections provided the infrastructure that linked producers to consumers and allowed for the mutual stimulation of supply and demand. Mapping out the full extent of these exchanges and networks is beyond the scope of this essay; we simply sketch in the range of

5. On the economic geography and definition of the Recôncavo region and the early planting of tobacco there, see Stuart B. Schwartz, *Sugar Plantations in the Formation of Brazilian Society, 1550–1835* (New York, 1985), 19, 85.

6. The early history of the arrival of sugar in the Caribbean is detailed in Genaro Rodríguez Morel, "The Sugar Economy of Española in the Sixteenth Century," in Stuart B. Schwartz, ed., *Tropical Babylons: Sugar and the Making of the Atlantic World, 1450–1680* (Chapel Hill, N.C., 2004), 85–114.

actors involved before focusing on how traders and planters from both England and Iberia came together in the early transatlantic trade in tobacco.

Trading relations between Iberians—the Portuguese especially—and the English were of long standing. Despite the war between England and Spain, trade carried on thanks to collaboration and even partnerships between nationals of both sides. When tobacco emerged as a new plantation crop in the 1590s, these relations guaranteed its vent in West Atlantic markets and funded the further spread of its cultivation. In the specific case of Virginia, Anglo-Iberian trade supplied English consumers with tobacco from the Spanish Caribbean in the lead-up to 1607, thus demonstrating the commercial viability of the crop to colonial promoters. Tobacco planting might have been seen as a means of challenging Spanish hegemony, but its impetus and roots come from the Iberian world. Nor did the founding of Virginia and other English plantations rupture the Anglo-Iberian trade. Tobacco continued to move across these national boundaries well into the seventeenth century and beyond. Portuguese merchants imported Virginia tobacco into Seville. English merchants relayed Brazilian tobacco to Amerindian markets via the Hudson Bay Company. These kinds of multinational ties, at least as much as international conflict, help explain the commodification of tobacco whether in Trinidad, Bahia, or the Chesapeake.[7]

Early Consumption and Commodification

The archaeological record shows that tobacco had long been produced, traded, and consumed by Amerindians from Paraguay to the Saint Lawrence Valley. It was a current enough practice to be noticed almost immediately by chroniclers of the European discoveries: in November 1492, Columbus dispatched two of his men on a reconnaissance expedition to the interior of Cuba. Upon their return, the emissaries told him about "the "many people going back and forth between their villages, men and women with a firebrand of weeds in their hands to take in the fragrant smoke to which they are accustomed." Normand traders to coastal Brazil reported its use as early as 1508. It appears first in print in Gonzalo Fernández de Oviedo y Valdés's *Historia general y natural de las Indias* (1535) and again in André Thevet's *Singularitez de la France antarctique* (1557).[8]

7. Linda Wimmer, "African Producers, European Merchants, Indigenous Consumers: Brazilian Tobacco in the Canadian Fur Trade, 1550–1821" (Ph.D. diss., University of Minnesota, 1996), 215–247.

8. Claude Chapdelaine, "Des 'cornets d'argile' iroquoiens aux 'pipes de plâtre' européennes," in Laurier Turgeon, Denys Delâge, and Réal Ouellet, eds., *Transferts cultu-*

Many of these early accounts describe tobacco as a ritualistic plant. It was potent and used intensely, reaching doses that led to hallucinations and stupor. During ceremonies led by shamans and priests, tobacco accompanied, if not precipitated, visions and revelations. Such practices led Europeans to lock their sights onto the religious uses of the plant, classing them among the "crimes and abominable customs and rites" of indigenous peoples, but tobacco served a much wider range of purposes and needs in Amerindian society. It was a medicinal and healing plant, for one. Ceremonial uses included processions of Mexica women bearing pouches of tobacco during the festival of *Ochpaniztli* (Sweeping of the Roads) that marked the beginning of harvest in Tenochtitlán; Mexica priests wearing gourds filled with mixed tobacco during ritual offerings; and the formalized smoking of pipes to aid Algonquin, Innu, and Iroquoian councillors in their diplomatic deliberations.[9]

Tobacco circulated within Amerindian societies through local exchanges and more regional patterns of trade. In Tenochtitlán, Bernal Diaz del Castillo noted that an entire section of a city market was dedicated to the sale of a "paper, which in Mexico they call *amal*, and some reeds that smell of liquidamber and are full of tobacco." The Tionnontate (or Petun) Nation of the Great Lakes traded the tobacco they produced to the Hurons of the Northeast, who then distributed it to their Algonquian partners to

<hr/>

rels et métissages Amérique / Europe, XVIe–XXe siècle ([Sainte-Foy], 1996), 189–208; Charles Heiser, "On Possible Sources of the Tobacco of Prehistoric Eastern North America," *Current Anthropology,* XXXIII (1992), 54–56; Oliver Dunn and James E. Kelly, Jr., trans., *The Diario of Christopher Columbus's First Voyage to America, 1492–1493* (Norman, Okla., 1989), 137–139; Willis H. Bowen, "The Earliest Treatise on Tobacco: Jacques Gohory's *Instruction sur l'herbe petum,*" *Isis,* XXVIII (1938), 351; Gonzalo Fernández de Oviedo y Valdés, *Historia general y natural de las Indias,* ed. Juan Pérez de Tudela Bueso (Madrid, 1992), I, 116–118; and see André Thevet, *Singularitez de la France antarctique* (Paris, 1558), 57–58, cited ibid. See also Johannes Wilbert, *Tobacco and Shamanism in South America* (New Haven, Conn., 1987), 10–11.

9. See Wilbert, *Tobacco and Shamanism in South America,* 10–11; Oviedo y Valdés, *Historia general,* ed. Tudela Bueso, I, 116–118; Fernando Ortiz, *Cuban Counterpoint: Tobacco and Sugar* (Durham, N.C., 1995), 111–183. For the Innus and Algonquins, see H. P. Biggar, ed., *The Works of Samuel de Champlain,* I, *Des sauvages* (Toronto, 1971), 100–101; for the Iroquois, see Robert D. Kuhn and Martha L. Sempowski, "A New Approach to Dating the League of the Iroquois," *American Antiquity,* LXVI (2001), 304. We thank Peter Cook for the information and references on the Amerindians of the Saint Lawrence Valley. For the Mexicas, see Inga Clendinnen, *Aztecs: An Interpretation* (Cambridge, 1991), 200–201; and Muriel N. Porter, "Pipas precortesianas,"*Acta anthropologica,* III (1948), 139–152.

the north, west, and east. Tobacco was also likely traded among Caribbean groups.[10]

After the arrival of Europeans, the picture of indigenous trade in the Caribbean becomes clearer. Amerindian nations, especially the Kalimas (Caribs) and Lokonos (Arawaks), traded between the islands of the Lesser Antilles and up the watersheds of the mainland, a regional commerce that drew from the advent of European goods and maritime techniques. Canoes were fitted with sails, greatly increasing their range and allowing certain nations to rove around the Caribbean. The Lokonos, for instance, came to be described as sea gypsies, "a vagabond nation," wrote one English observer, "finding no certain abode of their own." Goods obtained through trade with the Spanish, particularly metal tools, allowed the Lokonos to trade along the Venezuelan coast and deep into the Orinoco River basin. Their rivals, the Kalimas, would in time turn to the Dutch and the English for their supplies of tools and other wares. Tivitives of the Siawani Nation, reputed boatbuilders of the Venezuelan coast, traded their canoes for tobacco grown in Trinidad.[11]

The Caribbean was one of the first regions in which the cultivation and trade of tobacco moved from indigenous societies and into the European colonial sphere, an important step in the transformation of the plant into an Atlantic commodity. As early as the 1530s, tobacco was incorporated into the informal economy of survival and subsistence organized by African slaves working in the Spanish colonies. The Africans and Afro-Caribbeans of Santo Domingo were observed "cultivating this weed behind the fields of their masters . . . because they say that when they stop working and take the tobacco their fatigue leaves them."[12] The mention of slave gardens pro-

10. Bernal Díaz del Castillo, *The Conquest of New Spain,* trans. J. M. Cohen (Harmondsmith, 1963), 233; Bruce G. Trigger, *Children of Aataentsic: A History of the Huron People to 1660* (Montreal, 1987). Oviedo y Valdés noted that tobacco was "an esteemed barter good among the Indians" ("rescate muy estimado entre los indios") in describing the Caquetios of Venezuela (*Historia general,* ed. Tudela Bueso, III, 32).

11. Sir W. Raleigh, *The Discovery of the Large, Rich, and Beautiful Empire of Guiana . . .* , ed. Robert H. Schomburgk, Works Issued by the Hakluyt Society, no. 3 (London, 1848), 4; Arie Boomert, "The Arawak Indians of Trinidad and Coastal Guiana, ca. 1500–1650," *Journal of Caribbean History,* XIX (1982), 132; Neil Whitehead, *Lords of the Tiger Spirit: A History of the Caribs in Colonial Venezuela and Guyana, 1498–1820* (Dordrecht, 1988), 18; Cornelius Ch. Goslinga, *The Dutch in the Caribbean and on the Wild Coast, 1580–1680* (Gainesville, Fla., 1971), 76; H. Dieter Heinen and Alvaro García-Castro, "The Multiethnic Network of the Lower Orinoco in Early Colonial Times," *Ethnohistory,* XLVII (2000), 573.

12. Oviedo y Valdés, *Historia general,* ed. Tudela Bueso, I, 116.

vides a clue as to how the plant was transferred from indigenous milieux. Early Spanish settlements depended in large part on Amerindian laborers, either locked into the *encomienda* system or brought in as war captives, and therefore slaves, from societies across the Caribbean basin. Given that these individuals worked and lived side by side with African slaves, it is reasonable to assume that they passed on the knowledge and use of tobacco to their fellow laborers.

However they first took up tobacco, Africans and Afro-Caribbeans appear to have been an important factor in spreading it through the Spanish colonial settlements. Cultivation and sale of the crop followed the intercolonial movement of African and Creole slaves, from Santo Domingo to Cuba, then to Panama and the Venezuelan coast. For slaves, it was a reliable plant worth bringing along. The seeds were small, plentiful, and easy to plant. The leaf they produced was readily harvestable and sellable in the ports and markets of the colonies. In the mid-sixteenth century, the Spanish Crown attempted to prevent slave women from selling tobacco to the crews and passengers of the Indies' fleets. Prohibitions against the cultivation and marketing of tobacco met with stiff resistance and were never seriously put into effect. As officials in Santo Domingo noted, slaves viewed tobacco not as a commodity but as a necessity, both for their own consumption and as a source of cash from dockside vending, and would rebel if it were taken away from them. A final, more suggestive, note on the African role in the early formation of a consumption market in tobacco comes from coastal Venezuela. Originally, the region's economic fortunes had been founded on pearling. By the early seventeenth century, Crown official Diego Pinelo was stunned to see how far the conversion to tobacco had progressed. Moreover, it seemed a largely irreversible trend since, as Pinelo noted, even if the settlers could be convinced to return to pearling, the slaves would hear nothing of it.[13]

Sold informally on small urban markets of the colonies, tobacco was purchased not only by locals but also by migrants, travelers, and mariners. Havana, Panama, Veracruz, and Cartagena de Indias were major way stations for the flow of people traveling to and from the Spanish Indies. When the fleets arrived, fairs sprang to life, catering to the thousands of travelers coming ashore. Tobacco was just one of the many commodities they were

13. Fernando Ortiz, *Contrapunto cubano del tabaco y el azucar* (Barcelona, 1973), 310; Antonio Gutierrez Escudro, "El tabaco en Santo Domingo y su exportación a Sevilla (epoca colonial)," in Enriqueta Vila Vilar and Allan Kuethe, eds., *Relaciones de poder y comercio colonial: Nuevas perspectivas* (Seville, 1999), 119; Huguette Chaunu and Pierre Chaunu, *Séville et l'Atlantique,* 8 vols. (Paris, 1955-1960), IV, 576-577.

offered, but it was also distinct. It was a local plant and was associated with that peculiarly Creole or *indiano* habit—smoking. In the early periods of the colonies, newcomers learned to consume tobacco, especially as they gathered in taverns and other spaces of conviviality. And since these migrants and wayfarers were a notably mobile lot, they, in turn, introduced the practice farther afield. The return of colonial hands (indianos) and mariners to their homelands, tobacco in pouch, explains the spread of smoking and snuff to Iberia. As one wag put it, the hostels and inns of Seville were filled with "rogues *(bellacos)* forcing you to sneeze tobacco." The custom of "slaves, taverngoers and people of little consideration," tobacco quickly passed from port to port along the East Atlantic coast and appeared at roughly the same time, the 1570s, in Seville, London, and Flanders.[14]

It is from this moment on that tobacco became an Atlantic commodity. It circulated through an informal economy—grown in garden plots, sold by tavernkeepers and African market women in the Spanish Indies, and then carried to Europe by travelers to pay their passage and, in all likelihood, in the sea chests of mariners who regularly engaged in petty trading as a means of supplementing their dismal wages. The volume of tobacco moving across the ocean remained quite modest and was as yet untaxed by the Spanish Crown. For volumes to increase, tobacco would have to take one more step: incorporation into the plantation.[15]

Planting Tobacco

It is worth noting that, at this juncture, the transformation of tobacco into a crop that would be grown for overseas markets was far from apparent or inevitable. Commercial agriculture organized by planters in the Spanish Caribbean was a venture with narrow margins of profit. To commit land

14. Juan Castro y Medinilla, *Historia de las virtudes y propriedades del tabaco* (Cordoba, 1620), fol. 20v.; Quiñones de Benavente, "Entremés famoso: Dos gaiferos," quoted in José Nicolás Romera Castillo, "Los entremeses y el descubrimiento," in Ignacio Arellano, ed., *Las Indias (América) en la literatura del siglo de oro: Homenaje a Jesús Cañedo* (Kassel, 1992), 124; Matthias de l'Obel and Pierre Pena, *Nova stirpium adversaria . . .* (Antwerp, 1576), 252; Nicolás Monardes, *Primera y segunda y tercera partes de la historia medicinal: De las cosas que se traen de nuestras Indias occidentales, que se sirven en medicina* (Seville, 1574), fol. 117v.; Bowen, "Earliest Treatise," *Isis,* XXVIII (1938), 352.

15. Pablo E. Pérez Mallaína, *Spain's Men of the Sea: Daily Life on the Indies Fleets in the Sixteenth Century,* trans. Carla Rahn Phillips (Baltimore, 1998), 150; "Los Interessados mercaderes y personas vezinos . . . ," Archivo General de Simancas (hereafter cited as AGS), Dirección General del Tesoro, inventario 4, fols. 41v, 41r.

and labor to a relative unknown such as tobacco, a product associated with the gardens of African slaves and Amerindians, might have represented too high a risk. Colonists were much more disposed to hitch their fortunes to sugar. By the late sixteenth century, sugar had a long history as a plantation crop, its markets were assured and growing, and the organization of labor, techniques, and technology required for its commercial production had been tested by experience. It is true that sugar was not accessible to all colonists; the capital investments required to purchase land, slaves, and equipment were notoriously high. But even here, tobacco was not yet the entry-level crop, the poor planter's sugar, that it would become in subsequent years. Planters of modest means tried their hand at a number of different commodities that they hoped they might sell on the Atlantic market: indigo, peppers, ginger, canafistula, tanned leather, and other "products of the earth." Perhaps further slowing the incorporation of tobacco into this range of colonial export crops was its reputation as a plant of the Amerindians or of the garden plots of African slaves. It was a far cry from sugar.

Beginning in the early 1590s, however, tobacco moved out of the shadows of the informal economy and into prominence as one of the staples of the Atlantic trades. As they had done with rice, planters came to realize that a plant that had been long been under their noses could be grown intensively and reap considerable profits through export. Within the space of a few decades, plantations dedicated to tobacco production sprang up across the Greater Caribbean. It is at this juncture that we find the first mentions of tobacco as a plantation crop in Cuba, Santo Domingo, Barinas, Maracaibo, Cumana, and Trinidad. The expansion of plantation tobacco was remarkable, driving the settlement of new colonies and a sharp rise in cultivated acreage throughout the region. Consumption spread just as quickly. By the early seventeenth century, smoking and snuff were common practice in western Europe, the Maghreb, West Africa, and the eastern Mediterranean.[16]

16. Linda Carney, *Black Rice: The African Origins of Rice Cultivation in the Americas* (Cambridge, Mass., 2001). The English traveler R. Harcourt, in his *Relation of a Voyage to Guiana* (London, 1613), notes that tobacco was commonly smoked in Barbary and among Turks. See discussion in Ortiz, *Contrapunto cubano*, 166, 319, 335–336. In 1602, the king of Morocco issued a fatwa condoning the consumption of tobacco in his reign (Chouki El-Hamel, personal communication). Early observations of tobacco use and cultivation in West Africa include the following: Timbuktu in 1594, Sierra Leone in 1607, Senegambia in 1620, and the Kingdom of Kongo in 1620. See George E. Brooks, *Landlords and Strangers: Ecology, Society, and Trade in Western Africa, 1000–1630* (Boulder, Colo., 1993), 315; and Christopher R. DeCorse, *An Ar-*

The takeoff of tobacco production and consumption took place in the midst of an expansionary cycle that lifted colonial markets throughout the Spanish Indies beginning in the 1560s. Rising bullion production and capital flows, increased access to labor, and the multiplication of commodities all came together to drive the commercial expansion of local economies. In the Caribbean, this expansion revived the region's fortunes, which had sorely sagged since its heyday in the early sixteenth century—a downturn largely pushed by the demographic crisis sweeping through indigenous society. In the late sixteenth and early seventeenth centuries, new streams of colonists arrived to settle the islands and the coastline of Tierra Firme—the lands that stretched from modern day Colombia to the Guyanas. The number of immigrant laborers, both African slaves and, to a lesser extent, European servants, also rose at this time. Capital having become more accessible, Caribbean entrepreneurs invested into new ventures: pearling in Margarita and Cumaná, gold mining in the hinterland of Cartagena de Indias, and commercial agriculture everywhere.[17] In the case of agriculture, capital not only secured labor, provisions, and equipment but also funded the military campaigns required to "pacify" Amerindian territories and transform them into plantation zones.[18] Finally, the upturn in commercial activity led to a multiplication in the number of trading circuits linking colony to colony and colony to Europe. The transatlantic networks, in particular, were knit together by merchants of different European nations, thereby assuring that colonial products would be vented on a broad band of European markets.

The path that led to the formation of the early tobacco plantations illustrates how these different elements came together. The first tobacco plantations were established on the island of Trinidad between 1588 and 1591. Spanish officials encouraged the settlement of the island as a means of blocking the trade and possible settlement attempts of the French and the English in this strategic position at the mouth of the Orinoco River basin. The project triggered a snarl between competing Castilian and Portuguese factions of colonists, but ultimately the new colony fell under the governorship

chaeology of Elmina: Africans and Europeans on the Gold Coast, 1400–1900 (Washington, D.C., 2001).

17. Carlos Sempat Assadourian, El sistema de la economía colonial: Mercado interno, regiones y espacio económico (Lima, 1982); Juan Carlos Garavaglia, Mercado interno y economía colonial (Mexico, 1983); Antonino Vidal Ortega, Cartagena de Indias y la región histórica del Caribe, 1580–1640 (Seville, 2002).

18. The case of Cristobal Cobos's 1585 conquest of Cumanagoto, with Lokono allies, is illustrative. See Don José de Oviedo y Baños, The Conquest and Settlement of Venezuela, trans. Jeanette Johnson Varner (Berkeley, Calif., 1987), 256.

of the Portuguese Rodrigo Manuel Nunes Lobo. At this point in his career, Nunes Lobo had already made his fortune in the Santo Domingo sugar industry and had purchased the governorship of neighboring Cumaná before his bid for Trinidad. This background and experience afforded him critical resources for the business of planting. He had strong connections to other Portuguese merchants involved in the trade in African slaves, which he could activate to recruit fellow planters, many of whom were Portuguese, as well as Portuguese servants who could be put to work in the fields. Additionally, Nunes Lobo drew upon his relations with Portuguese, French, and English smugglers to assure the vent of the fledgling colony's produce. Many of these ties carried over from from his days in Cumaná, a period that saw the small settlement turned into what one Spanish official called "a bin of foreigners, traitors and other delinquents, all of whom are sheltered and provided for by the Governor [Nunes Lobo]." Trinidad's location at the gateway of the Indies—little over a fortnight's sail from the Canaries— placed it in the midst of a steady stream of smuggling vessels sailing from Portugal and other European kingdoms.[19]

Whether Trinidad was the epicenter of the spread of tobacco plantations in the Spanish Caribbean is difficult to say with certainty. What is clear is that, very soon after the settlement of the island, other mentions of tobacco planting or trading appear with increasing regularity. In 1591, for instance, Christopher Newport intercepted a frigate heading for Havana laded with "50 hogs-heads and two-hundred weight of excellent tobacco." Cuban planters would soon turn to tobacco themselves, slowly at first (the crop appears in only a handful of plantation inventories after 1602) but with alacrity thereafter, until Cuban tobacco came to account for close to 60 percent of Sevillian imports. The tobacco that Newport intercepted was clearly being grown in large enough quantities to comprise an important part of a ship's cargo. Aside from Trinidad, the other candidates for this tobacco's possible origins include Santo Domingo, Puerto Rico, and especially Venezuela, where tobacco plantations were springing up along the coast between Caracas and Cumaná, on the shores of the Maracaibo lagoon and the connecting valleys of Barinas. By the late 1590s, the region was already producing an estimated 150,000 to 200,000 pounds of tobacco a year.[20]

19. Domingo de Vera Ybargoien to Philip II, 1595, British Library, Additional Manuscripts (hereafter cited as BL, Add. MSS), 36315, fol. 264v; Consejo de Indias to Philip II, Dec. 31, 1591, ibid., fol. 286v–287r; Pedro de Liano to Philip II, Mar. 25, 1596, ibid., fol. 36r.

20. Richard Hakluyt, *The Third and Last Volume of the Voyages, Navigations, Traf-*

This first spate of tobacco planting was organized by Iberian colonists and took place in territories under de facto control of the Spanish monarchy. It would not take long, however, for other nations, both European and Amerindian, to join in this movement, extending the tobacco zone of the Greater Caribbean. The diversity of actors was quite remarkable. Within the first decade of the seventeenth century, the French, the Dutch, the English, and the Swedes had established plantations along the Guyanese coast and on the neighboring Windward Islands. Even more surprising, perhaps, was the extent to which different Amerindian nations, the Lokono Arawaks and Kalinago Caribs in particular, reoriented their own production of tobacco toward export markets.[21]

The Amerindian move toward the commercial cultivation of tobacco was made possible by the intensification of captive taking and slavery along the South American coast, a phenomenon that was itself associated with the multiplication of exchanges and alliances between Amerindians and Europeans. Iberian, and then English and Flemish, colonists looked to different Amerindian nations for support in their settlement projects. The Lokonos and the Kalinagos provided military service to their allies or acted as settlers of new colonies. In exchange, they received tools, ironware, cloth, and wine. But most important, they received European weapons, swords, arrowheads, and firearms. The influx of arms into indigenous society allowed allied nations to raid other Amerindian groups for captives, selling some to their allies and incorporating the others as dependents. Nor was the practice of raiding for captives restricted to the indigenous sphere. Amerindians also lured Europeans into ambushes and raided their settlements for captives; by the 1610s, European captives appeared across the Windward Islands and the Guyanas. They were joined by Africans and Afro-Caribbeans who likewise fell victim to Amerindian parties who raided plantation settlements or the pearling grounds of Margarita Island and Cumaná. Alternatively, raid-

fiques, and Discoveries of the English Nation (London, 1600), 569; Alejandro de La Fuente, "Población y crecimiento en Cuba (siglos XVI y XVII): Un estudio regional," European Review of Latin American and Caribbean Studies, LV (1993), 84–85 (the data on the estancia inventories come from La Fuente's own personal records); Mercedes Ruiz Tirado, Tabaco y sociedad en Barinas, siglo XVII (Mérida, 2000), 77; "Memorial de Lopez de Castro para el remedio de los rescates en la isla Espanola," Nov. 20, 1598, in Emilio Rodriguez Demorizi, Relaciones históricas de Santo Domingo (Ciudad Trujillo, 1945), II, 166; E. Arcila Farias, Economia colonial de Venezuela (Caracas, 1973), I, 113, 131.

21. 1602: French in Cayenne; 1604: Dutch and (1605) Swedes around Orinoco. See Whitehead, Lords of the Tiger Spirit, 84.

ing parties would steal upon Portuguese slaving ships at night, "cutting their cables, hauling them to the coast and there killing the Whites and capturing the Blacks to use them to till their fields." On other occasions, Amerindian nations obtained African slaves as laborers through exchanges, as the Lokonos of the Orinoco basin did from the Iberians in the early seventeenth century.[22]

Whatever the method, it is clear that the composition, and perhaps the scale, of the Amerindian workforce underwent important shifts during this period. In the early seventeenth century, Amerindian communities contained dependent workers who were from rival nations, Europe, and Africa. They labored together to produce the staffs of Amerindian life, cassava and maize, but also tobacco and cotton, valuable exchange goods. Tobacco was of particular importance because the growing demand for it allowed Amerindian producers access to a wide variety of transatlantic traders who connected them to European consumers. Were Carib and Lokono villages being transformed into plantations per se? It is difficult to say; but clearly, the broader transformations associated with the commodification of tobacco engaged both indigenous and colonial spheres of Caribbean society in the early seventeenth century.

Multinational Trade

At the turn of the seventeenth century, Atlantic tobacco consumption was expanding rapidly, and rising demand drove the spread of tobacco cultivation, whether by Amerindians or colonists, to wherever ecological conditions and reliable trading routes conjoined. This general context surrounded early English colonization projects in the Greater Caribbean, and it helps explain the central role tobacco would play in plantations like Virginia. From its beginnings in the 1570s, when it was restricted to the informal exchanges organized by seafarers, the domestic tobacco market absorbed steadily increasing volumes of the plant. The spread of tobacco consumption across regions and classes and its emergence as a piece of day-to-day English life assured that the first gluts in this market would not surface until well into the seventeenth century, some seventy years after tobacco was in-

22. Ibid., 85; Neil Whitehead, "The Crises and Transformations of Invaded Societies: The Caribbean (1492-1580)," in Frank Salomon and Stuart B. Schwartz, eds., *The Cambridge History of the Native Peoples of the Americas,* III, *South America,* part 1 (New York, 1999), 875; Tomas de Cardona, *Relacion . . . de lo sucedido en el descubrimiento de las perlas* (n.p., n.d.), 725.k.18 (43), 1r, BL; Juan de Haro to Philip IV, June 7, 1625, BL, Add. MSS, 36320, fol. 267r.

troduced to the kingdom. Clearly, this steadily rising demand cued entrepreneurs and promoters to the viability of this colonial commodity.

Yet, for most of this early period, tobacco consumed in England was not produced by English plantations but rather by Iberian ones. The volumes of these Iberian imports grew not only because of rising demand but also because of the commodification of tobacco and associated spread of plantations in the Spanish Caribbean. In 1611, Trinidad and eastern Venezuela alone accounted for more than one million pounds of all tobacco unloaded on London's docks. The first shipments of Virginia tobacco arrived in 1613, and it would be another fifteen years before the colony produced enough tobacco—500,000 pounds—to begin to raise fears about the saturation of the metropolitan market.[23]

The importance of Iberian tobacco imports, the rise of English tobacco consumption, and the role they played in motivating subsequent English colonial ventures raise the question of how Iberian producers were linked to English consumers in the late sixteenth and early seventeenth centuries. In the standard view, the Anglo-Spanish War deeply divided relations between England and the Spanish colonies. And, indeed, it was war against Spain that encouraged a steady stream of English privateers to sail into the Spanish Main. Some of them, such as the *Trial* of London in 1599, ransomed their prizes against tobacco that was then sold on English markets.[24]

Nevertheless, the privateers were ill suited to assure that sizable and regular shipments of tobacco moved across imperial boundaries and the line of war. Privateering was an enterprise that suffered from thin profit margins, principally because of the relatively large capital outlays required to contract, equip, and arm a ship capable of naval engagement. This encouraged captains and investors to seek out high-value commodities such as pearls, precious metals, and even sugar rather than tobacco, which had to be shipped in large quantities to turn a profit. Privateering was a risky business in which success was far from assured and "opportunities" had to be seized where and when they presented themselves. This last turned certain privateers into loose cannons who poached on Spanish, Portuguese, Flemish, French, and even English shipping with something approaching des-

23. Don Alonso de Velasco to Philip IV, Mar. 28, 1611, BL, Add. MSS, 36319, fol. 268r; petition of the Governor, Council, and Burgesses of Virginia to the king, Mar. 26, 1628, PRO, CO, I, 4 n. 44.

24. Kenneth R. Andrews, "English Voyages to the Caribbean, 1596 to 1604: An Annotated List," *William and Mary Quarterly*, 3d Ser., XXXI (1974), 243–254, esp. 248.

perate abandon. Piracy and privateering were highly notorious activities, and they attracted a great deal of attention from contemporaries (and from subsequent historians), but the overall economic flows that they set in motion were quite modest.[25]

Much more important, both in terms of yearly ship counts and global lading weights, were the traders. By the 1590s, the English *rescate,* or contraband trade, had become worrisome enough for Spanish officials in Santo Domingo to push for a ban on the cultivation of tobacco, sugar, and ginger and the firing of such lands where contraband was considered endemic. It is from this same period that we obtain the first reports on the number of English ships trading to various Caribbean settlements—an estimated average of ten ships per year. The rescate trade conjours up images of a clandestine and ephemeral trade in which English vessels surreptitiously roved around the Caribbean hunting for buyers and sellers willing to risk a quick barter with the enemy. Closer examination, however, reveals an entirely more regular and coordinated form of exchange. The arrival of English ships coincided with the agrarian calendar. Local "brokers" arranged for the gathering up of the harvest and negotiated a global price for the year. Conducting negotiations, squaring accounts, and unloading and loading the cargoes all took time, during which English ships berthed openly in local harbors. "There they were," wrote a Spanish official from Margarita, "for two or three months as if they were at home; dealing and conversing at their ease." Moreover, many transactions had already been arranged between merchants stationed in London, Lisbon, or Seville. Here, the work of gathering up the tobacco and lading it into the holds was simply the last stage in a complex, transatlantic movement in which orders were placed, ships outfitted and dispatched, and accounts squared between corresponding merchants. Such exchanges—seasonal, recurring, familiar, contractual—defined the main conduit that linked the tobacco fields of the Spanish Caribbean to consumers in England.[26]

25. Kenneth Andrews, *The Spanish Caribbean: Trade and Plunder, 1530-1630* (New Haven, Conn., 1978), 129-131; "Relation of Pedro Diaz," in David Beers Quinn, ed., *The Roanoke Voyages, 1584-1590: Documents to Illustrate the English Voyages to North America under the Patent Granted to Walter Raleigh in 1584,* 2 vols., Works Issued by the Hakluyt Society, 2d Ser., nos. 104, 105 (London, 1955), II, 786, 788.

26. "Memorial de Lopez de Castro," in Rodriguez Demorizi, *Relaciones históricas de Santo Domingo,* II, 166; Andrews, "English Voyages," *WMQ,* 3d Ser., XXXI (1974), 243-254; Lic. Pedro de Liano, Margarita, to Philip II, Mar. 25, Apr. 13, 1596, BL, Add. MSS, 36317, fol. 36r; Pedro de Salazar, Margarita, to Philip II, Oct. 8, 1595, ibid., 36316, fol. 182r.

This circuit was but one of a larger set of overlapping commercial circuits organized between producers, shippers, and merchants of many different nationalities. Tobacco grown in the Spanish Caribbean was not only sent to England but also to Portugal, France, Flanders, and, of course, Spain itself. The transatlantic trade was divided into a legal trade, freighted aboard the ships of the Spanish *Carrera de Indias* ("Route of the Indies") and the contraband trade carried by French, Flemish, English, and Portuguese ships. Though notoriously hard to quantify, records for Venezuela during the period 1594 to 1640 suggest that contraband traffic was double that of the Carrera (about ten to thirty ships per year against five to ten ships per year). This traffic, and the commercial associations that animated it, permitted not only the vent of Spanish tobacco across Europe but also the circulation of other Atlantic commodities, commercial signals, and capital. The multinational commercial system provides the context, and part of the explanation for, tobacco's career as a transatlantic commodity. The absence of such a system would have greatly restrained the links between production and consumption and curtailed tobacco's spread to the emerging colonial systems of the early seventeenth century.[27]

Among the different communities of merchants, certain relationships and overlaps played more determining roles than others. English traders interested in developing trading links to Spanish colonial markets turned to the Portuguese. Two factors explain Portuguese importance in the development of the early English transatlantic trade: the first was the long-standing nature of the Anglo-Portuguese commercial alliance; the second was the Portuguese infiltration of the Spanish Indies over the course of the sixteenth century, which proceeded apace with the progressive exclusion of English traders because of war and emergent state mercantilism. To appreciate the English engagement in the tobacco trade during the lead-up to Jamestown requires not only a geographically broad view of commercial multilateralism but also a focused historical examination of the relations between Portuguese and English merchants.

The Anglo-Portuguese commercial relationship originated in the Middle Ages, when it centered around the east Atlantic trade in wines, citrics, salt, wool, and cloths. In the late fifteenth century, English merchants resi-

27. On intercolonial trade, see Ortega, *Cartagena de Indias,* 183–186, 193–196. For the Carrera traffic, see Chaunu and Chaunu, *Séville et l'Atlantique,* VI, book 2, 600–612. For contraband trade, see Pedro de Liano, Margarita, to Philip II, BL, Add. MSS, 36317, fols. 36r, 38r, and Diego Suarez de Sandoval to Philip III, June 26, 1611, ibid., 36319, fol. 294.

dent in Lisbon were formally recognized as a "nation" by royal charter and accorded limited rights of self-governance. The English nation in Portugal would form an integral feature of the city's commercial landscape during the ensuing centuries. English traders also settled in Seville, the other major Iberian Atlantic trading port.The establishment of such commercial houses in Lisbon and Seville thus enabled English merchants to participate in the Iberian (Portuguese and Castilian) expansion into the Atlantic. In the early sixteenth century, English traders made direct voyages to the mid-Atlantic islands and a number of, albeit more sporadic, voyages to the Spanish Main itself. As the century progressed, however, the Spanish monarchy tightened the controls over the traffic moving across the Atlantic. By the 1550s, new laws forced ships to gather together in great convoys, the famous fleets of the Carrera de Indias. They were protected by the galleons of the admiralty, but in exchange for this protection, their cargoes and crew were closely monitored to assure the collection of duties and the exclusion of non-Castilians from the Indies. English merchants resident in Seville were able to continue their trade with the Indies but only indirectly, through agents who registered cargoes in their name. This restricted access would all but close with the eruption of war between the crowns of Spain and England and the imposition of embargoes on all English shipping to the Peninsula (1569–1573; 1585–1604).[28]

During this same period, the Portuguese succeeded in establishing themselves in the Castilian colonial sphere. Like the English, they, too, had settled an expatriate community in Seville in the late Middle Ages. Unlike their northern partners, however, their linguistic, cultural, and religious proximity to the Castilians allowed them to subsequently slip into the Spanish Indies. From the beginning of the sixteenth century, Portuguese traders, mariners, and settlers were a regular presence in the colonies. The Portuguese initially entered the Spanish Indies because of their control of the trade in African slaves; but Portuguese planters, artisans, mariners, and laborers followed. Local Spanish authorities petitioned the Crown to legalize Portuguese migration to their colonies because "they will bring great

28. Pauline Croft, "Trading with the Enemy, 1585–1604," *Historical Journal,* XXXII (1989), 281; George Connell-Smith, "English Merchants Trading to the New World in the Early Sixteenth Century," *Bulletin of the Institute of Historical Research,* XXIII, no. 67 (May 1960), 53–67. On the English nation in Portugal, see the compilation *Privilegios concedidos por los senores reyes de Portugal a los mercaderes alemanes, flamencos, y demas extrangeros residentes en la ciudad de Lisboa: Desde 1452 hasta 1589,* Museo Naval Madrid, colección navarete, XXIII, fol. 658–.

profit since, as planters and workers, they apply themselves more than the others." Indeed, the Portuguese drove the development of key sectors within the Spanish Caribbean economy: sugar, pearls, dyes, cattle, and, by the late sixteenth century, tobacco. By 1566, imperial officials estimated that there were more Portuguese than Castilians settled in the *audiencia* of Santo Domingo. In 1584, they outnumbered the Castilians by 500 to 150, giving rise to the Spanish fear that "some evil will come of this."[29]

Having pervaded the Castilian sphere and having maintained their connections to English and other northern trading communities, the Portuguese found themselves in the unique position of integrating the various markets of the Atlantic economy, despite the growing divisions of war. Indeed, in 1580, when the Spain incorporated the Kingdom of Portugal into its empire, Portuguese merchants made sure to obtain a constitutional guarantee that their trading relationship with England and other northern countries would be safeguarded. The English, for their part, lobbied hard to maintain an open trade with Portugal, even though the kingdom had formally passed over into the camp of the enemy. Drake himself would respect this distinction between allied and enemy Iberians. In his 1587 report to Sir Francis Walsingham, he gives a long list of the Spanish forts and ships attacked and destroyed but notes that care was taken to treat any Portuguese with customary kindness.[30]

Hence war only strengthened the bond between English and Portuguese merchants.[31] English exports of cloths and manufactured goods, directed at Seville but ultimately destined for exchange against bullion and colonial commodities from the Indies, passed through Portuguese intermediaries.

29. Lic. Larita to Philip II, Feb. 26, 1581, in Archivo General de Indias, Santo Domingo, 51, ramo 1, no. 55 (hereafter cited as AGI); and "Memorial de los vecinos de Santo Domingo," ca. 1570, in Genaro Rodriguez Morel, *Cartas de la cabildo de la ciudad de Santo Domingo en el siglo XVI* (Santo Domingo, 1999), 276; AGI, Santo Domingo, legajo 155, fol. 176r. The Portuguese numbered 200 by the early date of 1535 (ibid., legajo 49, ramo 1, no. 43). For quote, see Andrews, *Spanish Caribbean,* 38.

30. Fernando J. Bouza Álvarez, "Portugal en la monarquía hispánica (1580–1640): Felipe II, la Cortes de Tomar, y la génesis del Portugal católico" (Ph.D. diss., Universidad Complutense de Madrid, 1986); [John?] Hastings to Cecill, "Touching the Preservation of Amity and Increase of Trade with Portugal," 1569, *Calendar of State Papers,* Domestic Series (hereafter cited as *CSP,* Dom.), *Of the Reigns of Edward VI, Mary, Elizabeth and James I, 1547–[1625],* II, *1581–1590* (London, 1858), 358; Act of the Company of Merchants Trading to Spain and Portugal . . . , Aug. 31, 1580, ibid., 673; *Declaration of Certain Merchants Who Have Traded to Portugal* . . . , 1580, ibid., 698; ibid., 411 n. 33.

31. Croft, "Trading with the Enemy," *Historical Journal,* XXXII (1989), 281–284.

Many of these transfers were effected in Lisbon or in one of the numerous outports of the Portuguese coast and were not, strictly speaking, illegal, since the Portuguese had preserved the right to deal with the English.

The Portuguese would also play an important role in opening the Spanish Caribbean to direct English trade in the late sixteenth century. Portuguese pilots hired on aboard English ships bound for the Indies. The English Crown reciprocated these maritime courtesies, granting letters of safe passage to Portuguese settlers and traders in Santo Domingo so that they would be spared by English privateers. As the Caribbean tobacco sector developed, Portuguese proved to be key intermediaries between local planters and English traders. Nunes Lobo's settling of Trinidad was clearly motivated by the desire to horn in on a trade that English merchants and local Caribs had already established. Farther west along the Venezuelan coast, in Cumaná, Nunes Lobo's nephew Antonio Silveira brokered the trade with the English. Similar relations were established throughout the Spanish Caribbean—in Margarita, Maracaibo, Rio de la Hacha, Cuba, and Santo Domingo.[32]

During the first decades of the seventeenth century, the Anglo-Portuguese commercial partnership proved to be quite robust, weathering attempts by the Spanish and then English crowns to halt the imports of Caribbean tobacco into England. In 1604, the year of the peace, the Spanish Crown attempted to systematically monitor and control Lisbon's trade in order to put an end to the relay trade between the Indies and northern Europe. The effort failed spectacularly, as Portuguese merchants instigated a citywide riot against Castilian officials who dared to meddle with their constitutional right to free trade with the north. Lisbon was not the only hub where Portuguese and English merchants operated: the Algarve coast, Seville, the Canaries, the Azores, and Madeira all functioned as strategic transshipment points. Meanwhile, the direct trade between the Caribbean and England continued unabated.[33]

32. Pedro de Liano to Philip II, Mar. 25–Apr. 13, 1596, BL, Add. MSS, 36317, fol. 37r; Gregorio Palma Hurtado to the Consejo de Indias, June 15, 1610, cited in Chaunu and Chaunu, *Séville et l'Atlantique*, IV, 316; Sir William Chester to Sir William Garrad, Aug. 14, 1561, *CSP, Dom.*, 19. For cases of Portuguese pilots guiding French vessels, see AGS, Estado, Portugal, legajo 385 (1567–1568); AGI, Santo Domingo, 868, libro 3, fol. 113v; ibid., 70, ramo 1, no. 16, fol. 111r; "Declaration of Tome Rodrigues," 1596, ibid., ramo 1, n. 19; "Report by Lic. Juan de Prado on Behalf of Francisco de Vides," n.d., BL, Add. MSS, 36315, fol. 182v; Rodriguez Demorizi, *Relaciones históricas de Santo Domingo*, II, 168.

33. Luis de Vera to the consejo de estado, Nov. 21, 1604, AGS, Estado, legajo 435.

The ability of Portuguese and English merchants to bypass the official routes of the Spanish trading system forced Madrid to attack the problem at the source. In 1606, the Council of the Indies imposed a ten-year ban on the production of tobacco across the Caribbean. The success of the prohibition was fleeting at best, resulting in but a short year's lull in legal tobacco exports. The first breach came from Santo Domingo, where ships left loaded with tobacco for European markets in 1607. The following year, most of the major plantation zones shipped tobacco anew: Santo Domingo, Caracas, Margarita Island, Havana, Puerto Rico, and the Yucatan. Royal control broke down because settlers argued that they were dependent upon tobacco for their livelihood, and they appealed to the sovereign's responsibility to sustain his vassals and maintain the "necessities of the republic." Sancho de Alquiza, the official sent to investigate the situation in Trinidad, met a full assembly of settlers who, on bended knees, presented him with a signed petition admitting their guilt but pleading mercy given their great poverty. Faced with this collectively scripted act of contrition, Alquiza bade them all to rise and to return to their fields, because "to prosecute one would have required me, by justice, to prosecute them all"—an impossible move.[34]

Though the ban would not be formally lifted until 1612, tobacco cultivation in the Spanish Caribbean continued to develop. Production spread to new settlements, and the volumes of exports picked up once more. Additionally, the Portuguese now all but monopolized Venezuelan production. Even the smallest settlement along the coast had its resident Portuguese planters. The English, for their part, appear to have abandoned the rescate trade, but this did not sever their connections to England: as seen above, large quantities of "Spanish" tobacco continued to arrive in London in these same years.[35]

The end of the rescate trade made way for a more formal division of the transatlantic tobacco circuit. The Portuguese controlled production, gathered the crop, and arranged for its shipment to England. The routes varied

34. AGI, Contadurias, 4424; Sancho de Alquiza to the Audiencia de Santo Domingo, Feb. 15, 1612, BL, Add. MSS, 36319, fol. 256v. Plantations in Santo Domingo, Cuba, Margarita, Venezuela, Puerto Rico, Cumana, and Nueva Andalucia were prohibited from planting the following year's crop. See Real Cédula to the Audiencia de Santo Domingo, Aug. 26, 1606, AGI, Santo Domingo, 869, legajo 5, fol. 61v–61r.

35. Chaunu and Chaunu, *Séville et l'Atlantique,* IV, 572–573; "Relacion de los estrangeros flamencos yngleses franceses ytalianos portugueses que residen en la ciudad de Santiago de Leon y otras desta provinica de Venezuela," 1607, AGI, Santo Domingo, legajo 193, ramo 15, n. 50; Andrews, *Spanish Caribbean,* 230.

—an indication of the growing sophistication of these networks—but the connection between the tobacco fields of the Spanish Caribbean and the English consumption market remained strong. From his base in Cartagena de Indias, the Portuguese trader Jorge Fernandes Gramaxo orchestrated the shipping of substantial quantities of tobacco from Maracaibo to London. Other shipments went to Lisbon, and then, after a portion had been sold, were reexpedited north to Flanders and London. Still others were sent to Seville, legally this time, aboard ships registered by the officials of the Spanish House of Trade. Resident English merchants then transferred the tobacco to ships headed for England. The Anglo-Portuguese partnership took more immediate forms as well: in 1610, the Portuguese merchant Francisco Carrero sailed with his English partner, John Moore, from Trinidad to London, where he brokered the vent of subsequent shipments on the English market. English merchants invested, through local brokers, into the further expansion of tobacco fields in Venezuela.[36]

Bowing to the inevitable, the Spanish Crown switched tack and attempted to rein in the contraband tobacco trade by instituting a state monopsony in 1620. Growers along the Venezuelan coast were henceforth required to sell their crops at fixed prices to officials of the Crown. Though the Portuguese momentarily lost control over the local purchasing and exporting of tobacco, they quickly regained it; many of the principal Portuguese traders in the area were closely linked to Portuguese financiers, who leased the monopoly back from the Spanish Crown. By this time, the actors had changed and war had returned, but Portuguese and English merchants preserved their respective roles. Portuguese merchants continued to export sizable quantities of tobacco to Lisbon and London. They based themselves in England to receive these shipments or coordinated these exchanges from key entrepôts such as Seville. There were also personal continuities here: the nephew of Jorge Fernandes Gramaxo, Antonio Nunes Gramaxo, was one of the leading Portuguese merchants of Seville in the 1630s. Through his dealings with local English associates, Nunes Gramaxo supplied his nephew in Cartagena de Indias with English broadcloths and even

36. Chaunu and Chaunu, *Séville et l'Atlantique,* IV, 373, 575 (for further information regarding Jorge Fernandes Gramaxo and his network, see Vidal Ortega, *Cartagena de Indias,* 135–144); *Juan de Mendoza v. Gaspar Diaz,* 1614, AGI, Contadurias, 789, no. 17, fol. 3r; Joyce Lorimer, "The English Contraband Trade in Trinidad and Guiana, 1590–1617," in Andrews, Canny, and Hair, *Westward Enterprise,* 134; Real Cédula to Diego Gomez de Sandoval, May 29, 1612, AGI, Santo Domingo, 869, legajo 6, fol. 142r–143r.

French linens (relayed through London to evade yet another embargo). These goods never entered Seville but were instead discreetly transshipped off the Andalusian coast.[37]

The commercial relations between English and Portuguese merchants created and maintained the link between producers in the Spanish colonies and consumers in England, despite war, embargoes, and privateers. These merchants directed the bulk of their efforts at circumventing the various controls and checks imposed by the Spanish Empire, largely because, for the greater part of this period, it was Spain, rather than England, that stood to lose the most from these contraband operations. Beginning in the mid-1620s, however, the English Crown was called upon to halt the importation of Spanish tobacco in order to protect its own fledgling colonial possessions in Virginia, Barbados, St. Kitts, and Bermuda. In 1625, the importation of foreign or unlicensed tobacco into England was prohibited. Preserving the metropolitan market was critical, especially for Virginia, where tobacco production was booming and threatened to saturate the English market. But, as had been the case for Spain, the capacity of the English state to cut the flow of Caribbean and Venezuelan tobacco was limited. Still, the relations between English and Portuguese traders continued through this period of rising English protectionism.[38]

But in an ironic twist, the preservation of the Anglo-Portuguese partnership came to provide some succor to the needs of Virginia. At the very time when the Virginia Company was lobbying to free up the reexportation of colonial tobacco, Portuguese merchants running the Spanish tobacco monopoly began to import Virginia tobacco into the Sevillian market. When Spanish officials protested against these foreign imports, the Portuguese recurred to an ingenious bit of commercial sophistry: this tobacco should be admitted, they argued, because Virginia was still de jure

37. Chaunu and Chaunu, *Séville et l'Atlantique,* IV, 572–574, 576; Marcy Norton, "The Business of Tobacco in the Spanish Empire, 1590–1636," working paper presented at International Seminar on the History of the Atlantic World, 1500–1800, Harvard University, August 1999; Norton, *Sacred Gifts, Profane Pleasures: A History of Tobacco and Chocolate, 1492–1700* (forthcoming); *Antonio Nuñez Gramaxo contra los bienes de Luis Fernandez Suarez,* 1637, Archivo Histórico Nacional de Madrid, Inquisición, 1611, exp. 17.

38. James I to Solicitor General Heath, July 2, 1624, *CSP,* Col., I, 63; "Proclamation Forbidding the Importation of Tobacco," Apr. 9, 1625, *CSP,* Col., I, 72; "Proclamation for the Ordering of Tobacco," Aug. 9, 1627, ibid., I, 86.

part of the Spanish Empire and therefore fell within its economic patrimony. Matters had come full circle. Spanish mercantilism, which had long tried to prevent the internationalization of trade in the Atlantic, was now called upon to legitimate one of its products: the multinational trade in tobacco.[39]

39. La Junta del Real Almirantazgo de la ciudad de Sevilla . . . , n.d., BL, 765.i.3 (19).

Philip P. Boucher

REVISIONING THE "FRENCH ATLANTIC"

The goals of this essay are modest—to present a narrative-driven overview of the "French Atlantic" in the era 1550–1625 and to provide scholars of the Atlantic world with a summary of the most current literature. Modern scholarship has significantly affected our understanding of the ebbs and flows in French interests in the Atlantic basin.[1] This literature may not yet be easily accessible or well known to scholars of Iberian or British America or to colleagues in the broader field of Atlantic history. Scholars are handicapped by both a lack of reliable surveys of French America and by persistent myths bedeviling the field. It is all too typical to reduce the French presence in the Americas during that period to fish, furs, and the debacles in Brazil and Florida, as important as those topics are. This essay will provide a larger context about France in America before 1625.[2]

I would like to thank this volume's anonymous reviewer and Peter Mancall for their helpful suggestions.

1. I use quotation marks with "French Atlantic" to indicate the modest range of Gallic activities on and overseas. French scholarship recently has profited from using the Spanish archives to compensate for the relative poverty of French manuscript sources for the early period of the "French Atlantic": see, for example, Jean-Pierre Moreau, *Les Petites Antilles de Christophe Colomb à Richelieu, 1493–1635* (Paris, 1992).

2. For a detailed update about the last ten years in French language scholarship, see Mickaël Augeron and Laurent Vidal, "Du comptoir à la ville coloniale: La France et ses Nouveaux mondes américains. Bilan historiographique et perspectives de recherche," *Debate y perspectivas,* no. 2 (September 2002), 141–172. The classic survey of early French expansion into the Atlantic is still the best, despite its now-quaint proimperialist overtones: Ch. André Julien, *Les voyages de découverte et les premiers établissements (XVe–XVIe siècles)* (Paris, 1948). The many works of Frank Lestringant are crucial to knowledge of the sixteenth century "French Atlantic." See especially his *Le Huguenot et le sauvage: L'Amérique et la controverse coloniale, en France, au temps des*

Why have I chosen 1550 and 1625 as the beginning and terminal dates of this essay? They are of great importance in understanding the evolution of the *colonial* aspirations of France across the Atlantic. Both before 1550 and during the seventy-five years covered here, private commercial interests traded along a coast from Rio de Janeiro to the Gulf of Saint Lawrence. French fishermen in great numbers caught cod and other groundfish in the fabulously rich Grand Banks. Generally speaking, these commercial interests resisted sporadic state efforts to transplant settlers and missionaries in projects to establish colonies. Also, private and semiprivate (i.e., pirates and corsairs) military operations made the French presence felt in lands claimed by the Iberians, a persistent enemy of the French Crown from 1494 to 1659.[3] For example, in the 1540s and 1550s, French sea dogs, the most famous of whom was "Peg-Leg" François Le Clerc, made life miserable for colonists and traders in the Spanish Caribbean. None of these various private entrepreneurial activities had colonial intentions. The few, feeble French colonies in existence by 1625 were largely the product of private colonists working with and through the monarchy to acquire, legitimate, and defend colonial properties. These settlements largely evolved according to local conditions, interactions with Native American populations, and the agency of the colonists, with only a modicum of state interference. The various outposts in Acadia and along the Saint Lawrence were not in contact with those in the Greater Caribbean. Nevertheless, at crucial moments, royal policies, actions, and inactions did have repercussions on Frenchmen overseas.

This essay examines how forces promoting and inhibiting French maritime expansion, often simultaneously, shaped the evolution of the French Atlantic. These forces were the Crown, the commercial and piratical impulses of the maritime ports, and the Huguenot (French Calvinist) drive to survive and expand. At times, all three drove Atlantic expansion and at other times inhibited it. The ways in which these forces interacted were crucial to the character and rate of development of overseas French colonies.

---

guerres de religion (1555–1589) (Paris, 1990). He provides an invaluable chronology of events coupled with French and European writings on America between 1493 and 1615 (see 283–304).

3. The first known corsair attack occurred in 1523, when Jean Fleury of Honfleur succeeded in capturing some of Moctezuma's treasure that Cortés had dispatched to Emperor Charles V. See Mickaël Augeron, "Coligny et les Espagnols à travers la course (c. 1560–1572): Une politique maritime au service de la cause protestante," in Martine Acerra and Guy Martinière, eds., *Coligny, les protestants et la mer* (Paris, 1997), 157.

Metropolitan economic conditions, the region, class, and gender of the migrants overseas, and international rivalries are also critical to understanding the halting movement westward across the ocean. When French adventurers debarked in America, their motives for being there strongly shaped their actions and fortunes. Before the 1620s, those who intended to stay followed a Spanish model of empire building that proved counterproductive, as it did for the English. Exploiting rich mines while depending on Indian tribute of food and labor turned out to be a chimera.

The role of the Crown was, in an equally positive and negative sense, important to the establishment of a French position in the Atlantic. Before 1550, Francis I (1516–1547) had sponsored the reconnaissance voyages of Jacques Cartier to the Saint Lawrence and then, in the early 1540s, the sieur de Roberval's colonial enterprise, which proved a dismal failure. After 1550, Henri II and especially the first French Bourbon king, Henri IV (1589–1610), renewed royal support for the establishment of New Frances across the Atlantic. The latter's son Louis XIII allowed his chief minister, Richelieu, to control maritime enterprises. All three kings and the cardinal viewed French colonies in the Americas primarily as fortified bases to threaten Spain and Portugal's claimed hegemony there. On the whole, however, the Crown's dynastic and continental-oriented policies trumped colonial interests when a choice had to be made. Choices often occurred based upon the king's notoriously parlous finances in an age of soaring military expenditures. Examples of royal sacrificing of American interests (to be discussed at greater length below) include Catherine de Médicis's lukewarm and inconsistent support for the Florida enterprise (1562–1565) and Marie de Médicis's abandonment of the embryonic settlement at Saint Louis, Maragnan (currently São Luis in the bay of Maranhão) in the years 1612–1616. This essay critically examines the still-somewhat-current, if hoary, stereotypes of French America as primarily the product of state efforts, in contrast to the more laissez-faire English approach. Long ago and at a time when most French historians idolized the state, Prosper Cultru warned about exaggerating its role:

Nothing was done in the 17th century before Colbert, in the question of colonization, but by the actions of individuals, an action that was, to be sure, rather feeble and indecisive: the support of the state was primarily verbal, magnificent if one sticks to the preambles of edicts, but reduced to the simple act of granting deeds if one looks at the facts on the ground.

His wise admonition merits reiteration, even if this essay does attribute some role to the Crown and court.[4]

Commercial entrepreneurs and privateer captains in France's maritime ports, quite vital in this period, were very interested in exploiting the New World, from the lucrative North Atlantic fisheries to commodities provided by indigenous populations (i.e., furs, dyewoods, and sassafras, a supposed cure for the "pox").[5] The Norman ports of Rouen and Dieppe were especially active in all these trades and thefts and had connections with West Africa for gold, ivory, and a few slaves. The merchant prince Jean d'Ango of Dieppe prospered in Brazilian commerce, and his urban hôtel at Dieppe reflected his taste in Braziliana. His fleet in 1523 succeeded in capturing two ships of Cortés's containing looted Aztec gold. In 1537, his corsairs managed to capture nine ships of the annual Spanish treasure fleet. In the Caribbean itself, the first significant appearance of French interlopers occurred in 1543 and 1544, years of war between France and Spain. Where necessary, these merchants built trading posts, but they were not interested in bearing the costs of establishing permanent settlements.[6]

Huguenots also played a significant role in the shaping of an emerging French Atlantic. Constituting some 7 percent of the French population by the 1560s, they included powerful nobles such as Henri of Navarre and the admiral Gaspard de Coligny, and they had a strong presence in the maritime ports. They played a minor role in the Brazilian fiasco of the

4. Prosper Cultru, *Colonisation d'autrefois: Le commandeur de Poincy à St. Christophe* (Paris, 1915), 7.

5. By the mid-sixteenth century, Bordeaux, La Rochelle, and Rouen / Le Havre outfitted an average of 150 ships annually for the fisheries of the North Atlantic and to hunt whales in the Gulf of Saint Lawrence. See Laurier Turgeon, "Français et Amérindiens en Amérique du nord au XVIe siècle," in Frank Lestringant, ed., *La France / Amérique (XVIe–XVIIIe siècles): Actes du XXXVe Colloque international d'études humanistes,* Travaux du Centre d'études supérieur[e]s de la Renaissance de Tours (Paris, 1998), 220–221.

6. Charles Bréard, *Documents rélatifs à la Marine normande et à ses armements aux XVIe et XVIIe siècles pour le Canada, l'Afrique, le Antilles, le Brésil et les Indes* (Rouen, 1889); Philip Ainsworth Means, *The Spanish Main: Focus of Envy, 1492–1700* (New York, 1967), 59; Paul Butel, *Les Caraïbes au temps des flibustiers, XVIe–XVIIe siècles* (Paris, 1982), 34; Paul E. Hoffman, *The Spanish Crown and the Defense of the Caribbean, 1535–1585: Precedent, Patrimonialism, and Royal Parsimony* (Baton Rouge, 1980), 27. Jean d'Ango's tomb in Dieppe lies below a "stone frieze showing naked Brazilian men and women cavorting in their naked paradise." See John Hemming, *Red Gold: The Conquest of the Brazilian Indians* (Cambridge, Mass., 1978), 12.

1550s and a major one in the Florida debacle of the 1560s. Modern research has undermined the idea that Florida was to be a refuge for this minority threatened by persecution and religious war. The main motives for a French Florida were establishing a forward base to threaten Spain and exploiting illicit trade with the Spanish Caribbean, as well as searching for new Perus. The leader, Coligny, also hoped to unite all Frenchmen through war with the Spaniards. After the debacle in Florida, the Huguenots largely abandoned the idea of creating their own city on a hill overseas, if they had ever seriously entertained such a refuge.[7] The struggle was to be conducted in France, a conclusion reinforced by the apparent victory of the Edict of Nantes of 1598, which granted Huguenots a measure of religious toleration and some military guarantees. Goaded by hope of lucre, especially at the expense of the hated Iberians, Huguenot captains and privateers from La Rochelle and other ports scoured Brazil and the Greater Caribbean in search of prizes.[8] Under the tolerant rule of their former leader-turned–Roman Catholic, Henri IV, Huguenots and moderate Catholics combined in enterprises to establish trading posts in Acadia (Port-Royal, 1605), on the Saint Lawrence (Québec, 1608), at Cayenne in Guiana (1607), and in Maragnan, Brazil (1612–1616). It would not be until after 1626 that the Crown legally prevented Huguenots from overseas residence, not that the law was strictly enforced.

Brazil and Florida, 1552–1568

After the failure of the Cartier/Roberval expeditions, the next attempted settlement occurred in Brazil. This choice is not at all surprising, since a vibrant dyewood trade (brazilwood, which yields a red dye) sustained

7. In works to be cited throughout this essay, the prodigious scholar Frank Lestringant has promoted the idea of a Huguenot refuge. Although this idea on occasion might have played some role in Huguenot initiatives, I find that geopolitical and commercial motives were paramount in their thinking. For a recent article supporting this position, see Mickaël Augeron and Laurent Vidal, "Refuges ou réseaux? Les dynamiques atlantiques protestantes au XVIe siècle," in Guy Martinière et al., eds., *D'un rivage à l'autre: Villes et Protestantisme dans l'aire atlantique, XVIe–XVIIe siècles* (Paris, 1999), 32–61. They argue that "for the majority of Protestants who assaulted the American continent, motivated primarily by economic considerations, the notion of a refuge was, if not strange, at least secondary" (51).

8. The La Rochelle corsair who sabotaged John White's 1587 effort to resupply Roanoke demonstrates that any ship, however, was fair game. See David B. Quinn and Alison M. Quinn, eds., *The First Colonists: Documents on the Planting of the First English Settlements in North America, 1584–1590* (Raleigh, N.C., 1982), 112–113.

dozens of French ships a year on that long coast. To facilitate this lucrative commerce, trading posts were erected and young boys *(truchements)* left behind to learn Native languages. Indigenes, especially members of Tupinambá tribes, burned the bases of these hard trees, cut them with European axes, and prepared transportable timber. For these laborious tasks, they received ironware, bric-a-brac, and spirits. From the 1520s, the Portuguese fought these French incursions into lands claimed as a result of the Treaty of Tordesillas with Spain (1494). In 1530, a French ship captured the Portuguese post at Pernambuco, only to be captured itself off Portugal. It contained dyewoods, principally, but also cotton, six hundred parrots, and three thousand jaguar skins.[9]

By 1550, French ships had become so numerous that an estimate of one hundred thousand brazilwood tree trunks in the Rio area awaited them. In the same year, town magistrates of Rouen put together a spectacular show for the official entrée of Henri II and his much-neglected wife, Catherine de Médicis. Rouen desperately wished to reverse the king's prohibition of their shipping to Brazil. Two hundred Rouen veterans of the Brazil trade, appropriately underdressed for the occasion, and fifty real, naked *sauvages* performed Native combats and hunts for the royals in a re-created Brazilian village along the Seine. Monkeys and other exotic animals from Brazil sported in the trees and on land. This first "colonial exposition" was a marvelous and widely publicized success; the far-from-prudish Catherine returned for a second performance.[10]

The renewal of war with the emperor Charles V in 1551 opened the gates for revived interest in Iberian America, and Henri II became more receptive to schemes to challenge the Iberians. He reiterated the French argument that only territories occupied, not lands fleetingly discovered, legally

9. Olive Dickason, "The Brazilian Connection: A Look at French Techniques for Trading with Amerindians," *Revue française d'histoire d'outre-mer*, LXXI (1984), 129–146; Neil L. Whitehead, "Native American Cultures along the Atlantic Littoral of South America, 1499–1650," in Warwick Bray, ed., *The Meeting of Two Worlds: Europe and the Americas, 1492–1650* (New York, 1993), 204.

10. Augeron and Vidal, "Du comptoir à la ville coloniale," *Debate y perspectivas*, no. 2 (September 2002), 5. Rouen was the second biggest city in France with some seventy thousand people and, by far, the busiest port (Jean Meyer, "Nantes au XVIe siècle," in Philippe Masson and Michel Vergé-Franceschi, *La France et la mer au siècle des grandes découvertes* [Paris, 1993], 93). Henri II needed good relations with Portugal because of nearly continuous wars with Spain. On the spectacle, see Arthur Heulhard, *Villegaignon, Roi d'Amérique, un homme de mer au XVIe siècle* (Paris, 1897), 88; Ferdinand Denis, *Une fête brésilienne célébrée à Rouen en 1550* (Paris, 1850).

belonged to a European sovereign. Because wealth from the Indies under-girded the ambitions of the Iberians, Henri unleashed privateers such as the famous François Le Clerc and his lieutenant, the ferocious Jacques de Sores, who swarmed to the Spanish Caribbean. Le Clerc, for his part, armed ten ships out of Rouen and Dieppe to launch assaults on Hispaniola and Puerto Rico. The Huguenot de Sores wreaked havoc in Cuba, not sparing clerics or churches. He burned Havana to the ground after extracting every portable bit of wealth. In these same years, a complaint to the Spanish king claimed the French "are so numerous in these seas that a bird cannot fly without being seen." These events provide the context for the adventure to Brazil led by Nicholas Durand de Villegaignon that resulted in a French settlement in the bay of Rio de Janeiro between 1555 and 1560.[11]

It is useful here to examine the spectrum of distinctions between trad-ing/raiding adventures and true colonization. These factors are essential for colonization: a badly needed staple to export to the metropole; agricul-tural lands for long-term support; women for reproduction and social sta-bility; and official imprimaturs to legitimate land grants and inheritances. The trade in dyewoods called for trading posts, whereas that for sassafras in Low Country Georgia and Carolina did not. Raiding was most often sea-borne, and, if any enemy territory was occupied, it was not for any length of time. Raiding might be greatly facilitated by forward, heavily fortified camps, and some agriculture might be undertaken to help feed the soldiers, but such facilities were not very dependent on female colonists. Neverthe-less, such camps might evolve into more permanent settlements. These cri-teria will help us gauge whether the enterprises to Brazil and Florida (1555–1568) should be viewed as primarily colonial expeditions.

The motives of the Villegaignon expedition were many, but the estab-lishment of a Huguenot refuge was most definitely not one of them, at least at the outset. The orthodox Catholic Henri II, who secretly provided ten thousand livres tournois (lt) and two heavily armed ships in support of the expedition, intended to extirpate any whiff of "Lutheranism" in France.[12]

11. Bernard Grunberg, "Corsaires français et 'Luthéranisme' en Mexique en 1560," in Acerra and Martinière, eds., *Coligny, les protestants et la mer*, 85. Henri II ennobled Le Clerc upon his return in 1559. The complaint to the king is cited in Hoffman, *Spanish Crown*, 68.

12. In a 1557 letter to John Calvin asking for Calvinist colonists to come to Gua-nabara, Villegaignon claimed that his sole motive was "the promotion of the kingdom of Christ." The letter is in Charles W. Baird, *History of the Huguenot Emigration to America* (New York, 1885), I, 339. The lt was a unit of currency but not a coin. On paper, 3 lt equaled one silver écu.

Protection of French trading interests along the Brazilian coast, the establishment of a naval base for either a water or overland assault on Peru, and a challenge to Iberian claims motivated Henri and Coligny. Coligny, like Villegaignon and so many others trained in Erasmian humanism, despised the corruption of the Roman church but also regretted the split in Christianity that Luther and Calvin had deemed necessary. It was only in 1558, following his capture in battle and subsequent conversion to Protestantism, that Coligny moved closer to the Huguenot party. The commander Villegaignon, a tough-minded Knight of Malta—friend simultaneously of the zealously Catholic Guise family and of the reform-minded duchess of Ferrara, Princess Renée of France—accepted Catholics and reformers alike in his initial crew. While attempting to keep the expedition's goal a secret so as not to alert the Iberians, Henri, Coligny, and Villegaignon assembled some six hundred men, including criminals released from prisons when sufficient volunteers could not be found.[13]

Sailing into the bay of Rio, Villegaignon selected the island of Guanabara as his base, and there he established Fort Coligny. Endowed with little fertile land and inadequate water, the island nonetheless provided security from assault and helped contain volatile elements in the all-male crew. Villegaignon was, after all, a Knight of Malta, the monk / warriors who manned the rock fortress in the middle Mediterranean, guarding Christianity from the "infidels." He imposed iron discipline and a harsh work schedule on his men. Puritanical, authoritarian, and profoundly offended by Native American lifestyles, he refused to allow his men to visit the sirens on the mainland, the supposedly licentious Native American women made famous in writings attributed to Vespucci. He certainly did not believe in the evangelization of these "beasts possessed of human form."[14]

13. Villegaignon dispatched eighteen men to search for gold in the Plate River basin (Heulhard, *Villegaignon*, 162). Coligny was "Admiral of France," which is to say, admiral of those areas under the jurisdiction of the Parlement of Paris. There were also admirals for Brittany, Guyenne, and Provence. See Michel Vergé-Franceschi, "L'Admirauté de France dans la deuxième moitié du XVIe siècle: Un enjeu entre catholiques et protestants," in Acerra and Martinière, eds., *Coligny, les protestants et la mer*, 36. One could hold the office of admiral without ever leaving land; indeed, no sixteenth-century Admiral of France fought a sea battle. For an assessment of Coligny's closeness to the Reform in 1555, see Lilaine Crété, *Coligny* (Paris, 1985), 73–76. Loyalty to his Catholic king prevented an open espousal of reformed Christianity at that time. On Coligny's moving closer to the Huguenot party, see 104–106, 152; Crété cautions that he did not make an overt protestation of faith until July 1560.

14. According to Nicholas Barré, the island produced a little maize. See his *Copie*

These Tupinambás had become, over the previous two decades, fierce enemies of the Portuguese living to the north because of the latter's slave raids. Villegaignon, however, needed to truck with the Tupinambás for the foodstuffs he could not grow on his Brazilian Malta. But he failed to solidify alliances with the coastal Amerindians who had long been friends of the French—a crucial error, especially coupled with his alienation of the "licentious" French traders living in the coastal area.[15]

When some French refused to obey his authority, indeed, plotted to poison him, Villegaignon searched for solutions. Some neighboring Indians became overtly hostile, perhaps because they blamed him for the diseases afflicting them. In increasingly perilous circumstances, and without royal reinforcements, he wrote to his former law-school acquaintance John Calvin at Geneva, asking for support of his Brazilian enterprise. According to traditional Protestant historiography, the no-longer-extant letter proclaimed Villegaignon's intent to establish a refuge for persecuted Protestants. Though startling in hindsight, this episode must be understood in a context where religious lines were far from hardened. At the very least, Villegaignon was not unsympathetic to reform of the Catholic Church. At the same time, he had connections to the powerful Guise family, supporters of the Jesuits and opposed to a rapidly emerging Huguenot faction. Even Admiral Coligny, who would play such an important role in the Florida affair, had not in the later 1550s declared overtly for Protestant Christianity.[16]

Fourteen Calvinists, including the future famous chronicler Jean de Léry,

de quelques lettres sur la navigation du Chevalier de Villegaignon . . . (Paris, 1557), 20. Barré maintains that Villegaignon feared Native American assaults if he established a colony on the mainland. For an example of the Vespucci comments, see my Cannibal Encounters: Europeans and Island Caribs, 1492–1763 (Baltimore, 1992), 21–22. Villegaignon called them "whores." For his "beasts" comment, see Villegaignon to Calvin (1557), printed in Baird, History of the Huguenot Emigration, I, 338.

15. According to Barré, a friend of Villegaignon's, Villegaignon had not brought much provision from France (Copie, 31). Barré confirms that the commander imposed "incredible labor" amid food shortages (34).

16. Julien, Les voyages de découverte, 193; Andrea Daher, Les singularités de la France équinoxiale: Histoire de la mission des pères capucins au Brésil (1612–1615) (Paris, 2002), 34; Frank Lestringant, L'expérience huguenote au Nouveau Monde (XVIe siècle) (Geneva, 1996), 121. According to Barré (Copie, 35), some eight hundred Native Americans died, and Villegaignon was blamed. After a brief stay in Brazil, the Franciscan friar André Thevet had brought Henri II curiosities from Brazil including a Tupinambá headdress made of the yellow feathers of toucans. Thevet wrote an account of his Brazil sojourn; see Les singularitez de la France antarctique . . . (Paris, 1557). An English translation by Thomas Hacket appeared in London in 1568 (The New Found

and some three hundred colonists, including a few women, arrived in Brazil in 1557. At first, Villegaignon and the new arrivals got along famously. The two Calvinist ministers, in letters sent to Geneva sent on the returning ships, praised his rule and religious views. However, all too soon, disputes over the doctrine of the real presence of Jesus in the bread and wine broke out, dividing the colony and ultimately ending in death or dispersal for the Calvinists. In contrast to Villegaignon's belief in the real presence, the Calvinists believed in only a spiritual presence of Jesus at Communion.[17]

According to Protestant sources, the "Cain of America" now turned on the religious dissidents and soon exiled the Calvinists to the mainland, where they found refuge and hospitality among friendly indigenes. Eventually, early in 1558, all but five boarded a shabby vessel that made its return to France. These five Calvinists threw themselves on Villegaignon's mercy; after formal examination of their religious beliefs, he hurled three into the sea and imprisoned the other two. The emerging Huguenot party now had its first American martyrs.

Hearing rumbles from Paris concerning his religious beliefs, Villegaignon in late 1559 returned to defend his name and to gather new recruits, including Catholic missionaries.[18] Circumstances in France appeared propitious. With the accidental death of Henri II, the Guise faction dominated the young king Francis II and his wife Marie Stuart. No doubt Marie, a Guise, felt obligations toward Villegaignon, the courageous knight who had braved much to see her safely from Scotland to France. Villegaignon intended to return to Brazil in the summer of 1560, but unbeknown to him, the Portuguese had already conquered Guanabara Bay. Although not the only cause of the ultimate demise of "Antarctic France," the miniature war

---

Worlde or Antarctike . . .), and Frank Lestringant has brought out a modern edition (*Le Brésil d'André Thevet: Les singularités de la France antarctique* [Paris, 1997]).

17. Léry's book about his experiences in Brazil achieved a remarkable success in his own era, no doubt among a Protestant audience in particular, and has been a crucial source for twentieth-century anthropology (Léry, *Histoire d'un voyage fait en la terre du Bresil* . . . [La Rochelle, 1578]). Four other French editions and two Latin ones followed. For a modern French edition, use Frank Lestringant, *Jean de Léry; ou, L'invention du sauvage: Essai sur l'Histoire d'un voyage faict en la terre du Brésil* (Paris, 1999). A good English translation is by Janet Whatley (*History of a Voyage to the Land of Brazil, Otherwise Called America* [Berkeley, Calif., 1990]). The Calvinists' initial reaction to Villegaignon can be found in Baird, *History of the Huguenot Emigration*, I, 330–335.

18. At first, he approached the new, dynamic order of Jesuits, but their Portuguese brethren warned them that Guanabara was a nest of heretics. See Frank Lestringant, "Le Huguenot et le sauvage: Nouvelles hypothèses," in *La France / Amérique*, 135.

of religion at Fort Coligny would forever color that event. As mentioned above, the choice of Guanabara and alienation of local tribes also weakened the colony.

In France, the escalating tensions between Catholics and French Calvinists were what prevented Villegaignon's return to Brazil. Meanwhile, a Portuguese expedition led by the governor of Brazil, Mem de Sá, and his éminence noir, the famous Jesuit Manuel de Nóbrega, captured Guanabara in 1560 after a siege. The Portuguese blew up the fortress after carefully documenting the Protestant paraphernalia they supposedly found there. The Portuguese under Mem de Sá's son and nephew fought for more than a decade to subject the Tupinambás and Frenchmen living among them along the coast. In 1575, another Portuguese force destroyed the last French garrison, at Cabo Frio north of Rio.[19]

The polemical battle over the "loss of Brazil" had just begun. In 1561, Villegaignon himself fought a war of pamphlets with the Calvinist Richer, one of the ministers to reach Guanabara in 1557.[20] Villegaignon then played an active role on the Catholic side in the religious wars. He died in 1572, the year of the Saint Bartholomew's Day massacre, which ended any hopes for reconciliation between the religious parties.[21]

Villegaignon's Brazilian enterprise had colonial aspirations along the lines of the Spanish model: heavily armed Frenchmen intended to exploit Native American food and labor resources as a base for finding precious metals or looting such from Native American and Iberian sources. The same generalization applies to the enterprise of Florida in the 1560s. In both cases, the Spanish model proved disastrously flawed, as neither sufficient Amerindian food supplies nor intensely concentrated, submissive indigenous populations were available. As a result, French colonial aspirations suffered a crushing setback.

19. Julien, *Les voyages de découverte,* 208–210. Mem de Sá was mightily impressed by Villegaignon's fortifications.

20. Twenty-six pamphlets on the controversy printed in 1561 alone have been identified, with Villegaignon the author of about one-third (Lestringant, *L'expérience huguenote,* 126).

21. During a truce in the struggles between Catholic zealots and the Huguenots, queen mother Catherine arranged a marriage between her daughter Margherite and Henri of Navarre, leader of the Protestant cause. The chief Huguenot noblemen accordingly assembled in Paris. Pressured by the Catholic Guise faction, Catherine and Charles IX sanctioned the killing of Coligny and some other Huguenots. These killings turned into open season on all Protestants, first in Paris, then in the provinces. Well over ten thousand were murdered.

The years 1560–1562 were fraught with religious intrigue and struggle for control of two adolescent kings, Francis II and Charles IX (1560–1574). During the short reign of the former, the ultra-Catholic Guise family usurped power and bloodily enforced Henri II's laws against the reformers. The queen mother, Catherine de Médicis, became regent upon Charles's assumption of the throne. To counter the Guise clan, she supported the Huguenot Bourbon-Condé princes of the blood, as well as the related Châtillon brothers. One of these was Admiral Coligny. Though Catherine's attempt to straddle the religious fence ultimately failed, it provided two years of truce. During that time, Coligny schemed to establish a garrison / colony astride the return route of Spain's treasure fleet from Mexico (New Spain). For the next decade, until his assassination that initiated the infamous Saint Bartholomew's Day massacre, Coligny promoted hatred of Spain as a way to unite France. Before, during, and after the Florida affair, he encouraged corsair activities in the Atlantic, granting letters of marque on his own authority or through that of Henri of Navarre, the Admiral of Guyenne.[22]

Multiple motives underlay the three Florida expeditions of 1562–1565; the first voyage, in 1562, was a reconnaissance led by a respected Huguenot sea captain, Jean Ribaut of Dieppe, who, in his initial report, ascribed to Coligny the dual motivation of procuring riches for France and spreading the Gospel to the indigenes.[23] Coligny knew that an armed forward base would present a grave danger to the hated Spanish. Ribaut, his lieutenant René Goulaine de Laudonnière, and 150 heavily armed, mostly Protestant men left before the explosion of religious war in France in 1562. Before the

22. For details, see Augeron, "Coligny et les Espagnols," in Acerra and Martinière, eds., *Coligny, les protestants et la mer*. The chief port of the Guyenne admiralty was the Protestant stronghold, La Rochelle. Also, see Woodbury Lowery, *The Spanish Settlements within the Present Limits of the United States: Florida, 1562-1574* (New York, 1959), 25–26, for French privateer activities in the immediate years before Florida.

23. Crété, *Coligny*, 296. The similarities between the events described below, as well as their motives, will strike students of the Roanoke voyages: Coligny / Ralegh and the Calvinist / Puritan character of enterprises aimed to flank the Spaniards in America; the exploratory voyages; the failed first colony in part attributable to Laudonnière's and Ralph Lane's mishandling of Indian relations; the critical role of hurricanes in aborting these enterprises (September 13–15, 1565, and June 10–13, 1586); the monarchs' tepid support as immediate prospects were not particularly inspiring; and the difficulty of resupplying the settlements because of events in Europe. Also, in effect, those champions of a Protestant International, Coligny and Ralegh, were killed for their aggressive opposition to Spain. Finally, although the French had no Thomas Harriot to describe intelligently the land and people, they did have a rival to the great artist John White in Jacques Le Moyne de Morgues.

fleet's departure, the well-informed Spanish ambassador protested to the regent Catherine, who replied nonchalantly that his master, Philip II, would suffer no harm. Though there had been many Spanish attempts to settle in Florida, none had succeeded. In any case, Ribaut sailed directly across the Atlantic rather than took the traditional passage through the Caribbean to avoid giving the Spaniards pretext for reprisals. He sailed along the Florida coast, establishing contact with Native Americans hostile to the Spaniards. Leaving a crew of between twenty-six and thirty on present-day Parris Island, South Carolina (named Charlesfort), Ribaut returned to a France wracked by religious war.[24]

After he participated in a failed effort to defend Dieppe against a Catholic siege, Ribaut took refuge in Elizabeth's London, where he tried to persuade the young queen to support his enterprise. In France, Coligny and the harassed Huguenots could not consider immediately following up the Florida démarche. Meanwhile, the pitifully inept "colonists" at Charlesfort overly depended on the local population for supply while they wandered in search of treasure. Soon desperate and hungry, they constructed a rickety ship to launch a return voyage. An English ship finally picked up the starving survivors, but not before an act of cannibalism. Once refreshed, some of the survivors were brought to court to regale Elizabeth with tales of Florida. Meanwhile, a Spanish expedition found the site, destroyed the fortress, and dispatched its stone marker to Spain.[25]

After the promulgation of a religious truce in 1563, Coligny sponsored a second expedition to Florida. With Ribaut in jail in London for refusing to lead an English expedition to Charlesfort, his second-in-command, Laudonnière, captained the fleet of three ships carrying perhaps three hundred people, including a few women. That women took part is made manifest by the birth of eight children at Fort Caroline. Thus this expedition had some colonial intentions, as it also featured a significant number of artisans but not, however, farmers or fishermen. It further included criminals, foreigners, and "Moors." From the crew composition and from what happened

24. Jean Ribaut, *The Whole and True Discoverye of Terra Florida* (Deland, Fl., 1927), 53–60. This is a reprint of the 1563 English version (London), a presumed French original having disappeared. The Spaniard who later conquered and killed Ribaut, Pedro Menéndez de Avilés, called him "the most experienced sailor and corsair known, very skilful in this navigation of the Indies and of the Florida Coast" (cited in Lowery, *Spanish Settlements,* 200).The remains of the fort have recently been uncovered, adjacent to the United States Marines' old golf course.

25. Lestringant, *Le Huguenot et le sauvage,* 291; Jerald T. Milanich, *Florida Indians and the Invasion from Europe* (Gainesville, Fl., 1995), 144.

in Florida, it is clear that the expedition planned to depend on Native resources for basic needs while searching for instant riches, once again imitating the Spanish model.[26]

Taking what Laudonnière describes as the "customary" southern route through the Caribbean and on to Florida, the ships eventually stopped at the Saint Johns River near present-day Jacksonville. Laudonnière constructed Fort Caroline. After a good start, most everything went wrong as the fall of 1564 passed. The French depended on local Timucuan peoples for supplies, but the price was the diminution of their trading goods and demands to participate in indigenous conflicts.[27] Native surplus of maize and beans could not withstand the pressure of French demands. Nothing was immediately sown because the colonists not only arrived late in planting season but were distracted by gold fever.[28] A dilatory personality, Laudonnière was no John Smith. A bout with malaria further weakened the colony. Like Villegaignon, the moralistic Laudonnière attempted to prevent dalliances with Native women; though futile, these efforts disaffected many of his men.

In late November, some sixty disgruntled gold-seekers forced the commandant at pistolpoint to authorize them to take two ships for marauding in the Spanish Caribbean. These hunters became the hunted, and their capture meant that Madrid would soon hear of these "Lutheran" depredations. Their capture also undermined the French claim that colonization of unoccupied land was their right and not a casus belli. Philip authorized a punitive expedition against the French with an order to kill what he called pirates and heretics.

At Fort Caroline in the spring of 1565, the increasingly famished colonists raided Native American villages to find food. In response, the indi-

26. No names are known of these predecessors of Virginia Dare. See Charles E. Bennett, *Laudonniere and Fort Caroline: History and Documents* (1964; rpt. Tuscaloosa, Ala., 2001), 23. For a letter of Captain Giles de Pysière and the deposition of Robert Melenche, see 72–73, 88–89.

27. It is possible that the exceptionally dry conditions of the 1560s caused harvest problems for Native Americans and an inability to supply the hapless French. For those dry conditions, see Brian Fagan, *The Little Ice Age: How Climate Made History, 1300–1850* (New York, 2000), 96. Archaeologist Dennis B. Blanton argues that drought conditions similarly made life extremely difficult for both the Roanoke and early Jamestown colonists; see Blanton, "Drought as a Factor in the Jamestown Colony, 1607–1612," *Historical Archaeology,* XXXIV (2000), 74–81.

28. Several expeditions explored in every direction, with one perhaps reaching the Appalachians. See René de Laudonnière, *Three Voyages,* ed. and trans. Charles E. Bennett (1975; rpt. Tuscaloosa, Ala., 2001), 217 n. 12.

genes made life miserable for their tormentors. Laudonnière had resisted such actions until the famine became incredibly severe. Finally, the misery impelled him to construct a ship to bring the settlers home. Then the famous English sea dog and slave trader John Hawkins appeared in the Saint Johns River.[29] Elizabeth had advised Hawkins to reconnoiter the Florida coast in search of the colony after a slave-trading trip to the Spanish Caribbean. Hawkins assisted the colonists, mostly fellow Protestants and enemies of Spain, and sold one of his ships at a bargain discount to allow the French to return home. As they prepared to return, amazingly, almost deus ex machina, French ships appeared on the horizon.

In 1565, Coligny equipped a returned Ribaut with a force of about six hundred to find and relieve Laudonnière. Of these, soldiers were the majority, but also on board were some three hundred artisans, farmers, women, and children.[30] The admiral clearly now had colonial intentions, although whether the primary purpose was to establish a refuge for Huguenots or to establish a strong French presence along the lifeline of Spain's American empire is not entirely clear. Perhaps both purposes, not incompatible, motivated him.[31] Very well informed and alarmed, Philip II moved quickly to respond. He chose a man at least equal to Ribaut in maritime experience, personal strength, and religious zealotry as the captain general of the Florida armada: Pedro Menéndez de Avilés. The latter undertook to establish a permanent Spanish colony in Florida to stop further French depredations.[32]

Even though the admiral and Ribaut were aware of a Spanish fleet in preparation, Ribaut sailed the southern route and inexplicably proceeded at

29. Two decades later, Sir Francis Drake, fresh from a cruise in the Spanish Caribbean, sailed to Roanoke to resupply Ralph Lane and his men. After suffering losses due to a tropical storm in June (!), he wound up transporting Lane's colony to England, just days before a resupply ship arrived!

30. According to one of the participants, Nicholas Le Challeux, the miseries of the recent wars of religion, the unwillingness of disbanded soldiers to return to civilian life and descriptions of Florida as an earthly paradise made recruitment of volunteers easy for Ribaut. See Le Challeux, "Discours de l'histoire de la Floride," in Suzanne Lussagnet, ed., *Les Français en Amérique pendant la deuxième moitié du XVIe siècle: Les Français en Floride,* II (Paris, 1958), 211. Le Challeux himself was a carpenter. His account had four separate printings in 1566, and Thomas Hacket brought out an English translation in the same year.

31. There were some Catholics in the crew, so a religious litmus test had not been administered.

32. Menéndez warned Philip that the French posed a grave danger because they would liberate the Spanish slaves and turn them on the colonists. See his letter in Bennett, *Laudonnière and Fort Caroline,* 128–129.

a rather leisurely pace north along the Florida coast.[33] Fortunately for him, storms badly delayed most of Menéndez's fleet. Wishing to beat Ribaut to the Saint Johns River, the energetic captain general rushed to the Florida coast with but part of his force. In that, he failed, but he immediately attacked four of Ribaut's larger ships, which were unable to cross the bar into the Saint Johns. Failing, however, to catch the faster French ships, Menéndez brought his forces to what would become Saint Augustine and started to fortify the place.

Upon the return of his ships, Ribaut deposited the civilians and supplies at Fort Caroline. Against Laudonnière's warnings about late-summer weather dangers, the intrepid Ribaut moved quickly to assault Menéndez. However, a tempest in mid-September scattered Ribaut's fleet. Three ships were run onto the beaches near Ponce de Leon Inlet and Cape Canaveral, with the human remnants stranded on Florida beaches and tidal flats. Meanwhile, Menéndez force-marched his troops for four days through snake-infested swamps to Fort Caroline some fifteen leagues away. His assault at daybreak achieved total surprise. The captured soldiers were put to the sword or hanged, and about 50 women and children were captured. Only Laudonnière, the famous artist Jacques Le Moyne de Morgues, and perhaps 50 others escaped, including the future chronicler of these events, Nicholas Le Challeux. Subsequently, Menéndez systematically rounded up Ribaut's stranded men not far from Daytona Beach and slaughtered them in a grisly manner, according to Protestant accounts. Of approximately 140 soldiers abandoned on the Matanzas Inlet, all but about 10 were stabbed to death after capture. Ribaut and about 100 men surrendered in the vain hope that Menéndez would accept a ransom.[34]

33. Laudonnière lays heavy blame on Ribaut for the loss of Florida. We do not have Ribaut's version of events. See René de Laudonnière, *L'Histoire notable de la Floride* . . . (Paris, 1586). There are many English translations; see *Three Voyages,* ed. Bennett. Hakluyt collected accounts by Laudonnière, Ribaut, Jacques Le Moyne de Morgues, and others to stimulate English interest in these regions.

34. Julien, *Les voyages de découverte,* 24. Some seventeen were spared, including trumpeters, drummers, fifers, and four Catholics; see Lowery, *Spanish Settlements,* 199 n. 4. For Le Moyne de Morgues's drawings, see Paul Hulton, *The Work of Jacques Le Moyne de Morgues, a Huguenot Artist in France, Florida, and England* (London, 1977). Le Moyne de Morgues's *Brevis narratio* of his Florida experiences is the second part of Théodore de Bry's famous *Grands voyages.* For a modern translation, see Stefan Lorant, ed., *The New World: The First Pictures of America* (New York, 1946). According to Le Challeux, all the captured, including women and babes, were put to the sword (Le Challeux, "Discours de l'histoire de la Floride," in Lussagnet, ed.,

Frank Lestringant labels these events an "American St. Bartholomew's," with all the implications of cold and pitiless killing of ideological enemies. A more charitable view of Menéndez, a religious zealot so typical of that era, is that he massacred only the "Lutheran" pirates, and those in part out of military insecurity, as he did not have the forces to keep them as prisoners, the food to feed them, or the ships to transport them to Cuba. To be sure, "Lutherans" constituted the majority of the French enemy. Of the approximately one thousand French in Florida, as many as three-quarters perished, and most of these suffered "martyrdom." Philip enthusiastically applauded Menéndez for carrying out his orders so successfully. The French ambassador informed Catherine, "This court (Spanish) were more gladdened than if it had been a victory over the Turks."[35]

Catherine felt that court and country were too weak to go beyond vigorous verbal protests against this treatment of royal subjects. Philip had the whip hand as violent religious discord divided France. He protested French intrusions in La Florida so strongly to Catherine that she feigned ignorance of the Huguenot venture. When confronted with hard evidence, she complained to the Spanish ambassador that if "all the Huguenots resided in that place Florida," then there would be "peace in the kingdom." Catherine did, however, refuse Philip's demand that Coligny no longer have access to the Crown, and her continuing protests did lead to the release of forty-eight women and children prisoners taken from Florida. Her son Charles IX refused to grant letters of marque to attack the Iberians on the high seas, but Coligny and Henri of Navarre happily did so.[36]

Frenchmen in the Atlantic ports took private vengeance. In 1567, the Gascon corsair and inveterate hater of Spain Dominique de Gourgues assembled some two hundred mostly Huguenot soldiers who, with the assis-

Les Français en Amérique, II, 217). Spanish sources estimate that about 130 men were killed, but 50 women and children were spared. Le Challeux's charge is propaganda. See John T. McGrath, *The French in Early Florida: In the Eye of the Hurricane* (Gainesville, Fl., 2000), 145–146.

Modern, revisionist views based on Spanish archival evidence may be found in Lowery, *Spanish Settlements,* esp. 425–428; Eugene Lyon, *The Enterprise of Florida: Pedro Menéndez de Avilés and the Spanish Conquest of 1565–1568* (1974; rpt. Gainesville, Fl., 1983); McGrath, *French in Early Florida.*

35. Lestringant, *L'expérience huguenote,* 229–242; Lowery, *Spanish Settlements,* 303. McGrath, *French in Early Florida,* 149–154, explains Menéndez's actions in the charitable manner described.

36. Catherine's quotation in Paul Gaffarel, *Histoire de la Floride française* (Paris, 1875), 428; and see Lowery, *Spanish Settlements,* 322.

tance of Native Americans, destroyed three forts in Florida in early 1568. De Gourgues killed some two hundred Spaniards, most of whom had surrendered. It is said that he justified the massacre on an eye-for-an-eye principle. On his way home, De Gourgues captured three Spanish ships and threw the crews into the sea, his bloodlust apparently not yet satiated. De Gourgues appeared at court to relate his actions and to propose the reconquest of Florida. Charles IX, buffeted by religious factions, was far from amused. With the Guises wanting to collect the reward that Philip placed on de Gourgues's head, the avenger had to hide for a year.[37]

It should not be thought that the Florida debacle cowed Coligny. He was all too aware that Spain's American treasure fueled Philip II's drive to extirpate Protestantism throughout Europe. As a French royal navy barely existed, he continued to authorize and support corsair activities against the Iberians in the Canaries, the Azores, and beyond. Coligny used all of his persuasion to stop an angry king from punishing an unauthorized Huguenot corsair's sacking of Funchal in the Portuguese Madeiras in 1566.[38] Henri of Navarre also gave letters of marque to Huguenot corsairs out of La Rochelle, and it seems that the resulting prizes were an important source of Huguenot revenues.[39]

In other Huguenot thrusts, the daunting corsair Captain de Sores in 1565 and 1570 seized and unflinchingly killed forty-nine Jesuits on Portuguese ships on the Portugal/Brazil route. In 1568, the titular Huguenot leader, Louis, prince de Condé, had discussions with Elizabeth of England about a joint fleet to capture the Spanish Indies. In the same year, Coligny hoped to implement plans to capture Madeira as a forward base for corsair operations. Even his murder in 1572 did not stop Huguenot initiatives. In 1573, the pirate/corsair and mapmaker Guillaume Le Testu and a band of fellow Huguenots randomly encountered a squadron of Francis Drake's. They joined forces to ambush a Spanish silver mule train crossing the Isthmus of Panama. The raid was but a very modest success; in the melée, Le Testu

37. Lowery, *Spanish Settlements,* 334. A book about this escapade is *Histoire mémorable de la reprinse de l'isle de la Floride, faicte par les François, sous la conduite de Capitaine de Gorgues . . .* (n.p., 1568).

38. The king's first reaction was: "'I would make such an example of him (the corsair leader) that everyone would know that there is no consideration, not even the revenge of Florida, that would make me approve of these actions'" (cited in Heulhard, *Villegaignon,* 265).

39. Augeron, "Coligny et les Espagnols," in Acerra and Martinière, eds., *Coligny, les protestants et la mer,* 167. Huguenot corsairs not only paid the normal 10 percent of their prizes to the admirals but another 10 percent for the "cause."

fell dead and Drake escaped with some silver. Occurring one year after the Saint Bartholomew's Day massacre, this raid symbolizes England's overshadowing of France as premier enemy of Spanish America.[40]

As a result of the Florida affair, French and especially Huguenot ambitions to establish colonies in America received a devastating setback. For a long time, the matter of Florida played a crucial role in the development of the Black Legend. Protestant Europe lumped the French "martyrs" with the poor, slaughtered Native Americans as victims of the Spanish fury. Urbain Chauveton embroidered firsthand accounts by Laudonnière and Le Challeux, and foreign Protestants such as Theodore de Bry and Richard Hakluyt sought to never let the world forget the Matanzas Inlet. The cosmographer La Popélinière popularized Le Challeux's grisly depiction of Menéndez's desecration of Ribaut. Until recently, the Protestant version of events dominated English and French historiography.[41]

French merchants and corsairs did not cease to be interested in exploiting cross-Atlantic resources, despite internal turmoil and the real threat of Iberian reprisals. Jean-Pierre Moreau estimates that an average of twenty to thirty merchant / corsairs per year departed for the Indies in these years of nominal peace with Spain. Norman merchants seeking dyewoods still plied the Brazilian coast, and many suffered the consequences: in 1582 and 1583, the Spanish captured twenty-four Norman ships trading off the Brazilian coast. As early as the 1540s, Norman traders had encouraged the Potiguar Tupí tribe to resist Portuguese colonization of the area north of Pernambuco; the Potiguars, incensed by Portuguese slaving raids and armed by the French, successfully resisted for more than a half-century. During that time, French merchants and interpreters received good treatment in the area. Clearly, French traders also operated in the Maragnan area, and French merchants traded with indigenous suppliers of sassafras along the Georgia and Carolina Low Country coast.[42]

40. Paul Gaffarel, *Histoire du Brésil française au seizième siècle* (Paris, 1878), 355–357; Augeron, "Coligny et les Espagnols," in Acerra and Martinière, eds., *Coligny, les protestants et la mer,* 160.

41. Lancelot Voisin [sieur de la Popélinière], *Les trois mondes,* 2 vols. (Paris, 1582), II, 34.

42. Moreau, *Les Petites Antilles,* 57–58, 89; Hemming, *Red Gold,* 71–72. Charles Bréard reconstructed from notary documents in Honfleur an impressive list of ships going to "Pérou" starting from 1574 (*Documents rélatifs à la Marine normande,* 149–200). On the French traders and merchants, see Laudonnière, "L'histoire notable," in Lussagnet, ed., *Les Français en Amérique,* II, 41–42. For an overview, see Russell

Interlocking events around the year 1580 transformed the politics of Western Europe and the Atlantic. Drake's stunning around-the-world escapade, his queen's refusal to condemn his thefts in Spain's overseas empire, Philip II's capture of the Portuguese monarchy in 1580, and, in that same year, the Lowland rebels' formal rejection of him as their suzerain threw the European political system into turmoil.[43] Philip's Mediterranean-centered strategy of the 1560s and early 1570s shifted increasingly to an Atlantic one. Northern European heretics gradually replaced Moriscos, Berbers, and Turks as his principal enemy. In the 1580s, Philip increasingly restricted North European access to Lisbon and Seville and across the Atlantic strengthened Iberian defenses against both corsairs and merchants. In turn, European Calvinists launched a literary offensive against Spain and complemented that with a military offensive on the world's oceans.

In 1584, the last son of Henri II and Catherine died, leaving Henri of Navarre of the House of Bourbon as heir to the throne should Henri III (1574-1589) die heirless. Although it would be a decade before he could act, Navarre was interested in reviving French maritime activities to annoy Philip and to challenge Iberian hegemony in the Atlantic. Philip's assumption of the Portuguese monarchy in conjunction with an intense crusade against Protestant Europe set the stage for increasingly aggressive counterattacks by the English and Dutch and, to a lesser extent, by Huguenot captains.

In 1582, Catherine de Médicis, a distant claimant to the Portuguese throne, decided to support a Portuguese pretender. The Portuguese Azores had refused to declare for Philip II. She sponsored a fleet of some six thousand men on fifty-five ships commanded by her cousin, Philippe Strozzi, to attack the vital treasure route of Spain by gaining control of the Madeiras and the Azores. This was the largest French fleet up to that time and for a long time thereafter. But the price for her support of the pretender was Brazil. An initial assault against Iberian positions on the island of San Miguel in the Azores was successful; however, the advent of some thirty-seven large Spanish ships forced Strozzi to give combat. Owing to incompe-

Magnaghi, "Sassafras and Its Role in Early America, 1562-1622," *Terrae Incognitae,* XXIX (1997), 10-21.

43. Fernand Braudel once remarked that Philip's capture of the Portuguese throne was the greatest turning point in world history because an oceanic struggle replaced the Mediterranean struggle. Great historians can get away with such ex cathedra pronouncements.

tence, only twelve of his ships confronted the Spaniards, who administered a stinging defeat on the French. Strozzi and other prisoners, though not, for the most part, Huguenots, were summarily dispatched as pirates in the fashion of Menéndez. After this devastating defeat, large naval operations against Spain became the work of the English and then the Dutch, not the French. Equally, strengthened Spanish defenses in the Americas received challenges primarily from English corsairs and Dutch merchants prevented from trading for salt with Portugal.[44]

As French colonial initiatives in the last decades of the sixteenth century ceased, fierce ideological polemics rehashed the debacles in Brazil and Florida as part of an international Calvinist riposte to Castilian hegemonic pretensions.[45] Overwhelmingly, the Huguenot version of these events predominated.[46] However, polemical victories did not push Huguenots to new colonial endeavors or to the search for a "land of refuge." The very idea of a Protestant refuge overseas, which had not been in any case the dominant motive for either Brazil or Florida, weakened. Nicholas Le Challeux blamed the disaster at the Matanzas Inlet not only on the Spaniards but also on the French themselves. God punished him and his fellow colonists because "the father never does his duty in abandoning his vocation to search for adventure in foreign lands." The Huguenot poet Guillaume Du Bartas perhaps best captured the prevailing sentiment.

You, France, open your bosom to me, mother, you
Do not wish / That in strange countries, a vagabond
I grow old / You do not wish that a Brazil pride itself

44. Once again, Philip approved of the conduct toward the prisoners. His organization of an armada against England in 1588, which some historians treat as chimerical, appears less so in the context of this battle of 1582. For an overview of Dutch trade in the aftermath, see Cornelius Ch. Goslinga, *The Dutch in the Caribbean and on the Wild Coast, 1580–1680* (Gainesville, Fl., 1971).

45. This offensive reached its crescendo with the publication of de Bry's *Grands voyages* (1590-1634). See Michèle Duchet et al., *L'Amérique de Théodore de Bry: Une collection de voyages protestantes du XVIe siècle: Quatre études d'iconographie* (Paris, 1987).

46. I studied these polemics in my dissertation, "France 'Discovers' America: The Image of Tropical America in Sixteenth- and Seventeenth-Century France and Its Impact on Early French Colonialism" (University of Connecticut, 1974). Frank Lestringant has made a brilliant career analyzing them. See, inter alia, *Le Huguenot et le sauvage; André Thevet: Cosmographe des derniers Valois* (Geneva, 1991); *Le cannibale: Grandeur et décadence* (Paris, 1994); not to mention dozens of articles and other works cited above.

With my bones / A Cathay with my glory, a Peru with
My poetry: / You want to be my tomb as well as my
Home / O, pearl of Europe / France I salute you.[47]

Some Huguenots came to believe that Florida had been itself a mistake as every man was needed for the struggle at home.[48] In 1598, their former leader Henri IV issued the Edict of Nantes, guaranteeing significant religious freedom in many parts of France and the military means to back it up; in such circumstances, why look overseas to build a city on a hill? Certainly, individual Huguenots were involved in commercial and colonial activities in the decades between 1598 and 1625 and beyond, but whole communities did not migrate overseas. Thus, Huguenots did not play a role similar to that of their Calvinist brethren in England, the Puritans, in building English America.

Political / religious conflict in France and the touchy relationship with mighty Spain kept maritime activities at a relatively modest level before 1600, but other factors are relevant. In terms of the *mentalités* of those favoring maritime expansionism, the influence of the Hispanic model of empire dominated thinking in France (and also in England). Two paths to wealth emerged from the Spanish experience: the theft and / or mining of precious metals and the exploitation of the indigenous populations and African slaves to produce goods and provisions. As it turned out, France and England were unable, during the period discussed here, to emulate the Spanish model. Such notions had undermined the settlements in Brazil and Florida as well as Roanoke.

The sixteenth-century debacles overseas also inhibited future colonization schemes by reinforcing the notion that French national character was inappropriate for a task that required long-term effort. The mercurial French, so opinion held, were brilliant sailors, explorers, and adventurers. The gritty, grueling work of hewing settlements out of the wilderness was

47. Le Challeux, "Discours de l'histoire de la Floride," in Lussagnet, ed., *Les Français en Amérique,* II, 204–205; Guillaume de Salluste Du Bartas, *La seconde sepmaine* ... (Antwerp, 1591), book 7, 88. Le Challeux composed a poem on his return to Dieppe. Part of it reads: "Whoever wishes to go to Florida / he should go as I have been / and returned dry and arid / and struck down with poverty."

48. Lestringant, in his celebrated *Le Huguenot et le sauvage,* 108–116, argues that there was a resurgence in Huguenot support for colonization in the 1580s in conjunction with the international Protestant assault on Spain's record in the Americas. I do not find the argument convincing. Colonization is not the same thing as corsair raiding or trading with Native Americans for dyewoods and sassafras.

not a Gallic forte. Famously, Michel de Montaigne pronounced, "I fear that we have eyes bigger than our stomachs and more curiosity than capacity for colonization." The Huguenot duc de Sully, chief minister of Henri IV, opposed colonial schemes because "the experiences of the past have taught us only too well that the things which are separated from us by foreign lands or seas will be ours only through great expense and will yield little." Such was the legacy of Brazil and Florida. Future colonial failures would only reinforce this self-fulfilling prophecy.[49]

As Spain's growing dependence on France for food and manufactures for itself and for its American empire became well known to French thinkers, some responded by dismissing the need for France to cross the Atlantic at all. The famous political theorist Jean Bodin remarked: "The Spaniard, forced . . . to come here in search of wheat, cloth . . . and handcrafts, searches throughout the world for our benefit gold, silver and spices." Discussing the French cloth industry, one mercantilist thinker proclaimed that it "is one of the principal mines of France; for it Potosí vomits up almost all its silver." So colonization was beside the point.[50]

Henri IV and French Fortunes in the Atlantic

As Admiral of Guyenne, Henri had followed with interest the exploits of Francis Drake and, in 1588, had offered his small fleet to Elizabeth to help repel the Spanish Armada. So it is not surprising that the ever-curious king, with a particular fascination for the overseas world, sponsored voyages of exploration to many parts of the globe after the return of peace (Vervins, 1589).[51] Most famous of these voyages were those of Champlain in the area of Acadia, the Saint Lawrence, and the northeastern coasts of North America. Joining Champlain in 1606–1607 was Marc Lescarbot, who provided the first significant French "mercantilist" model of colonization. "The most beautiful mine that I know of is wheat and wine, with feed for beasts. He who has these, he has silver. We do not live by mines." Lescarbot advocated

49. Michel de Montaigne, *Oeuvres complètes,* ed. Arthur Armaingaud, 5 vols. (Paris, 1924), II, 234; Sully to Jeannin, Feb. 20, 1608, in Pierre Jeannin, *Négociations diplomatiques et politiques du Président Jeannin (1598–1620)* (Paris, 1875), 281.

50. Jean Bodin, *The Response of Jean Bodin to the Paradoxes of Malestroit,* trans. George Albert Moore (Washington, D.C., 1947), 12–13; Antoine de Montchrétien, *Traicté de l'oeconomie politique,* ed. Th. Funck-Brentano (Paris, 1889), 66.

51. Vergé-Franceschi, "L'Admirauté de France," in Acerra and Martinière, eds., *Coligny, les protestants et la mer,* 36–37. Jean Mocquet boasts of how Henri loved to spend his time listening to Mocquet's stories of his world travels. See his *Voyages en Afrique, Asie, Indes orientales et occidentales* (Rouen, 1645), dedication.

the establishment of monopoly fur companies to fund the expensive development of a true colony. This overt rejection of the Spanish model finally provided an alternative formula for French colonization.[52]

Henri IV also supported efforts to establish French trade and colonial settlements in various parts of northern South America, both for strategic reasons and to support French commerce in the area. These projects are far less known. For some three decades, from the 1590s to the 1620s, "Amazon fever" and the lust to find El Dorado, as well as the strong demand for tobacco and sugar, swept northern Europe. As noted earlier, French traders and truchements had strong ties with northern Brazil and connections with Native Americans there. In 1582, for example, a Portuguese fleet caught eight French ships trading with the Potiguars in the Paraíba River and destroyed five of them. Throughout the 1580s, the French actively assisted their Indian allies in defending against repeated Portuguese (and their allied Indians) sorties from Pernambuco; the Potiguars did not finally submit to Portuguese control until the end of the century. Indeed, in the culminating battle, fifty French musketeers fought with the Potiguars.[53]

After 1590, a series of French expeditions explored northern South America from the bay of Maranhão (Maragnan) to the Orinoco. French adventurers established outposts on the island of Maranhão, some three hundred miles south of the Amazon. They sought the precious dye and medicinal woods of the tropical forests, but they also explored potential settlement sites to grow tobacco and sugar, both crops in high demand from the 1590s. The Portuguese, however, were gradually spreading north from Pernambuco and demonstrating increasing military strength, which meant that any North European trading stations or settlements would have to be heavily fortified. Given the increasing restrictions on French trade with Lisbon and Seville, ports such as Rouen and Dieppe supported efforts to establish crop settlements in equatorial America.

In 1594, an expedition established an outpost at the site of Saint Louis, Maragnan. A small contingent of Frenchmen set up camp and established contact with local Tupinambá tribes, those old allies of the French. The last years of the religious wars prevented strengthening Saint Louis, but veterans of that expedition had a friend in Henri IV. By that time, the series of

52. Marc Lescarbot, *Histoire de la Nouvelle France* . . . (Paris, 1609), 16. Lescarbot was the closest French equivalent to Harriot.

53. Hemming, *Red Gold,* 162–163; Julien, *Les voyages de découverte,* 220. Reports exist of French traders at Spanish Trinidad loading tobacco. See, for example, James A. Williamson, *English Colonies in Guiana and on the Amazon, 1604–1668* (Oxford, 1923), 55.

expeditions undertaken by Ralegh and his captains, revealed in Sir Walter's trumpeted book, had taken Europe by storm. In 1602, the king granted a commission as lieutenant general of Guiana to René-Marie de Montbarrot, who, in turn, dispatched the experienced Huguenot naval captain, the sieur de La Ravardière, to explore the rivers of Guiana and to determine the best site to settle.[54]

Accompanying the reconnaissance expedition of some four hundred men was the royal collector Jean Mocquet, to gather parrots and other exotica for Henri's cabinet of curiosities. Another goal was to scout sites for precious dyewoods and medicinal plants, such as aloe leaves used for migraine headaches. The commander left a few men along the "wild coast" to plant some nicotiana seed. Upon his return in 1605, La Ravardière received the commission of lieutenant general "of America, between the Amazon and the island of Trinidad." In 1607, some four hundred men attempted a settlement at the island of Cayenne, only to succumb to attacks of local Caribs.[55]

It is not clear how much Ralegh's book claiming Guiana as the gateway to the city of Manoa, where reigned King El Dorado, influenced French interest in this coast. Its discovery could solve French financial woes and act as a counterweight to Potosí. Not only French but Dutch and English explorers and adventurers exhibited great interest in this wet and wild coast. La Ravardière led another reconnaissance in 1609 with a focus on the northern Brazilian coast. Still, the colonial project was not realized until two years after Henri's untimely death by assassination in 1610.[56]

Sixteen ten is a critical date in European and American history. The knife that killed Henri IV brought to power a weak female regent, Marie de Médicis. A devout Catholic, she was unhappy with her husband Henri's toler-

54. Moreau, *Les Petites Antilles,* 264. For the El Dorado legend, see, among others, John Hemming, *The Search for El Dorado* (1978; rpt. London, 2001).

55. Mocquet, *Voyages en Afrique,* book 2, 119–121; Moreau, *Les Petites Antilles,* 264; Arthur Percival Newton, *The European Nations in the West Indies, 1493–1688* (London, 1933), 134. The nicotiana seed was named for Jean Nicot, French ambassador to Spain who introduced tobacco to France before 1560.

56. Sir Walter Ralegh, *The Discoverie of the Large, Rich, and Bewtiful Empyre of Guiana* . . . (1596; rpt. Amsterdam, 1968). Louis de Pezieu, in his *Brief recueil des particularitez continues aux letters envoyées* (Lyons, 1613), 9, 21, indicates that the route to Peru was on some people's minds in the 1612 expedition. For the English explorers and adventurers, see Joyce Lorimer, *English and Irish Settlement on the River Amazon, 1550–1646,* Works Issued by the Hakluyt Society, 2d Ser., no. 171 (London, 1989); for the Dutch, see Goslinga, *Dutch on the Wild Coast.*

ant attitude to Huguenots. She favored religious orders committed to converting the Huguenots—Capuchins and Jesuits especially.

All these political upheavals had significant consequences for the evolution of a French Atlantic. In 1612, Marie forced the fur-trading interest in charge of Acadia to transport and support Jesuit missionaries. At Marie's insistence, La Ravardière accepted that his projected colonial expedition be joined to a syndicate headed by the devoutly Catholic Admiral François de Rasilly. The admiral was able to interest rich and powerful people in the enterprise, notably Henri de Harlay, sieur de Sancy. The act of association called for capitalization in the range of 70,000 lt. Rasilly asked Marie to solicit Capuchins to evangelize the indigenes of Maragnan. These were the Tupinambás who had found refuge from Portuguese attacks far to the north of their traditional homes. Four zealous Capuchins from the Paris convent were selected; two of these, Claude d'Abbeville and Yves d'Evreux, provide interesting firsthand accounts of the expedition and colony.[57]

Though far lesser known than the various explorations and settlements that led to a French presence in Acadia and the Saint Lawrence, the 1612–1616 project to colonize Maragnan was the French monarchy's most significant effort in the Americas before the ministry of Richelieu (1624–1642). Marie's sponsorship of the expedition meant that she did not anticipate the furious, if at first restrained, Iberian reaction. The important roles of the Capuchins and fervent Catholics like Rasilly at first protected the expeditions from the pro-Spanish faction at Court. In both Acadia and Maragnan, however, tensions plagued this forced condominium between fervent evangelists and Huguenot elements.[58]

In January 1612, François and his brother Isaac de Rasilly, La Ravardière, and Harlay de Sancy conducted a fleet with some five hundred colonists to Maragnan. At Saint Louis, Frenchmen constructed a stockade and attempted to raise support to reinforce the colony. Searches ensued to discover land appropriate for sugar cultivation, another indicator that the sugar

57. Bréard, *Documents rélatifs à la marine normande,* 207; Claude d'Abbeville, *Histoire de la mission des Pères Capucins en l'Isle de Maragnan . . .* (Paris, 1614); [Yves d'Evreux], *Suitte de l'histoire des choses plus memorables advenues en Maragnan, és années 1613 et 1614* (Paris, 1615). For a modern edition with notes by Hélène Clastres, see [Evreux], *Voyage au nord du Brésil: Fait en 1613 et 1614* (Paris, 1985).

58. Rasilly told the Tupinambás that he had come to Brazil only for their salvation. "I tell you that France is more beautiful than any country in the world . . . I left it and my family and my goods (which in truth are greater than any I could hope for here)." See Claude d'Abbeville, *Histoire,* 71–73.

boom of Portuguese Brazil was inspiring imitators. But the expedition's motives were multiple and contradictory. For the Capuchins, evangelization of the Tupinambás was paramount, but they argued that such could not occur without the support of a viable colony. A colony meant the need of a staple to pay for imports of food, drink, and manufactured goods such as weapons, textiles, and gifts for the Native Americans. Tobacco and sugar were the main possibilities. As one colonist said, sugar does "very well here." La Ravardière saw Maragnan as a base camp to raid the Iberians in Brazil and the Caribbean and to explore the Amazon as a possible route to Peru and El Dorado. The expedition leaders devoted energy to building Native American alliances and to preventing intertribal wars by focusing their hatred on the Portuguese.[59]

The expedition organizers understood the importance of sustained public support to resupply the colony and to transport artisans, farmers, and black slaves. Letters of the Capuchins Claude d'Abbeville and Arsène de Paris were published in Paris in 1612 and 1613.[60] These reveled in the Tupinambás' emotional reception of the Capuchins' evangelical message and their admiration for the French. To rally support, François de Rasilly and the sickly Father Claude returned to Paris in the spring of 1613, bearing the usual exotica such as parrots but also accompanied by six Tupinambás. Rasilly and Claude orchestrated a brilliant spectacle that had tout Paris entranced: the Tupinambá captain Itapoucou harangued the young king Louis XIII at court, and Louis and Marie participated in the very public baptism of the three sauvages who had survived the Atlantic passage and the cold northern French climate. Claude published an interesting account of these peoples and their "island" homeland. French settlers and missionaries, he argued, would transform Maragnan into a vibrant French colony.

59. Only six days after arrival, Father Arsène of Paris described the riches that would support a colony. Colonists hoped to produce large amounts of tobacco and dyes. Sugar grew on the island, and only fifty miles away was a gold mine. See Père Arsène de Paris, *Dernière lettre du reverend Père Arsène de Paris* (Paris, 1613), 1–5. It is clear that the colony depended on the Tupinambás for food; one of them worried that local provision for four hundred colonists could not be expected over the long term (Pezieu, *Brief recueil*, 5; and see 7 for his quote on sugar). According to Claude d'Abbeville, *Histoire*, 147, the French spread out to many villages to sustain themselves.

60. On public support for resupply and transport, see Claude d'Abbeville, *Histoire*, 19–20 (he averred that the Natives were too "lazy"). For the letters, see Claude d'Abbeville, *Lettre d'un père capucin* . . . (Paris, 1612). For a complete bibliography of the primary sources relating to this expedition, see Daher, *Les singularités de la France équinoxiale*, 315–326.

The Tupinambás would be valuable assets in this enterprise, and their conversion was the principal goal. At this point in 1613, the regent harbored no reservations about the enterprise, as she found 18,000 lt to support eleven more Capuchins to join their brothers in Brazil. The pope had explicitly authorized the Capuchin missions.[61]

The three surviving Tupinambás, dressed in court clothing festooned with medals and accompanied by French brides, returned in the spring of 1614 to Maragnan, along with some 1,300 recruits.[62] However, the publicity surrounding this enterprise led to protests from Madrid and Lisbon against the "interlopers." Already, a Portuguese force under Jerônimo de Albuquerque was preparing an attack, and a reconnaissance force had constructed a fort adjacent to Saint Louis. Meanwhile, Marie found it necessary to call a meeting of the Estates-General to deal with desperate financial problems of her own making. The meeting was a disaster in many respects and demonstrated publicly the growing tensions between the zealous Catholic faction at Court and the Huguenots.

Marie now made a major policy decision. In the summer of 1612, she had persuaded Spain's Philip III to sign a wedding contract between his daughter, Anne of Austria, and Louis. During ongoing negotiations over the marriage, Spain in 1614 raised the issue of the colony, so strategically placed between Portuguese Brazil and Spanish Venezuela. In Maragnan, meanwhile, hostilities between Huguenot and Catholic factions mirrored those that increased in France after the Estates broke up. The Huguenot lieutenant general La Ravardière, whom Rasilly had left in command, got along so badly with the Capuchins that most of them returned to France. Naturally, they complained bitterly to their patroness, Marie, which further undermined her support.

Two years after Philip III ordered the destruction of Saint Louis, a well-prepared expedition of Portuguese and Indian allies under the authority of the redoubtable Albuquerque confronted a stronger French force. The French commander left his fortress, with its bronze and iron cannon, to assail Albuquerque. Many Tupinambás, shocked by the ensuing Portu-

61. Claude d'Abbeville, *Histoire,* preface. According to Claude, some ten to twelve thousand Tupinambás lived in twenty-two villages (185). Legal ordinances provided for the death penalty for any colonist committing rape, adultery, or fornication with Native women (168–169). The Tupinambás were surprised at this puritanical attitude, given their previous experience with the truchements and complained that the Portuguese priests had acted similarly (72–73).

62. Ibid., 59.

guese victory, abandoned the French.[63] La Ravardière and the Portuguese commander arranged a one-year truce to allow adjudication of competing claims; even before the end of the truce, in early November 1615, a reinforced Portuguese army compelled the surrender of La Ravardière's abandoned forces. Those made prisoners, including the leader, received no support from Marie's ambassadors at Madrid or Lisbon. The commander languished for more than four years in the tower of Belém in Lisbon. The Bourbon monarchy, in effect, genuflected before Spain's assertions of sovereignty in America. Marie de Médicis and James I, La Ravardière and Sir Walter Ralegh make for telling analogies.[64]

This second, catastrophic French failure in Brazil led to a reorientation of French mercantile and colonial ambitions toward the north of America. Some French writers such as Lescarbot argued for greater concentration on Acadia and the Saint Lawrence, far distant from the Iberian sphere of control. The effort at Maragnan, at least partially motivated by the search for staple crops (sugar and tobacco), pointed toward the future of French colonization in the American tropics.

The continuing search for economic fortune in combination with political revenge motivated private French (as well as English and Dutch) entrepreneurs in sailing around the Caribbean. Much evidence points to a persistent French presence in these waters. Merchants, pirates, and privateers passed through these parts. Working extensively in the Spanish archives, Jean-Pierre Moreau has picked up numerous traces of the French presence in the Antilles, as reported by alarmed Spanish island officials. As will be indicated below, the founding father of the French Antilles, Pierre Blain d'Esnambuc, haunted Caribbean waters as a privateer long before he settled down as a habitant and governor at Saint Christopher in the later 1620s.

Shadowy evidence suggests that, during and after the debacle at Marag-

---

63. The French force consisted of four hundred well-armed soldiers accompanied by two thousand Native bowmen. For a Portuguese firsthand report on the battle, see Lorimer, *English and Irish Settlement,* 168. For a contemporary French account, see *Histoire veritable de ce qui c'est passé de nouveau entre les Français et Portugais en l'isle de Maragnan au pays des Toupinambas* (Paris, 1615).

64. The Iberians tried to exact a promise from La Ravardière that he would not return to Maragnan (Daher, *Les singularités de la France équinoxiale,* 289–293). Ironically, James I in 1619 had asked his ambassador in Lisbon to intercede on La Ravardière's behalf, presumably to enlist his help for the English Amazon Company. In 1621, the freed commander undertook a visit to London to thank James (Lorimer, *English and Irish Settlement,* 234 n. 3).

nan, small groups of Frenchmen attempted to establish settlements in Guiana between the Amazon and the Orinoco rivers, especially at the relatively dry island of Cayenne, one of the few accessible sites along that coast. Some indicators suggest the presence of 160 French there in 1613, perhaps to plant tobacco. The mainland Caribs are said to have destroyed the settlement. Some Normans in these years settled at the Sinnamary River. After failing, they found refuge in the tiny Lesser Antillean island of Saint Christopher, where they made a living as tobacco farmers among other European squatters and a small Island Carib outpost. In 1625, these fugitives from Guiana would give succor to a badly damaged ship and crew of fellow Normans whose captain was d'Esnambuc.[65]

A curious manuscript account of shipwrecked French corsairs at the Island Carib stronghold of Martinique in 1619–1620 has been edited and published by Jean-Pierre Moreau. It provides precious ethnographic details about a precolonial indigenous culture but one already being influenced by European contacts; remarkably, given contemporary stereotypes, these French visitors lived in perfect safety among these "cannibals." This rare account of freebooters who roamed the Caribbean in these years is a precious document that should receive an English translation.[66]

The French failure to establish tobacco farms in Amazonia and along the wild coast led them finally to settle in the Lesser Antilles. Northern Europeans had long been using these islands to refresh themselves with water, Carib foodstuffs, and tobacco and to hunt tortoises and manatees. These are the contexts to understand the history of d'Esnambuc and his fellow Normans in the founding of Saint Christopher, the mother island of the French (and English) Caribbean. Of an impoverished gentry family, the young d'Esnambuc sought his fortunes overseas on corsair ships starting as early as 1603. Records exist of another expedition to "the coasts of Brazil" in 1620. In 1624, he spent a few months on Martinique, and in 1625, Spaniards mauled his corsair ship, and the wreck put into Saint Christopher. He

65. Goslinga, *Dutch on the Wild Coast,* 417.
66. Jean-Pierre Moreau, ed., *Un flibustier français dans la mer des Antilles, 1618–1620* . . . (Paris, 1990). The parlous state of archaeological projects in the French Antilles, especially relating to the earlier historical period (ca. 1493–1660), has impoverished our understanding of that century and a half. Very little has been found that relates to the Island Carib villages of the historical period. See André Delpuech, "Historical Archaeology in the French West Indies: Recent Research in Guadeloupe," in Paul Farnsworth, ed., *Island Lives: Historical Archaeologies of the Caribbean* (Tuscaloosa, Ala., 2001), 23–24, 27–31.

found a welcome there by French survivors of an abandoned Guiana settlement.[67] The English inhabiting the island under Thomas Warner were also refugees from a failed Amazon settlement; these colonists grew tobacco and sporadically engaged in freebooting.

The current high prices for this plant, the charm of the island, and a cordial relationship with the English based on mutual antagonism to Spaniards and Island Caribs persuaded d'Esnambuc to return to France and organize a group to migrate there. Recognizing a need to establish legal claims to the land to be cultivated, the captain and his associates obtained Richelieu's support for a royally chartered company. Richelieu even invested money and ships in support of the new company and pressured clients to invest. Although terrible struggles characterized the next two decades, French colonies in the Antilles survived from 1625.[68]

By the mid-1620s, therefore, small and weak French settlements in the Caribbean and continental North America had emerged. France's position in America resembled that of England at the time. The English tobacco colony of Saint Kitts (Saint Christopher) and the emerging ones of Nevis, Antigua, and Barbados quite mirrored French settlements at Saint Christopher, Martinique, and Guadeloupe (1635). Indentured servants, as well as a sprinkling of African slaves brought either by the Dutch or as the profit of corsair prizes, worked alongside their masters to harvest a tobacco crop that still brought high prices through the mid-1630s. However, by then, these countries' colonial fortunes started to diverge. While France inched toward direct involvement in the Thirty Years' War (1635), so costly in men and money, the England of Charles I sent tens of thousands of people to her rapidly burgeoning colonies; some went in search of fortune in Barbados and the Chesapeake, and others, in the case of indentured servants, to leave behind misery at home. Many thousands came to New England in search of religious freedom and economic opportunity. Despite significant numbers of French indentured servant recruits for the islands in the 1630s and 1640s, Bourbon wars presented viable alternatives of employment for restless, sometimes desperate, young men who might have been migration material. Unlike their English counterparts, French mercantile entre-

67. This was a 1624 expedition to Cayenne led by one Captain Chantail. Once again, Carib Indians destroyed it. The thesis of the supposed ability of Frenchmen to conduct more benevolent relations with Native Americans does not withstand scrutiny of their conduct in Guiana in the first half of the seventeenth century.

68. For the charter, see Médéric Louis Élie Moreau de Saint-Méry, *Loix et constitutions des colonies françoises de l'Amérique sous le vent,* 6 vols. (Paris, 1784-1790), I, 18-19.

preneurs resisted the colonizing obligations of ill-conceived and ill-funded state-sponsored charter companies. In turn, company organizers such as Isaac de Rasilly expressed disdain for merchants who "had no other thought than to amass" wealth and who "do not care what happens in ten years." The Huguenot community, though interested in overseas trade and piracy, was not subject to the kind of harassment and persecution that the Puritans were. Richelieu was no William Laud. Finally, permanent or temporary French migration to Spain rather than to America was a realistic alternative to a life of poverty at home. Fernand Braudel estimates that some two hundred thousand took advantage of Spain's underpopulation and the trek across the Pyrenees. As a result of these and other factors, France never overcame this initial demographic disadvantage in America.[69]

This essay cannot pretend to give a definitive answer to the age-old question of why Britons migrated in far greater numbers to the Americas than did the French; nor can it answer the not-often-asked question of why French indentured servants might have been more likely to return home.[70] I cannot attest to the usefulness of K. G. Davies's argument that Britain had a "secret formula of colonization, the particular social chemistry that turned Englishmen, above all others, into willing or at least resigned colonists." That formulation does not help explain why it was in the 1630s that English migration to the Caribbean and continental North America exploded, whereas the number of Frenchmen, although not unimportant, especially in the Caribbean, increased only very gradually.[71]

This essay has employed a chronological framework to argue that the

69. The classic source on the French indentured servant recruits is Gabriel Debien, "La société coloniale aux XVIIe et XVIIIe siècles: Les engagés pour les Antilles (1634-1715)," *Revue d'histoire des colonies françaises,* XXXVIII, nos. 1, 2 (1951). Rasilly cited in Lucas A. Boiteux, *Richelieu: Grand Maître de la navigation et du commerce du France* (Paris, 1955), 219. For Braudel's estimate, see his *Capitalism and Material Life, 1400–1800* (New York, 1973), 23–24. In a 1635 letter to Richelieu, the Canadian Jesuit missionary Paul Le Jeune lamented that a "large percentage of artisans in Spain were French," thus strengthening the king of Spain. If these workers could be persuaded to go to Canada, they would remain French and strengthen France (cited in Michel Bideaux, "Le discours expansionniste dans l'histoire de la Nouvelle France," in Lestringant, ed., *La France / Amérique,* 181 n. 26).

70. Perhaps the relatively short indentured tenure of three years made it more possible or likely for the servants to do so. Peter Moogk estimates that two-thirds of indentured servants returned to France. See his *La Nouvelle France: The Making of French Canada — a Cultural History* (East Lansing, Mich., 2000), 105.

71. K. G. Davies, *The North Atlantic World in the Seventeenth Century* (Minneapolis, 1974), 329.

policies and actions (or inaction) of the royal court, the petty bourgeois ambitions of France's maritime centers, and the varying fortunes of the important, though small, Huguenot minority simultaneously worked to promote and to inhibit expansion across the Atlantic. In general, all three forces as often put barriers in the way of overseas colonization as they supported it. The court, the ports, and the Huguenots all sponsored a variety of endeavors across the Atlantic. However, in the few attempts to establish permanent settlements in Brazil and Florida, the predominant goal of acquiring wealth by robbing or trading with the Iberians, discovering and exploiting Native Americans in the (perceived) Spanish manner, and trading for Native American–produced commodities did not create suitable conditions for long-term colonization. Trading posts did not inevitably involve colonization. The few attempts to create fortified settlements in Guanabara, Fort Caroline, and at Saint Louis, Maragnan, depended too heavily on Native American support and suffered from the inevitable problems of resupply to survive in a hostile environment. In France, dynastic politics and religious turmoil further undermined these efforts. All of these factors explain the long gestation period of a "French Atlantic," its painful infancy, and its languid early childhood. Already by the 1630s, the British had planted and nurtured seeds of a more vibrant Atlantic position.

Peter Cook

KINGS, CAPTAINS, AND KIN

FRENCH VIEWS OF NATIVE AMERICAN

POLITICAL CULTURES IN THE SIXTEENTH

AND EARLY SEVENTEENTH CENTURIES

For most of the sixteenth century, French-language writing on the Americas tended to portray Native American societies as monarchies. There were two main sources for this particular representation of Native American polities. The first was the small but ever-growing body of literature on European encounters with New World peoples as related in early-sixteenth-century published accounts of discoveries and conquests. French editions of these works—such as those about Columbus and Cortés, for example— faithfully echoed the original accounts of exotic American kings and kingdoms. Later in the century, travel writing and official reports produced by explorers, colonizers, and cosmographers sponsored by the French state constituted a second source. These texts, which, in turn, flowed into the ever-growing river of European representations of the New World and its peoples, illustrate the pervasive nature of the trope of American kingship and its effects upon French-Native relations in a variety of concrete colonial situations. The problematic nature of these relations, in theaters as di-

Earlier versions of this essay were presented at the John Carter Brown Library in April 2001, at the Champlain–Saint Lawrence Seminar in Plattsburgh in February 2003, at the annual meeting of the Renaissance Society of America in Toronto in March 2003, and at the Early Canada Seminar in Toronto in February 2004. I am grateful to the John Carter Brown Library for providing both a research fellowship and the congenial atmosphere in which the ideas in this essay took root. As the argument has evolved over time, I have incurred many debts of gratitude to listeners and readers, who offered criticism, provided additional data, suggested other sources, and shared insights of their own. Rhys Isaac, Karen Spalding, Scott Manning Stevens, James Muldoon, Mark Meuwese, Catherine M. Desbarats, Toby Morantz, James Rice, Germaine Warkentin, and Joseph Hall all commented helpfully on earlier versions, and Peter Mancall and an anonymous reviewer offered invaluable criticism of a later incarnation.

verse as Canada, Brazil, and Florida, had important consequences for the history of colonial America. For France, like England, the sixteenth century was an era of failed efforts to establish lasting colonies in the Americas.[1] But, at the dawn of the seventeenth century, as France embarked on a series of new (and more enduring) colonial endeavors in Europe's New World, the tendency to view Native societies as monarchies was thoroughly eclipsed, and a new terminology took its place. Where sixteenth-century French observers saw American kings at the apex of American kingdoms, their seventeenth-century counterparts saw instead captains *(capitaines),* leading men or chiefs *(principaux),* and elders *(anciens)* guiding communities that seemed not to warrant the term "monarchy."[2]

Documenting and explaining this evolution are the primary goals of this essay. The former is achieved through a sampling of early-sixteenth-century French-language texts relating to the Americas or to Native Americans and a rather closer reading of narratives relating to French attempts to colonize Canada, Brazil, and Florida between the 1530s and the early 1600s. Accounting for the disappearance of representations of Native American kingship at the turn of the century is less straightforward. Although the reasons for the terminological shift were multiple, in the main they had less to do with the sociopolitical organization of the Native societies with whom the French interacted or observed from afar than with changing conceptions of kingship itself in late-sixteenth- and early-seventeenth-century France. In short, transformations of the meaning of kingship within France led, in turn, to an altered conception of the nature of Native American societies. A secondary goal of this study is to suggest how, as with any attempt to control experience through an act of naming, the invocation of familiar political taxonomies to understand the societies they encountered in the Americas attuned French colonizers to certain possibilities for interacting with Native peoples while simultaneously blinding them to others.[3] In seek-

1. Marcel Trudel thus subtitled the first volume of his narrative history of New France. See Trudel, *Histoire de la Nouvelle-France,* I, *Les vaines tentatives, 1524–1603* (Montreal, 1963).

2. For contemporary understandings of these terms and their English translations, see Randle Cotgrave, *A Dictionarie of the French and English Tongues* (London, 1611), s.v. "capitaine" and "principal."

3. In arguing thusly, I do not intend to embrace the extreme social constructivist conceit that people are prisoners of their language or that words rigidly limit and constrain thoughts and perceptions. Nor do I wish to imply that the practice of classification is always automatic and uncalculated. Rather, culturally determined schemes of perception evolve as culture bearers assess the consequences of their calculated appli-

ing to assimilate the unfamiliar, early modern French observers naturally drew on existing categories that seemed congruent with their perceptions of Native American societies. Partaking both of conscious rationalization and spontaneous recognition, this cognitive process was doubtless complex. But the choices early modern French observers made when describing Native polities were neither innocent nor epiphenomenal, for the classification of Native leaders as kings powerfully informed the policies and behaviors of French colonizers on the ground.

The same perspective could, of course, be brought to bear on the histories of other colonizing nations in the early modern period. Even as Norman fur traders established the basis of what would become a permanent French presence in Acadia and Canada in the early 1600s, English colonizers founded Jamestown in the midst of a powerful Algonquian polity on the western shores of the Chesapeake Bay. John Smith, briefly the leader of the Jamestown settlement, did not hesitate to translate the political arrangements of the Powhatan Confederacy by means of the vocabulary of monarchy. "The forme of their Common-wealth is a Monarchicall government, one as Emperour ruleth over many Kings or Governours," he wrote. Smith's *Generall Historie* also described Native kings in present-day New England.[4] By contrast, the nearly contemporaneous accounts of French travelers like Samuel de Champlain, Marc Lescarbot, Pierre Biard, and Gabriel Sagard eschewed, without exception, the vocabulary of kingship to describe the Algonquian and Iroquolan societies of early-seventeenth-century northeastern North America. To be sure, the French in Acadia and Canada encountered nothing quite like the Powhatan Confederacy and its "great King"; but in southern New England Smith saw kings where Champlain saw captains. And so we might ask: What was the conception of kingship in early-seventeenth-century English political culture that made it possible for Smith to categorize Native leaders in this way, and what consequences flowed from this categorization?[5] Although answers to these questions lie

---

cation of such schemes to external realities. In general, however, such schemes are enduring, and their evolution, unpredictable.

4. John Smith, *The Generall Historie of Virginia, New-England, and the Summer Isles* . . . (1624; facsimile rpt. Ann Arbor, Mich., 1966), book 2, 37, book 6.

5. In an essay that focuses principally on eighteenth-century British and Native conversations about and perceptions of kingship, Nancy Shoemaker argues (using Smith as an example) that in general early modern Europeans "used absolute monarchy as their frame of reference for understanding Indian systems of governance" and, consequently, as the basis for classifying Native leaders as kings (Shoemaker, *A Strange Likeness: Becoming Red and White in Eighteenth-Century North America* [New York,

beyond the scope of this essay, an interpretation bearing on the evidence from French America may usefully suggest some paths to follow.[6] Exploring the meanings of kingship at the time of France's earliest colonial enterprises is a good place to begin.

What kingship meant precisely to sixteenth-century French people is not easy to determine. In early modern French culture, kingship was a poly-

---

2004], chap. 2, esp. 45–47 [quotation on 45]). Shoemaker does not address the possibility of significant changes in the meaning of kingship within English political culture between Smith's time and the mid-eighteenth century. For historians of early modern France—some of whom have asserted the existence of a precocious absolutism under Francis I in the early sixteenth century—defining absolutism and pinpointing its onset remain matters for debate. In the present essay, I emphasize the multiplicity of meanings in early modern French conceptions of kingship rather than the highly simplified image presented by the ideologues of what later observers would term absolute monarchy.

6. The contrast between Smith's and Champlain's perceptions of Native leadership is intentionally overstated here. In general, as Eric Hinderaker has pointed out, early-seventeenth-century English writers "tended to regard Indians as natural men living in weak, stateless societies" and without kings ("The 'Four Indian Kings' and the Imaginative Construction of the First British Empire," *William and Mary Quarterly,* 3d Ser., LIII [1996], 487–526 [quotation on 488]). This view is echoed in French writing of the same period. Smith himself noted that the "[Virginian] word Werowance, which we call and construe for a King, is a common word, whereby they call all commanders" (*Generall Historie,* book 2, 38). Moreover, he noted that in New England "every *Sachem* is not a king" (book 6, 240). Nevertheless, Smith's willingness to use the vocabulary of kingship to describe at least some Virginian and New England leaders stands in contrast to his French contemporaries' refusal to do so, even when describing societies of comparable degrees of complexity. In the 1670s, Thomas Gorst, governor of the Hudson's Bay Company post at Rupert River, produced a journal that employed, without irony, the terms "king," "chancellor," and "prince" with reference to the Crees of Eastern James Bay (J. B. Tyrell, ed., *Documents Relating to the Early History of Hudson Bay* [Toronto, 1931], esp. 383–390). Gorst's counterparts in late-seventeenth-century New France never used such language when speaking of northern and eastern Algonquian hunter-gatherers. Such a contrast hints at the role of "national" political cultures in shaping colonial encounters. Without resorting to the simplistic overgeneralizations of an older historiography (one that saw the French embracing Native Americans while the English scorned and neglected them), studies like Patricia Seed's *Ceremonies of Possession in Europe's Conquest of the New World, 1492–1640* (Cambridge, 1995) show the promise of a comparative perspective that accounts for the varied symbolic expressions of Spanish, French, English, Dutch, and Portuguese colonialism. Any such endeavor must acknowledge that it is highly misleading to speak of coherent, bounded "national" cultures in early modern Europe.

valent symbol that collapsed an infinitude of meanings into a single term while simultaneously acting as a "root metaphor" for the explication of complex systems. If asked about the meaning of French kingship, one sixteenth-century jurist might have outlined the esoteric theory of royal bicorporality whereby the king was the result of a mystical union between the physical body of the monarch and the *corpus mysticum,* the intangible expression of the body politic. Another might have referred to the Salic Law, which had purportedly regulated the transmission of sovereignty down through the ages, ensuring the continuity and legitimacy of the monarchy. A historiographer of the old school, on the other hand, might have recounted how French kings were in fact descendants of refugees from fallen Troy who had migrated westward to establish themselves as the rulers of the Gauls. (Their leader, Francion, was said to be of the line of Priam, no less.)[7] For the pious, more meaningful was perhaps the tale of a dove bringing down from heaven an ampulla of oil for the timely baptism of the early-sixth-century king of the Franks, Clovis—a sign of divine favor that justified his successors' assuming the title of Most Christian King. A royalist ideologue might have begun by rattling off a litany of Roman legal maxims suggesting the absolute nature of kingly authority, whereas a writer might have played at length upon the well-known analogy in which the king was to the communities of his realm as a head is to the body that supports it. In the minds of the majority of his subjects, the king was imagined as a father, a shepherd, and a giver of justice. The first act in a popular anti-tax rebellion was to draw up a petition to the king, advising him that his treacherous ministers and self-serving favorites had unjustly conspired to make cruel exactions on the people in the sovereign's name, but without his knowledge. The king was also a healer, for God had given the legitimate king the power to cure scrofula, an ability that sixteenth- and seventeenth-century French kings

7. Sherry B. Ortner, "On Key Symbols," *American Anthropologist,* N.S., LXXV (1973), 1338–1346; Ernst H. Kantorowicz, *The King's Two Bodies: A Study in Mediaeval Political Theology* (1957; rpt. Princeton, N.J., 1997); Ralph E. Giesey, *The Royal Funeral Ceremony in Renaissance France* (Geneva, 1960); and Giesey, *Cérémonial et puissance souveraine: France, XVe–XVIIe siècle* (Paris, 1987); Sergio Bertelli, *The King's Body: Sacred Rituals of Power in Medieval and Early Modern Europe,* trans. R. Burr Litchfield, rev. and enl. (University Park, Pa., 2001) (on the ritual and ceremonial aspects of kingship); Colette Beaune, *The Birth of an Ideology: Myths and Symbols of Nation in Late-Medieval France,* trans. Susan Ross Huston, ed. Fredric L. Cheyette (Berkeley, Calif., 1991), 226–227, 245–282 (on Salic Law). Skeptical humanists of the mid-sixteenth century seem to have been increasingly doubtful of the accuracy of the story of Francion's lineage.

demonstrated to large crowds several times each year on religious holidays. Such images of a benevolent, just, and divinely sanctioned ruler formed the substratum of ancient and widely shared notions that overlapped and intertwined with the more esoteric conceptions embraced by elites.[8]

Popular conceptions of kingship in sixteenth-century France reflected to some extent the trickling down of classical and medieval intellectual dispositions. Among these was the tendency to view monarchy as an immanent feature of the natural world. This notion had long been part of the traditional justification for kingship, as Renaissance jurist Jean Bodin explained in his *Method for the Easy Comprehension of History* (1565): "If we should inspect nature more closely, we should gaze upon monarchy everywhere. To make a beginning from small things, we see the king among the bees, the leader in the herd, the buck among the flocks . . . and in the separate natures of things some one object excels: thus, adamant among the gems, gold among the metals, the sun among the stars, and finally God alone, the prince and author of the world."[9] The familiarity of the bee metaphor is

8. Marc Bloch, *The Royal Touch: Sacred Monarchy and Scrofula in England and France,* trans. J. E. Anderson (London, 1973), 14-21, 130-136, 177-179, 193-194, 203-206; Beaune, *Birth of an Ideology,* 78, 208, 214-215; William Farr Church, *Constitutional Thought in Sixteenth-Century France: A Study in the Evolution of Ideas* (1941; rpt. New York, 1969), 101-120. The corporeal metaphor of the political community emerged in the Middle Ages and endures to this day. Isabelle Flandrois points to the "extreme importance" of the traditional corporeal metaphor in the "mirror of the prince" literature of the early seventeenth century (*L'Institution du Prince au début du XVIIe siècle* [Paris, 1992], 14). On the antifiscal ideology of early modern peasant revolts in France, see Yves-Marie Bercé, *Histoire de Croquants: Étude des soulèvements populaires au XVIIe siècle dans le sud-ouest de la France,* 2 vols. (Geneva, 1974), II, 608-617, 634-636, 676-679, 696; and Jean Jacquart, "Immobilisme et catastrophes, 1560-1690," in Emmanuel Le Roy Ladurie, ed., *L'âge classique des paysans, 1340-1789,* vol. II of Georges Duby, ed., *Histoire de la France rurale* (Paris, 1975), 345-353. For a distillation of popular images of the king, see Pierre Goubert and Daniel Roche, *Les Français et l'Ancien Régime,* 2 vols. (Paris, 1984), II, 27-30.

9. Jean Bodin, *Method for the Easy Comprehension of History* [1565], trans. and ed. Beatrice Reynolds (1945; rpt. New York, 1969), 271. This passage is very close to one from a thirteenth-century treatise by Thomas Aquinas: "Now, every natural governance is governance by one. In the multitude of bodily members there is one which is the principal mover, namely, the heart; and among the powers of the soul one power presides as chief, namely, the reason. Among bees there is one king bee and in the whole universe there is one God, Maker and Ruler of all things" (*On Kingship, to the King of Cyprus,* trans. Gerald B. Phelan, ed. I. Th. Eschmann [1949; rpt. Toronto, 1982], 12). The editor notes that, in medieval opinion, the chief bee was considered to be male (12 n. 7). By the end of the seventeenth century, scientific observation had chal-

shown, too, in the opening pages of a late-sixteenth-century French novel in which the author, musing about the "barbarians" who live in distant Canada, notes that they "have chiefs and kings which they recognize more from natural inclination (like the bees) than through reason or through the knowledge that they are right to do so."[10]

As Roger Chartier has shown in a study of early modern French *littéra-ture de gueuserie,* even marginal social groups like beggars and thieves were understood to live in a kind of monarchy within the monarchy, under the rule of a king to whom all paid tribute. The motif of the beggar or thief king can be traced back to the fourteenth and fifteenth centuries, and by analogy the term "king" came to be applied to anyone who was the most skilled at any art, be it hen raising *(les rois des poules)* or barbering. Such popular usage even had its counterpart in law: a royal statute sanctioned in 1448 the existence of *rois merciers*—provincial "pedlar kings" whose lordship was to be exercised over the itinerant small-goods salesmen who hawked their wares at local fairs and throughout the countryside.[11]

Over the course of the sixteenth century, however, this late-medieval conception of kingship seems increasingly to have irritated the sensibilities of the Crown and the ideologues of royal power. Étienne Pasquier, a jurist, *parlementaire,* and loyal subject, bemoaned the proliferation of the term "king" among people who were manifestly not kings; doubtless he approved of the Crown's action in suppressing the office of the rois merciers (first in 1544 and definitively in 1588). Though such usages gradu-

---

lenged this assumption: Antoine Furetière's *Dictionaire universel* (1690) notes, under "roy," that the king bee was apparently a female. Until then, however, Aristotle's erroneous description of the queen bee and female workers as males endured. The solitary "king bee," who never used his powerful sting except against other "kings," and the efficient coordination of hive activity made bees a paradigm of monarchical perfection. See Jeffrey Merrick, "Royal Bees: The Gender Politics of the Beehive in Early Modern Europe," *Studies in Eighteenth-Century Culture,* XVIII (1988), 7–37 (esp. 10–18). The beehive model also proved attractive to early English colonial promoters; see Karen Ordahl Kupperman, "The Beehive as a Model for Colonial Design," in Kupperman, ed., *America in European Consciousness, 1493–1750* (Chapel Hill, N.C., 1995), 272–292.

10. "Ce n'est pas qu'ils n'ayent des chefs et des Roys qu'ils recognoisent plustost par une naturelle inclination (comme les mouches à miel) que par raison ny par cognoissance qu'ils ayent de bien faire; ces pauvres gens n'ayant rien de l'homme que la forme"; see Jacques Du Hamel, *The Earliest French Play about America: "Acoubar ou La Loyauté Trahie,"* introduction by Margaret Adams White (New York, 1931), ix.

11. Roger Chartier, "La 'monarchie d'argot' entre le mythe et l'histoire," in *Les marginaux et les exclus dans l'histoire,* Cahiers Jussieu, no. 5 (Paris, 1979), 275–311 (esp. 279–280, 291).

ally disappeared from official documents and elite discourses, Chartier argues that "these disappearances hardly affected collective representations. The monarchical principle remained alive as a conceptual framework allowing one to understand, and thus to assimilate within the universe of the already-known, new realities. The travel narratives reveal the same procedure; the Native societies encountered could not be conceived of except through the criteria which organized Western society."[12] And so they were, at least until the end of the sixteenth century. At that point, a rupture occurred as French travel writers discarded the terminology of their predecessors, consciously eschewing the model of kingship as a means of understanding Native American societies. Was it merely that these writers shared the evolving outlook of French elites who, as we have seen, gradually abandoned casual evocations of the monarchical principle? A closer examination of the trajectory of the representation of Native kingship in sixteenth-century texts suggests, instead, that a more definable set of circumstances played a role in its eclipse.

Before the first official French expedition in 1524, accounts of the exploits of Columbus, Cortés, and Pizarro circulated in French translation and provided French readers with glimpses of Native American kings in a variety of newly found lands.[13] Columbus's letter of 1493, published in seventeen edi-

12. "Ces disparitions d'institutions ne touchent guère aux représentations collectives. Le principe monarchique demeure vivace comme grille de lecture permettant de comprendre, et par là d'intégrer dans un univers de choses déjà connues, les réalités nouvelles. Les récits de voyages révèlent la même procédure: les sociétés indigènes rencontrées ne peuvent être pensées qu'à travers les critères qui organisent la société même d'Occident"; see Chartier, "La 'monarchie d'argot,'" *Les marginaux,* 292.

13. The works examined in the following paragraphs represent an informed sampling of a larger corpus of key works published in French on the Americas in the early sixteenth century. For relevant studies and bibliographies, see Gilbert Chinard, *L'exotisme américain dans la littérature française au XVIe siècle, d'après Rabelais, Ronsard et Montaigne* (Paris, 1911); Chinard, *L'Amérique et le rêve exotique dans la littérature française au XVIIe et au XVIIIe siècle* (1913; rpt. Geneva, 1970); Geoffroy Atkinson, *The Extraordinary Voyage in French Literature before 1700* (New York, 1920); Atkinson, *La littérature géographique française de la Renaissance: Répertoire bibliographique* (Paris, 1927); Atkinson, *Supplément au répertoire bibliographique se rapportant à la littérature géographique française de la Renaissance* (Paris, 1936); Philip P. Boucher, *Les Nouvelles Frances: France in America, 1500–1815, an Imperial Perspective* (Providence, R.I., 1989); Durand Echeverria and Everette C. Wilkie, Jr., *The French Image of America: A Chronological and Subject Bibliography of French Books Printed before 1816 Relating to the British North American Colonies and the United States,* 2 vols.

tions before the century was out (including one at Paris), initially cast doubt on the existence of kings among the Taínos of Hispaniola and Cuba: shortly after landfall on Cuba, Columbus ordered his men to look for kings, but none were found. By the end of the letter, however, things have changed: there are repeated references to kings and princes on the island of Hispaniola. Similarly, the fourth book of Mathurin de Redouer's *Le nouveau monde* (1516) asserted confidently that finding "Indian" kings in the Caribbean was merely a matter of asking: "Our people in examining their customs discovered through signs and gestures that among them they had a King, and after our people went ashore they were received honorably by the King." Indeed, there turned out to be many kings on Hispaniola, some of whom led the extermination of the troublesome sailors Columbus had left behind in 1493. Here, as in the 1532 French translation of Pietro Martire d'Anghiera's well-known *De orbe novo* (originally published in 1516), New World kings act very much like petty European princes: resenting their subordination, they instigate an uprising against the Spanish. The rebel leader, elected emperor, is captured, and his impassioned speeches to his people on the power and liberality of the Spanish help quell the resistance—for a time. Significantly, although the Indians are said to "live without weights, measures, ... without laws, judges, slanderers, books, [but] content with the law of nature," the narrator finds kings at every turn. The indigenous term *cacic* is invoked, but only as a synonym.[14]

(Metuchen, N.J., 1994). The most comprehensive reference is John Alden and Dennis Channing Landis, eds., *European Americana: A Chronological Guide to Works Printed in Europe Relating to the Americas, 1493–1776,* 6 vols. (New Canaan, Conn., 1980–1997).

Atkinson's bibliography and supplement list 33 examples of "geographical literature" on the Americas published in French between 1493 and 1609. My own enumeration, using the geographical indexes of *European Americana,* revealed 186 imprints of books relating to the Americas from French cities (principally Paris, Lyons, and Rouen) between 1493 and 1610. Not all of these works are in French, however, and French-language works published outside France (at Geneva, Antwerp, and Amsterdam, for example) in this period are not captured in my enumeration, although some appear in Atkinson's list.

14. Translation of *De Insulis nuper in mari Indico repertis* (Basel, 1494), in *The Columbus Letter,* Osher Map Library and Smith Center for Cartographic Education, University of Southern Maine, http://www.usm.maine.edu/maps/columbus/toc.html; *Le nouveau monde et navigacions faites p[ar] Emeric de Vespuce flore[n]tin des pays et isles nouvelleme[n]t trouvez auparava[n]t a nous incongneuz, ta[n]t en lethiope q[ue] arabie Calichut [et] aultres plusieurs regions estranges, translate de italien en la[n]gue francoyse par Mathurin de Redouer licencie es loix* (Paris, 1516), lxxxr ("Les nostres en

French-language accounts of the initial conquests of Mexico and Peru appeared ten or twelve years after those events took place. In these texts, the Spanish protagonists immediately recognize the leaders of the highly stratified states of early-sixteenth-century Mesoamerica and Peru as kings. For a reader of the French edition of Pietro Martire d'Anghiera, such classifications were integral to the rationale behind Cortés's treatment of the king of the Aztecs: not only was Montezuma a tyrant, demanding the children of his subjects for bloody sacrifices, but he himself recognized Cortés's master, Charles V, as the fabled lord in whose lands the Aztecs themselves had once lived and whose conquering return was foreseen in prophecies. In the end, it is Montezuma's scheming against Cortés, and hence against his recognized suzerain Charles V, that justifies his violent overthrow.[15]

Kingship similarly occupies a central place in the narrative of the conquest of Peru contained in *L'histoire de la terre neuve du Perù* (1545). The text accords Atabalipa, king of Peru, qualities appropriate to that status: "His speech was full of gravity and royal majesty." Yet it also insists that he usurped the position of his elder brother, Cusco, wresting the kingdom from him in a civil war and keeping Cusco in prison. Cusco, upon hearing of Pizarro's capture of Atabalipa, becomes hopeful of his own restoration. Fearful of just this eventuality, Atabalipa allegedly arranges to have Cusco assassinated from his prison, for "Atabalipa had made it his design to be the monarch of the country and wished to oust any who could block his enterprise."[16] Thus does the Spaniards' subsequent execution of Atabalipa become, in the eyes of the reader, an act of justice rather than of regicide: following Atabalipa's death by drowning, the Spanish install Cusco's eldest son as king, thereby reestablishing the legitimate line. Through the superimposition of European dynastic principles and strategies on the characters

---

chercheant leur coustumes trouverent par signes et actes que entre eulx ilz avoient ung Roy, et apres que les nostres furent descenduz en terre ilz furent receuz du Roy honorablement"), lxxxvi verso; Pietro Martire d'Anghiera, *Extraict ou recueil des isles nouvellement trouvés en la grand mer Océane* . . . (Paris, 1532), books 2, 3, 4 (esp. 11r, 13r).

15. Anghiera, *Extraict,* 156r, 171r.

16. *L'histoire de la terre neuve du Perù en l'Inde Occidentale, qui est la principale mine d'or du monde, nagueres descouverte, et conquise, et nommée la nouvelle Castille, traduitte d'Italien en Francoys* (Paris, 1545), G.iiii recto ("sa parolle estoit vrayement pleine de gravité et maiesté royalle"), H.iii recto ("Mais Atabalipa avoit fait son dessein d'estre monarque du pays et vouloit oster tout ce qui luy povoit donner quelque obstacle ou empeschement à son entreprinse"). The pages of this work are unnumbered; hence, I have adapted the printer's signatures for use as page references.

of the Sapa Inca and his brother, Pizarro's brutal conquest is explained as the justifiable overthrow of a vile usurper.

French texts revealed as well the existence of Native American kings well beyond the frontiers of the Aztec and Inca states. The semi-sedentary Tupinambás of coastal Brazil, some of whom had been in contact with Norman traders since the first decade of the sixteenth century, had their own kings— or so believed the creators of the royal entry festival held to honor Henri II's visit to Rouen in October 1550. One of the elaborate tableaux vivants prepared for the occasion by the Rouenese elite involved a re-created Brazilian village and a mock battle between two different groups of Tupinambás. The attackers were led by "their king otherwise called by them Morbicha," who, having previously inspired his men with an impassioned speech, was followed by them "with prompt obedience." The actors in this Brazilian episode were intended to evoke for the French king the military ideals of the old nobility of the sword. Other tableaux articulated the importance of reconciling these ideas with the humanist ideals of the newer nobility of the robe—urging, in effect, Henri II to temper the natural virtue of barbarians with the civilized arts of antiquity. For our purposes, the royal entry festival of 1550 is significant because it suggests that the chronicler saw little contradiction in portraying naked "savages"—*canyballes,* no less—as living under the rule of a king.[17]

By midcentury, these images of Native American kings circulating in printed works in France were joined by others appearing in the travel writing of French explorers and colonizers. Although relatively few in number, the accounts that emerged from France's three major sixteenth-century colonization efforts provide clear evidence for the continued recognition of indigenous monarchies. The first such effort, in the Saint Lawrence Valley in the early 1540s, was preceded by a number of exploratory expeditions that generated detailed reports on the lands and peoples of eastern North America. The surviving documents relating the colonization effort that followed are, unfortunately, few and fragmentary; they permit nonetheless the conclusion that the harsh climate, the disaffection of the Iroquoian-speaking

17. *L'entrée à Rouen du roi Henri II et de la reine Catherine de Médicis en 1550* (Rouen, 1885), fol. K.iv recto (the pages of this work are unnumbered; hence, I have adapted the printer's signatures for use as page references); Michael Wintroub, "Civilizing the Savage and Making a King: The Royal Entry Festival of Henri II (Rouen, 1550)," *Sixteenth Century Journal,* XXIX (1998), 465-494. Of the three hundred "Brisilians" acting in this pageant, some fifty were Native Brazilians brought to Rouen. The rest were Frenchmen familiar with Brazilian customs.

peoples inhabiting the region, and a lack of support from France compelled the two different groups of colonists to flee after only one winter. Following the abandonment of the short-lived Canadian colony in 1543, southern Brazil, long frequented by French traders in dyewood and exotica, became the focus of a second colonization attempt. Wracked by internal conflict, most of it religious in nature, the island colony at Rio de Janeiro was destroyed in 1560 by the Portuguese who claimed Brazil as their exclusive domain. A third major enterprise began only two years later, this time in territory claimed by Spain but well to the north of existing Spanish settlements. Envisioned in some circles as an American refuge for French Calvinists and in others as a convenient base from which to harry Spanish shipping, the French colony in *la Floride* lasted no longer than the others. Mutiny, poor relations with the local Timucuas, and near starvation weakened the colony before military intervention by Spain finally wiped it from the map. Of the three ventures, the Brazil colony generated the most printed works in France, in large part because the religious divisions between the colonists spurred a fierce debate among survivors and observers over whom to blame for the debacle. As we shall see, that debate continued well beyond the immediate aftermath of the failure and became bound up with the ideological turbulence of France's wars of religion (1562–1598). Because this essay's principal concern is the image of Native American kings and its evolution over time, it is crucial to bear in mind the date of composition of the travel writings examined, as opposed to their date of publication or the dates of the voyages and encounters to which they referred. For this reason, works stemming from the Brazilian venture will be examined after those relating to the Florida colony.[18]

The initial reports that resulted from French exploratory expeditions to eastern North America in 1524 and 1534 provided scant evidence of the existence of American monarchies. The first of these was a letter by the navigator Giovanni da Verrazano to his sponsor, Francis I. Verrazano, who had explored the North American coastline from the Carolinas to Cape Breton, described various landfalls and often fleeting encounters with Native peoples, frankly conceding on several occasions the paucity of information he was able to gather about them. The report says little about Native socio-

18. For a brief overview of sixteenth-century French colonialism, see Olive Patricia Dickason, "The Sixteenth-Century French Vision of Empire: The Other Side of Self-Determination," in Germaine Warkentin and Carole Podruchny, eds., *Decentring the Renaissance: Canada and Europe in Multidisciplinary Perspective, 1500–1700* (Toronto, 2001), 87–109.

political organization, but, in relating one extended encounter with the people of "Refugio" (present-day Narragansett Bay), Verrazano noted the presence of "two kings, who were as beautiful of stature and build as I can possibly describe." It was precisely the presence of these kings, along with (as art historian François-Marc Gagnon has insightfully observed) the "courtesy" they displayed and the embroidered stag skins they wore, that led the Florentine to assert that "these people are the most beautiful and have the most civil customs that we have found on this voyage." Other American peoples, especially those he met further north (in present-day Maine and Cape Breton Island, for example) were deemed, by contrast, "devoid of manners and humanity."[19] It was nonetheless to these northern regions that a second state-sponsored voyage of discovery was directed in 1534. It was led by Jacques Cartier, an experienced navigator from Saint-Malo who had made previous voyages to Brazil and was therefore presented to Francis I as a promising candidate for the leadership of the projected expedition. American kings were no more evident in his report than they were in Verrazano's. The Mi'kmaq, Innu, and Iroquoian groups Cartier encountered on the shores of the Gulf of Saint Lawrence are presented in the text as near homogeneous collectivities; there are men, women, and children but no other obvious differences in status or role. Only when the French raise a nine-meter-high cross at the entrance to the Gaspé Bay is this apparent homogeneity shattered and a leader or capitaine emerges from the crowd of Native peoples witnessing the event. The French recognize him as such, not because of dress or insignia or any special deference afforded him by his people, but rather because he acts as a spokesperson, addressing the newcomers in a long speech, accompanied by numerous gestures, which they cannot understand. Cartier, however, clearly interprets this speech as an objection to the cross, and so in return Cartier makes signs to assure the people that it is merely a navigational marker, not a claim of sovereignty. But Car-

19. Janus Verazanus to Francis I, July 8, 1524 [the Cèllere Codex], trans. Susan Tarrow, in Lawrence C. Wroth, ed., *The Voyages of Giovanni da Verrazzano* (New Haven, Conn., 1970), 134, 136, 137, 138, 140, 141. For Gagnon, Verrazano's observation that the kings of Narragansett Bay wore "a stag skin, skillfully worked like damask with various embroideries" (138) implies that he judged them according to a European sartorial code that placed embroidered fabrics above undecorated materials and subsequently viewed them as superior to other Native peoples along the Atlantic coast who were seen wearing unworked animal skins. See "L'image de l'Autre ou Verrazano 'ethnologue,'" in Philip P. Boucher, ed., *Proceedings of the Eleventh Meeting of the French Colonial Historical Society, Québec, May 1985* (Lanham, Md., 1987), 251–263 (esp. 254–258).

tier goes further: he lures this orator to his ship and then seizes two of his four companions, who Cartier believes are the captain's sons. He then releases the captain and remaining companion and sails away.[20]

If the narrative of Cartier's first voyage gave no indication that kings were to be found in northeastern North America, that of his second voyage of 1535–1536 revised the situation completely. In the opening passage of the narrative, the reader learns that the two young men kidnapped in 1534 remained with Cartier in France over the winter and are now returning with him to "Canada." In the interval, they have learned some French and serve Cartier as interpreters and guides, piloting the French ships directly to the hitherto unexplored Saint Lawrence River and to their home, the town of Stadacona (near present-day Quebec City). Upon arrival, the French are greeted by the same capitaine who harangued them the summer before—he is now, however, described as *seigneur,* or lord, of Canada. His indigenous title is *agouhanna;* his personal name, Donnacona. He governs a region—variously described as a province, a territory, or a kingdom—that includes several towns said to be subject to him. Donnacona invites the French to tarry at Stadacona, but Cartier has already noted the absence of precious metals and spices among the Stadaconans and so is anxious to press onward, toward the distant "kingdom of Saguenay" and Hochelaga to the west.[21]

20. Jacques Cartier, *Relations,* ed. Michel Bideaux (Montreal, 1986), 101–117. Bideaux's critical edition of the narratives emanating from Cartier's voyages is the most authoritative to date. Although there has been considerable debate over the authorship of these narratives, Bideaux is inclined to view Cartier as the author of the first and second Relations (64, 66).

On the significance of Cartier's expeditions for understanding early French-Native interaction, see, among others, Bruce G. Trigger, *The Children of Aataentsic: A History of the Huron People to 1660,* 2 vols. (1976; rpt., Montreal, 1987), chap. 4; Gilles Thérien, "Jacques Cartier et le langage des signes," and Bruno Roy, "Le 'Bref récit' d'une trahison," *Colloque Jacques Cartier: Histoire, textes, images* (Montreal, 1985), 229–265, 267–300; Michel Bideaux, "Introduction," in Cartier, *Relations,* ed. Bideaux, 9–83 (and see also the voluminous notes for elements of Bideaux's interpretations of the Relations); François-Marc Gagnon and Denise Petel, *Hommes effarables et bestes sauvaiges: Images du Nouveau-Monde d'après les voyages de Jacques Cartier* (Montreal, 1986); Ramsay Cook, "Donnacona Discovers Europe: Rereading Jacques Cartier's Voyages," in H. P. Biggar, trans. and ed., *The Voyages of Jacques Cartier,* rev. Ramsay Cook (Toronto, 1993), ix–xli (hereafter cited as *Voyages of Cartier*); and Réal Ouellet, "Gestualité et perception de l'Autre dans les *Relations* de Cartier," in Jaap Lintvelt, Ouellet, and Hub Hermans, eds., *Culture et colonisation en Amérique du Nord,* Nouveaux Cahiers du CÉLAT, no. 9 (Sillery, Quebec, 1994), 27–48.

21. *Voyages of Cartier,* 43, 50, 60. For Stadacona as a kingdom and subject towns,

Despite the objections of Donnacona and the desertion of his interpreters, Cartier continues upriver to Hochelaga (a town on present-day Montreal Island) where he and his small but well-armed party are given an elaborate welcome by the inhabitants. In the village itself, Cartier relates how nine or ten men carried in an older man on a deerskin and "made signs" that he was the "king and lord of the country"—an agouhanna like Donnacona. The text adds: "This Agouhanna, who was some fifty years of age, was in no way better dressed than the others except that he wore about his head for a crown a sort of red band made of hedgehog's skin. This leader was completely paralyzed and deprived of the use of his limbs."[22] Such details suggest the problem of classification facing Cartier at Hochelaga. This king wore a crown yet was otherwise clad no differently from the others. That he was borne in by attendants might have offered further evidence of his royal status, but for the physical condition that necessitated it. Had the agouhanna not been paralyzed, would he still have been honored in this manner?

The royal reception at Hochelaga lasts little more than an afternoon, for, despite the people's warm welcome, Cartier admits in the narrative to a dis-

---

see the wordlist of the second voyage (90, 95). Both Biggar's original translation published in 1924 and the slight changes made in the 1993 edition cited here contain some unfortunate renderings. A comparison with the sixteenth-century French variants of Cartier's narratives reveals that Biggar gives "chief" in most places where the original had *seigneur* (lord). Cook's edition, in turn, changes Biggar's "chiefs" into "leaders" or, in some cases, omits the title entirely. In seeking a translation more in accordance with the anthropologically correct terminology of their day, Biggar and Cook only obscure Cartier's understanding of Iroquoian political organization in 1535-1536. English readers seeking an appreciation of the sixteenth-century conceptual frameworks that structured this narrative are perhaps better served by the translation published by Richard Hakluyt in the second edition of his *Principal Navigations* . . . (London, 1598-1600). The phrase "roy et seigneur du pays" (Cartier, *Relations,* ed. Bideaux, 154) is more appropriately rendered as "the Lord and King of the countrey" (Hakluyt, *The Principal Navigations, Voyages, Traffiques, and Discoveries of the English Nation,* ed. Edmund Goldsmid, 16 vols. [Edinburgh, 1885-1889], XIII, 121) than as "the ruler and chief of this tribe" (*Voyages of Cartier* [1924], 163) or "the ruler and leader of the country" (*Voyages of Cartier* [1993], 63).

22. *Voyages of Cartier,* 63. As anthropologist William Fenton has pointed out, the rituals described in the narrative bear a structural resemblance to the Iroquois wood's-edge greeting that is well documented from the seventeenth century to the present. See "Structure, Continuity, and Change in the Process of Iroquois Treaty Making," in Francis Jennings et al., eds., *The History and Culture of Iroquois Diplomacy: An Interdisciplinary Guide to the Treaties of the Six Nations and Their League* (Syracuse, N.Y., 1985), 3-36.

comfort at being massively outnumbered by the Natives. Back at Stadacona, he and his crew hunker down for the winter, hoping to explore the kingdom of Saguenay with its hoped-for riches of gold and copper the following year. But the harsh winter, high mortality owing to scurvy, and deteriorating relations with the Stadaconans compel him to return to France in the spring. Before departing, however, the French become involved with what they perceive as Stadaconan court intrigues. Having learned that Donnacona has a rival named Agona, Cartier resolves to forcibly carry Donnacona and his two sons to France, ostensibly to provide Francis I with more information on the region but clearly also to allow Agona to set up as ruler. With the new lord of Canada owing the French a favor, what better foundations for further exploration and settlement?[23]

European politics prevented Francis I from sponsoring a third voyage until 1541. This time, however, a much larger expedition was planned, including several hundred colonists and soldiers along with an artillery train, the whole to be led by Jean-François de La Roque de Roberval, seconded by Cartier as pilot. The existence of Native seigneurs notwithstanding, Roberval was duly commissioned as lieutenant general in Canada and Hochelaga and given the power to "bring them into our possession" through friendship or force. The narratives of these colonizing expeditions are only available to us from Richard Hakluyt's *Principal Navigations* (1598-1600), the French originals having been lost. What is more, the surviving accounts are fragmentary, and the reasons for the ultimate abandonment of the colony established near Stadacona remain unclear. In any event, the narratives of Cartier's third voyage (1541-1542) and the Roberval expedition (1542-1543) clearly illustrate the tendency to situate Native government within the conceptual framework of lordship and monarchy. The first lines of the narrative of the 1541-1542 expedition inform the reader of Donnacona's death in France, styling him the "king of Canada." Returning to Stadacona, Cartier is greeted joyfully by the people there, including "he . . . which had the rule and government of the Countrey of Canada, named Agona, which was appointed king there by Donnacona, when in the former voyage we carried him [Donnacona] into France." To the narrative's author, Agona's subsequent actions made sense in light of his supposed triumph in acquiring the Crown of Canada through French intervention. "And hee [Agona] came to the Captaine's ship with 6 or 7 boates and with many women and children. And after the sayd Agona had inquired of the Captaine where Donacona and the rest were, the Captaine answered him, That Donacona was dead in

23. *Voyages of Cartier,* 82.

France, and that his body rested in the earth, and that the rest stayed there as great Lords, and were maried, and would not returne backe into their Countrey: the said Agona made no shewe of anger at all these speeches: and I thinke he tooke it so well because he remained Lord and Governour of the countrey by the death of the said Donacona." Following this, the author informs us, Agona took a piece of tanned leather edged with white shell beads "which was upon his head in stead of a crowne" and placed it on Cartier's head. Cartier then returned this "crowne of leather and put it againe upon his [Agona's] head, and gave him and his wives certaine small presents, signifying unto him that he had brought certaine new things, which afterward he would bestow upon him: for which the sayd Agona thanked the Captaine."[24]

These details allow us to guess at the ways in which Cartier and Agona might have misconstrued each other's actions in this critical encounter. Given the certain cultural affiliation between the sixteenth-century inhabitants of Stadacona and Hochelaga and other Native groups known to scholars as the Northern Iroquoians, the significance of Agona's actions can best be appreciated through comparison with the abundantly documented seventeenth- and eighteenth-century Iroquoian diplomatic rituals.[25] The latter, along with the numerous scholarly analyses they have inspired, make it clear that a gift given in council, especially of the white shell beads known as wampum, was meant to be kept, and another gift was to be given in return. To return a gift was to indicate a rejection of the proposal and sentiments that accompanied it. We can only guess what Agona intended by giving wampum to Cartier; presumably, it was an offer of friendship and alliance. For the French explorer, however, the shell beads themselves were relatively unimportant, even though Cartier was aware that they were "the thing which they esteeme most precious, as wee esteeme gold." Instead, what mattered was the "crowne of leather" to which they were sewn.[26] For a

24. *Voyages of Cartier,* 96, 98–99, 144–151 (Roberval's commission, Jan. 15, 1541). Hakluyt seems to have obtained French manuscript versions of the reports of Cartier's third voyage and of Roberval's expedition during several visits to France between 1583 and 1587 (Cartier, *Relations,* ed. Bideaux, 41).

25. On the Saint Lawrence Iroquoians, see James F. Pendergast and Bruce G. Trigger, *Cartier's Hochelaga and the Dawson Site* (Montreal, 1972); and Pendergast, "The Confusing Identities Attributed to Stadacona and Hochelaga," *Journal of Canadian Studies / Revue d'études canadiennes,* XXXII, no. 4 (1998), 149–167.

26. *Voyages of Cartier,* 99. See Jennings et al., eds., *History and Culture of Iroquois Diplomacy,* esp. the essay by Michael K. Foster, "Another Look at the Function of Wampum in Iroquois-White Councils," 99–114. See also Wilbur R. Jacobs,

French reader, Cartier's return of the crown might have implied that Agona had become a vassal of Francis I. But what to Cartier must have seemed a magnanimous gesture recognizing the rights of an indigenous vassal king to Agona might have been the equivalent of a brusque diplomatic rebuff.

Little is known of subsequent events. The French wintered again near Stadacona and departed in the spring for France, meeting the second half of the expedition under Roberval off the Newfoundland coast. Roberval's contingent continued on to Stadacona and likewise returned to France after a single winter in the Saint Lawrence Valley. Only a few pages of an account of the Roberval expedition survive, revealing little of the colony's history but underlining in passing the pervasive image of Native monarchy; in a passage describing the land and its inhabitants, we read that "they have a king in every Countrey, and are wonderfull obedient unto him: and they doe him honour according unto their maner and fashion." Later Spanish interrogations of French and Basque sailors revealed that the Stadaconans had attacked the fledgling colony and had boasted to fishermen of having killed thirty-five of Cartier's men. Native opposition—glossed in a later text as the "aloofness" of the inhabitants—was doubtless a primary cause for the failure of the French colonization effort in sixteenth-century Canada.[27] We can only wonder whether Cartier's classification and subsequent treatment of Donnacona and Agona as kings, rather than as headmen representing kin groups, had anything to do with the collapse of French-Native relations.

The images of North American kings embedded in the reports of the Cartier and Roberval expeditions were widely circulated in France and Eu-

"Wampum: The Protocol of Indian Diplomacy," *WMQ*, 3d Ser., VI (1949), 596–604; George S. Snyderman, "The Functions of Wampum," American Philosophical Society, *Proceedings*, XCVIII (1954), 469–494; André Vachon, "Colliers et ceintures de porcelaine chez les Indiens de la Nouvelle-France," *Cahiers des Dix*, XXXV (1970), 251–278; Vachon, "Colliers et ceintures de porcelaine dans la diplomatie indienne," ibid., XXXVI (1971), 179–192; Lynn Ceci, "Native Wampum as a Peripheral Resource in the Seventeenth-Century World-System," in Laurence M. Hauptman and James D. Wherry, eds., *The Pequots in Southern New England: The Fall and Rise of an American Indian Nation* (Norman, Okla., 1990), 48–63; Jonathan C. Lainey, *La "monnaie des sauvages": Les colliers de wampum d'hier à aujourd'hui* (Sillery, Quebec, 2004).

27. *Voyages of Cartier*, 112, 163, 166. According to an inscription on a 1550 map by Pierre Descellier, "As it was not possible to trade with the people of this country because of their aloofness and the intemperance of the land and small profits, they [the French] had returned to France and hoped to come back when it pleased the king." Quoted in Dickason, "Sixteenth-Century French Vision of Empire," in Warkentin and Podruchny, eds., *Decentring the Renaissance*, 96.

rope, less through the publication of an account of Cartier's second voyage in French in 1545 (which appears to have been virtually ignored) than through their inclusion in works authored or compiled by others.[28] A navigational tour of the Atlantic composed at midcentury confidently asserted that in the region between Newfoundland and Norumbega "there are cities [and the people] have a king as in the Indies." "The people," the author added, "are our size, somewhat black, and worship the sun and the moon. They have many furs."[29] Giovanni Battista Ramusio included the narratives of Cartier's first and second voyages in his *Terzo volume delle navigatione et viaggi* (1556) and, further, commissioned an engraving of the town of Hochelaga in which the house, court, and hearth fire of the king were clearly marked. Through Ramusio, the ethnographic and geographic information about Canada made its way into the works of French cosmographers like François de Belleforest and André Thevet, while Richard Hakluyt commissioned English translations of the accounts in their entirety for the benefit of his compatriots. No one disputed the classification of Native North American leaders as lords and kings. The royal cosmographer and prolific writer of geographic literature André Thevet reworked Cartier's material extensively (and often erroneously) for inclusion in his *Singularitez de la France antarctique* (1557) and *Cosmographie universelle* (1575); in the former work, he explained that, among the Canadians, "when it is a question of war their great *Agahanna* (which means like king or lord) commands his vassal lords, as each village to its superior, that they resolve to come and be before him." Thevet followed Cartier in calling Donnacona the lord of Stadacona and, in

28. *Brief récit et succincte narration de la navigation faicte es ysles de Canada . . .* (Paris, 1545). Only three copies of this work are known to exist. The account of Cartier's first voyage was not published in French until the end of the century: *Discours du voyage fait par le capitaine Jaques Cartier aux terres-neufves de Canadas, Norembergue, Hochelage, Labrador, et pays adjacens, dite Nouvelle-France, avec particulieres moeurs, langage, et ceremonies des habitans d'icelle* (Rouen, 1598).

29. "Il y ha villes. Ils ont un Roy comme aux Indes. Les gens y sont de nostre grandeur, entre-noirs, et adorent le Soleil et la Lune. Ils ont force pelleterie"; see *Les voyages avantureux du capitaine Jan Alfonce, sainctongeois; contenant les reigles et enseignemens necessaires à la bonne et seure navigation* (Poitiers, [1559]), 28v. Jean Alfonse was almost certainly dead when this work was written in the 1540s and so is unlikely to be the author. Moreover, the work curiously omits mention of actual voyages made by Alfonse or Cartier (Cartier, *Relations*, ed. Bideaux, 43). Cartier's narratives may not be the source for the American kings in the *Voyages avantureux*. The work nevertheless underlines the sixteenth-century French belief in the existence of North American kings.

a 1558 edition of the *Singularitez,* identified him in a marginal heading as the king of Canada. In a fictionalized episode in the later *Cosmographie,* the cosmographer recounted meeting "a certain kinglet" on the Norombegue River; elsewhere, he referred to a region on the great river of Hochelaga "where their king, whom they call in their jargon *Agouhanna,* usually resides."[30]

The vocabulary of lordship and kingship used by Cartier and Thevet demonstrated a much distorted understanding of Iroquoian sociopolitical organization. Other Northern Iroquoian polities, such as the Wendat (Hurons) or the Haudenosaunee (Iroquois) of the seventeenth century, were confederacies of autonomous villages whose various matrilineal clan segments each sent one or several headmen to the village council, which in turn sent delegates to nationwide or confederacy-wide councils. In addition to those upon whom were bestowed the titular leadership positions belonging to certain matrilineages, some individuals became leaders through personal achievement in war, diplomacy, or trade. But there was no institutionalized hierarchy that descended from a single individual—that is, no kingship.[31]

There was also no kingship as such in sixteenth-century Florida, although the Native polities of the day were perhaps closer in some instances to monarchies. French and Spanish sources as well as archaeological evidence lead modern anthropologists to label these societies as chiefdoms. Leaders claimed supernatural sanction for their authority and inherited their titles matrilineally (generally, from their mother's brother); rank in general (as well as access to resources) depended on "genealogical near-

30. *Voyages of Cartier,* unnumbered plate after xli (in this well-known engraving, reproduced countless times in modern publications, figure D indicates the "Casa del Re Agouana," and E, "La Corte della Casa del Re, et il suo fuoco"); Cartier, *Relations,* ed. Bideaux, 37–38; Roger Schlesinger and Arthur P. Stabler, trans. and eds., *André Thevet's North America: A Sixteenth-Century View* (Montreal, 1986), 14, 28, 34–35 (see also 39, 43, for reference to kings); André Thevet, *Les singularitez de la France antarctique* (Paris, 1557), 151v ("Dona-coua, A-guanna, Roy de Canada"). These marginal headings are not included in Schlesinger and Stabler's edition of Thevet's works.

31. Scholars continue to debate several issues concerning the political organization of the Northern Iroquoian confederacies, but the broad outlines of these polities are fairly clear. For the Wendat, see Trigger, *Children of Aataentsic.* For the Haudenosaunee, see Daniel K. Richter, *The Ordeal of the Longhouse: The Peoples of the Iroquois League in the Era of European Colonization* (Chapel Hill, N.C., 1992); William N. Fenton, *The Great Law and the Longhouse: A Political History of the Iroquois Confederacy* (Norman, Okla., 1998); and José António Brandão, *"Your Fyre Shall Burn No More": Iroquois Policy toward New France and Its Native Allies to 1701* (Lincoln, Neb., 1997).

ness" to the chief's lineage. Some achieved the status of paramount chiefs by extending their authority over neighboring villages.[32] Still, a great gulf existed between these polities and the monarchies of early modern Europe. Yet René de Laudonnière, in his account of French colonization efforts in the 1560s, did not hesitate to employ the vocabulary of kingship—and in an official communication that appeared directed toward the highest authorities in France.[33]

Beginning with the first casual mention of kings in the ethnographically oriented preface, Laudonnière allows his readers only the narrowest doubt about the status of Floridian leaders. Not only does the king have the privilege (alone of all men, it seems) of taking more than one wife, he also presides over Native councils and is honored posthumously with special funerary rites. Naturally, he leads his men in war.[34] The individual kings who appear throughout the narratives (of the expeditions of 1562, 1564, and 1565) that follow are accorded by Laudonnière the characteristic attributes of European royalty. They are gracious, generous, valiant, but also proud and fierce. Certain great kings have other kings as vassals. Their principal wives are queens, one of whom is rumored to be "the most beautiful of all

32. John H. Hann, *A History of the Timucua Indians and Missions* (Gainesville, Fla., 1996), 74, 75, 82; and John E. Worth, *The Timucuan Chiefdoms of Spanish Florida,* 2 vols. (Gainesville, Fla., 1998), I, 4–18 (see 5 on nearness to the chiefly lineage). Jerald T. Milanich has argued that the Timucuan polities were "simple" chiefdoms that occasionally "exercised complexity" by forming short-term regional alliances to meet an external threat; see Milanich, "Native Chiefdoms and the Exercise of Complexity in Sixteenth-Century Florida," in Elsa M. Redmond, ed., *Chiefdoms and Chieftaincy in the Americas* (Gainesville, Fla., 1998), 245–264.

33. Charles E. Bennett, "Introduction," in René Laudonnière, *Three Voyages,* trans. and ed. Bennett (Gainesville, Fla., 1975), xix. Readers of Bennett's English translation may be confused by Bennett's decision to consistently translate the Native term *paraousti* as "chief," despite Laudonnière's insistence (quoted later in this essay) that the term meant "king." As a result, Native individuals appear sometimes as chiefs (whenever they are called paraoustis in the original) and sometimes as kings (whenever the original text gives *roi*). In the original French text, Laudonnière never uses generic terms of leadership, like *chef* or *capitaine,* to describe the paraoustis or kings of Florida. As with Biggar's edition of Cartier's Relations, the anthropological presuppositions of the translator obscure the sixteenth-century interpretation of Native leadership.

34. René Goulaine de Laudonnière, *L'histoire notable de la Floride* . . . (Paris, 1586), 4v–7v. Although this account was published in 1586, it appears to have been written at an earlier date and to have circulated in manuscipt form. As Schlesinger and Stabler note, "Apparently Thevet possessed Laudonnière's narrative, which he suppressed in order to pose as an authority on Florida" (*Thevet's North America,* xxxi).

the Indian women" and is carried everywhere on her subjects' shoulders as a sign of respect.[35]

Lest skeptical readers entertain doubts about the nature of these "foreign kings," the text repeatedly strives to justify the use of the language of kingship. In one encounter, the French commander Jean Ribaut is greeted by a king who demonstrates "such constant dignity that he showed how deservedly he warranted the title of king."[36] Elsewhere, Laudonnière emphasizes that the Natives live in a ranked society, and that kings are surrounded by symbols of their status. In the account of the second voyage, the text introduces the indigenous terms *paraousti* and *paracousi,* insisting that they are appropriately understood to designate a "king" or a "monarch."[37]

As in the narratives relating to Cartier's voyages, the concept of Native kingship subtly determines French policies on the ground. Left in command of the French colony at Fort Caroline (on the present-day Saint John River) in 1564, Laudonnière outlines for the reader how he carefully and calculatedly cultivated the friendship of a dozen kings while gradually investigating potential sources of mineral wealth and assessing the geopolitical situation. Although he recognizes that the French have settled on the lands of King Satouriona, Laudonnière refuses that monarch's request for military assistance, instead hoping to mediate regional conflicts and establish a kind of *pax gallica.* But once the route to a promising source of gold is discovered, the French abandon this policy of restraint and instead resolve to take sides

35. Laudonnière, *L'histoire notable,* 25v–26r, 42v, 48v–49r, 75v. Laura Fishman asserts that Laudonnière's description of Timucuan kingship is largely "consistent with [the views] of modern anthropologists" (inasmuch as one could substitute the latters' "chiefs" for Laudonnière's "kings") and argues that, in viewing Timucuan political organization as akin to that of the French, Laudonnière "surprisingly" departed from prevailing European discourses of savagism and "sensed a common bond of humanity between himself and the Timucuans" ("Old World Images Encounter New World Reality: René Laudonnière and the Timucuans of Florida," *Sixteenth Century Journal,* XXVI [1995], 547–559 [esp. 552–553]). The evidence presented here suggests that Laudonnière's depiction of Timucuan kings should not be seen as especially surprising or original when placed in the broader context of sixteenth-century French travel writing.

36. Laudonnière, *L'histoire notable,* 23r ("ces Roys estrangers"), 9v ("une si constante gravité, qu'il feit paroistre qu'à bon et juste droict il portoit le tiltre de Roy").

37. Laudonnière, *L'histoire notable,* 36v ("leur *paraousti,* c'est-à-dire leur Roy et supérieur"), 38r ("il se nommoit *Paracousi Satouriona,* qui vaut autant que Roy *Satouriona*"), 39v–40r (rank), 49r ("le Paraousti *Satouriona,* monarque des confines de la Rivière May"). For symbols of kingly status, see, for example, King Oade's "white coverlet fringed in scarlet" (Laudonnière, *Three Voyages,* trans. and ed. Bennett, 43).

with the king who seems most able to guide them toward the metal. Sounding his men for their advice on the matter, the commandant learns that "most of them were of the opinion that I should send [military] aid to this *Paracousi*, because it would be more difficult to further explore the country without his help, and that the Spanish, when they were making their conquests, always allied themselves with some king, in order to bring down another." Later, as the thirst for gold is eclipsed by the prospect of starvation, Laudonnière (at the urging of his men) decides to kidnap his new ally, King Outina, to force the latter's subjects to provide the French with food. As successful as the policy of capturing the king might have appeared from earlier Spanish accounts of New World conquest, in Florida it proved a dismal failure: Outina's people respond by electing a new leader. Toward the end of the narrative, reflecting on the debacle that has led to the decision to abandon the colony in the summer of 1565, Laudonnière expresses regret for the conflict with Outina but congratulates himself for having retained the friendship of the other kings in the region.[38]

As with Cartier (and, perhaps, Roberval), the classification of Native leaders as kings led Laudonnière to contemplate and execute policies that assumed an extreme centralization of legitimate authority in one individual and his closest male family members. Within such a conceptual framework, wooing, controlling, replacing, or kidnapping indigenous kings was intended to produce predictable results. The failure of such policies was not solely a result of proceeding from wrong premises; the policies themselves were inherently heavy-handed and manipulative. But the act of classification itself might have foreclosed alternative conceptions and options for interacting on a more mutually beneficial basis with the Native leaders of Canada and Florida. Although climate, logistics, internal dissension, and (in the case of the Florida expedition) the aggression of a rival empire contributed to the demise of these sixteenth-century colonies, the alienation of local Native peoples also played a key role.

Over the course of the sixteenth century, Brazil, not Canada or Florida, most shaped French impressions of the Americas, a consequence of a long-standing French involvement in the brazilwood trade and of a brief but intense failed effort at colonization in the 1550s. The Tupinambás of the coast were famous in France for their ritual cannibalism—a sign of extreme bar-

---

38. Laudonnière, *L'histoire notable,* 77v ("La plus part fut d'opinion que je devois envoyer secourir à ce Paracousi, pour ce qu'il me seroit mal aisé de descouvrir plus avant pays sans son moyen, et que les Espagnols, lors qu'ils estoient sur les termes d'acquerir, s'estoient tousjours alliez de quelque Roy, pour ruiner l'autre"), 85r, 94r.

barism, in European eyes—but, as we have seen in the royal entry festival at Rouen in 1550, such barbarism did not preclude them from having proper kings. The image of an indigenous Brazilian monarchy in sixteenth-century French writing was largely the creation of André Thevet, who, as we have seen, also popularized the image of Canadian kings. At its center was Quoniambec, the physically impressive Tupinambá king and ally of the French in Brazil. As described in Thevet's *Cosmographie universelle,* Quoniambec is eight feet tall and immensely strong—so much so that he carries two culverins on his shoulders into battle—and possesses a booming voice and heroic demeanor. Yet he is no mere brute who commands through the use of force. Quoniambec spontaneously demonstrates the natural piety of royalty by falling to his knees when he sees the French at prayer and is remembered by his people after his death as a great leader. Where necessary, Thevet's writing compensates for the lack of obvious signs of kingship by careful substitution: thus does a typical *maloca* or longhouse become a palace once Quoniambec takes possession of it.[39]

The hyperbolic quality of Thevet's writing seems to provide ample positive evidence for William Sturtevant's hypothesis that many "American chiefdoms are an artifact of postmedieval European preconceptions"—in other words, that early modern Europeans' assumptions about the nature of human society led them to impose hierarchies and ranks upon groups where none in fact existed. Surveying the ethnographic data, Sturtevant finds that "the Tupinambá exhibit hardly any of the characteristics of chiefdoms and lack those considered crucial by most theorists."[40] Yet Thevet's portrait of the kingly Quoniambec was anything but a simple unconscious application of deeply rooted schemes of perception. As was the case with Cartier and Laudonnière, the classification of Native leaders as kings solved an important problem for the colonizer: how to legitimate the extension of French power over autonomous American polities. In inventing this portrait, Thevet was seeking to create a mirror of European kingship that would serve as the linchpin of the French colonial project in Brazil: Quoniambec's anticipated conversion to Christianity would lead ultimately to his incorporation within the French Empire as a vassal of the French king.[41]

39. Frank Lestringant, "The Myth of the Indian Monarchy: An Aspect of the Controversy between Thevet and Léry (1575-1585)," in Christian F. Feest, éd., *Indians and Europe: An Interdisciplinary Collection of Essays* (Aachen, 1987), 37-60 (esp. 40-42).

40. William Sturtevant, "Tupinambá Chiefdoms?" in Redmond, ed., *Chiefdoms and Chieftaincy,* 138-149 (esp. 139, 140, 146).

41. Lestringant writes: "The Indian monarchy represents the myth indispensable for the establishment of alliances with the new peoples and further for the installation

The matter of Brazilian kings might have remained unquestioned were it not for the religious turmoil of late-sixteenth-century France. Thevet had publicly blamed the failure of the French colony in Brazil on the insubordination of its Huguenot elements and so made enemies of Huguenot survivors like the Calvinist pastor Jean de Léry. When Léry published a second edition of his *Histoire d'un voyage fait en la terre du Bresil* (1580), he attacked Thevet by mocking the cosmographer's depiction of Quoniambec. Far from being majestic, Quoniambec becomes in Léry's view merely "funny," and the stories of his fantastic might, delusional. Thevet's response in his *Vrais pourtraits et vies des hommes illustres* (1584) was to up the ante, placing Quoniambec in a gallery with Julius Caesar, Charlemagne, and Tamerlane, intending thereby to indicate that the Brazilian monarch was on a par with the greatest princes of the Old World. The panegyric text completely overlooks the potentially disturbing elements of Tupinambá culture—cannibalism and nudity—that Thevet had acknowledged in the earlier *Cosmographie universelle,* emphasizing instead the king's virtues of strength and piety. Again, a calculated renaming assists in doing so: Quoniambec's feather diadem is interpreted as a crown and his war club becomes a scepter. Léry's fierce rebuttal came in the third edition of his *Histoire* (1585): Quoniambec's palace is revealed to be a "pig sty"; his kingdom, an expanse of wilderness. In fact, insists Léry, there are neither kings nor princes among the Tupinambás. No one leads, and yet the community functions in perfect harmony.[42]

To view Thevet and Léry as writers on opposite sides of the supposed

---

of jurisdiction over their territories. The isolation of a unique figure which marvelously realizes the monarchic principle transposed into Indian chieftainship considerably simplifies the transactions because the key to domination rests in a single individual, easy to convert and to corrupt" ("Myth of the Indian Monarchy," in Feest, ed., *Indians and Europe,* 47–48). Hinderaker echoes this notion in his study of the "Indian Kings" of 1710: "In cultural impact the episode was unique. In part this was a function of the social and political authority ascribed to the Indians by calling them 'kings.' . . . The idea of Indian kings had radical implications for Britons, who had previously tended to regard Indians as natural men living in weak, stateless societies. This new impulse to project political sovereignty onto Native leaders was entirely consistent, however, with the desire to extend English imperial authority in America: it posited the existence of Native peoples who were capable of serving as effective allies and agents of the crown in the empire-building process" ("Four Indian Kings," *WMQ,* 3d Ser., LIII [1996], 487–488).

42. Lestringant, "Myth of the Indian Monarchy," in Feest, ed., *Indians and Europe,* 42, 43–44, 46. For Léry's explicit rejection of the existence of kings or princes among the Tupís, see Jean de Léry, *History of a Voyage to the New Land of Brazil, Otherwise Called America,* trans. Janet Whatley (Berkeley, Calif., 1990), 113.

chasm between medieval and modern worldviews might be tempting. Is not Léry simply the more objective ethnographer, privileging direct experience over received wisdom, whereas Thevet remains a prisoner of unquestioned premises inherited from the authorities of antiquity? Such a conclusion would ignore the complex context of their feud. Léry's efforts to demolish the image of the Brazilian monarchy were not purely those of an indignant eyewitness anxious to set the record straight about the failure of the French colony and the true nature of indigenous society. Instead, Léry's sustained ridicule of Quoniambec was surely related to the increasingly antimonarchical Huguenot political discourses of the 1570s and 1580s. In the wake of the French king's involvement in the massacre of Saint Bartholomew of 1572—an episode of the wars of religion in which thousands of prominent Huguenots gathered at Paris were exterminated in an orchestrated purge—Léry could hardly view the institution of monarchy with equanimity or respect.[43] Demystifying Brazilian kingship by cutting through Thevet's rhetoric, Léry revealed in its place a naked savage in the forest. What might be revealed were the French king subjected to similar critical scrutiny? In assailing Thevet's underlying premise that people in a state of nature had kings, Léry was rejecting, in a fundamental way, the basis of monarchy in natural law. The debate between Thevet and Léry thus exposes the specific political and religious contexts in which the trope of the "savage" monarch became, in France, an ideological hot potato. The ridicule of a Brazilian king provided an altogether too obvious model for the degrading of a French king.

The vanishing Native American monarchy in early modern French rhetoric and perception thus reflected both the changing attitudes of sixteenth-century elites, as outlined earlier in this essay, and the new political order emerging from the wars of religion. As we have glimpsed in the debate between Thevet and Léry, the increasingly radical polemics that characterized the conflict contributed to a questioning of the taken-for-granted foundations of the French monarchy. The peculiar constellation of events that ended the civil wars, however, imposed a blanket of silence on the radical theses of the time of troubles. Briefly, a series of dynastic accidents led to the Protestant Henri de Navarre's becoming heir to the throne in 1584; the assassination of Henri III in 1589 then made Navarre the fourth king of that name according to the prevailing rules of dynastic succession. Thus, through the late 1580s and into the 1590s, did the Huguenot party now find itself supporting the monarchy while the ultra-Catholic opposition, em-

43. Lestringant, "Myth of the Indian Monarchy," in Feest, ed., *Indians and Europe,* 53-54.

bodied in the Holy League headquartered in Paris, sought the ideological and political means of undermining Henri IV's legitimacy. The king's timely conversion to Catholicism in 1593 took much of the wind out of those sails and made possible the rallying of moderate Catholic and Huguenot support around the figure of the king. By 1598, victory on the battlefield and the politics of religious toleration had secured Henri IV's throne. The French monarchy of the early seventeenth century enjoyed a fundamental legitimacy that was, to a large degree, the result of the atomization of France's elites during and after the wars of religion. In the opinion of historian Denis Richet, this was simply because no other political system or culture offered a viable alternative to the monarchy. The political apotheosis of Henri IV after his assassination in 1610 only further strengthened the ideological foundations of the new Bourbon dynasty. All the traditional rituals of and justifications for kingship—from the peculiar royal funeral ceremonies that enacted the theory of the king's two bodies to the king's touching for scrofula to the Roman legal maxims that made the king emperor in his own kingdom—were reinvoked and reinvigorated in support of a monarch who enjoyed what Jean Bodin had described as "absolute power."[44]

For French elites engaged in the promotion and execution of colonial ventures, the significance of the term "king" was now such that it no longer seemed reasonable to view Native leaders as belonging to this category. The late-medieval belief that all social groups, even those of animals, were microcosms of monarchy had given way to a conception of kingship that was rooted simultaneously in history and divine law. The French monarchy was known to be the result of a long, convoluted history and yet was deemed to be essentially a divinely sanctioned and pure expression of rational principles. Monarchy was no longer an immanent feature of the world but instead was proof of the triumph of religion and reason. Consequently, the benighted peoples of Europe's New World no longer appeared as other monarchies, but as others without monarchy.

Perhaps few other texts exemplify this change in the conception of kingship more explicitly in the early seventeenth century than the writings of Marc

44. Michael Wolfe, *The Conversion of Henri IV: Politics, Power, and Religious Belief in Early Modern France* (Cambridge, Mass., 1993); Denis Richet, *La France moderne: L'esprit des institutions* (Paris, 1973), 74, 102-103. For an excellent synthesis of the ritual meanings of the funerary and succession rites of Henri IV and Louis XIII, respectively, as well as of the political context in which they occurred, see Emmanuel Le Roy Ladurie, *L'absolutisme en vraie grandeur (1610-1715)*, vol. I of *L'Ancien Régime* (Paris, 1991), chap. 1.

Lescarbot, a Parisian lawyer who sojourned briefly in the French colony of Port-Royal in present-day Nova Scotia. In 1609, Lescarbot published a slim volume of poetry inspired by his twelve-month stay in the colony. One of the longer pieces in the book was a masque entitled the *Théâtre de Neptune en la Nouvelle-France*. Written three years earlier and performed at Port-Royal in November 1606, it was modeled on the pageants and tableaux vivants that were staged by early modern cities when receiving a king, a royal governor, an ambassador, a feudal lord, or any other important personage—precisely the type of event that had showcased a Brazilian king at Rouen half a century before.[45] In this case, the individual at the center of the masque was Jean de Biencourt de Poutrincourt, a French nobleman and commandant of Port-Royal. Lescarbot had written the work ostensibly to celebrate Poutrincourt's return from an expedition to explore the New England coast, but the masque as a whole spoke tellingly of the key political symbols that would consecrate and validate French claims to possess that part of North America.

The *Théâtre de Neptune* was structured as a series of speeches addressed to Poutrincourt by various mythological or allegorical figures. Neptune, god of the sea, appeared first, followed by a half-dozen Tritons who came forward to laud Poutrincourt's efforts on behalf of the Crown. The last to speak were four "savages" *(sauvages),* one of whom claimed to speak for all the nations of the country.[46] This leading "savage" faced Poutrincourt and declared:

45. Marc Lescarbot, *Théâtre de Neptune en la Nouvelle-France,* in *Les Muses de la Nouvelle-France* (Paris, 1609), reprinted in Lescarbot, *Histoire de la Nouvelle-France . . . ,* ed. Edwin Tross, 3 vols. (Paris, 1866). The *Muses de la Nouvelle-France* appear as unnumbered pages at the end of vol. III. On Lescarbot, see Rick Bowers, "*Le Théâtre de Neptune en la Nouvelle-France:* Marc Lescarbot and the New World Masque," *Dalhousie Review,* LXX (1991), 483–501; Éric Thierry, *Marc Lescarbot, vers 1570–1641: Un homme de plume au service de la Nouvelle-France* (Paris, 2001); and Paolo Carile, *Le regard entravé: Littérature et anthropologie dans les premiers textes sur la Nouvelle-France* (Sillery, Quebec, 2000), esp. chap. 3. On the royal entry ceremony, see Lawrence M. Bryant, *The King and the City in the Parisian Royal Entry Ceremony: Politics, Ritual, and Art in the Renaissance* (Geneva, 1986); and Edward Muir, *Ritual in Early Modern Europe* (New York, 1997), chap. 7.

46. We have no way of knowing whether these "savages" were played by the local Mi'kmaq, whom they were intended to represent, but it seems unlikely. The Mi'kmaq and the French communicated through a trade pidgin that probably could not accommodate the sentiments expressed in Lescarbot's French text. But, if the Mi'kmaq did not act in the play, some might well have attended its performance, given the proximity of several villages to Port-Royal and the tendency of the French to include Mi'kmaq leaders in ceremonies as confirmation of their alliance.

We come to give homage
Due to the holy fleur-de-lis
In your hands, which of your Prince
Represents his Majesty
Awaiting the day that this province
Shall flower with piety,
Civil customs, and all things
Which serve to establish
That which is good, and which repose
In a royal government.

In Lescarbot's masque, the "savages" are cast as supplicants, painfully aware of their need for piety, order, and good government and of the French ability to bestow these marvels upon them. According to the logic of this fantasy, the French have no need to conquer the Natives; instead, the latter will submit voluntarily, even cheerfully, to the beneficent suzerainty of the French king.[47]

Lescarbot was not the only French writer of his age elaborating fantasies of Native self-subjugation. In a fictional travel narrative published at Lyons in 1609, the pseudonymous sieur Des Combes related how a contrary wind pushed his ship to the land of Baccalaos, near Canada. There, Des Combes and his French companions encountered a village of poor barbarians who, "having considered the humour and ways of our Frenchmen, and seeing them so graceful compared to themselves, were as if spellbound, and wished to adore them as gods, making signs that if our Frenchmen would remain with them they would recognize them as kings and emperors of all their lands."[48] A similar indigenous response was presented in Jacques Du

47. "Nous venons rendre les homages / Deuz aux sacrées Fleurs-de-lis / Ès mains de toy, / qui de ton Prince / Représentes la Majesté, / Attendans que cette province / Faces florir en piété / En moeurs civils, et toute chose / Qui sert à l'établissement / De ce qui est beau, et repose / En un royal gouvernement"; see Lescarbot, *Théâtre de Neptune,* in *Les Muses de la Nouvelle-France,* reprinted in Lescarbot, *Histoire de la Nouvelle-France,* ed. Tross.

48. "Apres avoir contemplé l'humeur et la façon des nostres, les voya[n]t si addroits et de belle grace au prix d'eux, ils demeurerent comme ravis, et les vouloient adorer comme dieux, leur faisant signe que s'ils vouloient venir avec eux ils les constitueroient pour Rois et Empereurs de toutes leur terres"; see *Coppie d'une lettre envoyee de la Nouvelle France, ou Canada, par le Sieur de Co[m]bes, Gentilhomme Poictevin, à vn sien amy; en laquelle sont briesvement descrites les merveilles, excellences, et richesses du pays, ensemble la façon et moeurs de ceux qui l'habitent, la gloire des François, et l'esperance*

Hamel's play *Acoubar,* published at Rouen in 1603: the action is again set in Canada, where the valiant Frenchman Pistion not only wins the love of a beautiful Native princess but is also acclaimed king by the Canadian savages after rallying them in battle. The era's most elaborate representation of the French gift of kingship to indigenous Americans was not, however, a work of fiction nor a masque penned during idle hours at a northern fur trade post. In a series of carefully choreographed ceremonies modeled on the French royal entrance ceremony, François de Rasilly and other leaders of a large French expedition to the mouth of the Amazon River in 1612 enacted the arrival of Christianity and the establishment of French sovereignty over the Tupinambá peoples of Maranhão. As detailed by Claude d'Abbeville, the expedition's Capuchin chronicler, the French deliberately involved the Tupinambás themselves and conducted the ceremonies in a manner that demonstrated, according to French symbolic schemes, the people's joyful and willing acceptance of French political domination.[49]

The trope of the welcoming, awestruck, and worshipful Native, ripe for political or religious assimilation, is one of the oldest in European writing on America, having famously appeared in Columbus's description of the Taínos in his letter of 1493. And, although French political culture might have been especially prone to emphasize the consent of the ruled (as demonstrated through joyous celebration and a rhetoric of love), in Lescarbot's time the image of Native peoples spontaneously accepting, even seeking, the tutelage of the French had a special purpose: it was doubtless a calculated reaction to the Black Legend about Spanish atrocities in the Americas that had developed in the United Provinces and in Huguenot circles in France in the last decades of the sixteenth century. Lescarbot's *Histoire de la Nouvelle-France,* published in 1609, returns again and again to the theme of Spanish cruelty, providing a sharp contrast to the love the Mi'kmaq and other Native groups are said to bear the French.[50]

qu'il y a de rendre l'Amerique Chrestienne, facsimile ed., Americana Ser., no. 157 ([Boston], 1926), 9–10.

49. Du Hamel, *The Earliest French Play about America,* intro. Adams; Seed, *Ceremonies of Possession,* chap. 2. Seed identifies the leader of this expedition as the same Razilly who "would later found the French colony at Acadia" (41 n. 1), but this identification appears to confuse Isaac (the founder of Acadia) with François, his older brother and leader of the expedition to the Amazon. D'Abbeville's account is given in Claude d'Abbeville, *Histoire de la mission des pères capucins en l'isle de Marignan et terres circonvoisines* (Paris, 1614).

50. Translation of *De Insulis inuentis,* in *The Columbus Letter;* Seed, *Ceremonies of Possession,* 56–63. Lescarbot, in the dedication of *Histoire de la Nouvelle-France,* for

As with Columbus's ideology of "Christian imperialism," the underlying premise of such discourses is that Europeans are bringing to the Americas a gift of incalculable value: to be sure, hints the text of Columbus's 1493 letter, the Natives risk the loss of their autonomy, their land, even their bodies, but in return they will gain humanity and, above all, the chance of eternal salvation. In the context of the *Théâtre de Neptune,* the gift in question is not Christianity, or at least not only Christianity.[51] Instead, the playwright evokes the precious gift of all the elements of the ideal polity: law, justice, piety, civil order, and monarchy—all things that he believed the Mi'kmaq of Acadia to lack. For Lescarbot, the Native peoples of the Americas were without religion, without law, and without kingship—*sans foi, sans loi, sans roi.*[52]

In presenting the Mi'kmaq as being without kings and therefore in need of kingship—French kingship, to be precise—Lescarbot was quite conscious that he was departing from sixteenth-century discourses that *did* recognize the existence of Native kings. He insisted that Native leaders *not* be termed kings. In writing the *Histoire de la Nouvelle-France,* Lescarbot

---

example, grudgingly admits that the Spanish have hitherto been more zealous than the French in carrying civilization and Christianity to the New World, "mais il a esté cruel." By contrast, the humane treatment of the Mi'kmaq by the French at Port-Royal has earned the colonizers the love of the Natives (xii–xiii). Later, Lescarbot refers to the Spanish extermination of Native peoples and affirms that the French will act with grace, gentleness, pity, and mercy (xvii). See also references on 2, 5, 44, 60, 61, 113–118. Thomas Scanlan has identified a similar logic in Thomas Harriot's *Briefe and True Report of the New Found Land of Virginia . . .* (London, 1588); see Scanlan, *Colonial Writing and the New World, 1583–1671: Allegories of Desire* (Cambridge, 1999), chap. 2. The works of Lescarbot and Claude d'Abbeville make it clear that what Scanlan views as a distinctively Protestant discourse was also characteristic of early-seventeenth-century French colonial writing.

51. Stephen Greenblatt, *Marvelous Possessions: The Wonder of the New World* (Chicago, 1991), 70–72. Although Lescarbot was a fervent Catholic (his family supported the Catholic League during the wars of religion), that the 1606 expedition to Port-Royal lacked professional missionaries would have rendered undue exaltation of the evangelical enterprise somewhat awkward.

52. There are numerous variations of this formula in French writing of the sixteenth and seventeenth centuries; the form "ni foi, ni roi, ni loix" is from Chrestien Le Clercq, *Nouvelle relation de la Gaspésie . . .* (Paris, 1691), 378. This formula was but one iteration of the familiar rhetoric of lack that was a long-term characteristic of European discourse on the Native peoples of the Americas. For a discussion of the "negative formula" employed in descriptions of Native cultures, see Margaret T. Hodgen, *Early Anthropology in the Sixteenth and Seventeenth Centuries* (Philadelphia, 1964), 196–201.

cribbed extensively from the sixteenth-century French narratives relating to French colonization efforts in Canada, Brazil, Florida; yet, where his sources employed the term "king" in describing Native leaders, Lescarbot deliberately and systematically replaced this title with either the generic term *capitaine* or with an indigenous term such as *sagamo* (among the Mi'kmaq) or *paraousti* (among the Timucuas).[53]

The writings of the lawyer's contemporaries in early New France, and those of successive generations of colonial administrators, missionaries, and merchants, continued this trend: Native leaders in North America were everywhere designated as capitaines, *chefs,* or principaux (headmen), and never as kings.[54] To Rasilly and the Capuchin missionaries at the mouth of the Amazon in 1612, the local Tupinambás were led by a number of headmen and elders (anciens). (One principal, in particular, stood out from the others, but he was clearly not a king, for it was to an assembly of headmen and elders that Rasilly pronounced the crucial speech inviting them to offer their land to the French king.) To Samuel de Champlain, visiting the homeland of the powerful Wendat (Huron) Confederacy in 1615, the people he met—whose political organization was, from a modern ethnographic perspective, one of the most sophisticated in the Northeast—were "without religion, nor law, be it divine, political, or civil." Even those few leaders they recognized, he stated, were obeyed only in the midst of war.[55]

53. See, especially, Lescarbot, *Histoire de la Nouvelle-France,* ed. Tross, 41.

54. A rare exception to this assertion can be found in two different Jesuit Relations produced in the mid-1650s, when the missionaries were intent on advertising the triumph of a projected mission centered near the central council fire of the Haudenosaunee at Onondaga. One referred to an Onondaga headman named Agochiendagueté as being, "as it were, the King of the country." A subsequent Relation presented another man, Sagochiendagesité, who was said to possess "Royal power and authority over the whole Nation of Onontaghé [Onondaga], although he does not bear that title [of king]" (Reuben Gold Thwaites, ed., *The Jesuit Relations and Allied Documents: Travels and Explorations of the Jesuit Missionaries in New France, 1610-1791,* 73 vols. [Cleveland, Ohio, 1896-1901], XLII, 88, XLIII, 276-277).

55. D'Abbeville, *Histoire* (references to the principaux of the region are scattered throughout the work; see key passages on 57v, 58r, 67v, 98r-98v, 99, 101v, 105r, 160r-160v); Samuel de Champlain, *Voyages et descouvertures* (1619), in H. P. Biggar, ed., *The Works of Samuel de Champlain,* 6 vols. (Toronto, 1922-1936), III, 52 ("sans aucune Religion, ny Loy, soit divine, Politique, ou Civille"), III, 74 (for chiefs). Subsequently, Recollet and especially Jesuit missionaries would articulate a subtler understanding of Wendat leadership and the existence of hereditary titles; but they nevertheless did not employ the terminology of kingship or lordship.

Lacking kings in their own society, Native peoples were also deemed ill equipped to appreciate the true nature of kingship and, most gallingly, the immense distance that separated a savage captain from His Most Christian Majesty. The Tupinambás at Maranhão simply used their word for "headman" to refer to Louis XIII; it was the same word they used for the leaders of the French expedition. Lescarbot similarly reported that the Mi'kmaq headman Membertou "considered himself the same as the king and all his lieutenants, saying often that he was his friend, brother, companion and equal, indicating this equality by means of the joining of the two fingers of his hand."[56] The Jesuit Pierre Biard, in Acadia a few years after Lescarbot, similarly mocked a Mi'kmaq headman's pretension to equality with the royal house of France. Twenty years later, the Recollet lay brother Gabriel Sagard wrote nearly the same thing about the principal headman of the Bear nation of the Wendat: "He had no little esteem for himself, that he did not wish to call himself brother and cousin of the king of France, and of the same quality, as the two index fingers of his hands which he showed us joined together."[57] What Lescarbot, Biard, and Sagard found noteworthy about these episodes was the fundamental incommensurability between headmen and kings. No one needed to state what to their readers would have been obvious: neither Membertou nor the head of the nation of the Bear was a king in the sense in which that word was understood in the early seventeenth century.

For a time, the survival of the Indian monarchy was ensured, not in the firsthand accounts produced by explorers, traders, missionaries, and colonial officials, but rather in the ludic culture of the period—in literary works like Du Hamel's *Acoubar* and the fictional narrative of the sieur Des Combes or in the court ballets that featured feathered dancers playing exotic charac-

56. D'Abbeville, *Histoire,* 58r (term for king), 67v (term for Razilly); Lescarbot, *Histoire de la Nouvelle-France,* ed. Tross, 568–569. Lescarbot came closest to invoking the model of kingship in relation to the Mi'kmaq when he wrote that Membertou, "a sous soy plusieurs familles, ausquelles il commande, non point avec tant d'authorité que fait nôtre Roy sur ses sujets, mais pour haranguer, donner conseil, marcher à la guerre, faire raison à celuy qui reçoit quelque injure, et choses semblables." See Lescarbot, *La Conversion des sauvages qui ont esté baptizés en la Nouvelle-France* (Paris, 1610), 20.

57. A Mi'kmaq headman, upon hearing that the young king of France (Louis XIII) was unmarried, mused aloud the possibility of arranging a match with his daughter (Pierre Biard to Reverend Father Christopher Baltazar, Provincial of France at Paris, June 10, 1611, in Thwaites, ed., *Jesuit Relations,* I, 175). See Gabriel Sagard, *Le grand voyage du pays des Hurons . . .* (1632), ed. Edwin Tross (Paris, 1865), 391.

ters like "King Atabalipa." But as a means of conceptualizing Native leadership in North America, its day had passed.[58]

In turn, however, the eclipse of the notion of Native American monarchy opened new avenues for future intercultural relations—in particular, the possibility of an alliance premised on principles of kinship rather than those of kingship. The French fur traders who began frequenting Northeastern North America in increasing numbers after 1580 had little need for indigenous kings: seeking to turn a profit and not to extend French sovereignty, they more easily embraced indigenous modes of diplomacy.[59] The trade pidgins that emerged in the Northeast in the last decades of the sixteenth century provide clear evidence of the use of kinship terms as forms of address in French-Native diplomacy, signaling no doubt the influence of the political culture of Native trading partners. Foremost among these was the term "brother." As a new era of official French colonization began after 1598 (the year of the Treaty of Vervins, ending a decade of Franco-Spanish warfare), colonial agents in the Saint Lawrence Valley appropriated the protodiplomatic vocabulary and trade rituals that an earlier generation of fur traders had opportunistically embraced in their dealings with

58. King Atabalipa figured in Daniel Rabel's *Ballet Royal du grand bal de la Douairière de Billebahaut,* given before the public at the Hôtel-de-Ville in Paris by order of Louis XIII. See Margaret M. McGowan, *L'art du ballet de cour en France, 1581–1643* (Paris, 1963), 149–186 (see plate 17 for Rabel's sketch for the character of King Atabalipa). See also François Moureau, "Les Amérindiens dans les ballets de Cour à l'époque de Champlain," in Raymonde Litalien et Denis Vaugeois, ed., *Champlain: La naissance de l'Amérique française* (Sillery, Quebec, 2004), 43–49.

59. The sudden expansion of the North American fur trade around 1580 was the result of a confluence of factors. Declining whale harvests in the Strait of Belle Isle and less-abundant cod stocks along the coastlines argued for a diversification of activities: trading for furs was one way of topping up the profits on expeditions that now spent longer periods at sea in search of increasingly scarce maritime resources. As well, the increasing demand for furs, especially beaver for hatmaking, in western Europe had led importers to turn to distant sources, first Russia and then Canada. A brief stoppage in the supply of Russian furs in the early 1580s probably accounts for the sudden boom in the Canada trade. But the French fur trade in Canada collapsed just as quickly before the decade was out, owing in part to the slowing of commerce during the wars of religion and the related conflict between France and Spain. After the Treaty of Vervins, however, French traders reappeared in the Saint Lawrence Valley, some with royal commissions according them a monopoly on beaver exports from "New France." See Bernard Allaire, *Pelleteries, manchons et chapeaux de castor: Les fourrures nord-américaines à Paris, 1500–1632* (Sillery, Quebec, 1999), chap. 2.

coastal Algonquian-speakers. Thus did the French become, in Acadia, the brothers of the Mi'kmaq and in the Saint Lawrence Valley, the brothers of their Innu, Algonquin, and, later, Wendat allies. For Lescarbot, Champlain, and their contemporaries, there were no Native American kings—only captains and, in the ritual and language of indigenous diplomacy, kin.[60]

60. Peter Cook, "Vivre comme frères: Le rôle du registre fraternel dans les premières alliances franco-amérindiennes au Canada (vers 1580–1650)," *Recherches amérindiennes au Québec,* XXX, no. 2 (2001), 55–65. By the 1670s, however, the metaphor of French fatherhood had largely replaced images of brotherhood in French-Native diplomatic rhetoric.

Philip D. Morgan

VIRGINIA'S OTHER PROTOTYPE

THE CARIBBEAN

Early Virginia's roots have been traced to many places. Ireland, for one, ranks as an important prototype for Virginia's development. Many of the Englishmen who were prominent in the Virginia adventure participated in plantations in Ireland, that "famous Island in the Virginian Sea," as one Elizabethan put it. Through years of apprenticeship in Ireland, the English developed the techniques and rhetoric of colonial conquest, which were later put to good use in the New World.[1] A less apparent forerunner is the Arctic, which, in Joyce Chaplin's view, witnessed the true "forgotten" ventures of colonial America. "Important precedents were set in the icy north": the English would apply their generally positive speculations about the region's natural productions, the Natives' technological abilities, and their own bodily adaptability to other parts of America.[2] The famous lost colony of Roa-

I wish to thank Ida Altman, Michael Guasco, Michael Jarvis, Joyce Lorimer, Richard Price, David Ransome, Benjamin Schmidt, Daviken Studnicki-Gizbert, and the participants of a joint McNeil Center / Washington Area Early American History Seminar for their assistance.

1. David Beers Quinn, "Sir Thomas Smith (1513–1577) and the Beginnings of English Colonial Theory," American Philosophical Society, *Proceedings,* LXXXIX (1945), 543–560; Quinn, *Raleigh and the British Empire* (London, 1947); Quinn, "Ireland and Sixteenth-Century European Expansion," *Historical Studies,* I (1958), 20–32; and Quinn, *The Elizabethans and the Irish* (Ithaca, N.Y., 1966), 122 (quote from Fynes Moryson, *An Itinerary* . . . [London, 1617], III, iii, 156). See also the work of Quinn's natural successor, Nicholas P. Canny, *The Elizabethan Conquest of Ireland: A Pattern Established, 1565–76* (New York, 1976); Canny, *Kingdom and Colony: Ireland in the Atlantic World, 1560–1800* (Baltimore, 1988); Canny, *Making Ireland British, 1580–1650* (Oxford, 2001); Canny, "Writing Early Modern History: Ireland, Britain, and the Wider World," *Historical Journal,* XLVI (2003), 723–747; and Canny and Karen Ordahl Kupperman, "The Scholarship and Legacy of David Beers Quinn, 1909–2002," *William and Mary Quarterly,* 3d Ser., LX (2003), 843–860.

2. Joyce E. Chaplin, *Subject Matter: Technology, the Body, and Science on the Anglo-*

noke is the most obvious starting point of Virginia's history; a false start, to be sure, but for Edmund Morgan, Roanoke was the "failure of a dream; a dream on the verge of becoming reality, a dream in which slavery and freedom were not yet married, a dream in which Protestant Britons liberated the oppressed people of the New World from the slavery that the papist Spaniard had imposed on them."[3] One final candidate in the search for Virginia's origins is the Atlantic island of Bermuda. In 1585, it first came to the attention of those bent on founding Virginia when, sailing near Bermuda, Sir Richard Grenville captured a richly laden ship, the profit of which more than paid for his outward trip to Roanoke. Bermuda's usefulness, situated at the crossroads of the Atlantic world in the age of sail, where it could be "a thorn in [the Spanish king's] West Indies side," was immediately apparent. The early history of Bermuda remained intertwined with Virginia's, and in key ways the two colonies influenced each other and followed parallel, if competitive, tracks.[4]

American Frontier, 1500–1676 (Cambridge, Mass., 2001), 43–74, esp. 43. Chaplin mentions Martin Frobisher's 1578 voyage, with its "astonishing 397 men on 15 ships—the largest fleet in the history of maritime exploration" (47). Just for comparison, eight years later, Frobisher was with Drake's expedition, involving 34 ships and 2,000 men, which launched the famous attack on Santo Domingo. As his biographer notes, this 1585 expedition "was a truly impressive force, the largest English naval force to pass into the Atlantic to date": see James McDermott, *Martin Frobisher: Elizabethan Privateer* (New Haven, Conn., 2001), 301.

3. Edmund S. Morgan, *American Slavery, American Freedom: The Ordeal of Colonial Virginia* (New York, 1975), 6; see also Karen Ordahl Kupperman, *Roanoke: The Abandoned Colony* (Savage, Md., 1984), and David Beers Quinn, *Set Fair for Roanoke: Voyages and Colonies, 1584–1606* (Chapel Hill, N.C., 1985).

4. Neil Kennedy, "Imagining Arcadia and Conceiving Bermuda: The Reinvigoration of English Colonization, 1609–1624," paper presented at "The Atlantic World and Virginia, 1550–1624," conference, Williamsburg, Va., Mar. 6, 2004; Henry Wilkinson, *The Adventurers of Bermuda: A History of the Island from Its Discovery until the Dissolution of the Somers Island Company in 1684* (London, 1933); Wesley Frank Craven, *An Introduction to the History of Bermuda* (Williamsburg, Va., 1938); Wilkinson, ed., "Spanish Intentions for Bermuda, 1603–1615," *Bermuda Historical Quarterly,* VII (1950), 50–89; David B. Quinn, "Bermuda in the Age of Exploration and Early Settlement," *Bermuda Journal of Archaeology and Maritime History,* I (1989), 1–23; Michael J. Jarvis, "'In the Eye of All Trade': Maritime Revolution and the Transformation of Bermudian Society, 1612–1800" (Ph.D. diss., College of William and Mary, 1998); and I am especially grateful to Michael for sending me his "Planting the Somer Islands: A Global Enterprise," the first chapter of his forthcoming book, from which I have benefited greatly. The most obvious ways in which early Bermuda differed from early Virginia were in its small size, lack of Indians, low mortality, healthiness, and

Virginian prototypes can therefore be found in many locales, but surprisingly nobody has ever argued that the Caribbean was fundamental to the shaping of early Virginia. Some scholars—notably David Beers Quinn and his students and admirers Kenneth R. Andrews, Joyce Lorimer, and Karen Ordahl Kupperman—have identified connections and anticipations, but even they have made no systematic case for the salience of the West Indies to mainland North America. The nearest Andrews came was this passing comment: "Virginia came to have much in common with the Caribbean plantations, though it also had from the start the character of a full-scale settlement." By implication, then, early Virginia was different from the earlier Caribbean experience: one saw planting by land, the other, raiding by sea; one experienced colonization, the other, plunder. South Carolina, as is well known, was the colony of a West Indian colony, but Virginia seems, as its name implies, to be one of a kind, sui generis, more a progenitor than an outgrowth. This short essay is not the place to provide an elaborate case for the centrality of the Caribbean to early Virginia; it can suggest only some areas where the Caribbean experience was influential. But my broader argument, if space permitted a full accounting, would be no less than that the Caribbean was crucial to Virginia's founding and early growth, far more so than the other candidates already mentioned. The Caribbean experience was not merely epiphenomenal, an aside, a distraction, but was rather foundational for understanding early Virginia.[5]

---

therefore its radically different demographic profile. For one comparison, see Virginia Bernhard, "Bermuda and Virginia in the Seventeenth Century: A Comparative View," *Journal of Social History,* XIX (1985-1986), 57-70.

5. For some of Quinn's voluminous output, see footnote 1, above, and more will be mentioned below. For Andrews's key works, see Andrews, ed., *English Privateering Voyages to the West Indies, 1588-1595,* Works Issued by the Hakluyt Society, 2d Ser., no. III (Cambridge, 1959); Andrews, *Elizabethan Privateering: English Privateering during the Spanish War, 1585-1603* (Cambridge, 1964); Andrews, ed., *The Last Voyage of Drake and Hawkins,* Works Issued by the Hakluyt Society, 2d Ser., no. 142 (Cambridge, 1972); Andrews, "Caribbean Rivalry and the Anglo-Spanish Peace of 1604," *History,* LIX (1974), 1-17; Andrews, "English Voyages to the Caribbean, 1596-1604: An Annotated List," *WMQ,* 3d Ser., XXXI (1974), 243-254; Andrews, *The Spanish Caribbean: Trade and Plunder, 1530-1630* (New Haven, Conn., 1978); Andrews, "The English in the Caribbean, 1560-1620," in Andrews, N. P. Canny, and P. E. H. Hair, eds., *The Westward Enterprise: English Activities in Ireland, the Atlantic, and America, 1480-1650* (Liverpool, 1978), 103-123; Andrews, "Beyond the Equinoctial: England and South America in the Sixteenth Century," *Journal of Imperial and Commonwealth History* (hereafter cited as *JICH*), X (1981), 4-24; Andrews, *Trade, Plunder, and Settlement: Maritime Enterprise and the Genesis of the British Empire, 1480-1630* (Cam-

To conceptualize the early Caribbean is to think primarily in terms of islands—ranging from the Bahamas in the north to Tobago in the south and from Cuba in the west to Barbados in the east—but the area must also encompass adjoining coastal mainland areas to form an entire circum-Caribbean region. Islands were sites par excellence of encounters and transformations; they entered into the popular imaginary as places of sexual innocence and unspoiled cultural authenticity. The image of paradisical islands first centered in the Caribbean Sea before moving westward into the South Seas. The enchanted island was a liminal place, an encounter zone. In the age of sail, insularity was often thought to be a feature of mainlands, not islands: continents could be remote and isolated, outposts of islands, rather than the reverse. In the Caribbean region, the coastlines of the adjoining South American, Central American, and North American mainlands were in some ways extensions of Antillean islands. Contemporaries certainly thought in terms of islands and continents. When Thomas Warner received his royal commission in 1625 to settle Saint Christopher, Nevis, Barbados, and Montserrat, it mentioned these "fower severall Islands in the maine Ocean towards the continent of America." Guiana and Panama were the two mainland places within the circum-Caribbean region that most interested the English in this period and might seem to have the most relevance for another mainland locale in Virginia. But Roanoke and Jamestown were, after all, islands, and littoral settlements had much in common with islands in these early years of discovery and settlement.[6]

---

bridge, 1984), 357 (quotation); and Andrews, "Elizabethan Privateering," in Joyce A. Youings, ed., *Raleigh in Exeter, 1985: Privateering and Colonisation in the Reign of Elizabeth I* (Exeter, 1985), 1-20. Andrews has done more than any scholar to document English voyages to the Caribbean in the period 1560-1620, although the period 1604-1624 has been much less well-analyzed. Karen Ordahl Kupperman, *Providence Island, 1630-1641: The Other Puritan Colony* (Cambridge, 1993), is a powerful argument for the importance of the Caribbean to North American history, but it is, of course, outside the period of my essay. Joyce Lorimer, ed., *English and Irish Settlement on the River Amazon, 1550-1645,* Works Issued by the Hakluyt Society, 2d Ser., no. 171 (London, 1989), and her "Failure of the English Guiana Ventures, 1595-1667 and James I's Foreign Policy," *JICH,* XXI (1993), 1-30, are important statements about the relevance and importance of Guiana to North American history, but obviously Guiana is only one part of the story. I am going to use the terms *Caribbean, Antilles,* and *West Indies* interchangeably. *West Indies,* or *the Indies,* was the common term in this period. Spaniards referred to the Caribbean Sea as the "*Mar del norte.*"

6. CO 1/3, nos. 44, 45, as cited in James A. Williamson, *The Caribbee Islands under the Proprietary Patents* (London, 1926), 27; see also Aucher Warner, *Sir Thomas Warner, Pioneer of the West Indies: A Chronicle of His Family* (London, 1933), 27, 28-33;

During the period 1550–1624, the complex region of islands and adjoining mainlands that made up the circum-Caribbean area constituted something of a laboratory where the English first gained experience of the New World, learned about its promise and perils, gained knowledge of seaborne routes, experimented with plants, encountered others, rationalized procedures of conquest, honed systems of exploitation, and, perhaps above all, defined an important strategic role for the region. All of these elements would have a bearing on the founding and early development of Virginia.

The English not only learned firsthand from their Caribbean experiences but secondhand from their Iberian forerunners. Since they were latecomers, and the early Caribbean was a Spanish lake, the English both followed and repudiated Iberian precedents. In his first voyage to the Caribbean in 1562, John Hawkins relied on an experienced pilot, Juan Martínez, who was from Cádiz and could speak English; and Simon Fernandes, a Portuguese pilot from Terceira in the Azores, who claimed to have been in the Spanish service and familiar with Caribbean and Atlantic waters, was vital to the Roanoke voyages. English pirates and privateers captured by the Spanish inevitably gleaned useful information before they were ransomed. Nevertheless, some English people first learned about hurricanes, canoes, parrots, pineapples, mosquitoes, the Caribs, and the layout and names of islands from their reading of the Spanish Indies. Cosmographer Richard Eden was important for translating *A Treatyse of the Newe India* in 1553 and Peter Martyr's *Decades of the Newe Worlde, or West India* two years later, thereby publicizing Iberian exploits. In 1578, John Frampton published a guide to the ports of the West Indies, translated from Martin Fernández de Enciso's text, which was part rutter (or sailing directions) and part primitive ethnography. According to this work, for example, the islands between Trinity (Trinidad) and Saint John were the home of the "*Cannibals,* a people which eateth mans flesh" and "go to the sea in small botes called *Canoas.*" Daniel Elfrith, who sailed throughout the Caribbean from 1607 onward and produced his own rutter in 1631, not only knew the Spanish names for all the ports and islands and how to navigate among them but also everyday Spanish words such as *ingenio* (sugar mill), *estancias* (ranches), and *hatos* (cattle

<hr />

John R. Gillis, *Islands of the Mind: How the Human Imagination Created the Atlantic World* (New York, 2004), esp. 2–3; Martin W. Lewis and Kären E. Wigen, *The Myth of Continents: A Critique of Metageography* (Berkeley, Calif., 1997). For a classic account of how the Caribbean region was viewed in its early days, see Carl Ortwin Sauer, *The Early Spanish Main* ([1966]; Berkeley, Calif., 1992).

farms). The English described and identified species of fish, animals, and plants that they had read about in Spanish accounts of the Indies. Thomas Harriot relied on Nicholas Monardes's *Joyfull Newes out of the New Founde Worlde,* a Spanish account that had been published in English in 1577, for many of his botanical identifications. Sir Walter Ralegh, the best approximation to a conquistador that England produced, had Spanish examples in mind even as he tried to distance himself from Iberian methods. His account of El Dorado relied on the local traditions of Spanish colonists in Margarita as well as the explorations of Governor Antonio de Berrío, whom he captured at Trinidad. As Neil Whitehead has shown, Ralegh's *Discoverie of . . . Guiana* synthesizes a wide range of ethnographic information drawn primarily from the Spanish. His prediction that he would "see in London a Contratation house *[Casa de Contratación]* of more receipt for *Guiana,* then there is nowe in civil [Seville] for the West indies" reveals the source of his inspiration. John Brown's *Marchants aviso,* an instruction book for Bristol merchants first published in 1589 and reprinted a number of times thereafter, revealed how well briefed English merchants were on the spices, sugar, salt, and dyes obtained in Iberian trade, much of which was acquired in the Indies. For the English, imitation was the sincerest form of flattery.[7]

7. Harry Kelsey, *Sir John Hawkins: Queen Elizabeth's Slave Trader* (New Haven, Conn., 2003), 14 (see also 29 for the mysterious Llerena on Hawkins's second Caribbean voyage, who seems to have been a Portuguese black man who became a Jamaican merchant and/or pilot; and see 83 for information derived from Bartolomé González, a Spanish pilot); Quinn, *Set Fair for Roanoke,* 6, 22–23, 55, 274–279, 281–282; John Parker, *Books to Build an Empire: A Bibliographical History of English Overseas Interests to 1620* (Amsterdam, 1965), 36–53, 86–87 (he notes, too, on 231, Edward Grimeston's important translation of José de Acosta's *Naturall and Morall Historie of the East and West Indies . . .* [1604]); Nicholas Monardes, *Joyfull Newes out of the New Founde Worlde,* trans. John Frampton, 2 vols. (London, 1577); John Frampton, trans., *A Briefe Description of the Portes, Creekes, Bayes, and Havens, of the Weast India . . .* (London, 1578), 7; Daniell Ellffryth, *Guide to the Caribbean, 1631,* ed. Stanley McCrory Pargellis and Ruth Lapham Butler (Chicago, 1945), 29 (see also Pargellis and Butler, eds., "Daniel Ellffryth's Guide to the Caribbean, 1631," *WMQ,* 3d Ser., I [1944], 273–316); for other Caribbean rutters, see Richard Hakluyt, *The Principal Navigations, Voyages, Traffiques, and Discoveries of the English Nation . . . ,* 12 vols. (1598–1600; rpt. Glasgow, 1903–1905), X, 280–305, 306–337; Quinn, *Raleigh and the British Empire,* 80, 165–166, 174, 178; Quinn, ed., *The Roanoke Voyages, 1584–1590 . . . ,* Works Issued by the Hakluyt Society, 2d Ser., 104–105 (London, 1955), I, 329; Sir Walter Ralegh, *The Discoverie of the Large, Rich, and Bewtiful Empyre of Guiana,* ed. Neil L. Whitehead (1596; rpt. Norman, Okla., 1997), 108–109, 198; David B. Quinn and A. N. Ryan, *England's Sea Empire, 1550–1642* (London, 1983), 38–39. For the complex response to

Likewise, early Virginians both emulated and rejected the Spanish Caribbean model. Repudiation primarily emphasized the Black Legend and Spanish atrocities. Thus, in 1610, an Irishman claimed that Virginia Indians knew "those who are in West India treat the Natives very badly and as slaves" and that "the English tell them that those people are Spaniards, who are very cruel and evil disposed." The English also expressed their revulsion at alleged Spanish avarice, particularly their thirst for gold. Anti-Spanish in its very marrow, the English model in Virginia yet drew on Spanish archetypes. The emulation was evident in the aristocratic orientation of the earliest adventurers, the harsh military lines along which the experiment was initially run, the expectation of easy wealth, the plans for sociable living (hence James City, Charles City, and the like), the reliance on Indian labor, and the hope of plundering Spanish territories. In 1611, Sir Thomas Dale, as David Konig points out, "requested that the government send convicted felons to Virginia; his inspiration for the plan, he was not ashamed to say, was the Spanish Empire—a model unlikely to inspire a punctilious observance of individual liberties." John Smith—who was part Hispanophobe, part Hispanophile himself—awarded John Martin, one of Jamestown's first councillors, the sobriquet "refining Captain Martin" because of his lust for gold. Son of a London goldsmith, Martin was a member of Drake's fleet that had terrorized the Spanish Caribbean in 1585–1586. He got his first taste for easy riches in the Antilles; and perhaps he also learned about the region's agricultural potential, for in 1614 he reportedly experimented with tobacco seed from Trinidad. Early Virginia owed much to the Spanish Caribbean.[8]

the Spanish model, see J. N. Hillgarth, *The Mirror of Spain, 1500–1700: The Formation of a Myth* (Ann Arbor, Mich., 2000), esp. 351–479; Barbara Fuchs, *Mimesis and Empire: The New World, Islam, and European Identities* (Cambridge, 2001), esp. 118–138; and Ralph Bauer, *The Cultural Geography of Colonial American Literatures: Empire, Travel, Modernity* (Cambridge, 2003), esp. 77–117.

8. "Report of Francis Maguel," 1610, in Alexander Brown, *The Genesis of the United States . . .* , 2 vols. (1890; rpt. New York, 1964), I, 396; Eric Griffin, "The Specter of Spain in John Smith's Colonial Writing," in Robert Appelbaum and John Wood Sweet, eds., *Envisioning an English Empire: Jamestown and the Making of the North Atlantic World* (Philadelphia, 2005), 111–134; David Thomas Konig, "'Dale's Laws' and the Non-Common Law Origins of Criminal Justice in Virginia," *American Journal of Legal History,* XXVI (1982), 366; James P. C. Southall, "Captain John Martin of Brandon on the James," *Virginia Magazine of History and Biography,* LIV (1946), 21–67; Samuel M. Bemiss, "John Martin, Ancient Adventurer," ibid., LXV (1957), 209–221; and Konig, "Colonization and the Common Law in Ireland and Virginia, 1569–1634," in James A. Henretta, Michael Kammen, and Stanley N. Katz, eds., *The Transforma-*

This derivation should not be surprising, for in the sixteenth and early seventeenth centuries, the Caribbean attracted more attention than any other part of the extra-European world. In one historian's words, the region "was the cockpit of international maritime rivalry, and for long the lands around it were thought of as the greatest treasure-house in the world." Admittedly, by the middle of the sixteenth century, Europeans did not view the islands themselves as especially or intrinsically valuable, eclipsed as they had been by Mexico and Peru: what little gold there was had been exhausted, and output of the next most valuable products—pearls and sugar —declined over time. Tobacco output did rise, and the trade in hides and other commodities (dyewoods, salt, ginger) was fairly steady, if not spectacular, but the strategic importance of the region through which enormous riches passed made it an ever-present concern for Spain and highly attractive to interlopers. The Antilles were the gateway to the heart of the Indies; the French accurately termed them "the islands located at the entrance of Peru." The Caribbean's strategic significance explains why Elizabethan and later Jacobean adventurers floated alluring schemes for establishing a base there: in 1577, Humphrey Gilbert advocated the occupation of Cuba and Española; nine years later, Drake captured Cartagena; in 1598, the earl of Cumberland seized Puerto Rico; and in 1617–1618, Ralegh attempted his ill-fated Guiana expedition. It also explains why, between 1550 and 1624, London merchants invested more money in expeditions to the Caribbean than in any other form of long-distance, overseas business. During the war years, 1585 to 1604, English privateers brought home £100,000 annually in sugar, hides, logwood, indigo, silver, gold, and pearls from the Spanish Main. English interest in the region was long-lived: the first documented English voyage to the Caribbean was in 1527. Between 1550 and 1624, the English launched at least three hundred separate voyages to the region, involving about nine hundred ships and perhaps about twenty-five thousand sailors.[9]

tion of Early American History: Society, Authority, and Ideology (New York, 1991), 70-92, esp. 84-91. See also William S. Maltby, The Black Legend in England: The Development of Anti-Spanish Sentiment, 1558-1660 (Durham, N.C., 1971).

9. Arthur Percival Newton, The European Nations in the West Indies, 1493-1688 (London, 1933), ix (quote); Anne Pérotin-Dumon, "French, English, and Dutch in the Lesser Antilles: From Privateering to Planting, c. 1550-1650," in Pieter C. Emmer and German Carrera Damas, eds., General History of the Caribbean, II, New Societies: The Caribbean in the Long Sixteenth Century (London, 1999), 114-158, esp. 116; Theodore K. Rabb, Enterprise and Empire: Merchant and Gentry Investment in the Expansion of England, 1575-1630 (Cambridge, Mass., 1967), 61-66. Perhaps the best general account of the sixteenth-century Caribbean's economy, which strikes me as

In addition, English ships trading to Brazil or venturing to the mainland — particularly, of course, to Roanoke and Virginia—usually passed through Caribbean waters. The Roanoke expedition of 1585 spent a month on Puerto Rico, where its members established a temporary but fortified base camp; Ralph Lane constructed elaborate sand entrenchments, the design of which bears close affinities with the later construction of Fort Raleigh, while his men loaded salt from two mounds that he had discovered. Because of the prevailing winds of the northeastern Atlantic, English ships had trouble making it across the Atlantic without running short of food and water. English galleons were "fast, handy, and weatherly" but "lacked stowage." Furthermore, most ships, particularly if they aimed at colonizing, were grossly overcrowded and unable to carry the necessary victuals, so that they had to stop for fresh water, food, and wood on the Caribbean islands. In the

---

rather more successful than usually depicted, is in Andrews, *Spanish Caribbean,* esp. 1–30, 54–80, but also see the essays by Horst Pietschmann, in Emmer and Damas, eds., *General History of the Caribbean,* II, 1–28, 79–113, and, of course, the work of Pierre Chaunu, Enrique Otte, and others, all cited therein; F. A. Kirkpatrick, "The First Recorded English Voyage to the West Indies," *English Historical Review,* XX (1905), 115–124. For a 1540 voyage that saw action in the West Indies, see R. C. Marsden, "Voyage of the 'Barbara,' of London, to Brazil in 1540," *English Historical Review,* XXIV (1909), 96–100, esp. 99; and also Marsden, ed., "Voyage of the Barbara to Brazil, Anno 1540," in Sir John Knox Laughton, ed., *The Naval Miscellany,* II (London, 1912), 1–66, esp. 31–51. The English were latecomers to the Caribbean; the Portuguese seemingly made inroads by 1514 and the French perhaps even earlier. See Roland D. Hussey, "Spanish Reaction to Foreign Aggression in the Caribbean to about 1680," *Hispanic American Historical Review* (hereafter cited as *HAHR*), IX (1929), 286–302; but cf. Paul E. Hoffman, *The Spanish Crown and the Defense of the Caribbean, 1535–1585: Precedent, Patrimonialism, and Royal Parsimony* (Baton Rouge, 1980). Furthermore, the Dutch invasion of the Caribbean, at times, dwarfed the English: from 1599–1605, about 800 Dutch ships, most of them making for the Punta de Araya salt pan, entered the region. See Engel Sluiter, "Dutch-Spanish Rivalry in the Caribbean Area, 1594–1609," *HAHR,* XXVIII (1948), 165–196. The estimate of the number of English expeditions, ships, and men is based on Andrews, *Elizabethan Privateering,* 175; Andrews, *Spanish Caribbean,* 156–157; and Andrews, *Trade, Plunder, and Settlement,* 129, 283. Between 1562–1603, there were 94 known expeditions, involving 280 ships; I have more than doubled this number, based on Andrews's belief that such was easily the case. For 1604–1624, I estimate about 80–100 expeditions, which is pure speculation. In the early seventeenth century, merchant ships in Atlantic waters averaged 25 men; privateering ventures were more heavily manned, so the estimated number of sailors is conservative. When I say the Caribbean attracted more attention than most other overseas regions, I don't mean to suggest that this activity impinged all that much on the consciousness of even educated English people in this period; it obviously did not.

spring of 1607, Captain John Smith and company on the *Susan Constant, Godspeed,* and *Discovery* spent three weeks in the islands, recuperating, bathing, hunting, and fishing; they boiled pork in a heated pool in Guadeloupe, and on Nevis and the Virgin Islands they "daily feasted" on tortoises, pelicans, parrots, fishes, and caimans (crocodile-like animals). Smith had particular reason to remember Nevis, because there, his enemies erected a gallows intended for him, but, as he wryly noted, he "could not be perswaded to use" it. In 1620, an observer in Virginia noted that the *Bona Nova's* recently arrived passengers were "lusty and in good health. They came by way of the west Indyes, which passage at that season doth much to refreshe the people." By then, fresh citrus fruit was a well-known remedy for scurvy. In 1623, ten passengers on a Virginia-bound ship decided onboard conditions were so bad, and island life so attractive, that they remained on Saint Vincent. In the mid-1620s, Anthony Hilton, en route to Virginia, stopped at Saint Christopher. Impressed by the island's potential, he persuaded some Irish gentlemen, importers of Virginia tobacco, to invest in a tobacco-planting expedition. He returned to establish the first plantation on the windward side of the island. The Europeans' first experience of the Americas was usually Caribbean in flavor; and many of them were seduced.[10]

10. For a 1621 attack on a ship that was en route to Virginia, see "A Desperat Sea-Fight betwixte Two Spanish Men of Warre, and a Small English Ship, at the Ile of Dominica, Going to Virginia, by Capitaine Anthony Chester," in Lyon Gardiner Tyler, ed., *Narratives of Early Virginia: 1606–1625* (New York, 1907), 340–344. For ships, see N. A. M. Rodger, "Guns and Sails in the First Phase of English Colonization, 1500–1650," in Nicholas P. Canny, ed., *Oxford History of the British Empire,* I, *The Origins of Empire: British Overseas Enterprise to the Close of the Seventeenth Century* (Oxford, 1998), 79–98, esp. 88, 97; Rodger, *The Safeguard of the Sea: A Naval History of Britain,* I, *660–1649* (London, 1997), 218. For layovers in the Caribbean of early Virginia ships, see Susan E. Hillier, "The Trade of the Virginia Colony, 1606 to 1660" (Ph.D. diss., University of Liverpool, 1971), 105–107. The average number of days for seventeen ships that reached Virginia via the West Indian route (1606–1660) was 110. For the 1607 account, see "Observations by Master George Percy, 1607," in Tyler, ed., *Narratives of Early Virginia,* 6–7; Philip L. Barbour, ed., *The Complete Works of Captain John Smith (1580–1631),* 3 vols. (Chapel Hill, N.C., 1986), I, 205, II, 137, 139 n. 2, III, 236 (in 1598, John Ley, coming back from Guiana, took on wood and water at an island near Nevis, where he also "founde two extreame hot springes, which did boyle a peece of salt beef in a quarter of an houre": Lorimer, ed., *English and Irish Settlement,* 135). For the 1620 and 1623 examples, see Susan Myra Kingsbury, ed., *The Records of the Virginia Company of London,* 4 vols. (Washington, D.C., 1906–1935), III, 245, IV, 245; narrative by John Hilton, brother of Anthony, Egerton MSS, 2395, fols. 503–

An "Edenic island discourse" arose to describe the Caribbean that might later be transposed to or contrasted with other places. Antillean visitors generally described scenes of luminous simplicity and serene beauty. In 1607, en route to Virginia, George Percy described Dominica as "a very faire Iland, the Trees full of sweet and good smels." In the interior of Nevis, he "came into a most pleasant Garden, being a hundred paces square on every side, having many Cotton-trees growing in it with abundance of Cotton-wooll, and many *Guiacum* trees. Wee saw the goodliest tall trees growing so thicke about the Garden, as though they had been set by Art, which made us marvell very much to see it." On one of the Virgin Islands, his troop "cut the Barkes of certaine Trees which tasted much like Cinnamon . . . This iland in some places hath very good ground, straight and tall Timber." On the island of Monica, near Mona, fowl flew overhead "as thicke as drops of Hale," making such a noise that the men could not "heare one another speake." Fertility and natural abundance were the standard tropes; and traveling through the region was a sensory experience. Sir Walter Ralegh highlighted Guiana's wide plains, lush grass, groves of trees set apart "as if they had been by all the art and labour in the world so made of purpose," and deer feeding by the water's edge "as if they had beene used to a keepers call." He "never saw a more beawtifull countrey, nor more lively prospectes," the birds "singing on every tree with a thousand several tunes, cranes and herons of white, crimson, and carnation" perched by river banks; the air was "fresh," and "every stone" promised gold or silver. Often tending to think of the Caribbean and Chesapeake as one single climatic hot zone, early travelers thought the heat generated an abundance of both crops and precious stones. Writing after Virginia had been founded, however, Robert Harcourt thought Guiana a far more favorable environment than its northern counterpart. Virginia had "a sharpe Winter," whereas Guiana "is blest with a perpetuall Summer, and a perpetuall Spring." As a result, he thought, provi-

---

507, British Library (hereafter cited as BL), as cited in Williamson, *Caribbee Islands,* 66. For another account of a part-Caribbean trip obsessed in finding provisions, see Sir William Foster, ed., *The Voyages of Sir James Lancaster to Brazil and the East Indies, 1591–1603,* Works Issued by the Hakluyt Society, 2d Ser., no. 85 (London, 1940), 17–21, 25–30. Over time, more ships took a direct, shorter route (also entirely within the temperate zone) via Bermuda rather than through the West Indies, but the Caribbean route was most popular in the early seventeenth century. In 1611, Thomas Dale touted the West Indian route, saying it was the "most speedie" (not true) and "most convenient for our peoples refreshing and preserving of our Cattle" (which probably was true, although Bermuda had some of these advantages): Brown, *Genesis of the United States,* I, 488–494.

sions and products (cotton, dyes, gums, feathers, woods, precious stones, wax, honey, and tobacco) would be more abundant in Guiana than in Virginia.[11]

The pastoral aesthetic was complicated, even subverted, when Englishmen reflected on the healthiness of the Caribbean region. True, a Caribbean island-as-way station had restorative powers. Thus Nevis, Virginia-bound George Percy noted, was "so convenient for our men to avoid diseases which will breed in so long a Voyage," and he mentioned encamping there six days. Yet on a six-mile march into the interior of Mona, he later reported, many men fainted, and "Edward Brookes Gentleman" died in "great extreamitie" because his "fat melted within him by the great heate and drought of the Countrey"—presumably heatstroke. Sir Thomas Gates's wife died in the West Indies en route to Virginia. Those Englishmen who spent any time in the Caribbean soon recognized its unhealthiness. In 1585, about one hundred of Drake's men died of disease at Cartagena. With an ill contingent of men, Drake first postponed an attack on Panama and then decided to abandon the Caribbean altogether. Ten years later, both Hawkins and Drake died in the Caribbean: Hawkins became ill immediately after reaching Guadeloupe, perhaps from the water, and expired off Puerto Rico; bloody dysentery claimed Drake off Portobello. On this 1595 expedition, Thomas Maynard described the Panama isthmus as "the sickliest place of the Indies," revealing that the English were already aware of relative morbidity levels. Indians provided some of this information. Thus, in Guiana, an Indian informant told Robert Harcourt that the Englishman's present encampment on the Wiapoco River was "very unhealthful" and that his men "would there bee subject to sicknesse, and die"; the Indian suggested moving to his territory, which, by contrast, had "wholsome ayre" and was "healthfull." Guiana, in fact, as Joyce Lorimer has noted, might well have been healthier than Virginia at first, because yellow fever had not yet established itself, nor were the lower reaches of rivers significantly malarial. The Caribbean's promise and peril gradually became understood.[12]

11. Richard H. Grove, *Green Imperialism: Colonial Expansion, Tropical Island Edens, and the Origins of Environmentalism, 1600-1860* (Cambridge, 1995), 5, 24-42; "Observations by Master George Percy, 1607," in Tyler, ed., *Narratives of Early Virginia,* 5, 7, 8, 9; Ralegh, *Discoverie of Guiana,* ed. Whitehead, 163, 176; Robert Harcourt, *A Relation of a Voyage to Guiana . . . 1613,* ed. Sir C. Alexander Harris, Works Issued by the Hakluyt Society, 2d Ser., no. 60 (London, 1928), 64.

12. "Observations by Master George Percy, 1607," in Tyler, ed., *Narratives of Early Virginia,* 7-8; John Chamberlain to Sir Dudley Carleton, Dec. 18, 1611, in Karen Ordahl Kupperman, John C. Appleby, and Mandy Banton, eds., *Calendar of State Papers,*

The English also became aware of another quintessential Caribbean danger: the hurricane, which, although it was deadliest in the islands, could also move up the eastern seaboard, reaching Virginia on occasion. In July 1568, Sir John Hawkins left Cartagena in hopes that he had "escaped the time of their stormes . . . which they call Furicanos," but an "extreme storme" proved him wrong. In June 1586, Sir Francis Drake's offer to Ralph Lane of the use of his ship *Francis,* when he was moored off Roanoke Island, was cut short when a hurricane blew the fleet from its anchorage. One account described hailstones "as Bigge as Hennes egges" and "greate Spowtes at the seas as thoughe heaven and [earth] woulde have mett." In 1595, Drake saw a transformed Panama from the one he had seen more than twenty years earlier. He "never thought any place could bee so changed, as it were from a delitious and pleasant arbour, into a wast and desarte wildernesse, besides the variablenes of the winde and weather so stormie and blusterous as hee never saw it before." The famous shipwreck of the *Sea-Venture,* en route to Virginia in 1609, inspired Shakespeare to name his final play for the storm, although he chose a more familiar term than the word "hurricane" (despite the latter term's appearance in two of his earlier plays). William Strachey wrote a legendary firsthand account describing how the "swelling and roaring . . . did beat all light from Heaven; which, like an hell of darkness, turned black upon us, so much the more fuller of horror as in such cases horror and fear use to overrun the troubled and overmastered sense of all." Gabriel Archer, in the same fleet, described "a most terrible and vehement storme, which was a taile of the West Indian Horacano; this tempest seperated all our Fleet one from another, and it was so violent that men could scarce stand upon the Deckes, neither could any man heare another speake." In 1624, the first permanent English colonists in the West Indies had no sooner built a small fort and a house and planted their first tobacco crop on Saint Christopher when "upon the nineteenth of September came a Hericano and blew it away." Two years later—on September 4—"came such a Hericano, as blew downe all our houses, Tobacco, and two Drums into the aire we know not

Colonial Series (hereafter cited as *CSP,* Col.), *North America and the West Indies, 1574-1739,* I, *1574-1660,* CD-ROM (London, 2000), 12; Quinn and Ryan, *England's Sea Empire,* 89-90; Kelsey, *Sir John Hawkins,* 260-263; Kelsey, *Sir Francis Drake: The Queen's Pirate* (New Haven, Conn., 1998), 389; Thomas Maynarde's narrative, in Andrews, ed., *Last Voyage of Drake and Hawkins,* 100; Harcourt, *Relation of a Voyage to Guiana,* ed. Harris, 81; Joyce Lorimer, "The Failure of the English Guiana Ventures, 1595-1667, and James I's Foreign Policy," *JICH,* XXI (1993), 8. See Karen Ordahl Kupperman, "Fear of Hot Climates in the Anglo-American Colonial Experience," *WMQ,* 3d Ser., XLI (1984), 213-240.

whither, drove two ships on shore." The first appearance of the word "hurricane" in an English text seems to have been in 1555, when Richard Eden translated Columbus's and other Spanish accounts, but the term gained wider currency as sailors and later colonists encountered the phenomenon on what they gradually came to realize was a predictable basis.[13]

Exposure to some of the Caribbean's creatures also tended to heighten, rather than alleviate, fears. In 1585, when in the Caribbean, John White drew pictures of "a dangerous byting flye," threatening scorpions, and an open-mouthed, sharp-toothed "Allagatto." The anonymous author and illustrator of the "Histoire Naturelle des Indes," otherwise known as "The Drake Manuscript," created in the early 1590s, tended to be alarmist: the shark was "very vicious in the sea," tearing out a leg or arm of any sailor who entered the water; the "Egouge" was "a very dangerous fish," which, when "caught in a net it jumps at people's eyes"; the manta ray ate black pearl divers; a white snake was "very poisonous and dangerous"; a centipede was so poisonous that its victims died within twenty-four hours; mosquitoes were "small flies which are so small that one cannot see them, [and] are very dangerous. When there is no wind and the weather is calm, they come in droves attacking people, stinging them in such a manner that one would take them for lepers." In 1572, an English merchant familiar with Vera Cruz reported that "this town is inclined to many kinde of diseases, by reason of the great heat, and a certeine gnat or flie which they call a musquito, which

13. Clements Markham, ed., *The Hawkins Voyages during the Reigns of Henry VIII, Queen Elizabeth, and James I,* Works Issued by the Hakluyt Society, 1st Ser., no. 57 (London, 1878), 73; Kelsey, *Sir Francis Drake,* 277; Mary Frear Keeler, ed., *Sir Francis Drake's West Indian Voyage, 1585–1586,* Works Issued by the Hakluyt Society, 2d Ser., no. 148 (London, 1981), 210, 272–274; Andrews, ed., *Last Voyage of Drake and Hawkins,* 101; William Strachey, *A True Reportory of the Wreck and Redemption of Sir Thomas Gates, Knight, upon and from the Islands of the Bermudas* (London, 1625), in Louis B. Wright, ed., *A Voyage to Virginia in 1609* (Charlottesville, Va., 1964), 4; "August 31, 1609: Gabriel Archer's Account of His Voyage with the Virginia Fleet," in David B. Quinn, ed., *New American World: A Documentary History of North America to 1612,* 5 vols. (New York, 1979), V, 286; Barbour, ed., *Works of Smith,* III, 228–229. For the best account of this phenomenon, see Matthew Mulcahy, *Hurricanes and Society in the British Greater Caribbean, 1624–1783* (Baltimore, 2005), who reports that "hurricano" appears in both *King Lear* and *Troilus and Cressida.* He also notes that the first English text to provide readers with an extended description of a hurricane was John Taylor's *Newes and Strange Newes from St. Christophers . . .* (London, 1638). The first comparable Chesapeake account is *Strange Newes from Virginia, Being a True Relation of a Great Tempest in Virginia . . .* (London, 1667), for which information I am indebted to Matt Mulcahy.

biteth both men and women in their sleepe . . . [and] doth most follow such as are newly come into the country. Many there are that die of this annoyance." A generation later, an Englishman in Guiana concurred, describing the place as "full of Muskitas, which is a small Flie, which much offends a stranger comming newly into the Countrey." Exposure to the Caribbean prepared the visitor for the challenges posed by the Chesapeake region.[14]

The most direct way in which the Caribbean was critical to Virginia's founding concerned personnel. Just as many of the Virginia pioneers had experienced Ireland, Roanoke, or Bermuda, perhaps as many, or more, had a history, and a longer one at that, in the West Indies. Sir Walter Ralegh, Virginia's sponsor, went to the Caribbean (Guiana and Trinidad) twice, in 1595 and 1617–1618; he never once stepped foot in either Roanoke or Virginia. From 1590—when, at the age of thirty, he made his first West Indian voyage—to 1605, Christopher Newport voyaged at least thirteen times to the Caribbean Sea. His first voyage as captain was memorable, for off the northwest coast of Cuba he lost his right arm. In 1592, he tried to sell slaves at Puerto Rico; two years later, he returned with prizes of hides and blockwood. In 1598, he secured hides, ginger, pepper, tobacco, and logwood; four years later, he spent time on Nevis, building two small vessels to assist him in raiding Caribbean harbors; and in 1605, he returned to England with two young crocodiles (probably caimans) and a wild boar from Española. Perhaps no other English captain knew the Caribbean Sea as well. Thus, when the Virginia Company picked him, at age forty-six, to command its first expedition in 1606, they chose wisely. This veteran of Atlantic and West Indian waters, who commanded ships to the fledgling colony almost every year in its first six years, was crucial in securing England's toehold on the Chesapeake Bay. Another founding member of the Virginia Company, William Parker, was an old West Indian hand who had ventured to the region at least six times. In 1594, he engineered a major coup by capturing Puerto de Caballos in Honduras, a feat he repeated the following year, and he also obtained a valuable Spanish rutter of the West Indies for Ralegh. Sir George Somers and Amyas Preston, who made an important voyage together to the West Indies in 1595, both played a part in the foundation of Virginia.[15]

14. Paul Hulton and David Beers Quinn, eds., *The American Drawings of John White, 1577–1590, with Drawings of European and Oriental Subjects*, 2 vols. (London, 1964), II, plates 6, 9; Ruth S. Kraemer, trans., *Histoire Naturelle des Indes: The Drake Manuscript in the Pierpont Morgan Library* (New York, 1996), fols. 38, 41v, 47, 54, 58, 72, pp. 258–261; Hakluyt, *Principal Navigations*, IX, 379; Lorimer, ed., *English and Irish Settlement*, 143.

15. Andrews, *Elizabethan Privateering*, 86, 93; Andrews, "Christopher Newport of

Englishmen gained an intimate knowledge of Atlantic waters and routes by venturing to the Caribbean. In this way, English ships proved their capacity for long voyages, and sailors built up a reservoir of experience and technical know-how, which would be vital to ships plying their way up the North American coast. The lateness at which the English gained their knowledge is striking. As N. A. M. Rodger notes, "In 1558 there was probably not one Englishman capable unaided of navigating a ship to the West Indies, and in 1568, only one." Thereafter, they made up for lost time. In 1611, an English pilot even served the king of Spain in the West Indies. Word-of-mouth information must have spread among the maritime community before becoming inscribed on charts and rutters. Thomas Harriot had a collection of twenty-two rutters for "Brazil and the West Indies," dated 1590, in his possession. John White was hardly alone in sketching profiles of the Caribbean islands as viewed from ship. Daniel Elfrith, who provided his own guide for navigation throughout the Caribbean, warned of Indians on Dominica, recommended the fresh water at Martinique, advised loading salt at the great salt pan on the eastern end of Tortuga, and knew where the pearl boats left Margarita. He was conversant with scores of ports, although his "favorite stretch of coast was the southern one of eastern Santo Domingo [Española] which he describes as if he were completely at home there." He lived in Bermuda for eight years in the 1620s, visited Virginia at least twice in 1617 and in 1619, probably brought Africans into the colony, and later was actively involved in the Providence Island experiment. In 1660, a sixty-year-old Captain Simon Gordan recalled "about 40 yeares past sayleing in the West Indias" and landing upon "the Island now called the Barbadas, where he with others did hunt and take Hoggs without discovery or hearing of any people uppon the said Island." Surely Gordan did not wait forty years to tell his account, and news of Barbadian opportunities may help explain why that island was first settled in 1627.[16]

Limehouse, Mariner," *WMQ,* 3d Ser., XI (1954), 28–41; Andrews, *Spanish Caribbean,* 162. See also David B. Quinn, "Christopher Newport in 1590," *North Carolina Historical Review,* XXIX (1952), 305–316.

16. Rodger, *Safeguard of the Sea,* I, 244; Sir John Digbye to Lord Treasurer Salisbury, Nov. 4, 1611, item 55, IX (addendum 1574-1677), in Kupperman, Appleby, and Banton, eds., *CSP, Col.,* I, 41–42; E. G. R. Taylor, *Late Tudor and Early Stuart Geography, 1583-1650* (London, 1934), 201, no. 350; John W. Shirley, *Thomas Harriot: A Biography* (Oxford, 1983), 83–85, 227–229; Hulton and Quinn, eds., *American Drawings of John White,* II, plate 2; Ellffryth, *Guide to the Caribbean,* 5, 9, 19; Michael Jarvis and Jeroen van Driel, "The Vingboons Chart of the James River, Virginia, circa 1617," *WMQ,* 3d Ser., LIV (1997), 377–394, esp. 392–394; Kupperman, *Providence Island,*

Just as there was considerable overlap in the personnel connecting Caribbean and Chesapeake, so the same could be said of the motives driving the earliest Atlantic adventurers. In the early Caribbean, pillage was the dominant goal, although the line between trade and plunder was often difficult to draw. Raiding elided into trading, as with the *Elizabeth and Cleeve,* which, after taking various prizes in 1603, exchanged much of the cargoes for hides and *cassia fistula* at Guanahibes on Española. Five years earlier, the *Anne Frances* set sail with letters of reprisal but with an even more mundane task in prospect: on board were steel saws, and the crew cut "six score tun" of *lignum vitae* on Nevis. For the most part, this was a militant, bellicose, acquisitive imperialism. As N. A. M. Rodger puts it, "If empire, as Francis Xavier said, was little more than 'to conjugate the verb to rob in all its moods and tenses,' the English were the purest of imperialists." Their primary goal was predatory. Although the aim grew more muted over time (especially after James I made peace with Spain), it hardly disappeared. Roanoke was supposed to provide a base for strikes against the Spanish treasure fleets, and a strong element in early Virginia's and Bermuda's founding was to continue depredations on the Spanish Indies.[17]

Most investors in the Virginia Company, it is true, looked toward legitimate profits and sent settlers to produce whatever was useful. But Virginia was not initially meant to be an agricultural settlement. Why, otherwise, send military adventurers, gentlemen, and craftsmen rather than farmers? Why govern for so long through a military regime? The initial adventurers expected to get food not by dint of their own labor but, like their Elizabe-

---

25-28, 39-41, 72, 190, 211; CO 1/14, no. 25, as cited in Williamson, *Caribbee Islands,* 20. See also D. W. Waters, "The Art of Navigation in the Age of Drake," in Andrews, ed., *Last Voyage of Drake and Hawkins,* 259-265; and Waters, *The Art of Navigation in England in Elizabethan and Early Stuart Times* (London, 1958).

17. Andrews, "English Voyages to the Caribbean," *WMQ,* 3d Ser., XXXI (1974), 248, 253-254; Rodger, "Guns and Sails," in Canny, ed., *Oxford History of the British Empire,* I, 97; Andrews, "Elizabethan Privateering," in Youings, ed., *Raleigh in Exeter,* esp.3; Carole Shammas, "English Commercial Development and American Colonization, 1560-1620," in Andrews, Canny, and Hair, eds., *Westward Enterprise,* 151-174; Andrews, *Trade, Plunder, and Settlement,* 5, 9; John C. Appleby, "War, Politics, and Colonization, 1558-1625," in Canny, ed., *Oxford History of the British Empire,* I, 55-78. For more on early-seventeenth-century developments, see three key articles: David B. Quinn, "James I and the Beginnings of Empire in America," *JICH,* II (1974), 135-152; Appleby, "An Association for the West Indies? English Plans for a West India Company, 1621-29," ibid., XV (1987), 213-241; and Lorimer, "Failure of the English Guiana Ventures," ibid., XXI (1993), 1-30.

than counterparts in Ireland and the Spanish in the Caribbean, from the local population. All earlier trading company factories established in the midst of potentially hostile and numerically superior populations operated as military and commercial organizations rather than as agricultural societies. Early Virginia was in line with its predecessors. Admittedly, the Virginia Company was not wholly fixated on quick riches and was willing to settle for prosaic staples. Yet there, again, were Caribbean precedents and parallels: Charles Leigh's small settlement along the Wiapoco River in Guiana, which lasted from 1604-1606, showed serious interest in raising export crops such as flax, cotton, sugar, and tobacco; Robert Harcourt, who went out to Guiana in 1609 and whose small colony remained in being for three years, hoped sugar would be his mainstay, along with cotton, flax, and tobacco; and, also in 1609, an English syndicate sought to colonize the island of Grenada so as to produce tobacco.[18]

Even Virginia's name had Caribbean associations. In Western discourse about exploration, it was conventional to regard land as female, virginal. In 1493, Columbus had given the name "Virgin Islands" to a group of small islands in the northern part of the Antillean chain. The trope of a virgin land, unspoiled, intact, potentially fertile, waiting to be cultivated, was commonplace. In 1585, Sir Walter Ralegh named Roanoke "Virginia" in homage to his queen. Ten years later, on Trinidad, he reported telling five local Indian chieftains that he "was the servant of a Queene, who was the great *Casique* of the north, and a virgin," thereby proclaiming her virtue. In his famous concluding passage to his description of Guiana, he employed the metaphor of virginity to describe "a Contrey that hath yet her Maydenhead, never sackt, turned, nor wrought, the face of the earth hath not been torne, nor the vertue and salt of the soyle spent by manurance. . . ." Here is a "landscape of wish-fulfillment," in part a subversion of the "ethic of empire," as

18. W. Frank Craven, "The Earl of Warwick: A Speculator in Piracy," *HAHR,* X (1930), 457-479, esp. 457-465; Jack P. Greene, *Pursuits of Happiness: The Social Development of Early Modern British Colonies and the Formation of American Culture* (Chapel Hill, N.C., 1988), 8-9; James A. Williamson, *English Colonies in Guiana and on the Amazon, 1604-1668* (Oxford, 1923), 29-41; Lorimer, ed., *English and Irish Settlement,* 137-138; Andrews, *Spanish Caribbean,* 231, 240-242; Harcourt, *Relation of a Voyage to Guiana,* ed. Harris; Scott's "Description of Granada," in Sloane MSS, 3662, fols. 53b-49b, BL, as cited in Williamson, *Caribbee Islands,* 18-19; Carl Bridenbaugh and Roberta Bridenbaugh, *No Peace beyond the Line: The English in the Caribbean, 1624-1690* (New York, 1972), 9-24; G. V. Scammell, "'A Very Profitable and Advantageous Trade': British Smuggling in the Iberian Americas circa 1500-1750," *Itinerario,* XXIV, nos. 3-4 (2000), 135-172.

Stephen Greenblatt notes, even as it was an invitation to invade. At once a virgin land, passively female, Guiana would pass into masculine hands, which could be expected to exploit and despoil—a metaphorical rape of the land. As Greenblatt intuits, "a note of regret and dread" runs "counter to the dominant assertion" of conquest. Guiana's future, as Ralegh predicted it, would become Virginia's, although Samuel Purchas preferred a marital metaphor when he said that Virginia's "lovely lookes" were "worth the wooing and loves of the best Husband."[19]

The Caribbean was the source for many of the products with which the earliest settlers experimented on the North American mainland. When asked "what they were looking for in these islands," the first documented English ship's company in the Caribbean mentioned brazilwood. In 1585, Sir Richard Grenville brought roots of bananas, pineapple, mammee apples, and sugarcane to Roanoke Island. John White drew detailed pictures of many of these plants as he ventured through Caribbean waters. In the 1590s, Sir Walter Ralegh claimed to have discovered a red dye, presumably cochineal, in Guiana, and there were similar (as it happened, false) hopes of finding this valuable dyestuff in Virginia. In 1607, Gabriel Archer noted, "From the west Indies we brought a certain delicious fruite called a pina . . . this we rudely and carelessly sett in our mould, which fostereth it and keepes it greene, and to what Issue it may come I know not, our west Indy plantes of orenges and Cotten trees thrive well. . . . So the thing we crave is some skil-

19. Ralegh, *Discoverie of Guiana,* ed. Whitehead, 133–134, 196; Peter Hulme, *Colonial Encounters: Europe and the Native Caribbean, 1492–1797* (London, 1986), 136–173; Stephen J. Greenblatt, *Sir Walter Ralegh: The Renaissance Man and His Roles* (New Haven, Conn., 1973), 112; Philippa Berry, *Of Chastity and Power: Elizabethan Literature and the Unmarried Queen* (London, 1989), 148–149; John N. King, "Queen Elizabeth I: Representations of the Virgin Queen," *Renaissance Quarterly,* XLVII (1990), 30–74; Louis Montrose, "The Work of Gender in the Discourse of Discovery," *Representations,* XXXIII (1991), 1–41, rpt. in Stephen Greenblatt, ed., *New World Encounters* (Berkeley, Calif., 1993), 177–217; Jeffrey Knapp, *An Empire Nowhere: England, America, and Literature from "Utopia" to "The Tempest"* (Berkeley, Calif., 1992), 11–17, 149–158, 175–178, 189–204; Helen Hackett, *Virgin Mother, Maiden Queen: Elizabeth I and the Cult of the Virgin Mary* (New York, 1995); Stephen Orgel, "Gendering the Crown," in Margreta de Grazia, Maureen Quilligan, and Peter Stallybrass, eds., *Subject and Object in Renaissance Culture* (Cambridge, 1996), 133–165; Emi Hamana, "The Wonder of the Virgin Queen: Through Early Colonial Discourse on Virginia," in Yasunari Takahashi, ed., *Hot Questrists after the English Renaissance: Essays on Shakespeare and His Contemporaries* (New York, 2000), 37–52; Samuel Purchas, *Hakluytus Posthumus; or, Purchas His Pilgrimes . . . ,* 20 vols. (1625; rpt. Glasgow, 1905–1907), XIX, 242.

full man to husband sett plant and dresse vynes, sugar canes, olives rapes hemp flax, lycoris pruyns, currents raysons, and all such thinges, as the North Tropick of the world affordes." In 1610, Sir George Somers brought pumpkins, later identified as of the "west Indie kind," from Virginia into Bermuda. When Daniel Tucker was governor of Bermuda, he dispatched a ship to the West Indies to trade with "natives" for livestock, corn, and tropical plants. The ship returned in 1616 with plantains, sugarcane, figs, pineapples, and probably manioc, which Tucker cultivated on public lands. Five years later, a Bermudian ship supplied the white potato, the fig, peppers, prickly pears, papayas, "vines, oranges, lemons, sugar cane, cassava root, pine[apples], plantains . . . and sundry other West India fruits" to Virginia. In turn, Caribbean Indians and / or blacks helped Bermudians convert manioc into cassava, build crawls (ponds for the collection of fish), and make hammocks, mats, and baskets, plaited or woven from palmetto leaves. The Caribbean and its peoples, then, were a major source of plants and products for both Virginia and her sister colony, Bermuda.[20]

Within a decade after its initial settlement, Virginia shifted orientation to the production of a single agricultural staple—tobacco—the commercial possibilities of which can be traced directly to Caribbean antecedents. In the 1580s and 1590s, Englishmen traded for tobacco with Trinidad Indians. Indeed, in the late sixteenth century, "Trinidado" denoted tobacco in English common usage. The traffic in tobacco, or "freighting smoke", which encompassed Trinidad, the northern coast of Venezuela, Guiana, Cuba, and Española, and both Indians and Spanish settlers, developed out of Elizabethan privateering contacts in the Caribbean region. Of the roughly forty known merchants and ships' masters who participated in this contraband

20. "1527–1528. Gines Navarro Reports on the English Ship *(Mary Guildford)* Seen at Mona, in the West Indies," in Quinn, ed., *New American World,* I, 192; Quinn, *Set Fair for Roanoke,* 62, 179; Paul Hulton, *America 1585: The Complete Drawings of John White* (Chapel Hill, N.C., 1984), esp. on 47–50, plates 11–14, and 175; Hulton and Quinn, eds., *American Drawings of John White;* Amy Butler Greenfield, *A Perfect Red: Empire, Espionage, and the Quest for the Color of Desire* (New York, 2005), 165–167; Philip L. Barbour, ed., *The Jamestown Voyages under the First Charter, 1606–1609,* 2 vols., Works Issued by the Hakluyt Society, 2d Ser., nos. 136–137 (London, 1969), I, 100–101; Jarvis, "Planting the Somer Islands." See also William Strachey, *The Historie of Travell into Virginia Britania (1612),* ed. Louis B. Wright and Virginia Freund, Works Issued by the Hakluyt Society, 2d Ser., no. 103 (London, 1953), 38, 118, 120, for plants with West Indian connections. In addition, see Karen Ordahl Kupperman, "The Puzzle of the American Climate in the Early Colonial Period," *American Historical Review,* LXXXVII (1982), 1262–1289, esp. 1268–1269.

trade, about a half had previously engaged in Caribbean privateering. In the boom years of the first decade of the seventeenth century, English traders probably acquired about 60 percent of annual tobacco imports (then at about 100,000 lbs. per year) from Trinidad and the Orinoco, and almost all the rest from elsewhere in the Spanish Indies. English consumers preferred so-called "Spanish"-grown tobacco. But with the Spanish suppression of the trade and James I's unwillingness to aggravate Anglo-Spanish relations, the risks soon exceeded the returns. This context explains the fledgling attempts by English settlers throughout the region—whether in Guiana, Saint Lucia, or Grenada in the first decade of the seventeenth century or Saint Christopher and Barbados in the third decade—to grow the crop.[21] Bermudians also were fortunate that they found Spanish Varina tobacco (*nicotiana tabacum* rather than the North American *nicotiana rustica,* which was unpalatable to European tastes) growing on the island when they arrived. Apparently, shipwrecked Iberian sailors had planted this strain of tobacco in the 1580s and 1590s. In 1609, John Rolfe, Virginia's pioneer tobacco planter, spent ten months in Bermuda as a *Sea Venture* castaway and brought the commercially viable tobacco from island to mainland. Spanish Caribbean tobacco, then, was the basis for the English tobacco boom, first as a trade item, then as an export crop in Bermuda (which outproduced Virginia until 1624), and only later in Virginia and in the fledgling British Caribbean islands. William Strachey outlined the true source of this tobacco in his *Historie of Travell into Virginia Britania* (1612), where he contrasted native Virginia tobacco—which was poor, weak, "of a byting tast," and grew not a yard above ground—with "the best Tobacco of Trinidado and the Oronoque," which was "large sharpe and growing 2. or 3. yardes from the grownd." In 1614, Ralph Hamor touted the profitability of tobacco, particularly "west-Indie Trinidado," to prospective Chesapeake immigrants. That *Orinoco* became the name for a strain of profitable tobacco grown in Virginia was hardly accidental.[22]

21. Joyce Lorimer, "The English Contraband Tobacco Trade in Trinidad and Guiana, 1590–1617," in Andrews, Canny, and Hair, eds., *Westward Enterprise,* 124–150, esp. 134, 150; Sluiter, "Dutch-Spanish Rivalry," *HAHR,* XXVIII (1948), 165–196; Michiel Baud, "A Colonial Counter Economy: Tobacco Production on Española, 1500–1870," *New West Indian Guide,* LXV (1991), 27–49; Andrews, *Trade, Plunder, and Settlement,* 294–302; Andrews, *Spanish Caribbean,* 225–231. On Spanish-cured tobacco, see Jordan Goodman, *Tobacco in History: The Cultures of Dependence* (London, 1993), 136–137.

22. Tobacco was growing in Bermuda in 1603, and the first English-grown tobacco

Tobacco bridged cultures. If Indians in Trinidad and the Orinoco were the first people with whom the English traded for the weed, they were not the last. In the early 1590s, the anonymous illustrator of the Drake Manuscript drew the tobacco plant and promoted its value as both food and medicine. When Caribbean Indians were sick, the author noted, "they breathe in the smoke by mouth with a straw: soon the ill humour escapes by vomiting." The plant was also useful for toothache and as an eye-wash; mixed with balsam, it was said to cure wounds caused by poisoned arrows. When John Nicholl was a castaway on Saint Lucia in 1605, he and his men fought Natives but also took comfort in their mode of tobacco consumption. He described his men sitting all night "by greate fiers, drinking of Tobacc" (inhaling it, in Indian fashion). When Nicholl finally escaped and sailed to the mainland, tobacco became "the chiefe food I found to do me good, and did preserve my lyfe," he wrote, "and those which could take it downe, did keepe strongest, but those which could not take it all, died first." Just as the Drake Manuscript author had done, Nicholl highlighted tobacco's curative properties and sustenance value.[23]

Tobacco's spiritual qualities were also evident to the English. In 1596, Lawrence Keymis described how, in Guiana, the Indians "made small fyers, and sitting in their *Hamaccas*, . . . recounting amongst themselves the worthiest deeds, and deathes of their Ancestors. . . . Thus they sit talking, and taking *Tobacco* some two howers, and untill their pipes bee all spent (for by them they measure the time of this their solemne conference) no man must interrupt, or disturbe them in anie sorte: for this is their religion, and prayers, which they nowe celebrated, keeping a precise fast one whole day, in honour of the great Princesse of the North, their Patronesse and Defender [Queen Elizabeth I]." Tobacco served important functions, then—as medicine, ritual accompaniment, recreation, time measurement, diplomatic exchange, and, above all, spiritual aid. To the degree that the English could recognize these purposes and see their value, the product became an object

---

exported from the New World seems to have been the 170 pounds of rolled "pudding" tobacco shipped home in 1614 from the island (see Jarvis, "Planting the Somer Islands"). Strachey, *Historie of Travell,* ed. Wright and Freund, 123; Ralph Hamor, *A True Discourse of the Present State of Virginia* (1614; Richmond, Va., 1957), 24, as cited in Goodman, *Tobacco in History,* 135.

23. Kraemer, trans., *Histoire Naturelle des Indes,* fols. 4v, 92, pp. 253, 265; John Nicholl, *An Houre Glasse of Indian Newes* (London, 1607), C2v, Ev; Chaplin, *Subject Matter,* 208–209.

of cross-cultural appropriation. In spite of tobacco's demonic associations and claims that it was harmful, Europeans managed to domesticate its use.[24]

The circum-Caribbean was the first theater of European-Indian encounters. What happened there set the stage for later relations between the two groups. On the islands and adjoining mainland, the English gained their first impression of Indians, their appearance, their material life, their values. There, the English took the measure of Indians, traded with them, used them as guides, allied with them, and fought against them. When the English arrived in Virginia, they had decades of interactions with Indians behind them.

Early English accounts of the Caribbean Indians' appearance were often positive. The Indians impressed the English as "personable," "handsome," and "strong." Robert Dudley thought Trinidadian Indians "a fine shaped and a gentle people"; Captain Wyatt, a member of his expedition, described Guianan Indians as "tall of stature and of verie manlike visage"; Ralegh found the *"Tivitivas,"* or Waraos, "a verie goodlie people and verie valiant, and have the most manlie speech." The remarkable images of Indians (about 40 from a total of 199) contained in the so-called Drake Manuscript, which date to the early 1590s, are our best insight into Native life in the Caribbean region. The author and illustrator (and there might have been more than one in each case) were French Huguenots, seemingly members of Drake's ships; their views perhaps mirrored those of their English companions. Although hardly authoritative and certainly not widely available, these images are most interesting because they tell stories, revelatory of intimate encounters with Caribbean Indians. The images are often naïve, not in the class of John White's drawings of Roanoke Indians, but they share the same exuberance, vigor, and vivid colors. Like Harriot's sympathetic portrayal of the natives on Roanoke Island and John White's sensitive visual depictions, the tenor and tone are favorable. The Indians of Santa Marta—a representative is depicted with penis sheath, nose ring, anklets, and conical poison dispenser at his side—"are handsome and strong men, artful in war." Indian women scrubbed their children so well that they had no skin sores and were "clean all over their bodies"—a thing of wonder to Europeans. These women also "swim like fish in the sea." Indians are depicted as straight-limbed, lithe, well-muscled, and long-haired, but with no hair

24. Lawrence Keymis, *A Relation of the Second Voyage to Guiana* (1596; rpt. Amsterdam, 1968), C2v–C3; Peter C. Mancall, "Tales Tobacco Told in Sixteenth-Century Europe," *Environmental History,* IX (2004), 648–678.

elsewhere on the body or face. George Percy concurred, describing the hair of Dominican Caribs as "a yard long, all of a length pleated in three plats hanging downe to their wastes, [but] they suffer no haire to grow on their faces." The beardless Indian man so well known to European adventurers to the Caribbean (and to readers of Spanish accounts) was such an ingrained stereotype that only an exception would later elicit surprise. Thus, once in Virginia, Percy reported his astonishment at meeting an elderly, bearded Indian, describing it as "a Miracle to see a Savage have any haire on their faces. I never saw, read, nor heard, any have the like before." Percy's encounters with Caribbean Indians—not to forget his reading—had not prepared him for this "reasonable bigge beard, which was as white as any snow."[25]

The Caribbean Indians' material culture also made a generally favorable impression. On Saint Croix in 1587, John White found "potsheards . . . made of earth of that Island," which was his first indication of an Indian presence there. Later, one of his company saw Indians' "divers houses halfe a mile distant from the steepe, or toppe of the hill." Indians living near Sante Fe in present-day Colombia, according to the author of the Drake Manuscript, were "good workers with great skill and intelligence, . . . making beautiful cloth of fine wool," whereas those living in Borburata, in present-day Venezuela, were "ingenious" for fashioning "in gold relief several kinds of animals for their enjoyment, which is something unbelievable to us since they are taught only by nature." As the illustrations richly demonstrated, Caribbean Indians fished adroitly, gardened productively, made a "very nourishing bread," barbecued tastefully, caught parrots and rabbits inventively, medicated themselves ably, constructed canoes, nets and hammocks impressively, and spun cotton "with great diligence and speed." So skilled were the natives "that one could not show them any work they could not do." The paean of praise is striking. Hammocks and canoes (the Powhatan term *"Quintans,"* which Strachey reported as the equivalent of "the West-Indian . . . Canoas," never caught on) were two terms that entered the English language after these circum-Caribbean encounters.[26]

25. *A Summarie and True Discourse of Sir Frances Drakes West Indian Voyage . . .* (1589; New York, 1969), Diii; George F. Warner, ed., *The Voyage of Robert Dudley . . . to the West Indies, 1594–1595 . . .*, Works Issued by the Hakluyt Society, 2d Ser., no. 3 (London, 1899), 40, 70; Ralegh, *Discoverie of Guiana,* ed. Whitehead, 158; Kraemer, trans., *Histoire Naturelle des Indes,* fols. 81, 87, 110, 264, 269; "George Percy's Discourse," in Barbour, ed., *Jamestown Voyages,* I, 130, 142; Elliott Horowitz, "The New World and the Changing Face of Europe," *Sixteenth Century Journal,* XXVIII, no. 4 (1997), 1181–1201.

26. Quinn, ed., *Roanoke Voyages,* II, 518–519; Kraemer, trans., *Histoire Naturelle*

In the Caribbean, the English sometimes employed Indians, particularly those who had been subject to Hispanic assimilation, as guides and scouts. In the early 1570s, Francis Drake acquired an Indian named Pedro, a native of Margarita. When Drake returned to the region in 1586, he had Pedro alongside him as his "interpreter with the Indians, for [Pedro] knows English and Spanish and the language of the Indians of La Margarita, where he was born." At Cartagena, Drake ordered Pedro to become a "muleteer" so that he might learn the layout of the roads and the whereabouts of any treasure. In the same year, Juan Guillen, an aboriginal native of Cuba, said to have been "reared in [Havana] and its jurisdiction" and condemned to the galleys, fled to Drake and provided him with information on the surrounding countryside and harbors. Eleven years later, when Sir Anthony Shirley raided Jamaica, one of the island's Indians, another man named Pedro—who, according to Spanish accounts, fled to the English "of his own free will and accord"—served as a scout. In 1598, John Ley became "the first Englishman known to have entered the lower Amazon," thanks to an expert Indian pilot from the River Cawo who, "after such time the starrs appeare in the night can point directlie to anie countrie that ever he hath traveled by yt maine or Iland with such assurance that he hath caused us to admire oftentimes." When Christopher Newport insisted on guides for an overland expedition beyond the Virginia fall-line, or John Smith learned about far-off Indian villages from native scouts, they were doing what the English had long been doing in the Caribbean.[27]

---

des Indes, fols. 4v, 45, 83, 84, 86, 88, 92, 95v–96, 96v, 98–98v, 101, 108–109, 112, 114–123, pp. 253, 259, 264–267, 269–271; Strachey, *Historie of Travell,* ed. Wright and Freund, 81–82. The only commentaries on the Drake Manuscript of which I am aware are Hulton and Quinn, eds., *American Drawings of John White,* I, 7, 15, 34, 110–111, 132, II, plate 156a; William C. Sturtevant, "Views of a New World" and "America from Drake's Quarterdeck: Sixteenth Century Drawings from Sir Francis Drake's Voyages Recorded Important Intelligence for England in Spanish America," *American Heritage,* XXXVI, no. 5 (August/September 1985), 82, 85–92; and Frank Lestringant, "Le *Drake Manuscript* de la P. Morgan Library: Un document exceptionnel en marge des 'nouveaux horizons' français," *l'Homme,* XXXIV, no. 2 (1994), 93–104. From 1984 to 1988, William C. Sturtevant (and others, including Quinn, Hulton, and Lestringant) worked on an incomplete project on the manuscript. I have spoken to Bill Sturtevant about it. More generally, see Sturtevant, "First Visual Images of Native America," in Fredi Chiappelli, ed., *First Images of America: The Impact of the New World on the Old,* 2 vols. (Berkeley, Calif., 1976), I, 417–454.

27. Irene A. Wright, ed., *Further English Voyages to Spanish America, 1583–1594,* Works Issued by the Hakluyt Society, 2d Ser., no. 99 (London, 1951), 170, 213, 226;

Just as Namontack, one of Powhatan's men, traveled to England with Christopher Newport in 1608 and Uttamatomakkin made the trip with his sister-in-law Pocahontas in 1616, a number of Caribbean Indians had preceded them across the Atlantic. In fact, in 1590, John White learned that two young sons of a "chiefe Casiques" in Dominica got cold feet and jumped ship at Santa Cruz Island. Between 1584 and 1618, however, a score of Guianan Indians seem to have gone to England voluntarily—some living there a long time—and assumed Anglicized names, perhaps an indication of their religious conversion. On his first voyage to Guiana in 1595, Ralegh took along an "Indian interpreter," who presumably had been brought to England by Jacob Whiddon's scouting expedition the previous year. While in Guiana, Ralegh reported that a chieftain named "*Topiawari* . . . freely gave me his onlie sonne [Cayoworaco] to take with me into England," and three other Indians accompanied him. When, in 1604, Captain Charles Leigh attempted a settlement in Guiana, he encountered two Indians who "had beene before in England, and could speake some English"; he employed one of them, William, as his interpreter. Five years later, Robert Harcourt encountered an Indian named John who "could speake our language well, and . . . that sometimes had been in England, and served Sr. *John Gilbert* many yeeres." Accompanying Harcourt were two natives: Martyn had lived in England four years and Anthony Canabre had been away fourteen years. An Indian chief named Leonard Ragopo, who "hath been heretofore in England with Sr. *Walter Raleigh,* to whom hee beareth great affection . . . and loveth our Nation with all his heart," greatly aided Harcourt's explorations. When Ralegh finally returned to Guiana in 1617, he sought his "old sarvant Leonard the Indien who [had] bine with me in Ingland 3 or 4 yeers"; at another place, "the Cassique was also my sarvant and had lived with mee in the tower 2 yeers"; and elsewhere, he encountered "my [Indian] sarvant Harry . . . who had almost forgotten his Inglish." Indigenous leaders in Guiana had experienced decades of warfare, enslavement, and trade; had reshaped their own political structures as a result; and welcomed new European allies when it seemed in their interest.[28]

Wright, "The Spanish Version of Sir Anthony Shirley's Raid of Jamaica, 1597," *HAHR,* V (1922), 227–248, esp. 242; Lorimer, ed., *English and Irish Settlement,* 19, 24.

28. Quinn, ed., *Roanoke Voyages,* II, 602; Alden T. Vaughan, "Trinculo's Indian: American Natives in Shakespeare's England," in Peter Hulme and William H. Sherman, eds., *"The Tempest" and Its Travels* (Philadelphia, 2000), 49–59, esp. 53; Vaughan, "Sir Walter Ralegh's Indian Interpreters, 1584–1618," *WMQ,* LIX (2002), 341–376; Harald E. L. Prins, "To the Land of the Mistigoches: American Indians

When Christopher Newport dispensed prestige goods to the Powhatans and acted in a chieflike manner, he was building on extensive trading contacts with circum-Caribbean Indians in which he and other Englishmen had been engaged for decades. Thus, in 1592, Newport had bartered with Dominican Caribs for tobacco, fowl, and potato roots and had reportedly found the Calusa Indians of the Florida Keys "very courteous" and willing to trade precious metals for tools. In the Caribbean, English ship captains had learned the value of tribute networks if they were to acquire the provisions and water that they sought. An account of Drake's voyage to the Caribbean in 1585 described Dominican Caribs as "helping our folks to fill and carie on their bare shoulders fresh water from the river to our ships boats." English visitors traded for bananas, pineapples, plantains, nuts, sweet potatoes, cassava bread (or "Cassado, verie white and saverie, made of the rootes of Cassania"), parrots, and poultry (just as Newport did, indicating that Indians had adopted a Spanish import). Indeed, George Percy, en route to Virginia in 1607, noted how Dominican Caribs were willing to trade "Roane Cloth [in] abundance, which they had gotten out of certaine Spanish ships that were cast away upon that Iland." In return, the English soon recognized what the Indians most desired: knives, hatchets, saws, fishing hooks, combs, looking glasses, little bells, rosaries, and "liberall rewardes of glasse, coloured beades." Percy noted that Dominican natives also wanted "Copper Jewels which they hang through their nosthrils, eares, and lips, very strange to behold." Newport knew what to supply the Powhatan *weroances* when he sat down to negotiate with them.[29]

Traveling to Europe in the Age of Exploration," *American Indian Culture and Research Journal,* XVII, no. 1 (1993), 175–195; Harcourt, *Relation of a Voyage to Guiana,* ed. Harris, 6–8, 12–15, 71, 80; Keymis, *Relation of the Second Voyage to Guiana,* B2. For more on Guiana, see Neil L. Whitehead, *Lords of the Tiger Spirit: A History of the Caribs in Colonial Venezuela and Guyana, 1498–1820* (Dordrecht, 1988); Whitehead's notes to Ralegh, *Discoverie of Guiana;* and H. Dieter Heinen and Alvaro García-Castro, "The Multiethnic Network of the Lower Orinoco in Early Colonial Times," *Ethnohistory,* XLVII (2000), 561–579.

29. Andrews, ed., *English Privateering Voyages,* 189, 193–194, 383; *A Summarie and True Discourse of Sir Frances Drakes West Indian Voyage,* Diii; "Observations by Master George Percy, 1607," in Tyler, ed., *Narratives of Early Virginia,* 6. For other good accounts of trade with Caribbean Indians, see Wright, ed., *Further English Voyages to Spanish America,* 286, 289, 292, 293; Keeler, ed., *Sir Francis Drake's West Indian Voyage,* 66, 191–192; Quinn, ed., *Roanoke Voyages,* II, 600, 602; Warner, ed., *Voyage of Robert Dudley,* 22–23, 39; Andrews, ed., *Last Voyage of Drake and Hawkins,* 107; Nicholl, *An Houre Glasse of Indian Newes,* B3–C3, D3; Barbour, ed., *Jamestown Voyages,* I, 159. See Daniel K. Richter, "Virginia Algonquians and the Atlantic World,

If the English in the Caribbean often engaged in amicable relations with, and frequently had positive views of, the Indians, hostility and negativity were always present. The English frequently referred to Caribbean Indians as savages, as a naked people, "as redd as Scarlet," referring to a dye that many Caribbean Indians used to decorate themselves and that was often said to keep away mosquitoes. They were animal-like: "They will lap up mans spittle, whilst one spits in their mouthes, in a barbarous fashion like Dogges." They were pagan: "They worship the Devill for their God, and have no other beliefe." The Drake Manuscript identified this devil as "Athoua." Crying children, Caribbean Indians believed, had "the devil . . . in their body." Caribbean Indians did not "worship anything like the people of Barbary, Guinea, and Brasil." When a European told an Indian to believe in the crucified Jesus Christ, who would deliver him from "all his diabolical visions," the Indian replied that "the one up high was not good; he only sent cold, rain, and scorching heat while the one down on earth was good to them, giving them their daily food like bread, wine, meat, fish, fruits, and other goods from the soil itself and that when they die they are buried there." Seemingly, then, Caribbean Indians were not ripe for conversion. The English often encountered Indians as allies of the Spanish: a volley of poisoned arrows might be the initial greeting. Most obviously, the region was home to the Caribs. As early as 1565, John Hawkins reported Dominican "Canybals" eating sailors who ventured ashore. Describing a trading encounter twenty years later, another Englishman noted, "There manner is when they kill anie of there enemies they knocke owte the[ir] teethe and were them abowte there neckes like a chaine and eate [the] flesshe for meate." Another account of the same episode mentioned that Dominican Caribs were "greate devowrers and eaters of men." The Indians of Ihona (Guiana?), according to the Drake Manuscript, practiced cannibalism. When they defeated their enemies, they pounded them with a flat-edged sword or club but held back the blood once it flowed, "thinking that by this means the body will make a better roast for a solemn feast, calling this a deed of prowess." In 1627, a Virginia-bound ship that stopped in the Caribbean had several passengers killed by local Indians; their shipmates were so scared that they left sixteen survivors behind rather than risk a rescue.[30]

1560–1622" (unpublished paper, 2004), which contains the best account of the power of goods in the early Virginia context.

30. "Observations by Master George Percy, 1607," in Tyler, ed., *Narratives of Early Virginia*, 6; Keeler, ed., *Sir Francis Drake's West Indian Voyage*, 66, 164, 191, 192;

Come les yndiens ont ordinairement des Jausiona
Du Maling esprit

Ces yndiens sont fort tourmentés la nuit par disiona du
maling esprin quil appelle en leur langue athoua et
ne sem sortir de leurs maisons durant la nuit
et le jour ne sort dem en a leurs prouiem acaus... ...
... mille croianse ny enseignemens de nadoreus chose
quelz conreguent Comme peruent faire les nations de
barbarie guinee ny du bresil Et estans ving jour aultre
en la maison dun yndien les sortans di celle de nuit fust prie

PLATE I. *"How the Indians Usually Have Visions of the Evil Spirit [Athoua]."*
ca. 1590s. In Ruth S. Kraemer, trans., Histoire Naturelle des Indes: The Drake
Manuscript in the Pierpont Morgan Library *(New York, 1996), f. 111*

The penchant for dividing Indians Manichean fashion into good and bad—in a Caribbean context, into friendly Taínos (or Arawaks) and fierce Caribs—resonated far and wide. Sir Walter Ralegh's project in the Orinoco was premised on an alternative policy toward the Indian from that of the Spanish. Instead of decimating them by forced labor and brutality, the aim was to convert them into loyal and enthusiastic vassals by defending them against the Spaniards, by instructing them "in liberall arts of civility," and by teaching them "the use of weapons." Seemingly, Ralegh's treatment of particular Indian caciques, particularly Topiawari, won their goodwill. Ralegh usually referred to Guiana Indians as "naturals," and he keenly noted native terms, titles, and the personal names of leaders. Alternatively, Captain John Smith, as April Hatfield has pointed out, had a Spanish model in mind when he argued that Virginia colonists should have "forced the treacherous and rebellious Infidels to doe all manner of drudgery worke and slavery for them" to avoid their starving time. As he put it most directly, there are "twenty examples of the Spaniards how they got the West-Indies" by forcing the Indians to work for them. But even Smith subscribed to Powhatan political geography, seeing enemy Indians beyond the falls. The Powhatans, insofar as they cooperated with the English, could be considered friendly; the Monacans and Mannahoacs were the enemy.[31]

Indians and blacks mixed together in the islands, as they would later in Virginia. The first known English ship to venture into the Caribbean, in 1527, sent a boat and thirty men ashore near Santo Domingo, where they seized all the clothing belonging to Indians and blacks. Apparently,

Andrews, ed., *Last Voyage of Drake and Hawkins,* 90; Peter Hulme and Neil L. Whitehead, eds., *Wild Majesty: Encounters with Caribs from Columbus to the Present Day* (Oxford, 1992), 48–49, 53–54; Kraemer, trans., *Histoire Naturelle des Indes,* fols. 85, III–IIIv, and pp. 264, 269; H. R. McIlwaine, ed., *Minutes of the Council and General Court of Colonial Virginia* (Richmond, Va., 1979), 143–144.

31. Vincent T. Harlow, ed., *Ralegh's Last Voyage . . .* (London, 1932), 2; Joyce Lorimer, "The Location of Ralegh's Guiana Gold Mine," *Terrae Incognitae,* XIV (1982), 77–95, esp. 85, 92; Barbour, ed., *Works of Smith,* II, 299; Morgan, *American Slavery, American Freedom,* 77; April Lee Hatfield, *Atlantic Virginia: Intercolonial Relations in the Seventeenth Century* (Philadelphia, 2004), 16–17. For early European views of Caribs, see Philip P. Boucher, *Cannibal Encounters: Europeans and Island Caribs, 1492–1763* (Baltimore, 1992), 13–30. For an excellent summary of the variety of encounters between Europeans and Native Americans in various locales, see Neil L. Whitehead, "Native Society and the European Occupation of the Caribbean Islands and Coastal *Tierra Firme,* 1492–1650," in Emmer and Damas, eds., *General History of the Caribbean,* II, 180–200.

PLATE 2. *Beaded cotton zemi. ca. 1510s.*
Museo Nazionale Preistorico ed Ethnografico "Luigi Pigorini," Rome

their parting shot was, "Tell those saw-armed, Christ-killing Indian dogs that they shall pay!" By this point, Indians and blacks worked alongside one another as forced laborers in Española's homes, mines, and fields; one spectacular clue to their intimate associations is a cotton zemi, a recognizably Taíno artifact (deposited in a Rome museum), which is a synthesis of many styles and materials—not least the human face carved from an African rhinoceros horn, the symmetrically pointed corners of the eyes found on sub-Saharan sculptures, and the squat form atypical of Taíno, but

PLATE 3. *Beaded cotton zemi (back view)*

more akin to African, figures. This Taíno or possibly mixed-race craftsman must have known Africans well. Another spectacular example derives from Father Raymond Breton's dictionary of the Island Carib language, based on his fieldwork in the 1630s and 1640s. He gave as the derivation for the word *caiman* the Carib *Acayoûman*, but the term seems to derive from the Kongo, for a 1598 account in that region notes the word *caiman*. Perhaps enslaved Africans from the Kongo—possibly maroons from Española—had infiltrated Carib society so that their term had supplanted an older Carib word. Just as native Americans and blacks in the Caribbean learned from one another, so they would in the early Chesapeake, as is evident in the hybrid styles of the carvings on seventeenth-century tobacco pipes. Most of the black slaves from Española and Indians from the Cartagena area, whom Drake took aboard his ships in 1586 and who numbered in the hundreds, might have disembarked at Roanoke, where presumably they blended into the local population. Ten years later, when Drake returned to the Caribbean, his expedition landed at Jamaica, where, "by meanes of a Malatow and an Indian," they received forty bundles of dried beef. In 1616, Governor Tucker of Bermuda sent a ship to the Lesser Antilles to "trucke . . . for . . . negroes to dive for pearles"; it returned with "an Indian and a Negroe," the first Bermuda ever had, making it the first English colony to import African and Indian laborers, who, of course, had been intermixing on the Caribbean islands for more than a century.[32]

32. I. A. Wright, ed., *Spanish Documents concerning English Voyages to the Caribbean, 1527–1568,* Works Issued by the Hakluyt Society, 2d Ser., no. 62 (London, 1929), 56; but I have taken quotation from "Visit of the English Ship *[Mary Guildford]*," in Quinn, ed., *New American World,* I, 205. Lynne A. Guitar, "Cultural Genesis: Relationships among Indians, Africans, and Spaniards in Rural Hispaniola, First Half of the Sixteenth Century" (Ph.D. diss., Vanderbilt University, 1998); Dicey Taylor, Marco Biscione, and Peter G. Roe, "Epilogue: The Beaded Zemi in the Pigorini Museum," in Fatima Bercht, Estrellita Brodsky, John Alan Farmer, and Dicey Taylor, eds., *Taíno: Pre-Columbian Art and Culture from the Caribbean* (New York, 1997), 158–169. The zemi is also reproduced in Irving Rouse, *The Tainos: Rise and Decline of the People Who Greeted Columbus* (New Haven, Conn., 1992), 160; Raymond Breton, *Dictionaire français-caraibe* ([1666]; Leipzig, 1900), 96; and Georg Friederici, *Amerikanistisches Wörterbuch* (Hamburg, 1947), 152–154 (my thanks to Richard Price for kindly providing this information). For tobacco pipe carvings, see Philip D. Morgan, *Slave Counterpoint: Black Culture in the Eighteenth-Century Chesapeake and Lowcountry* (Chapel Hill, N.C., 1998), 21–22 (and references cited). The fate of the blacks and Indians captured (some say liberated) by Drake in 1586 is a mystery—for some key discussions, see Quinn, ed., *Roanoke Voyages,* I, 251, 254; David B. Quinn and Alison M. Quinn, *The First Colonists: Documents on the Planting of the First English Settlements in North America, 1584–1590* (Raleigh, N.C., 1982), 149; Quinn, *Set Fair for Roanoke,* 343–344; Kupperman, *Roanoke,* 88, 92; Quinn, "Turks, Moors, Blacks, and Others in Drake's West Indian Voyage," in Quinn, *Explorers and Colonies: America, 1500–1625* (London, 1990), 197–204; and Michael J. Guasco, "Encounters, Identities, and Human Bondage: The Foundations of Racial Slavery in the Anglo-Atlantic World" (Ph.D. diss., College of William and Mary, 2000), esp. 398–402, and see 350–405, which is the fullest account of black-English encounters in the early Caribbean; Andrews, ed., *Last Voyage of Drake and Hawkins,* 104; J. H. Lefroy, *Memorials of the Discovery and Early Settlement of the Bermudas, or Somers Islands, 1515–1685,* 2 vols. (London, 1878–1879),

Englishmen encountered blacks in all sorts of roles in the Caribbean, a wider array than anything that would exist in early Virginia and yet a harbinger of the flexibility that would characterize the Chesapeake colony's early race relations. On the one hand, blacks fought on the side of the Spanish against Englishmen in the Caribbean. In 1586, according to one Spanish report of Drake's expedition against Española, "the negroes of Santo Domingo, armed with nicking knives [a curved knife set at the end of a long shaft, used by herdsmen to hamstring cattle] and swords, seriously harass these English continuously and kill many, and do daring things, although the English with harquebuses kill some." Later, when Drake moved to Cartagena, he faced a company of at least twenty-five, perhaps fifty, free black and mulatto musketeers under the command of Captain Augustin, a free black. Augustin claimed that his company fought more bravely than others; he reported telling the general of the Spanish forces, "now is the moment for men to show themselves men . . . and let us die here fighting these dogs." On the other hand, blacks were sometimes allies and guides of the English. When, in 1567, Hawkins was at Río de la Hacha, "a mulatto and a negro" slave guided him to valuable goods that the Spanish had hidden (in return for their help, Hawkins allowed the Spanish to ransom these two slaves and then execute them for their disloyalty). In 1594, William Parker gained access to Puerto de Caballos in the Gulf of Honduras through the knowledge of Diego de los Reyes or Dieguillo el Mulato, described as a "mulatto oarsman." The following year, another mulatto, a cowherd named Amador, guided Thomas Baskerville's force about twenty miles inland from Nombre de Dios. In 1596, the earl of Cumberland's expedition employed a "black-Moore" guide on Puerto Rico. Blacks proved formidable opponents and useful allies of the English.[33]

The most dramatic alliance between the English and a group of blacks was that between Drake and the *cimarrones* at Panama. As Drake made diplomatic overtures to them in 1572, he acquired the services of "Diego, the Negroe," who provided valuable information about the military strength of

I, 115–116; [Nathaniel Butler?], *The Historye of the Bermudaes, or Summer Islands,* ed. J. Henry Lefroy (London, 1882), 84–85; Jarvis, "Planting the Somer Islands"; Virginia Bernhard, *Slaves and Slaveholders in Bermuda, 1616–1782* (Columbia, Md., 1999), 19.

33. Wright, ed., *Further English Voyages to Spanish America,* 30–31, 104, 127–129 (Augustin's deposition); Wright, ed., *Spanish Documents,* 117–118, 121–122, 156; Kelsey, *Sir John Hawkins,* 79–80; Andrews, ed., *English Privateering Voyages,* 309, 317, 320, 322; Andrews, ed., *Last Voyage of Drake and Hawkins,* 207, 220; Purchas, *Hakluytus Posthumus,* XVI, 59.

specific towns and the route most commonly traveled by Spanish treasure trains. Shortly thereafter, about twenty Englishmen managed to cross the Isthmus, only because they were shown the way by Pedro Mandinga and about forty cimarrones whom Spanish officials described as "expert in the bush," and whose bush-telegraph broadcast the arrival of the flota at Nombre de Dios. In the following year, a combined force of Englishmen, Frenchmen, and maroons captured a great haul of treasure. By 1577, if the Spanish are to be believed, the cimarrones were "as Lutheran as the English," crying, "I English; pure Lutheran," as they destroyed Catholic insignia. In that year, the Spaniards came across a camp of thirty Englishmen and more than eighty maroons "cooking a quantity of pork in kettles and amusing themselves together." A camaraderie had seemingly developed between corsair and maroon that, in Edmund Morgan's words, "went beyond the mutual benefits of the alliance." Thereafter, however, a powerful Spanish counteroffensive soured the maroons on the English to the point that they were said to "despise" them and viewed them as their mortal enemies. This volte-face strongly suggests the pragmatic quality of the earlier alliance. When Drake returned in 1596, the cimarrones actively opposed him. No doubt, occasional amicable encounters were still possible: in 1595, Robert Dudley mentioned trading with the "Simerones" of Trinidad. Nevertheless, Humphrey Gilbert's hope, expressed almost twenty years earlier—that the maroons, these "valiaunt men . . . will gladly receave ayde and libertie, and so they may be brought to do great service"—had proved illusory.[34]

This failure does not mean that Englishmen retreated from using black

34. I. A. Wright, ed., *Documents concerning English Voyages to the Spanish Main, 1569-1580*, Works Issued by the Hakluyt Society, 2d Ser., no. 71 (London, 1932), xxxviii-xxxix, 45, 49-50, 69, 113, 117-120, 129-130, 132-133, 176-177, 191, 201, 264-265, 269, 279-281, 293-295, 298, 305-307; Andrews, *Spanish Caribbean*, 134-146; Andrews, ed., *Last Voyage of Drake and Hawkins*, 196, 211, 212, 217-219; Hoffman, *Spanish Crown*, 197; Warner, ed., *Voyage of Robert Dudley*, 71; David B. Quinn, ed., *The Voyages and Colonising Enterprises of Sir Humphrey Gilbert*, 2 vols., Works Issued by the Hakluyt Society, 2d Ser., nos. 83-84 (London, 1940), I, 179 (Gilbert had in mind the maroons of Española). See also Morgan, *American Slavery, American Freedom*, 10-18 (quote on 13), which fails to consider the breakdown in the maroon-English relationship; for a more balanced account, see Guasco, "Encounters, Identities, and Human Bondage," 358-362, and for the best account, in a comparative framework, see Scott V. Parris, "Alliance and Competition: Four Case Studies of Maroon-European Relations," *Nieuwe West-Indische Gids*, LV (1981), 174-225, esp. 179-187. Perhaps the most intriguing piece of evidence is a report that, in 1581, a ship arrived in England from the Indies carrying "nine creoles of those parts, mulattoes, mestizos, and others" urging Drake to return and renew the alliance (ibid., 186).

skills. Bermudians, for example, secured the expert assistance of Caribbean blacks. Francisco, a black man from the Spanish Indies, brought to Bermuda in 1617, came to the attention of Robert Rich because "his judgment in the cureing of tobackoe is such that I had rather have him then all the other negers that bee here." James, another black man who made the journey from the Antilles to Bermuda, was said to be skilled in the "planting of west endy plants." With this expert help, Bermuda's tobacco crop grew quickly and improved in quality. In particular, these Spanish blacks instructed planters to coat tobacco with a brine solution before fermentation and twist it into tight rolls in the Spanish manner; Chesapeake tobacco, which did not have such assistance, suffered accordingly.[35]

Although some blacks were free and others occupied positions of skill, most blacks the English encountered in the Spanish Caribbean were slaves. The association between slavery and blackness took firm hold in the early Caribbean. The idea that slavery developed slowly in Virginia and that it was largely invented out of whole cloth fails to credit Caribbean antecedents. The Caribbean experience, with which many early Virginians were familiar, indicates the die was cast much earlier. In the 1560s, John Hawkins and associates mounted four slave-trading expeditions in which they brought about 1,300 African slaves into the Caribbean region. Seeing these Africans as legitimate prey, to be acquired by force (if necessary) and often sold with threat of force, the English viewed their human cargo as nothing other than "very good merchandize," as Richard Hakluyt put it. Hawkins's new coat of arms featured a black slave bound with a rope. His voyages were not especially successful, so thereafter English ship captains increasingly preyed on the slave ships of others and sold their captives to Spanish planters, or they raided plantations and then ransomed back the slaves to their owners. In the early 1590s, the Drake Manuscript depicted blacks entirely as slaves in two settings that focused upon degradation: first, as pearl divers near Margarita, with the emphasis that dives might last fifteen minutes, that divers were attacked by manta rays, and that they used conch hair as a cure for ear drums "hurt by frequent dives"; and, second, in the emerald mines of present-day Colombia and the gold mines of Panama, where lives were nasty, brutal, and short (blacks "die miserably" in the former and live "only a short time" in the latter). The illustrations of blacks in this manuscript contain none of the individuality and humanity with which Indians

35. Vernon A. Ives, ed., *The Rich Papers: Letters from Bermuda, 1615–1646* (Toronto, 1984), 58–59; Jarvis, "Planting the Somer Islands"; Bernhard, *Slaves and Slaveholders*, 20–21.

are depicted. When Englishmen saw blacks in the early Caribbean, they largely saw slaves, and for the most part they viewed them as a highly exploitable commodity. Iberian practices to which the English were exposed —most blacks were slaves, avenues to freedom were fairly widely available, and racial barriers were porous—help explain early Virginia race relations. That only thirty-two blacks, fifteen men and seventeen women, were in Virginia in 1620, all apparently recent arrivals—and seemingly mostly slaves but some destined for freedom—also helped produce a fluid racial order.[36]

In the sixteenth and early seventeenth centuries, the circum-Caribbean region was the hub of European activity in the New World. Aware of Spanish precedents, the English gradually took their measure of the place. They came to plunder and trade, exploit and settle. They imitated, preyed upon, and repudiated Spanish models. Captivated by the region's beauty, they were also repelled by its diseases, hurricanes, and wild creatures. The Caribbean became a way station where the English gained their first experiences of the New World. They learned to sail its waters, know its coastlines, and acquire a taste for its products. They encountered others—not just Spaniards, of course, but many others. The transnational quality of life in the Caribbean has been seriously underestimated in this essay; a larger study would explore interactions among English, Scots, Irish, Dutch, French,

36. Kelsey, *Sir John Hawkins,* 13–115; Wright, ed., *Spanish Documents,* 95–112; Andrews, *Trade, Plunder, and Settlement,* 116–134; Guasco, "Encounters, Identities, and Human Bondage," 355–356; Kraemer, trans., *Histoire Naturelle des Indes,* fols. 47, 57, 98–98v, 100–100v, and pp. 259, 261, 266–267. The authors of this manuscript also mentioned, but did not depict, black slaves in two other contexts: in describing the port of Nombre de Dios and the road to Panama, they referred to "runaway negro slaves who steal and plunder everything they find on the road belonging to the Spaniards." "These runaway negroes form bands for fear to be surprised by the Spaniards." In describing the Chagres River, they again referred to "the danger from the runaway negro slaves, commonly called thieves," and described how "barges are all laden with gold and silver and have only eight to ten negro slaves who swim when there is no proper wind, and one Spaniard, called Major-domo, who commands them" (ibid., fols. 97–97v, 106–106v, and pp. 266, 268). For the view that thirty-two blacks were already in Virginia in 1619, see William Thorndale, "The Virginia Census of 1619," *Magazine of Virginia Genealogy,* XXXIII (1995), 155–170; but for a persuasive argument that this census was actually made in 1620 (after the Dutch man-of-war landed its "20. and odd Negroes"), see Martha W. McCartney, "An Early Virginia Census Reprised," *Quarterly Bulletin of the Archaeological Society of Virginia,* LIV (1999), 178–196.

Portuguese, and so on. Still, the English undoubtedly drew valuable lessons from their interactions with Indians and Africans. The region was an important testing ground for maritime skills, agricultural repertoires, race relations—social and cultural encounters of all types—that in turn would help shape the Chesapeake experience.

From a Virginia perspective, perhaps the early Caribbean was most important for its strategic influence, which may be said to have pointed in two rather competing directions. First, the Caribbean region acted as a shield facilitating early Virginia's development. Precisely because so much attention was centered on the Caribbean, Virginia had the elbow room to establish itself. Virginia's very existence owed much to the war of attrition in the Caribbean. If Spain's officials had not been so preoccupied warding off European interlopers, they might have been able to quell the fledgling settlement on the Chesapeake Bay, much as they had managed to quash a previous French attempt in Florida.[37] Second, by the early 1620s, it was not at all clear that mainland ventures would be successful; islands, by contrast, looked a far more promising place as a model for the future. After all, consider the year 1622: the Amazon Company had just collapsed; Opechancanough had launched a surprise attack that killed nearly a third of Virginia's colonists; and Plymouth's few settlers had emerged from a long, starving winter that had killed half of them. Islanders themselves, the English might have been particularly attracted to islands; certainly, by the early 1620s, English overseas prospects seemed to reside in islands, as Ireland and Bermuda suggested, and as the first permanent establishment on Saint Christopher (in 1624) promised, soon to be followed by five other island settlements (Barbados, Nevis, Providence, Antigua, and Montserrat) in the next eight years. Islands had clear advantages over a mainland—they were knowable, they offered more coastline in relation to land mass, they could be more easily settled, their environments could be more readily transformed, and they seemed to pose fewer risks—and their most obvious disadvantage, the lack of available land, was not so evident in the beginning.

37. For similar thoughts about strategic importance, see Ruggiero Romano, "The Initial Linkage with America: A General Framework," in Emmer and Damas, eds., *General History of the Caribbean*, II, 43–61. Much could be said about contemporary fears that a Spanish attack on Virginia was imminent. In 1612, news reached London that the Spaniards had wiped out the Virginia colony by launching an attack from Havana. See John Digbye to Lord Edmondes, 1612, Edmondes Papers, Stowe MSS, 173, VIII, fol. 223, BL; see also Digbye to the king, Aug. 12, 1612, Aug. 15, 1613, in Kupperman, Appleby, and Banton, eds., *CSP*, Col., I, 45, 50.

In the early 1620s, the best model for colonization, it could be claimed, was island- rather than mainland-based. Thus, in the mid-1630s, the worldly-wise Thomas Bowdler identified the particular value of the West Indies as a place to "raise another England to withstand our new Spain in America." At that time, who would not have agreed with him?[38]

38. For the attractiveness of the island model, see B. W. Higman, "Economic and Social Development of the British West Indies, from Settlement to ca. 1850," in Stanley L. Engerman and Robert E. Gallman, eds., *The Cambridge Economic History of the United States,* I, *The Colonial Era* (Cambridge, 1996), 299–300; Grove, *Green Imperialism,* esp. 32–42; Gillis, *Islands of the Mind,* esp. 83–100. Thomas Bowdler, Commonplace Book, 1635–1636, Edinburgh University Library, Laing MSS, La III, fol. 532, as cited in Nicholas Canny, "The Origins of Empire," in Canny, ed., *Oxford History of the British Empire,* I, 19.

part four

INTELLECTUAL CURRENTS

Andrew Fitzmaurice

MORAL UNCERTAINTY IN THE DISPOSSESSION

OF NATIVE AMERICANS

Over the course of five hundred years from 1492, natural law emerged as the preeminent legal instrument for the dispossession of indigenous peoples. In the sixteenth century, in what is now a well-known story, the Salamanca School in Spain made the first use of natural law to consider the position of colonized peoples.[1] The Salamanca writers were widely read in Europe, and (outside Spain) nowhere more so than in England. Yet we have only a very sketchy understanding of the reception of the Salamanca School in England and, in particular, we know very little about how its writings were employed to consider the justice of English colonization. The Salamanca theologians had used natural law to argue that rights reside in the subject or individual, and on this basis they employed the idea of rights to defend Native Americans against Spanish colonization. The English, famously in the work of John Locke, used natural law to support the justice of colonization and to deny the rights of indigenous peoples. They inverted the force

I would like to thank David Armitage, Saliha Belmessous, Mark Goldie, and Duncan Ivison for assistance with this essay.

1. Five hundred years brings us from Columbus to 1992, the year in which the Queensland government in Australia argued against Aboriginal title on the basis of the Roman- and natural-law argument that the country was *terra nullius* when Europeans arrived. See *Mabo and Others v Queensland, Australian Law Journal Reports,* LXVI, no. 2 (1992), 408. This was not the first use of the argument in recent generations; see also International Court of Justice, advisory opinion of Oct. 16, 1975, *Western Sahara,* Reports of Judgments, Advisory Opinions, and Orders (The Hague, 1975) 12. On dispossession and the natural-law tradition, see Anthony Pagden, *The Fall of Natural Man: The American Indian and the Origins of Comparative Ethnology* (Cambridge, 1982); Robert A. Williams, *The American Indian in Western Legal Thought* (Oxford, 1990); James Tully, *An Approach to Political Philosophy: Locke in Contexts* (Cambridge, 1993); Barbara Arneil, *John Locke and America: The Defence of English Colonialism* (Oxford, 1996). The classic study on the Salamanca School's examination of Native Americans is Pagden, *Fall of Natural Man.*

of the Salamanca argument. As we remain ignorant of the reception of the Salamanca School writings in England, so the dramatic nature of this turn has not been clear to historians, nor have we understood how it was made. It was at the moment the English established the Virginia colony, I will argue, that rights were first used to dispossess indigenous peoples.

Reading backward from Locke, we might expect that the natural-law justifications of Indian dispossession in the generations before he wrote would share, if not his philosophical clarity, at least his certainty that dispossession was justifiable. Indeed, for Locke, there was no question of Indian dispossession because he did not believe Indians to be in possession of the lands upon which they lived. Locke's moral certainty was in no way typical of the discussion of the legal status of Indians in sixteenth- and seventeenth-century England. Early modern English people often acknowledged the rights of Indians and only overcame their consciousness of those rights with considerable difficulty. Even as they inverted the force of the natural-law discussion of Indian rights, they were unable fully to escape the polemical defense of indigenous rights for which that tradition had originally been employed.

My argument assumes that the concept of rights was not used by Francisco de Vitoria and his followers in the Salamanca School to justify the Spanish dispossession of indigenous peoples in the Caribbean, Mexico, and Peru. This is, of course, a contentious claim. In the late twentieth century, many historians have argued that the Salamanca School merely furnished a secularized and sanitized theory of conquest.[2] Thus the sixteenth-century Spaniards Vitoria and the Salamanca-influenced Bartolomé de Las Casas take their place alongside the seventeenth-century Englishman Locke and the eighteenth-century Swiss Emeric de Vattel in a unified and continuous justification of European expansion. The contours of history have been flattened under the weight of this revisionism.

I would like briefly to overview the theories of the Salamanca School in order to measure those claims. It was Francisco de Vitoria, a follower of the Aristotelian philosophy of Thomas Aquinas, who first introduced the question of rights to consider the position of conquered peoples. In his lectures at the University of Salamanca between 1534 and 1539, Vitoria addressed whether the peoples of the Americas had been justly dispossessed of their property, whether they had been justly enslaved and killed, and whether

2. See, for example, Williams, *American Indian in Western Legal Thought;* Tully, *Approach to Political Philosophy*. Anthony Pagden's work is an important exception to this trend. See, for example, Pagden, *Fall of Natural Man*.

their societies had been justly destroyed. He systematically analyzed, from the perspective of natural law, the claims by the conquistadors and subsequently by the Spanish Crown to have rightfully conquered. At the heart of the Salamanca defense of the rights of the American peoples was the Aristotelian metaphysic that all things exist in potential and that it is in the nature of man to release that potential through the recognition and exploitation of the laws of nature.[3] Thus all trees are potential chairs, and in making them into chairs, we realize our own humanity. To be just and therefore hold rights of possession, a society needs to have manifested the propensity to exploit nature in the creation of both physical and political structures. It was evident, Vitoria argued, that the peoples of the Americas had sufficiently understood natural law to be able to create societies. "They have," he declared, "properly organised cities, proper magistrates, marriages and overlords, laws, industries, and commerce, all of which requires the use of reason." In this case, the Indians had also established their humanity. "In the law of nations *(jus gentium),*" he continued, "a thing which does not belong to anyone [his term here is *res nullius*] becomes the property of the first taker." In Roman law, which was regarded as a codification of natural law, and to which Vitoria was referring, the statement of this principle was known as the law *ferae bestiae,* or the law of wild beasts. In the *Digest of Justinian,* the great compilation of Roman law, ferae bestiae was expressed: "What presently belongs to no one becomes by natural reason the property of the first taker"; thus "all animals taken on land, sea, or in the air, that is wild beasts, birds, and fish, become the property of those who take them." According to Vitoria, ferae bestiae clearly did not apply to the American lands, so that if the Spanish conquest was just, that justice must arise from one of a number of other legal bases: the Bulls of Donation made by Pope Alexander VI in 1493; or because the Indians were sinners; or because they were madmen. Vitoria rejected title based upon the Donation of Alexander because he contested the possibility that the church could hold the temporal power with which to make such a donation. He rejected the idea of Indians as sinners to justify conquest because that invoked the dangerous Protestant heresy that the only just society was a godly society. He rejected the notion that the Indians were madmen, because they clearly "had some order in their affairs." It was true, he observed, that some of their customs appeared obnoxious. But this was because of the Indians' barbarous education and not because they were not men and incapable of the use of reason. At this point, Vitoria raised the possibility that the Indians could be in the

3. See Pagden, *Fall of Natural Man.*

infancy of reason. If, and he emphasised "if," this were the situation, even such a state could not justify conquest. In that case, the relationship of the Spaniards to the Indians could be like that of a guardian to a child. Although the child requires protection, she maintains possession of her property.[4]

Vitoria then turned to the question of whether the Spaniards had fought a just war against the Indians and therefore had the right to appropriate the property of the vanquished. He concluded that a just war could only have been fought on the grounds that there had been a violation of the Spaniards' natural-law rights to "natural partnership and communication," that is, travel, friendship, trade, and the sending of ambassadors and missionaries. Of this stage in Vitoria's analysis, James Tully observes: "After advancing a number of objections to the standard justifications, Vitoria concluded his long discussion with a justification of conquest he believed to be invulnerable. Since both Spaniards and Amerindians are in the state of nature, if the Spaniards conduct themselves in accordance with the law of nature, then they have the right to defend themselves against any wrong committed by the Amerindians 'and to avail themselves of the rights of war.'" Similarly, Robert A. Williams concludes, "In Vitoria's discourse of New World conquest, reason as well as Rome were granted the right to initiate enforcement of Christian Europe's universally binding norms." "Francisco de Vitoria," he continues, "was the first articulator of a European discourse of conquest founded on secularly rationalisable norms and values. His Law of Nations justified the extension of Western power over the American Indians as an imperative of the Europeans' vision of truth." The problem with this interpretation is that Vitoria resisted the extension of Western power over the American Indians. For Williams and for Tully, because Vitoria argued that a violation of "the natural partnership of communication" would be grounds for just war against the Indians, he therefore justified the Spanish conquest. But Vitoria never stated—in "On Dietary Laws," in "On the American Indians," or in "On the Law of War"—that the Indians had violated the "natural partnership of communication" with the Spaniards. Indeed, it appears that the force of this natural-law argument for Vitoria was to demonstrate once again that there was *no* justification for the conquest and that perhaps it was the Spaniards who had violated natural law in this way. This was nowhere clearer than in his letter to Miguel de Arcos on

4. Francisco de Vitoria, "On the American Indians," in Vitoria, *Political Writings,* ed. Anthony Pagden and Jeremy Lawrence (Cambridge, 1991), 280; Theodor Mommsen, ed., and Alan Watson, trans., *The Digest of Justinian,* 4 vols. (Philadelphia, 1985), IV, 1–3, 41.

November 8, 1534. He commenced, "Very Reverend Father, As for the case of Peru, I must tell you, after a lifetime of studies and long experience, that no business shocks me or embarrasses me more than the corrupt profits and affairs of the Indies. Their very mention freezes the blood in my viens." He alluded to the political dangers of holding an opinion on the subject and then continued: "But if utterly forced to give a categorical reply, in the end I say what I think. . . . First, I do not understand the justice of the war . . . as far as I understand from eyewitnesses who were personally present during the recent battle with Atahuallpa [in the conquest of Peru], *neither he nor any of his people had ever done the slightest injury to the Christians, nor given them the least grounds for making war on them.*" "Other more recent conquests," he observed, "have, I think, been even more vile."[5]

The fact remains that the natural-law arguments of trade and friendship and, most important, ferae bestiae were used by Europeans to dispossess indigenous Americans and other indigenous peoples (ferae bestiae was reified in nineteenth-century international law by one of its terms: namely, as the doctrine of res nullius, or things belonging to no one). These arguments, while for Vitoria prohibiting invasion, provided a tool that could be and was turned against colonized peoples (and it is from that outcome that historians have anachronistically read the Salamanca School). Most famously, John Locke, the English philosopher, physician, and secretary to the lords proprietors of Carolina, employed natural-law arguments to contend that Native Americans did not possess their lands. The Swiss philosopher Emeric de Vattel employed similar arguments that perhaps achieved even greater popularity than Locke's. Both Locke and Vattel and, more broadly, the natural-law tradition were used from the eighteenth to the twentieth centuries to justify the dispossession of indigenous peoples in Africa, Canada, Australia, and New Zealand, among other colonial societies.[6]

5. Tully, *Approach to Political Philosophy,* 142–143; Williams, *American Indian in Western Legal Thought,* 105–107; Vitoria, *Political Writings,* ed. Pagden and Lawrence, 331–332 (my emphasis).

6. On Vattel, see Richard Tuck, *The Rights of War and Peace: Political Thought and the International Order from Grotius to Kant* (Oxford, 1999), 191–196; Anthony Pagden, *Lords of All the World: Ideologies of Empire in Spain, Britain, and France c. 1500–c. 1800* (New Haven, Conn., 1995), 78–79. On Locke's use of natural-law arguments to justify colonization, see Arneil, *John Locke and America;* Tully, *Approach to Political Philosophy,* 137–178. For the reification of ferae bestiae as res nullius in nineteenth-century international law, see, for example, Jean Louis Klüber, *Droit des gens* (Paris, 1831), 209; "Un état peut acquérir des choses qui n'appartiennent à personne *(res nul-*

There was, then, a turn. The question we are left with is when it happened—the historiography provides little sense of that. I will argue that the turn occurred in the English reception of the Salamanca writers. The most important event for that reception was the first twenty years of the foundation of the English colony in the Chesapeake. Why would promoters of the Virginia Company colony have troubled themselves with reading sixteenth-century Thomist philosophy? The Salamanca School had provided the most profound early modern account of the legality of colonization. Their writings, as we shall presently see, were felt to be directly relevant to concerns about justifying the Chesapeake colony.

There is, however, a prior question of how the promoters of the Virginia colony were able to read and obtain texts of the Salamanca School. Most of those people who wrote to promote the Virginia Company were university educated, and many were read in theology and so would have had access to the libraries of Oxford and Cambridge. The Oxford University library was, however, being created at this time by Thomas Bodley, and the Cambridge University library was weak. The college libraries were inferior to many private collections of books. It is instructive to consider the example of Saint John's College Library, Cambridge, particularly given that many members of the Virginia Company attended this college. Samuel Purchas, the great

---

lius) par l'occupation"—"A state can acquire things that belong to nobody (res nullius) by occupation." Many historians have anachronistically accepted the eighteenth- and nineteenth-century terms *res nullius* and *terra nullius* as descriptions of pre-nineteenth-century statements of ferae bestiae; see, for example, Andrew Fitzmaurice, *Humanism and America: An Intellectual History of English Colonisation, 1500–1625* (Cambridge, 2003), 137, 140; Pagden, *Lords of All the World,* 77–78; Hugo Grotius, *The Free Sea,* ed. David Armitage, Natural Law and Enlightenment Classics (Indianapolis, 2004), xv, derived from the post–1609 translation by Richard Hakluyt, MS 529, Inner Temple Library, London; Henry Reynolds, *The Law of the Land* (Ringwood, 1987), 67. For the dominance of natural-law arguments in the dispossession of colonized peoples, see *Annuaire de l'institut de droit international,* IX (1888), X (1889). In these two volumes of the *Annuaire,* the legal principles established in the Berlin conference of 1884 / 1885 by European colonial powers and the United States were articulated in terms of the doctrine of res nullius and, for the first time, *territorium nullius.* The Berlin conference brought the governments of colonial powers together to agree on rules by which they would partition territories that were deemed suitable for colonization, or as "protectorates." The occupation of Africa was the immediate motive for the conference. On natural-law arguments and the colonization of Australia, see Reynolds, *Law of the Land;* for Canada, see Brian Slattery, "French Claims in North America, 1500–59," *Canadian Historical Review,* LIX (1978), 139–169; L. C. Green and Olive P. Dickason, *The Law of Nations and the New World* (Edmonton, 1989).

compiler of voyage narratives, said that it was at Saint John's College that he "first conceived with this Travelling Genius."[7]

It is clear that, before 1626 (the period with which we are concerned), Saint John's College Library did not hold the books of the Salamanca Thomists because this was the date upon which they received the first part of an endowment that included those works (the aim of the endowment being to provide books that were not already held at the library). Could, therefore, the promoters of the Virginia Company have used private collections for their reading of the Salamanca authors? This appears undoubtedly to be the case, particularly if we believe Samuel Purchas's claim to have consulted seven hundred authors in the composition of the first edition of *Purchas His Pilgrimage* alone. Members of the Virginia Company had access to a number of private libraries. Henry Percy, the "wizard" earl of Northumberland, created one of the largest libraries in Jacobean England. His brother George Percy was one of the first Chesapeake colonists. Richard Hooker, the former tutor of Edwin Sandys, who was a leading figure in the Virginia Company, also collected a very large library. So did the great early modern lawyer and philosopher John Selden, who was associated with the Virginia Company and its members.[8]

There was, however, a library even closer to the circles of the Virginia Company. This one belonged to William Crashaw, preacher at the Middle Temple and later at Whitechapel and one of the many important but unexplored figures involved in the company.[9] Crashaw delivered a sermon promoting the Virginia colony, which was subsequently published, but more important, he organized other promotional efforts on behalf of the com-

7. On the education of these Virginia Company writers, see Fitzmaurice, *Humanism and America*, 62–67; on members and supporters of the Virginia Company who attended Saint John's College, see 66–67. For Purchas's quote, see epistle dedicatory, in Samuel Purchas, *Hakluytus Posthumus; or, Purchas His Pilgrimes . . .* , 4 vols. (London, 1625), III.

8. See P. J. Wallis, "The Library of William Crashaw," Cambridge Bibliographical Society, *Transactions,* II, part 3 (1956), 213–228; R. M. Fisher, "William Crashawe's Library at the Temple, 1605-1615," *The Library,* XXX, no. 2 (June 1975), 116–124; epistle dedicatory, in Samuel Purchas, *Purchas His Pilgrimage . . .* (London, 1613). Sandys also sponsored the publication of Richard Hooker's *Laws of Ecclesiastical Polity.* On Hooker and Sandys, see Theodore K. Rabb, *Jacobean Gentleman: Sir Edwin Sandys, 1561-1629* (Princeton, N.J., 1998).

9. Wallis, "Library of William Crashaw," Cambridge Bibliographical Society, *Transactions,* II, part 3; Fisher, "William Crashawe's Library at the Temple," *The Library,* XXX, no. 2 (June 1975). See also Peter John Wallis, *William Crashawe, the Sheffield Puritan,* Hunter Archaeological Society, *Transactions,* VIII ([n.p.], 1963).

pany, including tracts by William Symonds (another London preacher), an anonymous tract promoting the Bermudas, and the tract of the Chesapeake colonist William Whitaker (the son of the former master of Saint John's College). Further, Crashaw clearly had a part in commissioning *The Proceedings of the English Colonie in Virginia*.[10] He was closely associated with the Virginian plantation until his death in 1625.[11]

It was from Crashaw's library, via the patronage of the earl of Southampton (a leader of the Virginia Company), that Saint John's College received its new library in 1626 (both Crashaw and Southampton were former students at Saint John's College). By 1612, Crashaw had created the third largest library in England, exceeding four thousand books and manuscripts. At this time, only the library created by Bodley in Oxford and the library of Richard Bancroft, archbishop of Canterbury, were larger. Thus at the heart of the dominant colonial venture of early modern England was one of the greatest libraries of Jacobean England. It is clear, moreover, from Crashaw's letters and those of his contemporaries that he allowed his collection to be

---

10. William Symonds's letter concluding that tract begins: "Captain Smith I return to you the print of my labours, as Mr Croshaw requested me"; see W[illiam] S[ymonds], ed., *The Proceedings of the English Colonie in Virginia* . . . (Oxford, 1612), 110. Note that William Strachey also presented Crashaw with a copy of his *Articles, Lawes and Orders, Dyvine Politique and Martiall for the Colonye of Virginia;* see Wallis, *William Crashawe,* 42. As late as 1620, Crashaw was active in promoting the colony's affairs. The Virginia Company court minutes for June 23, 1620, record: "A writing being sent from Mr Crashaw intimatinge of one that will make Commodities in Virginia of good worth wch shalbe merchantable in all places of the world war referred to the said Mr Crashaw and Mr Deputy to confer wth him" (Susan Myra Kingsbury, ed., *The Records of the Virginia Company of London,* 4 vols. [Washington, D.C., 1906–1935], I, 370). In 1617, Crashaw published *Fiscus papalis* (London, 1617 and 1621), in which he declared, "Let covetous Merchants goe to the Indies, and Gallants to Guiana, let silly Catholicks goe dwell in Ireland, and fooles into Virginia" (sig. A3v). This comment could be taken as an illustration of the early modern English ambivalence about colonization except that it was made in a thickly ironic text. That irony is apparent from the Puritan Crashaw's declared purpose in "Laying downe the spiritual riches and infinite treasure which (as sure as the Pope is holy and true) are to be found in the Catholike Roman Church" (title page). The irony is also apparent in the continuation of the passage above: ". . . fooles into Virginia. Let us take a wiser course and post to Rome." My thanks to Karen Kupperman for alerting me to *Fiscus papalis*.

11. Crashaw remained in London during the plague of that year in order to care for the sick, but it is assumed he became one of its victims. For his death, see Wallis, *William Crashawe,* 51 n. 108. In his will, he employed the good offices of two leaders of opposing factions in the Virginia Company, Edwin Sandys and Robert Johnson (12).

used as a lending library. The catalogue of that part of Crashaw's collection which reached Saint John's College lists the complete works of Vitoria and also books by Vitoria's followers, including Domingo de Soto and Luis de Molina.[12]

If we appreciate that the early modern English were deeply skeptical of colonization, it becomes easier to understand why they were enthusiastic readers of the Salamanca School. Their zeal for the Salamanca authors has been conventionally, but weakly, attributed to the desire to propagate the Black Legend of Spanish colonization. The Salamanca defense of indigenous rights supported English anxiety about colonial dispossession. Minutes from one of the meetings of the Virginia Council held between 1606 and 1609 provide powerful testimony to this anxiety. The minutes record a debate held by the council—the colony's governing body—on whether "some form of justification of our plantation might be conceived, and pass . . . into many handes." After a long deliberation, the council decided against arguing for the justice of the colony for several reasons. First, it was noted that, when the Spanish monarch subjected the Spanish conquests to the consideration of the "Casuists, and Confesssors," the result was they "declyn'd him from that severe and unjust course" and concluded that there could be "gathered for him no title, of Dominion or property, but only a Magistracy, and Empire." The casuists and confessors here are, of course, the Salamanca School writers. Clearly, therefore, it was not only the promoters of the Virginia Company who grappled with the writings of the Salamanca School. The members of the company and the governing council itself had also found it necessary to read Vitoria and his followers and to discuss among themselves the implications of these writings for their enterprise. Moreover, this concern predates the promotion of the colony in print, so that the subsequent published discussion of the arguments of the Salamanca School would seem to arise from within the council. The second reason the council decided not to argue for the justice of the colony before 1609 was that they felt publicity would anger the Spaniards and put pressure on James I, who was equivocal about the question of colonies. And finally, it was held that "because therefore, we shal be putt to defend our title, not yet publiquely quarrelled, not only comparatively to be as good as the Spaniards . . . *but*

---

12. The endowment of Crashaw's books occasioned the construction of a new library building, which is the present-day rare books and manuscripts library. See Fisher, "William Crashaw's Library at the Temple," *The Library*, XXX, no. 2 (June 1975), 119; *Catalogus librorum bibliotecæ Johanensis*, MS U.4, Saint John's College Library, Cambridge.

absolutely to be good against the Naturall people: some thought it better to abstayne from this unnessisary way of provocation, and reserve ourselves to the defensive part." What the council clearly acknowledged here, with the Salamanca writings in mind, was that justifying the colony against the rights of the Native peoples of the Chesapeake would be difficult.[13]

This anxiety was expressed both negatively and positively. It was expressed negatively, for example, when John Smith, one of the first governors in the Chesapeake, and his supporters repeatedly complained about the Virginia Council's excessive concern about Native sensibilities. One of Smith's allies lamented that "the command from England was so straight not to offend them [the Chesapeake peoples] as our authority bearers (keeping their houses) would rather be anything than peace breakers." He continued, "The patient council, that nothing would move to warre with the Salvages, would gladly have wrangled with captaine Smith for his cruelty." War in America, as members of the council knew from their own reading of the Salamanca authors, would be extremely difficult to rationalize.[14]

This concern about dispossession was also expressed in promotional pamphlets when, in 1609, the Virginia Company changed its policy and began publishing in defense of its right to colonize. Many early modern English critics as well as promoters of colonies expressed the view that Native Americans lived in civil societies. On the first questions put by Vitoria, namely, is the country of the barbarians unclaimed and does ferae bestiae apply, promoters and critics of English colonization alike frequently agreed the colonizers could not be the "first takers" in Virginia. Native Americans were often represented as living in civil society and in possession of their land and goods. In premodern European cultures, the health of political systems was believed to depend as much on the character and spirit of a people—that is, upon the virtue of the citizens—as it did upon the strength of political institutions. It is important in this context that English reports frequently praised Indian virtues, particularly martial ones. The artist John White, governor of the short-lived Roanoke colony in 1585, represented Indians living in towns, cultivating fields, catching fish, and employing a number of familiar technologies. It was also clear to the English that

13. On early modern skepticism of colonization, see David Armitage, *The Ideological Origins of the British Empire* (Cambridge, 2000), 125–145; Fitzmaurice, *Humanism and America,* 2–4. For the council's debate, see "A Justification for Planting in Virginia," in Kingsbury, ed., *The Records of the Virginia Company of London,* III, 1–3, printed from Tanner Manuscripts, XCIII, fol. 200, Bodleian Library, Oxford.

14. S[ymonds], ed., *Proceedings of the English Colonie in Virginia,* 23–25.

the Indians possessed a political system for which many writers expressed admiration. As John Smith observed: "Although the countrey people be very barbarous, yet they have amongst them such government, as that their Magistrates for good commanding, and their people for due subjection, and obeying, excel many places that would be counted very civil. The form of the Common wealth is a monarchical government." His observation of the nature of rule by the "king" Powhatan would have struck a familiar chord with readers in Jacobean England: "The lawes whereby he ruleth is custome. Yet when he listeth his will is law." Of Powhatan's seat, Smith noted, "The great King hath foure or five houses, each containing four score or an hundred foote in length" overlooking a country in which lay "an hundred houses and many large plaines . . . together inhabited." Indians were also acknowledged to practice a religion, which for the natural-law theorists demonstrated civility. Similarly, Alexander Whitaker, one of the more negative writers on Indians, conceded that the Indians must be counted among those who exploit nature: "There is civill governement amongst them which they strictly observe, and shew thereby that the law of Nature dwelleth in them: for they have a rude kinde of Commonwealth, and rough governement, wherein they both honour and obey their Kings, Parents, and Governours . . . they observe the limits of their owne possessions, and incroach not upon their neighbours dwellings."[15]

From the perspective by which Indians were recognized to constitute a civil society, it was common that promoters of colonies would respond to the writings of the Salamanca School by observing that they would not dispossess the Native Americans. Samuel Purchas was one of the most emphatic writers on the injustice of dispossessing Native Americans, although he was generally referring to the Spanish conquests. But as for many English writers, criticism of the Spanish placed clear limits on what could be allowed the English. Purchas's observations on the injustice of dispossession are particularly trenchant in his essay in *Hakluytus Posthumus:* "Of the Propertie Which Infidels Have in Their Lands and Goods." Purchas has been described as "the early modern British writer who showed the greatest familiarity with Vitoria's writings" (although Alberico Gentili might challenge for that place), and it is certainly clear that Vitoria was

15. See Quentin Skinner, "Political Philosophy," in Charles B. Schmitt et al., eds., *Cambridge History of Renaissance Philosophy* (Cambridge, 1988), 389–452; Fitzmaurice, *Humanism and America,* 162–163; John Smith, *A Map of Virginia* . . . (Oxford, 1612), 34–35; Smith, *A True Relation* . . . (London, 1608), sig. B4v; Alexander Whitaker, *Good Newes from Virginia* (London, 1613), 26–27.

the main instrument he employed in the defense of indigenous rights. It is true that Purchas was at times sanguine about the Spanish dispossession of Native Americans. In a passage in which he cited Vitoria in the margin as his authority, he observed: "Innumerable are the compacts and contracts mentioned in Histories, whereby the rule of Countries and States have beene made over to new Masters." Accordingly, in the "Animadversions on the said Bull of Pope Alexander," he acknowledged that, however unjust the Spanish conquest might have been, with the passage of time, their title became just: "I question not the right of the Spanish Crowne in those parts. . . . The Castilian Industry I honour (as appears in the former relations) their Right may, for that which is actually in their Possession, without this Bull, plead Discoverie even before this [i.e. the Donation of Alexander] was written, the Sword Preseription, subjection of the Inhabitants, long and quiet possession; which, howsoever the Case was at first (wherewith I meddle not) must now, after so long Succession, be acknowledged Just. I quarrel the Pope only." Purchas's quarrel with the pope was over the Donation of Alexander, by which the Catholic Church granted possession of the New World to the Spanish. There was scarcely an English writer on colonization who did not make the same complaint. The legal basis of the objection concerned the temporal powers of the Roman church: "Christs Kingdome is not of this world, and properly neither gives nor takes away worldly properties, civill and political interests." This argument, as Purchas pointed out, is "cited by Vitoria" "largely proving these propositions, That the Pope is not Lord of the World, That the Temporall Power depends not of him, That it is not subject to his Temporall Power." [16]

In his quarrel with the pope, Purchas abandoned his claim that the Spanish conquests had become just. It is ungodly to "rob Kings of their supremacy and preheminence, subjects of their land and state, as if to convert to Christ were to evert out of their possessions, and subvert states." "The rights of men," he insisted, "by the royall or common lawes established (all derived from that of nature . . . are in conscience of Gods commandment to be permitted them." To deny those rights is a crime against nature of the same order as "filthy Sodomites, sleepers, ignorant beasts, disciples of Cham, Balaam, and fore, rockes, clouds without water, corrupt trees twice dead, raging warres, wandering stares, to despise government . . . spots and

16. Purchas, *Hakluytus Posthumus,* I, book 1, 14–16, esp. 15, and book 2, 20, 23; Armitage, *Ideological Origins,* 88; Fitzmaurice, *Humanism and America,* 148–157.

blots, wells without water, clouds carried about without a tempest, to whom the black darknesse is reserved for ever."[17] Again citing Vitoria, he asserted that infidels and, in this case, Native Americans could not be deprived of their property: "nor can Infidelitie which concerneth Divine Law, yea in matters supernaturall, take away that right which Positive or Naturall Law hath given; nor exclude from just title on Earth [in margin "Vict. de Ind," i.e. Vitoria "On the American Indians"]." Indeed, he argued, it would be unjust not only to challenge Native American dominion but even to breach sovereignty: "And for Ophir, long before inhabited (as appeareth Gen. 10) he [Solomon] did not for the discovery thereof, then new, challenge jurisdiction or sovereigntie, as Lord of that Sea or region by him discovered (no more than the Ophirians had been Lords of Israel, if they had then discovered it) but left things as he found them, the Countrey appropriate to the Inhabitants [Vitoria cited again in margin]." Purchas was not exceptional in his agreement with Vitoria on this point. In *Mare liberum,* the Dutch philosopher and statesman Hugo Grotius had made the same argument, and he had made it also on the authority of Vitoria: that the Indians could no more be dispossessed of their land than the Europeans dispossessed by the Indians. "Victoria therefore rightly saith that the Spaniards got no more authority over the Indians for this cause than the Indians had over the Spaniards if any of them had come formerly into Spain." Grotius's *Mare liberum* had been translated into English by Richard Hakluyt. Given that Hakluyt had left Purchas all his papers (which Purchas employed in composing *Hakluytus Posthumus*), we could also assume that Purchas was familiar with Grotius's work.[18]

Citing Vitoria, Purchas argued that even the preaching of Christianity could not justify the dispossession of the Indians: "And in his [Vitoria's] Relectiones of the Indians he sayeth, that it doth not appear to him, that the Christian Faith hath so beene preached to them, that they are bound sub novo peccato to beleeve it, having had no probable perswasion, as Miracles and examples of Religious life, but contrarie; yea, had the faith beene never so probably propounded, and they rejected it, yet might they not be spoyled of their Goods, or pursued by Warre." Alberico Gentili, the professor of law in Elizabethan Oxford, had made the same argument in *De jure belli libri tres.* In the chapter "Whether It Is Just to Make War for the Sake of Religion," Gentili cited "the learned Vitoria" for the argument that "religion

17. Purchas, *Hakluytus Posthumus,* I, book 1, 14.
18. Ibid., 16; Grotius, *Free Sea,* ed. Armitage, 15.

was not a just reason for the war of his Spanish countrymen against the Indians."[19]

Many of the Virginia Company promoters also warned of the problems of dispossession. One of the company's hired pens, Robert Gray, declared "that there is no intendment to take away from them by force that rightful inheritance they have in that Countrey." And William Crashaw, who kept the works of the Salamanca School in a room above the chapel at the Middle Temple, concluded: "A Christian may take nothing from a heathen against his will . . . We will take nothing from the Savages by power nor pillage, by craft nor violence, neither goods, lands nor libertie, much lesse life."[20] The Virginia Company's anonymous *True Declaration of the Estate of the Colonie in Virginia* paraphrased Vitoria in a further statement of these fears and explicitly acknowledged the debt to "Salamanca." According to the report, Christianity must be preached in Virginia in:

> one of these three waies: [1] Either meerly Apostolically, without the helpe of man, (without so much as staffe [2] (or meerly imperiallie, when a Prince hath conquered their bodies, that the Preachers may feede their soules; [3] Or mixtly, by discoverie, and trade of merchants; where all temporall meanes are used for defence, and security, but none for offence, or crueltie. For the first (to preach Apostolicallie) it is simplie impossible: except we had the gift of tongues, that every nation might heare the word of God in their owne language. . . . For the second, to preach the Gospell to a nation conquered, and to set their soules at liberty when we have brought their bodies to slaverie; It may be a matter sacred in the Preachers, but I know not how justifiable in the rulers, who for their mere ambition to set upon the glosse of religion. Let the divines of Salamanca, discusse that question, how the possessor of the west Indies, first destroyed and then instructed.

19. Purchas, *Hakluytus Posthumus,* I, book 2, 20; Alberico Gentili, *De jure belli libri tres* (1612), trans. John C. Rolfe, in *The Classics of International Law,* 2 vols. (Oxford, 1933), I, 39.

20. R[obert] G[ray], *A Good Speed to Virginia* (London, 1610), sig. [C4]r; William Crashaw, *A Sermon Preached in London before Right Honourable the Lord Lawarre* . . . (London, 1609), sigs. [D3]v–D4v. William Symonds, another company promoter, raised the same problem: "The countrey, they say, is possessed by owners, that rule and governe it in their owne right: then with what conscience, and equitie can we offer to thrust them, by violence out of their inheritances?" (William Symonds, *Virginia* [London, 1609], 10).

The author concluded that "The third belongs to us," referring to the third method of colonization ("by discoverie, and trade of merchants; where all temporal means are pursued for defence, and securitie, but none for offence, or crueltie").[21]

Here we see where English colonial promoters began to enter the door left open by Vitoria. They insisted that they would not conquer but that they had a right to enter the lands of the Indians for trade and to defend themselves in that situation if necessary. The right to trade also included the right to trade for land; thus the prominent colonist John Rolfe concluded his *Relation of the State of Virginia* observing that he had described the colonists' "several places of . . . abode." "Which places, or seates," he noted, "are all our owne ground, not so much by conquest . . . but purchased of the [Indians] freely, and they very willingly selling it." Similarly, William Strachey insisted that, in the "Law of Nations," the right of "Community betwixt man and man" permitted the English to trade with the Indians. It was but a short step to claim that the natural right of communication had been denied, and Strachey, along with many of his contemporaries, argued that, in that case, the Roman- and natural-law right to meet force with force would justify the use of violence against the Indians.[22]

It was clear, however, that the right to communication and commerce was not a right of dominion, far less sovereignty. It did not provide, that is, secure tenure for a colonizer. At this point, the legal profile of English colonization looked much more appropriate to Portuguese factories than to settler communities. Indeed, the argument of commerce implicitly assumes that rights reside in the persons with whom one is trading. The English insisted on the right to commerce with the Indians by using precisely the same arguments that they had used to insist on free trade (when they chose to insist on free trade) with other European nations, particularly the Spanish and the Dutch and their dependencies. It was no accident that Richard Hakluyt, the premier Elizabethan promoter of colonies, had chosen to translate Grotius's *Mare liberum,* of which the principal thesis was "It is lawful for any nation to go to any other and trade with it." Hakluyt's translation of Grotius (at some point between 1609 and 1616) might have been commis-

21. *A True Declaration of the Estate of the Colonie in Virginia* (London, 1610), 6–9; cf. Vitoria, "On the American Indians," in Vitoria, *Political Writings,* ed. Pagden and Lawrence, 278–281.

22. William Strachey, *The Historie of Travell into Virginia Britania (1612),* ed. Louis B. Wright and Virginia Freund, Works Issued by the Hakluyt Society, 2d Ser., no. 103 (London, 1953), 22–23; Fitzmaurice, *Humanism and America,* 144–147.

sioned by the English East India Company to help them in their struggles with both the Portuguese and the Dutch for the right to trade in the East Indies. Grotius had written *Mare liberum* in part to support the claims of the Dutch East India Company. Hakluyt was, at this time, working for the English East India Company (which shared leaders and membership with the Virginia Company, notably Thomas Smith). But Hakluyt could not have completed this translation without being mindful that it supported contemporary justifications for the Virginia Colony. The colonization of America had, after all, been the principal concern of his life's work. He had always placed that concern within a global context; in common with many of his contemporaries, he understood the colonization of America to be part of a political and religious struggle between European powers that was being conducted on an increasingly global scale. Grotius's *Mare liberum,* while specifically addressing the East, was also engaged with conflicts arising from that global competition.[23]

It was important that, just as freedom of the sea was interesting Hakluyt, Purchas titled his chapter on the rights of infidels "Of the Proprietie Which Infidels Have in Their Lands and Goods: Of Proprietie in the Sea, and of Solomon's Proprietie of the Sea and Shoare of Ezion Geber." The issue of property in the sea had been central to disputes about freedom of commerce. The two issues turned on the same principle. Freedom of the seas was based upon the right of communication and movement, and freedom of commerce was also understood to be an extension of the natural communication that should exist between men. To have the freedom of the sea was to have freedom of commerce. To demand these rights of Native Americans was to demand no more of them than other Europeans. Moreover, to do this was to recognize that Native Americans had a place at the legal table. The justification of colonies by commerce, therefore, was concerned much more with whether Native Americans would grant rights and less with whether they possessed rights (taking for granted that they did).[24]

Alberico Gentili had emphasized this disjunction between arguments from commerce and the justification of dominion in a passage that is not cited by historians (presumably because it does not fit his belligerent image):

No one doubts today that what we call the New World is joined to our own and has always been known to the remote Indi. And that is one reason why the warfare of the Spaniards in that part of the world seems to be

23. Grotius, *Free Sea,* ed. Armitage, 6.
24. Purchas, *Hakluytus Posthumus,* I, book 1, 14–16.

justified, because the inhabitants prohibited other men from commerce with them; and it would be an adequate defence, *if the statement were true*. For commerce is in accordance with the law of nations, and a law is not changed by opposition to it. But the Spaniards were aiming there, not at commerce, but at dominion. And they regarded it as beyond dispute that it was lawful to take possession of those lands which were not previously known to us; just as if to be known to none of us was the same thing as to be possessed by no one.

Skepticism on the same question was repeated in Hakluyt's translation of Grotius: "For they who pursue the barbarians with war, as the Spaniards do the people of America, are wont to pretend two things: that they are hindered from trading with them, or because they will not acknowledge the doctrine of true religion." As they sought a colony, rather than a factory, the English had to find a justification appropriate to a colony and one less vulnerable to the cynicism of their contemporaries.[25]

The most important innovation by the promoters of Virginia was not exploiting the gaps on communication opened by Vitoria. It was, rather, completely reversing the moral force of the argument of ferae bestiae, which was the strongest pillar in the Salamanca defense of indigenous rights. Once reversed, ferae bestiae (and, later, res nullius) would become the principal weapon in the attack upon indigenous rights. The nature of this turnaround was, of course, astoundingly simple, so simple that many historians, as we have seen, would like to conclude that it was Vitoria's intention all along. All that was required was a change in empirical description. Rather than recognize that Indians lived in civil societies, as they had done, the English needed to start describing Native Americans as devoid of society, closer in this respect to animals than humans, living off nature rather exploiting it. "Who will think," William Strachey demanded,

> it is an unlawful act, to fortefye, and strengthen our selves (as Nature requires) . . . in the wast and vast, unhabited groundes of their amongst a world of which not one foot of a thousand, do they either use or know how to turne to any benefit, and therefore lyes so great a Circuit vayne and idle before them?

The Natives had failed to create political societies. Significantly, these claims were made by reference to the natural-law theory developed by the Salamanca School and to Salamanca and Salamanca-influenced writers.

25. Gentili, *De jure belli*, trans. Rolfe, in *Classics of International Law*, I, 89 (my emphasis); Grotius, *Free Sea*, ed. Armitage, 11.

John Donne, glossing ferae bestiae, observed in his sermon before the Virginia Company: "In the law of Nature and Nations, a land never inhabited, by any, or utterly derelicted and immemorially abandoned by the former Inhabitants, becomes theirs that will possesse it." Neither, he argued, does a man "become proprietary of the Sea, because he hath two or three Boats, fishing on it." Whereas freedom of the sea had been used to support arguments for commerce with the Indians, now the idea of free seas was used to compare sea and land and to find that the land could also be void of ownership. The Native Americans had failed to turn trees into chairs. And, most damnably, they had failed to demonstrate their humanity. They were accordingly condemned as "participating rather of the nature of beasts than men" and as people who "doe but live like dear in heards."[26]

Gentili's writings clearly provided part of the context for these descriptions of men as beasts. In passages reminiscent of Juan Ginés Sepúlveda, the Spanish apologist for conquest, Gentili had argued that it is just to wage war against those "who wearing the human form, live the life of the most brutal of beasts," and citing Cicero's De officiis he observed that "some men differ very little from the brutes. They have the human form, but in reality they are beasts." In contrast to Sepúlveda, however, he was not specifically referring to the people of the New World in either case. In "Of an Honourable Reason for Waging War," Gentili exclaimed: "Why should Covarruvias [Vitoria's student, Diego de Covarrubias] reproach me and others for that other war, waged by the Spaniards against the violators of the law of nature and of common law, against cannibals, and monsters of lewdness." Here, and against many claims he made to the contrary, Gentili did accept an account of the peoples of the New World as having committed crimes against nature and a justification of conquest on that basis. But this was not equivalent to the descriptions, made by Strachey, Donne, Symonds, and Gray, of the people of the New World as brute beasts who did not possess dominion or sovereignty.[27]

Similarly, Gentili, in clear reference to the Roman and natural law ferae bestiae, declared that "the seizure of vacant places is regarded as a law of nature." "The ruling of our jurists," he argued, "with regard to unoccupied lands is, that those who take it have a right to it, since it is the property of no

26. Strachey, *Historie of Travell into Virginia Britania,* 25; John Donne, *A Sermon . . . Preached to the Honourable Company of the Virginian Plantation* (London, 1622), 25-27; Gray, *Good Speed to Virginia,* sigs. Br–Bv; and Symonds, *Virginia,* 15.

27. See Williams, *American Indian in Western Legal Thought,* 211, on parallels in Robert Gray and Gentili's descriptions of Indians. For Gentili's comments, see *De jure belli,* trans. Rolfe, in *Classics of International Law,* I, 7, 41, 122-123.

one. And even though such lands belong to the sovereign of that territory, as others maintain, yet because of that law of nature which abhors a vacuum, they will fall to the lot of those who take them." He included lands in the New World in this category. But he also included much of Italy, Spain, and Greece: "But are there today no unoccupied lands on the earth? Is it not, pray, being reduced more and more to the wilderness of primeval times, or in this decrepit old age is it more fruitful than ever before? What is Greece today, and the whole of Turkey? What is Africa? What of Spain? It is the most populous country of all; yet under the rule of Spain is not almost all of the New World unoccupied? Why should I name thee, Italy, in this connexion, and the country about Aquileia, Pisa, and Rome itself, unkempt and unwholesome because of the small number of its inhabitants?" Rather than provide a clear vindication of the dispossession of Native Americans based upon natural-law arguments, Gentili merely provided his audience with an uncomfortable reminder that, had Montezuma (or Powhatan, for that matter) conquered Europe, he might have exercised dominion (even around Rome, the center of Europe's greatest civilization) with perhaps more justice than Europeans had in America.[28]

The employment of the works of José de Acosta was far more important than the writing of Gentili for the reversal of the force of ferae bestiae found in writings on Virginia. Born in 1540 and educated partly at Salamanca, Acosta died in 1600 as rector of the Jesuit college in Salamanca. His "mind had been formed by Vitoria and his successors," but in contrast to the theologians of the Salamanca School, he spent sixteen years in the Americas, a missionary whose thoughts on the justice of colonization were shaped by long experience in Peru. Acosta was, like Vitoria, profoundly moved by the violence of the Spanish conquests. "Great harm," he argued, "has been done to the Faith in this region from the first from the great liberty taken to participate in violence." In the second book of his De procuranda Indorum (1588) concerning just and unjust war (De jure et iniuria belli), Acosta agreed with the Salamanca School that "in no way whatsoever" was infidelity a just cause to wage war: "God alone is judge and avenger of that." He also refuted the doctrine that war can be waged against those who commit crimes against nature. He pointed out that only God has the authority to punish sin, concluding: "The fact that a republic sins by making stupid and pernicious laws, or that its prince or its magistrates fall into bad habits, does not give the right to another neighbouring republic or its prince to promulgate better laws, nor the right to use force against them in order to

28. Gentili, De jure belli, trans. Rolfe, in Classics of International Law, I, 79–81.

apply such laws or make them be obeyed." Similarly, he agreed that commerce and preaching were just causes for "incursions into the lands of the barbarians."[29]

For Vitoria, however, the American Indian was an abstract and undifferentiated creation. Acosta's experience in the Americas led him to distinguish between Native Americans on the basis of cultural signs. He accordingly developed a progressive theory of barbarism (and civilization). In the "first class," he placed "those who do not depart greatly from true reason and the common way of life," for which the best example were the Chinese. Such peoples "have a stable form of government, legal system, fortified cities, magistrates," and prosperous commerce. Most important was that the barbarians of this first category had "the use and knowledge of letters, for where there are books and engraved monuments there the people are more human and civilised." In the "second class," he placed "Barbarians who did not achieve the use of writing nor the knowledge of philosophy or civil rights." Nevertheless, this second category of barbarians would have government, fixed settlements, leaders, law and order, military capability, and some form of religion. In this class, Acosta placed the Mexicans and Peruvians, "whose empires and republics, laws and institutions, are truly worthy of admiration." For these people to receive the Gospel, there was an argument, he claimed, that they should fall under the imperium of Christian princes but that they should not be deprived of dominion: "They are not to be deprived of the free use of their riches and inheritance." This argument was consistent with Vitoria. The sovereignty, or imperium, of a Christian prince over the second class of barbarians might be justified, but not dominion, not the dispossession of land and goods or the destruction of social systems. As we have seen, this second class of barbarism fitted many of the descriptions of "Virginian" Natives from the 1580s through to the first years of the Chesapeake colony.[30]

Where Acosta would prove particularly useful, however, was in his creation of the "third class" of barbarians. "There are," he argued, "many groups and nations of them in the New World. Amongst them are savages similar to wild animals, who hardly have human feelings—without law, without agreements, without government, without nationhood, who move from place to place, or if they live in one place they are more like

29. José de Acosta, *De procuranda Indorum salute,* trans. and ed. G. Stewart McIntosh, 2 vols. (Tayport, 1996), I, i–v, 41, 58, 63, 84–85; Pagden, *Fall of Natural Man,* 147.

30. Acosta, *De procuranda Indorum,* I, 4, 5.

wild animals' caves or animal cages." "The majority of those living in Brazil," he added, "and almost all those living in Florida are like that." Clearly, these people, who for Acosta included the Natives of the northern parts of America, could not be dispossessed because they did not possess. They had no *meum* and *tuum,* no mine and yours. In contrast to the second class of barbarians, they had failed to create dominion through the exploitation of the laws of nature.[31]

From 1609, writers redescribed Virginia in these terms, often employing Acosta's works. The reception of his writings made it possible to embrace Vitoria's attack on the Spanish conquests for the reason that the societies had already, at the time of subjugation, been "taken" (to use the terms of ferae bestiae), and at the same time these writings made it possible to describe the land in which North American Indian peoples lived as open to the first taker and therefore justly colonized. In 1604, Edward Grimstone translated Acosta's *Historia natural y moral de las Indias* into English with the title *The Naturall and Morall Historie of the East and West Indies.* In this work, Acosta demonstrated the progressive theory of barbarity established in *De procuranda Indorum* through an account of America in terms of its nature and, notably, its people and their "manners, ceremonies, lawes, governments, and warres." He argued that there was a great diversity of peoples in the Americas, and he showed how each corresponded to one of his classifications of barbarity through analyses of their political structures, commerce, customs, physical environment, and (most tellingly) their religions. This work, the original and translation, was enthusiastically received by promoters of early modern English colonization. It was first recorded to have been used in 1596 to support Walter Ralegh's voyages to Guiana and, in particular, to help prove the existence of El Dorado. In July of that year, Thomas Harriot, the Elizabethan scientist and employee of Ralegh, wrote to Sir Robert Cecil, the secretary of state, concerning "El Dorado which hath been showed your Honor out of the Spanish book of Acosta." Here we see Acosta's text employed not merely in curiosity or the pursuit of knowledge but, in the attempt to sway Cecil, as an instrument in the councils of state, a tool of colonial expansion.[32]

In the years after the foundation of Jamestown, Acosta's *Historie* was cited on matters of nature and custom in ways that supported his theory of progressive barbarism. Moreover, it was cited specifically in order to employ

31. Ibid., I, 5.

32. José de Acosta, *The Naturall and Morall Historie of the East and West Indies* (London, 1604), title page; Fitzmaurice, *Humanism and America,* 52.

that theory to redescribe Algonquin peoples of the Chesapeake as belonging to the third class of barbarism and so to justify the dispossession of those people—or, rather, to justify the possession of the lands on which they lived but from which they could not be dispossessed. William Strachey's *Historie of Travell into Virginia Britania* was typical of this use of Acosta. Strachey wrote his *Historie* during his time in Virginia as secretary of the colony between 1609 and 1612, and it is thought that he had a copy of Acosta's *Historie* with him in the Jamestown fort. If this was the case, Acosta's *Historie* is again revealed in a pragmatic light: as an instrument of a colonial secretary. The text served as an authority on New World cosmology and was therefore particularly useful in negotiating with the people and nature of that world.[33]

What Strachey learned from that cosmology is evident in his own *Historie*. He employed Acosta in his chapters "De origine, populi" and "Of the Religion amongst the Inhabitaunts." For Acosta, religion was the best measure of the state of a civilization. Strachey observed that the Virginian Indians were not so base that they were without religion: "There is as yet in *Virginia* no place discovered to be so savage and simple, in which the Inhabitants have not a religion." They were all the same, he argued, committed to devilish practices such as sacrifices, and it is clear he thought that the Virginian Indians, along with most Americans, belonged to the third class. On this matter, he referred the reader to Acosta: "That the Devill hath obteyned the use of the like offering in many other parts of *America, Acosta* hath observed and related in his morrall and naturall History." In the chapter on the origin of New World peoples, Strachey stated even more emphatically his view that those peoples belonged to the lowest category of barbarians; he asked, "What difference there may be betweene them and bruit beasts, nay things more vyle, and abhorring the inbredd motions of Nature yt self." As to how this "vagabond race of Cham" could have got itself into the New World, "lett me referre the reader to the search of *Acosta* in his [——] booke, Chap: [——] of his morrall and naturall History of the West-Indies." And Strachey left no doubt about his estimation of Acosta, who "hath so officiously laboured herein, as he should but bring Owles to Athens, who should study for more strayned, or new Aucthority Concerning the same."[34]

33. Strachey, *Historie of Travell into Virginia Britania,* xxvii.

34. Ibid., 55, 88, 90. For the use of Acosta, see also, for example, *True Declaration of the Estate of the Colonie in Virginia,* 8, 23. On Acosta, see also Joyce E. Chaplin, *Subject Matter: Technology, the Body, and Science on the Anglo-American Frontier, 1500–1676* (Cambridge, Mass., 2001), 120, 177.

The English author who most enthusiastically employed Acosta was Samuel Purchas. Indeed, Purchas was more profoundly indebted to Acosta (and more to Acosta than he was to Vitoria) than any other early modern English writer. In *Hakluytus Posthumus,* Purchas used Acosta's *De temporibus novissimus* (first published in 1590) and *De procuranda Indorum* to argue that the northern parts of the Americas were "thinly inhabited, and indeed in great part not at all." Chapters 2, 4, 5, and 6 of book 5, part 2 of *Hakluytus Posthumus* reprinted much of the first six books of Grimstone's translation of Acosta, from a total of seven. But it was in *Purchas His Pilgrimage* that this obligation was most clear, particularly in books 8 and 9 concerning the Americas. Nor did Purchas hide this debt to Acosta. In the first sentence of book 8, he acknowledged that his subject would allow contemplation of "such Philosophical Subjects, as the best Authors have thought worthie the first place in their Histories of these parts." The marginal note "b" cites "Joseph Acosta de procuranda Indorum salute, and hist indie *[The Naturall and Morall Historie of the East and West Indies]*" as well as Giovanni Botero, *Relationi universali,* and Francisco López de Gómara, *Historia general de las Indias.* The following two books of *Purchas His Pilgrimage* were abridgements of Acosta, Botero, and Gómara's histories. Purchas laboriously cut and pasted from the three texts, with assistance from many other minor sources, to weave a relatively seamless narrative of the history and customs of the New World. With regard to Acosta, Purchas drew most heavily upon *Naturall and Morall Historie,* specifically the books concerned with custom—"manners, ceremonies, laws, governments." Unravelling this complex fabric is extremely difficult, but it is clear, for example, that of the 100 pages in Acosta's fifth book, Purchas reproduced at least 30, and in the 150 pages of books 8 and 9 of the *Pilgrimage,* he cited Acosta sixty-three times. Purchas repeatedly and explicitly reverted to Acosta's voice: "They shewed me, (it is *Acostas* speech)"; "But to return to Acosta, he telleth."[35]

An indication of the availability and impact of Acosta's work in seventeenth-century England lies in the fact that Purchas used Grimstone's 1604

35. Purchas, *Hakluytus Posthumus,* I, book 1, 58–60 ("Of America, whether It Were Then Peopled"), and II, book 5, chaps. 2, 4, 5, 6. Book 5 of Acosta is numbered 329–430; the following thirty pages are reproduced in books 8 and 9 of Purchas's *Pilgrimage* (cross-referenced page numbers in the *Pilgrimage* are given in brackets): 340–341 (718); 345–347 (736); 348–350 (674); 360–361 (730); 365–366 (672); 368–369 (671); 391–393 (734–735); 393–396 (679); 398–400 (732); 402–406 (673); 406–407 (731); 408 (673). This list is not exhaustive. For quotations, see *Purchas His Pilgrimage,* 727, 728.

translation of the *Naturall and Morall Historie* and not the original in Spanish or de Bry's 1590 Latin version (although he did use the Latin version of *De procuranda Indorum,* which was not translated into English until the twentieth century). That it is Grimstone's translation and not Purchas's is rapidly evident from a comparison of any of the numerous transcribed passages. In the pages of the *Pilgrimage* and *Hakluytus Posthumus,* Grimstone almost achieved a second edition (which would come later), although, in contrast to Acosta, he received no acknowledgment. Through Purchas, we see Grimstone's text at work, but we also see Purchas at work with Grimstone's text. It was necessary to make adjustments to Acosta's account. It was important, for example, both for the Protestant Purchas and the Catholic Acosta, that heathen religion could corruptly imitate true Christian religion. In Acosta's progressive history, a people that believed in one god was more advanced than one that followed numerous gods. Book 5, chapter 25 of his *History* recorded the encouraging ways in which Mexican religious rites "laboured to imitate and counterfeit the sacraments of the Holy Church," albeit in ways corrupted by the devil. Purchas reprinted this chapter. But where Acosta concluded, "The Gospel of our Lord Jesus Christ thrust out all these superstitions" (to which Grimstone apparently did not object), Purchas felt obliged to add "till the Spaniards substituted in place thereof their Masse, a masse of more monstrous absurdities, (in their transubstantiation, bread-worshipping, God-eating . . .) then the former, notwithstanding the fairer pretexts of Christian and Catholike titles." Here Acosta's progressive theory of history is given a Protestant teleology.[36]

Acosta's importance to Purchas is not, however, revealed simply by the extent to which Purchas borrowed from Acosta's narrative of American history and culture. On the level of narrative, Purchas was almost equally indebted to Botero and Gómara. There was a more profound link between the Puritan Purchas and "that learned and judicious Author, *Josephus Acosta,*" a Jesuit. The *Pilgrimage,* first published in 1613 and the foundation of Purchas's subsequent work, was to a large degree *modelled* on Acosta's *Historia natural y moral de las Indias,* although Purchas was more ambitious than Acosta in scope, taking all time and all the world as his subject. Above all, Purchas conformed to Acosta's classes of barbarity and used Acosta's signs of classification to conduct his analysis, often citing Acosta to establish authority. Purchas's full title was illustrative of this debt: *Purchas His Pilgrimage; or, Relations of the World and the Religions Observed in All Ages and*

36. Purchas, *Purchas His Pilgrimage,* 734–735; Acosta, *Naturall and Morall Historie,* 391–393.

Places Discovered, from the Creation to the Present. Religion was the focus of Purchas's history of the world, in part because, as for Acosta, the state of religion was the best indicator of a culture's state of civilization or barbarity. As Purchas stated in dedicating the book to Archbishop Abbott, one of the two "lessons" of his work was "that law of Nature [has] written in the practise of all men (as we here in the particulars doe shew) the profession of some Religion." Books 8 and 9 of the *Pilgrimage* were concerned with the second and third classes of barbarians in the Americas (there being none of the first class). Citing Acosta, Purchas observed that the Mexicans belonged initially to the third class of barbarity: "Very barbarous and savage, which lived only by Hunting . . . They lived naked, solitarie in the Mountaines, without Tillage, Policie, or any Religious Ceremonies." He then went on, again employing Acosta, to describe the development of a complex religion, the following of an idol who led them to create Tenochtitlan, the creation of temples, ceremonies, priests, new idols, feasts, sacrifices, baptism, marriages, burials, colleges, schools, picture writing, and beliefs concerning life after death and the soul. By contrast, the Brazilians, who clearly conformed to the lowest form of barbarity, were later summarized with the sentence: "They have no use of three letters in the Alphabet, L, F, R, a reason whereof some have wittily given, they have no Law, Faith, nor Ruler." In this sense, they could possess no dominion, let alone sovereignty, and were "in summe, more like beastes then men."[37]

It was when Purchas turned to Virginia that he had the least need for Acosta's narrative, for Acosta had not written on this region. And yet it is on this point that Acosta's impact upon Purchas is most evident. Purchas described the Virginian Indians in terms of the third class, making his evaluation once again by appealing to Acosta's signs of civilization. Purchas found significance, for example, in the fact that Native Virginians, "having no letters," had no records. Their understanding of religion was presented as crude: "I may also here insert the ridiculous conceits which some Virginians hold, concerning their first originall . . . that a Hare came into their countrey and made the first men." He was therefore able to propose that "the Savage inhabitants, [are] unworthie to embrace with their rustike arms so sweet a bosome [as Virginia]." These judgments were echoed seventy years later in John Locke's famous dismissal, in the *Second Treatise of Government,* of the natural-law rights of Native Americans. Locke also echoed the use of Acosta's anthropology to justify his view, declaring: "If *Josephus Acosta's* word may be taken, he tells us, that in many parts of *America* there

37. Purchas, *Purchas His Pilgrimage,* epistle dedicatory and 610, 659–684, 705.

was no Government at all." Locke was drawing upon the intellectual innovation of the previous generations of English colonizers.[38]

In company with many of his contemporaries, Purchas employed natural-law assumptions derived largely from Vitoria's creation and defense of Indian rights to demonstrate that Native Virginians did not possess rights. And he did this by employing Acosta's writings to redescribe the state of the Virginians. One could conclude that English promoters of the Chesapeake colony therefore succeeded in completely inverting the Salamanca School's defense of indigenous rights, but that statement would be only partially true. The inversion was not coherent. In his 1617 expanded edition of the *Pilgrimage,* Purchas repeated his reliance upon Acosta and again described North American Indians in terms of the lowest form of barbarity. He added, however, a further chapter to this edition — "On the Present State of Virginia" — which was largely an edited version of John Rolfe's *Relation of the State of Virginia* (1616). He observed: "This peace hath yeelded many benefits, both opportunitie of lawfull purchase of a great part of the Countrey from the Natives, freely and willingly relinquishing and selling the same for Copper, or other commodities (a thing of no small consequence to the conscience, where the milde Law of Nature, not that violent Law of Armes, layes the foundation of their [the colonists'] possession." Here Native dominion was assumed in the act of selling the land. The Indians were acknowledged to have rights arising from the law of nature, and the author confessed to a troubled conscience on the part of the English.[39]

This question of conscience is vital to the contradictions in the legal descriptions of Native peoples. Indeed, *Purchas His Pilgrimage* is not the only place where contradictions and conscience were evident in discussions of these questions. The glaring contradictions in the tracts concerning colonization need hardly be pointed out. Almost routinely, the authors claimed, on the one hand, that the colony had purchased land from the Natives and that, on the other, the land was possessed by no one (and, therefore, presumably could not be sold). How can it be possible to trade with people who have no mine or yours, no concept of property? These contradictions were not merely between authors; they were also frequently embraced by the authors individually, in individual tracts, even on a single page. Strachey, for example, in response to the anxiety "surely Christian men, should not shew themselves like Wolves to devoure," answered that the land would not be

38. Ibid., 631, 636, 641; John Locke, *Two Treatises of Government,* ed. Peter Laslett (Cambridge, 1960), II, sect. 103.

39. Samuel Purchas, *Purchas His Pilgrimage . . . ,* 3d ed. (London, 1617), 946.

forcibly possessed: "and therefore even every foote of Land which we shall take unto our use, we will bargayne and buy of them for copper, hatchets, and such like commodities." Land would be purchased, and yet, as we have heard, Strachey also claimed that the Indians neither "use or know how to turne to any benefit" the environment in which they lived and therefore had no possessions, not even land, to trade. The tension is nowhere more evident than in Robert Gray's *A Good Speed to Virginia*. Gray raised the customary anxiety over possession: "The first objection is, by what right or warrant we can enter into the land of these Savages, and plant ourselves in their places." In accordance with Company policy, he disavowed any such intention: "The answer to the forsaid objection is, that there is no intendment to take away from them by force that *rightful inheritance* they have in that Countrey." Yet, having noted this rightful inheritance, a property right, it was Gray who described the Indians as "beasts and brutish savages, which have no interest in it [the land], because they participate rather of the nature of beasts than men."[40]

These tensions underline the ideological pressure on the promoters. Their inversion of the natural-law defense of the Native Americans was political rather than philosophical. It was in this quotidian and pragmatic context, rather than in philosophical discourse, that the natural-law tradition began to be turned to the purposes of dispossession. The moral certainty and relative coherence found in Locke's discussions of aboriginal rights were not characteristic of the vast majority of discussions of the legal status of Indians. One of the principal tools in overcoming the rights of Indians was the inversion of the polemical force of the natural-law arguments of the Salamanca School. But it was precisely the use and knowledge of that natural-law tool that nourished uncertainty and troubled consciences. Natural-law assumptions could be turned back in favor of indigenous peoples (as has happened in the recent past) as easily as they had been turned against them. In the subsequent history of European discussions of indigenous legal rights, that troubled conscience would be more often apparent in justifications of dispossession than Locke's philosophical rigor.

40. Strachey, *Historie of Travell into Virginia Britania,* 26; Gray, *Good Speed to Virginia,* sig.[C4]r (my emphasis).

David Harris Sacks

DISCOURSES OF WESTERN PLANTING

RICHARD HAKLUYT AND THE MAKING

OF THE ATLANTIC WORLD

Now the beginning must come from God, since our work, because of the excellent character of goodness in it, is manifestly from God, who is the author of all good and the father of lights. And in the operations of God, the beginnings, however slight, have a settled end. What is said of spiritual things, "the kingdom of God comes not with observation," is also found to be true in all the greater works of providence; so that all things move smoothly without sound or noise, and the thing is wholly done before men realize or notice that it is under way. Nor should we omit the prophecy of Daniel on the last times of the world: "many shall pass through, and knowledge will be increased," which obviously signifies enigmatically that it is in the fates, that is, in providence, that the through passsage of the world (which after so many long voyages now seems quite complete or on the way to completion) and the increase of knowledge should come to pass in the same age.

Francis Bacon, *Novum organum* (London, 1620), book 1, Aphorism XCIII

On October 5, 1584, Richard Hakluyt, already embarked on his extensive geographical researches, personally delivered to Elizabeth I a long memorandum, written in English, supporting Walter Ralegh's plan for a settlement in Virginia.[1] The modern title of this document, "Discourse of West-

---

1. Richard Hakluyt, *A Particuler Discourse concerninge the Greate Necessitie and Manifolde Commodyties That Are Like to Growe to This Realme of Englande by the Westerne Discoveries Lately Attempted* . . . , ed. David B. Quinn and Alison M. Quinn, Works Issued by the Hakluyt Society, Extra Ser., no. 45 (London, 1993) (a photographic facsimile of the original manuscript in the New York Public Library with transcriptions on facing pages); Hakluyt, "Discourse of Western Planting by Richard Hakluyt, 1584," doc. 46 in E. G. R. Taylor, ed., *The Original Writings and Correspondence of the Two Richard Hakluyts,* 2 vols., Works Issued by the Hakluyt Society, 2d Ser., nos. 76–77 (London, 1935), II, 211–326.

ern Planting," provides my own. On the same occasion, he also gave the queen an autographed copy, written in Latin, of his *Analysis* of the eight books of Aristotle's *Politics,* derived from his lectures in Oxford University, where he was a senior member of Christ Church College. On both documents, he identifies himself with the university; in the latter, he adds that he is *"verbi Dei Minister,"* literally, "servant of the word of God," a designation meant to indicate his ordination in the Church of England.[2]

Hakluyt was born to a merchant father in London, probably in 1552, the same year as Sir Walter Ralegh, and died as one of the senior canons of Westminster in 1616 after enjoying a highly successful career as an Oxford scholar; a student of Aristotle's philosophy and of classical literature; a promoter of geographical knowledge; an author, editor, and publisher; an ordained clergyman, parish preacher, and high ecclesiastical official; a consultant to commercial corporations and government ministers; and a sometime diplomat and spy.[3] Viewed superficially, this list gives the impression of a polymath jack-of-all-trades rapidly shifting his energies from workbench to workbench without apparent focus. But the learning he attained at Oxford and the high hopes he had for Virginia reinforced each other throughout the course of his active career and gave coherence to this array of callings.

Hakluyt often identified himself with Oxford, even long after he had left his university appointment for other parts and posts. Between 1598 and 1600, more than a dozen years after ending his academic tenure, he listed himself on the title pages of his three-volume second edition of *The Principal Navigations of the English Nation* as "Preacher, and sometimes student of Christ-Church in Oxford," an identification meant to convey the relationship between his ministerial calling and his scholarly learning.[4] He might

2. Richard Hakluyt's dedication to Elizabeth I, dated "Calendis Septembris [1 September] Ao Domini, 1583," in Hakluyt, *Analysis seu resolutio perpetua in octo libros Politicorum Aristotelis,* Royal MSS, 12 G. XIII, 2, British Library, London (hereafter cited as BL); there is a second manuscript copy of this work, dating from 1588, in Sloane MSS, 1982, BL.

3. D. B. Quinn, ed., *The Hakluyt Handbook,* 2 vols., Works Issued by the Hakluyt Society, 2d Ser., nos. 144–145 (London, 1974), II, 265; George Bruner Parks, *Richard Hakluyt and the English Voyages,* ed. James A. Williamson, American Geographical Society Special Publication, no. 10 (New York, 1928), 242–245; George J. Armytage, ed., *Allegations for Marriage Licenses Issued by the Bishop of London,* 2 vols., Harleian Society Publications, XXV (London, 1887), I, 286.

4. Title page of the second state of vol. I and of vols. II–III of Richard Hakluyt, *The Principal Navigations, Voyages, Traffiques, and Discoveries of the English Nation . . . ,* 3 vols (London, 1598–1600; STC 12626a), facsimile in Quinn, ed., *Hakluyt Handbook,*

equally have written "of Virginia" after his name, although he never actually landed on its shores. Along with being one of the earliest advocates of its settlement, in 1589 he also became one of the holders of the rights that Sir Walter Ralegh possessed there.[5] His name appears third in the first charter of the Virginia Company in 1606, whose foundation Emanuel van Meteren, his Dutch contemporary and friend, attributed to him.[6] He is there again in the second charter of 1609.[7] He remained an advocate of the colony and an investor in the company until his death. Two shares, valued together at twenty-one pounds, passed to Edmond, his son and heir, in 1616.[8]

These biographical facts frame the argument of this present essay. In it, I propose to examine the varied discourses—secular and philosophical, religious and exegetical—with which Hakluyt explained his purposes in *Principal Navigations* and justified his support for English colonial settlement in Virginia, and to demonstrate their convergence in his vision of temporal and spiritual history.

II, 501, 503, 505, 507, 509. Note that, on the cancelled first state of the title page to vol. I, Hakluyt appears as "Master of Artes, and sometime Student of Christ-Church in Oxford" (ibid., 499). The same designation was employed on the title page of the first edition of 1589 (Hakluyt, *The Principall Navigations Voiages and Discoveries of the English Nation* . . . [London, 1589], facsimile in Quinn, ed., *Hakluyt Handbook,* II, 479; STC 12625).

5. Hakluyt, *Principall Navigations* (1589), 815–817; see David Beers Quinn, *The Roanoke Voyages, 1584–1590: Documents to Illustrate the English Voyages to North America under the Patent Granted to Walter Raleigh in 1584,* 2 vols., Works Issued by the Hakluyt Society, 2d Ser., nos. 104–105 (London, 1955), II, 569–576.

6. Apr. 5, 1606, PRO, C66/1709, in Philip L. Barbour, ed., *The Jamestown Voyages under the First Charter, 1606–1609,* 2 vols., Works Issued by the Hakluyt Society, 2d Ser., nos. 136–137 (London, 1969), I, 24–34; Emanuel van Meteren, *Commentarien ofte memorien van-den Nederlandtschen staet, handel, oorloghen ende gheschiedenissen van onsen tyden* . . . (The Hague, 1610), entry for 1607, ibid., II, 270.

7. May 23, 1609, PRO, C66/1796/5, in *The Three Charters of the Virginia Company of London, with Seven Related Documents, 1606–1621,* Jamestown 350th Anniversary Historical Booklet, no. 4 (Williamsburg, Va., 1957), 32. "Richarde Hackluit" is designated "Clarke, Prebendarie of Westminster" in the 1606 charter (1) and "Richard Hacklewte" as "minister" in the 1609 charter (32); see Susan Myra Kingsbury, ed., *The Records of the Virginia Company of London,* 4 vols. (Washington, D.C., 1906–1935), IV, 364, 367, 368.

8. Kingsbury, ed., *Records of the Virginia Company,* I, 497, III, 63, 84, 326. See Richard Hakluyt, "To the Right Honourable, the Right Worshipfull Counsellors, and Others the Cheerefull Adventurors for the Advancement of that Christian and Noble Plantation in Virginia," Apr. 15, 1609, in Hakluyt, *Virginia Richly Valued* . . . (London, 1609; STC 22938), sigs. A2r–A3[b]v.

Despite the fact that Hakluyt was a prolific producer of books, his main work was that of an editor and publisher. Along with his *Divers Voyages Touching the Discoverie of America* (1582) and the two editions of his *Principal Navigations* (1589, 1598–1600), he was responsible for seeing into print at least six other texts concerned with navigation and discovery as well as promoting or influencing the publication of more than twenty others. But he left behind very few of his own words either in print or manuscript. In fact, the manuscript "Discourse of Western Planting" represents one of the few sustained pieces of his own writing that survives. This lack has made it easy for him to be treated in different lights.[9]

Hakluyt has variously been identified as a Christian apologist; an anti-Catholic Protestant propagandist; an anti-Spanish English nationalist; a latter-day Aristotelian, or Thomist; a humanist scholar and moralist; an exemplar of capitalist imperialism; and a learned geographer. None of these designations is untrue. Nevertheless, he was no mere rhetorician, moving from paradigm to paradigm without commitment to any overarching vision. His work has a coherence of its own in which the settlement of Virginia played a major role. How should we characterize its unity and its basis?

From the 1840s, when renewed interest in Hakluyt resulted in the founding of the Hakluyt Society, two competing positions have dominated the scene. As David Beers Quinn has put it, one school saw Hakluyt as "a typical expression of Free trade Optimism" and the other as "the protagonist of nationalistic empire." According to L. E. Pennington, this distinction persisted well into the twentieth century, with scholarly assessment largely divided between "those who have seen his thinking as essentially concerned with the high strategy of international politics, usually with religious overtones, and those who have viewed him as essentially a pragmatist interested in promoting the economic advancement of England." Falling between these positions, however, there have been several important writers —G. B. Parks, E. G. R. Taylor, R. A. Skelton, and David Quinn himself—

9. Richard Hakluyt, *Divers Voyages Touching the Discoverie of America, and the Ilands Adjacent unto the Same, Made First of All by Our Englishmen, and Afterward by the Frenchmen and Britons* (London, 1582; STC 12624), sig. 2v; Hakluyt, *Principall Navigations* (1589); Hakluyt, *Principal Navigations* (1598–1600). For a listing of other texts Hakluyt saw into print, see D. B. Quinn, C. E. Armstrong, and R. A. Skelton, "The Primary Hakluyt Bibliography," in Quinn, ed., *Hakluyt Handbook,* II, 461–575. For the corpus of Hakluyt's surviving writings (letters, prefaces, and several shorter memoranda on imperial themes), see Taylor, ed., *Original Writings.*

for whom the history of navigation and discovery is seen as advancing geographical knowledge as well as promoting confessional, national, and material interests.[10] Richard Helgerson has even more explicitly characterized Hakluyt's *Voyages* as located at the nexus of "intersecting communities," helping to propagate Christianity as well as expand trade and empire. Mary Fuller, in her *Voyages in Print,* endorses a related view by considering Hakluyt the author of an epic, here following J. A. Froude, who called Hakluyt's *Principal Navigations* "the prose Epic of the modern English nation."[11]

In some measure, Hakluyt lends credence to the view that his *Principal Navigations* is modeled on epic, classical if not also religious. Writing in 1582 to his friend Jean Hotman, by then secretary to the earl of Leicester, Hakluyt called Sir Edward Dyer, from whom he had received much assistance with his researches, "my best Maecenas," implicitly comparing his own project to Virgil's *Aeneid.*[12] Elsewhere, he drew freely on episodes from Virgil's epic in analyzing his own historical moment, in effect equating his epoch with the first great age of empire under Rome.[13] In 1587, in

10. D. B. Quinn, "Hakluyt's Reputation," in Quinn, ed., *Hakluyt Handbook,* I, 147–148; L. E. Pennington, "Secondary Works on Hakluyt and His Circle," ibid., II, 588–589; Richard Helgerson, *Forms of Nationhood: The Elizabethan Writing of England* (Chicago, 1992), 175–176; Parks, *Richard Hakluyt and the English Voyages,* ed. Williamson; E. G. R. Taylor, *Late Tudor and Early Stuart Geography, 1583–1650: A Sequel to "Tudor Geography, 1485–1583"* (London, 1934), 1–38; see also Taylor, *Tudor Geography, 1485–1583* (London, 1930), 12, 34, 46–48, 88, 124, 127, 133–136; R. A. Skelton, "Hakluyt's Maps," in Quinn, ed., *Hakluyt Handbook,* I, 48–73. Quinn's views have been expressed in numerous publications devoted to Hakluyt's work; see, for example, Hakluyt, *A Particuler Discourse,* ed. Quinn and Quinn, xv–xxxi; David Beers Quinn and Raleigh Ashlin Skelton, "Introduction," in Richard Hakluyt, *The Principall Navigations Voiages and Discoveries of the English Nation . . . , 1589,* ed. Quinn and Skelton, 2 vols., Works Issued by the Hakluyt Society, Extra Ser., no. 39 (London, 1965), I, ix–lx.

11. Helgerson, *Forms of Nationhood,* 153; Mary C. Fuller, *Voyages in Print: English Travel to America, 1576–1624* (Cambridge, 1995), 141–174, esp. 142, 144, 251. Elsewhere, Helgerson insists that "to dismiss such religious claims as mere humbug would surely be wrong" (*Forms of Nationhood,* 167).

12. Richard Hakluyt to Jean Hotman, undated (August or September 1582), Oxford, in François Hotman and Jean Hotman, *Francisci et Joannis Hotomanorum patris ac filii et clarorum virorum ad eos epistolae* (Amsterdam, 1700), 292.

13. See, for example, Richard Hakluyt, "To the Right Honorable My Singular Good Lord, the Lord Charles Howard, Erle of Notingham," Oct. 17, 1598, London, dedicatory letter to vol. I of the second edition of *Principal Navigations* (1598–1600), in Hakluyt, *The Principal Navigations, Voyages, Traffiques and Discoveries of the English Nation . . . ,* 12 vols. (Glasgow, 1903–1905), I, xxxiii.

dedicating his edition of Peter Martyr's *Decades* to Sir Walter Ralegh, he extended the epic analogy to Homer, likening Ralegh to Achilles and Martyr to Homer (and himself to Martyr).[14]

Some of Hakluyt's contemporary readers also regarded his book of epic significance, reading it not only for the knowledge it imparted but also for edification as literature and as a spur to heroic action. Michael Drayton, for example, speaks of Hakluyt in just such terms in his ode "To the Virginian Voyage," first published in 1606. Addressing the adventurers about to make their historic colonizing voyage—those "brave Heroique Minds . . . That Honour still pursue"—Drayton invokes the presence of "Industrious Hackluit, / Whose Reading shall inflame / Men to seeke Fame" and asks him to attend their voyages and commend them "to after-Times" in the manner of a singer of tales.[15] To William Warner, writing in the complete *Albions England* of 1612, Hakluyt was "fames sweet Trumpetor," worthy of "*English* Garlands," whose pen assured continued life to the deeds of the discoverers.[16] In 1611, the East India Company sought to use *Principal Navigations* to encourage its own factors residing in the Indies in similar terms. They sent Hakluyt's three volumes to them, along with editions of Foxe's *Book of Martyrs* and William Perkins's *Works*. These titles, taken together, were to be read as remembrances of the purpose of their mission,

14. Richard Hakluyt, "Illustri et magnanimo viro, Gualtero Ralegho, equiti anglo . . ." ("To the Illustrious and Right Worthy Sir Walter Ralegh, Knight"), Feb. 22, 1587, Paris, in Pietro Martire d'Anghiera [Peter Martyr d'Anghera], *De orbe novo*, ed. Hakluyt (Paris, 1587), hereafter cited as Hakluyt, epistle dedicatory to Sir Walter Ralegh, 1587 (also cited in Taylor, ed., *Original Writings*, II, 364, 369); Andrew Fitzmaurice, *Humanism and America: An Intellectual History of English Colonisation, 1500–1625* (Cambridge, 2003), 110–111.

15. See D. B. Quinn and A. M. Quinn, "A Hakluyt Chronology," in Quinn, ed., *Hakluyt Handbook*, I, 317, 320, 321, 322, 324–326, 327, 329, 330–331; Michael Drayton, "To the Virginian Voyage," lines 1–3, 67–72, in J. William Hebel, ed., *The Works of Michael Drayton*, 5 vols. (Oxford, 1961), II, 363–364. For commentary on Drayton's literary debts to Hakluyt, see Joseph Quincy Adams, "Michael Drayton's *To the Virginian Voyage*," *Modern Language Notes*, III (1918), 405–408; Robert Ralston Cawley, "Drayton and the Voyagers," *PMLA*, XXXVIII (1923), 530–556; Gerhard Friedrich, "The Genesis of Michael Drayton's Ode 'To the Virginian Voyage,'" *Modern Language Notes*, LXXII (1957), 401–406.

16. William Warner, *Albions England: A Continued Historie of the Same Kingdome, from the Originals of the First Inhabitants Thereof* . . . (London, 1612; STC 25084), 288; Quinn and Quinn, "Hakluyt Chronology," in Quinn, ed., *Hakluyt Handbook*, I, 321; for commentary on Warner's use of Hakluyt, see Robert Ralston Cawley, "Warner and the Voyagers," *Modern Philology*, XX (1922–1923), 113–147.

with Hakluyt specifically intended for the "better confort" of the company's agents, and "to recreate their spirittes with varietie of historie." By the early 1630s, George Hakewill was asking to have *Principal Navigations* translated into Latin not just for "the benefit that might redound to other *Nations*" but "for the honour of the *English* name" that it would spread on the Continent.[17]

James Anthony Froude acknowledged this reception by speaking of the *Principal Navigations* as a compendium of "the heroic tales of the exploits of the great men in whom the new era was inaugurated; not mythic like the Iliads and the Eddas, but plain broad narratives of substantial facts, which rival legend in interest and grandeur. What the old epics were to the royally or nobly born, this modern epic is to the common people." For Froude, the story had a providential religious character. He equated the Elizabethan seamen who "went out across unknown seas fighting, discovering, colonizing, and graved out the channels . . . through which the commerce and enterprise of England . . . flowed out over all the world" with the "few poor fishermen from an obscure lake in Palestine," who, during the time of the apostles, "assumed, under the Divine mission, the spiritual authority over mankind." When challenging the Spanish in America, the English navigators did so, Froude said, "as the armed soldiers of the Reformation, and as the avengers of humanity." To Froude, therefore, Hakluyt's big book was not just an epic in prose, and modern and forward-looking in its theme, but explicitly a Protestant epic, colored by a godly vision of history and its progress.[18]

Historians have now abandoned Froude's romanticized whiggery and jingoistic triumphalism. But some scholars have also come to doubt the religious basis of Hakluyt's project and its importance to his concept of En-

17. "Directors of the East India Company to John Sairis, Chief Commander, and Gabriell Towerson, Captain of the *Hector*," Apr. 4, 1611, in George Birdwood and William Foster, eds., *The Register of Letters etc. of the Governour and Company of Merchants of London Trading into the East Indies, 1600–1619* (London, 1893), 419; Quinn and Quinn, "Hakluyt Chronology," in Quinn, ed., *Hakluyt Handbook*, I, 324–326; George Hakewill, *An Apologie or Declaration of the Power and Providence of God in the Government of the World*, 3d ed. (London, 1635; STC 12613), 310–311; Quinn, "Hakluyt's Reputation," in Quinn, ed., *Hakluyt Handbook*, I, 136–137.

18. James Anthony Froude, "England's Forgotten Worthies," in Froude, *Short Studies on Great Subjects*, 4 vols. (London, 1886), I, 446–447, 471–472. Froude's essay first appeared in the *Westminster Review* in 1852; see Quinn, "Hakluyt's Reputation," in Quinn, ed., *Hakluyt Handbook*, I, 147–148; Helgerson, *Forms of Nationhood*, 175–176, 187.

gland's imperial destiny. Several historians now maintain, as Richard Tuck has put it, "that Hakluyt on the whole completely eschewed any religious justification for colonization." David Armitage has argued similarly. Hakluyt, he says, "made only the most glancing references to the schemes of church history; and . . . presented no apocalyptic justification for English trade and settlement." On this view, Hakluyt's "intellectual projects owed more to his Oxonian Aristotelianism and Thomism than they did to any supposedly unmediated Protestant experience of scripture." For Hakluyt, "who had no conception of the supposed place of England in the scheme of divine election," Armitage says, "religion shaped little, if any, of [his] corpus, either generically or rhetorically." Hakluyt's "English nationalism," he concludes, "may therefore have owed more to his classicism than to his Protestantism."[19]

We can agree that Hakluyt's writings are not the product of systematic religious exegesis. He was too much of a literary man for that—too ready to draw analogies, to rely on similes and metaphors, and to gesture at his arguments through allusion. His work resists reduction to any simple model. Nevertheless, Hakluyt's classicism did not compete with his Protestantism. Like many other learned figures in his day, he read ancient Greek and Roman texts in light of his Christianity, not in opposition. The relationship was what mathematicians might call commutative, since the final result is independent of the steps taken to reach it. Whether he started with the Bible or an ancient moral epistle of epic poem, he drew on the other and ended up in the same place.

Among Oxford Aristotelians especially, figures like Richard Hooker of Corpus Christi College and John Case of Saint John's as well as Hakluyt—thinkers who read their Aristotle through the lens of their Christianity—there was no contradiction between their belief in the direct influences of a personal God on their lives and their most deeply held philosophical views. Rather than focusing on God exclusively as the unmoved mover—the first and final cause of events—their eclectic Aristotelianism interpolated into Aristotle's thought a concept of the divine will derived from the Hebrew and Christian traditions and then treated God effectively as the efficient cause

19. Richard Tuck, *The Rights of War and Peace: Political Thought and the International Order from Grotius to Kant* (Oxford, 1999), 110; David Armitage, *The Ideological Origins of the British Empire* (Cambridge, 2000), 71, 76–77, 81, 85; see also Fitzmaurice, *Humanism and America*, 50–55, 138–139. Although Fitzmaurice acknowledges that Hakluyt had a religious goal, he argues that it was remote and understood to be insufficient to move the project forward.

of all events as well. "According to Aristotle," the philosopher John Case said, "there is Divine Providence in individual events." Seen in this light, therefore, Hakluyt's views, linking Scripture to ancient philosophy and literature, formed in much the same way as Thomas More's and Desiderius Erasmus's as well as Richard Hooker's and John Case's. These figures, too, mixed their classical learning with their religious understanding in ways that defy the working of distinct paradigms in their thinking.[20]

Admittedly, however, Hakluyt has not made it easy for us at this distance to discern the roots of his thought, since they lie deep in the soil. They bring nutrients to the upper branches of his considerable learning without directly revealing their workings. But nothing is purposely concealed, only taken for granted. And enough survives to make the processes by which he worked and thought apparent on close inspection.

As Hakluyt saw it, the work of navigators and explorers moved, as did everything, under the power of God and subject to his judgment. In the pursuit of new discoveries, as in every worldly endeavor, virtue would be blessed and sin punished. "Wee forgotte," he told Philip Sidney, his near classmate at Christ Church, Oxford, and his sometime patron,

> that Godlinesse is great riches, and that if we first seeke the kingdome of God, al other thinges will be given unto us, and that as the light accompanieth the Sunne, and the heate the fire, so lasting riches do waite upon them that are zealous for the advauncement of the kingdome of Christ, and the enlargement of his glorious Gospell: as it is sayde, I will honour them that honour mee.[21]

Seen in this light, Hakluyt's works are not just (and not simply) anti-Spanish diatribes provoked by fears of what Spanish tyranny might do to the liberty of the English and the fate of Protestantism. Neither are they only examples of his Aristotelian and Ciceronian convictions on the nature of human society and personal virtue. They also have—and quite centrally—a religious message, although, as I shall argue, not exactly the one Froude thought they did and some modern commentators have argued they did not.

---

20. Johanne Caso [John Case], *Thesaurus oeconomiae seu commentarius in oeconomica Aristotelis* . . . (Oxford, 1597; STC 4765), 45; Charles B. Schmitt, *Aristotle and the Renaissance* (Cambridge, Mass., 1983), 94–95; Schmitt, *John Case and Aristotelianism in Renaissance England* (Kingston, 1983), 77–80, 106–138, 160–162. The concept of "eclectic Aristotelianism" is Schmitt's; see *Aristotle and the Renaissance,* 89–109.

21. Hakluyt, *Divers Voyages,* sig. 2v. The final clause alludes to 1 Sam. 2:30.

There is no doubt, however, that Hakluyt's writings were meant in part to answer Spanish Hapsburg pretension to be the "last descendants of Aeneas," heirs to the imperial powers of the emperor Augustus and his successors as "Lords of All the World." In the hands of Spanish propagandists, and of Philip II himself, this claim to universal monarchy was connected with its own form of messianic or apocalyptic eschatology, which, as Geoffrey Parker has emphasized, saw the establishment of Spanish imperial power in Europe and the Americas to be the holy mission of Philip's divinely ordained and absolute rule. The imagery of an exalted imperialism, equating universal earthly monarchy with God's eternal rule over the world, followed Philip II nearly everywhere he went. Nowhere was it more abundant than in the Escorial, Philip's palace-monastery, designed specifically as a "re-creation" of Solomon's Temple.[22]

This imperial understanding took on a new force for the Spanish in the early 1580s, when Philip II inherited a claim to the title of king of Portugal and then made good on it. For the English, Hakluyt especially, this union—making a reality of Spain as "the first empire upon which the sun never set"—was especially frightening.[23] When Philip II was crowned in Lisbon

22. Marie Tanner, *The Last Descendant of Aeneas: The Hapsburgs and the Mythic Image of the Emperor* (New Haven, Conn., 1993); Anthony Pagden, *Lords of All the World: Ideologies of Empire in Spain, Britain and France, c. 1500–c.1800* (New Haven, Conn., 1995), esp. 1–62. For Geoffrey Parker's most recent statement of Philip II's messianism, see Parker, "The Place of Tudor England in the Messianic Vision of Philip II of Spain," Royal Historical Society, *Transactions*, 6th Ser., XII (2002), 167–221. On the Escorial, see Tanner, *Last Descendant of Aeneas*, 162–182; José de Sigüenza, *La fundación del monasterio de el Escorial* (Madrid, 1986); George Kubler, *Building the Escorial* (Princeton, N.J., 1982); José Luis Cano de Gardoqui y Garcia, *La construcción del monasterio de el Escorial: Historia de una empresa arquitectónica* (Valladolid, 1994); Rosemarie Mulcahy, *The Decoration of the Royal Basilica of El Escorial* (Cambridge, 1994); Jean Babelon, *Jacopo da Trezzo et la construction de l'Escurial: Essai sur les arts á la cour de Philippe II, 1519–1589* (Paris, 1922); Catherine Wilkinson-Zerner, *Juan de Herrara: Architect to Philip II of Spain* (New Haven, Conn., 1993); Agustín Ruiz de Arcaute, *Juan de Herrera, arquitecto de Felipe II* (Madrid, 1936); Eusebio Julián Zarco-Bacas y Cuevas, *El monasterio de San Lorenzo de Real de el Escorial, y la casita del príncipe,* 7th ed. (El Escorial, 1949).

23. Geoffrey Parker, "David or Goliath? Philip II and His World in the 1580s," in Richard L. Kagan and Parker, eds., *Spain, Europe, and the Atlantic World: Essays in Honour of John H. Elliott* (Cambridge, 1995), 245; Richard Hakluyt, "A Discourse of the Commodity of the Taking of the Straight of Magellanus," PRO, SP 12/229/97, rpt.

in 1581, he concluded, along with Philippe Duplessis-Mornay and Phillipe de Marnix (ardent Calvinist supporters of William the Silent, with whom Hakluyt was in communication), that Spain's New World treasure fueled not only its war in the Netherlands but its capacity to threaten England and France.[24] Like Duplessis-Mornay, he saw this fact as a point of strategic vulnerability for the Spanish.[25] In his "Discourse," Hakluyt presented a chap-

---

in Taylor, ed., *Original Writings,* I, 139–146. *The Calendar of State Papers,* Domestic Series, incorrectly suggests that the discourse dates from 1589; Taylor and Quinn date it a decade earlier, from soon after news reached England of the death of Henry of Portugal on Jan. 30, 1580; see Taylor, ed., *Original Writings,* I, 16–18; Quinn and Quinn, "Hakluyt Chronology," in Quinn, ed., *Hakluyt Handbook,* I, 272.

24. Philippe de Mornay, "Discours au Roy Henry III, sur les moyens de diminuer l'Espaignols," in de Mornay, *Mémoires et correspondence de Duplessis-Mornay . . . ,* 12 vols (Paris, 1824), II, 580–593; [Philips van Marnix van St. Aldegonde], *A Pithie, and Most Earnest Exhortation, concerning the Estate of Christiandome . . .* (Antwerp, 1583; STC 17450.7). The printer was Robert Waldegrave. Marnix's work was first published in Latin at Middelburg in 1583 and by 1584 was also available in Italian, French, Dutch, and English. Hakluyt does not directly cite Duplessis-Mornay in the "Discourse," but he does cite this work of Marnix's; see Hakluyt, *A Particuler Discourse,* ed. Quinn and Quinn, 40–45; Hakluyt, "Discourse of Western Planting," in Taylor, ed., *Original Writings,* II, 245, 248–249. During Hakluyt's service in Paris between 1583 and 1588, he also seems to have been familiar with similar thought of Achille de Harlay, the French *politique,* who had become first president of the Parlement of Paris in 1582. In 1599, Hakluyt referred to him as "the reverend and prudent Counseller Monsieur Harlae, the lord chiefe Justice of *France*" and indicated, in connection with his account of publishing the work of Laudonnière on French Protestant explorations in Florida, that he already knew Harlay in 1587; see Hakluyt, "To the Right Honorable Sir Robert Cecil Knight, Principall Secretarie to Her Majestie," Oct. 24, 1599, London, in Hakluyt, *Principal Navigations* (1903–1905), I, lxviii. Harlay was the brother-in-law of the historian Jacques Auguste de Thou, which only reinforced Hakluyt's affinity to him. Writing in 1594 to Henri IV, Harlay made arguments similar to those presented by Duplessis-Mornay to Henri III a decade earlier; see Achille de Harlay, "Harangues du Premier Président Achille de Harlay," ed. Albert Chamberlain, in *Documents d'histoire (de Henri IV à nos jours),* troisième année, no. 4 (December 1912), 531–539; see also Frank Lestringant, *Le Huguenot et le sauvage: L'Amérique et la controverse coloniale, en France, au temps des guerres de religion, 1555-1589,* 3d ed. (Geneva, 2004), 344– 356; Elie Barnavi and Robert Descimon, *La sainte ligue, le juge, et la potence* (Paris, 1985), 175–179. For Harlay's career, see Jacques De La Vallée, *Discours sur la vie, actions et mort de tres-illustre seigneur, Messire Achilles de Harlay: En son vivant conseiller du Roy en ses Conseils d'Estat et Privé, premier président du Sénat de Paris, et Comte Beaumôt et Gatinois* (Paris, 1616).

25. "[B]y this treasure," he says, Philip "hathe hired at sondry times the sonnes of

ter demonstrating "the mischefe that the Indian Treasure" had wrought, as he put it, to the "unrevocable annoye of this Realme" and advocated the establishment of colonial settlements in North America as the best means to exploit it and thereby thwart the Spanish threat.[26]

Hence, responding to a dire moment of crisis for international Protestantism, when religious war was returning to its fever pitch in Europe and Spain was organizing to crush the English, Hakluyt argued that colonies in America would be the cure for multiple ills. They would bring the English into mutually advantageous exchange with Native peoples yearning to shed the yoke of bondage imposed by the Spanish. They would provide a base for harassing the Spanish silver fleets and thereby cut off the wealth that Spain was using to dominate Europe. And they would assure the wealth necessary for England to maintain itself as an independent commonwealth.

There was already an idea of English empire before Hakluyt's time, of course. In medieval legal and political discourse, to say that a kingdom is an "empire" means that it is subject to no earthly power but exists as an independent political community under God alone. This concept took on important new scope and significance with the Reformation in England, since Henry VIII's break from Rome and the royal supremacy over the church were grounded on it. The critical statute—the Act in Restraint of Appeals of 1533—had declared "that this realm of England is an empire, and so hath been accepted in the world, governed by one supreme head and king" who possessed "whole and entire" authority within the realm. An "empire" in this understanding is a free state governed entirely by its own rulers and laws.[27] Hence, when Hakluyt brought his "Discourse of Western Planting" to the queen in 1584, he was arguing as a good Church of England clergyman that, if England was to remain an empire in this older sense and, there-

---

Beliall to bereve the Prince of Orange of his life"; see Hakluyt, *A Particuler Discourse,* ed. Quinn and Quinn, 38–41; Hakluyt, "Discourse of Western Planting," in Taylor, ed., *Original Writings,* II, 245. Indeed, almost at the moment Hakluyt was writing this very line, William the Silent, having miraculously escaped such a death in 1582, in fact had fallen the fatal victim to just such an assassin's bullet.

26. Hakluyt, *A Particuler Discourse,* ed. Quinn and Quinn, 36–39; Hakluyt, "Discourse of Western Planting," in Taylor, ed., *Original Writings,* II, 243, 245.

27. Act in Restraint of Appeals, *St. Realm,* 24 Hen. VIII, c. 12 (1533). See Walter Ullmann, "'This Realm of England is an Empire,'" *Journal of Ecclesiastical History,* XXX (1979), 175–203; Quentin Skinner, "Classical Liberty and the Coming of the English Civil War," in Martin van Gelderen and Skinner, eds., *Republicanism: A Shared European Heritage,* 2 vols. (Cambridge, 2002), II, 11–13.

fore, if it was to keep control over its church and state against the prospects of conquest by Catholic Spain, it now needed to plant colonial settlements in America.[28]

Given the assassination of William the Silent in July 1584, and the renewal of the wars of religion in the Low Countries and in France in the months following, the year 1584 was an especially propitious moment for the expression of such thoughts. In October of that year, a fortnight after Hakluyt delivered his "Discourse," along with his *Analysis* of Aristotle's *Politics,* to the queen, the Privy Council, guided by Lord Burghley and Sir Francis Walsingham and fearing Elizabeth's assassination, met at Hampton Court to sign and seal their copy of the Bond of Association—that striking instrument of Protestant propaganda and what Patrick Collinson has called "monarchical republicanism." By endorsing it, the privy councillors and other members of England's ruling elite vowed to avenge the assassination of the queen, should it occur, and gave their sacred oaths to prevent its perpetrators from benefiting from it. Viewed in this context, Hakluyt's "Discourse" appears as a Protestant and neo-Aristotelian pendant to the Bond: the "Discourse" offering an ambitious, outward-looking, aggressive, Atlantic strategy for reducing the Spanish and Catholic threat to England and to international Protestantism; the Bond an equally ambitious, inward-looking, defensive, home-island strategy for coping with a grave moment of danger to the queen, the realm, and true religion at home and abroad.[29]

Endeavoring to secure the autonomy of England and the liberties of the English through territorial aggrandizement in this manner was fraught with potential problems. As ancient Roman thinkers and their Renaissance followers well knew, actions necessary for successful expansion could all too easily destroy the liberty and corrupt the virtue of the citizens of the very state whose interests were being protected and advanced.[30] However, in 1584, the Spanish threat was too immediate and palpable for Hakluyt to dwell on such worries. As we shall see, there was also a Hakluytian answer to them, grounded in Hakluyt's high expectations regarding future history.

28. See Armitage, *Ideological Origins,* 63–65.

29. Royal MSS, 12 G. XIII, 1–47, BL; Quinn, ed., *Hakluyt Handbook,* I, 286; Patrick Collinson, "The Monarchical Republic of Queen Elizabeth I," *Bulletin of the John Rylands Library,* LXIX (1987), 394–424; PRO, SP 12/174/1.

30. On this point, see David Armitage, "Empire and Liberty: A Republican Dilemma," in van Gelderen and Skinner, eds., *Republicanism,* II, 29–36; Armitage, *Ideological Origins,* 125–145.

Viewed in the most immediate terms, Hakluyt's motives in promoting the plantation of colonial settlements in North America were material and economic. Colonies, he argued, would supply England with exotic commodities hitherto acquired at the second hand in European markets; would furnish raw materials for its finishing industries; would give employment to the hands of clothworkers and other artisans made idle by the dislocations of religious war; would raise customs revenues for the Crown and offer encouragement to mariners and shipwrights essential for the growth and maintenance of the navy; would become places to which criminals and the indigent could be sent to live productive lives; and, by thus improving economic conditions, would furnish incentives for the growth of population, which Hakluyt saw as "the honor and strengthe of a Prince."[31]

Through his family ties in the London merchant community and the patronage he received from privy councillors who favored England's commercial expansion, Hakluyt was closely connected with the country's new commercial ventures to Muscovy, the Levant, and the Barbary Coast. For almost a decade, he also received a pension from the Company of Clothworkers of London. These ties gave him access to detailed information about trading conditions on the Continent and the state of the cloth industry at home, as well as a strong bias in favor of the development of new trades and industries and against the Merchant Adventurers' monopolistic program.[32]

Although Hakluyt did not offer a systematic critique of the Merchant Adventurers' monopoly, many of his economic points are best understood to advance the interests of the newer trades and of the leading clothworkers against it. He praises the trade to Russia, Barbary, Turkey, Persia, and the like because, unlike dealings in the Low Countries, where the Merchant Adventurers had their privileges, all the cloth passing to those parts is "full wrought by the poore naturall subjectes of this Realme." American colonial enterprise, he argued, would have the same benefit. "Nowe if her Ma[jes]tie take these westerne discoveries in hande and plante there, yt is like that in a shorte time wee shall vente as great masse of clothe yn those partes as ever

---

31. Hakluyt, *A Particuler Discourse,* ed. Quinn and Quinn, 32–33; Hakluyt, "Discourse of Western Planting," in Taylor, ed., *Original Writings,* II, 238.

32. See G. D. Ramsay, "Clothworkers, Merchants, Adventurers, and Richard Hakluyt," *English Historical Review,* XCII (1977), 517–521, esp. 520–521; Quinn and Quinn, "Hakluyt Chronology," in Quinn, ed., *Hakluyt Handbook,* I, 268–269, 271–273, 292–293.

wee did in the netherlandes, and in tyme moche more," keeping for England the profits of the vast finishing trades. He also believed that, in this American trade, the English would find "gold and spicerie" north of the equator equal to what the Spanish and Portuguese had found to the south.[33]

Both predictions were widely off the mark, of course. Tobacco and sugar eventually would prove the equivalent of "gold and spicerie" to North America, but until a sufficiently large labor force could be recruited to clear the land and produce these commodities in quantity—something that would take decades (and eventually would also require the introduction of chattel slavery)—America provided hardly more than a fraction of England's market in the Low Countries. Nevertheless, it is clear that Hakluyt envisioned the American trade as answering England's condition as a relatively backward economy vis-à-vis its European trading partners, exporting raw materials and unfinished or semifinished wares with low profit margins and receiving in return high-priced finished goods. Hakluyt understood that if the English were to have a measure of security in their own prosperity, they needed to liberate themselves from this subordination to the more developed economies of their European neighbors, some of them also England's dire enemies.

Opposition to monopoly—of the sort manifested by the London Cloth-workers and implied in Hakluyt's support for them—links liberty to Adam's obligation to labor for his bread. This paradigm treats Adam's curse as the antithesis of slavery—bondage to God being the condition of freedom from bondage to others—and conceives society thus to be a commonwealth of free persons who exchange their skills and the products of those skills for mutual benefit and the public good. This scripturally informed understanding of civilized life stresses—as a starting place—the community's need for sufficient material resources if its members are to live well and do well. It also implies the human capacity to find the best means for producing the desired ends. And it makes the just and proper performance of one's calling a duty in conscience that one rightly should fulfill in a spirit of generosity and goodwill—giving the commonwealth the gift of one's skills—not out of greed and narrow self-regard.[34]

33. Hakluyt, *A Particuler Discourse,* ed. Quinn and Quinn, 31–33; Hakluyt, "Discourse of Western Planting," in Taylor, ed., *Original Writings,* II, 237.

34. David Harris Sacks, "Parliament, Liberty, and the Commonweal," in J. H. Hexter, ed., *Parliament and Liberty from the Reign of Elizabeth to the English Civil War* (Stanford, Calif., 1992), 93-101; David Harris Sacks, "The Countervailing of Benefits: Monopoly, Liberty, and the Benevolence in Elizabethan England," in Dale Hoak, ed., *Tudor Political Culture* (Cambridge, 1995), 272-291; Sacks, "The Greed of Judas:

In the "Discourse," and more generally, Hakluyt relies on a similar understanding of the rational workings of the soul in naturally free persons. Take, for example, his arguments about poverty. If England can send its wares to America and elsewhere in a finished state, he says, and bring back raw materials to be worked at home, "there nede not [be] one poore creature to steale, to sterve, or to beg as they doo." The passage, which echoes Thomas More's analysis in *Utopia,* treats crime in some measure as a rational response to poverty and places the blame for it partly on failings in the structure of English overseas trade. Hakluyt recognizes that the poor, lacking work, seek their sustenance from theft, because the merchants, necessarily seeking their own advantage, choose to export unwrought and import wrought commodities because market conditions prevent them from profiting from the alternative. Change the state of the market, make it possible to export finished products and import unfinished ones at profitable prices, and the problem will correct itself.[35]

"And if this come aboute that worke may be had for the multitude," he says, "where the Realme hath nowe one thousande for the defence thereof, the same may have fyve thousande: for when people knowe howe to lyve, and howe to maynetayne and feede their wyves and children, they will not abstaine from mariage as they now doe." "I dare truly affirme," he goes on, "that if the number in this Realme were as greate as all Spaine and France . . . the people beinge industrious, industrious I say, there shoulde be founde victuals ynoughe at the full in all bounty to suffice them all." This analysis attributes to the artisan and the husbandman, and to the wandering poor as well, the same rational capacities as shown by experienced merchants. What, then, gave Hakluyt his confidence in the industriousness of the people?[36]

Part of the answer again lies in his Aristotelianism, in which he shares much with the views of those sixteenth-century social commentators who, like Sir Thomas Smith, read not only their Livy but their Aristotle through the lens of a hardheaded anti-Utopianism. Like Smith, Hakluyt saw eco-

Avarice, Monopoly, and the Moral Economy in England, ca. 1350–ca. 1600," *Journal of Medieval and Early Modern Studies,* XXVIII (1998), 263–307.

35. Hakluyt, *A Particuler Discourse,* ed. Quinn and Quinn, 32–33; Hakluyt, "Discourse of Western Planting," in Taylor, ed., *Original Writings,* II, 238; and see Thomas More, *Utopia,* trans. Ralph Robynson (1556), ed. David Harris Sacks, The Bedford Series in History and Culture (Boston, 1999), 100–104. More attributed the structural causes of crime to the increase of poverty resulting from enclosure.

36. Hakluyt, *A Particuler Discourse,* ed. Quinn and Quinn, 32–33; Hakluyt, "Discourse of Western Planting," in Taylor, ed., *Original Writings,* II, 238–239.

nomic exchange as a reciprocating feedback system in which particular actions produce predictable results. He also understood human nature to be intrinsically acquisitive as well as political and social. The flourishing life of civilization required getting the things necessary to live and to live well and then using them productively in social interchange. Hence, Hakluyt held that human rationality, i.e., the capacity to deliberate about and choose the best means to achieve desired ends, had a calculating, advantage-driven character aimed toward matching causes to their wished-for effects.[37]

As an Aristotelian writing on the *Politics,* Hakluyt also was bound to consider the issue of slavery. To a remarkable degree, he did so by replicating the views of Bartolomé de Las Casas, from whose *Brief Relation of the Destruction of the Indians* he quoted liberally in the "Discourse." Like Las Casas, Hakluyt saw the Amerindians as fully rational and treated their seeming barbarism, not as a sign of their permanent condition as natural slaves, but as evidence that they stood at an early stage in their social development as a civilized people. Distinguishing between natural slaves who have justly been put into bondage and persons of honor who are unjustly enslaved, he counts the Natives of the Americas among the latter, the naturally free, i.e., as a people fully capable of forming beneficial allegiances and measuring their actions to their ends. The Natives, Hakluyt was confident, possessed the instincts for trade and would prove good trading partners.[38]

The condition of natural freedom assumes the capacity of free persons to know their own best interest and to seek it. Their freedom also implies their natural resistance to coercion of any kind. The peoples of the Spanish colo-

37. See David Harris Sacks, "The Prudence of Thrasymachus: Sir Thomas Smith and the Commonwealth of England," in Anthony T. Grafton and J. H. M. Salmon, eds., *Historians and Ideologues: Essays in Honor of Donald Kelley* (Rochester, N.Y., 2001), 89–122; and see Hakluyt, *Analysis,* Royal MSS, 12 G. XIII, fol. 4v, BL; [Thomas Smith], *A Discourse of the Commonweal of This Realm of England . . . ,* ed. Mary Dewar (Charlottesville, Va., 1969), 96; see also 59.

38. Hakluyt, *A Particuler Discourse,* ed. Quinn and Quinn, 52–59; Hakluyt, "Discourse of Western Planting," in Taylor, ed., *Original Writings,* II, 257–261; Bartholomew [Bartolomé] de Las Casas, *The Spanish Colonie, or Briefe Chronicle of the Acts and Gestes of the Spaniardes in the West Indies, Called the Newe World . . . ,* trans. M. M. S. (London, 1583; STC 4739). *The Spanish Colonie* is a translation from the French of Bartolomé de Las Casas, *Tyrannies et cruautez des Espagnols, perpetrees ès Indes occidentales . . . ,* trans. Jacques de Miggrode (Anvers, 1579). On Las Casas's views about Amerindians as rational beings, see Anthony Pagden, *The Fall of Natural Man: The American Indian and the Origins of Comparative Ethnology* (Cambridge, 1982), 119–145; for Hakluyt's commentary on Aristotle's view of slavery, see Hakluyt, *Analysis,* Royal MSS, 12. G XIII, fol. 5v, BL.

nies in the Americas, Hakluyt states, "are kepte by greate tyrannie, and *quos metuunt oderunt*": whom they fear, they hate. "And the people kepte in subjection desire nothinge more than freedome." He is certain, therefore, that given the opportunity, "the people . . . in every forrein territorie" belonging to Philip, bearing on their shoulders "the most intollerable and insupportable yoke of Spaine," would "revolte . . . and cutt the throates of the proude hatefull Spaniardes their governours." He even suggests that Sir Francis Drake was already of "so greate credit" among the South American Natives whom he had met during his circumnavigation that he might himself incite and lead such a rebellion. Hakluyt concludes, *"Multorum odijs nulla respublica stare diu potest"*: no state can stand long by the hates of many.[39]

In these passages, Hakluyt offers a stunningly hard-headed (almost Machiavellian) reading of Cicero on love and fear. "But, of all motives," Cicero said, "none is better adapted to secure influence and hold it fast than love. Nothing more foreign to that than fear. For . . . [w]hom they fear they hate. And whom one hates, one hopes to see . . . dead. For fear is but a poor safeguard of lasting power, while benevolence . . . may be trusted to keep it safe forever." Machiavelli thought Cicero's trust in love to be naïve, but in Hakluyt's hands, this argument not only gives the concept of liberty a certain toughness but shows the Amerindians in respect of their reason to be just like us, i.e., to possess the same instincts for sociability and exchange and the same resistance to slavery as all rational human beings.[40]

Preacher of the Word of God

Hakluyt was a man equally at home in studies of ancient writers on politics and civil life and of the Bible, the Church Fathers, and the history of the Church and the practical necessities of European politics, international trade, and global exploration. Throughout his long career, he saw himself as simultaneously advancing the causes of civilization and of Christianity, which to him, as to Las Casas, were interrelated. Although Hakluyt was involved intimately in temporal matters and secular affairs, his was essentially

39. Hakluyt, *A Particuler Discourse,* ed. Quinn and Quinn, 40–43, 54–55, 60–63; Hakluyt, "Discourse of Western Planting," in Taylor, ed., *Original Writings,* II, 246, 248, 257–258, 265. Hakluyt also says, *"Nullum violentum est diuturnum, et malus diuturnitatis custos est metus":* "Nothing violent is long lasting, and fear is a bad guardian of stability." See *A Particuler Discourse,* 60–61; "Discourse of Western Planting," 264.

40. Cicero *De officiis* 2.23–24; Walter Miller, trans., *Cicero, "De officiis,"* The Loeb Classical Library (1913; rpt. Cambridge, Mass., 1956), 191. Note that Erasmus had dealt with this point in *Adages* 2.9.62; see Margaret Mann Phillips, trans., *The Collected Works of Erasmus: Adages* (Toronto, 1982–), XXXIV, 114–115, 354–355.

an ecclesiastical career. An ordained Church of England clergyman, Hak-luyt was educated at Westminster School and at Christ Church, Oxford, deeply immersed in Scripture and in the languages and literatures of the ancients.[41] In 1574, he became a student of Christ Church, i.e., a fellow, and continued his official membership until 1586, when he vacated his place on being installed to a prebendal chair in Bristol Cathedral. While at Oxford, he became a licensed preacher and pursued, but did not complete, a Bache-lor of Divinity degree; and he made the teaching of Aristotle and of geogra-phy in the modern style his areas of expertise. In 1583, he departed for ser-vice in Paris as chaplain and secretary to Sir Edward Stafford, Elizabeth I's ambassador, a post he continued to hold until 1588. Along with collecting geographical information, he served as a diplomat and intelligence officer, observing from close quarters the course of Europe's wars of religion.[42]

On his return from Paris, Hakluyt moved into a series of clerical posts. He was instituted in 1590 as rector of Wetheringsett with Blockford in Suf-folk and subsequently in 1599 was granted the reversion of a chaplaincy in the Hospital of the Savoy, a post he came to fill sometime before 1604. Later, in 1612, he also became rector of Gedney in Lincolnshire. Having dedicated the second and third volumes of *Principal Navigations* to Sir Robert Cecil, he entered into the principal secretary's circle of favored church figures. In 1601, he referred to himself in a dedication to Cecil as "Your Honors Chap-lein," a position that brought him not only within a circle of major cleri-cal figures but also into intimate communication with the most influential Crown official of the early Jacobean period. It was Cecil's patronage in 1599 that brought him his opportunity at the Savoy, over which the Cecil family had long acted as a patron. In 1602, again with Cecil's patronage (along with that of the earl of Nottingham), he became a canon of Westminster, where he served the chapter until his death in 1616 in a variety of impor-

41. See John Sargeaunt, *Annals of Westminster School . . .* (London, 1898), 36–43; Lawrence Edward Tanner, *Westminster School: A History* (London, 1934), 6–10; for the character of classical education for schoolboys in Elizabeth's reign, see T. W. Bald-win, *William Shakspere's Small Latine and Lesse Greeke,* 2 vols. (Urbana, Ill., 1944), I, esp. 380–407. For this section and the following, see David Harris Sacks, "Richard Hakluyt's Navigations in Time: History, Epic, and Empire," *Modern Language Quar-terly,* LXVII (2006), 37–48.

42. Quinn and Quinn, "Hakluyt Chronology," in Quinn, ed., *Hakluyt Handbook,* I, 267–298; see n. 37 for Hakluyt's mission in Paris; see also Gordon Bruner Parks, "Hak-luyt's Mission in France, 1583–1588," *Washington University Studies,* IX (1922), 165–184; Parks, *Richard Hakluyt and the English Voyages,* ed. Williamson, 99–122; Lestrin-gant, *Le Huguenot et le sauvage,* 311–356.

tant offices including archdeacon, steward, and treasurer. As much as we remember him for his publications in the history of geography and navigation, before all else he was a clergyman, and a learned and scholarly one at that. Twice in his career, in 1585, while he was still connected with Oxford, and again in 1612, he was identified in official documents as "professor of theology."[43]

Hakluyt was not a writer of treatises, even on navigation and discovery, and none of his surviving writings presents a systematic statement of his theological position.[44] Despite his official standing as a licensed preacher, and the fact that he served as a parish minister as well as an ecclesiastical official for most of his adult life, no sermon has survived of the many dozens, perhaps hundreds, that he must have delivered between his ordination in 1580 and his death in 1616. Instead, his religious views shape and are embedded in his cosmography. From what has survived, it is clear that he was no conventional Calvinist, and, although he possessed apocalyptic views of a kind, he also was no conventional millenarian. Like his patron Sir Robert Cecil, Hakluyt's religious outlook evolved rapidly away from the conventions of Elizabethan Protestantism toward a position that had more in common with the rationalist providentialism of his friend and sometime patron Sir Walter Ralegh; with the neo-Aristotelian thinking of his Oxford contemporary Richard Hooker; with Francis Bacon's advanced apocalyptic views on the significance of overseas discovery to the history of the world; and, most of all, with the spirituality of Sir Robert Cecil himself.[45]

43. Quinn and Quinn, "Hakluyt Chronology," in Quinn, ed., *Hakluyt Handbook*, I, 303-304, 313, 320, 326; Hakluyt, "To the Right Honorable Sir Robert Cecill Knight, Principall Secretarie to Her Majestie," Oct. 29, 1601, London, dedicatory epistle to Hakluyt's translation and edition of Antonie Galvano, *The Discoveries of the World from Their Originall unto the Yeere of Our Lord, 1555* (London, 1601; STC 11543), sig. A2[c]v; William Mount, master of the Savoy, to Sir Robert Cecil, Nov. 23, 1599, Cecil MS 74/97, paraphrased in Historical Manuscripts Commission, *Calendar of the Manuscripts of the Most Honourable the Marquess of Salisbury, Presented at Hatfield House, Hertfordshire*, 24 vols. (London, 1883-1976), IX, 397-398; on the patronage of the Cecils at the Savoy, see Robert Somerville, *The Savoy: Manor, Hospital, Chapel* (London, 1960), 67, 152, 222, 239. This thumbnail sketch of Hakluyt's career is derived from Quinn and Quinn, "Hakluyt Chronology," in Quinn, ed., *Hakluyt Handbook*, I, 263-331, esp. 288, 311, 327.

44. For Armitage's suggestions regarding the possible significance of this fact, see his *Ideological Origins*, 71, 76-77.

45. On Ralegh, see Katharine R. Firth, *The Apocalyptic Tradition in Reformation Britain, 1530-1645* (Oxford, 1979), 180-199. On Hooker, see Peter Lake, *Anglicans and Puritans? Presbyterianism and English Conformist Thought from Whitgift to Hooker*

Among the ecclesiastical institutions on which Cecil left the mark of his religious outlook, Westminster Abbey was perhaps the most important. Although not itself a cathedral, in the Elizabethan and early Stuart era, it was what Diarmaid MacCulloch has called "a showcase for the English cathedral ethos."[46] Under Gabriel Goodman as dean, it had already "enshrined the most conservative aspects of the Elizabethan church" before Hakluyt's arrival.[47] In addition to emphasizing sacramentalism, ceremony, and church music in its practices, its chapter also was peopled by many of the early leaders of the theological and ecclesiastical movement later associated with Archbishop William Laud. Lancelot Andrewes was its dean when Hakluyt joined the chapter, and Richard Neile succeeded Andrewes. During

(London, 1988), 145-238, esp. 225-230; Lake, "The 'Anglican Moment?' Richard Hooker and the Ideological Watershed of the 1590s," in Stephen Platten, ed., *Anglicanism and the Western Christian Tradition: Continuity, Change, and the Search for Communion* (Norwich, Conn., 2003), 90-121; Richard Bauckham, "Hooker, Travers, and the Church of Rome in the 1580s," *Journal of Ecclesiastical History*, XXIX (1978), 37-50; Patrick Collinson, "Hooker and the Elizabethan Establishment," in Arthur Stephen McGrade, ed., *Richard Hooker and the Construction of Christian Community* (Tempe, Ariz., 1997), 149-181; Diarmaid MacCulloch, "Richard Hooker's Reputation," *English Historical Review*, CXVII (2002), 773-812. Hooker, born in Exeter in 1554, became a fellow of Corpus Christi College, Oxford, upon receiving his M.A. in 1577; he had entered Corpus Christi in 1569, within a year or so of Hakluyt's beginning at Christ Church, and received his B.A. in 1573, a year before Hakluyt. For Bacon's views, see Francis Bacon, *The Advancement of Learning*, ed. Michael Kiernan, The Oxford Francis Bacon, IV (Oxford, 2000), 71 [sig. 2D3v], discussed further below. On Cecil's spirituality, see Pauline Croft, "The Religion of Robert Cecil," *Historical Journal*, XXXIV (1991), 773-796; see also Croft, "The New English Church in One Family: William, Mildred, and Robert Cecil," in Platten, ed., *Anglicanism and the Western Christian Tradition*, 83-89.

46. Diarmaid MacCulloch, review of Stanford E. Lehmberg, *Cathedrals under Siege: Cathedrals in English Society, 1600-1700, Journal of Ecclesiastical History*, XLVIII (1997), 581; see, more generally, MacCulloch, "The Church of England, 1533-1603," in Platten, ed., *Anglicanism and the Western Christian Tradition*, 30-31, 40-41; MacCulloch, "Putting the English Reformation on the Map: The Prothero Lecture," Royal Historical Society, *Transactions*, 6th Ser., XV (2005), 75-95.

47. J. F. Merritt, "The Cecils and Westminster, 1558-1612: The Development of an Urban Power Base," in Pauline Croft, ed., *Patronage, Culture, and Power: The Early Cecils*, Studies in British Art, VIII (New Haven, Conn., 2002), 235; Merritt, *The Social World of Early Modern Westminster: Abbey, Court, and Community, 1525-1640* (Manchester, 2005), 80; see also A. Tindal Hart, "Westminster College: Elizabethan and Stuart Times," in Edward Carpenter, ed., *A House of Kings: The History of Westminster Abbey* (London, 1966), 133-136.

this same period, Hadrian Saravia, William Barlow, and Christopher Sutton occupied prebendal stalls.[48] At Westminster, therefore, as in the Cecil household, Hakluyt found himself engaged with some of the most important figures in the Church of England, promoting what has been called "avant-guard conformity" in its liturgical practice and theology.[49]

As Pauline Croft has demonstrated, to be among Cecil's ecclesiastical clients was to be associated with the main spokesmen of the early Jacobean era advancing such a viewpoint in the church, figures such as Lancelot Andrewes and Cecil's chaplains Samuel Harsnett and Richard Neile. Through Cecil's patronage as high steward and bailiff of Westminster, Andrewes became dean of Westminster in 1601; Neile succeeded Andrewes in 1605. At Westminster, Hakluyt worked closely with its deans in the business of the chapter.[50] He is particularly evident in the chapter's records during Neile's very active tenure, assisting him in the projects he undertook to support ceremonial order and reverence for the sacraments in the Abbey.[51] With Andrewes, there seems also to have been a personal affinity, not just

48. J. F. Merritt, "The Cradle of Laudianism? Westminster Abbey, 1558–1630," *Journal of Ecclesiastical History,* LII (2001), 623–646; Merritt, "Cecils and Westminster," in Croft, ed., *Patronage, Culture, and Power,* 237–238; see also Merritt, *Social World of Early Modern Westminster,* 119–121. In 1611, William Laud, a protégé of Neile's at the time, acquired the reversionary right to a stall, although he did not actually come to hold it until ten years later.

49. Peter Lake, "Lancelot Andrewes, John Buckeridge, and Avant-Garde Conformity at the Court of James I," in Linda Levy Peck, ed., *The Mental World of the Jacobean Court* (Cambridge, 1991), 113–133.

50. C. S. Knighton, ed., *Acts of the Dean and Chapter of Westminster, 1543–1609,* 2 vols., Westminster Abbey Record Series (Woodbridge, 1997–1999), II, 183; Croft, "Religion of Robert Cecil," *Historical Journal,* XXXIV (1991), 791–794; Merritt, "Cecils and Westminster," in Croft, ed., *Patronage, Culture, and Power,* 233, 234, 237; Quinn and Quinn, "Hakluyt Chronology," in Quinn, ed., *Hakluyt Handbook,* I, 317–318.

51. Knighton, ed., *Acts of the Dean and Chapter of Westminster,* introduction, I, xlvii–xlviii, II, 200ff; Hart, "Westminster College," in Carpenter, ed., *A House of Kings,* 144–147; Andrew Foster, "Richard Neile, Dean of Westminster, 1605–1610: Homegrown Talent Makes Its Mark," in C. S. Knighton and Richard Mortimer, eds., *Westminster Abbey Reformed, 1540–1640* (Aldershot, 2003), 190–192, 196–197; see also Foster, "The Function of a Bishop: The Career of Richard Neile, 1562–1640," in Rosemary O'Day and Felicity Heal, eds., *Continuity and Change: Personnel and Administration of the Church of England, 1500–1642* (Leicester, 1976), 33–54; Nicholas Tyacke, *Anti-Calvinists: The Rise of English Arminianism, c. 1590–1640* (Oxford, 1987), 106–124; Foster, "Archbishop Richard Neile Revisited," in Peter Lake and Michael L. Questier, eds., *Conformity and Orthodoxy in the English Church, c. 1560–1660* (Woodbridge, 2000), 159–178.

because the two of them came from London-based merchant families but also because they both had strong interests in geography and cartography.[52]

Although the surviving evidence is too limited to allow us to establish the degree with which Hakluyt shared doctrinal positions with these churchmen, his accommodationist views on relations with Roman Catholicism alone place him at a distance from the "Calvinist hegemony" in the English church in the late Elizabethan and early Jacobean periods.[53] On this point, Hakluyt was closer to Hooker in the 1580s, as well as to William the Silent and his supporters in the Netherlands, than he was even to Sir Francis Walsingham, from whose patronage he greatly benefited in those early years.[54] He was no Elizabethan "Puritan" in any of the varied senses in which the term was used.[55]

From the Map to the Bible

The publication of the second edition of *Principal Navigations* concluded a project that first stirred Hakluyt's imagination, we learn from him, when he was "a youth" and one of the queen's scholars at Westminster School. His often-cited account contains an implicitly providential view not only of his own biography but of world history in general.

A year or two before entering Christ Church, Hakluyt had occasion, he tells us, to visit the Middle Temple chambers of his older cousin Richard, "at

52. D. D. C. Chambers, "A Catalogue of the Library of Bishop Lancelot Andrewes (1555-1626)," Cambridge Bibliographical Society, *Transactions,* V (1970), 103, 111; "Demands of (Lancelot Andrewes) Bishop of Chichester, for Stuff Left by Him (When Quitting the Deanery of Westminster) . . . circa 1605," in Westminster Abbey MSS 41119, Westminster Abbey Library, London; Paul A. Welsby, *Lancelot Andrewes, 1555-1626* (London, 1958), 88-89. I thank Christine Reynolds, Assistant Keeper of the Muniments at Westminster Abbey, and Dr. Peter McCullough of Lincoln College, Oxford, for their assistance in tracing Andrewes's intellectual interests.

53. For further discussion of this point, see below at note 85.

54. See P. G. Lake, "Calvinism and the English Church, 1570-1635," *Past and Present,* no. 114 (February 1987), 34; Patrick Collinson, "England and International Calvinism, 1558-1640," in Menna Prestwich, ed., *International Calvinism, 1541-1715* (Oxford, 1985), 202-203; Bauckham, "Hooker, Travers, and the Church of Rome," *Journal of Ecclesiastical History,* XXIX (1978), 37-50; see also Lee W. Gibbs, "Richard Hooker and Lancelot Andrewes on Priestly Absolution," in McGrade, ed., *Richard Hooker,* 261-274.

55. See Patrick Collinson, *The Elizabethan Puritan Movement* (London, 1967); Collinson, "A Comment: Concerning the Name Puritan," *Journal of Ecclesiastical History,* XXXI (1980), 483-488; Peter Lake, *Moderate Puritans and the Elizabethan Church* (Cambridge, 1982).

a time when I found lying open upon his boord certeine bookes of Cosmographie with an universall Mappe." Being "somewhat curious in the view therof," the young man became the pupil of his kinsman, who, observing his interest, "began to instruct my ignorance." His cousin, Hakluyt says, first showed "me the division of the earth into three parts after the olde account and then according to the latter, and better distribution, into more." Hakluyt refers in the first instance to the tripartite Ptolemaic worldview centered on Jerusalem and depicting only Europe, Africa, and Asia in a medieval *mappa mundi* or in a stylized T–O form. The new worldview took into account the discoveries in the Americas and elsewhere. Reviewing this modern map—we do not know which—the elder Hakluyt "pointed with his wand to all the knowen Seas, Gulfs, Bayes, Straights, Capes, Rivers, Empires, Kingdomes, Dukedomes, and Territories of ech part, with declaration also of their speciall commodities, and particular wants, which by the benefit of traffike, and entercourse of merchants, are plentifully supplied." The world according to Ptolemy and the other ancient geographers, such as Strabo and medieval mapmakers, was revealed to be more complex than they had thought—richer and more varied in structure and also an amalgamation of the civic and the economic with the natural.[56]

The elder Hakluyt was suggesting to his young cousin that the new discoveries made in recent times gave the modern age some advantages over past epochs, especially perhaps in confirming that God had so disposed the world to balance scarcities in one place with abundance in another and to promote exchange between regions. Despite the Fall, the course of history was not the story of uniform decline from a golden age of perfection but had unveiled more and more of the truths of God's creation and brought peoples into communication with one another. This view implied that the restoration of ancient learning, useful as it was, would not be enough to provide the knowledge or the guidance necessary for a flourishing life of virtue in the present age.[57]

56. "To the Right Honorable Sir Francis Walsingham, Knight . . . ," Nov. 17, [1589], dedicatory epistle to the first edition of Hakluyt, *Principal Navigations* (1903–1905), I, xvii. For the date and circumstances of this visit, see Richard Hakluyt to Emanuel van Meteren, Dec. 6, 1594, in Taylor, ed., *Original Writings,* II, 419; Quinn, ed., *Hakluyt Handbook,* I, 265. Taylor and Skelton speculate that the map might have been Abraham Ortelius's cordiform world map published in Antwerp by Christofell Plantin in 1564 and supplied in many copies to London booksellers; see Taylor, ed., *Original Writings,* I, 77–78 n. 2; R. A. Skelton, "Hakluyt's Maps," in Quinn, ed., *Hakluyt Handbook,* I, 48.

57. Armitage, *Ideological Origins,* 77; and see Stephen Gaukroger, *Francis Bacon and the Transformation of Early-Modern Philosophy* (Cambridge, 2001), 110–111.

The instruction did not stop here, however. "From the Mappe," the elder Hakluyt brought his young cousin "to the Bible, and turning to the 107 Psalme, directed mee to the 23 and 24 verses, where," Hakluyt says, "I read, that they which go downe to the sea in ships, and occupy by the great waters, they see the works of the Lord, and his woonders in the deepe." As Hakluyt retold the tale, this move from map to Bible was life determining:

[the] words of the Prophet together with my cousins discourse . . . tooke in me so deepe an impression, that I constantly resolved . . . I would by Gods assistance prosecute that knowledge and kinde of literature, the doores whereof (after a sort) were so happily opened before me.

Hakluyt's project became his calling. He represented it as a mission given to him in his cousin's study by God's command.[58]

This brief narrative provides no systematic religious exegesis, of course, but there is also nothing "disingenuous" about it. Using the art of literary representation and relying on scriptural allusion, the passage vividly conveys a significant religious message. Take, for example, Hakluyt's reference to his youthful curiosity. As is now well documented, curiosity was far from being an undisputable virtue in the late sixteenth century. According to the ancient ethical philosophers, *curiositas* is a moral failing—an excessive or obsessive inquisitiveness into the affairs of others or into forbidden matters. To early Christians, it is a sin, a form of lust, a violation of the admonition to "love not the world, neither the things that are in the worlde." To Saint Augustine, this "concupiscence of the eyes," as he called it, was the greedy desire to see, to possess, and to devour what should remain hidden; it was contrasted with the awe or wonder a true Christian should show in experiencing God's creation. However, as with Saint Augustine himself, curiosity could also be the starting place on a long pilgrimage to God, provided the soul was, or became, turned toward his guiding light.[59]

58. "To the Right Honorable Sir Francis Walsingham, Knight," Nov. 17, [1589], in Hakluyt, *Principal Navigations* (1903-1905), I, xvii–xviii.

59. 1 John 2:15-16, quoted from 1560 Geneva Version; cf. Armitage, *Ideological Origins,* 71, 77; and see Saint Augustine of Hippo, *Confessions,* 10:30, 35, with 5:3, Saint Augustine, *Confessions,* trans. William Watts, 2 vols. (London, 1912), I, 210-215, II, 150-151, 174-181; Henri Irénée Marrou, *Saint Augustin et la fin de la culture antique,* 4th ed. (Paris, 1958), 149-157; André Labhardt, "Curiositas: Notes sur l'histoire d'un mot et d'une notion," *Museum helveticum,* XVII (1960), 206-224; André Cabassut, "Curiosité," in Marcel Viller et al., eds., *Dictionnaire de spiritualité* (Paris, 1937-1994), II, cols. 265-462; Jean Céard, ed., *La curiosité à la Renaissance: Actes* (Paris,

Hakluyt was not praising himself in telling us of his curiosity and of his cousin's response to it, but picking out the divinely ordained moment in which he was turned around—converted—from his intellectual self-indulgence as a young student and brought to his godly calling. It was this move from map to Bible, and his cousin's instruction on the new knowledge of God's creation revealed by the recent voyages of discovery, that saved him from the lust of his eyes.

The verses his cousin chose from Psalms make the point allusively but nonetheless with some precision to those familiar with the exegetical tradition connected with these verses. The text as quoted by Hakluyt comes from the Geneva Bible—itself a book filled with maps marking the places where God's will had been worked in the world. In the Geneva Version, safe passage on the high seas is connected in the accompanying marginal note with God's love and the redemption from the wages of sin that comes with faith in him. The note, itself dependent on commentaries by Saint Augustine and Cassiodorus, reads: "He sheweth by the sea what care God hathe over man, for in that he delivereth the[m] from the great dangers of the sea, he delivereth them, as it were, from a thousand deaths." In their allegorical interpretations, Augustine and Cassiodorus equated going down to the sea with the descent into hell, and identified the wonders of the deep with baptism and the resurrection.[60]

Read in the context Hakluyt himself provides, the passage serves to equate the journey from the Old World to the New not just with the journey from ignorance to knowledge but with that from sin to salvation. Taken together, these two movements formed the twin pillars of God's plan for the world. They moved human history itself, as it were, from the map to the Bible, from a focus on the material things necessary for survival in this world to a concentration on divine imperatives for deliverance in the next, with experience of the former leading to, and dependent on, knowledge of the latter.

Hakluyt believed that God had revealed the existence of the Americas for

1986); Caroline Walker Bynum, "Wonder," *American Historical Review,* CII (1997), 1–26; Lorraine Daston and Katharine Park, *Wonders and the Order of Nature, 1150–1750* (New York, 1998), esp. 92, 122–125, 218, 273–274, 303–316; see also Barbara M. Benedict, *Curiosity: A Cultural History of Early Modern Inquiry* (Chicago, 2001).

60. Pss. 107:23–24, 1560 Geneva Version; P. G. Walsh, ed. and trans., *Cassiodorus: Explanation of the Psalms,* 3 vols., Ancient Christian Writers: The Works of the Fathers in Translation, nos. 51–53 (New York, 1990–1991), III, 89–90; Saint Augustine, *Expositions on the Psalms,* translated for Christian Classics Ethereal Library (http://www.ccel.org/fathers2/NPNF1-08/npnf1-08-104.htm#P2469_2437254).

his own divine purpose. As the world's creator, he had disposed the world to balance scarcities in one place with abundance in another and so had promoted exchange between regions, and he had instilled in us the desire to seek our own happiness and self-sufficiency, giving us what Adam Smith would later call a natural "propensity to truck, barter, and exchange one thing for another."[61] But in punishment for human arrogance at the time of the Tower of Babel, God had scattered the world's peoples, inflicted a confusion of tongues on them, and cut off one hemisphere from knowledge of the other. Seen in this light, therefore, the "discovery" of the New World, which now was drawing the dispersed nations back into mutually beneficial exchange, represented the inception of a new age.

Hence, just as the young Hakluyt was liberated from his sinful curiosity and drawn into harmony with God's will through learning of the true nature of the world, so, too, the world was gradually being freed from the ignorance into which it had sunk at the Fall and brought back step-by-step through the voyages of discovery and the exchanges of goodwill and mutual benefit that they encouraged to its divinely ordained reunification. Indeed, in Hakluyt's account, the one process is constitutive of the other, since the cleansing of the individual soul of its ignorance prepares it to participate in returning the world to its unity.

Thyestean Tragedies

Hakluyt's underlying theme in his public actions as well as his publications is not just the redemption of individual souls—his own and those of others—but the restoration of the world to its original wholeness. This concentration on what we might call the healing of the world found expression nowhere more profoundly or suggestively than in his high hopes for England's colonial enterprise in Virginia.

In 1599, anticipating the end of war with Spain, for which he knew Sir Robert Cecil had been striving, Hakluyt argued to his patron that with "Gods assistance" the queen's support for the colony would quickly "worke many great and unlooked for effects, increase her dominions, enrich her cofers, and reduce many Pagans to the faith of Christ." To "reduce," derived from the Latin *reducere,* means literally "to lead back." In this case, its use implies that, for the Natives of North America, the forward course of his-

61. See Adam Smith, *An Inquiry into the Nature and Causes of the Wealth of Nations,* ed. R. H. Campbell and A. S. Skinner, 2 vols. (Oxford, 1976), I, book 1, chap. 2, par. 1; Jacob Viner, *The Role of Providence in the Social Order: An Essay in Intellectual History* (Philadelphia, 1972), esp. chaps. 2 and 3; cf. Armitage, *Ideological Origins,* 77.

tory represents a return to lost truth. A similar idea is stated more substantively in the dedication to Sir Walter Ralegh of the edition of Peter Martyr d'Anghera's *De orbe novo* that Hakluyt published in Paris in 1587. There, he treated the historical processes at work in Virginia as a response and recompense to the "tragedies" of religious war in Europe, equating them with the workings of human passion and divine fate in classical Greek and Roman drama. Brief though the passage is, it deserves our close attention.[62]

In the dedication, Hakluyt told his patron that success in Virginia would "leave to posterity an imperishable monument" to Ralegh's "name and fame."

> For to posterity no greater glory or honor can be handed down than to subdue *[domare]* the barbarian, to recall *[revocare]* the wild and the pagan to life in civil society, to lead the savage back *[reducere]* within the orbit of reason, and to imbue *[imbuere]* the atheist and those alienated from God with reverence for divinity.[63]

Although such achievements would be noble in any epoch, Hakluyt believed them even more virtuous "in our present wretched and more than disasterous age, when, to the increase and advantage of the followers of Mahomet, the greater part of the Christian princes fiercely intent on their own domestic dissensions heap up civil tumults and Thyestean tragedies day by day, and without any end."[64] These remarks reflect the deep knowledge of Europe's wars of religion that Hakluyt gained from his watching post in Paris, and they convey a profound understanding of the providential significance of Ralegh's Virginia venture.

Hakluyt's conclusion that the religious wars benefited the spread of Islam closely parallels arguments made by François de La Noue, the Huguenot

62. Hakluyt, "To the Right Honorable Sir Robert Cecil Knight, Principall Secretarie to Her Majestie," Oct. 24, 1599, London, in Hakluyt, *Principal Navigations* (1903–1905), I, lxvii; Hakluyt, epistle dedicatory to Sir Walter Ralegh, 1587, cited in Taylor, ed., *Original Writings*, II, 357–358, 360, 361 (translation provided by Taylor, 363–364, 367, 368, 369).

63. "Nihil enim ad posteros gloriosius nec honorificetius transmitti potest, quàm Barbaros domare, rudes et paganos ad vitae civilis societatem revocare, efferos in gyrum rationis reducere, hominésque; atheos et à Deo alienos divini numinis reverentia imbuere"; Hakluyt, epistle dedicatory to Sir Walter Ralegh, 1587, in Taylor, ed., *Original Writings*, II, 361, 368. I have adapted Taylor's translation to be closer to the original Latin. I am grateful to Professor James Muldoon for his assistance on this reading of the passage.

64. Ibid., 361, 368.

nobleman and general, a figure well known to Sir Francis Walsingham and other English councillors and, in the 1570s, one of the leading aides to the duc d'Anjou and supporters of William the Silent in the Netherlands. Captured and incarcerated by the Spanish in 1580, La Noue spent his long imprisonment writing reflective essays on current affairs. He renewed contacts with the English upon his release in 1585 and, probably with their assistance, published *Discours politiques et militaires* in Basel and Geneva in 1587 and in an English translation in London the following year. Since Edward Aggas, their English translator, almost certainly was working with Hakluyt on another publishing project at the same time, it seems highly likely that the *Discours* themselves, or their substance, came to Hakluyt's attention from the earliest moments—indeed, Hakluyt himself might well have been behind its translation into English in 1588. Making texts on navigation and discovery available to readers both in their original languages and in translations is a role Hakluyt regularly played in London and on the Continent; he clearly had good connections with printers and publishers, especially in London.[65]

La Noue shared political ideas with the French *politiques* and theological doctrines with staunch Calvinists. A strict moralist in his outlook and personal life, he also held that religious convictions could never be coerced and

65. The French editions of La Noue's *Discours* bear a dedicatory epistle to the "Roy de Navarre," Apr. 1, 1587, signed "De Fresnes," i.e., Philippe Carnaye, sieur de Fresne, one of Navarre's principal servants. The *Discours* saw two editions in French in 1587, one published in Basel and the other in Basel and Geneva; another was published in Basel in 1588, and subsequent French editions in 1590, 1595, 1596, and 1597; further versions appeared in the seventeenth century. On the wide circulation and success of La Noue's *Discours,* see Henri Hauser, *François de la Noue (1531-1591)* (1892; rpt. Geneva, 1970), 201-206. The work appeared in 1588 in an English translation by Edward Aggas (La Noue, *The Politicke and Militarie Discourses of the Lord de la Nouue* [London, 1587 (1588); STC 15215]). Aggas entered this work on Nov. 11, 1587, in the *Stationers' Register,* but its publication was later turned over to William Ponsonby (Edward Arber, ed., *A Transcript of the Registers of the Company of Stationers of London, 1554-1640 A.D.,* 5 vols. [London, 1875-1894], II, 478). Earlier in the year, Aggas had also entered into the *Stationers' Register* his intention to publish *New Mexico; Otherwise, The Voiage of Anthony of Espejo . . .* (London, 1587; STC 18487) (ibid., 469). Hakluyt had arranged for publication of this book in Spanish both in Madrid and Paris in 1586 under the title *El viaie que hizo Antonio de Espejo en el anno de ochenta y tres;* see Quinn, Armstrong, and Skelton, "Primary Hakluyt Bibliography," in Quinn, ed., *Hakluyt Handbook,* II, 468-469. In the end, it was Thomas Cadman who published the English translation, which was by Francesco Avanzi, not Aggas (ibid., 572). I am grateful to Professor Philip Benedict for his assistance in identifying La Noue as one of Hakluyt's sources.

was in consequence a tolerationist on matters of belief. In his *Discours,* he returned repeatedly to an analysis of the wars of religion as resulting from human sinfulness: "the mallice of man," as he put it, "who loveth darknes more than light." It was the passion of rage and the lust for revenge in the wars, he believed, that made the factions "grow savage one to another." Elsewhere, he spoke of the wars as the consequence of "evill will." "Must it not needes be," he argued, "that there is some furie hidden in the bowells of France that thus intangleth us? sith so many preparations to unitie and concord cannot any whit profite us, or bring us to the injoying of . . . felicitie?"[66]

According to La Noue, both parties in the conflicts—Protestants and Catholics—confessed "that they worship one selfesame God: that they advowe one selfesame Jesus Christ to be their Saviour: and that the Scriptures and foundations of their faith bee all one." As "true Christians," they should therefore have been able to compound their confessional differences on peaceable terms, unite for the "universal good," and permit those who would not conform "to live after their owne rites and consciences." Nevertheless, they "esteeme one of another as of Turkes." "It is a lamentable matter," he said, "to see those that worship one self[-same] Christ thus to pursue each other with fire and blood like wild beastes, and the whiles to suffer these Mahumetistes to tryumph over the lives, lands, and spoyles of . . . poore Christians." The need of Christians to resist the Turks, whom La Noue regarded as the true enemies of Christ, and to rid Europe of their menace is one of the recurring themes in his career.[67]

In offering his analysis, La Noue was following Stoic views of human agency and the role of Providence in human history.[68] His analysis of the

66. According to Henri Hauser, La Noue stood between "Calvin and Montaigne"— he was "un Montaigne chrétien et huguenot" (Hauser, *François de la Noue,* 141, 145). For some of La Noue's comments on liberty of conscience, see, for example, La Noue, *Politicke and Militarie Discourses,* trans. Aggas, 24–25, 65–66, 255. For La Noue's analysis of the wars of religion, see ibid., 36 (compare Thuc. 3:82–85), 50, 55, 251. La Noue's fourth *Discourse* also offers a similar analysis; see ibid., 53–70. For an overview of La Noue's philosophy, see Hauser, *François de la Noue,* 139–206.

67. La Noue, *Politicke and Militarie Discourses,* trans. Aggas, 3, 24–25, 48–49, 249, 254 (note that the book is partly mispaginated, and some page numbers are duplicated; here, at pages 48–49, I refer to what would sequentially be pages 38–39); La Noue also devoted his twenty-first and twenty-second *Discourses* to relations between Christians and Turks (ibid., 244–300, esp. 234–290). In addition, see *Domini de la nue galli . . . disputatio de bello Turcicum excitantur,* in Joachim Camerarius, *De rebus Turcicis commentarii duo accuratissimi* (Frankfurt, 1598), 93–123. La Noue refers to this *Disputatio* as an earlier work; see *Politicke and Militarie Discourses,* trans. Aggas, 246.

68. For the importance of Stoicism in France during the era of its sixteenth-century

place of rage in shaping events draws on the discussion in Seneca's *Of Anger,* and his conception of the remedy for it also parallels the thought of the Roman philosopher, poet, and statesman and his Renaissance followers such as Justus Lipsius. Instead of permitting the mind to be buffeted by every event and to suffer the stings of every misfortune, La Noue believed that we "ought constantly to beare whatsoever in honestie [we] maye or shoulde, to the ende that by preservation of order and tranquilitie, the natural course of mans life may with more facilitie be performed."[69]

Along with drawing on Seneca's moral theories, La Noue took something more from him. La Noue viewed the France of his day as a "theatre" in which the actors are seized of a "cursed passion" and where, in consequence, a "tragedie have bene plaied." Elsewhere, he spoke of the events of religious warfare as a "bloodie tragedie." The model he had in mind was revenge tragedy of the type made famous by Seneca and widely imitated in sixteenth-century France and elsewhere.[70]

The key feature of revenge tragedy is its intense focus on the unbounded anger of the protagonists. An almost unquenchable appetite for the cruelest and most sordid vengeance overtakes them, wipes away all constraints of reason or compassion, and rages on without regard to social relations, civil order, or personal well-being. In the hands of Seneca himself and of his

religious wars, see Léontine Zanta, *La renaissance du stoïcisme au XVIe siècle* (1914; Geneva, 1975); Jason Lewis Saunders, *Justus Lipsius: The Philosophy of Renaissance Stoicism* (New York, 1955), esp. 21–41, 59–116; Jean Jehasse, *La renaissance de la critique: L'essor de l'humanisme érudit de 1560 à 1614* (Saint-Étienne, 1976), 247–314, 449–530; Jacqueline Lagrée, *Juste Lipse et la restauration du stoïcisme: Étude et traduction des traités stoïciens "De la Constance," "Manuel de philosophie stoïcienne," "Physique des stoïciens" (extraits)* (Paris, 1994). See also Anthony Levi, *French Moralists: The Theory of the Passions, 1585 to 1649* (Oxford, 1964), 7–73; Gerhard Oestreich, *Neostoicism and the Early Modern State,* ed. Brigitta Oestreich and H. G. Koenigsberger, trans. David McLintock (Cambridge, 1982); Mark Morford, *Stoics and Neostoics: Rubens and the Circle of Lipsius* (Princeton, N.J., 1991), 3–55. I am grateful for the advice of Professors Anthony Grafton and Mark Greengrass on these points. There also was considerable interest in Stoicism and in Lipsius in England in the same period, especially in Ralegh's work; see Adriana McCrea, *Constant Minds: Political Virtue and the Lipsian Paradigm in England, 1584–1650* (Toronto, 1997), xix–xxxi, 3–70.

69. See Lucius Annaeus Seneca, *Moral Essays,* ed. and trans. John W. Basore, 3 vols. (Cambridge, Mass., 1928–1935), I; La Noue, *Politicke and Militarie Discourses,* trans. Aggas, 50 [actually, 40; see note 67 for an explanation]. Here, La Noue is virtually summarizing the central thought in such essays of Seneca's as *De constantia* and *De tranquillitate anima.*

70. La Noue, *Politicke and Militarie Discourses,* trans. Aggas, 36, 254.

latter-day followers, this kind of uncontrolled and uncontrollable fury represents a form of "autarkic selfhood," to adopt Gordon Braden's phrase.[71] The enraged protagonist stands alone, in isolation from all but his or her own irate passion, and anger appears in full control of the self. For the ancients, following Aristotle's paradigm, this autarkic individuality represented the antithesis of what it meant to live as a rational and political being. For Christians, the acting out of unrestrained anger shows human beings in profound alienation not only from kin, neighbors, and friends but also from God. In this light, the unbounded fury portrayed in revenge tragedies represents humankind in an unalloyed state of original sin.

In construing the religious wars of his day as tragedies, Hakluyt was offering Ralegh an analysis very similar to La Noue's. But in calling those tragedies "Thyestean," Hakluyt also added a significant historical insight of his own. The use of this unusual adjective associates the wars of religion not just with one of the most compelling myths of the ancient world but with a powerful vision of the ultimate triumph of civility, reason, and justice over humankind's most savage and uncontrolled passions. In the myth, Thyestes betrays his brother Atreus and sullies his own lineage when he seduces Atreus's wife and steals the golden ram whose fleece assured his family's prosperity and power. Atreus then avenges himself by murdering Thyestes's sons and serving up their flesh to his brother at a feast. This gruesome deed leads in turn to a further cycle of revenge—punctuated by bloody acts of regicide and matricide—that ends only when Athena, goddess of wisdom and of the arts of good government, halts the incessant sequence of murder, rage, and retribution by introducing a regime of disinterested, dispassionate public justice.[72]

The meaning of this often-retold story was sufficiently familiar in ancient Rome for the adoption of the adjectival form "Thyestean" by a number of writers. We read of "Thyestean curses," "Thyestean prayers," and "Thyestean feasts."[73] A theory of history was implicit in this usage, as Ovid

71. Gordon Braden, *Renaissance Tragedy and the Senecan Tradition: Anger's Privilege* (New Haven, Conn., 1985), 2.

72. See Aeschylus, *The Oresteia,* trans. Hugh Lloyd-Jones (Berkeley, Calif., 1979); Aeschylus, *The Oresteia,* trans. Robert Fagles, rev. ed. (Harmondsworth, 1979); Jean-Pierre Vernant, *The Origins of Greek Thought* (Ithaca, N.Y., 1982); Hugh Lloyd-Jones, *The Justice of Zeus* (Berkeley, Calif., 1971).

73. Cicero *Oratio in pisonem* 19.43; Lucan *De bello civili* 1.544; Horace *Epodi* 5.56; Ovid *Metamorphoses* 15.462, *Ars amatoria* 1.327, and *Epistulae ex ponto* 4.6.47; Seneca the Elder *Controversiae* 1.1.21. See also Athenagoras the Athenian, *Legatio pro Christianis* 3.1.31–32. A number of ancient pagans believed the early Christians also com-

made clear in speaking in one place of an age of "Thyestean feasts" to which human beings might return.[74] In the distant past, the theory goes, our actions were dominated by dark, Thyestean impulses. Over time, and with the growth of civil order, these bloody passions had come under the control of reason, without, however, entirely disappearing from the human soul. If human beings withdraw themselves from the civilizing constraints of established institutions, if they reject the requirements of social custom and religious tradition, they—we—shall revert to our earlier Thyestean state.

The reference to Thyestes, whose very identity is embodied in the eating of human flesh, also calls forth parallels with Montaigne's "Of Cannibals," first published in 1580, and even more with Jean de Léry's *History of a Voyage to the Land of Brazil,* first published in 1578. In Montaigne, the cannibalism encountered in America, itself identified as a form of "extreme and inexpatiable revenge," is compared to the barbarism of Europeans, who "mangle by tortures and torments a body full of lively sense" and roast their "neighbours and fellow-citizens under pretence of pietie and religion."[75] Léry is even more explicit. "During the bloody tragedy [note that word again] that began in Paris on the twenty-fourth of August [Saint Bartholomew's Day], 1572," he says,

> among other acts horrible to recount, which were perpetrated at that time throughout the kingdom, the fat of human bodies . . . was it not publicly sold to the highest bidder? The livers, hearts, and other parts

---

mitted Thyestean acts of cannibalism; see Robert L. Wilken, *The Christians as the Romans Saw Them* (New Haven, Conn., 1984), 17–25. I am grateful to Professor Anthony Grafton for advice and suggestions on this point.

74. Ovid *Epistulae ex ponto* 4.6.41–50, in Arthur Leslie Wheeler, ed. and trans., *Ovid, with an English Translation: Tristia, Ex Ponto,* The Loeb Classical Library (London, 1924), 444–445. I have amended the translation slightly to bring it closer to the Latin. Wheeler translates *tempora* as "age," the equivalent of "era." The precision of Hakluyt's reference to Thyestes points strongly to Seneca's play by that title as his main source.

75. Michel de Montaigne, *Essais: Reproduction photographique de l'édition originale de 1580,* ed. Daniel Martin, 2 vols. (Geneva, 1976), I, 316–318; the initial edition was published with royal privileges in Bordeaux by S. Millange, printer ordinary to the king. I have followed John Florio's translation, first published in 1603 (STC 18041) (Michel Montaigne, *The Essayes of Montaigne,* ed. J. I. M. Stewart, trans. John Florio [New York, 1933], 166). For a useful commentary bringing out the importance of Stoic thought in Montaigne's essay, see David Quint, "A Reconsideration of Montaigne's *Des Cannibales,"* in Karen Ordahl Kupperman, ed., *America in European Consciousness, 1493–1750* (Chapel Hill, N.C., 1995), 166–191.

of these bodies—were they not eaten by the furious murderers, of whom Hell itself stands in horror? Likewise, after the wretched massacre of one Coeur de Roy, who professed the Reformed Faith in the city of Auxerre—did not those who committed this murder cut his heart to pieces, display it for sale to those who hated him, and finally, after grilling it over coals—glutting their rage like mastiffs—eat of it?[76]

Hakluyt similarly viewed the peoples of Europe as effectively devouring one another and falling back into the age of Thyestean feasts. But he also saw Ralegh's Virginia project as an opportunity to advance God's "glory" through the "salvation of countless souls, and the increase of the Kingdom of Christ."[77] By thus bringing religion, reason, and civility to the peoples of North America, who remained in, or not far from, a Thyestean state, he would thereby counter the descent back into barbarity being witnessed in Europe's civil wars and carry forward God's plan for the ultimate salvation of the world.

There was something instrumental in this view—something focused on the material processes of historical cause and effect, and therefore something that linked Hakluyt's high hopes for the world's future with his strategy for thwarting Spanish power and improving the English economy. The successful civilizing of the Indians not only would make America a strong market for English wares, he thought, but also would provide a secure strategic base against the Spanish. In this, however, there was no inconsistency with Hakluyt's larger goal. The establishment of naval bases and the growth of a market were the means God had provided for achieving it. Or so Hakluyt believed. The end remained clear: the restoration of the world to its original condition.

Answering the Spanish, who claimed great successes in bringing the indigenous peoples of America to Catholicism, a goal for the Virginia colony

76. Jean de Léry, *History of a Voyage to the Land of Brazil, Otherwise Called America,* ed. and trans. Janet Whatley (Berkeley, Calif., 1990), 132–133. There were three French editions as well as a Latin edition before 1587: French in 1578, 1580, and 1585, and Latin in 1586. There were subsequent editions in 1594 (Geneva, French); 1594 (Geneva, Latin); 1600 (Geneva, French); and 1611 (Geneva, French). His work also appeared in Latin in the third volume of the *Grands voyages,* published in 1583 by the de Bry family. For discussion, see Frank Lestringant, *Cannibals: The Discovery and Representation of the Cannibal from Columbus to Jules Verne,* trans. Rosemary Morris (Berkeley, Calif., 1997), 74–80, and more generally 51–111; Lestringant, *Le Huguenot et le sauvage,* 77–128, 205–225.

77. Hakluyt, epistle dedicatory to Sir Walter Ralegh, 1587, cited in Taylor, ed., *Original Writings,* II, 361, translation at 368.

at its inception was the conversion of its Native population to the truths of Protestant Christianity. Since the region's inhabitants already possessed a conception of the divine, Thomas Harriot, one of Ralegh's servants and a member of the Virginia expedition of 1585, expected them to be "reformed" to true religion within a short time. Harriot's verb "reformed" refers to the renewing or restoring of what had once existed, or to converting or bringing back something to its original form or state or previous condition. As we have already noted, Hakluyt presented the same idea to Sir Robert Cecil in 1599. He had long held it. In 1587, in his dedicatory letter to Ralegh, he developed the conception briefly but in some depth, as we can see if we concentrate on the Latin verbs he employed: *domare, revocare, reducere,* and *imbuere.*[78]

Taken together, these verbs describe a process of spiritual transformation in their subjects. *Domare,* which might mean to subdue, master, or conquer, carries the implication of taming, as in bringing a wild beast under control. It entails the disciplining or educating of animals or persons to habits of good order but not the transformation of their natures. The trainer or teacher brings out what is already there in potential. As employed by Hakluyt, the word also represents the beginning of a long-term process. *Imbuere,* at the end of the sequence, signifies its goal. Although it can carry the sense of "giving initial instruction in a task or subject," its core meaning is "to wet," "to soak," or "to dip." As Hakluyt uses it, therefore, it associates the proselytizing activities of missionaries to the Natives of the Americas with the sacrament of baptism, the sacrament, that is, by which individuals are incorporated into the Christian community of believers. We are meant to see that the successful catechizing of the Natives brings a fitting end in the Aristotelian sense to the civilizing process that Hakluyt also describes.

The essence of that civilizing process is conveyed in the verbs *revocare* and *reducere.* The Indians are to be recalled from savagery to civility and reduced from ignorance to reason. This usage reflects the view that the Natives of the Americas, along with the rest of humankind, have suffered the consequences of the Fall but can be freed from the burdens of sin and returned—recalled and led back, i.e., reformed—to a state of righteousness

78. Thomas Har[r]iot, *A Briefe and True Report of the New Found Land of Virginia* ... (London, 1588; STC 12785), sig. E2v. On Harriot's religion, see Scott Mandelbrote, "The Religion of Thomas Harriot," in Robert Fox, ed., *Thomas Harriot: An Elizabethan Man of Science* (Aldershot, 2000), 246–279. For Hakluyt's letter, see Hakluyt, epistle dedicatory to Sir Walter Ralegh, 1587, cited in Taylor, ed., *Original Writings,* II, 361, 368. I have adapted Taylor's translation to be closer to the original Latin.

Adam and Eve. Engraving by Theodore de Bry. In Thomas Harriot, A Briefe and
True Report of the New Found Land of Virginia . . . *(Frankfurt, 1590; STC 12786).
De Bry's brief commentary on this image stresses how the way of life of the "savage
nations" of Virginia demonstrates that, "although . . . man by his disobedience, weare
deprived of those good Gifts wher with he was indued in his creation, yet he was not
berefte of wit to provyde for hym selfe, nor discretion to devise things necessarie for
his use." The passage offers the hope, also expressed by Thomas Harriot and Richard
Hakluyt (who translated de Bry's comments), that the Virginia natives would soon
receive what pertained to the "soules healthe" and be reformed. By permission of
The Huntington Library, San Marino, California*

and reason, the potential for which is in their God-given nature. The process moves from taming to civilizing to baptizing and assumes that the Native peoples must be removed from their state of near-savagery to civil order before their conversion to Christianity can be completed. In this regard, Hakluyt appears to be following an understanding similar to the ideas of Spanish missionaries, derived from Aristotle and especially Cicero, to the effect that true conversion depended in the first instance on bringing savage peoples to civility.[79] In this brief passage, therefore, Hakluyt is not just laying out a providential mission for Ralegh, important though he believes it to be, but is describing the providential history of the world. Hakluyt exhibits a sense of history as proceeding inexorably from the Fall to the recovery of Grace, and from the beginning of history to its end.[80]

Dueling with Antichrist

There can be no doubt that Hakluyt saw the history of mankind as following a plan ordained by God. Was he also an apocalyptical thinker? It has been said that he was not—that the debt he acknowledged to John Foxe, John Bale, and Richard Eden resided mainly in following his use of personal narratives rather than in adhering to the apocalyptic model of salvation or reprobation Foxe set forth, following Bale.[81] On this view, Hak-

79. Pagden, *Fall of Natural Man,* 119–197; Armitage, *Ideological Origins,* 73–74; Fitzmaurice, *Humanism and America,* 139. See José de Acosta, *De procuranda Indorum salute,* ed. Luciano Pereña, 2 vols. (Madrid, 1984–1987), esp. Pereña, "Proyecto de sociedad colonial: Pacificación y colonización," I, 1–48; see also Walter D. Mignolo, "Introduction to José de Acosta's *Historia Natural y Moral de las Indias,*" in José de Acosta, *Natural and Moral History of the Indies,* ed. Jane E. Mangan, trans. Frances M. López-Morillas (Durham, N.C., 2002), xxi; René de Laudonnière, *L'histoire notable de la Floride situee es Indes occidentales . . . ,* ed. Martin Basanier (Paris, 1586), which uses similar language; see sig. [a v]r–[a vii]r.

80. Cf. Armitage, *Ideological Origins,* 76; Fitzmaurice, *Humanism and America,* 140.

81. Armitage, *Ideological Origins,* 78. See "Richard Hakluyt to the Favourable Reader" (1589), in Hakluyt, *Principal Navigations* (1903–1905), I, xxiv. John Foxe's *Actes and Monuments* went through four editions during Foxe's own lifetime: Foxe, *Actes and Monuments of These Latter and Perillous Dayes Touching Matters of the Church* (London, 1563; STC 11222 and 11222a); Foxe, *The First Volume of the Ecclesiasticall History Contaynyng the Actes and Monuments of Thynges Passed in Every Kynges Tyme in This Realme . . .* (London, 1570; STC 11223); ibid. (London, 1576); Foxe, *Actes and Monuments of Matters Most Speciall and Memorable, Happening in the Church, with an Universall History of the Same . . .* (London, 1583; STC 11225). For

luyt's expression of apocalypticism was conventional and *pro forma,* its logic contradicted by his apparent willingness to accept as genuine the conversions to Christianity accomplished by Catholic missionaries in America.[82] It is true, despite his one reference to the "greate Antichrist of Rome," that he never viewed the Catholic Church as an utterly false church, whose corruption overthrew its true foundation of faith.[83] As Hakluyt made clear in his "Discourse," he recognized that the conversions by Catholic missionaries of American Natives had benefited the latters' souls, even though their knowledge of Christ was fraught with error. The Catholics, Hakluyt suggested, had taken the American Natives from Scylla to Charybdis, which, according to the adage, meant from a worse danger to a lesser one, but not to death itself. In other words, Hakluyt considered that the Natives' conversion to Catholicism had left them open to ultimate salvation with the removal of error, whereas continuance in paganism carried the certainty of eternal damnation.[84]

In expressing these views, Hakluyt allied with English Protestants of diverse persuasions by distinguishing those who, in accepting popish superstitions, had sinned ignorantly and therefore could be saved, from those who, like the pope himself, had acted willfully to overthrow the foundations of Christian truth, remained unrepentant, and would be eternally damned.

John Bale, see, for example, Bale, *The Ymage of Both Churches after the Moste Wonderful and Heavenly Revelacion of Saincte John the Evangelyst* . . . (London, 1550; STC 1299); Leslie P. Fairfield, *John Bale: Mythmaker for the English Reformation* (West Lafayette, Ind., 1976). For Eden, see Franklin T. McCann, *English Discovery of America to 1585* (New York, 1952), 113–137; John Parker, *Books to Build an Empire: A Bibliographical History of English Overseas Interests to 1620* (Amsterdam, 1965), 36–53; Fitzmaurice, *Humanism and America,* 32–35, 38, 43–46, 109–110.

82. Armitage, *Ideological Origins,* 76–78.

83. Hakluyt, *A Particuler Discourse,* ed. Quinn and Quinn, 116–117; Hakluyt, "Discourse of Western Planting," in Taylor, ed., *Original Writings,* II, 315. On this characteristic of English apocalypticism, see Richard Bauckham, ed., *Tudor Apocalypse: Sixteenth-Century Apocalypticism, Millennarianism, and the English Reformation: From John Bale to John Foxe and Thomas Brightman* (Oxford, [1978]); Firth, *Apocalyptic Tradition;* see also Andrew Cunningham and Ole Peter Grell, *The Four Horsemen of the Apocalypse: Religion, War, Famine, and Death in Reformation Europe* (Cambridge, 2000), esp. 1–91, 137–151.

84. Hakluyt, *A Particuler Discourse,* ed. Quinn and Quinn, 40–41; Hakluyt, "Discourse of Western Planting," in Taylor, ed., *Original Writings,* II, 217. The ultimate source for the commonplace is Homer's *Odyssey* 12.235–246 as interpreted in Erasmus's *Adages (Adagia* 1.5.4); see Erasmus, *Adages,* trans. Phillips, XXXI, 387–389.

On this point, Hakluyt was one with Richard Hooker and with William Fulke, the Cambridge Puritan.[85] What Hakluyt added was application of this principle to the Catholics' conversions of the Natives in America. Hence Hakluyt did not seek the extirpation of the Chuch of Rome but believed —like William the Silent and his followers such as La Noue, and like Sir Robert Cecil—that a means could be found to accommodate Protestants and Catholics to one another. In this respect, Hakluyt did not adhere to the standard model of apocalyticism articulated by Foxe or Bale, since he saw no irreconcilable opposition between the True Church of Christ and the False Church of Rome, the Whore of Babylon. Nevertheless, there was much else that Hakluyt took from his models.[86]

Much as Hakluyt believed—"hoped," perhaps, would be the better word —that the end of the present world order was near, he was not expecting it to happen in a divine lightning flash. But neither was Foxe. Instead, Foxe's eschatological scheme, like those of numerous medieval thinkers, allowed for a final age between the expected defeat of the Roman Antichrist and the Second Coming—a last age that witnessed the gradual turning of the tide of history away from Satan toward God. During this period, which Foxe held to have been under way since around 1300, the light of truth gradually reasserted itself and knowledge grew in the battle against falsehood and error. Eventually, a "this-worldly . . . time of peace and victory" would prevail, and Turks, Jews, and the heathen would all be converted to true religion. Hakluyt held an analogous view. For him, not only was the steadily successful

85. Bauckham, "Hooker, Travers, and the Church of Rome," *Journal of Ecclesiastical History,* XXIX (1978), 42–50; and see Richard Hooker, *Two Sermons upon Part of S. Judes Epistle,* ed. Henry Jackson (Oxford, 1614; STC 13723), 26–29; Hooker, *A Learned Discourse of Justification, Workes, and How the Foundation of Faith Is Overthrowne,* ed. Henry Jackson and John Spenser (Oxford, 1612; STC 13708); Hooker, *The Works of That Learned and Judicious Divine, Mr. Richard Hooker,* ed. John Keble, 7th ed., 3 vols. (Oxford, 1888), III, 482–596, 674–680; and William Fulke, *A Retentive, to Stay Good Christian, in True Faith and Religion against the Motives of Richard Bristowe* (London, 1580; STC 11449), 100–102. See also [Oliver Carter], *An Answer Made by Oliver Carter, Bacheler of Divinitie: Unto Certain Popish Questions and Demaundes* (London, 1579; STC 4697), fols. 41v, 42r–v.

86. See Croft, "Religion of Robert Cecil," *Historical Journal,* XXXIV (1991), 780–785. Sir Edwin Sandys, Hakluyt's colleague in the Virginia Company, had somewhat similar views. Compare La Noue, *Politicke and Militarie Discourses,* trans. Aggas, 3, with Hakluyt, *A Particuler Discourse,* ed. Quinn and Quinn, 8–12; Hakluyt, "Discourse of Western Planting," in Taylor, ed., *Original Writings,* II, 215–218; and see, for example, Bale, *Ymage of Both Churches.*

evangelizing of non-Christians already in process but the new knowledge of the created world unveiled—revealed—by the voyages of discovery also was a sign of the progressive growth of knowledge in the present age.[87]

Paralleling Foxe, Hakluyt brings out the this-worldly side of the Antichrist's satanic menace. He condemns the pope because, in pretending to rule over the temporal and spiritual world rather than simply ministering to souls, the pope became a tyrant and served the interests of Satan. Similarly, Hakluyt condemns the Spanish for their pretension "to be Lordes and onely seigniors of all the earthe." To Hakluyt, this claim to universal monarchy revealed no more than the "puffed upp and inflamed . . . pride" of the "ambitious and insatiable" Spaniards. They exercised, he says, the "most outragious and more than Turkishe crueltie in . . . the west Indies." They showed "satanicall arrogancie and insolencies." Here we have the Antichrist, but replayed in a new key, in which the Spanish together with the pope, not the pope alone, perform the part of the Roman Antichrist, their joint enslavement in body and soul of naturally free peoples revealing their opposition to God and his purposes.[88]

In regard to Spain's support for Rome, the remedy (as with the Indians) was to reduce its king to reason, in this case to a realistic grasp of his own material interests and the limits of his power. Spoiling "Phillipps Indian navye," Hakluyt argued, would "deprive him of yerely passage of his Treasure into Europe" and "consequently . . . abate the pride of Spaine and of the supporter of the greate Antechriste of Rome, and . . . pull him downe in equallitie to his neighbour princes, and consequently . . . cutt of the common mischefes that comes to all Europe by the peculiar abundance of his Indian Treasure."[89]

87. See Palle J. Olsen, "Was John Foxe a Millenarian?" *Journal of Ecclesiastical History,* XLV (1994), 600–624, esp. 604, 609–611, 622–624; see also Robert E. Lerner, "Refreshment of the Saints: The Time after Antichrist as a Station for Early Progress in Medieval Thought," *Traditio,* XXXII (1976), 97–144.

88. See, for example, Richard Hakluyt, "An Aunswer to the Bull of the Donacion of All the West Indies Graunted to the Kinges of Spaine by Pope Alexander the VIth Whoe Was Himselfe a Spaniarde Borne," in Hakluyt, *A Particuler Discourse,* ed. Quinn and Quinn, 96–113; Hakluyt, "Discourse of Western Planting," in Taylor, ed., *Original Writings,* II, 297–313. For Hakluyt's condemnation of the Spanish, see Hakluyt, *A Particuler Discourse,* ed. Quinn and Quinn, 4–5, 52–53, 60–61, 112–113; Hakluyt, "Discourse of Western Planting," in Taylor, ed., *Original Writings,* II, 212, 257, 264, 311; and see Pagden, *Lords of All the World,* 23, 27, and 29–62.

89. Hakluyt, *A Particuler Discourse,* ed. Quinn and Quinn, 116–117; Hakluyt, "Discourse of Western Planting," in Taylor, ed., *Original Writings,* II, 315.

Pride, ambition, and insatiable desire, the terms Hakluyt used to characterize Spanish oppression, cast universal monarchy as a form of tyranny in
the Aristotelian sense—an oppression imposed on free persons on behalf of
the despot's bottomless lust for more of everything than is his due. In this
analysis, Hakluyt the Aristotelian is matched by Hakluyt the preacher. The
Spanish might have fancied that "God hath geven [them] these Indies to
the intente that [its King] shoulde be the universall and onely monarch of
the world," but

> god that sitteth in heaven laugheth . . . them . . . to scorne, and he will
> abase and bringe downe their proude lookes, and humble ther faces to the
> duste, yea he will make them at his goodd time and pleasure to confesse
> that the earthe was not made for them onely . . . And nowe no doubte
> many of them remember that the threateninge of the prophet hath taken
> holde upon them, whoe pronounceth an heavie woe againste all suche as
> spoile, because they themselves shall at length be spoiled.[90]

The final sentence in this passage derives from Jeremiah 30:16: "Therefore
all they that devoure thee, shall be devoured, and all thine enemies every
one shal go into captivitie: and they that spoyle thee, shalbe spoyled, and
all thei that robbe thee, wil I give to be robbed." This verse appears in the
first of the two chapters of Jeremiah known traditionally as the "Book of
Consolation," where the Lord promises through his prophet that he will restore his people, living under the Babylonian yoke, to their birthright and
bring about the restoration of Solomon's Temple.[91]

Here Hakluyt effectively equates the Spanish with the Babylonians, and
by extension with the ancient Romans, as oppressive tyrants and destroyers
of God's Temple. He treats those they oppress (for example, the peoples of
the Netherlands and the Natives of America) as the equivalent of the Jews
of Jeremiah's day, many of them sinners to be chastised but who ultimately
will be redeemed. The English, Hakluyt implies, will be God's instrument
in breaking the bondage imposed by Spain on their imperial subjects, and
the regime they uphold at home and establish in America will be a godly
form of rule, fitting the natural freedom of its peoples—the very antithesis
of Spanish despotism. As in Foxe, there is a distinctly progressive view of

90. Aristotle's main discussion of tyranny is to be found in *The Politics* 5.10.1310a40–
5.11.1315b10. For Hakluyt's quote, see Hakluyt, *A Particuler Discourse,* ed. Quinn and
Quinn, 112–113; Hakluyt, "Discourse of Western Planting," in Taylor, ed., *Original
Writings,* II, 312.

91. Jer. 30:3 (1560 Geneva Version).

history as godly rule itself is spread throughout the world and human felicity comes to reign over it in its penultimate age.[92]

The image of Solomon's Temple, which played so a great part in Philip
II's self-presentation at the Escorial, also loomed large for Hakluyt, as his
reference to Jeremiah 30 was meant to indicate. Hakluyt did not foresee its
physical restoration but imagined its symbolic resurgence in the material
processes of exchange. As revealed by his *Principal Navigations,* its rebuilding occurs metaphorically in the processes of discovery he describes. It is
also embedded in the structure of his book. Taken in sequence, the tales
move toward their ordained end, in this case the uniting (or reuniting) of
the scattered or dispersed peoples of the world in common belief and mutually beneficial exchange under God.

In particular, the opening to East Asia, toward which Christopher
Columbus and John Cabot had set their sails at the outset of the era of
discovery, had long loomed large in Hakluyt's thinking as a fitting culmi-
nation to England's godly mission. In the 1580s, he had equated the promotion of "common trade" with China's merchants and the carrying there
of "the incomparable treasure of the trueth of Christianity, and of the Gospel" with Solomon's building of the Temple, and he associated the ships
that Elizabeth might send into Asia with the "golden voyadge to Ophir . . .
by Salomon," which, as readers of Scripture would know, not only brought
back great quantities of gold but "almug wood" to provide supports for the
Temple and lyres and harps for the singers.[93] The reference to the Temple
is omitted in *Principal Navigations,* but not the thought that, in creating
its empire and engaging in free exchange with the far corners of the world,
England was erecting a godly edifice—a unified whole composed of inter-
dependent parts.

In Hakluyt's view, God was inexorably lifting the veil that had descended
on the world after the Fall. In this apocalyptical history, there would be no
Armageddon, at least not from England's confrontation with the Spanish.
Hakluyt was envisioning a different, more peaceable end, one that would
call to a halt the violent succession of regimes that had characterized past

92. See William M. Lamont, *Godly Rule: Politics and Religion, 1603-1660* (London, 1969), 7-35; cf. Olsen, "Was John Foxe a Millenarian?" *Journal of Ecclesiastical
History,* XLV (1994), 600-601, 620-621.

93. "To the Right Honorable Sir Francis Walsingham, Knight," Nov. 17, [1589], in
Hakluyt, *Principal Navigations* (1903-1905), I, 21; Hakluyt, *A Particuler Discourse,*
ed. Quinn and Quinn, 86-87; Hakluyt, "A Discourse of Western Planting," in Taylor,
ed., *Original Writings,* II, 289; see I Kings 9:26-28; 10:11-12.

history, would continue the increase in knowledge of God's creation already under way, and would bring the world into harmony, restore it to reason, and permit it to proceed by orderly means to its ordained end. Just as the great navigators had moved in their explorations from the Old World to the New, bringing the possibility of salvation with them, Hakluyt saw the sea-borne discoveries he so carefully recorded as God's sign that he was bringing the human community back into balance. Providence was replicating, in the history of the world, what he fervently believed it had already produced: conversion of his own soul. The plantation of an English colony in Virginia, which first became a mission for Hakluyt in 1584 and which the founding of Jamestown brought to fruition, represented a significant step toward the fulfillment of this divine plan.

Reading Hakluyt, and perhaps also similar collections of narratives of discovery such as Ramusio's *Delle navigationi e viaggi,* Francis Bacon also saw the new geographical discoveries that he and others had made available as evidence that this grand accommodation was already in progress. "Proficience in navigation, and discoveries," Bacon said in 1605, citing the Book of Daniel, had planted "an expectation of the furder proficience, and augmentation of all scyences, because it may seeme they are ordained by God . . . to meete in one Age."[94] This passage depends on the angel's prophecy in Daniel 12:4: "But thou, O Daniel, shut up the wordes, and seale the boke til the end of the time: many shal run to and fro, and knowledge shalbe increased." Bacon took the comings and goings of the many in exploration of the earth's seas and lands to mark the inception of the endtime, "as if," he said, "the opennesse and through-passage of the world, and the encrease of knowledge were appointed to be in the same ages"[95]

94. Giovanni Battista Ramusio, *Delle navigationi e viaggi . . .* , 3 vols. (Venice, 1554–1606); Ramusio, *Navigationi et viaggi: Venice, 1563–1606,* ed. R. A. Skelton, 3 vols. (Amsterdam, 1967); Bacon, *Advancement of Learning,* ed. Kiernan, 71 [sig. 2D3v].

95. Bacon, *Advancement of Learning,* ed. Kiernan, 71 [sig. 2D4r]. Bacon reiterated this view in *Novum organum* (1620); see book 1, Aphorism XCIII, in Lisa Jardine and Michael Silverthorne, eds., *The New Organon* (Cambridge, 2000), 78; translation amended in part according to the rendition in Bacon, *Novum organum,* trans. and ed. Peter Urbach and John Gibson (Chicago, 1994), 104. Bacon also uses Dan 12:4 in "Valerius Terminus of the Interpretation of Nature, with the Annotations of Hermes Stella," fragmentary MS dating from ca. 1603, in James Spedding, Robert Leslie Ellis, and Douglas Denon Heath, eds., *The Works of Francis Bacon,* 15 vols (Cambridge, Mass., 1863), VI, 32; see Stephen Gaukroger, *Francis Bacon and the Transformation of Early-Modern Philosophy* (Cambridge, 2001), 9 n. 8; Charles Webster, *Great Instauration: Science, Medicine, and Reform, 1626–1660* (New York, 1976), 22–23. The same

For Bacon, as for Hakluyt, the world was illuminated by individual acts of discovery from beyond the limits of received learning, guided by the benevolence of royal government, not the pretended wisdom of an absolute ruler. Taken together, these new discoveries would increase human knowledge voyage by voyage, observation by observation, and piece by piece, gradually—but inevitably—restoring the dominion over the true order of nature that had been lost by humankind at the Fall.[96]

---

point is vividly made in Simon van der Passe's engraving for the title page of Bacon's *Novum organum* (1620); see Bacon, *Francisci de Verulamio / Summi Angliae cancellarii / Instauratio magna* (London, 1620; STC 1162), title page. The volume, which includes *Novum organum* along with several other shorter commentaries on natural philosophy and natural history, constitutes the second part of the never-completed main work that was meant to carry the overall title *Instauratio magna*. On the frontispiece, see Ralf Konersmann, "Die Umdeutung des Unsichtbaren," in Ralf Konersmann, *Der Schleier des Timanthes: Perspectiven der historischen Semantik* (Frankfurt, 1994), 56–83.

96. For further discussion of the issues discussed in this section, see Sacks, "Richard Hakluyt's Navigations in Time," *Modern Language Quarterly,* LXVII (2006), 48–61; Sacks, "Rebuilding Solomon's Temple: Richard Hakluyt and the 'Age of Discovery,'" paper presented at "States and Empires," seventy-fourth Anglo-American Conference of Historians, London, July 8, 2005; Sacks, "Rebuilding Solomon's Temple: Richard Hakluyt's Advancement of Learning," plenary address presented to the conference on "New Worlds Reflected: Representations of Utopia, the New World, and Other Worlds, 1500–1800," Birkbeck College, University of London, Dec. 10, 2005.

Benjamin Schmidt

READING RALEGH'S AMERICA

TEXTS, BOOKS, AND READERS IN THE EARLY

MODERN ATLANTIC WORLD

Though hobbled by bad knees, Sir Walter Ralegh was blessed with a good stomach. It may seem striking to us today that the illustrious soldier, energetic explorer, and exquisite courtier who easily leaps to the top of any list of quintessential "Elizabethan gentlemen" had limited mobility and, from as early as his forties, horrible difficulty simply walking. The greatest conquistador of Renaissance England was not much of a hiker. On the other hand, Ralegh had a superb constitution for another of his vocations—digesting a stunning quantity of texts—and he gained a reputation already in his early years as a dedicated oceanic reader. In truth, he loved to read, whether by land or at sea, a fact that may surprise students of the Elizabethan court and of early modern reading alike, since courtiers of Ralegh's stature were generally not known to be bookworms. Real Elizabethan courtiers—especially of the virile and dashing sort—did not do books.[1]

Much of the research for this essay was done at the Huntington Library, San Marino, and I would like to acknowledge the generosity of the Andrew W. Mellon and W. M. Keck foundations, which supported my work there. I would also like to thank David Armitage, Scott Black, Dan Carey, Richard Johnson, Peter Mancall, Louise Townsend, and the members of the Pacific Northwest Early Americanist Seminar for their very helpful comments. I am grateful, too, for the support of Roy Ritchie at the Huntington, Ron Hoffman at the Omohundro Institute of Early American History and Culture, and the Howard and Frances Keller Endowed Fund of the University of Washington.

    1. Ralegh's seaworthiness is confirmed by John Aubrey, in *Aubrey's Brief Lives,* ed. Oliver Lawson Dick (London, 1949), 254, whose comments are echoed by most of the leading Stuart biographers—Robert Naunton and William Winstanley, for example. Ralegh's physical appearance was widely admired and discussed among the gossipy court-watchers, yet altogether less commented upon were the daring soldier's gimpy knees, which Ralegh himself owned up to. Never one to turn down a challenge, Ralegh at first begged off an excursion into the hinterland of Guiana "to view the strange overfals of the river Caroli . . . being a very ill footeman," even if he later assented to the trip:

Ralegh, happily, did. In fact, he both read voraciously and was himself ravenously devoured in textual form, for Ralegh was also a prodigious writer. Here, too, he distinguishes himself from the rest of the courtier pack, both in terms of the quantity he wrote and published (the latter a relatively rare career move for political figures of his day) and the wide range of literary forms he capably handled: poetry, of course, in its multiple Elizabethan guises, yet also the innovative genre of travel narrative, sacred and secular history (most remarkably, the colossal *History of the World*), pamphlet literature (or what we might call political journalism), the essay (a literary style only lately refined by Michel de Montaigne and Sir Francis Bacon), and even "scientific" prose (chiefly pertaining to naval and military topics).[2] The range of these texts suggests not only a breadth of competence on the part of the author, the incomparable Sir Walter Ralegh, but also a span of skills—of reading practices—mastered by Ralegh's not-insubstantial audience. Ralegh read and was read exceptionally, and this offers the historian of early modern Europe, the Elizabethan court, and, not least, the Atlantic world—the enduring object of Ralegh's attention—a windfall of data.

Reading practices play a critical, yet largely unexamined, role in the encounter of the Old World and the New. Original texts, it hardly needs pointing out, are essential to our understanding of the early modern Atlantic world, since assimilating new worlds in this period was largely a textual affair. As imperative as it may be to trace the path of the actual voyagers and to smell the salty sea air they inhaled, it is equally vital to trace those texts produced by the voyagers (as well as their stay-at-home sponsors) and to handle the books through which most Europeans imbibed America. Yet if schol-

------

Sir Walter Ralegh, *The Discoverie of the Large, Rich, and Bewtiful Empyre of Guiana,* ed. Neil L. Whitehead (1596; rpt. Norman, Okla., 1997), 176. On his second voyage and now in his sixties, Ralegh made no bones about his creaky physical well-being, as he now required his soldiers to carry him on land (along with the deterioration of earlier conditions, he was seriously injured during the raid on Cádiz of 1596). For difficult forays upriver, he declined altogether to participate and remained confined to the rear boat—he also had an indeterminate illness for much of the voyage—and this left him tragically absent when his son was killed in an attack against the Spanish in San Thomé. For further details of the second Guiana voyage and the relevant documents, see V. T. Harlow, *Ralegh's Last Voyage* (London, 1932).

2. Philip Edwards notes the "profuseness and variety" of Ralegh's literary production and the daunting and "formidable" challenges that his oeuvre presents to a reader: *Sir Walter Ralegh* (London, 1953), 127. Another simple testament to this productivity and range is the difficulty contemporaries had in categorizing him, as is commented upon by Anthony à Wood, *Athenae Oxonienses,* 2 vols. (London, 1691–1692), I, 371.

ars have done much to help us analyze New World narratives, they have paid only meager attention to the manner in which those texts were tangibly consumed: to books as material objects and to the reading practices of both the authors and readers of early Americana. The actual delivery of American reports is taken for granted. This should not be the case. The study of reading and of book history more generally has been pioneered by scholars of the early modern period—influential contributions of Lucien Febvre and Henri-Jean Martin, Robert Darnton, Roger Chartier, and Adrian Johns have helped shape the field.[3] And the study of published volumes on early America in particular has been enhanced by heroic bibliographic labors of the late twentieth century—notably, the monumental, six-volume *European Americana* and the other major tomes produced in wake of the Columbian Quincentenary.[4] For all of our efforts to locate and explicate the meaning of early modern texts on America, however, little has been done on the production and consumption of those books that served as the primary medium for these texts. We lack a history of reading Americana.

The modest contribution that this essay makes toward filling this lacuna pertains to the inveterate reader and eloquent conquistador Sir Walter Ralegh. Ralegh, as Christopher Hill once put it, was "no mere courtier." He was a gallant who explored—an exceedingly precarious occupation at the time—and a conquistador who read, not simply romances and geography, but a full scholarly range of genres. "He founded the first English colony in America, in Virginia, though it failed to survive," Hill reminds us, which should render him a topic of vital importance for the study of Anglo-America's first successful colony.[5] (It should also prompt the lingering, yet never squarely addressed, historiographic question: why do we tradition-

3. Lucien Febvre and Henri-Jean Martin, *The Coming of the Book: The Impact of Printing, 1450-1800,* ed. Geoffrey Nowell-Smith and David Wootton, trans. David Gerard (London, 1976); Robert Darnton, *The Literary Underground of the Old Regime* (Cambridge, Mass., 1982); Roger Chartier, *The Order of Books: Readers, Authors, and Libraries in Europe between the Fourteenth and Eighteenth Centuries,* trans. Lydia G. Cochrane (Cambridge, 1994); and Adrian Johns, *The Nature of the Book: Print and Knowledge in the Making* (Chicago, 1998). See further footnote 22, below.

4. John Alden and Dennis C. Landis, eds., *European Americana: A Chronological Guide to Works Printed in Europe Relating to the Americas, 1493-1750,* 6 vols. (New York, 1980-1997). Along with the numerous, updated critical editions of New World literature, see further the volumes collected in the *Repertorium Columbianum* (Berkeley, Calif., 1993-).

5. Christopher Hill, "Ralegh—Science, History, and Politics," in Hill, *Intellectual Origins of the English Revolution* (Oxford, 1965), 131-224 (quotations on 131).

ally start the clock on U.S. colonial history with Jamestown or Plymouth Rock rather than Roanoke?) For scholars of the book and of the early modern textual experience, Ralegh serves as an excellent case study for reading America. He provides an example of reading practices of Americana, namely the reading he undertook in preparation for his expeditions to Roanoke (in which case he served as chief sponsor) and Guiana. And Ralegh's own works, on America and otherwise, offer contrasting samples of early modern textual consumption: of the varying media of textual delivery, if you will, that illustrate the diverse manner in which early modern readers consumed America. The practice of reading Americana can be greatly improved by a firmer understanding of early modern reading habits more generally. Texts interest critics, yet bona fide readers contend with something inherently different: books. As material objects, books are handled by readers in specific ways; identical texts, moreover, can reach readers in greatly varied forms, and it is incumbent upon historians (and literary critics, for that matter) to account for these differences and their effects. There was (and is) no single way to read Ralegh, just as there was no single way Ralegh read; it is inaccurate to talk about Ralegh's *Discovery of Guiana* as if it were a textual puzzle for which a singular solution can be found. On the contrary, there were various forms of *Discovery of Guiana* in circulation, both in England and abroad, and acknowledging as much offers valuable insight into this critical record of, and moment in, early American and Atlantic world history.

Ralegh Reading

How Sir Walter Ralegh (ca. 1554–1618) first learned to read is not well known—although he came from a prominent and mildly prosperous West Country family, the future courtier's youth and early education are only dimly documented—yet it can be established that he landed in Oriel College, Oxford, by 1572 and there read admirably enough to earn a reputation as "the ornament of the Juniours . . . worthily esteemed a proficient in Oratory and Philosophy."[6] Ralegh also attended what had become the fashion-

6. The scholarship on Ralegh is immense and incessantly expanding. For a fine literary biography, which contains a good bibliography of Ralegh's own writings, see Steven W. May, *Sir Walter Ralegh* (Boston, 1989). Two recent and outstanding editions of Ralegh's poetry and letters, respectively, are Michael Rudick, ed., *The Poems of Sir Walter Ralegh: A Historical Edition,* Renaissance English Text Society, 7th Ser., XXIII (Tempe, Ariz., 1999); and Agnes Latham and Joyce Youings, eds., *The Letters of Sir Walter Ralegh* (Exeter, 1999). On the immense body of Raleghana, see Christo-

able finishing school for young Protestant Englishmen of his day, namely the battlefields of France and the Netherlands, where the Reformation's hottest wars of religion raged. For Ralegh, France served as "the school of life," as the Renaissance cliché had it. His military service spanned as many as five years (mostly before, yet possibly also after, his Oxford tour of duty) and left him not only more "seasoned" than his peers and a reputable soldier but also fluent in French, a language he capably read throughout his life.[7] Ralegh next surfaces in 1574, at the Inns of Court, where he received further polish—less so in legal training than in the pleasures of London life, which were considerable for young and ambitious gentlemen. It is in these years (the mid-to-late 1570s) that Ralegh began to dabble in, then publish or otherwise circulate, lyric verse. This placed him in the circle of George Gascoigne, the most important English poet of the day, and in contact with other leading literary figures of Elizabethan London, including Sir Philip Sidney. Ralegh would compose the majority of his original, datable verse in these early years (not uncommon for a courtier), although his habit of poetry continued throughout his life: his great work of prose, *History of the World* (1614), contains numerous samples of verse translations that demonstrate how well Ralegh had paid attention to the poetic mentors of his youth.

Between his early poems and later magnum opus, Ralegh led an astonishingly eventful life, which spanned an impressive range of early modern vocations and social stations, a life that gives sharp and tangible meaning to that dulled expression "Renaissance man." "Authors are perplex'd (as some are pleased to say) under what topick to place him," wrote an early biographer who tried to do just that, "whether of Statesman, Seaman, Souldier,

---

pher M. Armitage's *Sir Walter Ralegh: An Annotated Bibliography* (Chapel Hill, N.C., 1987). Among the latest of the innumerable Ralegh biographies (in this case by a "kinsman") is Raleigh Trevelyan, *Sir Walter Raleigh* (London, 2002). The quotation on his early years at Oxford comes from Wood, *Athenae Oxonienses,* I, 369.

7. Richard Hakluyt attests to the Francophone aptitudes of Ralegh in his 1587 translation of René de Laudonnière's *L'histoire notable de la Floride* (Paris, 1586), which Hakluyt dedicated to Ralegh—a client's gesture of flattery, to be sure, yet revealing all the same. Note also that Ralegh owned a full library's worth of French books, which, if not necessarily proving linguistic competency, does seem to suggest, in this case, the owner's literary proficiencies. In his working library in the Tower, Ralegh possessed scores of volumes in Latin, French, and Spanish, which he regularly cited; by contrast, of the considerable, relevant titles available in Dutch or German—on geography and history, for example, both of which were among Ralegh's favorite subjects—none turn up in Ralegh's collection. See Walter Oakeshott, "Sir Walter Ralegh's Library," *The Library: Transactions of the Bibliographical Society,* 5th Ser., XXIII (1968), 285–327.

Chymist, or Chronologer [historian]; for in all these he did excell."[8] He excelled in much more—accomplished poet, master of Elizabethan prose, patron of Renaissance literary figures including Edmund Spenser—though he was admired, above all, as a courtier; and soon after his introduction at court and following a distinguished military service in Ireland, he became the dashing favorite of the queen. Ralegh occupied an enviably privileged place in Elizabeth's entourage. Although never a member of the Privy Council, he served as the queen's inseparable companion throughout the 1580s, exchanging witty poems, performing gallant deeds (even if the cloak-over-puddle episode is likely apocryphal), and gaining royal rewards, both financial and social. Knighted in 1585 and made captain of the guard two years later, Ralegh received a series of lucrative appointments and grants from the queen that transformed him from a provincial gentleman into one of the most powerful (and wealthy) men of the realm and certainly the leading figure in the West Country, which Ralegh represented in Parliament (Devon) through the end of Elizabeth's reign. He inhabited the sumptuous Durham House in London and there hosted some of the leading scholars of the day: the Oxford mathematician Thomas Harriot; Britain's great polymath (and the queen's astrologer), John Dee; the foremost advocate of the colonial enterprise, Richard Hakluyt, who would produce under Ralegh's patronage that "epic" of English expansion, *The Principall Navigations;* and many others with whom Ralegh carried on his lifelong habits of learning and, of course, reading. Among the favorite topics of scholarly discourse in Ralegh's circles was geography, particularly as it pertained to the New World, and overseas exploration became another lifelong pursuit for Sir Walter Ralegh. In 1584, Ralegh received a patent for the discovery of foreign lands, and later that year he sponsored the Roanoke voyages, the first large-scale English colonial project in America. Ralegh directed a second expedition in 1587 to those lands now christened Virginia in honor of the queen (who forbade him to make the voyage himself); and, despite the intervention of the Armada in 1588, he remained intensely interested in the region and the New World more generally for the rest of his life. He devoured literary works on the New World as quickly as they appeared, and he ultimately composed a fair amount of prose on the topic, including one of the enduring samples of English Americana, *The Discovery of Guiana.*

His ample training, literary preparations, and intellectual explorations aside, the fundamental question remains: how did Ralegh read? How does one trace, more generally, the reading habits of early modern Europeans,

8. Wood, *Athenae Oxonienses,* I, 371.

whose literary practices—elusive though they may be—differ substantially from our own? The short answer to this long question is, with great difficulty, supreme luck, and much ingenuity (probably in that order). I can hardly claim, for my part, to have an abundance of the last; nor was Ralegh particularly cooperative, for his part, in bequeathing an archive of annotated texts (thus reducing the difficulty quotient). Although we have inherited a small commonplace book that lists some five hundred volumes believed to have shared space with Ralegh in the Tower of London (our measure of luck), none of these books has actually been identified and made to yield the prized marginalia that can sometimes provide a more direct trail to the owner's reading routines and bibliographic concerns.[9] We have a limited sense, then, of what Ralegh read at this stage in his life (ca. 1610), though not very much on how he read.

We do have scattered clues, though, most of which tend to emphasize the sheer profusion of Ralegh's reading. Virtually the entire roster of court observers who, in the decades following the queen's death, penned their biographies of the illustrious Elizabethans comment on Ralegh's reading, its pervasiveness, and its stupendous volume. Their unanimity is striking. "He studied most in his Sea-Voyages, where he carried always a Trunke of Bookes along with him, and had nothing to divert him," wrote the great Stuart biographer John Aubrey, establishing Ralegh's bona fides as a sea-sturdy scholar. Sir Robert Naunton, a contemporary of Ralegh's and fellow Parliamentarian, observes in his *Fragmenta Regalia* that Ralegh "was an indefatigable reader, whether by sea or land." When by land, "five hours he slept, four he read, two he discoursed, allowing the rest to do his business and necessities," according to David Lloyd. Although certainly "a great soldier . . . an excellent courtier [and] an accomplished gallant," Lloyd reminds us, Ralegh was ultimately "a bookish man." He was relentless, too, in his

9. If there is a trick to tracing readers' methods and thought processes, it would probably lie in marked books, as they are known: volumes that have been annotated by their original (or otherwise known) owners and possess rich marginalia. On this critical and relatively fresh area of research, see Lisa Jardine and William Sherman, "Pragmatic Readers: Knowledge Transactions and Scholarly Services in Late Elizabethan England," in Anthony Fletcher and Peter Roberts, eds., *Religion, Culture, and Society in Early Modern Britain: Essays in Honour of Patrick Collinson* (Cambridge, 1994); William H. Sherman, *John Dee: The Politics of Reading and Writing in the English Renaissance* (Amherst, Mass., 1995); Anthony Grafton, "Is the History of Reading a Marginal Enterprise? Guillaume Budé and His Books," *The Papers of the Bibliographical Society of America*, XCI (1997), 139–157; and Kevin Sharpe, *Reading Revolutions: The Politics of Reading in Early Modern Europe* (New Haven, Conn., 2000).

pursuit of books. Aubrey notes his habit of sailing with a generous store of volumes, a comment substantiated by evidence from the 1596 raid on Cádiz, following the sack of which Ralegh emerged with "a chest of books" (among his otherwise meager spoils). Ralegh himself records his "want of books" upon commencement of his second tour of duty in the Tower, a deficiency rectified following a fervent request to Robert Cotton for "any of thes old books or any manuscrips wherein I cann [sic] reade." One gets the impression of a restless intellect, easily bored, and a compulsive bibliophile. More to the point, whether by land or at sea, in the comfort of Durham House or the confines of the Tower, Ralegh always read.[10]

Ralegh's Tower request—honored, as we know from the commonplace book, by the eventual attainment of a quite impressive library of sixteenth- and early-seventeenth-century tomes—speaks volumes about his dedication to acquiring books, which was apparently inexhaustible. He bought, borrowed, and even stole books as the situation demanded, the illicit behavior less a reflection of malice than of Ralegh's relentless desire to lay hands on the latest available literature. In his early years in London, he purchased books with an almost obsessive zeal. "At his trial," we learn from Philip Edwards's biography, "when questioned about his possession of a suspicious writing, by one Snagge, which [Henry Brooke, Lord] Cobham had borrowed from his library, he protested that there was no book published in those days, when he was a young man, that he did not buy."[11] Ralegh also made free use of books in the possession of his patrons—the immense library of Northumberland, for example, from which he regularly took volumes home.[12] And Ralegh enjoyed access to the collection of Lord Burghley, Elizabeth's powerful privy councillor. In the latter case, we know the general purpose, if not specific titles, that piqued Ralegh's bibliographic interest. At Ralegh's trial in November 1603, Robert Cecil, son of the late

10. On Ralegh's oceanic literacy, see Aubrey, *Aubrey's Brief Lives,* ed. Dick, 254 (and cf. the remarkably similar comment in William Winstanley, *England's Worthies: Select Lives of the Most Eminent Persons from Constantine the Great, to the Death of Oliver Cromwel Late Protector* [London, 1660], 252); and Robert Naunton, *Fragmenta Regalia; or, Observations on Queen Elizabeth, Her Times and Favorites,* ed. John S. Cerovski (Washington, D.C., 1985), 73. David Lloyd is cited in Edwards, *Ralegh,* 48. The quotations of Ralegh come from his *History of the World* (London, 1614), II, xxiii, 4 (cited in Oakeshott, "Ralegh's Library," *The Library,* 5th Ser., XXIII [1968], 285); and from a letter, ca. 1610, to Sir Robert Cotton, in Latham and Youings, eds., *Letters of Sir Walter Ralegh,* 319.

11. Edwards, *Ralegh,* 48.

12. Robert Lacey, *Sir Walter Ralegh* (London, 1973), 111.

privy councillor, leaped to his feet when his father's library was identified as the source of a "notorious libel":

> After my father's death, Sir Walter Ralegh desired to search for some cosmographical description of the Indies which he thought were in his [Burghley's] study and were not to be had in print. Which I granted, and would have trusted Sir Walter Ralegh soon as any man. . . . But I must needs say, Sir Walter Ralegh used me a little unkindly to take the [illicit] book away without my knowledge.

Ralegh found this digression sufficiently irrelevant—and insulting—to explain that he had "no purpose in taking that book. But amongst other books and maps it seems it was cast in."[13] He wanted the good stuff on the Indies, in other words, not the libelous political tract—which was easy enough to come by, he claimed, that he had no need to pilfer a copy from the privy councillor. He went out of his way and even took risks, the exchange suggests, to hunt down all obtainable Americana.

Ralegh plainly read a lot and had an apparent weakness for books. But this still does not explain how he read—and what this has to do with the early modern Atlantic world. Bearing in mind his status as a literate discoverer and bookish conquistador, a few comparisons with his peers may be useful. The parallel case of Hernán Cortés (1485–1547) makes for an obvious starting place, since Ralegh himself was particularly keen to note how he measured up to the great Castilian warrior, the gold standard of the conquistador class.[14] As both John Elliott and Anthony Pagden have pointed out, Cortés, who otherwise gets a bad rap as a hardened and even boorish thug, did display literary leanings, if meager ones. His muscular prose (as showcased in the *Cartas de relación*) betrays a fondness for the ballads and romances of chivalry that were exceedingly popular in his day and in which he was apparently steeped—yet does not suggest much else. There is little by way of Latin citations (pretentiously invoked or not), scholarly

13. For an overview of the trial, see ibid., 303; and see also T. B. Howell, ed., *Cobbett's Complete Collection of State Trials, and Proceedings for High Treason and Other Crimes and Misdemeanors from the Earliest Period to the Present Time* (London, 1809–1828); and David Jardine, *Criminal Trials, Supplying Copious Illustrations of the Inportant [sic] Periods of English History during the Reigns of Queen Elizabeth and James I . . .* , 2 vols. (London, n.d.).

14. See Ralegh, *Discovery of Guiana,* ed. Whitehead, 136, 149, and 194, where the author pronounces his ambition to challenge and surpass the great Castilian conquistador both in terms of valorous deeds and profitable returns (on which score he also invoked Pizarro).

musings (on historical or classical antecedents to his conquests), or just plain yearnings for something good to read. If he did read, he did so casually rather than purposefully.[15] Closer to Ralegh's temperament might have been Christopher Columbus, who cited all manner of literature and made much of his self-acquired erudition. Columbus was indeed well read—this, moreover, in an age when printed matter was harder to come by—yet his writings suggest an undisciplined approach to reading (and to writing). His not-terribly-focused letters, both published and not, and his highly spiritual journal entries offer something for everyone. He tended to allude to texts rather than cite them methodically; he demonstrated a broad familiarity with geographic and religious literature yet hardly a command of specific books. Unlike Vespucci's (or Ralegh's), his prose badly wanted editing.[16]

Ralegh's pattern of reading is more striking even than Columbus's— more wide-ranging, more vigorous, more concentrated—and perhaps it merits comparison with a contemporary made famous less for his geographic explorations than for his literary ones: the Cambridge scholar Gabriel Harvey, who forms the subject of Anthony Grafton and Lisa Jardine's seminal essay on reading, "'Studied for Action.'"[17] A onetime secretary in the household of Leicester, Harvey is described by Grafton and Jardine as a model of "active" reading, by which is meant, first, one who reads for another, generally well-born patron (in his case, the earl of Leicester) and assists especially in the explication of classical texts; second, one

15. See J. H. Elliott, "The Mental World of Hernán Cortés," in Elliott, *Spain and Its World, 1500-1700: Selected Essays* (New Haven, Conn., 1989), 27-41; and Anthony Pagden, "Translator's Introduction," in Hernán Cortés, *Letters from Mexico,* ed. and trans. Pagden, 2d ed. (New Haven, Conn., 1986). Pagden notes Cortés's affinity for the typical fare of the hidalgo class, namely romances, whereas Elliott underscores the opportunistic way that Cortés handled "learned" literature, which he acquired mostly secondhand, and the process by which Cortés constructed a convincing facade of bookish knowledge. Still, he "cannot be described as learned or well-read," Elliott concludes (32), and his literary background certainly did not match that of the humanist-trained and amply well-read Ralegh.

16. For the Columbian oeuvre, see Cecil Jane, ed. and trans., *Select Documents Illustrating the Four Voyages of Columbus,* 2 vols., Works Issued by the Hakluyt Society, 2d Ser., nos. 65, 70 (London, 1930-1933). On the author's literary methods and makeup, see Valerie Flint, *The Imaginative Landscape of Christopher Columbus* (Princeton, N.J., 1992); and Margarita Zamora, *Reading Columbus* (Berkeley, Calif., 1993). For the contrasting case, see Amerigo Vespucci, *Letters from a New World: Amerigo Vespucci's Discovery of America,* ed. Luciano Formisano, trans. David Jacobson (New York, 1992).

17. Lisa Jardine and Anthony Grafton, "'Studied for Action': How Gabriel Harvey Read His Livy," *Past and Present,* CXXIX (1990), 30-78.

who reads in the company of others and energetically debates with this coterie of readers the meaning and purpose of texts; and third, one who comprehends the act of reading as a road to action—one who not only reads actively but also sees reading literature (not unlike seeing a dramatic performance) as a prod to action.[18] Although Ralegh overlapped and even intersected with Harvey—one of Harvey's reading mates, Sir Humphrey Gilbert, was Ralegh's kinsman and close associate, and both men counted themselves friends of Edmund Spenser—the two cases are more illustrative for their differences than similarities. Ralegh probably never served as a professional reader or "facilitator" in the mode of Harvey—he ranked significantly higher than Gabriel Harvey on the Elizabethan sociopolitical food chain—but he did gather around him a group of other readers that came to be called (after his London residence) the Durham Set. Since Ralegh himself engaged in the same sort of collaborative disputation, as described by Grafton and Jardine, as Harvey—vigorous scholarly give-and-take, not unlike Talmudic "pilpul": a form of Jewish scholarly debate popularized in Eastern Europe precisely during the heyday of "active" reading in the fifteenth and sixteenth centuries—his circumstances seem to defy understood convention. He was neither a professional reader per se nor personally reliant on other such readers but one who read with the would-be facilitators and probably as their intellectual equal. In fact, Ralegh often read on his own and then instigated "secretaries" and other members of his circle to act —the reverse of Harvey's pattern—as, for example, in the case of his earliest New World ventures. He personally devoured the literature on America, and this moved him (in part) to outfit the Roanoke expeditions.

There is also evidence to suggest that Ralegh was a better reader than others who served him—if by "better" is meant more closely replicating the nervously energetic, ambitiously polyvalent, humanist-inflected model of reading described by Grafton and Jardine. Compare, in this regard, two texts produced in the final years of the sixteenth century, one by the reader-turned-writer who composed *Discovery of Guiana* (1596)—Sir Walter Ra-

18. Jardine and Grafton, "'Studied for Action,' *Past and Present,* CXXIX (1990), 32. A fascinating illustration of this habit of reading can be seen in Peter Paul Rubens's famous painting of *Four Philosophers (Self-Portrait with Friends)* (ca. 1610, Palazzo Pitti, Florence), which shows the exceedingly well-read artist (who was Ralegh's exact contemporary) reading in the company of friends—Filips Rubens, the artist's brother and a well-regarded humanist; Justus Lipsius, the leading philosopher of the period; and Johannes Woverius, a humanist follower of Lipsius—exactly as one might imagine Harvey (or Ralegh) doing with their colleagues. See, on this topic, Prosper Arents, *De bibiotheek van Pieter Paul Rubens* (Antwerp, 2001).

legh—and the other by a member of Ralegh's entourage (and his Guiana lieutenant), Lawrence Keymis. Larded with learned citations and literary allusions, Ralegh's *Guiana* narrative demonstrates a broad knowledge of the Spanish prose of discovery, an easy mastery of classical sources, and a flair for rhetorical disputation. It dissects the earlier Guiana narratives, and it makes a powerful case—rhetorically and politically—for England in America. It is, in brief, precisely the product that one might expect from someone "studied for action." Meanwhile, the *Relation of the Second Voyage to Guiana* (1596) by Keymis, who was an Oxford mathematician before joining Ralegh in London, offers a dry and uninspired description of the region. "We cannot denie that the chiefe commendation of vertue doth consist in action," intones Keymis in the rousing preface.[19] Yet the narrative thereafter lacks all of the vim and vigor of Ralegh's. A travelogue mostly of the wind-and-weather variety, it possesses nary a rhetorical sign of the active reading that one might anticipate from a bona fide scholar and an Oxbridge colleague of Gabriel Harvey.

If the Grafton and Jardine model does not pertain particularly to the Ralegh who authored—and did the preparatory reading for—*Discovery of Guiana,* it does illuminate Ralegh's literary practices in other regards. For Ralegh appears to have employed scholarly eyes in other instances. Although the vast library in Ralegh's quarters in the Tower must have greatly assisted him in the composition of *History of the World* (1614), it did not, apparently, suffice. For some subjects, Ralegh availed himself of hired readers. As it turns out, one of them, the ornery Ben Jonson, left record of his efforts in the form of a complaint that Ralegh failed properly to credit him for his work on the Punic Wars. Jonson, who served as tutor to Ralegh's beloved son Wat, did not get much traction in his day from this after-the-fact grumbling—the materials on the Punic Wars were not so terribly original. Yet his objections are valuable for the evidence they provide, first, of the practice of having assistants read and write for a patron and, second, of Ralegh's recourse to this assistance for his massive *History of the World.* For that typically humanist work, most scholars agree, the author relied on numerous such readers who undertook important literary services for their patron. Ralegh, however, did not leave evidence of such assistance in his other notable work of prose, which happens also to be a seminal sample of early English Americana. There is no sign that Ralegh hired eyes, that is, for his *Discovery of Guiana.*

19. Lawrence Keymis, *A Relation of the Second Voyage to Guiana* (London, 1596), sig. Ar ("To the Reader").

The case for reading Ralegh's America, it must be confessed, offers purely evidence of absence: there is no sign of Ralegh's employing a reader for the *Discovery of Guiana,* whereas there are signs for another major work, the *History of the World.* Yet it is suggestive all the same, which counts for a lot in pursuit of that rare prey, early modern reading practices. The data point to the differing ways that Ralegh read in preparation for different forms of composition, and, insofar as they help us to understand how Ralegh read, they beg an obvious question: why did Ralegh approach disparate literary tasks in dissimilar ways? More to the point, why did reading and writing Americana induce in Ralegh a different set of literary practices? Here I want to offer an admittedly conjectural answer, which points to a factor perhaps not adequately acknowledged in histories of reading, namely genre. Reading and writing different genres have different conventions, different demands, and different traditions. Ralegh set about to work on the *History of the World* in the manner of a historian; he followed a prescribed and recognizably humanist tradition. Yet America and Americana presented novel challenges, and Ralegh improvised accordingly. It is worth pointing out that, from a formal standpoint, the *Discovery of Guiana* was sui generis. Even as a specimen of Americana, it fell between the cracks: of history (compare Peter Martyr's *De orbe novo*), of epic (compare Alonzo de Ercilla's *La Araucana*), of epistolary reportage (compare Cortés's *Cartas de relación*), or of prose advertisement for colonialism (which would be the format of so many editions of English Americana in the decades to come).[20] Travel literature represented a relatively new, innovative genre for which accepted rules had not yet been established (for Europeans, at least). Ralegh consequently experimented in the *Discovery of Guiana*—he did not even think to publish it initially—and this led to a new mode of writing and, by extension, reading on America.

Reading Ralegh

Grafton and Jardine make a simple yet important point about the nature of early modern reading and our critical interpretation of those materials we so casually lump under the broad rubric of "texts." We cannot assume the "point" of any given text, they argue—"a tidily univocal interpretation"—since individual readers (as opposed to the more traditionally studied com-

20. Pietro Martire d'Anghiera [Peter Martyr d'Anghera], *De orbe novo . . . decades* (Alcalá de Henares, 1516); Alonzo de Ercilla y Zúñiga, *Primera, segunda, y tercera partes de la Araucana* (Antwerp, 1597); Cortés, *Letters from Mexico,* ed. and trans. Pagden.

munity of readers) bring to a text their own particular purposes.[21] I would like to nuance their argument in a way that approaches the issue from a slightly different perspective. We cannot assume the point of any particular text, even allowing for the individuality of its reader, since the very form in which it is delivered affords distinctive reading experiences. Once it leaves the hands of an author, that is to say, a text has a life of its own. Most essentially, it becomes a book; and, as so much recent scholarship on the history of the book has reminded us (particularly work on early modern history of science), even printed texts can be highly unstable.[22] I do not have in mind here the mistakes that printers can introduce to a text, the variations that may exist among pirated editions of a text, and the slew of other "dangers" inherent to the publishing process (as recently described, for example, by Adrian Johns).[23] Nor am I concerned with what Anna Beer calls "the public production of meaning," by which she means the way the interpretation of a text, once in book form, can be shaped by the patterns of its reception (rather than authorial intent).[24] All of these observations are highly relevant, of course. Yet what I am after in this instance, by contrast, is the way different forms of the book itself—different artifacts that land in readers'

21. Jardine and Grafton, "'Studied for Action,'" *Past and Present,* CXXIX (1990), 32.

22. See David McKitterick, *Print, Manuscript, and the Search for Order, 1450–1830* (Cambridge, 2003), which describes the distinctions that developed in the early modern period between book and text and the collective production of the former versus the singular authorial role in making the latter. The literature on early modern reading and on the history of the book, more generally, has expanded vastly in recent years. Two excellent points of departure are Robert Darnton's germinal essays "Toward a History of Reading," *Wilson Quarterly,* XIII, no. 4 (Autumn 1989), 86–103, and "How to Read a Book," *New York Review of Books,* XLIII, no. 10 (June 1996), 52–58. A very useful bibliographic sketch, with a focus on the Renaissance and England more particularly, is Cyndia Susan Clegg, "History of the Book: An Undisciplined Discipline?" *Renaissance Quarterly,* LIV (2001), 221–245. See also Kevin Sharpe and Steven N. Zwicker, eds., *Reading, Society, and Politics in Early Modern England* (Cambridge, 2003); Jennifer Anderson and Elizabeth Sauer, eds., *Books and Readers in Early Modern England: Material Studies* (Philadelphia, 2002); Sharpe, *Reading Revolutions;* Zachary Lesser, *Renaissance Drama and the Politics of Publication: Readings in the English Book Trade* (Cambridge, 2004); and Marina Frasca-Spada and Nick Jardine, eds., *Books and the Sciences in History* (Cambridge, 2000), which addresses volumes of early modern science, including geography.

23. Johns, *Nature of the Book.*

24. Anna R. Beer, *Sir Walter Ralegh and His Readers in the Seventeenth Century: Speaking to the People* (New York, 1997), 8.

hands—invite different processes of reading. Early modern travel literature lent itself exceptionally to processes of transformation. As a relatively new genre, it was unusually unstable and relatively more pliable in terms of its printed presentation. Fewer conventions existed for the genre, especially for its American variant, which meant that more options remained open in terms of its delivery. If early modern texts encouraged more (or less) active methods of reading, then early modern travel literature encouraged an outstanding level of what might be called bibliographic manipulation. If readers could be active, so, too, could genres.

Back to Ralegh. Ralegh's two major prose works, the *History of the World* and the *Discovery of Guiana,* represent two utterly distinct categories of book, the first an immensely popular volume of humanist history, the second among the earliest and, as it would turn out, most widely circulated samples of English Americana.[25] The two books do not perfectly exemplify their genres—what literary text ever does?—though they are fairly good samples of early modern historical prose and travel narrative, respectively, and they afford contrasting strategies of bookmaking from a single author. Juxtaposing the pair grants a superb view into early modern textual production and the practices of reading, modes of writing, and forms of publishing that they induced. This, in turn, provides critical insight into methods of reading America circa 1600.

To grasp the difference between these volumes requires only to possess them; for to grasp both of these titles in their original form (a significant caveat, it will be argued) is to handle two seemingly different media. The immense *History of the World* requires two sturdy hands (or perhaps a solid bookstand, as might have been the case), whereas the *Discovery of Guiana* fits neatly into one's pocket. Yet these texts share a great deal, as well; what separates them is both much and little. For starters, both are written from positions of disadvantage: the earlier work was composed

25. Sir W. Ralegh, *The Discoverie of the Large, Rich, and Bewtiful Empyre of Guiana, with a Relation of the Great and Golden Citie of Manoa (Which the Spanyards Call El Dorado): and the Provinces of Emeria, Arromaia, Amapaia and Other Countries, with Their Rivers Adjoyning* (London, 1596), and *The History of the World* (London, 1614). Evidence of the former's success in print can be found in Alden and Landis, *European Americana,* I–III: three English editions came out in 1596, four in Latin and German in 1599, and several more (in multiple languages) over the coming quarter-century (see also discussion below). For the popularity of the latter—at least twenty editions in the seventeenth century alone—see C. A. Patrides's excellent essay, "Ralegh and *The History of the World:* An Introduction," in Sir Walter Ralegh, *The History of the World,* ed. Patrides (Philadelphia, 1971).

PLATE I. *Original editions of the* History of the World *(on the right) and* Discovery *of* Guiana. *The calf binding of the* History *is from the turn of the twentieth century, done in "antique style" with gilt edges by the London firm of Riviere and Son (1882– 1939). The* Discovery *is in contemporary binding. By permission of The Huntington Library, San Marino, California*

by a just-released-from-prison yet still-in-hot-water courtier (Ralegh had just emerged from the proverbial frying pan for secretly marrying one of Elizabeth's ladies-in-waiting, Elizabeth Throckmorton, and many cast aspersions on his voyage as a publicity stunt); the later work was launched by a long-imprisoned yet soon-to-be-released fallen idol of the earlier regime (out of the frying pan and onto the chopping block, as it turned out). The author of both works must at once acknowledge, or at least gesture toward, this awkward state of affairs, and both therefore have elements of polemic in them (vigorously and persuasively argued cases, appeals to and beyond the court, and so on), especially in their prefatory materials. Despite the plain difference in genre, moreover, both texts have certain generic overlap: both contain large passages of history (a full third of the *Discovery of Guiana*), digressions on theology, and elements of natural history. Both history and travel narrative, it turns out, could be quite capacious literary forms. Both of these works also rely, extensively even, on outside authorities (rather than the "I-witness," otherwise typical of contemporary travel accounts and the memoirlike tropes of political history), which means that both generously cite other sources to substantiate their evidentiary claims. Finally, both of these titles appeal to a wide audience and enjoyed significant popularity. They have both gone through multiple printings and multiple editions; and the *Discovery of Guiana* appears, moreover, in multiple translations. Both books, in short, circulated widely.

But the formats in which the *History of the World* and *Discovery of Guiana* were delivered—the original and in many regards determinative configuration that the texts took upon their first English publication—differ so substantially, they result in two wholly different products, and these, in turn, produce two drastically different reading experiences (Plate 1). So dissimilar are the experiences of the two that it is arguably inaccurate to place them under the same rubric of "reading." Indeed, the *History of the World* may rank among the most popular books never read; it is simply unreadable in the common sense of the word. A large folio encompassing 1,571 pages, it daunts its reader from start (a 40-page table of contents) to finish (more than 120 pages of accompanying lists and charts). *History of the World's* famous prefatory essay—another two-score dense folio pages of prose, "famous" since it is, in all likelihood, the only portion of the book regularly read—is nearly the length of the entire *Discovery of Guiana*. The latter volume, by contrast, originally appeared in small quarto and, after that, in ever more slender and manageable formats. In its slightness, it resembles the modern paperback. But the distinctions between the books amount to more than just size and shape; there are qualitative differences as well. *History of the World* offers a full graphic package that includes well-executed illustrations, detailed maps, elaborate diagrams, dense tables, and the somewhat uncommon genre of engraved battle scenes (which, in *History of the World,* are not terribly successful: the dreadful two-page spread, depicting certain ancient battles of the Romans, possesses all of the sophistication of naïve stick-art) (Plate 2).[26] An allegorical frontispiece, perhaps the single most impressive image in *History of the World,* is accompanied by its own verse description. Meanwhile, *Discovery of Guiana* lacks all manner of illustration—which does not necessarily follow from its meager size, since many pamphletlike books of this period came with extensive graphic material. In-

26. *History of the World,* 452–453, and see also 454–455.

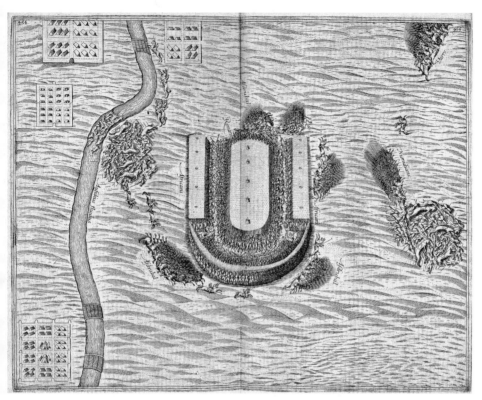

PLATE 2, *"A Scene of Battles of the Romans."* Two page engraving in Ralegh,
History of the World *(London, 1614), I (between 454–455). By permission of*
The Huntington Library, San Marino, California

deed, the 1596 edition of *Discovery of Guiana* contains no decorative matter
at all apart from a Mannerist scroll on the lower half of the title page and
the embellished letters that launch the dedication, preface, and body of the
text. A florid description of the American tropics and a thrilling adventure
story of colonial intrigue, Ralegh's *Discovery of Guiana* makes an austere
bibliographic impression nonetheless.

There is a final visual distinction between these two works that merits
mention: *History of the World* offers readers a thick foliage of marginalia
on which to rest their eyes as they flit through the text, whereas *Discovery
of Guiana* offers nothing of the kind. The extensive side notes of *History of
the World,* which provide explanatory synopses of the narrative and a running tally of its author's impressive source base, point to certain bookish
devices that might have shaped the exercise of "reading" such an impos-

ing work.[27] To overcome its stunning dimensions and challenging proportions, *History of the World* includes a series of what might be called textual apparatuses—"paratexts" is the word used by the eminent French critic
Gérard Genette—to help usher the reader through the volume.[28] The table
of contents, for example, not quite standard for books circa 1600, breaks
the narrative down to the level of "chapters, paragraphes, and sections"
and thus, over the course of its forty pages, distills *History of the World*
into its elemental parts. In practice, there are in the body of the text only
chapter and section divisions, so this service goes beyond the call of taxo-
nomic duty. More generally, *History of the World* is exquisitely subdivided,
the very design of the volume encouraging the reader to pick and choose
his or her spots: "parts" (two, though the second was never completed),
"books" (five), "chapters" (nearly thirty), and "sections" (scads). If readers
did not care to scan this perhaps overly liberal summary, they could also
turn to the slimmer (if still fairly substantial) "Chronological Table," which
runs twenty-six pages and comes with its own explanatory note. And if still
stymied, they had recourse to yet another level of metadescription, delivered in two separate indices, one for the first two books, the other for the
following three. In more than thirty carefully designed pages, these supply
readers with yet another means to survey the volume's contents and to alight
upon the narrative branch of their choosing.

The options for the reader of the *Discovery of Guiana* were not nearly as
generous. It is not simply that the *Discovery of Guiana* streams its words
along in a forceful rush of prose—the result, no doubt, of Ralegh's kinetic
literary style and his imperative call (in this case) to colonial action. It is, further, the very bibliographic design of the volume, which compels a strategy
of reading that is as brisk and urgent and linear as a perusal of *History of
the World* is not. The layout of *Discovery of Guiana* offers nary a graphic
break and little by way of textual apparatus. It does contain a brief dedication and a preface ("To the Reader"), to be sure, both of which serve as
apologia of sorts, promoting Ralegh's case at the royal court and the court
of public opinion, respectively. Yet after these are dispensed with, the nar-

27. Cf. Ann Blair's discussion of "bookish methods of research," a phrase she em-
ploys to describe those early modern bibliographic devices (such as commonplacing)
that were enlisted as a means to comprehend the vast, growing amounts of literature
lately available: Ann Blair, "Annotating and Indexing Natural Philosophy," in Frasca-
Spada and Jardine, eds., *Books and the Sciences,* 69–89.

28. See Gérard Genette, *Paratexts: Thresholds of Interpretation,* trans. Jane E.
Lewin (Cambridge, 1997).

rative carries the reader swiftly along the currents of Guiana's history, its colonial experience with Spain, and the course of Ralegh's exploration. The 1596 edition possesses a distinct urgency. It does not allow for chapter or section breaks, it provides no marginal summaries, and it permits no systematic skimming. It is meant to be consumed, one imagines, in a single, gustatory gulp.

As a gulp is to a sip, so is the experience of reading Ralegh's *Discovery of Guiana* to that of *History of the World*. Ralegh's two major prose publications—far and away his most impressive and substantial works, aside, perhaps, from his fragmentary *Ocean to Cynthia*—offer two contrasting models of books and point to two very different experiences of early modern reading. They also give two varying answers to the question of how Ralegh was read. The books' array of apparatuses, their distinct bibliographic frames, and their interior designs would have encouraged, not a singular type of reading, but multiple textual experiences. The format of *History of the World* allows for—indeed, all but requires—skimming and skipping by providing the reader with multiple mechanisms to move from the body of the text to those accessories that so expertly adorn it. *History of the World* might also stimulate, paradoxical though this may seem, a more leisurely pace of consulting and lingering: taking more time with a particular table or illustrated scene, for example, which might have been otherwise subsumed in the grander narrative. Some of the bibliographic devices speed the reader up, whereas others slow him or her down. And despite their purpose in ordering the volume for a potentially overwhelmed reader, the apparatuses of *History of the World* can also have a disorienting effect. When readers arrive at a critical juncture, they may be lured by the ancillary materials and thrown off course. Thus, the presumably central story of the Trojan War is illustrated with an otherwise incongruous scene of Hannibal's military tactics, placed by the publisher expressly in this section of the book.[29] No such danger for the consumer of *Discovery of Guiana*. That book propels its reader forward in the most breathless, direct manner imaginable, offering hardly a respite from the thrust of Ralegh's prose. Even the transitional passages, where the printer might been expected to insert a section break or chapter heading, convey the audience headlong to the next scene of action: as, for example, when Ralegh moves from the background narrative (on the

29. The image appears right before the chapter "Of the Grecians Journey, and Embassage to Troy, and of Helenaes Being Detained in Aegypt; and of the Sacrificing of Iphigenia." The plate itself is marked unambiguously in the upper corners "452" and "453," meaning its placement was not a printer's error.

Spanish *Doristas*) to the foreground plot of his own expedition. This occurs precisely one-third of the way into the book—yet without any indication of a change of scene or tempo. The experience of reading *Discovery of Guiana* is intense where that of *History of the World* is mild; the slighter of the two books makes far more strenuous demands on the reader, whereas the preposterously challenging *History of the World*—even the title is overwhelming—lets its reader off easy.

The Discovery *Abroad*

The *Discovery of Guiana* and the *History of the World* each experienced a considerable afterlife: once they left their author's hand, they both went through multiple editions and enjoyed notable popularity.[30] Yet they parted company once they left the London print shop—or rather, once *Discovery of Guiana* ventured abroad, since *History of the World,* its titular claims notwithstanding, would remain a distinctly provincial text. That is, although both books had fairly comparable appeal to English readers, *History of the World's* popularity was consistently and exclusively British: the work came out only in English-language editions and, if the form of the text did change somewhat over the years, its heft and geopolitical orientation did not.[31] The same can hardly be said of *Discovery of Guiana,* which embarked on a major bibliographic journey almost immediately following its initial English launch. The variations of *Discovery of Guiana* that appeared beyond the borders of England, moreover, offered consumers fundamentally different textual and bibliographic flavors, which could be imbibed in utterly distinct ways. The issue was less a matter of sipping and gulping than of sampling altogether different concoctions that had been mixed from Ralegh's original ingredients: geographic and literary cocktails that might scarcely have retained the taste of Ralegh's original recipe.

Such literary mixing began more or less at once, as Ralegh's American treatise was promptly appropriated by publishers on the Continent. *Discovery of Guiana* turned out to be enormously popular in Latin, German, and Dutch; it appeared more frequently in those languages, ultimately, than that of its original composition. Yet these derivative editions often bear

30. *The Discovery of Guiana* appeared in three separate editions in 1596 alone, while *History of the World,* although the more expensive publishing proposition, appeared in fresh editions throughout the seventeenth century: 1614, 1621, 1634, 1652 (twice), 1666 (twice), 1677 (thrice), and 1687.

31. For its none-too-subtle critique of "tyrannical" princes, *History of the World* earned the enduring admiration of those who would challenge Stuart rule; it was a hit, fittingly, during the run-up to the Civil War and the early years of the Protectorate.

little resemblance to Ralegh's initial product. It is not only that the text has been substantially altered, abbreviated, and reframed in many of these non-English versions in order to make Ralegh's work fit into the various other contexts of its production and consumption—which is emphatically the case. It is also that the book itself takes on a whole new appearance, and this effectively produces a different message—a different "read"—than the muscular, imperial, Elizabethan one that is generally affiliated with it. The swiftly generated (and widely consumed, to judge by number of editions) versions that first appeared in Latin and German translation came from the prestigious firm of Levinus Hulsius; both were published in Nuremberg in 1599.[32] The slender Hulsius volumes (which, although separate translations, are otherwise similar in form) make for a much briefer book than the original—a scant twelve pages in Latin and sixteen in German—yet one that is much nicer to look at.[33] They bear six identical, full-page plates, along with a separate pull-out map (signed by Hulsius yet based on and elsewhere attributed to the Dutch cartographer Jodocus Hondius) and a striking title-page illustration. This means that, in the Latin version, for example, there is a two-to-one ratio of text to image. If not quite coffee-table books per se, these editions fit most sensibly under the rubric of picture books. The emphasis of both editions, moreover, is on wonders and marvels, a point made from the outset—right from the volume's opening "portal," as it were (Plate 3). Thus, the title page announces the "admiranda"/"wunderbare" contents of the volume; and the title-page vignette displays enticing samples of the same. Three far-fetched figures fill the foreground—two headless men, or acephali, shown in frontal and rear views, and a fully armed and naked Amazonian woman—and two wondrous animals scamper through the engraved background (an armadillo and a tapir-like quadruped), with the entire cast of characters staged in the peaceful, pastoral countryside of Guiana. The reader of the Hulsius editions hardly glimpses Ralegh's Anglo-Spanish war zone.[34]

These images effectively provoke wide-eyed amazement, if not incredu-

32. [Walter Ralegh], *Brevis et admiranda descriptio regni Guianae auri abundantissimi, in America* (Nuremberg, 1599), and *Kurze wunderbare Beschreibung de goldreichen Königreichs Guianae in America* (Nuremberg, 1599).

33. The original English version, which came out in three editions distinguishable by minor typographical differences, ran 112 pages.

34. Note that all of these title-page images correlate to "creatures in the map," namely in the Hondius pull-out map, which was also published separately as a sheet map. See the discussion below, and cf. Charles Nicholl, *The Creature in the Map: A Journey to El Dorado* (London, 1995).

Brevis & admiranda defcriptio
REGNI GVIANÆ, AVRI
ABVNDANTISSIMI, IN AMERICA,
SEV NOVO ORBE, SVB LINEA ÆQVINOCTILIA
fiti: Quod nuper admodum, Annis nimirum,
1564.1595&1596.
Per Generofum Dominum,
Dn. GVALTHERVM RALEGH EQVI-
tem Anglum detectum eſt: paulò poſt juſſu ejus
duobus libellis comprehenſa:
Ex quibus
IODOCVS HONDIVS TABVLAM GEO-
graphicam adornavit, addita explicatione
Belgico fermone fcripta:
Nunc verò in Latinum fermonem tranflata, & ex variis
authoribus hinc inde declarata.

NORIBERGAE,
Impenfis LEVINI HVLSII, D. M, XCIX.

PLATE 3. *Frontispiece of the Latin edition of* Discovery of Guiana
(Brevis et admiranda descriptio regni Guianae *[Nuremberg, 1599])*.
By permission of The Huntington Library, San Marino, California

lous amusement. They also induce in the putative reader—or, better, gazer —a wholly different reaction than that presumably prompted by the direct, vibrant, purposeful, and solemn text authored by Ralegh. One ponders the images rather than the text. Above all, the Hulsius editions, and especially their title-page illustrations, are entertaining—they provide "diversion" in the literal sense of the word—and this is also the thrust of the volumes' full-page engravings, which are truly fabulous. Collectively, the images convey the alluring enchantment and attractiveness of America. In one image, a charming land-cum-seascape displays Native canoes and indigenous tree houses (Plate 4); while exotic flora and fauna decorate another engraving, with Native Indians hunting the bizarrely formed beasts. In another illustration, the capital city of Manoa beckons with its European-modeled towers, turrets, and spires; European and Native vessels moored in its harbor suggest the city's easy accessibility. Two striking images of Amazon women —in one, they picnic and couple with their (male) suitors (Plate 5); in the other, they attack, entrap, and execute their (male) enemies—suggest a classical context for the New World; whereas dual views of the headless people of Guiana's hinterland (which recapitulate the title-page image of acephali) suggest a plethora of otherworldly marvels.[35] Hondius's pull-out map is embellished with more of the same—or rather a distilled version of the same: a headless man, a warrior woman, exotic animals, and so forth. Always sensational, sometimes even sensual, and rarely bearing the sensible message of Ralegh's original call to imperial arms, the images in the Hulsius editions transform *Discovery of Guiana* into a collage of marvels. They offer an altogether different read than the text-driven treatise Ralegh published in London in 1596.

And this, more generally, is the effect of the *Discovery* abroad: Ralegh's imperial message is supplanted by the publisher's impression of marvels. It is a process that is repeated in the numerous variations of the text produced by Hulsius and others, which circulated extensively, both anthologized and on their own, well into the seventeenth century. As late as 1663, the Dutch publisher Gillis Joosten Saeghman issued a pamphletlike compilation of the "rare and monstrous races of men that can be found in the

35. Many of these 1599 images had a considerable afterlife in other published Americana, and it is worth singling out the exotic fauna, which adumbrate the equally fabulous creatures that illustrate Arnoldus Montanus's triumph of imaginative geography, *America* (Amsterdam, 1671). The latter was a folio work (as opposed to the quarto editions of Hulsius) that appeared in several editions around 1670 and served as the model for much of the exotica of the late seventeenth century.

PLATE 4. *Engraving of landscape with Indians, in Hulsius's Latin edition of*
Discovery of Guiana (Brevis et admiranda descriptio regni Guianae), *facing page 6.*
By permission of The Huntington Library, San Marino, California

kingdom of Guiana," offering much the same views—now rendered in inex-
pensive woodcuts—for what had passed for Ralegh's geopolitical reportage
in 1596.[36] The Hulsius presentation of Guiana also appeared in that publisher's lengthier anthologies of Americana, the so-called *Sammlung,* and in
this form had an arguably wider reach than the original English edition.[37]
It is thus through these "texts" that most European consumers (and, con-
ceivably, most consumers of the wider Atlantic world) assimilated the news
and formulated their image of Ralegh's Guiana. The differences between
the variant renditions of the New World are considerable. Ralegh's original
text has an imperial context, a court audience, and a personal agenda that
pertained to the queen and her fickle favor. Yet all of this is absent from the
more enticingly fabulous, lushly pictorial, and frankly exotic presentation

36. *Korte en wonderlijcke beschryvinge van de seltsame wanschepsels van menschen,*
die ghevonden worden in het coninckrijck Guianae, aen het Meyr Parime (Amsterdam,
[166-?]).

37. Levinus Hulsius, ed., *[Sammlung von sechs und zwanzig Schiffahrten in ver-*
schiedene fremde Länder] (Nuremberg, 1602–1650).

PLATE 5. *Engraving of Amazons coupling, in Hulsius's German edition of* Discovery of Guiana (Kurtze wunderbare Beschreibung: Desz goldreichen Königreichs Guianae im America *[Nuremberg, 1599]), facing page 12.* *By permission of The Huntington Library, San Marino, California*

of the New World that was pervasively promoted by the continental editions of *Discovery of Guiana.* The titular author, Walter Ralegh, has been all but subsumed in these editions of the *Discovery,* which are the product of enterprising publishers wholly untroubled by Ralegh's courtly concerns.

Visual images shape *Discovery of Guiana* when issued beyond the borders of England. Whether engraved in copper or cut in wood, whether printed in folio or in quarto, the illustrations of the non-London editions greatly influence the experience of "reading" a book by now only nominally ascribed to Ralegh. In some cases, the images are the book: Hulsius's volumes and their direct descendants make an almost purely visual impression, the meager text serving as backdrop for the pictures. Yet even when the text is substantial and the images relatively few, the visual component can have a way of shaping the textual. *The Discovery of Guiana* came out, perhaps most famously during the seventeenth century, in the deluxe editions issued by the firm of de Bry. The Liège-born yet by this time (following the Dutch Revolt) Frankfurt-settled Theodore de Bry headed one of Europe's most prestigious printing houses. Trained as an engraver, the elder de Bry combined expert draftsmanship with superb printing techniques (he came from a family of goldsmiths) to create some of the finest and best illustrated books of his day. The firm of De Bry and Sons lavished attention on the New World, including early English travel literature pertaining to America, and its editions of *Discovery of Guiana,* like those of Hulsius, were instrumental in dispersing Ralegh abroad. The de Bry volumes, likewise, appeared in German and Latin; they carry the imprint of de Bry's widow and sons, since the paterfamilias had died the year before their publication in 1599.[38] (There were second editions in 1624 and 1625, respectively.) In de Bry's publications, Ralegh's text appeared as part of the *Americae* anthology (the eighth volume), and this gave it yet another quality. *The Discovery of Guiana* is one of many narrations of the New World, its exploration, and its imperial conquest. Since all of the texts in the volume describe English voyages, one might be tempted to read into them the same patriotic message that is imparted by Richard Hakluyt's *Principall Navigations*—or by Ralegh's original work. Yet other volumes of the series are also organized along national lines, and this dilutes any particularly English flavor of the whole. The German and Latin editions are not identical—the order and arrangement of plates, for example, are idiosyncratic—yet they have a similar feel. Both are intended for the luxury market and printed in folio, with excellent typesetting and engravings; they thus offer consumers a far more sumptuous product than Hulsius's lean publications. Yet they also supply, much as the lower-end books do, a visually attractive product that underscores the books' apparatuses and, above all, their images. De Bry's editions bear extensive marginalia and have separate pagination for different narratives; their respective title pages advertise Ralegh's text, even though it is one of several texts in the volume. They also position the Hondius pull-out map of Guiana prominently, which foregrounds the "creatures on the map" that were similarly publicized in Hulsius's editions (Plates 6, 7). The de Bry plates come in different arrangements and according to slightly different publication strategies—in the Latin edition, they appear in a separate section at the end, and in the German, they are interspersed throughout the

38. *Americae achter Theil, in welchem erstlich beschrieben wirt das machtige vnd goldtreich Konigreich Guiana, zu Norden dess grossen Flusses Oronoke, . . . gelegen* (Frankfurt, 1599); and *Americae pars VIII: Continens . . . duo itinera, nobilissimi et fortissimi domini Gualtheri Raleigh equitis et designati gubernatoris Regij in Anglia praesidij, nec non fortissimi Capitanei Laurentii Keyms. Quibus itineribus describitur auriferum et potentissimum regnum Guiana, ad septentrionem fluminis Orenoque* (Frankfurt, 1599).

PLATE 6. *"How the nobility in Guiana would cover themselves in gold when feasting,"* in Theodore de Bry, Americae pars VIII . . . *(Frankfurt, 1599), plate XV.* By permission of The Huntington Library, San Marino, California

narrative. Yet they are comparably lavish and beautifully engraved and accomplish the same result. Both de Bry editions give pride of place to their visual content by drawing readers' attention to their outstanding illustrations, and this lends them the feel of a coffee table book. The pictures alone are worth the price of the volume—and certainly more than the proverbial thousand words.

Another notable edition of Ralegh prompts another proverbial wisdom, in this case the chestnut on judging books by their covers. Early modern printers placed great stock in their equivalent of the book cover; the engraved title page or frontispiece was an admired art form and much valued device in the business of bookselling. In the first Dutch edition of *Discovery of Guiana,* printed in 1598 by Cornelis Claesz, the title page plays a pivotal role in framing the volume's contents (Plate 8).[39] The actual title, rather extensive for the slim volume, advertises Guiana's riches and geopolitical

39. Sir Walter Ralegh, *Warachtighe ende grondige beschryvinge van het groot ende goudt-rijck Coninckrijck van Guiana* . . . (Amsterdam, 1598).

PLATE 7. *"How the Guianans cast gold,"* in *Theodore de Bry,*
Americae pars VIII . . . *(Frankfurt, 1599), plate XVII.*
By permission of The Huntington Library, San Marino, California

value; and an engraved map of the North Atlantic world (Mare des Nort),
covering the lower half of the page, underscores a similarly colonial theme.
Yet like the title itself—which gets around to mentioning Ralegh's role in
the narrative almost as an afterthought—the cartographic précis on the title
page effectively marginalizes the English: "Anglia" barely makes it onto the
map. Still more graphically, the two figures who abut the map in separate
architectonic niches—heraldic devices, as it were, representing a cannibal
and an Amazon—privilege precisely those marvelous narrative details that
Ralegh himself, preoccupied with his credibility at court, was at pains to
minimize. Ironically, in view of the book's Dutch origins, these title-page
figures come from an altogether different set of engravings that are related
to ancient British history: the Amazon is based on a de Bry engraving of
an ancient Pict (Plate 9). In all events, the volume's devices and presentation move Claesz's book in yet another direction away from the original.
The Dutch *Discovery of Guiana* offers a hybrid edition: it carries some of
the attractive, wonder-filled images of the Latin and German editions, yet
it also bears in its fiercely partisan and imperial-minded prefatory material

a vigorously Dutch slant on the narrative. The framing texts underscore Ralegh's claim that Guiana's Natives would welcome a colonial alternative to Spain, yet they argue—sensibly enough, given the political context and colonial ambitions of the Dutch Republic circa 1600—that the Netherlands, not England, represented the single best hope for the region. Dutch publishers appropriated the *Discovery,* in other words, for Dutch agendas that had scarcely anything to do with Ralegh's primary intentions.

The Dutch *Discovery's* disconnect is typical. Editions of Ralegh's seminal Americana appearing outside of England often bear only a tenuous connection to the original. The text, quite simply, was handled differently in the diverse contexts of its republication. From these various strategies of production, moreover, one can deduce competing patterns of consumption, models of bibliographic use that suggest contrasting processes of "reading" Ralegh. To read of tropical marvels is not to read of English challenges to

PLATE 9. *De Bry engraving of Pict woman, based on John White drawings, in Thomas Har[r]iot,* A Briefe and True Report of the New Found Land of Virginia *(Frankfurt, 1590). By permission of The Huntington Library, San Marino, California*

Spanish arms. And to gaze on headless men and warrior women is not to read at all. The effect on the reader of the more visual treatments that characterize editions of Ralegh published abroad—and the consequent influence of the fantastic engravings on prevailing notions of England's Atlantic-world enterprise—must have been significant. These non-English editions of the *Discovery* encourage yet another sort of engagement with Guiana and with the New World more generally that would have been quicker and more emblematic in nature. In fact, this emblematic style of representation enjoyed increasing popularity in printed Americana of this period. It was the wildly successful format adopted by de Bry and the Amsterdam-based Claesz for their influential editions of Bartolomé de Las Casas's *Brevíssima relación de la destruyción de las Indias* (Seville, 1552)—perhaps the single most influential publication on America in the early modern period.[40] De Bry, in all events, by anthologizing, illustrating, and, not least, upgrading (in terms of the category and cost of publication) Ralegh's *Discovery of Guiana* produced yet another form of the text. Along with the Hulsius and Claesz editions, it should register as a different product than the original English and be handled by critics accordingly.[41]

Reading Ralegh's America

Reading Ralegh's America is a trickier proposition than might, at first blush, appear to be the case. Along with the rigorous and close readings that such early modern texts demand, Ralegh's New World prose requires an equally rigorous investigation of the media of its delivery—of its biblio-

40. Bartolomé de Las Casas, *Narratio regionum Indicarum per Hispanos quosdam devastatarum verissima . . .* (Frankfurt, 1598), and *Spieghel der Spaenscher tyrannye in West-Indien* (Amsterdam, 1607). On the work's phenomenal popularity, see Alden and Landis, *European Americana,* I-II; and Benjamin Schmidt, "The Purpose of Pirates; or, Assimilating New Worlds in the Renaissance," in Willem Klooster and Alfred Padula, eds., *The Atlantic World: Essays on Slavery, Migration, and Imagination* (Upper Saddle River, N.J., 2004), 160-175.

41. Note, finally, that *Discovery* came out, perhaps most prominently for English readers, in Richard Hakluyt's *Principal Navigations, Voyages, Traffiques and Discoveries of the English Nation . . . ,* 3 vols (London, 1598-1600), and that this version—like the others reviewed in this section—would have provided an altogether different look, prompting an altogether different effect, than Ralegh's original. Ralegh's text was one of many in this sometimes overwhelming volume; and one imagines readers consulting this version of the *Discovery* rather than reading it—much as readers might have consulted passages of the similarly gargantuan *History of the World.*

graphic forms and of its strategies of textual representation. Any analysis of *Discovery of Guiana* (or, for that matter, any other leading sample of early Americana) demands that we first comprehend, most basically, what ended up in readers' hands. *The Discovery of Guiana* was both a popular and a pliable text; it took on myriad forms that would ultimately have imparted multiple messages. Historical processes of reading—or better, consuming—texts, so notoriously difficult to trace, can be better illuminated by paying attention to methods of production and by tracing the forms as well as meanings of texts. The case of Sir Walter Ralegh demonstrates the complex exercise of making, distributing, and assimilating literature: Ralegh read and was read, wrote and was rewritten, in a fascinating variety of ways. He offers a highly instructive example of literary engagement from the perspectives of both the producer and the consumer.

Ralegh (in collaboration with his printer: a fairly important caveat) produced two notably different books in *Discovery of Guiana* and *History of the World,* and these books would have induced two dissonant experiences of reading. *History of the World* would likely have appealed to the Gabriel Harvey set: it embodies precisely the sort of text that a humanist-trained reader, "studied for action," would have delved into and dissected in the company of learned colleagues, who would have picked their passages and cross-referenced their arguments with the ample assistance of the bibliographic devices. *Discovery of Guiana* invited a more "extensive" reading pattern in the sense that historians of reading use that expression with reference to the *Lesewut* (reading craze) of the eighteenth century.[42] The original text of *Discovery of Guiana* is designed to be read rapidly and in its entirety; reading bits and pieces with the goal of textual pilpul makes little sense. It is not, of course, that *Discovery of Guiana* is an avatar of the eighteenth-century "reading revolution" but rather that the genres of travel literature and colonial polemic invited this sort of treatment—just as they invited different strategies of reading from Ralegh himself, when he took his preparatory literary paces for his New World excursions.

All of which is not to conclude that Ralegh's Americana induced a new kind of reading—or, more broadly, that the literary treatment of America

42. See, for example, the discussion in Roger Chartier, *Forms and Meanings: Texts, Performances, and Audiences from Codex to Computer* (Philadelphia, 1995), 17; and cf. Rolf Engelsing, "Die Perioden der Lesergeschichte in der Neuzeit: Das statistische Ausmaß und die soziokulturelle Bedeutung der Lektüre," *Archiv für Geschichte des Buchwesens,* X (1970), 945-1002.

from this period was designed to be read rapidly and expeditiously, while the genre of history was best enjoyed in small and intensive bursts. There are certainly samples of early Americana that replicate the format of *History of the World*—Johannes de Laet's comparably sized *Nieuwe wereldt ofte Beschrijvinghe van West-Indien* (Leyden, 1630) comes to mind, as does Caspar Barlaeus's magnificently illustrated history of Brazil, *Rerum per Octennium in Brasilia* (Amsterdam, 1647), both products of the Dutch publishing trade—just as there were polemical brands of history composed with the same relentless intensity as *Discovery of Guiana*. This bibliographic opposition makes sense only for the case of Ralegh. In fact, the translations of *Discovery of Guiana*—promptly into Latin, German, and Dutch, the latter to become the single most durable language of its publication over the whole of the early modern period—suggest wholly different forms of book, text, and reading: often briefer and streamlined texts, decorated with fabulous illustrations, and commonly accompanied by the widely distributed pull-out map of Jodocus Hondius, which featured some of the more Mandevillean creatures gleaned from Ralegh's imagination. These formats highlighted a different set of themes than the 1596 English edition; and they would have stimulated a different mode of engagement with their consistently less sharp, less politically charged, and more sensational product. They underscore how difficult it is to speak of a singular text that accords with Ralegh's *Discovery of Guiana*.

And this is really the point: an inquiry into Ralegh's Americana—both the works on America that Ralegh read and Ralegh's own writings on America as they were read by others—illustrates the multiple manners of reading, consuming, and appropriating texts. It suggests the broader necessity of rethinking our tendency to speak about *the* text, as if all forms of a text function the same way and can be treated alike—as if individual texts have a singular way to be read. It may also serve to shift our attention to the actual form in which the text was delivered—the book—and to how this particular medium might have been handled and read in the early modern world. Most important, it points to the role of genre in the process of reading: how genre compelled reading habits and induced disparate writing and publishing practices in the production of early Americana. The history of reading cannot focus merely on the action of the reader (Grafton and Jardine's "studied for action") but must further endeavor to study the form of the text. It should not attend only to the physicality of the text, for that matter (Chartier's "forms and meanings"), but also to the literary genres and conventions of their delivery. Ultimately, an inquiry into Ralegh's reading of America should provoke new ways of thinking about those signal Americana that we routinely discuss and critique to comprehend the earliest encounters with the New World. And better understanding textual encounters should allow for a smoother sailing in the rough waters of real-life encounters—such as those that took place between the Atlantic world and Virginia from 1550 to 1624.

David S. Shields

THE GENIUS OF ANCIENT BRITAIN

What does Captain John Smith's life mean four hundred years after his landing in Jamestown? The answer is complicated. If one were to judge by the Commonwealth of Virginia's gala "America's 400th Anniversary," it would appear not much. In the welter of tall ship cruises, Native America symposia, democracy fora, African-American cultural events, artifact displays, and teacher lesson plans, the captain proves an elusive presence, meriting a quarter of a sentence in the school instructional packet "Arrival at Jamestown: The Need for Leadership." In Jamestown's archaeological center, the star attraction is the exhumed leader of the colony, "Bartholemew Gosnold," and the bulletins from archaeologist Bill Kelso and company have promoted Gosnold as the force for civil order—at the expense of Smith. Yet the Library of America did not prepare a commemorative volume of thoughts of Bartholemew Gosnold; it added an anthology of Captain John Smith's writings to its library of American classics. If one turns to mass culture, the old image of Smith as cross-cultural suitor, the boyfriend of Pocahontas, retains its centuries-long grip on the popular imagination. Even Terence Malick's cinematic meditation on the 1607 encounter between the English and the Natives, "A New World," could not escape the fascination. What is a Captain John Smith reenactor to do? Is he fated forever to play the awkward martial suitor (a Lincolnshire version of Sir Darby O'Bluster) to the Native princess, or the small-scale Anglo conquistador, a vainglorious white man bullying his way into history?

Part of the problem lies with Smith's own self-presentation. I don't refer to his penchant for bragging or the incredibility of his adventures. I speak of a more fundamental problem, a difficulty perhaps more visible to literary historians than to other scholars. Smith's persona has suffered from being projected through two genres that are at cross-purposes. When putting "I" on the paper or "Captain Smith" (he had a penchant for speaking of himself in the third person), Smith found himself torn between framing himself as the hero of epic history and as the man of ideas of Diogenes Laertius's biographies of ancient worthies, between imagining himself an actor and envisioning himself a thinker.

His biographers have complicated matters further, by viewing him as a romantic misadventurer. But the circumstances that shaped Smith's messy and energetic self-fashioning explain, in a way, his peculiar oscillation between the roles of action hero and imperial sage in his writings from 1612 to 1631. Emphasizing the Laertian strain will suggest how Smith's durability through the ages has depended on his binding of his life to a set of ideas with a political future. As a sage, he was more prophet than philosopher, more politician than historian. In short, I propose a new way of looking at his life from his departure from Virginia in 1609 to his death in 1631.

Memory tends to frame the Elizabethan adventurers—the royal suitors, sea dogs, projectors, and explorers—in one of two literary modes: epic or romance. Sir Francis Drake appeared so much the figure of imperial destiny and providential victory that he was enshrined in epic. Even his Spanish enemies sang his deeds to Calliope's measure—Lope de Vega's *Dragontea* (1598) and Martín Barco de Centenera's *Argentina y conquisto del Río de la Plata* (1602) present much the same monster of energy found in Charles FitzGeffrey's *Sir Francis Drake, His Honorable Lifes Commendaton, and His Tragical Deathes Lamentation* (1596). In contrast, the histories of Sir Walter Ralegh—Margaret Irwin's *That Great Lucifer: A Portrait of Sir Walter Raleigh* (1960), Ralegh Treveleyan's *Sir Walter Raleigh* (2002)—have tended to that discourse associated with chronicling frustration and failure, the romance. Smith's memorializers have disagreed on how to speak of him from the first. Is he epic hero, fraudulent buffoon, or romantic failure?[1] To this day the dilemma continues. Leo Lemay exalts him as the creator of the American Dream. Dennis Montgomery reviles him as a self-serving political bullyboy. And his most widely read biographer, Philip Barbour, a victim of providence and the English class system. Barbour's standard biography, *The Three Worlds of Captain John Smith,* is a romance of failure and exerts an influence even among New Historicist expositors of the Captain's career.[2]

Smith is the victim of mendacious reprobates in the Virginia Company who quash his testimonies and projects to cover their lies and maladminis-

1. The epic-romance distinction here is one of the findings of David Quint, *Epic and Empire: Politics and Generic Form from Virgil to Milton* (Princeton, N.J., 1993).

2. Dennis Montgomery, "Captain John Smith," *Colonial Williamsburg,* XVI, no. 3 (Spring 1994), 42–52; J. A. Leo Lemay, *The American Dream of Captain John Smith* (Charlottesville, Va., 1991); Philip L. Barbour, *The Three Worlds of Captain John Smith* (Boston, 1964)—the most informative biography of Smith, by the editor of his collected works.

PLATE I. *Captain John Smith. Detail from John Smith's* Map of New England.
Portrait attributed to Simon van de Passe. Courtesy of The Library of Virginia

tration. His dreams of creating New England are dashed by pirates, muti-
neers, harsh weather, empty promises, undercapitalization, and misinfor-
mation floated by his enemies. When New England is finally planted, Miles
Standish and John Endicott, not Smith, serve as the plantation's valorous
knights. Landless, loveless, and seemingly useless, Smith sublimates his
enormous energy into writing and rewriting accounts of Virginia in which
his own role in the colony's preservation swells to monstrous proportions.

Before he dies, he encounters Pocahontas in court dress in London, her face marred by pox and her soul cankered by the misdeeds of Smith's successors in her homeland. She pleads for him to return and restore order. Smith must disappoint her by refusing. It is not in his power. Nothing is in his power before he dies.

That was not how his associates saw the "Sometime Governor of Virginia and Admiral of New England" when they laid him to rest in June 1631 in Saint Sepulchre's Church in London. To the writer of his epitaph Smith's life had to be elegized in heroic measure:

> Here lyes one conquered that hath conquered Kings.
> Subdu'd large Territories, and done things
> Which to the World impossible would seem,
> But that the Truth is held in more esteem.
> Shall I report his former Service done
> In honour of his God and Christendom?
> How that he did divide from Pagans three
> Their Heads and Lives, Types of his Chivalry?
>
> . . . .
>
> Or shall I tell of his Adventures since,
> Done in Virginia, that large Continent?
> How that he subdu'd Kings unto his Yoke,
> And made those Heathen flee, as Wind doth Smoke:
> And made their land, being of so large a Station,
> An Habitation for our Christian Nation,
> Where God is glorify'd, their Wants supply'd;
> Which else, for Necessaries must have dy'd.
> But what avails his Conquests, now he lyes
> Interr'd in Earth, a Prey to Worms and Flyes?
> O! May his Soul in sweet Elysium sleep,
> Until the Keeper that all Souls doth keep,
> Return to Judgment; and that after thence,
> With Angels he may have his Recompence.[3]

He was to his memorialist a chivalrous Christian knight, an evangelist, crusader, and nation builder—a man whose exploits verged on the incredible. This was no isolated testimony. Smith was the rare Elizabethan who saw his own life celebrated on the stage. Richard Gunnell's *Hungarian Lion*

3. "Original Epitaph in St. Sepulchre's Church, London," in Philip L. Barbour, ed., *The Complete Works of Captain John Smith,* 3 vols. (Chapel Hill, N.C., 1986), III, 390.

(1623) celebrated Smith's service on behalf of the prince of Hungary in the war against the Ottoman Turks. If some filmmaker of the future wished to break the thrall of Pocahontas on the popular imagining of Smith's life and present a new film narrative, the opening scene would be Smith in the audience of the New Fortune playhouse witnessing with profound discomfort his representation as a miles gloriosus, inventing signal systems and beheading Turks. From the remarks of one of the poets prefacing a New England tract, we know Smith had mixed feelings about the play. His pride as a martial man was gratified, yet he knew that he had ceased to be that man. He struggled toward another identity, that of a man of learning.

Smith reckoned prose, not dramatic poetry, the proper medium for presenting the meaning of his life. His one confessed model for his writing, Julius Caesar's *Gallic Wars,* combined a matter-of-fact chronicle of extraordinary actions with lessons learned from a broad experience of the world. Smith, however, lacked Caesar's clarity of expression and mastery of circumstance. The Captain's histories tended at times to antic self-assertion and bald rhetoric. And there was the inescapable problem that action in Smith's life never led to satisfaction but led to frustrations of various sorts. He chose the wrong genre. Neither romantic history nor action-adventure memoir was appropriate for framing Smith's meaning, though prose was and is the proper medium. During Smith's lifetime there existed a form of memoir more suitable than Caesar's for capturing what Smith was about. Diogenes Laertius's *Lives of the Eminent Philosophers* viewed life as a process of shaping an enduring idea, doctrine, argument, or way of speaking. Of early modern prose genres, it is the most apt for presenting a life that began in action but transmuted to idea. Like Diogenes Laertius, we can first inspect in a bald abstract the intellectual telos of John Smith's life, then review certain episodes and ideas in detail.[4]

A Brief Narrative

The November 1609 injury that forced Smith's departure from Virginia (the matchlock dropped into his lap that ignited a powder bag dangling from his belt) destroyed Smith's genitals.[5] Deprived by accident, or per-

---

4. Diogenes Laertius's *De vita et moribus philosophorum* became available to the learned world in Europe through Ambrosius Traversarius's 1435 Latin edition prepared for Cosimo Medici.

5. Lemay, *American Dream of Captain John Smith,* 105. Smith's narrative: "accidentallie, one fired his powder bag, which tore his flesh from his bodie and thighes, 9. or 10. inches square in a most pittifull manner" (*Complete Works of Captain John Smith,* I, 272).

haps by an assassination attempt in the guise of an accident, of the chance of founding a family, the honor of having his memory blessed by his posterity, he was forcibly displaced from the dynastic preoccupations of the governing class of his time and place. The accident conditioned all of Smith's subsequent career in letters. Once one is cognizant of the fact of Smith's emasculation and exclusion from the reproductive economy, certain quirks of his prose take on sense—his compensatory masculine posturing, his preoccupation with the virile body—that of the Susquehanna Indians particularly—and his repeated and poignant references to "posterity": those descendants who bless the labor of the virtuous patriarch. Indeed Smith's justification for all colonial enterprise derives from a notion of paternal legacy:

> Noah and his family began againe the second plantation, and their seed as it still increased, hath still planted new Countries, and one Country another, and so the world to that estate it is; but not without much hazard, travell, mortalities, discontents, and many disasters: had those worthy Fathers and their memorable off-spring not beene more diligent for us now in those ages, than wee are to plant that yet unplanted for after-livers. Had the seed of Abraham, our Saviour Christ Jesus and his Apostles, exposed themselves to no more dangers to plant the Gospell wee so much professe, than we, even we our selves had at this present beene as Salvages, and as miserable as the most barbarous Salvage, yet uncivilized. The Hebrewes, Lacedemonians, the Goths, Grecians, Romans, and the rest, what was it they would not undertake to inlarge their Territories, inrich their subjects, and resist their enemies. Those that were the founders of those great Monarchies and their vertues, were no silvered idle golden Pharisies, but industrious honest hearted Publicans, they regarded more provisions and necessaries for their people, than jewels, ease and delight for themselves; riches was their servants, not their masters; they ruled as fathers, not as tyrants; their people as children, not as slaves.[6]

Smith's appearance in prose, his invocations of posterity and plantations, would be his worldly immortality. He turned to literature rather than progeny and property for his reputation's futurity. While some commentators have noted his connection to the literary world of the theater (a world in which Ben Jonson and William Shakespeare were creating a new myth of

6. John Smith, *Advertisements for the Unexperienced Planters of New England, or Any Where; or, The Path-way to Experience to Erect a Plantation* (London, 1631), in *Complete Works of Captain John Smith*, III, 274–275.

belletristic immortalization), Smith did not embrace this model of enduring fame, so much as the older tradition of learning. The learned in 1610 England were dominated by William Camden, the historian, and his disciples, the circle of antiquaries. These figures had absorbed the Italian humanist fascination with geography as a register of national history, and cartography as its modern expression. Smith crafted his first post-Virginia literary work to speak directly to these concerns, *A Map of Virginia, with a Description of the Countrey, the Commodities, People, Government, and Religion* (1612), published at Oxford, not London. Smith successfully secured the notice of the Camdenites by joining their world. In particular, he became attached to Camden's protégé, Sir Robert Bruce Cotton, the scholar, sometime member of Parliament, and government official who collected the corpus of Anglo-Saxon writings and whose library, located next to the Houses of Parliament, became the meeting place of the opposition to Charles I's attempt to institute absolute monarchy.[7]

In this circle the myths of the antiquity of Parliament, a Gothic heritage of personal liberty, and the cultural value of the yeomanry were promulgated. Cotton regarded Smith as a modern embodiment of ancient valor and prompted him to write his memoirs, *The True Travels, Adventures, and Observations of Captaine John Smith* (1630). Smith in turn absorbed the political philosophy of the Cotton circle, yet instead of locating liberty and the self-fulfillment of the commonality in an ancient English past, Smith projected it to an American futurity. In sum, Smith's politics were absorbed directly from John Selden, John Pym, Edward Coke, and Cotton—the framers of the 1628 Parliamentary Petition of Right, the early theoreticians of the parliamentary revolution—and were translated to America by means of his works of the 1620s. His ideas have proved sufficiently potent to accomplish what he wished. They keep the captain's name alive and distinct from the multitude who bore that commonest of English names.[8]

7. H. R. Trevor-Roper, *Queen Elizabeth's First Historian: William Camden and the Beginnings of English 'Civil History'* (London, 1971); Richard Helgerson, "The Land Speaks," in Helgerson, *Forms of Nationhood: The Elizabethan Writing of England* (Chicago, 1992), 107–147. Kevin Sharpe has written the standard account of Cotton's career: *Sir Robert Cotton, 1586–1631: History and Politics in Early Modern England* (Oxford, 1979).

On Oxford publication: there is no evidence that the presses in London had been closed to Smith through the influence of the Virginia Company.

8. Matthew A. Fitzsimons, "Politics and Men of Learning in England, 1540–1640," *Review of Politics,* VI (1944), 452–483; J. A. Guy, "The Origins of the Petition of Right Reconsidered," *Historical Journal,* XXV (1982), 289–312. John Selden (1584–1654), a

To understand the context of Smith's installation into Sir Robert Bruce Cotton's circle, we must briefly review the chronology of Smith's activities from 1623 to 1630. In 1623, Richard Gunnell, master of the New Fortune playhouse, staged *The Hungarian Lion,* banking on the enduring popular interest in the contest of the Ottoman Turks with Christendom. A caricature of Smith appeared conspicuously in the action. In 1624, Smith's *Generall Historie of Virginia, New-England, and the Summer Isles* appeared coincidentally with the resumption of animosity between England and Spain and the abrogation of the Virginia Company's charter, and its publication vested Smith with some celebrity. The prefatory poems of the *Generall Historie* played up two heroic ideas. One, punning Smith's name, emphasized Smith as one who forges nations into being, shaping raw material into useful form by will and skill. The other emphasized the scope of Smith's travel and experience, arguing that few matched Smith's worldly wisdom because few had seen and worked in so much of the world.[9]

-----

graduate of Hart Hall, Oxford, and member of Clifford's Inn, began his career as a legal scholar copying records for Cotton in the Tower of London. A legal and political historian, he wrote on the early history of the law, preconquest civil administration, and the status of titles. His treatise *On Tithes* irritated the Established Church, which sought the work's repression. Selden entered politics in response to this censorship. He drafted (perhaps at Edward Coke's request) the 1621 parliamentary declaration of rights and privileges and was arrested for his contributions. After release, he won election to the Commons from Lancaster and sat with Coke and Pym on the committee deciding the election of Sir John Glanville. He was a mover in the impeachment of Buckingham and a coauthor of the Petition of Right, for which he was incarcerated in the Tower for eight months and Marshalsea Prison for a shorter term. Upon release he sought peace, retiring to the earl of Kent's estate and compiling at Cotton's suggestion a catalog of the Arundel marbles. Later in his career he served as keeper of the records in the Tower.

John Pym (1583–1643) was educated at Broadgates Hall, Oxford, and became a member of the Middle Temple. A member of Parliament in 1621, he was in the group promoting Selden's declaration. He, like Selden, was arrested. A Puritan and staunch anti-Catholic, he worked with Edwin Sandys (of the Virginia Company) in drafting legislation denying Roman Catholics legal privileges. He coauthored with Selden the Petition of Right in 1626, drawing heavily on Cotton's scholarship. Legend has it that Pym, after Charles I's assumption of personal rule in the wake of Buckingham's assassination, planned to emigrate to New England with Cromwell and Hampden, but was restrained by royal decree. Whatever the truth to this rumor, from 1629 onward Pym displayed a marked interest in colonial ventures, serving as a patentee for Providence Island and Connecticut. A great parliamentary speaker, Pym was the leader of the Short Parliament.

9. Philip Barbour, "Captain John Smith and the London Theatre," *Virginia Magazine of History and Biography,* LXXXIII (1975), 277–279.

During the following year, a manuscript that Smith had prepared treating his early career as a soldier in Europe, including his beheading three Turks outside Alba Regis in solo tournament combat, saw print in Samuel Purchas's *Hakluytus Posthumus*. Smith then banked on his name by publishing two works on the language and practice of seamanship just as the Anglo-Spanish war stimulated interest in maritime power. In these works, which offered a survey of the language of the sea as a "Path-way to Experience," Smith moved from epic nation maker to Laertian sage. Wye Saltonstall, who wrote a prefatory commendation, dubbed Smith the master of navigational science, who first ordered its terms of art: "Now th' untraveld land-man may with ease / Here know the language both of ships and Seas." Physician Edward Jordan exalts Smith for giving order to a body of terms so obscure in their origins and odd in their usage that it would have challenged "Camden, Clenard, Ramus, Lilly," and even the grammarian Scaliger. His first tract, *An Accidence; or, The Path-way to Experience* did so well in the market place that the expanded and more systematic *Sea Grammar, with the Plaine Exposition of Smiths Accidence for Young Sea-men* issued quickly from John Haviland's press. It particularly attracted the notice of Camden's followers.[10]

In 1626, James I died, and Charles I took the throne. The succession galvanized Puritan efforts to move overseas for protection. John Winthrop and the Puritan leaders negotiated with Smith but decided against incorporating him into their colonization effort. By 1628, he knew that his years of effort to found New England would not personally benefit him. He would govern no English colony again. Forestalled from future glory as defender of New England, he sought to fix his experience in the minds of posterity as expositer of the meaning of colonization.

When keeping one's name lustrous, it is good to have a curator of reputations as a champion. At the end of his life, Captain John Smith had the greatest. "That most learned Treasurer of Antiquitie," Sir Robert Bruce Cotton, appears in the first pages of Smith's memoirs as the instigator of *The True Travels, Adventures, and Observations of Captaine John Smith*. Cotton had urged Smith to record an authentic account of his life to counteract the fancies that Gunnell had staged. Cotton was singularly concerned with

10. Samuel Purchas, *Hakluytus Posthumus; or, Purchas His Pilgrimes* (London, 1625), part 2, 1361–1370; W[ye] S[altonstall], "In Authorem," in *A Sea Grammar, with the Plaine Exposition of Smiths Accidence for Young Sea-men* (London, 1627), in *Complete Works of Captain John Smith*, III 52; Edw[ard] Jorden, "To His Friend Captaine Smith, on His Grammar," ibid., 51–52.

the issue of misrepresentation at the time, attempting to counter Charles I's contention that English kings in ancient times ruled without the advice and consent of Parliament. Cotton's library was the most telling witness against the royal claim. Cotton's shelves supported the most extraordinary collection of early English manuscripts ever assembled: the Anglo-Saxon charters, King Alfred's verse translation of Boethius's *Consolation of Philosophy*, two copies of the Magna Carta, Alcuin's letters, Aelfric's homilies, *The Anglo-Saxon Chronicle, The Battle of Malden, Sir Gawain and the Green Knight,* the sole surviving text of *Beowulf.* The materials certified the antiquity of Parliament and the reign of law. And in the library the parliamentary opposition to the king met—John Pym, John Selden, and Cotton himself—until Charles I had Cotton and the others arrested in 1629 and seized the library.[11]

Cotton's library came into being because that of the College of Antiquaries did not. At some juncture during the 1580s, a group of William Camden's colleagues and followers petitioned for a charter to Queen Elizabeth to form an academy devoted to the study of English antiquities "of which the Universities, being busy in the arts take little care of or regard." Enabling the work of this company would be a library "well furnished with diverse ancient books and monuments of Antiquities." While the society came into existence, the library failed to materialize. The society proved to be an intellectual force of a decidedly political bent. Each meeting explored two questions posed by the membership. The members (twenty of twenty-seven known participants) were lawyers, including eminent figures such as William Hakewill and Sir Henry Spelman. (Spelman, who prepared portions of the charter for Massachusetts Bay, might have been the intermediary in the interviews that took place between Captain John Smith and the leaders of the planned Puritan colony.) Many of the society's inquiries revolved around the history of English law, particularly whether the customs and precedents that made up the English common law were continuous with the feudal law of postconquest England and the civil law of early modern humanism. John Selden summarized the antiquarians' conclusion in *The Reverse or Back-face of the English Janus:* William the Conqueror's

11. John Smith, *The True Travels, Adventures, and Observations of Captaine John Smith, in Europe, Asia, Affrica, and America, from Anno Domini 1595 to 1629* (London, 1630), in *Complete Works of Captain John Smith,* III; Joseph Planta, *A Catalogue of the Manuscripts in the Cottonian Library Deposited in the British Museum* (London, 1802). On Cotton: *DNB,* s.v. "Cotton, Sir Robert Bruce." The library was seized in 1629. Coke was appointed by the Crown to examine its contents. After Cotton's death in 1631, the crown restored the collection to his son. His grandson bequeathed the collection to the nation in 1700.

sword severed any governmental and legal continuity from Anglo-Saxon England and the laws of Edward the Confessor. Antiquarian Cotton glossed Selden's conclusion with his observation, "The people brought under by the Sword of William and his followers to subjected vassalage could not possess . . . the right of their former liberties." There was only one means of recovering those liberties, and that was by recovering the customs and precedents of immemorial justice contained in the English common law. This required a heroic antiquarian recovery of those texts that preserved the customs (poetry) and precedents (chronicles, charters, histories, ancient judgments, findings) of preconquest England. The original antiquarians were disbanded in 1614 before a library could be gathered, because their politics offended James I. But Robert Bruce Cotton, ex-antiquarian, realized that a private library abutting the halls of Parliament might ensure the continuance of ancient English liberty and had begun assembling manuscripts in the 1590s. It was the most assiduous user of Cotton's library, Sir Edward Coke, who identified the common law with Parliamentary prerogative and sought to systematize and adapt the common law to the emerging commercial nation in the *Institutes of the Lawes of England* (1608).[12]

Coke believed that preconquest law was the "best inheritance" an English subject possessed. His defense of Anglo-Saxon liberties conflated with a defense property against nonparliamentary taxation. As Christopher Hill has argued, Coke saw the parliamentary franchise itself as a property right, and for this reason Charles I would not allow the later parts of Coke's Institutes to be published. John Pym during the debate over the 1628 parliamentary Petition of Right against Charles's imposition argued that the Anglo-Saxon legal legacies "were of that vigour and force as to overlive the Conquerer; nay, to give bounds and limits to the Conqueror." Coke fretted, "I fear that many want true knowledge of this ancient birth-right." Sir Robert Bruce Cotton's library was where the true knowledge was preserved, where the historians and lawyers convened to gather up the legacies, and where politicians conspired to frustrate the rule by monarchs who wished to revive the absolute rule that William the Conqueror had imposed on England.[13]

12. Sir Richard Gough, "An Historical Account of the Origin and Establishment of the Society of Antiquaries," *Archaeologia,* I (1779), i–xliii; Hope Mirrlees, *A Fly in Amber, Being an Extravagant Biography of the Roman Antiquary Sir Robert Bruce Cotton* (London, 1962), 104–139; John Selden, *The Reverse or Back-face of the English Janus* (London, 1682), gathered also in *Tracts Written by John Selden of the Innter-Temple, Esquire* (London, 1683); James Howell, *Cottoni Posthuma: Diverse Choice Pieces of That Renowned Antiquary, Sir Robert Cotton* (London, 1679), 20.

13. Christopher Hill, *Intellectual Origins of the English Revolution Revisited* (Ox-

Captain John Smith belonged to the company that came to Cotton's library. Why did Cotton, arguably the most bookish and past-obsessed man of his generation, take a shine to Smith so much as to encourage him to write a narrative of his life? Smith explained, "Cotton . . . having by purusall of my Generall Historie, and others, found that I had likewise undergone divers other as hard hazards in the other parts of the world, requested me to fix the whole course of my passage in a booke by it selfe." The man of books was entranced by the tales of action and adventure. Smith seemed a Beowulf incarnate—an avatar of ancient energy—at times a martial Roman, at others a freedom-loving Saxon, or, in his more refined moments, a latter-day member of Arthur's round table, an embodiment of knightly virtue. The story of Smith's beheading three Turks in single tournament combat outside the city of Alba Regis in Transylvania, a fragment of Smith's early career that appeared in Purchas and on stage, recounted what might have been the last recorded deed of knightly chivalry in the West. Its resonance would not have been lost on the discoverer of the manuscript of *Sir Gawain and the Green Knight*.[14]

We should not underestimate what meeting an avatar of primitive virtue meant to Cotton and his circle. Cotton's mentor, William Camden, had lauded Roman Britain as the grounds of English civility and political maturity. Yet Cotton and his fellow antiquaries of the younger generation saw Anglo-Saxon England as the seedbed of English liberty. Camden's contemporary William Lambarde, who expounded the pre-Norman genesis of the English legal code in his *Archaionomia* (1568), and the antiquity of the judiciary in *Eirenarcha; or, Of the Office of the Justices of Peace* (1581) and *Archeion; or, A Discourse upon the High Courts of Justice in England* (1635), exerted a more potent influence on the political understanding of the habitués of Cotton's library. In particular, Lambarde's elaboration of the origins of Parliament in the witenagemot, which stressed that the "Witena"—the wise heads—"doth include the *Nobilitie* and *Commons*," was adopted by Cotton as the premise of his understanding of government. From Lambarde, Cotton elaborated a picture of the Anglo-Saxons in which commons did not differ greatly from the nobility, and both had a say in forming the

ford, 1997), 363; *A Declaration of the Grievances of the Kingdome Delivered in Parliament by John Pym, Esquier,* in *A Second Collection of Scarce and Valuable Tracts . . . of Lord Somers . . .* , part 2 (London, 1750), vi, 161; Edward Coke, "Proeme," *Third Part of the Institutes of the Lawes of England, concerning High Treason, and Other Pleas of the Crown and Criminal Causes* (London, 1644).

14. Smith, *True Travels,* in *Complete Works of Captain John Smith,* III, 141.

laws of the land. In the mid-1610s, Cotton composed his own meditation on the Saxon creation, Parliament.[15]

For Cotton the Anglo-Saxons lived ideals, acted values. There was no separation between action and philosophy. Parliament itself was where action and thought coalesced into nation and national character. Parliament remained for Cotton the one vehicle by which an England suffering from the growing influence of George Villiers, first duke of Buckingham, and aristocracy might revert to its primordial liberty and character. In the early 1620s, Cotton celebrated parliamentary power and the conjoint authority of king and Parliament. With the accession of Charles I to the throne and the elevation of Buckingham to executive power, the challenge to parliamentary authority turned critical. The monarch preferred to rule with the aid of his council, not with the advice and consent of Parliament. Against this titled cabal, this rule by courtiers, Cotton, Pym, Selden, and Oliver St. John asserted the ancient liberties of the nation and the ancient jurisdiction of Commons. In Smith they glimpsed one of the heroic ancients in their midst, a Saxon man of action, a pragmatic wise head, a warrior of Roman energy. Richard James, Cotton's librarian and Camden's student, wrote that Smith's "sword and pen in bold, ruffe, Martiall wise, / Put forth to try and beare away the prize, / from Caesar." Like Caesar's recollections, like the sagas sung in the mead halls of the North Atlantic, like the chivalric romances told by minstrels, Smith's tales of derring-do in Europe, Africa, and America resounded with a spirit bolder and larger than that of the moment. As librarian James remarked, "our age / Is now at large a Bedlem or a Stage."[16]

Smith's valor was wonderfully ambiguous. It could be stoically Roman, bardicly bumptious and violent, or chivalric and contemplative. The last style played directly to Cotton and his circle's mystification of things Elizabethan in the face of Charles's and Buckingham's innovations. Elizabeth had cherished chivalric nostalgia, encouraging the Accession Day tilts and neochivalric pageants of the 1590s. In one episode written specifically for *True Travels* and Cotton, Smith revived a potent emblem of chivalric nostalgia: the hermit knight. Smith in this story is eighteen years old, having experienced war and won a reputation on the field:

---

15. William Lambarde, *Archeion; or, A Discourse upon the High Courts of Justice in England,* rev. and enl. (London, 1635), 2; Egerton MS 2975, fols. 30–32v, British Library. William Dunkel, *William Lambarde, Elizabethan Jurist, 1536-1601* (New Brunswick, N.J., 1965), is the best summary view of this thinker and his influence.

16. Rich[ard] James III, "To My Worthy Friend, Captaine John Smith," in Smith, *True Travels,* in *Complete Works of Captain John Smith,* III, 147.

After much kinde usage amongst those honest Scots at Ripweth and Broxmoth, but neither money nore meanes to make him a Courtier, he returned to Willoughby in Lincoln-shire; where within a short time being glutted with too much company, wherein he took small delight, he retired himself into a little wooddie pasture, a good way from any towne, invironed with many hundred Acres of other woods: Here by a faire brook he built a Pavillion of boughes, where only in his cloaths he lay. His studie was Machiavills Art of warre, and Marcus Aurelius, his exercise a good horse, with his lance and Ring; his food was thought to be more of venison than any thing else; what he wanted his man brought him. The countrey wondering at such an Hermite; His friends perswaded one Seignior Theadora Polaloga, Rider to Henry Earle of Lincolne, an exellent Horse-man and noble Italian Gentleman, to insinuate into his wooddish acquaintance, whose Languages and good discourse, and exercise of riding drew him to stay with him at Tattersall. Long these pleasures could not content him, but hee returned againe to the Low-Countreyes.[17]

Certain features of this account fascinate. His contemplative reading, Machiavelli and Marcus Aurelius, played to the intellectual commitments of the Camden group within the Antiquaries, who were significant in promoting both neostoicism and Italian humanist inquiry in England. The encounter with the old knight, Polaloga, a collateral descendant of Constantine XI (the last Byzantine emperor), who refined Smith's skills in both Italian and Greek and taught him the ancient arts of arms and horsemanship, gave him access to the last master of traditional martial arts in the land. Modern learning, languages, ancient ethics, and archaic skills: the paradox precisely suited the curious amalgam of contemporary politics and imaginative traditionalism that Cotton and the Antiquaries cultivated.

Smith knew what the learned read, but in all probability he did not venture into Cotton's library to burnish his rusty Latin or peruse the *Anglo-Saxon Chronicles*. Rather, he absorbed the intellectual atavisms through conversation. Yet there was one body of texts on the bookshelves that Smith desired greatly to study, Cotton's ample collection of writings in manuscript and print, ancient and modern, concerning the sea. Cotton and Smith were

17. Smith, *True Travels,* in *Complete Works of Captain John Smith,* III, 155–156. The Arthurian romance celebrated the figure in Sir Baudwin of Britayne, known to English readers since Caxton published Malory's *Morte d'Arthur* in 1485. In that same year Caxton published a translation of the handbook of theoretical chivalry, beloved of Elizabethans, the Catalan Ramon Llull's *True Order of Chivalry,* "attributed . . . to a hermit who was once a knight."

drawn together by a conviction that England's future lay in mastering the ocean. Both believed that consolidating naval power would ensure national greatness and that an armed state fleet was essential to the preservation of trade and the security of the homeland.[18] Cotton first manifested an interest in the navy in a tract of 1604, arguing for peace with Spain, entitled "Reasons to Maintain Navigation of the English Merchants with the East and West Indies," prepared for his patron, Henry Howard, earl of Northampton. It foresaw England's wealth accruing from maritime commerce with America. Its wealth of information led to Cotton's appointment to the commission investigating abuses in the navy in 1608–1609. In December 1626, during the revival of animosity with Spain, he was a moving force in the commission impaneled to reform the navy. In this year, Smith published *An Accidence; or, The Path-way to Experience, Necessary for All Young Sea-men.* Given Cotton's fascination with etymology as a historical tool—a legacy of his training with Camden—as well as his maritime interests, it was not remarkable that he made the acquaintance of the first lexicographer of England's maritime life to venture into print.

Once we grasp the shared faith in maritime power, we can see that Smith's autobiographical *True Travels* was designed for Cotton's library in two senses. Its first section, the memoir of Smith's rise to arts and arms, fulfilled Cotton's wish that the genius of ancient Britain be reborn in the age of the corrupt arch courtier, Buckingham. The second section, styled "The Continuation of the Generall Historie of Virginia," was something more than that. It argued from experience the necessity of a navy to support colonization, particularly since war with Spain had turned the imperial imagination toward the West Indies. Simultaneously, it projected anxiety at the possibility that English colonization efforts would be directed toward the Caribbean away from New England. John Pym was organizing the Providence Island venture as Smith wrote. Puritans in 1630 were migrating to the western Caribbean as well as Massachusetts Bay. Consequently, Smith examined England's colonization efforts in South America and the islands in chapters 21 through 27. In an account of his time in Nevis, Smith declared that all the get-rich-quick schemes of tropical plantations were doomed because the islands were "so open to any enimie." Only a navy in which the surplus of England's able seamen were well paid and well employed would prevent that restless population from turning pirate and trou-

18. And not just Smith and Cotton. John Selden would write the great defense of the liberty of the ocean in *Mare Clausum* (1635). See David Armitage, *The Ideological Origins of the British Empire* (Cambridge, 2000), 111–122.

bling the seas of the Old World and the New. Only a navy could protect the vulnerable colonies that might grow up in those places about which Drake had set England dreaming. The final chapter of the *True Travels* presented an either/or: piracy or honest service as seaman or soldier in America— anarchy or a standing navy.[19]

History would provide an odd fulfillment of Smith's projections when Cromwell's failed invasion of the Indies in 1656 left the Caribbean awash with unemployed sailors and surplus men of arms such as Captain Henry Morgan, who took up the cutlass and became the admiral of the buccaneers.

Cotton was a champion of an English maritime empire, for Smith was a prophet as well as the conservator of the nation's ancient liberty. Cotton's importance for Smith may be gauged in the forthrightness of his confession that the antiquary instigated the *True Travels.* At the time of the memoir's publication in 1630, Cotton was persona non grata at the court after his arrest. His librarian, Richard James, whose laudatory poem prefaced the *True Travels,* was also in bad odor for writing in defense of Buckingham's assassin. John Selden languished in jail along with Oliver St. John on suspicion of sedition. Smith in his acknowledgment asserted his solidarity with a man whose life as a politician was over and with a circle whose prospects looked dire. Cotton would die of grief, bereft of his books and manuscripts, in 1631.[20]

Smith by 1630 had come to believe that books themselves were acts, and libraries the memory of peoples preserved for posterity. This understanding complicated and enriched his original intuition that he might achieve personal immortality by being the interlocutor of a learned book. Camden's and Cotton's reconstruction of Roman imperial Britain and valorous Anglo-Saxon England showed that ancient ideals, primitive rights, great deeds, and great persons would not be forgotten. They were the very stuff of nationhood. The library itself was the message. The written past had the power to make a king quake. The king's seizure of Cotton's library could not quash the truths that had been read therein. More books would be written, more libraries gathered. Indeed, Smith set himself to this task, translating the political ideals to an America that was yet to come, rather than

19. Karen Ordhal Kupperman, *Providence Island, 1630-1641: The Other Puritan Colony* (Cambridge, 1993), 271-274, 321; Smith, *True Travels,* in *Complete Works of Captain John Smith,* III, 237.

20. Catherine Drinker Bowen, "Historians Courageous," American Philosophical Society, *Proceedings,* CI (1957), 253-254.

to an England that was. Smith's final years were spent furiously installing himself in print to fix himself in memory and renovate the ideals of the Cotton circle by dislodging them from their dangerous place in the realm of precedent.

When the *True Travels* issued from the press in 1630, Smith lived in the house of Sir Samuel Saltonstall. There he heard tidings of the success of Winthrop's settlement of Massachusetts. In unsure health but personally secure, he prepared his summary reflection on colonization, *Advertisements for the Unexperienced Planters of New England, or Any Where; or, The Pathway to Experience to Erect a Plantation* (1631). Though he spoke of undertaking a "History of the Sea" (the book that surely would have been the fruit of Smith's study in the libraries of his two patrons, Purchas and Cotton), *Advertisements* was his final book, and a valedictory tone sounded throughout the narrative. Smith spoke with the voice of hard wisdom. The political animus of his message remained, but enriched with a novel ecclesiological dimension.

Advertisements was dedicated to George Abbot, the archbishop of Canterbury, whose stand against the assertions of unlimited monarchial right had caused him to be deprived of his primacy in the Church of England in 1627 and enabled the elevation of his enemy William Laud, archbishop of London, to preeminent power. Just as Smith's dedication of the *True Travels* to Cotton during Cotton's eclipse attested a solidarity with the political principles of the framers of the parliamentary Petition of Right, so his dedication of *Advertisements* to Abbot during the archbishop's eclipse signaled Smith's support of the prelate's stand against untrammeled prerogative. In 1626, Buckingham attempted to promote support within the Church of England for the "Forced Loan," an extraparliamentary extraction of money from persons, corporations, and towns that masqueraded as a loan but would never be paid back. A substantial number of persons refused to pay the highly unpopular levy. The earl of Lincoln and seventy-six gentlemen were arrested for their refusal. Five knights in this company petitioned the Court of King's Bench for a writ of habeas corpus. The court did not find in their favor, thereby touching off a public opinion storm. Into this disturbance Buckingham wished to inject the calming voice of religious authority on behalf of royal prerogative and convinced Roger Maynwaring and Robert Sibthorp to deliver sermons proclaiming that the king, as God's earthly representative, should be obeyed cheerfully in all things not directly contradictory to the word of God. The king directed Abbot to license the printing of Sibthorp's sermon; Abbot refused, criticizing the ideal of absolute nonresistance to royal prerogative. For his action, Abbot was rusticated.[21]

Abbot projected into the realm of religion the principle of sovereign conscience, a sense of warranted personal righteousness that enabled resistance to unchecked executive power. Yet Abbot's ecclesiology contained other elements that appealed to Smith. The archbishop of Canterbury was well disposed to the Calvinist doctrines of sin and redemption and tolerated Puritans in pulpits so long as they conformed to the Church of England's orders of worship. Smith's own sympathies for nonseparating Reformed Christians, expressed in his respect for and support of the founders of Massachusetts Bay, made him endorse Abbot's inclusive view of the church. As the *True Travels* made clear, the experience of fighting Islamic forces in Africa and southeastern Europe and pagans in the New World made him aware that Christianity as a world force needed unity. Such unity was necessary for the integrity of nationhood and for the framing of public peace. In *Advertisements* Smith expatiated on the problem of Christian divisiveness in the world and nation:

> He that will but truly consider the greatnesse of the Turks Empire and power here in Christendome, shall finde the naturall Turkes are generally of one religion, and the Christians in so many divisions and opinions, that they are among themselves worse enemies than the Turkes, whose dis-joyntednesse hath given him that opportunity to command so many hundred thousand of Christians as he doth, where had they beene constant to one God, one Christ, and one Church, Christians might have beene more able to have commanded as many Turkes, as now the Turkes doe poore miserable Christians.[22]

Consequently, he recommends to would-be colonizers of the New World adherence "to the prime authority of the Church of England, for such an orderly authority as in most mens opinions is fit for you both to intreat for and to have." Abbot had the breadth of vision to see Christendom, the world, the nation, and the Church of England as unities embodying disparities. When Archbishop Laud in 1628 began the persecution of Calvinists and the exclusion of Puritans from pulpits to secure the theological dominion of Arminian doctrine, he fostered division. Laud imposed a new orthodoxy centered upon the Book of Common Prayer and an internal church disci-

21. "The Archbishop of Canterbury's Speech to His Majesty," MS Eng 1266.2, fol. 138, Houghton Library, Harvard University.

22. Smith, *Advertisements,* in *Complete Works of Captain John Smith,* III, 296–297.

pline Roman in its hierarchical rigor. There was nothing inclusive, tolerant, or demotic about his campaign. Smith would have had it otherwise.

The *Advertisements* was as close to a utopian vision as a man of hard experience could manage. Its idealisms were tempered by knowledge of the world and a sense of the costs of creating anything memorable. Yet there is nowhere in the text any sense that the fundamental aspirations of humans for a better existence, the rule of God in human affairs, or the virtue of nationhood are dubious. Instead, there is often a painful insistence upon what is right and honorable, heroic and memorable. One cannot help read certain of the "true reasons for plantations" in chapter 4 without a sense of the extraordinary personal resonance of his arguments. "Adam and Eve did first begin this innocent worke to plant the earth to remaine to posterity, but not without labour, trouble, and industry"—an arresting sentence for a man incapable of producing posterity who fought with gold-besotted dreamers all his adult life in America. The mythos of the Cotton library spoke loudest when Smith proclaimed that the past spurs the present on to be worthy of a future. "Seeing honour is our lives ambition, and our ambition after death, to have an honourable memory of our life: and seeing by no meanes wee would be abated of the dignitie and glorie of our predecessors, let us imitate their vertues to be worthily their successors, or at least not hinder, if not further them that would and doe their utmost and beast endeavour."[23]

Nation was the frame of reputation. By using the biblical patriarchs as his exemplar of history, Smith folded familial posterity into national legacy. Fathering New England out of Old England was the most honorable and virtuous cause for Smith's being remembered. Several scholars have detailed how Smith projected the possibility of re-creating the common people into virtuous and memorable founders of civilization in America —how Smith invented a version of the American dream. I think of J. A. Leo Lemay's *American Dream of Captain John Smith* particularly. Smith's, however, was a resolutely English dream. The after-livers have made it American. Smith's last published words—the final paragraphs of *Advertisements* —make clear his allegiance and intentions: he recalled the names and deeds of the great sea captains of Elizabeth's reign: the commoners Drake, Cavendish, Hawkins, Frobisher—and the great peers—the earl of Cumberland, the earl of Essex, lord high admiral the earl of Nottingham, and the earl of Southampton. This is no roll call of heroes from the Anglo-Saxon Age, from the Arthurian mists, or from the age of chivalry. They date from the 1580s on—the men who projected nation beyond the Three Kingdoms (En-

23. Ibid., 276–277.

PLATE 2. *Coat of Arms of New England, prefacing Smith's* Advertisements
for the Unexperienced Planters of New England . . . *(London, 1631).*
Courtesy of the John Carter Brown Library at Brown University

gland, Scotland, and Wales) to the oceans of the world. They were more than simply men of arms: they were explorers who brought new worlds to view; they were men of commerce, expanding trade and imperial dominion round the globe; they were institution builders, preparing for the consolidation of the Royal Navy and an English colonial world. Smith here claimed his patrimony. These were the names worthy of books and commemoration. He would add his own to the lineage.

This heroic ancestry stood parallel to that roll of learned men proclaimed in his prefaces and dedications. Smith would never resolve the disparities between his dual patrimonies. His proposed Coat of Arms for New England, prefacing the *Advertisements,* distilled the tension—a shield bearing the Stuart Arms and ocean waves is surmounted by a helmet upon which Neptune, riding a seahorse, brandishes his triton. The shield is flanked by twin muses, one bearing a book, the other a mason's rule. Captain John Smith is more historically compelling for his mixture of identities and purposes.

Here in this scholarly collection commemorating the founding of Jamestown, the man who would not be forgotten has called himself into cognizance again. Now he claims his posterity. Not as the romantic failed adventurer. Not as the braggart and bully and martial law dictator. Not as Caesar redivivus. But as the man who found a place in the library and in this volume finds it once again. It was and is in the end where, after he could no longer get to America or command a ship on the high seas, he most wanted to be.

part five

THE ATLANTIC WORLD
AND VIRGINIA, 1550–1624

James Horn

IMPERFECT UNDERSTANDINGS

RUMOR, KNOWLEDGE, AND UNCERTAINTY IN EARLY

VIRGINIA

"Casacunnakack, peya quagh acquintan uttasantasough?" In how many
days will more ships come? Opechancanough, chief of the Pamunkeys, had
been watching the white men encamped at Paspahegh (Jamestown Island)
for some time. He had seen their numbers steadily dwindle during the summer and fall and the ever more desperate efforts of starving survivors to
get corn from peoples nearby. Now, after tracking one of the *tassantasses'*
(strangers') leaders along the Chickahominy River for several days, he decided to find out why the men had stayed behind at Paspahegh when their
ships had left in the summer and whether more ships would be arriving
soon. The white man his warriors had captured, frozen to the bone after
falling into the river, was ready to talk. He flourished a small round object,
flailing his arms and gesturing to the sky and his surroundings as he spoke.
The chief's men soon tired of the man's incomprehensible ranting, however,
and raised their bows to dispatch him, but at that moment Opechancanough
intervened. The stranger might yet have valuable information.[1]

I am especially grateful to Fredrika J. Teute and Peter Mancall for their helpful suggestions and encouragement. Earlier versions of this chapter have been presented at several seminars and I would like to thank participants for their thoughtful comments. I am
grateful also to Kathy Burdette for her expert work as copy-editor and to the staff of the
Omohundro Institute of Early American History and Culture for preparing this chapter
for publication. Finally, I would like to thank Basic Books for permission to use sections
from *A Land as God Made It: Jamestown and the Birth of America* (New York, 2005).

1. John Smith, *A True Relation . . . (1608),* in Philip L. Barbour, ed., *The Complete Works of Captain John Smith (1580–1631),* 3 vols. (Chapel Hill, N.C., 1986), I,
39–47; Smith, *A Map of Virginia . . .* (1612), ibid., 137; Smith, *The Generall Historie
of Virginia, New-England, and the Summer Iles . . .* (1624), ibid., II, 146–147. Fewer
than half of the original 104 settlers who had landed at Jamestown Island in mid-May
1607 were still alive seven months later, when John Smith was sent to the lands of the

In the winter of 1607, far upriver in a "vast and wilde wilderness," Captain John Smith was captured by a large hunting party of several hundred Indians, who carried him to their chief, an old, imperious-looking man. In fear for his life and playing for time, Smith took from his pocket an ivory compass. He talked about whatever came into his head: the "roundnesse of the earth, and skies, the spheare of the Sunne, Moone, and Starres, and how the Sunne did chase the night round about the world continually." He described "the greatnesse of the Land and Sea, the diversitie of Nations, [and] varietie of complexions" of their peoples. His ploy seemed to work: the chief stopped the warriors from killing him. Smith knew then that his survival depended on persuading his captors that he might be of use to them.[2]

At Rasawek, a hunting camp nearby, Opechancanough quizzed Smith about English ships and how they sailed the seas, and about the white people's God. Smith's answers confirmed the chief's opinion that the Englishman had information that his brother, Wahunsonacock, paramount chief of the Powhatans, would want to hear. A couple of weeks later, Opechancanough brought his prisoner to Werowocomoco, Wahunsonacock's principal residence on the Pamunkey (York) River, where Smith was straightaway taken to the "Kings-howse." After a few pleasantries, Wahunsonacock came to the point: why had the English come? Smith concocted a story that they had been in a fight "with the Spaniards our enemie" and had been forced to put into the Chesapeake Bay by bad weather and the need to refill their water casks. After they were directed upriver by friendly Kecoughtans, their pinnace sprang a leak, so they encamped temporarily at Jamestown to make repairs and wait for the return of their leader, Captain Christopher Newport, whom Smith described as his father. He added that they had subsequently gone upriver into the interior to "the other side the maine, where was salt water," to revenge the slaying of Newport's child by the Monacans, ancient enemies of the Powhatans. Wahun-

Chickahominies to trade for corn (Helen C. Rountree, *Pocahontas, Powhatan, Opechancanough: Three Indian Lives Changed by Jamestown* [Charlottesville, Va., 2005], 30, 67–68). Rountree argues that Opechancanough was chief of the Youghtanunds but was also accounted chief of the Pamunkeys.

2. Opechancanough was in his early sixties at the time of the encounter. He is treated at length in Rountree, *Pocahontas, Powhatan, Opechancanough*. See also J. Frederick Fausz, "Opechancanough: Indian Resistance Leader," in David G. Sweet and Gary B. Nash, eds., *Struggle and Survival in Colonial America* (Berkeley, Calif., 1981), 23. For Smith's oration, see his *Generall Historie,* in Barbour, ed., *Complete Works of Captain John Smith,* I, 45, II, 147.

sonacock must have known Smith was lying but chose not to press him on it.[3]

Instead, after a pause, perhaps weighing what to tell the Englishman, the chief began a lengthy description of peoples who lived in or visited lands beyond Tsenacommacah (Virginia). To the north, where a great river flowed into the bay that issued from "mightie Mountaines betwixt the two Seas," lived warriors who shaved their heads and carried swords "like Pollaxes." Farther north lived men "with short Coates, and Sleeves to the Elbowes, that passed that way in Shippes," and to the south of Tsenacommacah lay the countries of "Mangoge," "Chawwonock," and Roanoke and a land called "Anone," where "they have abundance of Brasse" and walled houses like those of the English. Smith took careful note of Wahunsonacock's description, "seeing what pride hee had in his great and spacious Dominions, seeing that all hee knewe were under his Territories." In additional conversations, the two men eventually reached an accord, and Smith was sent home to Jamestown on New Year's Day to fulfill his side of the bargain.[4]

Of course, Smith's account cannot be taken at face value—besides projecting conventional assumptions of European superiority, Smith took pains to fashion himself as a resourceful and self-reliant leader, fully capable of managing the Powhatans as well as fractious English colonists. Nevertheless, his exchanges with Opechancanough and Wahunsonacock are revealing. Both sides, Indian and English, were intent on finding out as much as they could about each other—information that might reveal the newcomers' intentions to the two Powhatan chiefs and that, for the English, might unlock the secrets and wealth of the new lands they had entered.

Nearly forty years had passed since white men (the Spanish) had first tried to settle in the region, an attempt that had brought unanticipated and tragic consequences to peoples of the James River. For their part, although the English had learned a good deal about Indian peoples of the mid-Atlantic from voyages of the previous two decades, no one who sailed

3. Smith, *True Relation,* in Barbour, ed., *Complete Works of Captain John Smith,* I, 49, 50–55, esp. 53; Smith, *Generall Historie,* ibid., II, 150–151; William Strachey, *The Historie of Travell into Virginia Britania (1612),* ed. Louis B. Wright and Virginia Freund, Works Issued by the Hakluyt Society, 2d Ser., no. 103 (London, 1953), 57. It is unlikely Strachey ever met the paramount chief. His description is derived from other eyewitnesses, such as John Smith. Wahunsonacock was the chief's personal name, but the English called him "Powhatan," which was his official name. Rountree discusses his titles, family, and origin in *Pocahontas, Powhatan, Opechancanough,* 25–33.

4. Smith, *True Relation,* in Barbour, ed., *Complete Works of Captain John Smith,* I, 55.

with the first Jamestown expedition had encountered the Powhatans before or knew what to expect of them. In an environment of uncertainty and shifting relations during the months following initial encounters, knowledge was vital if opportunities were to be realized and potential threats averted.

First Contacts

Indian peoples of the Chesapeake region first heard of white men in the 1520s and 1530s, when news reached them that strangers had appeared to the south along the coast of modern-day Georgia and South Carolina as well as far to the north in Canada. The Florentine Giovanni da Verrazano, in the service of the French king, Francis I, coasted the Outer Banks and Chesapeake Bay in 1524, and the following year the Spaniard Pedro de Quejo was likely the first European to enter the bay during an exploratory voyage in search of a passage to the Orient. Fifteen years later, in the mid-1540s, a storm forced a French ship to take shelter in the Chesapeake Bay for several days, during which the crew traded for pelts in exchange for "knives, fishhooks, and shirts."[5]

More frequent contact between Europeans and peoples of the Chesapeake did not occur for another generation, when the Spanish began to take an interest in the region. In 1561, a caravel entered the bay and carried off two Indians from the James River, giving one of them, Paquiquineo (described as "a young *cacique*"), the name Don Luis de Velasco in honor of the viceroy of Mexico. The Spanish took Don Luis to live at the court of Philip II in Madrid, where the king, high nobility, and churchmen befriended him. On returning to America, he lived in Mexico City and Havana and converted to Catholicism, living first with the Dominicans and subsequently with Jesuits.[6]

On his travels, Don Luis became acquainted with Pedro Menéndez de Avilés, who in 1565 was appointed *adelantado* (governor) of La Florida in charge of Spanish interests in North America. With the help of Menéndez, an intensely devout man, Don Luis was eventually able to return to the

5. David B. Quinn, *North America from Earliest Discovery to First Settlements: The Norse Voyages to 1612* (New York, 1977), 154-155; Paul E. Hoffman, *A New Andalucia and a Way to the Orient: The American Southeast during the Sixteenth Century* (Baton Rouge, 1990), 55-56; Clifford M. Lewis and Albert J. Loomie, *The Spanish Jesuit Mission in Virginia, 1570-1572* (Chapel Hill, N. C., 1953), 13.

6. Hoffman, *New Andalucia*, 181-187; Charlotte M. Gradie, "The Powhatans in the Context of the Spanish Empire," in Helen C. Rountree, ed., *Powhatan Foreign Relations, 1500-1722* (Charlottesville, Va., 1993), 154-172; Lewis and Loomie, *Spanish Jesuit Mission*, 13, 156, 179.

James River as a member of a Jesuit mission sent to establish a settlement in the region. Besides bringing his own people to the true church, Don Luis told Menéndez and the vice-provincial of the Jesuit order in Florida, Father Juan Baptista de Segura, of a passage that would lead to "the discovery of great kingdoms such as Tartary" and others adjoining it. The small group of Jesuits, made up of Segura, seven others, and a boy, Alonso de Olmos, arrived in the Chesapeake Bay in the summer of 1570 and settled near Kiskiack on the Pamunkey River. Soon after, Don Luis abandoned them and went to live with his own people about thirty or forty miles away, returning several months later with a group of warriors to kill the fathers, leaving only the boy alive.

Following more than a year with no word of the Jesuit mission, Menéndez decided to investigate what had happened and led an expedition to the James River in the summer of 1572. He managed to recover Alonso, whereupon he learned of the fathers' murder and went in search of Don Luis. Unable to find him, the Spaniards eventually left the river after hanging nine Indians from the rigging of Menéndez's ship and killing dozens of others. The "country remains very frightened from the chastisement the Governor inflicted," it was reported, "for previously they [the Indians] were free to kill any Spaniard who made no resistance. After seeing the opposite of what the Fathers were, they tremble." Don Luis, meanwhile, had disappeared without a trace.[7]

Menéndez's "chastisement" might well have been the first time Indians of the James River had witnessed the terrible, destructive power of European weaponry, and it was long remembered. Peoples of the region must have wondered whether the Spanish would return to renew their attempt to settle the land and whether more ships would come to their rivers, leaving havoc in their wake. In the early 1580s, two pinnaces carrying fifty men, commanded by the Spaniard Vicente Gonzáles, visited the Chesapeake Bay in search of a French fort rumored to be in the area, and a few years later, Wahunsonacock might have heard about the white strangers who had settled to the south on Roanoke Island in 1585. Chesapeakes, Nansemonds, and several other unidentified peoples made contact with an expedition sent by the English from Roanoke to the southern shore of the

7. Eugene Lyon, *The Enterprise of Florida: Pedro Menéndez de Avilés and the Spanish Conquest of 1565-1568* (Gainesville, Fla., 1976); David B. Quinn, ed., *New American World: A Documentary History of North America to 1612,* 5 vols. (New York, 1979), II, 400-401, 415, 457-458, 535; Lewis and Loomie, *Spanish Jesuit Mission,* 39-57, 89-92, 109-111, 134-139, 159, 180-185.

Chesapeake Bay in the winter of 1585–1586. Over the next two decades, a couple of dozen Spanish and English ships skirted the coast or put into the bay briefly, but no soldiers or settlers returned to plant a colony.[8]

Early European encounters with the peoples and lands of the mid-Atlantic region stimulated a persistent vein of hearsay about untold wealth yet to be discovered somewhere in the interior. In the 1560s, Guale Indians told French colonists belonging to a short-lived Huguenot settlement in Florida of gold "in the mountains of Appalesse [Appalachians]," and Menéndez reported to Philip II that he had heard stories of silver and gold as well as turquoises and emeralds "near the mountains" inland from the Chesapeake Bay. Spanish and English accounts of the 1580s derived from Indians of the Outer Banks and Virginia confirmed these stories, none more intriguing from an English point of view than those related to Roanoke.[9]

Lost Colonies

In 1584, Walter Ralegh dispatched two small ships to reconnoiter the mid-Atlantic coast as a preliminary to establishing a colony that would serve both as a privateering base for English fleets and a beachhead from which colonists could explore inland. An unnamed Englishman captured by the Spanish in the West Indies testified that the English had discovered a large freshwater bay "with some islands" (most likely Albemarle Sound of the Outer Banks of North Carolina), which, the Indians had told him, was the largest inlet along the coast and "a channel to the other sea." He reported that the master pilot of the expedition, the Azorean Simon Fernandes (whom Ralegh engaged because of his knowledge of the waters and peoples

8. Lewis and Loomie, *Spanish Jesuit Mission*, 111; Quinn, ed., *New American World,* V, 165; Quinn, *England and the Discovery of America, 1481–1620* (New York, 1974), 405–430; Paul E. Hoffman, *Spain and the Roanoke Voyages* (Raleigh, N.C., 1987), 16–40. Two earlier expeditions to Roanoke were possibly sent out by Ralegh in 1599 and 1600, but no information about them has survived. Samuel Mace might have explored the Chesapeake Bay in 1603 during an expedition also sponsored by Ralegh. If so, that might explain why the Virginia Company thought it unnecessary to send a reconnaissance voyage three years later in advance of the Jamestown expedition. Mace might have left a small holding party in Virginia, expecting to return the following year (see the remarks of the Spanish ambassador in August 1607, in Philip L. Barbour, ed., *The Jamestown Voyages under the First Charter, 1606–1609,* 2 vols., Works Issued by the Hakluyt Society, 2d Ser., no. 134 [Cambridge, 1969]).

9. Sarah Lawson, *A Foothold in Florida: The Eye-Witness Account of Four Voyages Made by the French to That Region and Their Attempt at Colonisation, 1562–1568* (East Grinstead, 1992), 5, 94–95, 127; Quinn, ed., *New American World,* II, 400–401, 415, 457–458, 535.

of the Atlantic coast), asked a group of friendly Indians whether there was gold or silver in their land. The Indians replied that "there was much, and gave him four pounds of gold and a hundred [pounds] of silver, buffalo-skins [queros de ante] and many other valuable things."[10]

Following Fernandes's successful exploratory voyage, the English established a colony of approximately 107 men on Roanoke Island in the summer of 1585. During the first six months, the colonists surveyed the surrounding area and made contact with local peoples. In the spring, the commander, Ralph Lane, led an expedition up one of the major rivers of the region, the "River of Morotico" (Roanoke), his interest sparked by information current among neighboring Indians, "most notorious to all the countrey," that somewhere upriver "a marveilous and most strange Minerall" existed. It was known to Indians of the interior such as the Mangoags and Chowanocs, and its mine was located in the fabled province of "Chaunis Temoatan." He described the mineral, called by Indians "Wassador," as copper, but he went on to say that the metal was "very soft, and pale." The Mangoags had such large quantities "that they beautifie their houses with great plates of the same."[11]

Lane was impressed by the size and strength of the Roanoke River (which he compared to the Thames) but even more impressed by Moratico (Moratuc) Indians' reports of "strange things" at the head of the river, thirty to forty days from their principal village. They said that the head-waters "springeth out of a maine rocke . . . and further, that this huge rocke standeth nere unto a Sea." Here was a story to whet the appetite of the English commander: not only had he possibly discovered news of gold mines, but also near the mountains where the mines were said to be located was a great sea that could only be the Pacific.[12]

10. David Beers Quinn, ed., *The Roanoke Voyages, 1584–1590,* 2 vols., Works Issued by the Hakluyt Society, 2d Ser., no. 104 (London, 1955), I, 80–81, 108. Except for a brief reference to a "broad plate of golde, or copper" worn by a local chief, Granganimeo, no mention of gold appears in the published account of the voyage of 1584 by Arthur Barlowe, one of the commanders of the 1584 expedition (see ibid., 102).

11. Ibid., 268–270.

12. Ibid., 263–264. The Chowanoc chief, Menotonon, informed Lane that three days up the Chowan by canoe and another four days overland to the northeast lay a province bordering the sea, ruled by a powerful king whose seat was on an island in a bay. This king had such great quantities of pearls that he adorned not only himself with them but also his chief men and followers, and his "beds, and houses are garnished with them . . . that it is a wonder to see." The king apparently traded with white men (Menotonon did not specify whom) and the chief advised Lane to go only with a strong

Lane had no further opportunity to pursue explorations into the interior. When he returned to Roanoke Island, hostilities with neighboring Secotans intensified over the next few months, leading to several pitched battles and the killing of the chief, Wingina. Without the support of local Indians, the English could not survive on the island for long, and in June 1586 Lane decided to abandon the settlement. It was a frustrating end to the colony, but Lane remained convinced that the Roanoke River promised "great things" and would perhaps provide a passage either to the Gulf of Mexico or the South Sea.[13]

The sort of gossip that might have begun circulating in London and Plymouth following the return of Lane's colony to England can be surmised from the account of Pedro Morales, a Spanish deserter (or prisoner) taken by Sir Francis Drake from San Augustín. Morales asserted that sixty leagues (about two hundred miles) north of the Spanish garrison of Santa Elena (near present-day Savannah) "are the mountaines of golde and Chrystall Mines, named Apalatci." He claimed to have seen "a rich Diamond which was brought from the mountaines that lye up in the countrey Westward" from Santa Elena—either the "Apalatci" or the "hils of Chaunis Temoatam, which Master Lane had advertisement of [learned of]."[14]

Nicholas Burgoignon, a Frenchman captured by the Spanish in 1580 on the coast of Florida, also rescued during Drake's raid on San Augustín, confirmed Morales's story and embellished it by adding sensational details. In the mountains inland from Santa Elena was to be found "great store of Christal, golde, and Rubies, and Diamonds." The gems gleamed so bright in places that the Indians "cannot behold them, and therefore they travell unto them by night." Fifty leagues from the Spanish garrison, Burgoignon

force and plenty of provisions, for "that king would be loth to suffer any strangers to enter into his Countrey, and especially to meddle with the fishing of any Pearle there." News of a powerful chiefdom and pearls suggested to Lane the possibility of riches, and that was another reason he came to believe the Chesapeake held greater promise than the Outer Banks. What he could not have known was that the king Menotonon referred to was the chief of the Powhatans, Wahunsonacock, at that moment consolidating his hold over the peoples of the Virginia tidewater.

13. Karen Ordahl Kupperman, *Roanoke: The Abandoned Colony* (Totowa, N.J., 1984), 84–87; Quinn, ed., *Roanoke Voyages,* I, 273–274.

14. Quinn, ed., *Roanoke Voyages,* II, 761–763. The mountains Morales called "Apalatci" (Appalachian) derive from Jacques Le Moyne's *Floridae Americae provinciae: Recens et exactissima descripto* (n.p., 1591) and Theodore de Bry's *Collectiones Peregrinationum in Indiam Orientales . . . ,* part 2 (Frankfurt, 1591).

continued, the Spanish had encountered Indians "wearing golde rings at their nostrels and eares."[15]

Whether such stories influenced Ralegh's decision to make another attempt to plant a colony in the region is uncertain, but he did not favor returning to the Outer Banks, which had proved unsuitable for oceangoing vessels owing to shallow and treacherous waters. Deepwater harbors about seventy or eighty miles to the north on the southern shore of the Chesapeake Bay, discovered by the English in the spring of 1586, held greater promise, and he directed that the new colony be established there.

Departing Plymouth in early May 1587, three ships carrying 117 colonists arrived off the Outer Banks in mid-July, where the governor, John White (who had participated in both previous Roanoke expeditions), was to inquire about the fate of fifteen men left the summer before by a relief expedition led by Sir Richard Grenville. Grenville had arrived a few weeks after the departure of Lane's colony and left the small garrison to ensure the English continued to have a presence on the island, albeit a token one. Apart from the bleached bones of one of the men, White found no evidence of what had happened to them, but in any event, he soon faced a more urgent problem.

On reaching the Outer Banks, Simon Fernandes, once again the pilot, refused to take White's colonists any farther, claiming his mariners wanted to get back to the Caribbean to prey on Spanish shipping as soon as possible. The settlers tried to establish themselves on Roanoke, but when it became clear the Secotans remained hostile, they decided that White should return to England to alert Ralegh to their situation and raise fresh supplies. In the meantime, they would move fifty miles inland, where they might find Indians willing to help them and be able to support themselves through the winter until White returned. As it turned out, despite his best efforts, White was unable to return until three years later, by which time the colonists had vanished.[16]

White was not the only one who wanted to find the colonists. Although the Spanish had abandoned efforts to settle the Chesapeake following the

15. Quinn, ed., *Roanoke Voyages,* II, 763–765.

16. Ibid., 517–536, 608–622; Kupperman, *Roanoke,* 105–133. White believed they had gone to the island of Croatoan, where the friendly Indians of that name lived. When he returned to Roanoke in 1590, he found carved on a tree near the fort the letters "CRO" and a short distance away, on "one of the chiefe trees or postes," the word "CROATOAN." Owing to worsening weather, however, and the loss of his ship's anchors, White was unable to get to the island to confirm the settlers had moved there.

destruction of the Jesuit mission, they remained deeply concerned about English activities along the mid-Atlantic coast and were determined not to allow the northern littoral to become a haven for pirates or fall into the hands of heretics. In the summer of 1588, an expedition commanded by Vicente González arrived in the Chesapeake Bay to look for an English settlement thought to be in the region. He had visited the bay on several occasions, the last time in 1582, when he encountered a chief wearing many gold rings and a golden crown. The chief told him of a mountain within three days' travel that "has nothing else [but gold]." Six years later, near the head of the bay, González saw another Indian chief wearing a necklace of "fine gold" but apparently learned nothing more about the mountain where mines might be found.[17]

Leaving the Chesapeake and heading southward, González encountered strengthening winds and sought shelter in the Outer Banks, where, quite by chance, he discovered evidence he had been looking for—the English had settled not in the Chesapeake Bay but on Roanoke Island. The Spaniards reported that they found a slipway for small vessels (used to transport supplies to the fort) and barrels placed in the ground to collect rainwater. They saw no sign of the English colonists themselves, however, and opting not to linger any longer, returned to San Augustín.[18]

González picked up valuable information from the Indians during the voyage. They told him that the English were established on a river from which "there is a passage to the South Sea," perhaps a reference to the Chesapeake Bay, or inland from the Outer Banks. His assessment was confirmed shortly after by the testimony of Pedro Diaz, who had been a prisoner (or so he said) of the English between 1585 and 1588. In the spring of 1586, he had sailed with the fleet commanded by Sir Richard Grenville, mentioned earlier, that had been dispatched to reinforce Lane's colony. Arriving off the Outer Banks in July or August, Diaz described the deserted fort and commented: "The reason why the English have settled here is . . . because on the mainland there is much gold and so that they may pass from the North [Atlantic] to the South Sea, which they say and understand is nearby; thus making themselves strong through the discovery of great wealth."[19]

17. A full account of Spain's response to the Roanoke voyages can be found in Quinn, ed., *Roanoke Voyages,* II, 717–825; Hoffman, *Spain and the Roanoke Voyages,* 30–57; Lewis and Loomie, *Spanish Jesuit Mission,* 186.

18. Quinn, ed., *Roanoke Voyages,* II, 810–811. The English had left Roanoke Island no later than by the spring of 1588.

19. Quinn, ed., *Roanoke Voyages,* II, 791, 825.

Throughout the 1590s, stories about the continued existence of an English settlement in the mid-Atlantic region and of valuable mines in the interior circulated between San Agustín, Havana, and Madrid. The Spanish knew far more about the coastline north of Santa Elena—the bays, inlets, and rivers—and Chesapeake region than any other Europeans but were unable to secure the area. The Spanish annexation of Portugal and its overseas possessions in 1580 transformed Philip II into the lord of the Indies, East and West, creating a vast empire on which the sun never set. Yet it also saddled the imperial monarchy with huge bureaucratic and military expenses. Despite an increasing flow of bullion from the silver mines of Peru and Mexico, there was never enough money to pay for the armies fighting the Dutch in Flanders, protecting the empire's sprawling East European flank against the Turks, prosecuting a ruinous sea war against England, and managing the elaborate machinery of government and trade on a global scale. The Crown's bankruptcy in 1596 signaled the end of Philip's imperial dreams for the time being and thwarted any plans to expand Spanish colonies in Florida.[20]

The "Greatnes and Bowndes" of Tsenacommacah

Sometime in the 1570s, Wahunsonacock inherited six regions located between the upper James and York rivers—"the Countryes *Powhatan, Arrohateck, Appamatuck, Pamunky, Youghtamond,* and *Mattapanient*"—which together with lands along the lower York River comprised the historic core of his paramount chiefdom. The settler William Strachey later described him as a "strong and able salvadge [savage], synowie, active, and of a daring spiritt, vigilant, ambitious, subtile to enlarge his dominions," for apart from those lands he inherited, "all the rest of the Territoryes . . . have bene either by force subdued unto him, or through feare yeilded." During the 1590s and opening years of the seventeenth century, the Kecoughtans and Piankatanks had been conquered and the Chesapeakes, who lived near the mouth of the bay, destroyed. By the time he encountered John Smith, Wahunsonacock ruled over some thirty or so peoples spread across the Virginia tidewater, from south of the James River to the Potomac.[21]

20. Hoffman, *Spain and the Roanoke Voyages,* 58–70; Quinn, *North America,* 298–321; J. H. Elliott, *Imperial Spain, 1469–1716* (Harmondsworth, 1970), 249–287; Elliott, *Spain and Its World, 1500–1700: Selected Essays* (New Haven, Conn., 1989), 7–26; Geoffrey Parker, *The Grand Strategy of Philip II* (New Haven, Conn., 1998).

21. Strachey, *Virginia Britania,* 36, 43–44, 56–58. Following the defeat of the Kecoughtans, which historians estimate might have occurred in 1596 or 1597, the remnants of the people were transported over the Pamunkey River and settled "amongst

The arrival of the English in 1607 posed a conundrum for Wahunsona-cock and Opechancanough. In themselves, the newcomers were not a threat —there were too few of them, and their chronic dependence on the Indians for food made them vulnerable—but if they attempted to settle in larger numbers or to forge alliances with unfriendly peoples on the Powhatans' borders, they might cause trouble. On the other hand, the strangers might possibly be of use (if they could be controlled) in repulsing raids from the west and north and might be useful also in implementing an altogether more ambitious strategy to expand their territorial conquests.

Wahunsonacock needed more information. "Watchful he is over us," one contemporary remarked, "and keeps good espiall upon our proceedings, Concerning which he hath his Sentinells, that at what tyme soever any of our boates, pinaces or shippes, come in, fall downe, or make up the river, give the Alarum." During May and June 1607, he kept the English under close surveillance, and when Newport set off to explore the James River, to seek "the Sea againe, the Mountaynes Apalatsi, or some issue," Wahunsonacock seized his chance.[22]

About fifty miles upriver from Jamestown at Arrohateck, as Newport's men were being entertained by the chief "Arahatec," news came that the "greate kyng Powatah had arrived." After the English presented gifts, the great chief appointed five men to guide Newport to his own habitation, which the English called "Pawatah's Towre [Town]," the pallisaded settlement of Powhatan, the great chief's birthplace. There, the English were feasted by the chief, who told them of all the peoples of the region who were "one with him or under him." Newport affirmed that they were friends "with all his people and kyngdomes," at which the chief offered a "leauge of fryndship" with the newcomers, "laying his hand in his breast saying Wingapoh Chemuze (the most kynde wordes of salutatyon that may be)."[23]

Several days later, at the falls of the James River, the English once again met the great chief, who sought to dissuade them from going into the in-

his owne people." Loyal supporters were moved into the Kecoughtans' former lands, under the rule of the paramount chief's son. See Rountree, *Powhatan Indians of Virginia,* 7-15, 118-121; Frederic W. Gleach, *Powhatan's World and Colonial Virginia: A Conflict of Cultures* (Lincoln, Neb., 1997), 22-34; J. Frederick Fausz, "Patterns of Anglo-Indian Aggression and Accommodation along the Mid-Atlantic Coast, 1584-1634," in William W. Fitzhugh, ed., *Cultures in Contact: The Impact of European Contacts on Native American Cultural Institutions, A.D. 1000-1800* (Washington, D.C., 1985), 226-236.

22. Strachey, *Virginia Britania,* 58; Barbour, ed., *Jamestown Voyages,* I, 81.

23. Barbour, ed., *Jamestown Voyages,* I, 85-86.

terior to the lands of the Monacans. So as not to give offense, Newport agreed to go no farther, but before turning back, he set up a cross with the inscription "Jacobus Rex. 1607," which he later told the chief confirmed their accord—"the two Armes of the Crosse signifyed kyng Powatah and himselfe, the fastening of it in the myddest was their united Leaug [league]." From the falls, Newport and his men made their way downriver, stopping off at Arrohateck, Appomattoc, and the rich lands of the Pamunkeys, where they met another chief (but not Opechancanough) who entertained them lavishly.[24]

The English had been duped. Newport and his men had not met Wahunsonacock at Arrohateck or at the falls but one of his sons, Parahunt. The hospitality extended to the English during the voyage was merely a ruse to keep them upriver long enough for an alliance of five tribes (Quiyoughcohannocks, Weanocs, Appomattocs, Paspaheghs, and Kiskiacks), numbering about two hundred warriors, to launch "a very furious Assault" on the men who had remained at Jamestown. They beat off the attack after an hour of intense fighting, largely owing to the murderous effect of small shot fired from the two ships moored near the island, but nevertheless the sudden strike very nearly succeeded in overwhelming the settlement and left two colonists dead and a dozen wounded.[25]

From Newport and other English leaders on the expedition, the Indians gathered something of the newcomers' intentions. Newport had hinted that the English had come "to Plant" in their country and had shown considerable interest in the mountains to the west where the Monacans lived and from whence the Powhatans derived their *caquassan* (copper). At Arrohateck and Appomattoc, at the request of the Indians, the English had demonstrated firing their muskets. Finally, the attack on the English encampment at Jamestown had underlined (as had the Spanish incursion thirty-five years earlier) the effectiveness of firearms and cannon. The size of the English contingent might be small, but their ships and weaponry were deadly. As long as the newcomers could be confined to Jamestown Island, Wahunsonacock might have concluded that the best course was to continue to watch and wait.[26]

Neither containment nor outright destruction of the English was the chief's ultimate objective, however. Following the departure of Newport and two of the largest ships in late June and the settlers' declining num-

24. Ibid., 87–95, 98–102, 141.
25. Ibid., 95.
26. Ibid., 85, 87–88, 91–95.

bers during the summer, there was ample opportunity to overrun the ailing settlement if Wahunsonacock wished. Hence the significance of the capture of John Smith in the winter of 1607; only during the protracted discussions between Smith and Wahunsonacock did the chief reveal what he wanted from the intruders.

In *A True Relation,* written shortly after the event, Smith mentioned that Wahunsonacock was willing to bargain with him for English copper and tools, highly prized commodities that would underline the chief's status among his own peoples and neighbors. The chief "desired mee to forsake Paspahegh, and to live with him upon his River, a Countrie called Capahowasicke" (a few miles downriver from Werowocomoco). "[H]ee promised to give me Corne, Venison, or what I wanted to feede us, Hatchets and Copper wee should make him, and none should disturbe us." Smith and the rest of the English would be guaranteed food and safety if they acknowledged the great chief as their lord and became a subordinate people within his chiefdom. A day or two later, having assured Wahunsonacock he would "performe" his request, Smith was released and allowed to return to the fort.[27]

But many years later, in the *Generall Historie* (published in 1624), Smith recounted another condition of the agreement. Before they released Smith, the Powhatans took him to a large house in the woods outside Werowocomoco, where Wahunsonacock told him to send "two great gunnes, and a gryndstone" (for sharpening knives and swords) to seal their accord. The chief repeated his offer to give Smith Capahowasick, with the significant addition of creating him a son and *weroance.* The Powhatan chief wanted guns and swords as well as copper and truck. With two "great gunnes," his warriors could easily breach English defenses at Jamestown or anywhere else along the river. More important, if they could secure a regular supply of weapons and powder from the English "people" they had absorbed as fellow Powhatans, they would not only prove a match for subsequent new arrivals but also for their enemies to the south, west, and north: the Tuscaroras of the North Carolina interior, Monacans and Mannahoacs in the piedmont, and Susquehannocks and Massawomecks at the head of the bay.[28]

What followed over the next nine months was an uneasy standoff. Wahunsonacock might have been disturbed by the return of Newport and

27. Smith, *True Relation,* in Barbour, ed., *Complete Works of Captain John Smith,* I, 57.

28. Smith, *Generall Historie,* ibid., II, 151.

about a hundred settlers early in the new year but continued to negotiate with the English. He appointed a "trustie servant," Namontack, sometimes described as his son, to go to England and return a "true report therof" and throughout 1608 encouraged regular visits to the fort — to trade but also to keep an eye on the settlers. By fall, with the arrival of another group of settlers (which brought the number at Jamestown to about two hundred), more expeditions into the interior, and raids on Indian peoples along the James River to get corn, Wahunsonacock and Opechancanough concluded that the effort of absorbing the English into the Powhatans under the chiefdom of Smith was futile. Instead, they developed another strategy, one that would undermine the colony from within and allow them to get rid of the troublesome intruders once and for all.[29]

The Second Supply that arrived in October 1608 included several "Dutch-men" (Germans) who had been recruited specifically to set up sawmills and woodworking in the colony. Around Christmas, with the English settlement once again short of provisions, Wahunsonacock offered to freight one of Smith's barges with corn if, in return, Smith would send men to build him a house, provide fifty swords, some muskets, a grindstone, beads, and copper. Smith agreed, and several of the Germans together with a couple of English were sent to Werowocomoco to make a start on the house.[30]

What Smith could not have foreseen was that, once at the chief's capital, the Germans decided to throw in their lot with the Indians and informed Wahunsonacock that the colony was on the verge of collapse owing to lack of food. Two of the Germans were dispatched by Wahunsonacock back to Jamestown with a story about needing tools, clothing, and weapons and were able to make off with "a great many swords, pike-heads, peeces, shot, powder, and such like." They also persuaded six or seven other settlers to join them, who likewise managed to get away with as much as they could carry, so that Wahunsonacock quickly amassed some three hundred hatchets, fifty swords, eight pikes, eight cannon, and some muskets. Over the next

29. Alden T. Vaughan, "Powhatans Abroad: Virginia Indians in England," in Robert Appelbaum and John Wood Sweet, eds., *Envisioning an English Empire: Jamestown and the Making of the North Atlantic World* (Philadelphia, 2005), 51-54. For an account of this period, see James Horn, *A Land as God Made It: Jamestown and the Birth of America* (New York, 2005), 73-83, 99-127.

30. John Smith, *The Proceedings of the English Colonie in Virginia since Their First Beginning from England in the Yeare of Our Lord 1606, till This Present 1612* . . . (1612), in Barbour, ed., *Complete Works of Captain John Smith*, I, 237-243.

six months, as Smith struggled desperately to hold the settlement together, the chief was able to use his German confederates and other disaffected settlers to smuggle out of the fort all the weapons and tools he wanted. When the Germans could bring over sufficient colonists to ensure the Powhatans would be able to maintain their weapons and be trained in the use of firearms, he could finally rid himself of the rest of the settlers.[31]

Virginia Britannia

While Wahunsonacock was plotting the overthrow of the English, wide-ranging discussions about the future of the colony were under way in London. The new treasurer of the Virginia Company, the great merchant and financier Sir Thomas Smythe, was well aware that the colony "went rather backwards than forwards" and convened a series of meetings with the company's governing members, inviting those knowledgeable about Virginia such as Richard Hakluyt, the propagandist and translator, and Thomas Harriot, one of the few Englishmen still alive who had explored the region. What emerged was a fresh start, involving a new charter that reorganized the company into a joint stock venture, a vigorous campaign of recruitment, a fresh approach to the Powhatans, and a new vision of the colony itself. Backed by powerful courtiers, nobles, merchants, and the Church of England, Virginia transformed from a private colony into a national undertaking.[32]

Confidential instructions delivered by the company to the deputy governor, Sir Thomas Gates, shortly before he was about to leave England in May 1609 itemized four principal ways "of enrichinge the colonies and providinge returne of commodity." The "first is the discovery either of the southe seas or royall mines . . . the second is trade whereby you recover all the commodities of those countreys that ly far of[f] and yet are accessable by water; the third is tribute . . . [and] the fourth is labour of your owne men in makinge wines, pitche, tarre, sope, ashes, steele, iron, pipestaves, in sowing of hempe and flaxe, in gatheringe silke of the grasse, and providinge the [silk]worme and in fishinge for pearle, codd, sturgion, and such like." Jamestown was to be reduced to a small garrison, "because the place is unwholesome" and vulnerable to enemy warships. Gates was to select a site for the colony's new seat away from major rivers, accessible only by small

31. Ibid., 250–256.

32. Horn, *A Land as God Made It*, 132–138; Wesley Frank Craven, *The Southern Colonies in the Seventeenth Century, 1607–1689* (Baton Rouge, 1970), 82–92; Alexander Brown, *The First Republic in America* (Boston, 1898), 73–74.

boats or from overland, such as above the falls of the James River, "whither no enemy with ease can approache nor with ordinance [cannon] at all but by land."[33]

The company, however, had another proposal for the site of a new capital. "Foure dayes journey from your forte southewardes," they informed Gates, was a town "called Ohonahorn," and inland, at Ocanahowan, was "a brave and fruiteful" country, well watered and "every way unaccessable by a straunger enemy." Nearby were the rich copper mines of Ritanoe, and at Peccarecamicke lived four "of the Englishe" left by "Sir Walter Rawely, which escaped from the slaughter of Powhaton of Roanocke, uppon the first arrivall of our Colonie." Roanoke was to be incorporated into a new Virginia that would stretch from the piedmont of North Carolina to the falls of the James River.[34]

John Smith had heard of "Oconohowan" in conversations with Opechancanough and Wahunsonacock. Their lack of reticence to tell the Englishman what they knew of the whereabouts of Roanoke survivors (if that is who they were) suggests the fate of the lost colonists was common knowledge among local peoples. Smith, eager to bolster his own influence in the colony and with the company, was anxious to discover more specific reports of their whereabouts. What he was able to find out was summarized in a sketch map he sent back to London in the summer of 1608. Written on the lower left-hand side were the following notes: (1) on the southern bank of the James River, "here paspahegh and 2 of our men landed to go to panawiock"; (2) near the Roanoke River, "here the king of paspahegh reported our men to be and went to se[e]"; and (3) at Pakerakanick, "here remay[n]e the 4 men clothed that came from roonock to okanahowan." Also included were a number of place names: "chisiapiack," "imhamoack," "Roanock," "Chawanoac," "Uttamuscawone," "panawiock," "ocanahowan," and so on. It was sensational news, the first seemingly reliable information about the lost colonists in nearly twenty years.[35]

Much of the specific information came not from Wahunsonacock or Opechancanough but from another source. An expedition led by the Paspahegh chief, Wowinchopunck, which included two Englishmen, had set off from Warraskoyack (probably the Pagan River) on the south bank of the James River in January 1608 to look for a place "beyond Roanoke," where it was

33. Samuel M. Bemiss, *The Three Charters of the Virginia Company of London . . . with Seven Related Documents . . . , 1606-1621* (Williamsburg, Va., 1957), 66–67.

34. Ibid., 59–60.

35. Barbour, ed., *Jamestown Voyages*, I, 236–240.

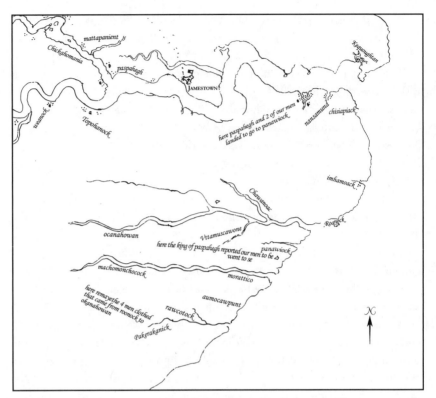

Detail from John Smith's sketch map of 1608. Drawn by Rebecca L. Wrenn

reported many "apparelled" men lived. Although, according to Smith, Wo-winchopunck played the villain "'and deluding us for rewards,' returned within three or four dayes," the notes on the map indicate the small search party traveled a good way to the south, possibly as far as the Neuse, and had some success in finding out where a few of the colonists might be. Despite being unable to make contact with the survivors themselves, Smith might have wondered whether a future expedition led by a more reliable guide would fare better.[36]

The passage in Gates's instructions was clearly derived from Smith's sketch map and description of 1608, but it also included additional information about lands to the south and the lost colonists' slaughter. Who had informed the London Company about the fate of the lost colonists? The most

36. Smith, *True Relation,* in Barbour, ed., *Complete Works of Captain John Smith,* I, 63; Horn, *A Land as God Made It,* 100–103.

likely candidate is a shadowy Indian called Machumps, who might have heard of the killings from his sister, Winganuske, one of Wahunsonacock's favorite wives, or from other relatives close to the great chief. Machumps went to England at the behest of Wahunsonacock late in 1608 and remained there (probably in London) until returning with Gates the following summer. Little is known about his stay in the capital, but sometime during the first few months of 1609, he met William Strachey. Strachey had probably already decided to try his luck in the colony, having no better prospects at home, and had been thinking about writing an official account of Virginia. Hearing of Machumps's arrival, Strachey might have wondered whether the Indian could provide information about the Powhatans that Strachey intended to include in the first part of his book. Why Machumps might have told Strachey about the slaughter is unknown; possibly he was boasting about Wahunsonacock's influence over peoples of the Roanoke region, or perhaps the information came out indirectly in questioning about rumors, commonplace among peoples on the south side of the James River, telling of strangers who lived in the interior.[37]

Strachey quickly passed the information to the company, who in turn relayed it in the form of a report (now lost) to the king. The news was devastating. The "men women, and Children of the first plantation at Roanoak," Strachey wrote, "(who 20. and od yeares had peaceably lyved and intermixed with those Savadges, and were out of his Territory)," were "by practize and Comaundement of Powhatan [Wahunsonacock] (he himself perswaded thereunto by his Priests) miserably slaughtered without any offence given him." Machumps provided also a description of the "high-land," the piedmont of North Carolina, where at "*Peccarecanick,* and *Ochanahoen* . . . the People have howses built with stone walls, and one story above another, so taught them by the English who escaped the slaughter at *Roanoak.*" In this same region, at "Ritanoe, the Weroance *Eyanoco* preserved 7. of the English alive, fower men, twoo Boyes, and one young Maid, (who escaped and fled up the River of Chaonoke) to beat his Copper, of which he hath certayn Mynes."[38]

In other discussions held by the company, Thomas Harriot provided details of the area surrounding Roanoke Island. Indians had told him many times that, southwest of "our old fort in Virginia" (on Roanoke Island), there were great deposits of "red mettall," and more recently Jamestown

---

37. The following paragraphs are based on *A Land as God Made It,* 143–149.
38. Strachey, *Virginia Britania,* 34, 91.

settlers had learned from local Indians of a "rich mine of copper or gold" at a "towne called Ritanoe, neere certaine mountaines lying West of Roanoac."[39]

According to Strachey, although grieved by news of the slaughter, James I—because he was a "most just and most mercifull Prynce"—had "given order that Powhatan [Wahunsonacock] himself with his Weroances, and all his people shalbe spared, and revenge only taken upon his *Quiyoughquisocks* [priests], by whose advise and perswasions was exercised that bloudy Cruelty." Countless sermons that rang out from English pulpits during the spring and summer of 1609 underlined the Anglican Church's mission to redeem the Indians of Virginia and bring them to the true faith. The Powhatans could yet be saved, the English believed, if removed from the baleful influence of their priests, "being the ministers of Sathan."[40]

Wahunsonacock was to be spared, but company leaders instructed Gates to take the Indian prisoner or render him a "tributary," for, they asserted, "it is clere even to reason beside our experience that he loved not our neighbourhood." Lesser chiefs would be required to acknowledge no other lord but James I, "and so we shall free them all from the tirrany of Powhatan." Each weroance would provide corn at every harvest, baskets of dye, and skins, as well as laborers "to worke weekely" for the English. This tribute would be much less onerous than that exacted by Wahunsonacock, and in return the Indians would be protected from their enemies and enjoy many "commodities and blessings" from the English "of which they are yet insensible." Priests would be imprisoned or executed, and to better convert the Indians, the company recommended the colony take into custody those "which are younge and to succeede in the[ir] governement" to be educated "in your manners and religion." In this way, the company anticipated, the "people will easily obey you and become in time civill and Christian."[41]

The company saw itself as the liberator of Indian peoples who had been conquered by the Powhatan chief. Company leaders were confident that oppressed peoples would most willingly submit to English rule because they would be treated much better by the English than by the Powhatans, enjoying "freely the fruictes of their owne Territoryes" and partaking in "a peaceable and franck trade with the English." Indians would become "Cittizens with the English," protected from their enemies and allowed to live in free-

39. Edward D. Neill, *History of the Virginia Company of London* (1869; rpt. New York, 1968), 26–27.

40. Strachey, *Virginia Britania,* 89, 91.

41. Bemiss, *Three Charters,* 62–63.

dom and safety. The company would profit from Indian tribute, and the Indians would become better off from working the land and engaging in English trade. Replacing Wahunsonacock with an English overlord would unlock the natural bounty of Virginia, break the military dominance of the Powhatans, turn Indian warriors into farmers, and convert Native peoples to Christianity. Peace would bring prosperity to English and Indians alike.[42]

Until Wahunsonacock and his priests could be removed from the people, the company advised the colonists to proceed cautiously. Alliances were to be made only with peoples outside the region that were hostile to the Powhatans. Establishing a garrison above the falls of the James River would strengthen relations with the Monacans and Mannahoacs, just as locating a settlement at Ocanahowan, several days' journey to the south of Jamestown, would situate the English among peoples unfriendly toward Wahunsonacock and open up a new front against the Powhatans.[43]

If survivors of the Powhatans' slaughter could yet be found in the North Carolina piedmont, they might provide invaluable information about lands in the interior. Having lived in the region for nearly twenty years, lost colonists and their children must have established extensive contacts with the local peoples who had sheltered and traded with them.[44] In the "warme Vallyes" near *"Peccarecanick,"* Strachey believed it would be possible to grow sugarcane, oranges, lemons, and "all sortes of Southren fruites" as cultivated in Mediterranean latitudes. Friendly peoples of "South Virginia" might know of copper or silver mines in the mountains, have heard of a river passage to the great sea in the west, and, because of their intimate knowledge of the region, be able to "open the womb and bowels of this country,"

42. Strachey, *Virginia Britania,* 91–93.

43. Bemiss, *Three Charters,* 62–64, 66–67.

44. Two further expeditions were sent to the south by John Smith in the winter and spring of 1608–1609: Michael Sicklemore had returned from the Chowanocs in January or February with "little hope and lesse certaintie of them [that] were left by Sir Walter Rawley," and Nathaniel Powell and Anas Todkill, sent by Smith to search in the lands of the Mangoags, learned nothing of the lost colonists apart from "they were all dead" (Smith, *Proceedings,* in Barbour, ed., *Complete Works of Captain John Smith,* I, 265–266). The company's *True and Sincere Declaration,* however, states that two men (probably Powell and Todkill) were "sent out to seek them . . . , found crosses and letters, the characters and assured testimonies of Christians, newly cut in the barks of trees" but were "denied by the savages speech with them" (Edward Wright Haile, ed., *Jamestown Narratives: Eyewitness Accounts of the Virginia Colony, The First Decade: 1607–1617* [Champlain, Va., 1998], 367).

to the inestimable benefit of the company, its financial backers, and the nation.[45]

The new Virginia was to be located deeper in the interior, from the falls of the James River to the rapids of the Roanoke River, where colonists would be safe from attack by the Spanish, live close to Indian peoples hostile to the Powhatans, and be well placed for further expeditions inland where perhaps great wealth yet remained to be discovered.

The Voyage of Captain Francisco Fernández de Écija

About the same time Sir Thomas Gates's great fleet of nine ships and five hundred settlers left Plymouth Sound for Virginia, a small vessel (a *zabra*, frequently used by the Spanish to explore inshore waters and rivers) slipped away from San Augustín on June 11, 1609, bearing north. Besides the crew and Captain Francisco Fernández de Écija, *La Asunsión de Cristo* carried twenty-five officers and soldiers, a Guale Indian woman ("a native of Santa Elena and interpreter for that country"), and two pieces of artillery. Écija's mission was to gather information in preparation for a larger expedition should Philip III decide to follow the advice of his ambassador in London and the Council of State in Madrid and confront the English interlopers in America. The council had earlier expressed the opinion that the "matter of Virginia is not to be remedied by any negotiation, but by force, punishing those who have gone there" and recommended an armada "be assembled, with all possible speed, to go hunt them and drive them out from wherever they may be, punishing them exemplarily." Before taking action, however, the king demanded more details about the English colony, the settlers' intentions, and what they had accomplished.[46]

Écija adopted a leisurely pace as he proceeded up the coast. Nearly three weeks passed before they reached the Rio Jordán (Santee River), three hundred miles from San Augustín and less than halfway to their destination. After sending a small party ashore with an Indian interpreter—Alonso, a Christian convert they had picked up along the coast—the captain was informed by local peoples that, thirteen days earlier, a ship had anchored two leagues (seven to eight miles) to the south. They understood it "had been to the village or fort of the English." Écija learned also that, four or five days' journey away, the English had settled "in a village called Guandape" by "a river that runs to the sea." On an island "surrounded by water," apart from

45. Strachey, *Virginia Britania,* 34; Haile, ed., *Jamestown Narratives,* 367; Bemiss, *Three Charters,* 59–61; Horn, *A Land as God Made It,* 149–150.
46. Horn, *A Land as God Made It,* 153–154.

a narrow strip that connected it to the mainland, the English had built a fort made of wood. They had made alliances with "neighboring caciques" (chiefs), Alonso said, who provided them with food in return for clothes and tools, because the colonists "did not bother with sowing but with fortifying." Ships reportedly "came and went every day," and three months before, seven had sailed from the settlement, six to the north and one to the south, the latter flying colors and beating a "war-drum."[47]

Proceeding cautiously around Cape San Roman (Cape Fear) and along the Outer Banks, the Spanish saw great smoke signals rising from the coast. As they passed by one of the islands, they spotted six Indians running along the beach, "continually blowing on some pipes and shouting to us," Écija recounted. "And we got the idea from what we heard that they were playing on those pipes in some harmony, and judging by the sound they were pipes made by foreigners." The Spaniard concluded the music "was a signal they had for ships that passed, they were so diligent"; but whether a warning or welcome was unclear.[48]

Finally, at five o'clock in the afternoon on July 14, the Spanish arrived off Cape Henry, where they spotted a ship "in the bay." Opting not to risk an engagement late in the day, they dropped anchor and posted a guard for the night. At dawn, the lookout reported the ship had not moved, which led Écija to believe it must be an enemy, since it appeared to be guarding the entrance to a large river. After waiting for a favorable wind, the Spanish hoisted sail and set a course directly toward the ship. As they approached, Écija realized that the ship he faced was much larger than his own and began to have second thoughts about a battle. If his vessel was badly damaged in action, he might be unable to get back to Florida and therefore unable to report the valuable information he had learned from the Indians en route to the Chesapeake Bay.[49]

While the Spanish stood off, the English ship headed into the interior, showing the way up the river where, Écija surmised, Jamestown was located. When the Spanish did not follow, the English ship returned and

47. Barbour, ed., *Jamestown Voyages,* II, 282, 291–301. The Indians' account reveals how information about Jamestown had spread to peoples some three hundred miles away.

48. John H. Hann, "Translation of the Ecija Voyages of 1605 and 1609 and the González Derrotero of 1609," *Florida Archaeology,* II (1986), 34; Barbour, ed., *Jamestown Voyages,* II, 307. I am grateful to Philip Evans for bringing this passage to my attention.

49. Barbour, ed., *Jamestown Voyages,* II, 307–308.

began bearing down on them. Upon consulting with his officers, Écija decided not to fight or attempt to slip past (for fear of becoming trapped) and ordered a hasty retreat with as much sail as possible. The English ship gave chase the rest of the day, but under cover of darkness, the Spanish managed to evade her and headed back along the coast to San Augustín.[50]

On the return journey, Écija questioned a captive Frenchman, "Juan Corbe [Jean Corbet]" of Le Havre, whom he had picked up earlier on the Jordan River from Indians living at a village called "Sati" deep in the interior. Corbet had learned from three Indians who had been to the English settlement that the fort and village were made of wood and that "they had two large ships mounted like castles on guard at the fort, and two more on guard as sentinels by the sandbank [at the entrance to the bay], without counting others that went and came." One of the Indians was an interpreter for the English and "served as, executioner." In late August, Écija put in at the Bay of Cayuga and anchored off the mouth of two large rivers (the Cooper and Ashley), where quite by chance he encountered one of the Indians Corbet had mentioned, who confirmed the Frenchman's testimony. The English, the Indian said, had "a lot of people and one fort . . . and a very large house where the English cacique lived."[51]

To follow up, Écija persuaded Alonso to go to the English settlement and then report back to him directly. More than a month later, Alonso returned to San Augustín. He told Écija that they had traveled five days from his village when they reached a village called "Guaño," where the Indians quarreled a great deal because "they [Alonso and his companion] had told the Spaniards that there was an English settlement near there, and this ended in a great fracas." The "Guaño" Indians said "they did not need to go any farther, that there was nothing to see, and for them to go back for they were afraid for their lives." Although Alonso asserted "that the English have won the Indians over as far as there," Écija might have reached a different conclusion: the English were viewed by the people of "Guaño" as extremely dangerous.[52]

In his report to the king, Écija included an assessment by Don Diego de Ibarra, governor of Florida, who asserted that the English planned to use Jamestown as a base for exploring inland waterways to New Spain and the

50. Ibid., 307–319; Irene A. Wright, "Spanish Policy toward Virginia, 1606–1612: Jamestown, Écija, and John Clark of the Mayflower," *American Historical Review,* XXV (1920), 450–452.

51. Barbour, ed., *Jamestown Voyages,* II, 303, 312, 315.

52. Ibid., 316–319.

rich silver mines of Zacatecas as well as finding a river passage to the west coast, where they would fortify themselves, build fleets, "and overrun the whole coast of New Spain, Tierra Firme, Peru, and China, to the great damage of the crown and subjects of Your Majesty." Given the gravity of the threat, the Council for War in the Indies urged Philip III to send four or five thousand men to drive the English out of Virginia as soon as possible, "before they take more root and possess themselves of more land . . . [and] extend through other regions, as they will go on to do, since none other is their design." Yet Philip chose not to do anything, believing that the colony was on the brink of collapse as a result of disease, starvation, and Indian attacks.[53]

A "Lande, Even as God Made It"

During the summer of 1608, John Smith carried out two extensive explorations of the Chesapeake Bay. What he learned had been almost wholly discouraging. He was unable to discover news of gold or silver mines in the interior, and mention by the Powhatans of a sea somewhere far beyond the mountains turned out to be a reference to the Great Lakes, not the Pacific. His exploration of the Potomac and headwaters of the bay confirmed no large river existed that would carry the English through the mountains to the other side of the land mass.[54]

Smith might have been skeptical that Virginia held hidden treasures as early as September 1608, when he took over the presidency of the colony, but by the time of the publication of his *Proceedings of the English Colony* four years later, he had given up hope of finding riches. Virginia was not England's "Spanish" colony, a rival to Mexico or Peru. In the *Proceedings,* three of his old companions—Richard Wiffin, William Phettiplace, and Anas Todkill—put into words what were surely Smith's sentiments:

> It was the Spaniards good hap to happen in those parts, where were infinite numbers of people, whoe had manured the ground with that providence, that it afforded victuall at all times: and time had brought them to that perfection, they had the use of gold and silver, and the most of such commodities, as their countries afforded, so that what the Spaniard got, was only the spoile and pillage of those countrie people, and not the

53. Wright, "Spanish Policy toward Virginia," *AHR,* XXV (1920), 463–466. The Council for War's report was not forwarded to Philip III until the spring of 1611.

54. Smith, *Proceedings,* in Barbour, ed., *Complete Works of Captain John Smith,* I, 224–233; Smith, *Generall Historie, ibid.,* II, 162–180.

labours of their owne hands. But had those fruitfull Countries, beene as Salvage, as barbarous, as ill peopled, as little planted, laboured and manured as Virginia, their proper labours (it is likely) would have produced as small profit as ours. But had Virginia bin peopled, planted, manured, and adorned, with such store of pretious Jewels, and rich commodities, as was the Indies: then, had we not gotten, and done as much as by their examples might bee expected from us, the world might then have traduced us and our merits, and have made shame and infamy our recompence and reward.

But we chanced in a lande, even as God made it. Where we found only an idle, improvident, scattered people; ignorant of the knowledge of gold, or silver, or any commodities; and carelesse of any thing but from hand to mouth, but for ba[u]bles of no worth; nothing to encourage us, but what accidentally wee found nature afforded.[55]

The English failed to discover rich gold or silver mines in the interior or to locate the lost colonists or a passage to the South Sea, although rumors of their existence lingered on for decades. Hostilities with the Powhatans, which erupted in the fall of 1609 shortly after Smith's departure, rendered impossible plans to convert Indians to Christianity and to establish English settlements in the piedmont of North Carolina, where survivors of Roanoke were thought to be. When Gates arrived at Jamestown in May 1610 after being shipwrecked for ten months on Bermuda, any prospect of finding the lost colonists and creating a new Virginia extending from the falls of the James to the Roanoke River had long since perished.

War and the urgent necessity to shift the capital from Jamestown to Henrico forty miles upriver kept the English fully occupied over the next five years, and by the time hostilities between the settlers and Indians ended, English planters had discovered a new source of wealth in the guise of tobacco and Indian lands that made the search for riches in the interior no longer attractive. As buoyant demand for Virginia leaf in England stimulated growing profits for the company and planters alike, so the lure of gold mines and a passage to the Pacific rapidly faded.[56]

55. Smith, *Proceedings,* ibid., I, 257.

56. In fact, the English did discover silver mines in Monacan territory about twenty miles above the falls of the James River, but these were evidently insufficient to warrant the labor of developing. See Strachey, *Virginia Britania,* 131–132. On the tobacco boom, see Edmund S. Morgan, *American Slavery, American Freedom: The Ordeal of Colonial Virginia* (New York, 1975), 108–130.

For their part, the Powhatans were unable to acquire English firearms and other weapons in the quantities they desired or expel the intruders from Tsenacommacah. Wahunsonacock and Opechancanough missed their best chance to finish off the colony in the winter and spring of 1608–1609, when the ailing settlement at Jamestown was in complete disarray, undermined by internal dissension, food shortages, and the renegade Germans in league with the Powhatans. Why did the chiefs not strike? There is no clear answer. Whether they, like the Spanish, thought the colony would soon collapse or could not agree on a strategy, the two chiefs failed to coordinate a large-scale attack and focused instead (unsuccessfully) on trying to kill Captain John Smith.

The consequence of their failure was catastrophic. Devastation caused by the war of 1609–1614 and spread of English settlements in its aftermath brought misery and hardship to many Indian peoples of the James River valley, who were driven off their lands or moved away. A massive uprising orchestrated by Opechancanough in March 1622, although leading to the deaths of hundreds of settlers, proved too little too late and only led to more attacks on the Powhatans by vengeful colonists. In July 1624, Sir Francis Wyatt, the English governor, together with sixty men in full armor, sailed up the Pamunkey River into the heartland of Opechancanough's territory, where they were confronted by approximately eight hundred bowmen and an unspecified number of allies. The battle continued for two days but despite their courage, which even Wyatt acknowledged, the Pamunkeys were beaten back by the sheer firepower of the soldiers. Eventually, after sustaining heavy losses, the Indians stopped fighting and "dismayedly, stood most ruthfully [ruefully] looking on while theire Corne was Cutt downe" by the English.[57]

The defeat of the flower of Opechancanough's fighting forces was decisive. Over the next two decades, the English arrived in ever larger numbers, taking up the best lands and dispossessing local peoples. In 1644, Opechancanough launched a last assault that claimed the lives of about four hundred settlers, but by then, any attempt to oust the English from Virginia was hopeless. Blind, feeble, and near a hundred years old, the great Pamunkey

57. Susan Myra Kingsbury, ed., *The Records of the Virginia Company of London,* 4 vols. (Washington, D.C., 1906–1935), II, 482, IV, 507–508; J. Frederick Fausz, "The Powhatan Uprising of 1622: A Historical Study of Ethnocentrism and Cultural Conflict" (Ph.D. diss., College of William and Mary, 1977), 493, 509–511; Helen C. Rountree, *Pocahontas's People: The Powhatan Indians of Virginia through Four Centuries* (Norman, Okla., 1990), 78.

chief died a prisoner in a squalid Jamestown jail two years later, shot in the back by one of the guards. The Powhatan chiefdom had collapsed.[58]

The Spanish also failed to prevent the English from settling in Virginia. Their best opportunity had passed with Écija's reconnaissance mission. Had he arrived a few days earlier and not been blocked at the entrance to the James River by Captain Samuel Argall's ship, *Mary and John,* the Spanish might have seen for themselves Jamestown's disunity, which might have encouraged them to test the fort's defenses. Even a small-scale attack might have proved successful. Mutinous Englishmen might have rebelled and joined forces with Écija or have brought Powhatan warriors into the fray on the side of the Spanish to overwhelm the fort. The destruction of Jamestown could have discouraged further English efforts to settle in the region for a generation, or perhaps permanently. As it was, Jamestown's survival signified an end to any remaining hope that the Spanish might eventually populate the vast regions north of Florida or at least prevent other Europeans from doing so.[59]

Early-seventeenth-century Virginia / Tsenacommacah was an unpredictable place. Despite their best efforts to find out as much as they could about each other, none of those involved—the Powhatans, English, or Spanish— was able to penetrate much beyond the half-baked impressions they had initially formed of one another. Only the experience of living together side by side along the James River valley finally revealed to English settlers and Indians the irreconcilable differences in their lifestyles and cultures, and only after the passing of many years did it become clear to the Spanish that they had long since missed their chance to get rid of the English. Indian and Spanish claims to Virginia persisted, but by 1625, a new power had arisen in North America.

58. Rountree, *Pocahontas's People,* 82–86; Rountree, *Pocahontas, Powhatan, Opechancanough,* 232–233.

59. Horn, *A Land as God Made It,* 153, 155.

J. H. Elliott

THE IBERIAN ATLANTIC AND VIRGINIA

From the standpoint of European history, the story of early colonial Virginia is the story of the intrusion of an alien group of English men and women—totaling some 200 in 1609 and 843 in 1621—into an Iberian Atlantic world. From the standpoint of the history of the indigenous peoples of America, it is equally the story of an intrusion—that of one more set of strangers into an area inhabited by Algonquian-speaking peoples of the eastern seaboard. From the standpoint of African history, it is the story of how yet another European-American community developed an interest in a combined Afro-European slave trade that had acquired over the past century a profitable transatlantic extension.[1]

These three stories are not easily integrated—a problem that I fear confronts every practitioner of Atlantic history. But insofar as they are capable of being inserted into a single framework, that framework is the Iberian Atlantic, and it is this Iberian Atlantic that I shall primarily be discussing to suggest the ways in which its fortunes and character affected the establishment and hesitant growth of the Jamestown settlement.

In the first volume of his *Shaping of America,* D. W. Meinig identifies three oceanic systems in the sixteenth century extending Europe's reach across the Atlantic, "one to Northern America and two to distinct national and geographical sectors of Tropical America." These were shaped by the winds and currents. The North Atlantic system developed out of the interest of Atlantic Europeans, northerners and southerners alike, in exploiting the Newfoundland fishing banks; it gradually acquired extensions along the North American coast, beginning with the French forts and trading posts at Port-Royal and Quebec, which were established in the years when the

1. Kenneth R. Andrews, *Trade, Plunder, and Settlement: Maritime Enterprise and the Genesis of the British Empire, 1480–1630* (Cambridge, 1984), 318, 323; and see Frederic W. Gleach, *Powhatan's World and Colonial Virginia: A Conflict of Cultures* (Lincoln, Neb., 1997); and John Thornton, *Africa and Africans in the Making of the Atlantic World, 1400–1800,* 2d ed. (Cambridge, 1998).

Virginia project was being launched. The first of the two Iberian systems spanning the mid-Atlantic was the Spanish *Carrera de Indias,* which linked Seville to the Caribbean and thence to Mexico and Panama to supply Spanish settlers in the Indies and carry back the silver mined by an indigenous labor force in the viceroyalties of New Spain and Peru. The second, more southerly, system was the Portuguese one, linking Lisbon to the Portuguese coastal settlements in Brazil. Although the crowns of Spain and Portugal were united under Philip II in 1580, these two systems remained distinctive while becoming interconnected as Portuguese merchants shipped increasing numbers of African slaves across the Atlantic in response to growing demand in the Americas. The growth of this slave trade, in turn, spawned a Portuguese subsystem in the late sixteenth and early seventeenth centuries as bilateral routes developed that linked Angola directly to the Brazilian ports without exposing living merchandise to the risks and higher costs of shipment through Lisbon.[2]

Atlantic history should be a history at once of connections and comparisons, and if Virginia is to be successfully inserted into the wider history of the Atlantic world, both need to be explored. In practice, colonial Virginia was to be a meeting point of the three Atlantic systems—northern, Spanish, and Portuguese. The colony owed something to each but developed its own distinctive characteristics in response to local conditions and to the attitudes and initiatives of the colonists and their sponsors.

In their eyes, that world was dominated by the power of Spain—a Spain that was bent on universal monarchy and acted as the right arm of the church of Rome. Throughout the early stages of their colonization of the Americas, the English tended to define themselves in relation to Spain, which they looked upon as both an example and a menace. Take, for instance, these words from the *True and Sincere Declaration* issued by the Council and Governors of the Virginia Company in 1609, when their project was at a low ebb: "If we cast our eye upon the *Spanish Conquest* of the *Indyes,* how aboundant their stories are of Fleets, Battailes, and Armies lost: eighteen upon the attempt of *Guiana,* and more than seventy in both the *Indyes,* and yet with how indefatigable industry, and prosperous fate, they have pursued and vanquished all these, their many Armies maintained in *Europe,* can witnesse, with too lamentable an experience. If we compare the *beginnings,* they were meaner than ours, and subject to all the same and

2. D. W. Meinig, *The Shaping of America,* I, *Atlantic America, 1492–1800* (New Haven, Conn., 1986), 60; Luiz Felipe de Alencastro, *O trato dos viventes: Formação do Brasil no Atlántico sul, séculos XVI e XVII* (São Paulo, 2000), 28–29.

much more uncertainty. If the *Religion,* which shall crown the success, it admits no controversy nor comparison, among those to whom we write: if the *Commodities,* they, which we have in assurance and knowledge, are of more necessity, and those in hope equally rich and abondant."[3]

Although the defeat of the Armada in 1588 would greatly increase the confidence of the English that, with divine assistance, they could check and ultimately overcome the power of Spain, experience had made them painfully conscious of that power's reach and depth. Francis Drake might have exposed the vulnerability of Spain's Caribbean outposts, but attacks by English and other northern privateers and marauders induced Philip II to embark on a program designed to improve the defenses of the American ports and set up coastal patrols to protect the shipping lanes.[4] Although the desirability of establishing a transatlantic base from which to launch attacks on Spain's American territories and the returning silver fleets ranked high among the motivations for the colonizing projects of Elizabeth's reign, those involved were well aware of the risk. The brutal extinction of the French colony in Florida by Pedro Menéndez de Avilés in 1565 had etched itself deeply into the collective consciousness of northern Europeans. What had happened once could all too easily happen again.

The foundation and extinction of the French settlement in Florida in the early 1560s was indeed a defining moment in the history of the Iberian Atlantic. The Florida massacre sharply intensified Protestant Europe's hatred for the Spain of Philip II and provided an unpleasant warning of the risks run by those who attempted to gain a foothold in Spain's American territories. On the Spanish side, the French attempt at colonization provoked Philip II into establishing at Saint Augustine in 1565 what was to be the first permanent European settlement on the eastern coast of North America.[5]

But Saint Augustine did not represent the first Spanish intrusion into North American territory. The story, as told by Paul Hoffman in his *New Andalucia and a Way to the Orient,* began in 1521 with a Spanish caravel sighting a previously unknown land north of the Bahamas and weighing anchor at Winyah Bay. This sighting of a land initially called Chicora by the Spaniards led in 1526 to an expedition organized by Lucas Vázquez

3. Alexander Brown, *The Genesis of the United States* (London, 1890), I, doc. 114, 348.

4. See Paul E. Hoffman, *The Spanish Crown and the Defense of the Caribbean, 1535–1585* (Baton Rouge, 1980).

5. For Florida, see David B. Quinn, *Explorers and Colonies: America, 1500–1625* (London, 1990), chap. 16 ("The Attempted Colonization of Florida by the French, 1562–1565").

de Ayllón to settle a region that he believed would be fertile and rich. He christened it New Andalusia, claiming that Andalusia and the Chesapeake Bay, which his ships entered but did not seriously explore, shared the same latitude. They do not.[6] The failure of Ayllón's expedition turned the Spaniards away from further exploration of the northern coastline, and the reports of the survivors of Hernando de Soto's famous expedition of 1539–1543 did nothing to encourage the belief that the coastal region was suitable for settlement. But the legend of the fertile land of Chicora made its way into the European literature of discovery. Here it became associated with Verrazano's tale of a North American isthmus and a route to the Orient, providing one source of inspiration for the colonizing dreams of the French and the British.

French interest in the region in the 1550s, at a time when France and Spain were at war, led to renewed Spanish interest and a decision in 1557 to establish a chain of Spanish settlements running as far north as the Point of Santa Elena, on today's Parris Island, South Carolina. Only the vaguest notions existed about the true extent of the coastline and the nature of the hinterland between the Gulf of Mexico and Newfoundland, a vast area called La Florida by the Spaniards, which they claimed under the terms of the Treaty of Tordesillas of 1494. In the discussions surrounding the Franco-Spanish peace settlement at Cateau-Cambrésis in 1559, the French refused to accept any prohibition on their ships' sailing to areas other than those under Spanish occupation. In response, Philip II ordered the immediate establishment of a Spanish colony at Santa Elena. The intention was to ward off any French attempt to colonize the Florida peninsula, of the kind that, in fact, Jean Ribaut would undertake in 1562.[7]

To the north of Santa Elena, a reconnaissance expedition ordered by the viceroy of New Spain, Don Luis de Velasco, led to the chance rediscovery in 1561 of the bay of Santa María—the Chesapeake Bay—by Antonio Velázquez, the captain of a Spanish caravel. When it left, it carried on board two young Indians, one of them a person of standing, who gave them to understand that the land was known as Ajacán. This, it seemed, could be the fabled New Andalusia. In the light of Velázquez's report on the land and its inhabitants, the governor of Florida, Menéndez, concluded that the Chesapeake was a more promising region than Santa Elena for a Spanish settlement.

6. Paul E. Hoffman, *A New Andalucia and a Way to the Orient: The American Southeast during the Sixteenth Century* (Baton Rouge, 1990), 35–36, 60–83.

7. Ibid., 166.

This is not the place to recount the extraordinary story of the young Algonquian-speaking Indian—called Don Luis de Velasco by the Spaniards, in honor of the viceroy—who went to Mexico and then to Spain, where he was presented at court to Philip II and was taken up, first by the Dominicans and then by the Jesuits, as a God-given instrument for the evangelization of the Atlantic coast Indians.[8] But by encouraging the Spaniards to devote their attention to Ajacán, perhaps primarily in the hope of returning to his homeland, he played a crucial role in the subsequent history of the Chesapeake region. He participated in the abortive Dominican attempt of 1566 to establish a mission on the Chesapeake and then in the more serious 1570 Jesuit mission sponsored by Menéndez and led by Father Juan Baptista de Segura, the vice-provincial of the Jesuit order in Florida. He came with them to a land very different from the one he had left in 1561—a famine-stricken land depopulated by the epidemics that the earlier Spaniards must have brought along with them.[9]

We do not know whether the sight of this terrible transformation played a part in his decision to leave the mission and rejoin his own people or in his subsequent decision to lead the party that massacred the Jesuits in February 1571.[10] Life is always complicated for inhabitants of the "middle ground." But the impact of his actions was momentous. His initial desire to return to his native country, and perhaps to Christianize his people, brought the land of the Powhatan into the orbit of the Iberian Atlantic. His murder of the Jesuits called forth a punitive expedition led by Menéndez in 1572, which gave the Powhatans a sharp taste of European ruthlessness. But the whole experience also discouraged the Spaniards from further attempts to found a settlement in Ajacán, thus leaving the land clear for Spain's rivals and the later Jamestown enterprise. Finally, if indeed, as has been suggested, Don Luis, once back among his own people, was metamorphosed into Opechan-

8. For differing versions of the story of Don Luis de Velasco and Spanish evangelization of Ajacán, see Clifford M. Lewis and Albert J. Loomie, *The Spanish Jesuit Mission in Virginia, 1570-1572* (Chapel Hill, N.C., 1953); Charlotte M. Gradie, "Spanish Jesuits in Virginia: The Mission That Failed," *Virginia Magazine of History and Biography*, XCVI (1988), 131-156; Hoffman, *New Andalucia*, 183-187, 262-266.

9. "We find the land of Don Luis in quite another condition than expected, not because he was at fault in his description of it, but because Our Lord has chastised it with six years of famine and death" (Luis de Quirós and Juan Baptista de Segura to Juan de Hinistrosa, in Lewis and Loomie, *Spanish Jesuit Mission,* 89).

10. For an attempt to interpret Velasco's behavior, see Gleach, *Powhatan's World,* 90-97.

canough, then the English colonists of Virginia would have been confronted by an Algonquian leader intimately versed in European ways.[11]

The prelude to the English intrusion into Ajacán in 1607 was Sir Walter Ralegh's Roanoke venture of 1584-1586. Roanoke brought together, in a concentrated effort, the various strands of motivation behind the privateering, trading, and colonizing projects of the England of Elizabeth: the desire for a base for attacks on Spain's empire of the Indies and the Spanish silver fleets; the hopes of a route to the Orient by way of the supposed Verrazzano Sea; the search for raw materials and mineral wealth and for new markets for English commodities; the desire for an outlet for surplus population; and the hopes of extending the Gospel and acquiring national glory.[12] The failure of the Spaniards to establish permanent settlements north of Santa Elena made this part of the coast potentially a good area for an English colonial venture. While Spain might claim possession, the nearest Spanish settlements were far away, and the Spanish Crown had failed to make good its territorial claims.

Although Roanoke Island turned out to be unsuitable, a more promising alternative began to suggest itself in the shape of the Chesapeake Bay, which Philip Amadas entered on his 1584 expedition (only to encounter hostile Indians who—presumably mindful of the treatment they had received at the hands of Spaniards twelve years earlier—killed some of his crew). Shortage of money and the outbeak of war with Spain in 1585 prevented further attempts at settlement, but the deepwater harbor of the Chesapeake and its navigable waterways suggested a base that would be secure from Spanish attacks. By 1587, when the remaining Roanoke colonists moved into the area and settled among the Chesapeake Indians, the Spaniards already had some idea of English intentions and made plans to seize the bay. In the event, no attack was launched. The efforts of the Spaniards, like those of the English, were diverted from the Chesapeake to the European conflict, and the Armada campaign and its aftermath gave the Powhatans twenty years' reprieve.[13]

The timing of events on the North American fringe of the Iberian At-

11. See the account in chapter 2 of Carl Bridenbaugh, *Jamestown, 1544-1699* (New York, 1980). Bridenbaugh's identification of Velasco with Opechancanough is much contested. See Helen C. Rountree, *Pocahontas's People: The Powhatan Indians of Virginia through Four Centuries* (Norman, Okla., 1990), 18-19.

12. The most comprehensive account of the Roanoke project is to be found in David Beers Quinn, *Set Fair for Roanoke: Voyages and Colonies, 1584-1660* (Chapel Hill, N.C., 1985).

13. Ibid., 42-43, 142, 343; Hoffman, *New Andalucia*, 303-305.

lantic was therefore dictated by the course of international events in Europe. How, then, do we explain the return of the English to the Chesapeake region and the colonizing venture of 1607? Again, the same holds true: the international conjuncture was decisive. By the late 1590s, the strain of war was taking its toll on both Spain and England.[14] With the Spanish Crown finances collapsing, Philip II made peace with France during the last months of his life in 1598 and laid the ground for a possible future settlement with the Dutch. His young son, Philip III, however, began his reign on a bellicose note and in 1601 launched an unsuccessful attack on Ireland in an attempt to support the Catholic rebellion in Ulster.

Ireland, that laboratory for English colonizing experiments in the Atlantic world, had long been on the front line in the struggle between Spain and England and between Reformation and Counter-Reformation Europe. The defeat of the Spanish invading force at Kinsale in 1601 ended the danger of a Catholic Ireland's becoming a Spanish satellite and left the road clear for the definitive imposition of English rule and for large-scale colonization of Ulster by the English and the Scots. But the war in Ireland had imposed a massive additional strain on English resources, already stretched by the naval war and by support for the Dutch and the French. By the start of the new century, England, like Spain, was exhausted. The death of Elizabeth in 1603 and the accession of the pacifically inclined James VI of Scotland to the English throne opened the door to a peace settlement between two profoundly war-weary countries.[15]

The new monarchs, Philip III and James I, were both faced by divided councils, but they moved hesitantly towards a rapprochement. Peace was concluded at the Somerset House Conference of 1604. Under the Treaty of London, it was agreed that free trade should be restored between the two countries where it had existed before the war, but the English delegates tried and failed to secure recognition from the Spaniards that this included the right to trade with the Indies.[16]

14. For the Anglo-Spanish conflict in the 1590s, see R. B. Wernham, *The Return of the Armadas: The Last Years of the Elizabethan War against Spain, 1595–1603* (Oxford, 1994).

15. On Ireland, see, in particular, David Beers Quinn, *The Elizabethans and the Irish* (Ithaca, N.Y., 1966); and Nicholas Canny, *Kingdom and Colony: Ireland in the Atlantic World, 1560–1800* (Baltimore, 1988). For the costs of maintaining the English army in Ireland—£1,800,000 over the nine years of war—see J. McGurk, *The Elizabethan Conquest of Ireland: The 1590s Crisis* (Manchester, 1997), 203.

16. Roland Dennis Hussey, "America in European Diplomacy, 1597–1604," *Revista de historia de América,* XLI (1956), 1–30; Paul C. Allen, *Philip III and the Pax His-*

In spite of this, the advocates of a new colonizing venture in the New World—ambitious or land-hungry gentry, and merchants with no personal involvement in the Spanish trade—detected enough ambiguity in the clause about the resumption of prewar Anglo-Spanish trading relations to find encouragement.[17] But in James I, they had to reckon with a monarch who cast himself in the role of peacemaker of Christendom and placed a high priority on an Anglo-Spanish reconciliation, to be sealed by a dynastic union between the two crowns. The shadow of an Anglo-Spanish match—which would only be dispelled by the failure of the Prince of Wales's 1623 journey to Madrid to sue in person for the hand of Philip III's daughter—therefore hung over the whole early history of the Virginia project. James's desperate anxiety to avoid any new confrontation with Spain set him firmly against Elizabethan-style privateering ventures. On the other hand, the reversion to the Crown of Ralegh's charter rights in 1603 following his imprisonment for treason made the king an interested party in any future colonization projects. James's comments and behavior make it clear that, like the French, he had no intention of recognizing a territorial division of the world based on papal arbitration. Instead, he believed in the applicability to America of the Roman law doctrine of *res nullius*—that land not viewed as occupied or used was open to firstcomers. In 1604, the Spanish ambassador reported him as saying that "he had no wish to permit his subjects to go to the Spanish Indies and places already reached by [the king of Spain's] forces, but to many other parts of America."[18]

The effect of government policy under James I was therefore to move English colonial enterprise away from the Spanish Caribbean to those regions, like the coastal region north of the Florida peninsula, where Spaniards had failed to settle. Further probings by English captains of the Atlantic coastline, including the Chesapeake, gave a new impetus to plans for colonization, which began to mature in 1605. These plans looked back to the colonial

---

panica, 1598-1621 (New Haven, Conn., 2000), 135-136; Kenneth R. Andrews, *The Spanish Caribbean: Trade and Plunder, 1530-1630* (New Haven, Conn., 1978), 216-220.

17. Theodore K. Rabb, *Enterprise and Empire: Merchant and Gentry Investment in the Expansion of England, 1575-1630* (Cambridge, Mass., 1967), 35-42.

18. For the English appropriation of the doctrine of res nullius, which could be turned against the indigenous population as well as against European rivals, see Anthony Pagden, *Lords of All the World: Ideologies of Empire in Spain, Britain, and France, c. 1500-1800* (New Haven, Conn., 1995), 76. Quote cited by Andrews, *Spanish Caribbean,* 218-219, from a letter from Juan de Tassis to the constable of Castile, Mar. 6, 1604, Archivo General de Simancas, E. 842, no. 5.

ventures of the period leading up to the Anglo-Spanish War, particularly those of Ralegh and his circle, but they also carried with them into the new century the imperial and anti-Spanish sentiments of the Elizabethan age. An ex-privateer like Christopher Newport spanned the two ages in person, and the virulently anti-Spanish gentry and merchants of the west country, who had been so heavily involved in the sea war against Spain, were also to play a prominent part in the new colonizing venture. Chief Justice Popham worked to merge their interests with those of the London merchants, and Sir Thomas Smythe used his influence in the city to ensure that the necessary capital was raised. Government interest in the project was reflected in the part played by Robert Cecil, earl of Salisbury, in shaping the Virginia Company, which received its royal charter in April 1606, but the interest had to be discreet because of James's fear of offending Spanish sensibilities. Any colonizing initiatives would have to be firmly associated with private enterprise, like that which now emerged under the umbrella of the Virginia Company. In December 1606, the company's fleet, under the command of Christopher Newport, set sail, and it entered the Chesapeake in April 1607 to found the Jamestown settlement.[19]

By inserting themselves into the Iberian Atlantic with what was intended to be a permanent settlement, the English directly challenged the Spanish definition of territorial rights based on papal donation. Why, then, did the Spain of Philip III not follow the example of the Spain of Philip II in Florida and wipe out the colony during the first precarious years of its existence? Although Spain's resources in the late sixteenth and early seventeenth centuries were clearly overstretched, and Ralegh and others were busily asserting that Spain's power was in decline, the answer would appear to lie more in the priorities of Spanish policy than in the practicalities of power.[20] The principal concern of Spanish ministers was, and remained, the Dutch Revolt. James I had committed himself in the 1604 treaty to ending English assistance for the Dutch and to working for a reconciliation between the rebel provinces and Spain. Spain was therefore anxious not to jeopardize its understanding with England. The need for such an understanding was greatly enhanced by the growing evidence that France under Henri IV was

19. K. R. Andrews, "Christopher Newport of Limehouse, Mariner," *William and Mary Quarterly,* 3d Ser., XI (1954), 28–41; Philip L. Barbour, ed., *The Jamestown Voyages under the First Charter, 1606–1609,* 2 vols., Works Issued by the Hakluyt Society, 2d Ser., nos. 136–137 (London, 1969); Andrews, *Trade, Plunder, and Settlement,* 308–314.

20. William Oldys and Thomas Birch, eds., *The Works of Sir Walter Ralegh, Kt. . . . ,* 8 vols. (Oxford, 1829), VIII, 309 ("A Discourse Touching a War with Spain").

rapidly recovering from its civil wars and was once again asserting itself as a major power. It was as important, therefore, to Philip III as it was to James I to prevent any incident in the Americas from souring the new Anglo-Spanish relationship. Virginia was to be the beneficiary of this uneasy entente.

At the same time, the Spanish government, alerted by a stream of letters from successive ambassadors in London, remained deeply preoccupied by reports of English activities in the Chesapeake. These activities coincided not only with moves by the French to establish settlements in the Saint Lawrence region but also with a massive influx of Dutch shipping into the Caribbean after 1598 and growing Dutch activity off the coasts of Venezuela and Brazil.[21] This international challenge to the Iberian monopoly of the New World in the opening years of the seventeenth century made Spanish ministers acutely sensitive to any fresh piece of information about developments in Virginia, and at several moments in the course of his reign, Philip III received recommendations from bodies of ministers that force should be used against the colony.

But on each occasion, Spain took no action, partly out of deference to the requirement of maintaining good relations with England but also because there were good reasons for thinking that the new colony was unlikely to survive. Perhaps encouraged by distant memories of Ayllón's abortive expedition in search of a new Andalusia in 1526, a leading Spanish minister argued in 1612 that Virginia was of no value and had neither gold nor silver. A consensus seems to have been reached in Madrid that, if the English wanted to pour more money into their struggling colony, so much the better. It was money down the drain.[22]

Ironically, therefore, we could say that early Virginia's weakness was its greatest source of strength. Why bother about an enterprise so clearly doomed to failure? But there was, of course, a further irony in all this. Growing numbers of English were coming to share the sentiments of the Spanish ministers. There were all too many reasons for thinking that Virginia was doomed.

Assumptions of failure are closely linked to the expectations that precede them, and it is at this point that I want to move from Atlantic history in

21. Jonathan I. Israel, *Dutch Primacy in World Trade, 1585–1740* (Oxford, 1989), 62–66.

22. See Irene A. Wright, "Spanish Policy toward Virginia, 1606–1612: Jamestown, Ecija, and John Clark of the Mayflower," *American Historical Review,* XXV (1920), 448–479.

terms of connections to Atlantic history in terms of comparisons. Although the English had gained their own experience from colonizing ventures in their kingdom and colony of Ireland, their American expectations and to some extent also their behavior in America were heavily shaped by Spanish experience. "If we compare the *beginnings*," as the *True and Sincere Declaration* of 1609 had said in its bid to raise morale and drum up new investments, "they were meaner than ours, and subject to all the same and much more uncertainty." It was, in fact, true that Columbus's settlement on Hispaniola had lived on a knife-edge in its early years, and there were moments when he feared that the Spanish Crown would abandon an enterprise that had led to many disappointments.[23]

Spain's enterprise of the Indies was saved by the discovery and conquest of Mexico and Peru, with their large settled populations and what turned out to be amazingly rich deposits of silver. Although from the beginning there was a strong entrepreneurial and commercial component in Spain's colonization of the Indies, the subjugation, evangelization, and exploitation of the indigenous populations and the extraction of American mineral resources were the dominant elements in the Spanish colonial enterprise. The wealth of the Indies was regarded as the key to Spanish power in Europe, and by the time of the Virginia enterprise, a considerable literature was available in English about the history of Spain's empire of the Indies. This included a shortened version of *Historia general de las Indias,* by Cortés's secretary, Francisco López de Gómara, translated into English in 1578; and among the books in the reference library of the Virginia Company was Richard Hakluyt's translation of the account by the gentleman from Elvas of Hernando de Soto's Florida expedition, published in 1609 under the title *Virginia Richly Valued.*[24]

This makes it hardly surprising that early participants in the Virginia project were imbued with similar expectations to those of the conquerors of Mexico and shared their conquistador mentality. One of them, William Brewster, wrote in 1607: "Nowe is the kinge[s] majesty offered, the most Statlye, Riche kingedom in the woorld, nevar posseste by anye Christian prynce; be you one meanes among manye to Further our Secondinge, to Conquar this land." This was the language of Cortés and his men. There

23. Brown, *Genesis of the United States,* I, doc. 114, 348; Juan Pérez de Tudela, *Las armadas de Indias y los orígenes de la política de colonización, 1492–1505* (Madrid, 1956), 67–68.

24. John Parker, *Books to Build an Empire* (Amsterdam, 1965), 87; "A List of Books Purchased for the Virginia Company," in Quinn, *Explorers and Colonies,* 385.

was the same frenzied search for precious metals and the same reluctance of gentleman colonists to turn their hands to hard labor. Prospects of finding in the empire of Powhatan a more northerly version of the empire of Montezuma raised questions similar to those confronted by Cortés about securing and legitimizing a formal recognition of European overlordship. In 1519, Cortés skillfully stage-managed a "voluntary" transfer of empire from Montezuma to Charles V, and Powhatan's "coronation," ordered by the Virginia Company to the indignation of Captain Smith, looks like a conscious echo of the Mexican charade.[25]

All the expectations, as we know, proved fallacious. "Silver and golde," reported Dudley Carleton in August 1607, "have they none." Powhatan proved more astute than Montezuma in his dealings with the European intruders and resolutely refused to place himself in their power by coming to Jamestown for his coronation ceremony. Above all, his empire could not begin to compare with that of Montezuma. Although he collected some tribute from his lesser chiefdoms, his tribute system was incapable of sustaining a settler community that was not prepared to work for a living, and his people proved to be "unusable" Indians who could not be transformed into a submissive labor force like those of Central Mexico. Consequently, the early seigneurial dreams of the Virginian colonists vanished when confronted with North American realities, and the colonists themselves, without the benefit of acclimatization to a new environment enjoyed by conquistadores who had lived in the Antilles, died in their scores.[26]

It was fortunate that, although William Brewster and his kind might talk in terms of conquest of the land, there was another dimension to the Virginia project—the desire to develop a settled colony capable of promoting and expanding the power and prosperity of a newly unified Britain as a commercial empire. Cortés, who had seen for himself the destruction of the Antilles, was always insistent on the need to settle the Spaniards and de-

25. Barbour, ed., *Jamestown Voyages,* I, 107; Edmund S. Morgan, "The Labor Problem at Jamestown, 1607–18," *AHR,* LXXVI (1971), 595–611, and *American Slavery, American Freedom: The Ordeal of Colonial Virginia* (New York, 1975), chap. 4, "The Jamestown Fiasco"; Sigmund Diamond, "From Organization to Sovereignty: Virginia in the Seventeenth Century," *American Journal of Sociology,* LXIII (1958), 457–475; John Smith, *The Proceedings of the English Colonie in Virginia since Their First Beginning from England in the Yeare of Our Lord 1606, till This Present 1612 . . .* (1612), in Philip L. Barbour, ed., *The Complete Works of Captain John Smith (1580–1631),* 3 vols. (Chapel Hill, N.C., 1986), I, 236–237.

26. Barbour, ed., *Jamestown Voyages,* I, 113; April Lee Hatfield, *Atlantic Virginia: Intercolonial Relations in the Seventeenth Century* (Philadelphia, 2004), 16.

velop the resources of the land, and with his sugar plantations and his trading ventures he practiced what he preached.[27] But where the seigneurial elements came to predominate over the commercial in the value systems of New Spain and Peru as a result of the presence of large subject populations and the discovery of silver, the Virginia project, lacking both these assets, had no option but to move in a contrary direction if it were to survive.

Although such a move was dictated by the harsh facts of life in the Chesapeake, both the national and the international climate at the turn of the sixteenth and seventeenth centuries helped to create a predisposition in its favor. Although the silver of the Indies still possessed a hypnotic fascination for Europeans, more perceptive Spaniards were beginning to ask whether it had not diverted the attention of their compatriots from the true sources of wealth, which were to be found in the development of agriculture, trade, and industry. At the same time, the extraordinary achievements of the nascent Dutch Republic were stimulating a new appreciation, in England and on the Continent, of the interdependence of profit and power. The Dutch, with their East India Company and their lucrative overseas trading ventures, were offering a new formula for national success in an expanding and competitive world. This formula was deeply attractive to an English merchant community that had grown in importance, wealth, and self-confidence during the reign of Elizabeth but was still struggling to assert its own values against the more traditional values of an aristocratic society.[28]

This "commercializing of colonization" found its expression in the establishment of the Virginia Company on the model of the Dutch and English East India Companies and its promotion of the Jamestown settlement. In turn, this form of company organization for overseas enterprise had important implications for the kind of colony that developed. Cortés and Pizarro turned to merchant capital to finance their expeditions, but a joint-stock company could mobilize much larger funds than single individuals or small groups of merchants. This greatly enhanced the prospects for a long-term mercantile commitment to enterprises that got off to a shaky start and lacked

27. Richard Konetzke, "Hernán Cortés como poblador de la Nueva España," *Estudios cortesianos* (Madrid, 1948), 341–381; France V. Scholes, "The Spanish Conqueror as a Business Man: A Chapter in the History of Fernando Cortés," *New Mexico Quarterly,* XXVIII (1958), 5–29.

28. John H. Elliott, *Illusion and Disillusionment: Spain and the Indies,* The Creighton Lecture (London, 1992); Charles Wilson, *Profit and Power* (London, 1957); B. E. Supple, *Commercial Crisis and Change in England, 1600–1642: A Study in the Instability of a Mercantile Economy* (Cambridge, 1959); Richard Helgerson, *Forms of Nationhood: The Elizabethan Writing of England* (Chicago, 1992).

effective support by the state. Because Mexico and Peru proved to be so rich in people and resources, the Spanish Crown was quick to intervene and take command of colonization. The British Crown, faced with such disappointing reports of Virginia's prospects, had no inducement to become actively involved in this way and was perfectly happy to leave the enterprise to shareholders willing to bear the risks. Insofar as the shareholders spoke for the wider community, this was the community of the nation, not the state. As a result, Virginia in its critical formative years was to reflect many of the values and aspirations of the national community and in the course of time was able to develop, after the uncomfortable experiment with military government, in a relatively libertarian direction untrammelled by close royal control.[29]

But, as a business organization, the company's first priority was to satisfy investors and attract new infusions of capital, and this again had implications that differentiated the Virginia enterprise from the Iberian pattern of New World colonization. Because Mexico and Peru had large populations that could be mobilized to produce tribute and labor, there was no need to resort in the Iberian Peninsula to the kind of promotional campaigns that the Virginia Company was compelled to employ in order to persuade investors to part with more capital and English men and women to cross the Atlantic. Virginia had to be made attractive to potential investors and emigrants. This required the preaching of sermons and the production of tracts that dwelled insistently on the religious and patriotic character of the enterprise and presented a relentlessly upbeat picture of the indigenous population and Anglo-Indian relations, although William Symonds, in his 1609 sermon, used God's command to Abraham to issue a warning against the dangers of consorting with Indian women. "They may not marry nor give in marriage to the heathen, that are uncircumcised. And this is so plaine, that out of this foundation arose the law of marriage among themselves. The breaking of this rule, may breake the necke of all good successe of this Voyage." For reasons that are likely to have had more to do with deep-rooted English fears of cultural degeneration than with God's admonition to Abraham, Virginia would not develop a racially mixed society along the lines of of Iberian America.[30]

29. Carole Shammas, "English Commercial Development and American Colonization, 1560–1620," in K. R. Andrews, N. P. Canny, and P. E. H. Hair, eds., *The Westward Enterprise: English Activities in Ireland, the Atlantic, and America, 1480-1650* (Liverpool, 1978), 151–174, esp. 173; Rabb, *Enterprise and Empire,* 29.

30. Wesley Frank Craven, *Dissolution of the Virginia Company: The Failure of a*

The colonization of Virginia was therefore cast by its promoters in terms of a national enterprise that would spread the Gospel, enhance the power and wealth of the English nation, and improve the waste spaces of the earth. Before the successful cultivation of the tobacco plant, there seemed little chance of realizing these visionary prospects. But the success of the first tobacco exports acutely raised the problem of labor supply. The Spaniards, faced with the need to work the fields and mines of Mexico and Peru, and the Portuguese, with the need to develop the rapidly expanding sugar plantations of Brazil, initially solved this problem of labor supply by exploiting the services of the indigenous population and using Indian slaves captured in "just wars." Then, as this indigenous population was devastated and drastically reduced by European epidemics, growing numbers of African slaves were imported as a substitute.

In the later sixteenth century, the provision of slaves to Spanish America —to which some 150,000 had been shipped by 1600—was wrested by Portuguese merchants from the hands of the Genoese. Following the union of the crowns of Spain and Portugal in 1580, these merchants became the subjects of Philip II, and they had the advantage over native Spaniards of being in a position to tap into the slave trade of the African interior from Portuguese enclaves along the West African coast. Following the negotiation with the Spanish Crown of the Angola *asiento,* or contract, in 1587, Portuguese traders and businessmen successfully penetrated the Spanish Atlantic commercial system. Between the 1590s and 1640, when Portugal recovered its independence from Spain, Portuguese traders had shipped a minimum of 250,000 Africans to the Spanish Indies. During the same period, a further 150,000–200,000 were shipped to Brazil.[31]

The early settlers of Virginia, excluded from the Iberian Atlantic and lacking an indigenous labor force, had to look elsewhere for the provision of labor for the plantations. Their answer came with the development of

---

Colonial Experiment (New York, 1932), 24; Loren E. Pennington, "The Amerindian in English Promotional Literature, 1575-1625," in Andrews, Canny, and Hair, eds., *Westward Enterprise,* chap. 9; Brown, *Genesis of the United States,* I, 290; David D. Smits, "'Abominable Mixture': Toward the Repudiation of Anglo-Indian Intermarriage in Seventeenth-Century Virginia," *VMHB,* XCV (1987), 157-192; John Elliott, *Britain and Spain in America: Colonists and Colonized,* The Stenton Lecture (Reading, 1994).

31. David Eltis, "The Volume and Structure of the Transatlantic Slave Trade: A Reassessment," *WMQ,* 3d Ser., LVIII (2001), 17-46, esp. 24; Enriqueta Vila Vilar, *Hispano-America y el comercio de esclavos* (Seville, 1977), chap. 1 (statistics, 197-211); Alencastro, *O trato dos viventes,* 191.

the headright system and recourse to white indentured servants. But although indentured service was to provide the dominant form of labor for the next half-century, an alternative option made its appearance as early as 1619, when John Rolfe reported the purchase of "20. and odd Negroes" from a Dutch man-of-war. The nature of the commodities supplied was not the only portent for the future. There was portent, too, in the nationality of the supplier. The Dutch were staking out their position in the Atlantic world, not only as colonizers in their own right in the Caribbean and on the American mainland but also as intermediaries, winding their way, sometimes openly, sometimes surreptitiously, through the interstices of an increasingly internationalized network of Atlantic connections. They would soon move in to organize the marketing of Virginian tobacco in continental Europe, providing the settlers in return with European commodities, and on occasions, as in 1619, with a consignment of African slaves.[32]

By 1624, therefore, the Atlantic world was transformed when compared with that of the mid-sixteenth century. The Iberian monopoly had been finally, and definitively, broken. The Caribbean, formerly the destination of privateers, had in effect become an open sea. The three mid-sixteenth-century Atlantic systems of the North Atlantic, the Spanish Atlantic, and the Portuguese Atlantic had become far more porous, as licit and illicit traders infiltrated to exploit the possibilities and, in the process, to link one system to another. The Spaniards had failed to find and settle their New Andalusia and as a result had left the coastal expanse of the northern mainland open to settlement by their European rivals, the French, the English, and the Dutch. Above all, a vast new space had been created and defined, a supranational space in which Europe, Africa, and America were brought into conjunction and collision.

In this new supranational Atlantic world, the Virginia of the early 1620s, with its thousand English settlers expanding into the territory of a dwin-

32. For a comparison of Brazilian and Virginian labor systems, see Richard R. Beeman, "Labour Forces and Race Relations: A Comparative View of the Colonization of Brazil and Virginia," *Political Science Quarterly,* LXXXVI (1971), 609–636; Alden T. Vaughan, "Blacks in Virginia: A Note on the First Decade," *WMQ,* 3d Ser., XXIX (1972), 469–478; Ira Berlin, *Many Thousands Gone: The First Two Centuries of Slavery in North America* (Cambridge, Mass., 1998), 29; Claudia Schnurmann, "Atlantic Trade and Regional Identities: The Creation of Supranational Atlantic Systems in the Seventeenth Century," in Horst Pietschmann, ed., *Atlantic History: History of the Atlantic System, 1580–1830* (Göttingen, 2002), 179–197. See also Schnurmann, *Atlantische Welten: Engländer und Niederländer im amerikanisch-atlantischen Raum, 1648–1713* (Cologne, 1998), 25–40, for Anglo-Dutch commercial relations in this period.

dling indigenous population with which it had failed to live in peace, was still at best a minor player. But it had joined the game, and, like all the other players, was already showing distinctive characteristics. Some options had already been foreclosed; others still remained open. In economic terms, it was becoming a plantation society, with resemblances to those of the Caribbean and Brazil but with the nature of its labor system still to be decided. Socially, it showed signs of becoming seigneurial, like New Spain and Peru, although—reflecting its commercial origins—with a greater emphasis on commercial values. Racially, unlike the Iberian world, it was moving down the path of segregation. Politically, its adoption of a system of government that included a representative assembly anchored it in a world of English liberties that set it on a different road from the one followed by the colonial societies that the monarchies of continental Europe had established. There was, however, nothing yet to indicate that—in the words of the promise to Abraham, as quoted in William Symonds's *Nova Britannia*—"God will make him a great Nation."[33]

33. Brown, *Genesis of the United States,* I, 290.

Stuart B. Schwartz

VIRGINIA AND THE ATLANTIC WORLD

At the birth of the tiny settlement on the Virginia shore at the dawn of the seventeenth century, Spain, like Banquo's ghost, hovered over those woodlands and provided an unseen but always-present context for much of what was decided both in London and in the fledgling colony itself. The original settlers had stopped first in the Spanish Canary Islands (already well known to the English for their wines and sugars) to take on supplies before crossing the Atlantic, and they had then proceeded to the Caribbean and up the chain of the Lesser Antilles before arriving at the Virginia shore. Their itinerary was unconsciously symbolic; it recognized the complex international reality in which the new colony would be situated. John Elliott's elegant essay in this volume makes that reality convincingly clear.

The first settlers had not crossed a tranquil sea. In 1624, while the little colony was passing through its first crisis, other great events were taking place in the Atlantic. A Dutch fleet seized Salvador, capital of Portugal's flourishing sugar colony in Brazil, and within a year, a joint Spanish-Portuguese armada of fifty-six ships, eleven hundred canons, and twelve thousand Spanish, Portuguese, and Neapolitan troops—the largest force ever to have crossed the Atlantic—retook the city from the Dutch. There was war in the Atlantic, and the various countries and crowns of Europe were seeking advantage.[1] Momentous events like the fall and recapture of Salvador caught the imagination of contemporaries and have tended to overshadow other, less dramatic events or to leave unnoticed the structural crises that lay beneath those events. The Atlantic economies had suffered a general contraction between 1619 and 1621, which also served as the context and background of Virginia's own troubles.[2]

1. See Stuart B. Schwartz, "The Voyage of the Vassals: Royal Power, Noble Obligations, and Merchant Capital before the Portuguese Restoration of Independence, 1624–1640," *American Historical Review*, XCVI (1991), 735–762.

2. Ruggiero Romano, "Tra XVI e XVII secolo: Una crisi economica, 1619–22," *Revista storica italiana*, LXXIV (1962), 480–531. See also Barry Emanuel Supple,

At the moment of Jamestown's foundation and the establishment of a handful of settlers on Virginia's shore, a whole world of rivalry, colonial settlements, migrations, dynastic affairs, cultural encounters, and biological and military conquests had already existed in the Atlantic for a century. Europeans knew of each other's activities, and Africans and Native Americans would also become aware of events that might impinge on their worlds or serve as precedents for their own actions. In 1580, when Philip II "bought, inherited, and conquered" Portugal and became master of a truly global empire, the Iberian kingdoms were the greatest power in Europe, but by 1650, their dominion was diminished and their primacy challenged by the maritime power of England and the Netherlands and the growing strength of continental France. Virginia played simply a small part in a great global story. As these essays make clear, that story can no longer be told only from the court at Westminster, the palace of the Buen Retiro, or the counting houses of Amsterdam. We must now also tell it from Benin and Mbanza Kongo, Maracaibo and Bahia, Senegambia, and Tsenacommach as well. How we should think about this world in formation and about the processes, contradictions, and contingencies of its creation is the underlying theme of this volume.

In the historiography of what we might call the Greater South Atlantic, there are three intersecting paradigms that have oriented most studies to date, each of which predominates, but does not exclusively shape, the study of three different subfields. Although scholars primarily interested in Europe and Europeans still speak of expansion and colonization, that field has changed considerably and is not the base camp for triumphalist, positivist accounts of voyages, landfalls, and maritime technologies that it used to be. Yet it has not died out because its questions still remain pertinent and provocative: "Why did certain countries of western Europe adopt a policy of armed trading and colonization often based on the displacement of indigenous people from positions of power and dominance?" Why and how, in the face of tremendous challenges and opposition, did the Europeans succeed in most places?[3] Braudelian and Wallersteinian structuralists in the 1960s

Commercial Crisis and Change in England, 1600–1642: A Study in the Instability of a Mercantile Economy (Cambridge, 1959); Romano, Coyunturas opuestas: La crisis del siglo XVII en Europa e Hispanoamérica (Mexico City, 1993); Geoffrey Parker and Lesley M. Smith, eds., The General Crisis of the Seventeenth Century, 2d ed. (London, 1997).

3. K. N. Chaudhuri, "Politics, Trade, and the World Economy in the Age of European Expansion: Themes for Debate," in Hans Pohl, ed., The European Discovery of

and 1970s did overturn the celebratory narratives of the voyage-by-voyage accounts, but their search for explanation also made European expansion once again the center of the story and Europe the protagonist of global interaction.[4] Newer approaches reveal the shortcomings of an overemphasis on Europe. Africanists and Afro-Americanists have found in diaspora a concept better suited to their concerns and focus because, by shifting the viewpoint to Africa and emphasizing the diffusion of African peoples and cultures, they can construct a story far less celebratory but no less impressive.[5] Historians of the colonial Americas have worked on themes and from viewpoints within both the expansion and the diaspora models, but they have been increasingly drawn to the idea of encounter or frontier as a framework to describe social and cultural interactions within colonial contexts.[6] Needless to say, those interested in Native Americans have been especially drawn to this approach and to its often close association with ethnohistorical methods. These three paradigms represent different lines of inquiry, and although many scholars and books do not fit any one of them comfortably,

---

the World and Its Economic Effects on Pre-industrial Society, 1500–1800: Papers of the Tenth International Economic History Congress (Stuttgart, 1990).

For twenty-first-century takes on Atlantic history, see Alison Games, "Atlantic History: Definitions, Challenges, and Opportunities," AHR, CXI (2006), 741–757; Bernard Bailyn, Atlantic History: Concept and Contours (Cambridge, Mass., 2005).

4. Fernand Braudel, The Mediterranean and the Mediterranean World in the Age of Philip II, trans. Siân Reynolds, 2 vols. (New York, 1972); Immanuel Wallerstein, The Modern World-System (New York, 1974–).

5. For a starting point for the diasporic approach, see John Thornton, Africa and Africans in the Making of the Atlantic World, 1400–1680, 2d ed. (Cambridge, 1992); Paul Gilroy, The Black Atlantic: Modernity and Double Consciousness (Cambridge, Mass., 1993); David Eltis, The Rise of African Slavery in the Americas (Cambridge, 2000). For collections of work in a Black Atlantic perspective, see Michael A. Gomez, ed., Diasporic Africa: A Reader (New York, 2006); Paul E. Lovejoy, ed., Identity in the Shadow of Slavery (London, 2000).

6. The rapidly growing literature of the encounter/frontier approach in North American studies can be seen in Richard White, The Middle Ground: Indians, Empires, and Republics in the Great Lakes Region, 1650–1815 (Cambridge, 1991); David J. Weber, Bárbaros: Spaniards and Their Savages in the Age of Enlightenment (New Haven, Conn., 2005); Andrew R. L. Cayton and Fredrika J. Teute, eds., Contact Points: American Frontiers from the Mohawk Valley to the Mississippi, 1750–1830 (Chapel Hill, N.C., 1998). That this approach is not limited to cultural contact but can be employed to understand other historical processes is underlined by the essays in Christine Daniels and Michael V. Kennedy, eds., Negotiated Empires: Centers and Peripheries in the Americas, 1500–1820 (New York, 2002).

these categories do allow us to group and summarize the current trends of study.[7]

The essays in this volume all roughly fall within the three approaches that I have just described, but many point in new directions as well. Moreover, it is particularly interesting that the former ethnic association or political predictability of the three historiographical traditions is no longer so clear or predictable. Diaspora may now be a way to describe and evaluate European impacts on Africa as well as vice versa. Ethnohistorical methods now allow us to make some sense of African and Native American intellectual responses to European challenges; conquest and colonization can also serve as frameworks in which to discuss African or Native American polities. Above all, many of the chapters included here emphasize cultural changes and hybridities that have destabilized our fixed images of religion, identity, ethnicity, and nationality. Europeans, for example, who sought out Native American herbalists and African "sorcerers" were demonstrating the permeability of various types of boundaries, and that fluidity could be found in many kinds of interactions.

The value of having numerous methodologies and disciplinary approaches also emerges from this collection. The discussions at the lively conference from which this volume grew demonstrated a desire to enrich the historical record by using evidence drawn from archaeology, oral tradition, anthropology, linguistics, and legal studies. A number of the essays show, for example, a healthy concern for etymology and for precision in language, as well as attention to changing meanings and to "discourse." "Savage" is a term of the seventeenth century that needs to be carefully defined, and "slavery" and "indenture," often conflated in that era, did not necessarily mean then what they mean today. In a similar fashion, it is also necessary to examine the techniques of archaeology, oral history, linguistics, and anthropology, all of which bring new insights to history and all of which are subject to similar methodological, epistemological, and interpretative challenges as history.

The idea that Virginia is the northern flank of a circum-Caribbean region that extended from the Potomac to Rio de Janeiro, as though someone had placed a compass point on Barbados and drawn a great arc, was borne out in a number of the conference contributions. Philip Morgan confronts this issue head-on by arguing that Virginia drew on models and experience of a century of earlier contacts with the Caribbean, and the colony's raison

7. Stuart Schwartz, "Expansion, Diaspora, Encounter: Approaches to the Historiography of the South Atlantic," *Itinerario,* XIX (1995), 48–59.

d'être had as much to do with the continuing rivalry with Spain and the patterns of Caribbean trade and plunder as it did with schemes of settlement or colonization. As others have argued in the case of mainland Spanish America, Morgan notes that the Caribbean was a crucible where plants and products were first encountered or their cultivation first tried and where relations with Indians were defined. Indeed, slavery developed in Virginia out of the Caribbean experience, particularly the Spanish Caribbean. English colonists and adventurers knew what the Spanish had done, how they had acted, and what they had accomplished, and they tried to emulate the dons at the same time as they sought to dispossess them. Morgan's essay also makes another important point: the Caribbean colonies of England served as a buffer or shield for Virginia because they drew the envy and aggression of foreign competitors away from the little colony at Jamestown. Even at the outset, Virginia did not stand alone, and it must be seen alongside outposts like Barbados or Bermuda's small settlement, places that offered alternative models of social organization and, in the latter case, as a food supplier, became something of a colony of the Virginian settlement.

The Virginia colony also had a Hispanic prehistory. The region had been part of a Spanish missionary province before the English arrived, and Spain's experiences there and elsewhere with indigenous peoples provided a guide to English aspirations and ambitions. Work done on the publishing projects of Samuel Purchas, David Harris Sacks's essay on the Hakluyts, and Benjamin Schmidt's piece on the reading habits of men like Sir Walter Ralegh make it clear that the founders of the early North American settlements knew the Spanish experience well.[8] That knowledge gave the English a marginal advantage over their Native American hosts. The English operated in an Atlantic world of information that was, for the most part, unavailable to Native Americans and to most Africans, for whom information flows were slower and intermittent. One is struck, reading James Rice's close historical, ethnopolitical account of the peoples around the Powhatans, that the indigenous relations and diplomacies in the face of a new external presence resembled in many ways the situation that had existed in Central Mexico a century before. But the lessons to be learned from that earlier invasion remained unknown to the Algonquins. For Europeans, there was an Atlantic world of information that made the exploits of the "Spainyards" in the New World or the "Portugals" in Asia available as a strategic re-

8. L. E. Pennington, ed., *The Purchas Handbook: Studies of the Life, Times, and Writings of Samuel Purchas, 1577–1626*, 2 vols. (London, 1997).

source that the English could draw upon. Native Americans had to depend on their own experience or what little they could glean by oral transmission from their neighbors. Englishmen, on the other hand, could compare their actions to the Spanish in Mexico, their fisheries to the wealth of Potosí, or their legal justifications to the school of Salamanca.

In fact, although policies and practices differed, the goals of Spaniards and Englishmen were probably not very different. The gentlemen of Virginia would have loved to discover another Mexico, but, alas, Powhatan was not Montezuma, there were no cities or mines, and the Virginians would have to seek other livelihoods. In 1983, James Lockhart and I suggested that comparisons of European attitudes, policies, and cultural differences were, in fact, not the best strategy for understanding the differences in the colonization of the New World.[9] We suggested instead that the key was in the nature of the indigenous societies encountered and in the economic possibilities that each region presented. It made little sense to compare Spanish experiences amid great indigenous empires in Mexico or Peru, based on populous sedentary peasantries and economies capable of producing great surpluses, with English dealings with the semi-sedentary Algonquins of the Chesapeake. When, however, one compares the English experience to the Spanish contacts with the Taínos of the Caribbean or to Portuguese contacts with the Tupinambás of Brazil, then the actions of the Spanish, English, and Portuguese become far more similar. A pattern in European–Native American contact emerges: alliance, conflict, demographic disaster, European farming and appropriation of land, the search for a staple crop, the introduction of a new and often coerced labor force. This outline can be found in many places throughout the circum-Caribbean. Virginia, for all its specificity and peculiarity, seems not so different from the other contemporaneous projects in the region.

This, of course, was a world tied together not only by information and European ambition but by goods as well. The essay by Marcy Norton and Daviken Studnicki-Gizbert reveals how English contacts with Portuguese merchants who had often positioned themselves within the Spanish Empire laid the foundations for a tobacco trade and eventually opened up new markets for Virginia's product. Tobacco was both Virginia's salvation and its damnation, its path to a slave society. Norton and Studnicki-Gizbert demonstrate that there was already an Iberian axis of trade that provided a

9. James Lockhart and Stuart B. Schwartz, *Early Latin America* (Cambridge, 1983).

stepping-stone for Virginia's success; nor should we ignore the point, made at the conference in a paper by Claudia Schnurmann, that tobacco also brought Virginia into the world of Dutch capital and commerce.[10] With tobacco, Virginia entered a world of international competition. Just how international is made clear by the subsequent market for tobacco in the interior of North America. By the eighteenth century, agents of the Hudson's Bay Company were visiting Lisbon, where they bought Brazilian tobacco, produced of course by enslaved Africans and Afro-Brazilians, from the returning Brazil fleets. These agents then reshipped it back across the Atlantic to Canada, where it competed with Virginia tobacco in the fur trade on the upper Great Lakes; its sweet flavor, painted with molasses, made it a favorite among its Native American consumers.[11]

Of course, the Spanish and English were not alone in the business of empire. Philip Boucher explains the broad scope of French activity from Rio de Janeiro to the Grand Banks and also the private nature of French actions during a century when the Crown's continental interests continually trumped its colonial ambitions. The French experience was marked by this private sector orientation and by religious divisions that were mostly absent in the Spanish or English colonization efforts. The lack of royal support and the religious conflicts help to explain the failure of the various French colonizing attempts in Brazil, but in the Caribbean and in North America, the French turned out to be as good or better than the Spanish and the English in dealing with Native Americans, and they were able to establish small settlements in the Lesser Antilles and in Canada. Still, the overall record was not positive. Above all else, France remained distracted by Catholic-Protestant conflict and continental wars at the very moment that England began to colonize in earnest.

Peter Cook's description of the French encounter with Native Americans and French representations of indigenous polities and society nicely complements Boucher's more political description. Europeans generally demonstrated a preference for certain kinds of Native American polities, seeking out and settling first among fully sedentary Native American peoples when they could find them. Cook's essay also shows us that a similar hier-

10. Claudia Schnurmann, "A Comparison of Colonizing Propaganda in England, France, and the Netherlands, ca. 1580–1624," paper presented at "The Atlantic World and Virginia, 1550–1624," conference, Williamsburg, Va., Mar. 6, 2004.

11. This important trade is discussed in Linda Wimmer, "African Producers, European Merchants, Indigenous Consumers: Brazilian Tobacco in the Canadian Fur Trade, 1550–1821" (Ph.D. diss., University of Minnesota, 1996).

archy of preference existed in terms of representing indigenous societies, and that, once having learned and mastered the kinship terminology and the social relationships it represented, the French projected their own understanding of cultural hierarchy on the Native inhabitants. As the French increasingly perceived the Native peoples as "savages," they refused to use the term "kingship" to refer to indigenous polities and rulers. Most important, Cook points out how political and religious changes in France altered the nature and meaning of the discourse about rule, and this, in turn, changed the way in which the French perceived Native American leaders. Similar concerns appear in the article by Andrew Fitzmaurice, as the English also sought to reconcile moral and legal questions and exigencies of empire with their dispossession of Native Americans. Perhaps I have a jaundiced view of lawyers and legal argument, but I suspect that the well of Justinian precedents and scholastic justifications was never in danger of running dry. Even when Native Americans were clearly not savages, as in the case of the Inca empire, Spanish civil lawyers could find in legal arguments against tyrants —that is, against illegitimate rule—just as much reason for dispossession as the mere reduction of Indians to the category of savages. One argument worked just as effectively as another, and the defenders of imperial expansion could use legal precedent in infinite ways.

Many of the essays in this collection demonstrate that the contact between Europeans and Native Americans had a history that changed over time and that both sides sought to adjust their understandings and actions as circumstances demanded. Cultural encounters were never the meeting of two essentialisms. On each side, there was a dynamic relationship between cultural perceptions and assumptions—implicit ethnographies or understandings of what characteristics "others" were supposed to have— and actual observations and experience. As the relationship between these elements changed on each side of a cultural encounter, so too did the nature of the contact. Encounters, then, are fluid historical processes in which change is an inherent part of the model.

That dynamic process emerged clearly in the original conference and in this volume in a number of papers on the early contacts between Native Americans and the English in Virginia. Tsenacommach really received excellent and thorough treatment. Daniel Richter's essay sets the stage and inverts the usual tale of Atlantic crossings by looking at the Algonquins who traveled to Europe; but by concentrating on the importance of "goods from afar," he demonstrates the ritual and spiritual as well as the economic role that Europeans and their things could have on indigenous cultures. Used by Spaniards, English, and French, these indigenous go-betweens became the equivalent of "Atlantic creoles," brokers and facilitators of the formation of a broader Atlantic world.[12] Richter's study further shows that indigenous travelers applied what they had observed and learned to their own encounters. Just as Cook's paper demonstrates how the French eventually refused to apply the concept of kingship to indigenous leaders, Richter demonstrates how those leaders insisted on their authority and demanded that it be recognized by gift or alliance. Indian leaders who went to England knew how kings were supposed to act and be treated, and they took offense when their own treatment did not meet those expectations.

In Joseph Hall's essay, the Native peoples of Spanish Florida reoriented the ritual and economic aspects of long-range trade in prestige items and incorporated the "foreign" sources of such goods into existing structures of trade and dependency. Although Native Americans might have been at an informational disadvantage, as suggested above, there is little evidence in this volume of Indian peoples overwhelmed and overawed or left speechless and defenseless by European military or informational technologies. The once-popular paradigm of Tzvetan Todorov would seem no longer very useful for understanding the dynamic of European–Native American interaction.[13] Instead, we see indigenous adaptability in difficult circumstances. Here, even more comparative work could bear fruit. Scholars who work on the chieftainships of the North American southeast might derive considerable theoretical and comparative benefit from incorporation of the extensive literature on chiefdom-level societies in South America, where there are striking parallels to social and political organization and where the historical record of contact is often quite detailed.[14]

Work in this anthology and at the conference demonstrates that the impact of America and its peoples on the English was varied and not predictable. John Elliott once observed that cognizance of and concern for America

12. The term was developed in Ira Berlin, "From Creole to African: Atlantic Creoles and the Origins of African-American Society in Mainland North America, *William and Mary Quarterly,* 3d Ser., LIII (1996), 251–288.

13. Tzvetan Todorov, *The Conquest of America: The Question of the Other,* trans. Richard Howard (New York, 1984).

14. See Juan Villamarín and Judith Villamarín, "Chiefdoms: The Prevalence and Persistence of 'Señoríos Naturales,' 1400 to European Conquest," in Frank Salomon and Stuart B. Schwartz, eds., *South America,* The Cambridge History of Native Peoples of the Americas, III (Cambridge, 1999), part 1, 577–667; Neil L. Whitehead, "The Crises and Transformation of Invaded Societies: The Caribbean (1492–1580), ibid., 864–903.

came slowly to Europe.[15] The lands of Barbary with their pirates, rene-gades, and treasure rather than Virginia with its savages and sotweed cap-tured the popular imagination and the attention of the playwrights. The Mediterranean still predominated as the preferred reference point for En-glish "otherings," but as David Sacks demonstrates, in the hands of an effec-tive and zealous propagandist like Richard Hakluyt, the western planting could take on salvific, if not apocalyptic, importance. By the early seven-teenth century, America was rising on the horizon of English consciousness.

Lastly, the fine essays herein that center on Africa emphasize that, as in the triangular trade, so too in the triangulation of culture, Africa must play a significant role in our understanding of the Atlantic world. But one must examine that seeming truism with care and avoid the all-too-common ten-dency to read the eighteenth century, the great century of the slave trade, backward in time. The slave trade to America was slow in starting, and even early plantation economies like that of northeastern Brazil shifted to enslaved Africans gradually, as warfare, disease, and missionary activities made the forced labor of Native Americans more difficult. As David North-rup points out, the slave trade before 1650 was only a small part of the trade in the Gulf of Guinea. In the seventeenth century and into the eighteenth, the slave trade remained a tiny fraction of Africa's total domestic product, but as Robin Law reminded us at the conference, slavery and the slave trade were not experienced continentally but locally, and from that perspective their impact could still be devastating.

Whereas an earlier generation of Africa-oriented and Afrocentric schol-arship emphasized how Africans transferred their cultures to the Americas as part of the formation of the Atlantic world, Robin Law, following Ira Berlin, emphasized the importance of the early presence of culturally hy-brid, often Lusophone "Atlantic creoles," and the impact of European ways and European agents on African statecraft, economies, and cultures. Linda Heywood and John Thornton's provocative description of Central Africa stresses African cultural appropriation. The usual direction of diaspora is inverted, and Africa here is cultural recipient as much as donor. Their essay opens up new directions but also raises new questions. The first is the ques-tion of the court versus the country: the evidence of European cultural im-pact seems to be much stronger on the former, and the effect of European cultural penetration outside the royal courts of Africa or outside the capital cities like Mbanza Kongo still remains to be demonstrated. Then, too, the

15. J. H. Elliott, *The Old World and the New: 1492–1650,* The Wiles Lectures (Cam-bridge, 1970).

continual debates among Jesuits and other missionaries over the validity of baptisms performed in Africa should make us wary about the nature and profundity of Catholicism of the majority of the African population, even in regions where royal conversions were made. Second, we must also keep in mind that what Africans thought they were doing in adopting European religion or other cultural attributes was one thing, and how Europeans perceived Africans was quite another. Despite courts, dukes, and embassies that imitated European usages, Europeans often continued to see Africans according to other categories and preconceptions. When, in 1673, the governor of Angola sent several African princes to Brazil who were then to continue to Lisbon as part of a diplomatic mission, the governor of Brazil, Afonso Furtado, sent a receipt saying: "I received six slaves, I mean black princes . . . to be sent to the Overseas Council." This was a slip of the pen (or the tongue) that should make us careful about placing too much emphasis on the significance of Europeanization or the acceptance of Africans as equals whatever their status.[16]

Whereas the essay by Heywood and Thornton underlines the hybridity of African polities and cultures in Africa, the papers by David Northrup and James Sweet are more concerned with the way in which African identities and patterns shaped interactions with Europeans both in Africa and in the Americas. Northrup's reading of African ethnicities seems to follow the path laid out by anthropologists Richard Price and Sidney Mintz.[17] Africans might have re-created Africa in the Atlantic spaces beyond their original continent, but to a large extent that process was made possible by pidgin languages, creole go-betweens, and the creation of new identities that were amalgams; the result, not of cultural re-creation, but of cultural creation. James Sweet looks for ethnic identities and solidarities in cases of resistance. He examines the well-known cases of the Angolares on the island of São Tomé and the runaway community, or *quilombo*, of Palmares in northeastern Brazil. He retraces what has been established in the literature for a while: that the use of the term *kilombo*, which in Angola had referred to a specific ritualized military organization and encampment, became over time, for the Portuguese in Africa, a way to speak about certain African

16. Stuart B. Schwartz and Alcyr Pécora, eds., *As excelências do governador: O panegírico fúnebre a d. Alfonso Furtado, de Juan Lopes Sierra (Bahia, 1676)* (São Paulo, 2002), 32.

17. Sidney Wilfred Mintz and Richard Price, *The Birth of African-American Culture: An Anthropological Perspective,* 2d ed. (Boston, 1996). Price has reviewed his original position and the criticism of it in "The Miracle of Creolization: A Retrospective," *New West Indian Guide,* LXXV (2001), 35–64.

polities *(reino e quilombo de Matamba)*. In Brazil, it became a generic term applied widely to any escaped slave community. Surely, all kinds of people, Native Americans, Africans of various origins, Brazilian-born blacks *(criou-los)* all ran off to join these communities and participate in this form of resistance. At the same time, it is only fair to note that Native Americans, black and mulatto slave catchers, and militia contingents were also usually the very forces that destroyed these runaway communities as well. For these instruments of the colonial state, ethnic identity and solidarity seemed to be less important than a colonial identity or perception of personal advantage. Finding the balance between resistance and accommodation and between multiple ethnic, religious, cultural, and political identities is a task that much of the new scholarship on the Black Atlantic has challenged us to consider.

Our categories of analysis must be less rigid, our understanding of ethnic and cultural boundaries more fluid, and our expectations about the perceptions and prejudices of peoples in the past less definitive. If we can do this, we may be surprised and our histories reinvigorated. We need to be willing to break out of our geographic and historiographic boundaries of study and to be as willing to cross frontiers as were the people whom we study. Many of the essays in this volume suggest that the history of Virginia as part of the circum-Caribbean world was never predetermined and that the choices open to all the actors—Europeans, Native Americans, Africans, and their descendants—were many. With the emphasis on human actions and choices, speaking of the contingent nature of history and downgrading structural constraints have become fashionable; and we are sometimes given to wonder whether there were moments when the history of the Atlantic world might have been set in a different direction. Identifying and understanding those moments is difficult. When dealing with the actions and dynamics of other cultures across a span of centuries, separating our own expectations and understandings from theirs is always a challenge. Let me close, then, with two vignettes that touch on the question of cultural interpretation and on the limits of historical contingency in the Atlantic world of which Virginia had become a part.

On Columbus's first voyage, after his landfall on the island of the Bahamas he named San Salvador, he began to explore other islands. On October 15, only three days after his first contact with the peoples of the islands, as he headed for Long Island (Fernandina), his ship overtook a Taíno canoe at sea. Columbus discovered that its occupant carried Spanish beads and even Castilian coins bartered from the Spaniards on San Salvador and was probably on his way to trade them a few islands over before the Europeans could arrive. How to explain this behavior? Was this a transfer of prestige goods with high ritual value, or just a Taíno homo economicus with natural understanding of supply and demand and a sharp eye for profit? The story is curious, and it suggests that perhaps Native American actions and motives were not always so strange or different from those of the Europeans. And the story is not so singular as it first appears.[18]

Adventurer John Lawson, in his 1709 account of the Indians on the Carolina coast, wrote that the local Indians noticed that the English ships always arrived at one place, and this made them confident that they could sail from that point directly back to England. Lawson then explains:

> And seeing so many Ships coming thence, they believ'd it could not be far thither, esteeming the *English* that were among them, no better than Cheats, and thought, if they could carry the Skins and Furs they got, themselves to *England,* which were inhabited with a better Sort of People than those sent amongst them, that then they should purchase twenty times the Value for every Pelt they sold Abroad, in Consideration of what Rates they sold for at home.
>
> . . . After a general Consultation of the Ablest heads amongst them, [they began] building more Canoes, and those to be of the best Sort, and biggest Size as fit for their intended Discovery. . . . The Affair was carry'd on with a great deal of Secrecy and Expedition, so as in a small Time they had gotten a Navy, Loading, Provisions, and Hands ready to set Sail."

A Native American merchant fleet on its way to England? Could the history of the Atlantic world have been reversed? But history, it turns out, is never quite that contingent.

> The wind presenting, they set up their mat-sails and were scarce out of sight when there arose a tempest which its supposed carried off one part of these Indian Merchants by way of the other world, whilst the others were taken up at Sea by an English ship and sold for slaves to the islands.[19]

18. Samuel Eliot Morison, trans. and ed., *Journals and Other Documents on the Life and Voyages of Christopher Columbus* (New York, 1963), 70.

19. John Lawson, *A New Voyage to Carolina,* ed. Hugh Talmage Lefler (Chapel Hill, N.C., 1967), 18-19.

SESSION I. Native American Settings. Chair: Kathleen Bragdon, College of William and Mary. Daniel K. Richter, McNeil Center for Early American Studies, University of Pennsylvania, "Tsenacommacah and the Atlantic World, 1550–1624." Kathleen DuVal, University of North Carolina, Chapel Hill, "A Bordered Land: Mississippian Foreign Relations, 700–1600." Joseph Hall, Bates College, "Between Old World and New: Native American Adaptations to the Spanish Southeast, 1540–1624." James D. Rice, State University of New York, Plattsburgh, "Escape from Tsenacommacah: Chesapeake Algonquians and the Powhatan Menace, 1300–1624." Commentators: J. Frederick Fausz, University of Missouri, St. Louis, and Kathleen Bragdon.

SESSION 2. Native American Oral Traditions. Chair: Helen Rountree, Old Dominion University, Emerita. Chief Kenneth Adams, Upper Mattaponi Tribe. Chief Stephen R. Adkins, Chickahominy Tribe. Gene Adkins, Assistant Chief, Chickahominy Tribe, Eastern Division. Councilman Fred Bright, Nansemond Indian Tribal Association. Councilman John Johns, Monacan Indian Nation. Linwood Custalow, Mattaponi Tribe. Danielle Moretti-Langholtz, American Indian Resource Center, College of William and Mary. Edward Ragan, Syracuse University. Chief Anne Richardson, Rappahannock Indian Tribe. Keith Smith, Nansemond Indian Tribal Association.

SESSION 3. Recapturing Lost Landscapes of the Emerging Atlantic World. Chair: Warren Billings, University of New Orleans. William Kelso, Association for the Preservation of Virginia Antiquities, Jamestown Rediscovery. Crandall Shifflett, Virginia Polytechnic Institute and State University. William Thomas, University of Virginia.

Keynote Address. The Atlantic World and Virginia. Sir John Elliott, University of Oxford, Emeritus.

SESSION 4. Negotiating along the Mediterranean and Atlantic Littoral. Chair: Paul E. Lovejoy, York University. Daniel Goffman, DePaul University, "The Malleability of Identity: Being English in the Eastern Mediterranean Borderlands." Chouki el Hamel, Arizona State University, "Moroccan Slavery in the Atlantic World in the Sixteenth Century." Ann McDougall, University of Alberta, "'The Caravel and the Caravan':

Reconsidering Received Wisdom in the Sixteenth-Century Sahara." David Northrup, Boston College, "Coastal West African Institutions and Identities, 1550-1624." Commentator: Joseph C. Miller, University of Virginia.

SESSION 5. Africa, Europe, and the Atlantic. Chair: Stephanie Smallwood, University of California, San Diego. Linda M. Heywood, Boston University, and John K. Thornton, Boston University, "Central Africans and the Appropriation of European Culture: Kongo and Ndongo, 1560-1624." Innocent Pikirayi, University of Zimbabwe, "Gold, Slaves, and Palaces: The Consequences of Early African-European Contact during the Sixteenth and Seventeenth Centuries." James La Fleur, Universiteit Leiden, "The Globalization of African and Atlantic Foodways." Robin Law, University of Stirling, "West Africa in the Atlantic World in the Early Seventeenth Century." James H. Sweet, Florida International University, "African Resistance in the Portuguese Atlantic, 1550-1624." Commentator: Stephanie Smallwood.

SESSION 6. Market Exigencies. Chair: Nicholas Canny, National University of Ireland, Galway. Martin Quitt, University of Massachusetts, Boston, Emeritus, "Free Trade and Monopoly in Jacobean England and Virginia: Connecting Commons, the Company, and the Colony." Nuran Çinlar, Simmons College, "Banks, Bankruptcy, and the Risk of Virginia." Emily Rose, University of Cambridge, "'Seminary for a Seditious Parliament': The Virginia Company and the House of Commons, 1621." Daviken Studnicki-Gizbert, McGill University, "Imperial Rivalries and Commercial Collaboration: Portuguese and English Merchants and the Formation of an Atlantic Tobacco Trade, 1550-1650." Thomas Cogswell, University of California, Riverside, "Mr. Anys's Virginia: Whitehall, Entrepreneurs, and a Tobacco Monopoly, 1626-1627." Commentator: J. Craig Muldrew, Queen's College, University of Cambridge.

SESSION 7. Colonial Rationales. Chair: Alison Games, Georgetown University. Andrew Fitzmaurice, University of Sydney, "Moral Uncertainty in Virginian Dispossession." Ken R. Macmillan, University of Calgary, "Sovereignty, the Law of Nations, and Settlement of Virginia." Neil Kennedy, Brock University, "Imagining Arcadia and Conceiving Bermuda: The Reinvigoration of English Colonization, 1609-1624." Claudia Schnurmann, Hamburg Universitaet, "A Comparison of Colonizing Propaganda in England and the Netherlands, ca. 1580-1624." Commentator: Carla Pestana, Miami University.

SESSION 8. Comparative Models on the Ground. Chair: Kris E. Lane, College of William and Mary. Philip D. Morgan, Johns Hopkins University, "The Caribbean and the Atlantic World, 1550-1624." Ida Altman, University of New Orleans, "Rebellion and Response in the Early Spanish Empire." Philip P. Boucher, University of Alabama, Huntsville, "New Perspectives on the French Atlantic, 1550–1630." Peter Cook, Nipissing University, "Kings, Captains, and Kin: The Encounter of Native American and French Political Cultures in the Atlantic World, 1534-1650." John M. Monteiro, Universidade Estadual de Campinas, Brazil, "Converts, Slaves, and Rebels: Tupi Indians in the Making of the Portuguese Atlantic, 1550-1650." Commentator: Richard Price, College of William and Mary.

SESSION 9. Settling Jamestown. Chair: James Horn, Colonial Williamsburg Foundation. Cary Carson, Joanne Bowen, Willie Graham, Martha McCartney, and Lorena S. Walsh, Colonial Williamsburg Foundation, "New World, Real World: Improvising English Culture in Seventeenth-Century Virginia." Karen Bellinger Wehner, New York University, "Crafting Selves and Crafting Society in Seventeenth-Century Jamestown." Michael A. LaCombe, New York University, "Feasting and Foodways as Cultural Mediators: Jamestown, 1607-1624." Commentators: Martha Zierden, Charleston Museum, and Tom Davidson, Jamestown Settlement.

SESSION 10. Intellectual Currents. Chair: Alden T. Vaughan, Columbia University, Emeritus. Benjamin Schmidt, University of Washington, "Reading Ralegh's America." David Harris Sacks, Reed College, "Discourses of Western Planting: Richard Hakluyt and the Making of the Atlantic World." Jean Howard, Columbia University, "Fictions of Contact: Adventure Drama and the Ethnographic Imagination in Early Modern England." David S. Shields, University of South Carolina, "The Genius of Ancient Britain." Commentator: David Armitage, Columbia University.

SESSION 11. Concluding Observations. Chair: Thad W. Tate, College of William and Mary, Emeritus. Karen O. Kupperman, New York University, and Stuart B. Schwartz, Yale University.

INDEX

Angolares, 235–236
Anne Frances (ship), 358
Antilles, 302
Antiquarians, 498–499, 502
Antonio, Pedro, 203
Antonio, prior of Crato, 209
Apalachee peoples, 92
Aqit family, 156
Aquinas, Thomas, 284
Araucana (Ercilla), 466
Arawaks, 256, 262–263. *See also* Taínos
Archaionomia (Lambarde), 500
Archeion (Lambarde), 500
Archer, Gabriel, 44–48, 354, 360–361
Arcos, Miguel de, 386–387
Argall, Samuel, 64, 97–98, 128, 132, 540
Argentina y conquisto del Río de la Plata (Barca Centenera), 490
Aristotle, 446
Armitage, David, 417
Arrohateck, 44, 524
Atabalipa, 316
Aubrey, John, 460–461
Augustin, Captain, 375
Axtell, James, 48
Ayllón, Lucas Vázquez de, 80, 543–544, 550
Aztecs, 316–317

Bacon, Francis, 429, 452–453, 455
Bale, John, 446, 448
Bancroft, Richard, 390
Bandera, Juan de la, 72
Barbarism: progressive theory of, 402–404, 407, 437; cannibalism versus, 442–443; and Virginia project, 443–446
Barbour, Philip, 490
Barbuda, Francisco, 208
Barca Centenera, Martín del, 490
Barlaeus, Caspar, 487
Barlow, William, 431
Barry, Boubacar, 151–152, 154
Baskerville, Thomas, 375

Beads, 59–60, 115–117, 172, 182–183
Beer, Anna, 467
Bellarmino, Roberto, 194–195
Belleforest, François de, 325
Benin, Kingdom of, 177–179; and trade goods, 170–171, 178, 182–183; and trade relations, 170–171, 175–176, 177; described, 177–179; and slave trade, 185; Christian missionaries in, 191; and comparison to Central Africa, 224
Bermuda, 374, 377
Berrío, Antonio de, 347
Beverley, Robert, 8–9
Biard, Pierre, 339
Black Legend of the Spanish conquest, 292, 336, 348, 391
Bodin, Jean, 296, 312, 333
Bodley, Thomas, 388, 390
Bond of Association, 422
Book of Consolation, 450
Book of Martyrs (Foxe), 415
Books, influence of, 388–389, 402, 456, 504–505. *See also* Libraries; Reading
Borburata Indians, 365
Botero, Giovanni, 405–406
Bowdler, Thomas, 380
Braden, Gordon, 441
Braudel, Fernand, 305
Brazil: slavery in, 237–242, 555; and dyewood trade, 278–279, 292, 329; French colonization of, 278–284, 297–301, 331; and Native American kingship model, 329–332; and progressive theory of civilization, 407
Breton, Raymond, 373
Brevíssima relación de la destruyción de las Indias (Las Casas), 426, 485
Brewster, William, 551
Bridenbaugh, Carl, 37
Brief Relation of the Destruction of the Indians (Las Casas), 426, 485
Brookes, Edward, 353
Brown, John, 347
Brun, Samuel, 220–221, 223
Bry, Theodore de, 292, 406; engrav-

ings by, *60, 98,* 139, *445, 481, 483;* as
    publisher, 479–480, 485
Burghley, William Cecil, first Baron,
    422, 461–462
Burgoignon, Nicholas, 520–521
Burial practices: Algonquian, 36, 58–59;
    of Southeast tribes of North America,
    72, 76

Cabot, John, 451
Cacique Juan, 89–90, 95
Cacique María, 89, 95
Cadornega, Antonio de Oliveira, 201
Caesar, Julius, 493
Calusa Indians, 368
Calvert, George, 139
Calvin, John, 282
Calvinists, 282–283
Camden, William, 495, 498, 500, 503
Canabre, Anthony, 367
Cannibalism, 206, 303, 329–331, 346,
    369, 442
Caporelli, Francesco, 195, *197,* 198
Capuchins, 299–302, 336, 338
Cardoso, Mateus, 216
Caribbean: and tobacco trade, 256, 269–
    270, 351, 361–364; and shaping of
    colonial Virginia, 343–346, 348, 358–
    362, 374–375, 377–379; as enchanted
    island, 345, 351–355; geography of,
    345; travel writing on, 346–348;
    strategic importance of, 349–351, 379–
    380; trading and raiding in, 349,
    356–358; weather in, 354–355; ani-
    mals of, 355–356; blacks in, 372–378;
    slavery in, 377–378; transnational
    quality of life in, 378–380
Caribbean Indians: description of, 364–
    366, 369; English relations with,
    364–369; language appropriation
    and, 365, 373–374; as interpreters,
    366–367; as guides, 366; travel of, to
    England, 367; and tribute networks,
    368; religious beliefs of, 369, *370;*
    relationship of, with blacks, 372–374

Carleton, Dudley, 552
Carmelites, 199, 214–217, 220–221
Carrera, Juan de la, 40–41
Carrera de Indias, 542
Cartagena, 375
Cartas de relación (Cortés), 462, 466
Cartier, Jacques, 276, 319–325, 330
Case, John, 417–418
Cassiodorus, 435
Castillo, Bernal Diaz del, 255
Catharina, queen of Portugal, 202–203
Catholic Church, 394, 447–449. *See also*
    specific religious orders
Catholicism: in Kingdom of Kongo, 194–
    198, 201–206, 212–217; in Kingdom of
    Ndongo, 218–219; Henri IV's conver-
    sion to, 333. *See also* Christianity
Cecil, Robert, first earl of Salisbury,
    403, 428–430, 436–437, 444, 448,
    461–462, 549
Cecil, William. *See* Burghley, William
    Cecil, first Baron
Central Africa: naming practices in,
    196; imports and exchanges in, 198–
    199; tobacco trade and, 199, 200,
    201; and identity formation, 244. *See*
    also Kongo, Kingdom of; Ndongo,
    Kingdom of
Champlain, Samuel de, 296, 338
Chaplin, Joyce, 342
Charles I (king of England), 251, 304,
    495, 497–499, 501
Charles I/V (king of Spain), 279, 316,
    552
Charles IX (king of France), 285, 290–
    291
Charlesfort, 285–286
Chartier, Roger, 313–314
Chauveton, Urbain, 292
Chesapeake Bay: early exploration of, 2,
    543–544, 546, 548–549; agriculture
    of, 1300s, 102–105; and Jesuit coloni-
    zation, 517. *See also* Native Americans,
    Chesapeake Bay area
Chicacoans, 133–134

Chickahominies, 110, 124-126

Chicorana, Francisco, 73

Chiefdoms: definition of, 31-32, 71; and lineage, 34, 113-114, 326-329; colonization and collapse of, 81-82, 95; Saint Augustine's position in, 83, 88-89; paramount, 102, 118; nation-states versus, 111; tribal societies versus, 111; and priests, 114; comparison of kingship model to, 326-329. *See also* Wahunsonacock (Powhatan); *individual tribes*

Choapock, 124

Chowanocs, 519

Chozas, Fray Pedro de, 83-86, 90, 91, 95

Christianity: and Southeast tribes of North America, 78, 82, 83-86; in West Africa, 189-191; African naming practices and, 196; and literacy in Central Africa, 220-221; in santidades communities, 238-239; revenge tragedies in, 440-446; divisiveness in, 506-507. *See also* Catholicism; *specific religious orders*

Christina, Dona, 223

Cicero, 400, 427, 446

Civilization, progressive theory of, 402-404, 407

Claesz, Cornelis, 482-483, 485

Clement VIII, 203

Cobham, Henry Brooke, 461

Cofitachequi chiefdom, 72, 76

Coke, Edward, 495, 499

Coligny, Gaspard de, 277, 281-282, 285-286, 288, 290, 291

College of Antiquaries, 498

Collinson, Patrick, 422

Colombia, 377

Colonization: requirements for, 280; Spanish model of, 284, 295, 305, 329, 348, 371; mercantilist model of, 296-297, 553; Virginia Company defense of, 392, 396-397; Acosta on, 401-402; Hakluyt's works as religious justification for, 414-422; Smith's justification for, 494

Columbus, Christopher, 314-315, 336-337, 359, 451, 463, 551

Commerce, freedom of, 397-400

Communication, right of, 386, 398-399

Company of Clothworkers of London, 423

Coosa chiefdom, 72, 75, 76

Copper: as prestige good, 34, 50; trade in, 48, *49, 50*; spiritual qualities of, 115-117; and African long-distance trade, 172; demand for, in sub-Saharan Africa, 181-182; Powhatan mining of, 525, 531-532

Corbet, Jean, 534-537

Cornell, Vincent, 145

Correa, Bras, 213

Correia de Sousa, João, 209, 214

Cortés, Hernán, 316, 462, 466, 552-553

Cosmographie universelle (Thevet), 325, 330-331

Cotton, Robert Bruce, 461, 495-505, 507

Counterblaste to Tobacco (James I), 251

Cowrie shell currency, 173

Crashaw, William, 389-391, 396

Creoles, 225-226

Croft, Pauline, 431

Cromwell, Oliver, 504

Croshaw, Raleigh, 134-136

Cuba, 261, 280, 315

Cultru, Prosper, 276

Cultural identity, 4-5

Cumberland, earl of, 349, 375

Currency, 173, 323

Cusco, 316

D'Abbeville, Claude, 299-301, 336

Dale, Thomas, 61, 63, 121, 348

D'Ango, Jean, 277

Da Silva, João (Chrachafusus), 202

Davidson, Basil, 180

Davies, K. G., 304-305

Decades of the Newe Worlde (Peter Martyr). See *De orbe novo* (Anghiera)

Dee, John, 459
De jure belli libri tres (Gentili), 395
De la Warr, Lord, 123
Delle navigationi e viaggi (Ramusio), 452
De officiis (Cicero), 400
De orbe novo (Anghiera), 6-7, 8, 315, 346, 437, 466
De procuranda Indorum (Acosta), 401, 403, 405
De Sá, Mem, 284
Desert Frontier (Webb), 154
D'Esnambuc, Pierre Blain, 302, 303-304
De Sores, Jacques, 280
De temporibus novissimus (Acosta), 405
Devisse, Jean, 151, 153
D'Evreux, Yves, 299
Dias de Novais, Paulo, 207-208, 218-219
Diaz, Pedro, 522
Diogenes Laertius, 489-490, 493
Diogo I, 202, 212
Diplomatic relations: gift giving and, 117, 123, 208, 323-324; ritual in, 255-256, 323-324; French fur trade and, 340
"Discourse of Western Planting" (Hakluyt), 410-411, 413, 420-421, 425
Discours politiques et militaires (La Noue), 438-439
Discovery of Guiana (Ralegh), 347, 459, 464-466, 468-474, 485-488; and binding, 469; translations of, 474-485
Disease, infectious, 3-4
Divers Voyages Touching the Discoverie of America (Hakluyt), 413
Dominicans (Natives), 368
Dominicans (religious order), 39, 213, 215, 516, 545
Donation of Alexander, 394
Donnacona, 319-326
Donne, John, 400
Dragontea (Vega), 490

Drake, Francis, 291; report of, to Walsingham, 268; influence of, on European politics, 293; in the Caribbean, 349, 353-354, 375-376; Native Americans employed by, 366; trade networks of, 368, 374; Hakluyt on, 427; and literary modes, 490; and Roanoke Island colony, 520-521
Drayton, Michael, 415
Du Bartas, Guillaume, 294
Dudley, Robert, 364
Du Hamel, Jacques, 335-336, 339
Duplessis-Mornay, Philippe, 420
Dutch: and Gulf of Guinea trade relations, 175-177, 182-183; and Kingdom of Kongo alliance, 206-207; and slave trade, 241-242, 556; trade relations of, 256, 553; Salvador seized by, 559
Dutch East India Company, 397-398, 553
Dutch Revolt, 549
Dutch West India Company, 206
Dyer, Edward, 414

Écija, Francisco Fernández de, 534-537, 540
Economie de l'empire portugais (Magalhães-Godinho), 151
Eden, Richard, 346, 355, 446
Edict of Nantes, 278, 295
Edwards, Philip, 461
Eirenarcha (Lambarde), 500
Elfrith, Daniell, 346, 357
Elizabeth I, 422, 498; Ribaut and, 286; Hawkins and, 288; Louis, prince de Condé, and, 291; Hakluyt and, 410-411, 428; Ralegh and, 459, 501
Elizabeth and Cleeve (ship), 358
Elliott, J. H., 462
Eltis, David, 186
Enciso, Martin Fernández de, 346
Endicott, John, 491
England: tobacco cultivation and trade by, 253, 256, 264-267, 270-272, 304, 361-364; private libraries in, 389

—colonization: Spanish settlement model used in, 295, 348, 371, 393; in Caribbean, 304; effect of war on, 304–305, 546–550; of Ireland, 342, 547; and island-based model, 380; and Salamanca School texts, 388–393; justification for, 392–393, 397–400; and methods of Virginia Company, 396–397; and progressive theory of barbarism, 403–404, 407–408; and necessity of navy, 503–504; rumors of gold and, 518–523; Spanish challenge to, 534–537, 540, 546–660; expansion of, 539; under *res nullius,* 548; commercializing of, 553. *See also* Jamestown; Roanoke Island
—trade relations of: with Benin, 170–171, 177; in Gulf of Guinea, 170, 176–177, 182; and racial bias, 176; and Caribbean Indians, 367–368
English East India Company, 397–398, 415, 553
English Royal African Company, 160–163
Erasmus, Desiderius, 418
Ercilla, Alonzo de, 466
Escamaçus, 79, 87
Escobedo, Alonso Gregorio de, 84–86
European Americana (Alden and Landis, eds.), 456
Exchange networks. *See* Trade networks

Fausz, J. Frederick, 43, 46, 58
Ferae bestiae, 385, 392, 399–402
Fernandes, Simon, 346, 518–519, 521
First Anglo-Powhatan War. *See* Anglo-Powhatan War (1609–1614)
FitzGeffrey, Charles, 490
Fleet, Henry, 137
Florida. *See* La Florida, colonization in
Fonseca, Jacome de, 202
Fort Caroline, 80, 286–288, 289, 328–329
Fort Coligny, 281
Fort Nassau, 177

Fort Raleigh, 350
Foxe, John, 415, 446, 448–449, 450
Fragmenta Regalia (Naunton), 460
Frampton, John, 346
France: piracy and privateering by, 275; and forces affecting maritime expansion, 276–278; and Catherine de Médicis's assault against Spain, 293–294; and tobacco cultivation, 304; and understanding of kingship, 310–314; and fur trade, 340
—colonization: indigenous populations' acceptance of, 88, 329, 334–337; 1550–1625, 275–276; in Brazil, 278–284, 297–301, 318, 331; Portuguese response to, 279, 283–284, 297–302, 318; the Tupinambás and, 279, 297–301, 329–331; Spanish settlement model used in, 284, 295, 305, 329; and Lesser Antilles, 303–304; in Guiana, 303; effect of war on, 304–305; elements undermining efforts of, 304–306, 329; in Caribbean, 304; in Canada, 317–324; and the Saint Lawrence colony, 320–324. *See also* La Florida, colonization in
Francis I, 276, 319, 322, 516
Francis II, 283, 285
Franciscans, 81–88
Francisco de Tolomato, 86–87, 89
Frankenstein, Susan, 32
French Atlantic: and forces shaping development, 276–278; Henri IV and, 296–305
Fried, Morton, 31–32, 34
Froude, James Anthony, 414, 416, 418
Fulke, William, 448
Fuller, Mary, 414

Gagnon, François-Marc, 318
Gallic Wars (Caesar), 493
Garcia I, 207
Gascoigne, George, 458
Gates, Thomas, 123, 528–532, 538; wife of, 353

Hakluyt Society, 413
Hakluytus Posthumus (Purchas), 395, 405–406, 497
Hall, Joseph, bishop of Exeter, 25–26
Hamor, Ralph [Raphe], *60*, 61–63, 97–99, 134, 136, 362
Harcourt, Robert, 353, 359, 367
Harlay, Henri de, 299
Harriot, Thomas, 364, 459, 528; as explorer, 357; on El Dorado, 403; on conversion of Natives, 444; and knowledge of area around Roanoke, 531–532
Harsnett, Samuel, 430
Harvey, Gabriel, 463–464, 485–488
Hatfield, April, 121, 371
Haviland, John, 497
Hawkins, John, 176, 288, 346, 353, 369, 375, 377
Helgerson, Richard, 414
Helms, Mary, 32
Henri II, 276, 279–280, 283, 317
Henri III, 293, 332
Henri IV (Henri Navarre), 276–278, 285, 290, 293, 295–305, 332, 333, 549–550
Henry VIII, 421
Henry the Navigator, 148
Heyn, Piet, 206–207
Hill, Christopher, 456, 499
Hilton, Anthony, 351
Hispaniola, 315
Histoire de la Nouvelle-France (Lescarbot), 336–338
Histoire de la terre neuve du Perù, 316
Histoire d'un voyage fait en la terre du Bresil (Léry), 331
Historia general de las Indias (López de Gómara), 405, 551
Historia general y natural de las Indias (Oviedo y Valdés), 254
Historia natural y moral de las Indias (Acosta), 403–404
Historie of Travell into Virginia Britania (Strachey), 362, 404

History and Present State of Virginia (Beverley), 8–9
History of a Voyage to the Land of Brazil (Léry), 442
History of the World (Ralegh), 455, 458, 465–466, 468–474, 485–488
Hodges, Cornelius, 160–163
Hoffman, Paul, 543
Hondius, Jodocus, 475, 487
Hooker, Richard, 389, 417–418, 429, 432, 448
Hope, James Barron, 9
Hotman, Jean, 414
Howard, Henry, 503
How Europe Underdeveloped Africa (Rodney), 180
Huguenots, 277–278, 280–285, 290–296, 331–332, 364
Hulsius, Levinus, 475–478, *479,* 485
Hungarian Lion (Gunnell), 492–493, 496

Ibarra, Diego de, 536–537
Ibarra, Pedro de, 91
Imbangala (Jagas), 206, 210, 219, 221, 241
Incas, 316–317
Indigenous peoples: French relationship with, 88, 279, 297–301, 320–324, 329–331, 334–337; on Martinique, 303; Purchas on rights of, 393–395. *See also* Native Americans; Southeast tribes of North America; *individual tribes*
Institutes of the Lawes of England (Coke), 499
Iopassus, 97–98, 113, 132–133
Ireland, 342, 547
Iron, demand for, 181–182
Iroquois, 106–107, 255, 319–326
Iroquois Great League of Peace and Power (the Five Nations), 106–107
Irwin, Margaret, 490
Islamic culture and scholarship, 156–158, 168, 189

Itapoucou, 299–300
Itoyatin, 121, 129, 132–133
Ivory, trade in, 183

Jaguaripe, 238–239
Jamaica, 374
James, Richard, 501, 504
James I/VI, 547; Uttamatomakkin and, 63; colonial intentions of, 251, 358, 391; tobacco and, 251, 362; as peacemaker, 391, 532, 546–547, 549–550; death of, 497; antiquarians disbanded by, 499
Jamestown: historical survey of, 1–13; and significance of settlement, 2; anniversary celebrations of, 9–12; scholarship on, 9–12; 1607 attack on, 46–47, 123, 126, 130, 133, 524–525; and starvation strategy of Wahunsonacock, 46, 124, 132, 513, 527; and strategies of exploitation, 119–131; and incorporation into Powhatans, 120–121; and tribute relationships with Anglo-Native peoples, 120–121, 126; and colonists' attack on Natives, 125–126, 527; Wahunsonacock's negotiations with, 526–527; and support from Virginia Company, 528–531; Spanish challenge to colonization of, 534–537, 540, 546–550. See also Anglo-Powhatan War
Jardine, Lisa, 463–466
Jesuits: in Chesapeake, 30, 40–43, 79, 517, 545; Paquiquineo and, 30, 40, 516–517, 545; in Cartagena, 190; in Ndongo, 207–208, 218; in Kongo, 213, 217; on runaway slave communities, 237; Huguenot massacre of, 291; in Acadia, 299
Jobson, Richard, 185
Johns, Adrian, 467
Jolof slaves (Islamic), 226–227, 229–233, 243, 245
Jonson, Ben, 465, 494
Jordan, Edward, 497

Joyfull Newes out of the New Founde Worlde (Monardes), 347

Kalimas (Caribs), 256, 303
Kalinagos (Caribs), 262–263
Kane, Omar, 153, 166
Kecoughtans, 109–110, 125, 514, 523
Keller, Georg, 97–99
Kelso, William, 489
Keymis, Lawrence, 363, 465
Kingship, French understanding of, 310–314
Kingship model. *See* Native American societies, kingship model in
Kongo, Kingdom of: relations of, with Portugal, 189, 199, 201, 206, 220–224; Catholicism in, 194–198, 201–206, 212–217; and diplomatic relations' appropriation of European style, 194–198, 201–207; literacy levels in, 196, 220–221; and appropriation of European culture, 198–199, 222–224; and weapons trade, 199, 201; and Dutch alliance, 206–207; and Kingdom of Ndongo relations, 207–209; language of, and appropriation by Caribs, 373–374
Konig, David, 348
Kunta clan, 157–158, 168

Laet, Johannes de, 487
La Florida (Escobedo), 84
La Florida, colonization in: and Spanish population growth, 69; Native hostility to, 70, 78–80; Spanish-French conflict over, 79–80, 284–293, 318, 543–544; rumors of gold and, 518
Lambarde, William, 500
Lane, Ralph, 350, 519–520
Language, appropriation of, 190–191, 240–241, 365, 373–374
La Noue, François de, 437–440, 448
La Popélinière, 292
La Ravardière, sieur de, 298–302
Las Casas, Bartolomé de, 284, 426, 485

Laud, William, 305, 430, 505–507
Laudonnière, René Goulaine de, 285–289, 292, 327–329, 330
"Law of Nations" (Strachey), 397
Le Challeux, Nicholas, 289, 292, 294
Le Clerc, François "Peg-Leg," 275, 280
Leigh, Charles, 359, 367
Lemay, J. A. Leo, 490, 507
Le Moyne de Morgues, Jacques, 289
Leo X, 202
Léry, Jean de, 282–283, 331–332, 442
Lescarbot, Marc, 296–297, 302, 333–338
Lesewut (reading craze), 486
Lesser Antilles, 303
Lestringant, Frank, 290
Le Testu, Guillaume, 291–292
Lewis, Clifford M., 36–37
Ley, John, 366
Libraries, 498–499, 502–505, 507, 551. *See also* Reading
Lipsius, Justus, 440
Liquor, West African importation of, 182
Little Ice Age, 104–105
Lives of the Eminent Philosophers (Diogenes Laertius), 493
Lloyd, David, 460
Locke, John, 383–384, 387, 407
Lok, John, 176–177
Lokonos. *See* Arawaks
Loomie, Albert J., 36–37
Lopes, Duarte, 199, 209, 222
López de Gómara, Francisco, 405–406, 551
Lorimer, Joyce, 353
Louis I de Bourbon, prince de Condé, 291
Louis XIII, 276, 299–300, 339

MacCulloch, Diarmaid, 430
Machiavelli, Niccolò, 427
Machumps, 56, 531
Madison, Isaac, 135–136
Magalhães-Godinho, Vitorino, 151

Malick, Terence, 489
Mandinga, Pedro, 376
Mangoags, 519
Manit, 113
Mannahoacs, 110, 371, 526, 533
Manuel, Antonio, 194–197, 204–205, 212, 214, 221
Map of Virginia (Smith), 495
Marchants aviso (Brown), 347
Marees, Pieter de, 175–176, 181, 191–192
Mare liberum (Grotius), 395, 397–399
Margarita Indians, 366
Marnix, Phillipe de, 420
Marrón, Francisco de, 83
Martin, John, 129–130, 348
Martínez, Bartolomé, 38
Martínez, Juan, 346
Martinique, indigenous culture on, 303
Massawomecks, 107, 117, 123, 130–131, 526
Matchumps. *See* Machumps
Maynard, Thomas, 353
Maynwaring, Roger, 505
Médicis, Catherine de, 276, 279, 285, 290
Médicis, Marie de, 276, 298–301
Meinig, D. W., 541
Membertou, 339
Mendes de Vasconcelos, Luis, 209
Méndez de Canzo, Gonzalo, 83, 87–90, 95, 292
Menéndez de Avilés, Pedro, 38–40, 43, 78, 288–290, 516–518, 543, 545
Merchant Adventurers, 423
Meteren, Edmond van, 412
Meteren, Emmanuel van, 412
Method for the Easy Comprehension of History (Bodin), 312
Mexico/Mexican people, 255, 316, 402, 407, 551, 554–555
Mi'kmaqs, 334, 337, 339
Miller, Joseph, 243–244
Mission San Pedro, 82, 88–89
Mission Santa Isabel, 92, 93

Mocamas, 79, 83, 89–90
Mocambo communities, 240
Mocquet, Jean, 298
Moctezuma. *See* Montezuma
Molina, Luis de, 391
Monacans, 110, 371, 514–515, 525, 526, 533
Monardes, Nicholas, 347
Montaigne, Michel de, 296, 442, 455
Montbarrot, René-Marie de, 298
Montezuma (Moctezuma), 316, 552
Montgomery, Dennis, 490
Morales, Pedro, 520
Moratucs, 519
More, Thomas, 418, 425
Moreau, Jean-Pierre, 292, 302–303
Moreno, Diogo de Campos, 240
Morgan, Edmund S., 342, 376
Morgan, Henry, 504
Morocco, 145–146, 148–153, 155, 158–160, 165–168
Muslims: enslavement of, by Portuguese, 226–227, 229–233, 243
Mvemba Nzingo, Henrique, 212, 221
Mwenge a Kiluanje, Francisco, 222–223

Nacotchtanks, 134–138
Namontack, 30–31, 51–53, 56, 58–59, 61, 367, 527
Nansemonds, 517
Native Americans: and infectious diseases, 3–4; capture of, and removal to Europe, 97–99, 132, 516; stereotypes of, 99, 365; and tobacco, 255–256, 262–263; and slave trade, 262–263; and arms trade, 262; portrayal of, in France, 279, 317; as guides, 366–367, 376; as interpreters, 366–367, 536; natural-law rights of, 383–393, 396–397, 402, 407–408; and progressive theory of civilization, 402–404. *See also* Southeast tribes of North America; *individual tribes*
—Chesapeake Bay area: and influx of

material goods, 38; and Jesuit mission, 40–43, 79, 517, 545; history of, 1300–1600, 102; political hierarchy of, 102; population of, in sixteenth century, 102; and reasons for migration, 105–108; and basis for chiefly power, 110–119; and evidence of post-1624 English disengagement, 139; and progressive theory of civilization, 402, 404, 407–408; religion practiced by, 404; and Hakluyt's project for civilizing, 443–446; and first contact with white men, 515–518; and violence model of subjugation, 517; and war with English, 538. *See also individual tribes*
—dispossession of: justification of, by eternal salvation, 337; natural law and, 383–393, 396–409; *ferae bestiae* and, 385, 392–393, 399–402, 408–409; Purchas on, 393–395, 405–408; justification of, by right of commerce, 397–400; Gentili on, 400–401; Acosta on, 401–404.
—Oconee Valley, 69–71, 89–92; exchange networks in, 75; instability and collapse of chiefdoms in, 76–77, 96; Franciscans and, 83–86, 92; and Guale revolt, 87–90; consolidation and relocation of, 91–92, 95–96. *See also* Southeast tribes of North America
Native American societies, kingship model in: and prestige goods, 35; travel writing on, 308, 314–331; evolution of, 309, 314–315; Columbus on, 314–315; Anghiera on, 315; and Peruvians, 316–317; and Mexicans, 316; portrayal of, in France, 317, 334–336; in Iroquois, 319–326; and comparison of chiefdoms, 326–329; in Brazil, 329–332; Léry's rejection of, 331–333; and replacement by Native self-subjugation model, 333–338; and replacement by kinship model, 340–

Pasquier, Étienne, 313
Patawomecks, 99, 130-139
Paul V, 194-196, 202
Pearl trade, 34
Pedro (interpreter), 366
Pedro I, 202
Pedro II, 206, 213-214
Pennington, L. E., 413
Pepiscunimah, 123-124
Pepper, trade in, 170-171, 183
Percy, George, 352, 353, 365, 368, 389
Percy, Henry, 389
Pereira, Manuel Cerveira, 209
Perkins, Francis, 51
Perkins, William, 415
Pernambuco, 292
Peru/Peruvian people, 186-187, 316-317, 386-387, 402, 551, 554-555
Peter Martyr. *See* Anghiera, Pietro Martire d'
Phettiplace, William, 537
Philip I, 239
Philip II: and presentation of Paquiquineo at court, 38, 516, 545; and support for Menéndez de Avilés, 78; and order for gift giving, 80; colonial intentions of, 288, 543, 544; goals of, 291; Catherine de Médicis and, 293; claim of, to universal monarchy, 419; and rumors of gold, 518; and annexation of Portugal, 523, 542, 555, 559; death of, 547
Philip III, 206, 301, 537, 547, 550
Piankatanks, 109, 126, 523
Picts, *483*
Pinelo, Diego, 257
Piracy and privateering: tobacco trade and, 265, 270-272, 361-362; Huguenot, 278, 290-292; French colonists and, 287; by French, in Caribbean, 302-303; by Grenville, 343; by English, 349
Piscataways, 109-110, 113, 130-131, 137-138
Pizarro, Francisco, 316-317, 553

Platform mounds, 72, 91
Plymouth colony, 379
Pocahontas: travel of, to England, 30, 52, 97-99, 132, 367; end of Anglo-Powhatan War and, 52, 60, 132; Smith and, 492
Poole, Robert, 135
Popham, Sir John, 549
Portugal: and attempted trans-Saharan trade takeover, 145-146; and conquest of Morocco, 145; and gold trade, 145, 148, 172-173; and Gulf of Guinea trade relations, 172-175; Spanish annexation of, 186, 522, 547, 555; and slave trade, 187, 206, 226-234, 241, 243, 282, 284, 292, 542, 555; imports and exports of, 193; Kingdom of Kongo and, 199-209, 220-224; and Central Africa trade relations, 199, *200*, 201; and tobacco trade, 199, *200*, 266-272; and weapons trade, 199, 201; Kingdom of Ndongo and, 201, 207-211, 218-219; and French colonization in Brazil, 279, 283-284, 297-302, 318; and resistance of colonization attempts, 292; and Indian relations in Brazil, 301-302
Potiguars (Tupís), 292, 297
Potter, Stephen, 34
Poutrincourt, Jean de Biencourt, sieur de, 334-335
Powhatan (chief). *See* Wahunsonacock (Powhatan)
Powhatan Nation: political units in, 32-34; kinship relationships in, 34; tribute networks and expectations in, 34, 120; burial practices in, 36, 58-59; Newport's relations with, 44-48; and 1607 Jamestown attack, 46-47, 123, 126, 130, 133, 524-525; and strategies of exploitation, 119-131; and Jamestown incorporation ceremony, 120; and English plan to liberate, 121, 123, 532-533; colonists' attacks on, 125-126, 527; scholarship on, 139-140;

Smith on social hierarchies of, 309; and weapons trade, 526–528, 539; and alliance with Germans, 527–528; defeat of, 539–540. *See also* Anglo-Powhatan War; Wahunsonacock (Powhatan)

Prestige goods, 32–33; in Powhatans' songs, 29–30; and Namontack's voyage to obtain, 30–31, 51–53, 56; and power, 32–36, 44–48, 50–54, 56–59, 61–65; examples of, 33–34, 55, 57, 59, 61; and Paquiquineo's voyage to obtain, 36–43; and burial practices, 36, 58–59; and barter, 42, 47–48; and alliance with English, 44–48, 50–54, 56–59, 61–63; Thomas Savage as, 50–51, 61; and tracing chiefly authority, 115–116. *See also* Rare goods; Trade goods; *specific types*

Preston, Amyas, 356

Principall Navigations of the English Nation (Hakluyt), 322, 411, 413–417, 428, 432, 451, 459, 480

Privateering. *See* Piracy and privateering

Proceedings of the English Colonie in Virginia (Symonds), 390

Proceedings of the English Colony (Smith), 537

Providence Island, 357, 503

Purchas, Samuel, 497; on Uttamatomakkin, 61, 63; influences on writings of, 388–389, 405–408; on rights of indigenous peoples, 393–395, 405–408; on Smith, 500. *See also specific works*

Purchas His Pilgrimage (Purchas), 389, 405–408

Puritans, 497–499, 503

Pym, John, 495, 498–499, 501, 503

Quejo, Pedro, 516

Quilombo communities, 240–243

Quinn, David Beers, 413

Quirós, Luis de, 40–43

Quitt, Martin, 43

Quiyoughcohannocks, 123–124, 128

Quiyoughcosughs, 112–113

Quoniambec, 330–332

Quo Vadis? (Hall), 25–26

Ragopo, Leonard, 367

Ralegh, Walter, 298, 356, 459; and Guiana expedition, 349, 352, 360, 367, 371, 403; Virginia named by, 359; Tivitivas described by, 364; Hakluyt and, 410, 412, 429, 437, 444–446; as reader, 454–455, 457–466; health of, 454; as writer, 455, 458, 465–466; background of, 457–458; career of, 459; Elizabeth I and, 459, 501; marriage of, 469; portrait of, *491;* and early colonial settlement, 518–519, 521, 546; and Roanoke expedition, 518–519 —works of: influences on, 347; *Discovery of Guiana,* 347, 459, 464–466, 468–474, 485–488; *History of the World,* 458, 465–466, 468–474, 485–488; comparison of printed presentations of, 468–488; generic overlap in, 469–470; *Ocean to Cynthia,* 473

Ralegh, Wat, 465

Ramusio, Giovanni Battista, 325, 452

Rare goods: and social organization, 69–74, 78, 82–84, 89–96; and exchange networks, 74–75; incorporation of, into ritual, 75, 94; and conversion, 78; power of, 78, 80–81, 91–93; geographic migration of, 94. *See also* Prestige goods; *specific types*

Rasilly, François de, 299–301, 336, 338

Rasilly, Isaac de, 299, 305

Rawawek, 514

Reading: Ralegh's habits of, 454–455, 457–466; study of, 456; nature of early modern, 466–467; reader's role in, 466–467; effect of presentation on, 466–486; illustrations' role in, 475, 477–485; and *Lesewut,* 486; and role of genre, 487. *See also* Books, influence of; Libraries; Travel writing

Reading craze. *See Lesewut*

Santissimo Sacramento, Diego de, 217, 223

Santo Domingan Indians, 375

Santo Domingo, 371

São João Bautista (ship), 225

São Jorge da Mina, 173, 174–175, 177

São Tomé, 227, 233–237

Saravia, Hadrian, 431

Savage, Thomas "Newport," 30, 43, 51, 61, 129

Sea Grammar (Smith), 497

Sebastião, duke of Mbamba, 223

Second Anglo-Powhatan War. *See* Anglo-Powhatan War (1622)

Second Treatise of Government (Locke), 407–408

Secotans, 520, 521

Segura, Juan Baptista de, 40, 517, 545

Selden, John, 389, 495, 498–499, 501, 504

Seneca, 440–441

Senegambia, 149, 151–154, 229–230

Sepúlveda, Ginés, 400

Service, Elman R., 31–32, 34

Shakespeare, William, 354, 494

Shamans, 111, 117

Shaping of America (Meinig), 541

Shell-based currency, 173, 323

Shirley, Anthony, 366

Sibthorp, Robert, 505

Sidney, Philip, 418, 458

Silva, João de, 202

Silva Manuel, Pedro da, 208

Silver, discovery of, 552–553

Singularitez de la France antarctique (Thevet), 254, 325–326

Sir Francis Drake (FitzGeffrey), 490

Sir Gawain and the Green Knight (Smith), 500

Sir Walter Raleigh (Treveleyan), 490

Slave Coast, 179

Slaves and slavery: in Peru, 186–187, 555; in colonial America, 186–191, 225–226, 377, 556; identity formation in, 186–191, 229–233, 243, 245–247;

in Kingdom of Kongo, 189, 206; and women as sexual partners, 192; and "20. and odd Negroes," 225, 556; and Muslims, 226–227, 229–233, 243, 245; and runaway communities, 227, 233–242; and escape attempts, 229–232; sugar and, 233–234; in Brazil, 237–242, 555; in Spanish colonies, 256–257, 555; tobacco and, 256–257, 259–262, 555–556; in Caribbean, 374–378; in Colombia, 377; Hakluyt on, 426–427; in Mexico, 555

Slave trade: trans-Saharan trade and, 153–154; Tajakant involvement in, 157; role of salt in, 160–161; Saharan perspectives on, 161; statistics for, 184–186, 227–228, 234, 555; Portugal and, 187, 206, 227–233, 241, 282, 284, 292, 542, 555; and women as sexual partners, 192; beginnings of Atlantic, 227–233; Dutch and, 241–242, 556; Native Americans and, 262–263; England and, 377–378

Smith, James Morton, 12

Smith, John, 139; Newport compared to, 44, 52, 57; in Caribbean, 350–351; Spanish model of colonization advised by, 371; as knight chivalrous, 459, 500–502; and self-presentation, 489–492, 494, 501–502, 513–515; characterization of, 490–493, 495, 501; and epitaph, 492; and matchlock accident, 493–494; influences on, 493–495, 504–505; and justification for colonization, 494, 507; Cotton and, 495–496, 500, 502–505, 507; activities of, 1623–1630, 496–509; Abbott and, 505–506; idealism of, 507–509; and coat of arms proposed for New England, *508;* and search for Roanoke survivors, 529–530; and Chesapeake Bay exploration, 537–538

—capture of, by Wahunsonacock, 125; and declaration of dependence, 46–48, 50, 52–53, 57–58, 120–121, 526;

description of, 513–515; and conditions of release, 526

—comments by: on lineage in determining chiefdoms, 34; on Uttamatomakkin, 63; on Algonquian spirit world, 113; on Accomacks, 128; on Powhatan society, 309; on concern for Native welfare, 392; on Native Americans' form of government, 393; on Christian divisiveness, 506–507

—works of: *True Relation,* 47, 526; *Map of Virginia,* 495; *True Travels,* 495, 498, 501–503; *Generall Historie of Virginia,* 496, 526; *Accidence,* 497, 503; reviews of, 497; *Sea Grammar,* 497; *Sir Gawain and the Green Knight,* 500; *Advertisements,* 505–508; idealism in, 507–509; *Proceedings of the English Colony,* 537

Smith (Smythe), Sir Thomas, 398, 425–426, 528, 549

Soba Songo, 218

Solomon's Temple, 450–451

Somers, George, 356, 361

Songhay Empire, 159–160

Sores, Jacques de, 291

Soto, Domingo de, 391

Soto, Hernando de, 70, 71, 75, 76–77, 92, 544

Sousa, Fernão de, 211

Sousa, João Correia de, 206

Southeast tribes of North America: and rare goods, 69–74, 78, 82–84, 89–96; chiefdoms of, 72–73, 76–77, 81–83, 88–89, 96; rituals and ceremonial acts of, 72–73, 75, 94; Spanish and, 74–75, 80–83, 87–90; evangelizing and conversion of, 78, 82, 83–86; consolidation and relocation of, 91–92, 95–96. *See also* Native Americans: Oconee Valley

Spain: Virginia settlement challenged by, 67, 534–537, 540, 546–550; Portugal's annexation by, 186, 522, 547, 555; and diplomatic relations with Kingdom of Kongo, 202; tobacco cultivation and trade by, 256–257, 260–261, 264–271; Catherine de Médicis's assault against, 293–294; and claim to universal monarchy, 419, 449–450; and removal of Natives to Europe, 516; and Chesapeake Bay exploration, 516, 543–544

—colonization: violence model of, 70, 292, 336, 371, 401, 426–427, 449–450, 517; in Southeast, 78–80, 87–88, 93, 96; Black Legend of, 292, 336, 348, 391; and Salamancans' argument, 383–387; Purchas on justice of, 394–395; and Donation of Alexander, 394; Gentili on justice of, 395–396, 398–399; rumors of gold and, 522; effect of war on, 522, 523, 544, 546–550; dominance of, 542–543, 551–552, 559; and international challenge to monopoly, 550. *See also* La Florida, colonization in

Spelman, Henry, 58, 132–134, 136, 498

Spenser, Edmund, 459, 464

Stadaconans, 320–324

Stafford, Edward, 428

Standish, Miles, 491

Strachey, William, 139; warrior chant transcribed by, 29–30; on importance of prestige goods, 34–35; Powhatan relations with, 123; on hurricanes, 354; on tobacco, 362; on dispossession of Native Americans, 397, 399–400, 408–409; on Wahunsonacock, 523; and knowledge of Roanoke survivors, 531–534. *See also specific works*

Strozzi, Philippe, 293–294

Stuart, Marie. *See* Guise, Marie de

"Studied for Action" (Grafton and Jardine), 463

Sturtevant, William, 330

Sugar cultivation, 233–234, 259, 299–300

Susquehannocks, 107, 117, 123, 131, 526

Sutton, Christopher, 431

126, 368; of Wahunsonacock and his weroances, 127

Trinidad/Trinidadians, 253, 260–261, 264, 269–270, 364

True and Sincere Declaration (Virginia Company), 542, 551

True Declaration of the Estate of the Colonie in Virginia (Virginia Company), 396

True Discourse of the Present State of Virginia (Hamor), 97

True Relation (Smith), 47, 526

True Travels . . . of Captaine John Smith (Smith), 495, 498, 501–503

Tuck, Richard, 417

Tucker, William, 137, 361, 374

Tully, James, 386

Tupinambás: French and, 279, 297–301; Portuguese and, 282, 284; kingship model of, 317, 329–331, 339; and acceptance of French domination, 336

Tuscaroras, 526

Tyler, Lyon G., 11

Utopia (More), 425

Uttamatomakkin (Tomocomo, Tomakin), 30–31, 59–64, 367

Vasconcelos, Luis Mendes de, 205

Vatican, 194–198, 201–206

Vattel, Emeric de, 284, 387

Vega, Lope de, 490

Velasco, Luis de (Paquiquineo), 30–31, 36–43, 516–517, 544–545

Velázquez, Antonio, 37, 544

Venezuela, 257, 264, 266, 270–271, 377

Veráscola, Francisco de, 83–86

Verrazano, Francis I., 318

Verrazano, Giovanni da, 38, 318–319, 516

Vespucci, Amerigo, 463

Vieira, Antonio, 202–203, 204

Villegaignon, Nicholas Durand de, 280–284, 287

Villiers, George, 501

Virginia: Spanish challenge to settlement of, 67, 534–537, 540; slavery in, 225–226, 377, 556; tobacco and, 251–254, 361–363, 555–557; prototypes for, 342–344; shaping of Caribbean role in, 343–346, 348, 358–362, 374–375, 377–379; and settlement model, 348; Spain's role in defining, 348, 542–543, 552–553; Caribbean compared to, 352–353; founding of, 358–359, 528–534, 558–559; naming of, 359–360; race relations in, 375, 378, 557; Hakluyt's belief in, 410, 412, 420–427, 436–437, 443–446, 452; commercializing of, 553–555; and libertarian development, 554

Virginia Company, 356–359, 388–393, 396–397, 399, 412, 549

Virginia Richly Valued (Hakluyt), 551

Vitoria, Francisco de, 383–387, 391–399, 401–403, 408

Vives, Juan Baptista, 206

Voyages in Print (Fuller), 414

Vrais pourtraits et view des hommes illustres (Thevet), 331

Wahunsonacock (Powhatan), 517, 522, 523; envoys of, 30–31, 36–43, 51–53, 56, 58–64, 527, 531; chiefly authority obtained through, 34, 35, 58–59, 109–110, 123–124, 127–128, 130–132, 523; and exchange of prestige goods, 44–48, 50–54, 56–59, 61–63; Newport and, 44–48, 50–54, 61–63, 121, 524–525; Newport and Smith compared by, 52, 57; coronation of, 53–54, 55, 121, 552; Hamor's embassy to, 60, 61–63; growth of territories under, 109–110, 129–132, 526–528; lineage of, 113–114; tributary relationships of, 127; death of, 132; and kingship model, 393; on his dominions, 515; planned replacement of, by English, 532–533. *See also* Smith, John, capture of

Walsingham, Francis, 268, 422, 432, 438

NOTES ON THE CONTRIBUTORS

Philip P. Boucher is Distinguished Professor of History at the University of Alabama in Huntsville. He is the author of *France and the American Tropics to 1700* (forthcoming).

Peter Cook is Visiting Assistant Professor of History at Nipissing University. He is the author of "Vivre comme frères: Le rôle du registre fraternel dans les premières alliances franco-amérindiennes au Canada (vers 1580–1650)," *Recherches amérindiennes au Québec*, XXX (2001).

J. H. Elliott is Regius Professor Emeritus of Modern History and Fellow of Oriel College at the University of Oxford. He is the author of *Empires of the Atlantic World: Britain and Spain in America, 1492–1830.*

Andrew Fitzmaurice is Senior Lecturer in History at the University of Sydney. He is the author of *Humanism and America: An Intellectual History of English Colonisation, 1500–1625.*

Joseph Hall is Assistant Professor of History at Bates College. He is the author of "Confederacy Formation on the Fringes of Spanish Florida," *Mediterranean Studies,* IX (2000).

Linda Heywood is Professor of History at Boston University. She is the author of *Contested Power in Angola, 1840s to the Present.*

James Horn is Vice President of Research and Abby and George O'Neill Director of the John D. Rockefeller Library at the Colonial Williamsburg Foundation. He is the author of *A Land as God Made It: Jamestown and the Birth of America.*

E. Ann McDougall is Professor of History at the University of Alberta and Director of Middle Eastern and African Studies. She is the author of "Discourses and Distortions: Critical Reflections on Studying the Saharan Slave Trade," *Revue française d'histoire d'Outre Mer* (December 2002).

Peter C. Mancall is Professor of History and Anthropology at the University of Southern California and the Director of the USC-Huntington Early Modern Studies Institute. He is the author of *Hakluyt's Promise: An Elizabethan's Obsession for an English America.*

Philip D. Morgan is Harry C. Black Professor of History at Johns Hopkins University. He is the author of *Slave Counterpoint: Black Culture in the Eighteenth-Century Chesapeake and Lowcountry.*

David Northrup is Professor of History and of African and African Diaspora Studies at Boston College. He is the author of *Africa's Discovery of Europe, 1450–1850.*

Marcy Norton is Associate Professor of History at The George Washington University. She is the author of *Sacred Gifts, Profane Pleasures: A History of Tobacco and Chocolate, 1492–1700* (forthcoming).

James D. Rice is Associate Professor of History at State University of New York, Plattsburgh. He is the author of *Ahone's Waters: Nature and Culture in Potomac Country, 700–1800* (forthcoming).

Daniel K. Richter is Richard S. Dunn Director of the McNeil Center for Early American Studies and Professor of History at the University of Pennsylvania. He is the author of *Facing East from Indian Country: A Native History of Early America*.

David Harris Sacks is Richard F. Scholz Professor of History and Humanities at Reed College. He is author of *The Widening Gate: Bristol and the Atlantic Economy, 1450–1700*.

Benjamin Schmidt is Associate Professor of History at the University of Washington. He is the author of *Innocence Abroad: The Dutch Imagination and the New World, 1570–1670*.

Stuart B. Schwartz is George Burton Adams Professor of History at Yale University. He is the author of *In Their Own Law: Salvation and the Roots of Tolerance in the Iberian Atlantic World*.

David S. Shields is McClintock Professor of Southern Letters at the University of South Carolina. He is the author of *Civil Tongues and Polite Letters in British America*.

Daviken Studnicki-Gizbert is Assistant Professor of History at McGill University. He is the author of *A Nation upon the Ocean Sea: Portugal's Atlantic Diaspora and the Crisis of the Spanish Empire, 1492–1640*.

James H. Sweet is Associate Professor of History at the University of Wisconsin, Madison. He is the author of *Recreating Africa: Culture, Kinship, and Religion in the African-Portuguese World, 1441–1770*.

John Thornton is Professor of History at Boston University. He is the author of *Warfare in Atlantic Africa, 1500–1800*.